Emerging Trends in Cloud Computing Analytics, Scalability, and Service Models

Dina Darwish
Ahram Canadian University, Egypt

IGI Global
PUBLISHER of TIMELY KNOWLEDGE

A volume in the Advances in Computer and Electrical Engineering (ACEE) Book Series

Published in the United States of America by
IGI Global
Engineering Science Reference (an imprint of IGI Global)
701 E. Chocolate Avenue
Hershey PA, USA 17033
Tel: 717-533-8845
Fax: 717-533-8661
E-mail: cust@igi-global.com
Web site: http://www.igi-global.com

Library of Congress Cataloging-in-Publication Data

Names: Darwish, Dina (Dina Gamal), 1981- editor.
Title: Emerging trends in cloud computing analytics, scalability, and service models / edited by Dina Darwish.
Description: Hershey, PA : Engineering Science Reference, [2024] | Includes bibliographical references and index. | Summary: "This book covers a variety of topics pertaining to Cloud computing and how it is utilized within organizations to improve resource utilization"-- Provided by publisher.
Identifiers: LCCN 2023049089 (print) | LCCN 2023049090 (ebook) | ISBN 9798369309001 (h/c) | ISBN 9798369309018 (ebook)
Subjects: LCSH: Cloud computing--Technological innovations. | Cloud computing--Industrial applications. | Big data--Industrial applications.
Classification: LCC QA76.585 .E545 2024 (print) | LCC QA76.585 (ebook) | DDC 004.67/82--dc23/eng/20240314
LC record available at https://lccn.loc.gov/2023049089
LC ebook record available at https://lccn.loc.gov/2023049090

This book is published in the IGI Global book series Advances in Computer and Electrical Engineering (ACEE) (ISSN: 2327-039X; eISSN: 2327-0403)

British Cataloguing in Publication Data
A Cataloguing in Publication record for this book is available from the British Library.

All work contributed to this book is new, previously-unpublished material. The views expressed in this book are those of the authors, but not necessarily of the publisher.

For electronic access to this publication, please contact: eresources@igi-global.com.

Advances in Computer and Electrical Engineering (ACEE) Book Series

Srikanta Patnaik
SOA University, India

ISSN:2327-039X
EISSN:2327-0403

Mission

The fields of computer engineering and electrical engineering encompass a broad range of interdisciplinary topics allowing for expansive research developments across multiple fields. Research in these areas continues to develop and become increasingly important as computer and electrical systems have become an integral part of everyday life.

The **Advances in Computer and Electrical Engineering (ACEE) Book Series** aims to publish research on diverse topics pertaining to computer engineering and electrical engineering. **ACEE** encourages scholarly discourse on the latest applications, tools, and methodologies being implemented in the field for the design and development of computer and electrical systems.

Coverage

- VLSI Design
- Algorithms
- Sensor Technologies
- Digital Electronics
- Power Electronics
- Chip Design
- Applied Electromagnetics
- Programming
- Analog Electronics
- Computer Architecture

IGI Global is currently accepting manuscripts for publication within this series. To submit a proposal for a volume in this series, please contact our Acquisition Editors at Acquisitions@igi-global.com or visit: http://www.igi-global.com/publish/.

The Advances in Computer and Electrical Engineering (ACEE) Book Series (ISSN 2327-039X) is published by IGI Global, 701 E. Chocolate Avenue, Hershey, PA 17033-1240, USA, www.igi-global.com. This series is composed of titles available for purchase individually; each title is edited to be contextually exclusive from any other title within the series. For pricing and ordering information please visit http://www.igi-global.com/book-series/advances-computer-electrical-engineering/73675. Postmaster: Send all address changes to above address.

Titles in this Series

For a list of additional titles in this series, please visit:
www.igi-global.com/book-series/advances-computer-electrical-engineering/73675

Discovering the Future of Data Storytelling Key Technologies and Innovations
Mohammad Daradkeh (University of Dubai, UAE)
Engineering Science Reference • copyright 2024 • 300pp • H/C (ISBN: 9781668494417) • US $270.00 (our price)

Principles and Applications of Quantum Computing Using Essential Math
A. Daniel (Amity University, India) M. Arvindhan (Galgotias University, India) Kiranmai Bellam (Prairie View A&M University, USA) and N. Krishnaraj (SRM University, India)
Engineering Science Reference • copyright 2023 • 237pp • H/C (ISBN: 9781668475355) • US $275.00 (our price)

Design, Optimization, and Applications of Underwater Acoustic Sensor Networks
Bhumika Gupta (G.B.Pant Institute of Engineering & Technology, India) Kamal Kumar Gola (COER University, India) Brij Mohan Singh (COER University, India) Mridula . (COER University, India) and Rohit Kanauzia (COER University, India)
Engineering Science Reference • copyright 2023 • 340pp • H/C (ISBN: 9781668456866) • US $270.00 (our price)

NeutroGeometry, NeutroAlgebra, and SuperHyperAlgebra in Today's World
Florentin Smarandache (University of New Mexico, USA) and Madeline Al Tahan (Abu Dhabi University, UAE)
Engineering Science Reference • copyright 2023 • 264pp • H/C (ISBN: 9781668447406) • US $270.00 (our price)

Principles and Theories of Data Mining With RapidMiner
Sarawut Ramjan (Thammasat University, Thailand) and Jirapon Sunkpho (Thammasat University, Thailand)
Engineering Science Reference • copyright 2023 • 319pp • H/C (ISBN: 9781668447307) • US $255.00 (our price)

Energy Systems Design for Low-Power Computing
Rathishchandra Ramachandra Gatti (Sahyadri College of Engineering and Management, India) Chandra Singh (Sahyadri College of Engineering and Management, India) Srividya P. (RV College of Engineering, India) and Sandeep Bhat (Sahyadri College of Engineering and Management, India)
Engineering Science Reference • copyright 2023 • 389pp • H/C (ISBN: 9781668449745) • US $270.00 (our price)

Artificial Intelligence Applications in Battery Management Systems and Routing Problems in Electric Vehicles
S. Angalaeswari (Vellore Institute of Technology, India) T. Deepa (Vellore Institute of Technology, India) and L. Ashok Kumar (PSG College of Technology, India)
Engineering Science Reference • copyright 2023 • 342pp • H/C (ISBN: 9781668466315) • US $260.00 (our price)

IGI Global
PUBLISHER of TIMELY KNOWLEDGE

701 East Chocolate Avenue, Hershey, PA 17033, USA
Tel: 717-533-8845 x100 • Fax: 717-533-8661
E-Mail: cust@igi-global.com • www.igi-global.com

Editorial Advisory Board

Table of Contents

Detailed Table of Contents

Cloud computing has transformed corporate and consumer lives. Cloud computing may save startups and businesses money and improve services. Independent developers may build global apps and services, share, and analyze data at scales formerly reserved for well-funded projects. Internet users may quickly create, share, and preserve digital content beyond their devices' computing capabilities. The cloud provider owns and maintains computer resources in cloud computing. Browser-based apps like Netflix, third-party data storage for images and other digital files like iCloud or Dropbox, and third-party servers used to support a company, research, or personal project's computer architecture are examples of such resources. This chapter discusses many topics related to cloud computing, such as: Cloud computing term, entities, technologies, delivery models, environments, and platforms, advantages and disadvantages of cloud computing, benefits of cloud computing, using cloud computing, risks and security concerns, cloud computing ethics, challenges, and costs, and research directions.

Amidst an era marked by a relentless surge in digital data and computational demands, the imperative for eco-conscious and sustainable computing solutions has reached unprecedented significance. This study delves into the emerging realm of green cloud computing (GCC), a pivotal catalyst in cultivating a greener digital tomorrow. To nurture a sustainable digital frontier, this research investigates various GCC strategies encompassing efficient data center designs, resource optimization techniques, and innovative virtualization practices. Additionally, the authors scrutinize real-world instances of industry leaders embracing sustainable energy sources. Furthermore, they shed light on the obstacles within eco-friendly cloud computing while illuminating forthcoming trends for the triumphant integration of sustainable and eco-friendly technologies. This study offers profound insights for researchers, students, and stakeholders alike.

Yogita Yashveer Raghav, K.R. Mangalam University, India
Ramesh Kait, Kurukshetra University, India

Edge computing is a revolutionary approach that enables processing and decision-making in close proximity to data sources, reducing latency and optimizing bandwidth usage. This paradigm involves various components such as edge devices, servers, and networks, integrating sensors, actuators, and IoT devices with real-time analysis enabled by edge processing units and containerization technologies. Edge networks, facilitated by edge routers and gateways and diverse communication protocols, ensure seamless data flow. Network edge computing (NEC) further minimizes latency and supports critical network functions. In conclusion, edge computing is reshaping the computing landscape, fostering innovation across industries. The chapter also addresses challenges, potential solutions, and promising trends for future research.

Renuka Devi Saravanan, Vellore Institute of Technology, Chennai, India
Shyamala Loganathan, Vellore Institute of Technology, Chennai, India
Saraswathi Shunmuganathan, Sri Sivasubramaniya Nadar College of Engineering, Chennai, India

Cloud computing is a recent technology that facilitates wide access and storage on the internet. Cloud computing faces few challenges like data loss, quality issues, and data security. Data security became a major concern in the cloud domain as the demand for cloud services is increasing drastically due to its scalability and allowance of concurrent access to users for using various cloud resources. As a consequence, malicious attacks and data breaches happen which also affect other cloud users. Cloud security is made possible with cryptography, which protects from malware and unauthorized users. Traditional cryptographic algorithms are often used to provide data privacy, integrity, and confidentiality. Most recently, a new data encryption scheme was proposed for cloud computing that uses quantum cryptography to improve security. The proposed chapter will provide the complete details about need of data security in cloud computing, significance of cryptography in cloud, existing cryptographic solutions, and proposes a generic model for cloud data security.

Veera Talukdar, D.Y. Patil International University, India
Ardhariksa Zukhruf Kurniullah, Institut Tazkia, Indonesia
Palak Keshwani, The ICFAI University, India
Huma Khan, Rungta College of Engineering and Technology, India
Sabyasachi Pramanik, Haldia Institute of Technology, India
Ankur Gupta, Vaish College of Engineering, Rohtak, India
Digvijay Pandey, Department of Technical Education, IET Lucknow, Government of Uttar Pradesh, India

In a cloud framework, conveyed figuring is a flexible and modest area. It permits the development of a strong environment that supports pay-per-view while taking client demands into account. The cloud is a grouping of replicated approaches that collaborate as one computing system with constrained scope. Spread management's main goal is to make it simple to provide consent to distant and geographically distributed resources. Cloud is taking little steps in the direction of a turn while dealing with a massive array of issues, among them organizing. There are many methods for determining how to correspond with the volume of work that a PC structure is expected to complete. According to the evolving scenario and such an effort, the scheduler modifies the occupations' coordinating situation. The suggestion for thinking Improvements to the assignment movement combination planning estimate have been made for assessment with FCFS and least fulfillment time booking and expert execution of initiatives.

In this chapter, there are very novel techniques in which, by deleting nodes that are either overloaded or underloaded and then reassigning the total load to the collective system's nodes, it is possible to maximise the usage of resources and the amount of time it takes for tasks to be completed. The approaches that are utilised for dynamic load balancing are based on the behaviour of the system as it is being utilised right now, as opposed to the behaviour of the system as it was being utilised in the past. When constructing an algorithm of this kind, the most essential considerations to give attention to are the estimation and comparison of load, the stability and performance of the system, the interaction between nodes, the amount of work that needs to be transmitted, and the choice of nodes.

Cloud computing has evolved as an innovation that facilitates tasks by dynamically distributing virtual machines. User has to pay for the resources as per the demand. This is a challenging task for cloud service providers. The problems caused in load balancing are selecting random solutions, low speed convergence and picking up the original optima. To attain the best result, a mutation-based glow worm swarm optimization (MGWSO) technique is proposed. With this method, the makespan is reduced for a single work set across multiple datacentres. The work is motivated to decrease the consumption of resources in dynamic contexts while simultaneously increasing their availability. The simulated result shows that the suggested load balancing method dramatically reduces makespan in comparison to mutation-based particle swarm optimization.

This chapter takes the reader on a journey through the world of cloud scalability, showing how crucial it is in today's digital world. It starts with the basics and then dives deep into understanding scalability, from how we measure it to new ways of building scalable systems. It also explores the balance between scalability, security, and following the rules. When it comes to real-world problems, the chapter offers practical solutions based on industry knowledge. Finally, it looks to the future, suggesting exciting new areas for research in the ever-changing digital landscape. Whether you're an IT pro, a business leader, or a researcher, this chapter offers valuable insights into the world of cloud scalability.

A wide range of applications, many of which need ever-increasing processing capability, may now be supported by smartphones. Smartphones are resource-constrained devices with limited computation power, memory, storage, and battery; therefore, this presents a hurdle. Fortunately, dynamic resources for processing, storage, and service supply are nearly endless thanks to cloud computing technologies. In order to get beyond the limitations of smartphones, experts foresee expanding cloud computing services to mobile devices. Cloud computing, software as a service, community networks, online stores, and other application models have grown rapidly over the past several years as a result of developments in network -based computing and applications on demand. Since 2007, the scientific and business sectors have turned to studying cloud computing, an important application model in the Internet era. Since mobile cloud computing is still in its infancy, it is essential to have a complete understanding of the technology in order to identify the course of future research.

The advent of cloud computing has dramatically transformed our perceptions of IT infrastructure, software rollouts, and the scaling of services. As the cloud's prominence has risen, organizations can now sidestep hefty investments in tangible hardware and sideline extensive capacity planning concerns. This chapter embarks on a journey through the predominant platforms of cloud computing, exploring their distinct features, and guiding on the selection process tailored to individual requirements. The emergence of cloud technology has ushered in a new era in how we approach IT infrastructures, software implementations, and the expansion of services. With cloud computing taking center stage, companies are relieved from sinking large sums into on-premises hardware and are granted more flexibility in their resource allocation strategies. This chapter sheds light on the leading cloud computing ecosystems, their characteristic advantages, and offers insights into making an informed choice that aligns with specific needs.

This chapter delves into the multifaceted aspects of cloud security, highlighting unique challenges posed by the cloud environment, such as multi-tenancy and virtualization, and the critical need for robust data privacy measures. It explores advanced security protocols and measures, emphasizing the importance of encryption and threat mitigation strategies. The discourse extends to the dynamics of mobile cloud computing security, underscoring pertinent considerations. The chapter culminates with insights into future research directions, advocating for continuous innovation in cybersecurity mechanisms to pace with evolving threats.

Big data helps organizations of all sizes track performance, detect issues, and find growth opportunities. Big data has advantages, but supporting it with computer resources and software services may cost even the biggest organizations. Sales, IoT sensors, and user feedback give analytics, and clouds can handle big data. Cloud computing changed computer infrastructure, since all services are cloud-based. Cloud computing is great for massive data storage, administration, and analytics due to its flexibility, pay-as-you-go or pay-per-use strategy, and minimal upfront cost. This chapter examines big data and its analytics with cloud computing for businesses and end users and discusses the key concepts of big data and cloud computing; the advantages, benefits, and disadvantages of big data analytics; cloud service types for big data analytics; security challenges; differences between big data and cloud computing; applications of big data analytics; choosing the cloud deployment model; and security and research issues in big data.

Cloud analytics is the process of using cloud computing resources and technologies to analyze and gain insights from large and complex data. Cloud analytics has become increasingly popular in recent years due to its scalability, cost-efficiency, and accessibility. It enables organizations to process large datasets, perform complex analytics, and make data-driven decisions more effectively and affordably. This book chapter provides a comprehensive overview of cloud analytics, covering its fundamental principles, significance in today's data-driven landscape, benefits and challenges of adoption, critical tools and technologies, data management in cloud environments, and promising future directions and emerging trends. By the end of this chapter, readers will have a deep understanding of cloud analytics and its potential to revolutionize the way organizations analyze and leverage data.

Preface

Cloud computing refers to on-demand Internet access to computer resources stored in a remote data center and maintained by a cloud services provider (or CSP), such as programs, data storage, servers (physical and virtual), development tools, and networking capabilities. The CSP offers access to these resources through a monthly subscription fee or a usage-based model.

Compared to traditional on-premises Information Technology (IT), cloud computing enables the following, depending on the cloud services chosen:

Lower IT costs: The utilization of Cloud technology enables the possibility of transferring a portion or the entirety of expenses and work related to the acquisition, implementation, setup, and management of in-house infrastructure.

Improve your agility and time-to-value: By utilizing cloud technology, organizations can quickly implement business applications, procure and configure equipment, and install software, as opposed to waiting for IT to respond to requests, which can take weeks or even months. Furthermore, the cloud allows to provide self-service access to software and support infrastructure to developers and data scientists.

Scale more simply and affordably: The cloud's elasticity can be leveraged to adjust capacity in response to fluctuations in traffic, thereby avoiding the acquisition of excess capacity that remains underutilized during periods of low demand. One may leverage the global network of their cloud provider to enhance the proximity of their applications to a diverse user base across the globe.

The nomenclature 'cloud computing' also denotes the technological infrastructure that facilitates the functioning of cloud computing. The aforementioned encompasses a type of IT infrastructure that has been virtualized, comprising servers, networking, operating system software, and other infrastructure that has been abstracted through specialized software. This virtualized infrastructure may be consolidated and divided across physical hardware boundaries. As an illustration, it is feasible to divide a single physical server into numerous virtual servers.

The utilization of virtualization technology enables cloud service providers to optimize the utilization of their data center resources. It is a common practice for numerous organizations to opt for the cloud delivery model for their on-premises infrastructure, with the aim of optimizing utilization and cost savings in contrast to traditional IT infrastructure. This approach enables them to provide their end users with the same level of self-service and agility.

The categorization of cloud computing is comprised of four distinct types, namely public, private, hybrid, and community. In the realm of cloud computing, a ***public cloud*** refers to a category of cloud computing services that are offered by a cloud service provider to users via the public internet. These services include, but are not limited to, software as a service (SaaS) applications, virtual machines (VMs), physical computing hardware, as well as enterprise-grade infrastructures and development platforms.

The aforementioned resources could potentially be accessible to the general public, or alternatively, they may be provided through a subscription model or a fee-based system.

Commonly, it furnishes a network linkage with ample bandwidth to guarantee maximum effectiveness and swift collection of applications and data.

Private Cloud denotes a cloud computing environment in which all cloud infrastructure and computing resources are dedicated to a single client and are restricted to that specific customer only. The integration of access control, security, and resource customization of on-premises infrastructure with the advantages of cloud computing, such as elasticity, scalability, and service delivery simplicity, results in the creation of a private cloud.

The infrastructure of a private cloud is often located within the boundaries of the client's data center. A ***private cloud*** deployment can be executed through either the utilization of a third-party cloud service provider's infrastructure or through the leasing of equipment situated in an external data center.

Private cloud is often preferred by numerous organizations due to its ability to fulfil regulatory compliance requirements, which may not be feasible with public cloud. Some individuals may opt for a private cloud deployment due to their professional obligations that entail the handling of intellectual property, confidential documents, medical records, personally identifiable information (PII), or financial data.

The hybrid cloud is a cloud computing paradigm that combines the functionalities of both public and private cloud infrastructures. The principal aim of a hybrid cloud is to integrate an organization's private and public cloud services into a cohesive and flexible architecture that can execute applications and workloads. This solution is widely regarded as optimal.

The target of ***hybrid cloud*** is to integrate public and private cloud resources, with a certain level of coordination, to allow enterprises to select the most appropriate cloud for each application or workload. Additionally, this facilitates the smooth transfer of workloads between the two clouds as circumstances change. The utilization of a hybrid cloud infrastructure enables the organization to effectively and efficiently achieve its technological and commercial goals, surpassing the capabilities of solely relying on either public or private cloud services.

The community cloud refers to a cooperative computing approach where a shared infrastructure is utilized by multiple organizations within a particular community who share similar concerns such as security, compliance, and jurisdiction. This infrastructure may be managed either internally or by a third-party and may be hosted domestically or internationally. This is implemented and utilized by a consortium of entities with comparable objectives. The cost-saving potential of cloud computing is not fully realized due to the fact that the expenses are distributed among a smaller number of users compared to a public cloud, but a larger number of users compared to a private cloud.

The community cloud is made accessible to a group of users from different organizations that have comparable concerns (for example, application, security, policy, and efficiency needs).

In terms of cloud computing services, the three most frequent types are IaaS, PaaS, and SaaS, and it is not unusual for one organization to employ all three.

SaaS, an acronym for Software-as-a-Service, pertains to cloud-hosted application software that can be accessed via a web browser, a specialized desktop agent, or an Application Programming Interface (API) that links to a desktop or mobile operating system. The majority of Software as a Service (SaaS) consumers remunerate a periodic fee, either monthly or annually. Nevertheless, certain providers may offer a "pay-as-you-go" pricing model, which is contingent upon the actual usage. Software as a Service (SaaS) provides automated updates and safeguards against data loss, while also delivering benefits such as cost efficiency, rapid deployment, and the ability to easily scale operations.

The market offers a vast array of Software as a Service (SaaS) solutions, encompassing industry-specific and departmental applications, as well as corporate software databases and Artificial Intelligence (AI) software.

Platform-as-a-Service (PaaS) provides software developers with a readily available platform to develop, deploy, and manage applications, thereby eliminating the expenses, intricacies, and rigidity associated with maintaining the platform on-site.

The cloud service provider assumes responsibility for hosting all components, such as servers, storage, networks, middleware, operating system software, and databases, within their data center through the utilization of Platform as a Service (PaaS). Developers initiate the servers and environments required for application operations, creation, testing, deployment, management, updating, and expansion by selecting their preferences from a menu.

Platform as a Service (PaaS) is typically constructed using containers, which represent a virtualized processing model that is one level higher than virtual servers. Containers facilitate operating system virtualization, allowing programmers to merge a software application with only the essential operating system services required for its execution on any given platform, without necessitating any modifications or middleware.

The Infrastructure-as-a-Service (IaaS) model in cloud computing offers users the ability to access essential computing resources such as virtual and physical servers, networking, and storage on a pay-per-use basis, with the provision of on-demand availability. Infrastructure as a Service (IaaS) enables users to dynamically scale their resources as needed, thereby obviating the necessity for significant upfront capital expenditures or superfluous on-premises or proprietary infrastructure. Additionally, IaaS eliminates the need to over provision resources to accommodate occasional spikes in utilization.

Compared to Software as a Service (SaaS) and Platform as a Service (PaaS), and even more contemporary PaaS computing models such as containers and server-less, Infrastructure as a Service (IaaS) offers users the highest level of control over cloud-based computing resources.

During the early 2010s, the Infrastructure as a Service (IaaS) model was extensively embraced as the predominant cloud computing paradigm. The adoption of SaaS and PaaS is expanding at a faster rate, although the cloud model still persists for many application categories.

There is some important research direction in Cloud Computing that needs to be studied. So, This book contains twenty one chapters, and focuses on the following Trending Cloud Computing Topics, like; fundamental concepts of Cloud computing, Green Cloud Computing, Edge Computing, Cloud Cryptography, Load Balancing, Cloud Analytics, Cloud Scalability, Cloud Service Models, Cloud Computing Platforms, Mobile Cloud Computing, Big Data and cloud computing, Cloud Deployment Models, Cloud Security, and real world implementation of cloud computing new technologies inside organizations and in real life applications.

Green Cloud pertains to the potential ecological benefits that can be derived from environmentally friendly IT services delivered through the internet, which may have positive implications for both businesses and society. The aforementioned expression amalgamates the words 'green', signifying eco-friendliness, and 'cloud', which is the conventional emblem for the internet and a truncated form for cloud computing.

There is some ambiguity surrounding the definition of green cloud (or green cloud computing, in its extended form). In some cases, it is used to describe the environmental benefits of extensive cloud migration of IT systems. For example, in certain organizations, the cloud reduces the overall number of data centers and better accommodates a remote workforce, resulting in lower resource utilization and lower greenhouse gas emissions.

Green Cloud Computing is a comprehensive topic that conserves energy by virtualizing data centers and servers. The IT services consume so many resources, resulting in a scarcity of resources.

In this context, ***"green cloud computing"*** refers to the measures taken by service providers to enhance the environmental profiles of their data centers by utilizing green computing strategies. Green clouds produced can also contribute to larger environmental, social, and governance (ESG) programs at cloud service providers and organizations that use their services. Greener IT is a typical component of ESG activities, which strive to reduce firms' environmental and social effect while also ensuring ethical and equitable business practices.

Green Cloud Computing offers numerous solutions that make IT resources more energy-efficient and reduce operational expenses. It also handles electricity management, virtualization, sustainability, and environmental recycling.

In Edge Computing, data is processed at the network's edge rather than in a data warehouse. Here, data is processed closer to its origin. ***Edge Computing*** is a new and emerging discipline that optimizes cloud computing resource utilization. Additionally, it enhances the system's security.

It is feasible to enable content caching, service delivery, permanent data storage, and Internet of Things (IoT) management by shifting services to the network's edge, resulting in faster response times and transfer rates. Furthermore, as discussed in the next sections, spreading the logic to other network nodes brings additional issues and impediments such as privacy and security, scalability, dependability, speed, and efficiency.

Security and privacy: The decentralized characteristic of this paradigm modifies the security protocols of cloud computing. In edge computing, data may traverse through various distributed nodes connected to the Internet, necessitating encryption techniques that are not reliant on cloud infrastructure. Resource limitations of edge nodes may limit the range of security measures that can be implemented. Moreover, there is a necessity to transition from a centralized infrastructure to a decentralized trust architecture. The implementation of edge computing enables the enhancement of privacy through the minimization of sensitive data transfer to the cloud. Moreover, the transfer of ownership of obtained data to end users is executed by service providers.

Scalability: A dispersed network encounters distinct challenges. The recommendation for a solution must consider the diverse range of devices with varying performance and energy constraints, the dynamic nature of the environment, and the reliability of connections compared to the more robust architecture of cloud data centers. Moreover, the requirements for security may introduce additional latency in the establishment of node connectivity, thereby constraining the scalability of the system.

The utilization of cutting-edge scheduling techniques enhances the efficiency of edge resources and enables the scaling of edge servers through the allocation of minimal resources to each offloaded task.

Reliability: In order to maintain a service's viability, the management of failovers is crucial to its reliability. If a single node fails and becomes unreachable, consumers should still have uninterrupted access to a service. In addition, periphery computing systems must provide recovery actions and user notification in the event of a failure.

To do this, each device must preserve the network topology of the whole distributed system so that error detection and recovery may be accomplished with reasonable simplicity. Other aspects that may impact this feature include the connection technologies used, which may give various degrees of dependability, and the correctness of the data provided at the edge, which may be inaccurate owing to unique environmental circumstances. For example, during failures of cloud services or the internet, an edge computing device, such as a voice assistant, may continue to offer service to local customers.

Speed: Edge computing can improve the responsiveness and throughput of applications by bringing analytical computational resources closer to the end consumers. A well-designed edge platform would outperform a traditional cloud system by a significant margin. Edge computing is a substantially more practical option than cloud computing for applications that require quick response times.

Efficiency: Because analytical resources are close to end users, complex analytical tools and Artificial Intelligence tools may work at the system's edge. This positioning near the system's edge improves operating efficiency and adds to the system's numerous advantages.

Furthermore, the usage of edge computing as an intermediate step between client devices and the larger internet leads in efficiency advantages, as proven by the following scenario: a client device needs other servers to execute computationally demanding processing on video files.

By utilizing servers located on a local edge network to perform these computations, only local transmission of video files is required. Avoiding Internet transmission results in significant bandwidth savings and increases productivity.

Regarding ***cloud encryption***, Cloud Computing provides clients with a virtual environment in which they can store data and conduct a variety of duties. It can transform plain text into an illegible format. With the aid of Cryptography, we can transfer content securely by restricting document access.

Cloud cryptography is a set of techniques used to protect data stored and processed in cloud computing settings. It ensures data privacy, integrity, and secrecy by employing encryption and secure key management methods. Among the most common cloud cryptography techniques are:

- *Symmetric encryption*: encrypts and decrypts data using the same key.
- *Asymmetric encryption*: makes use of two unique keys, one for encryption and one for decryption.
- *Hash functions*: generate a message's unique digest to guarantee its integrity.
- *Key management*: stores and manages encryption keys in a secure manner to ensure the confidentiality of encrypted data.

Concerning ***Load balancing***, load Balancing is the process of distributing the burden across multiple servers so that work can be completed efficiently. This allows the demands of the workload to be distributed and managed. There are a number of advantages to load balancing, including a decrease in the likelihood of a server failure, enhanced security, and enhanced overall performance.

Optimizing parameters such as execution time, response time, and system stability, ***load balancing*** enhances the performance, availability, and dependability of cloud applications. ***Load balancing*** can refer to both the distribution of cloud-based applications and the cloud-based load balancers themselves. ***Load balancing*** in the cloud can be provided as a pay-as-you-go, as-a-service model that facilitates scalability and agility. In cloud computing, load balancing techniques differ based on workload and traffic characteristics, as well as the cloud provider's policies.

The load balancing techniques are simple and inexpensive to implement. Additionally, the issue of sudden disruptions is mitigated.

As a result of the proliferation of data analytics and cloud computing technologies, ***cloud analytics*** can become an intriguing area of study for academics. Cloud analytics is advantageous for both small and large organizations.

It has been observed that the market for cloud analytics is expanding rapidly. Additionally, it can be delivered via a variety of models, including public, private, hybrid, and community models.

This topic's analysis has a vast scope due to the various researchable topics. Some of the market segments include enterprise information management, business intelligence tools, governance, analytics solutions, enterprise performance management, risk and compliance, and complicated event processing.

In terms of ***Cloud Scalability***, Significant progress may be achieved if extensive study on scalability is undertaken. Many limitations may be reached, and jobs such as infrastructure burden can be maintained. Scalability allows for the expansion of current infrastructure. Scalability may be horizontal or vertical.

The applications may be scaled up or down, removing the resource constraints that impede performance.

There are three ***cloud service delivery models***. Platform as a Service (PaaS), Software as a Service (SaaS), and Infrastructure as a Service (IaaS). Because IaaS offers customers with storage, virtual devices, and a network, these are the broad research and development topics that may be investigated. The user installs and executes extra software and apps. The customer gets software services in software as a service.

The client may supply and investigate a number of software services. PaaS also provides infrastructure services through the internet, which customers may install on top of their current infrastructure.

Platforms for cloud computing include diverse applications run by organizations. There is a large number of platforms on which we may undertake a wide range of study. We may do research on an existing platform, such as IBM Computing, Amazon's Elastic Compute Cloud, Google AppEngine, Microsoft Azure, Salesforce.com, and so on.

In ***mobile cloud computing***, the mobile device serves as the console, while data storage and processing occur remotely. It is one of the principal research topics in Cloud Computing.

Today's sophisticated mobile applications are capable of authentication, location-aware functions, and the delivery of targeted content and communication to end users. Consequently, they necessitate voluminous computational resources such as memory, processing power, and data storage capacity. ***Mobile cloud computing*** alleviates the burden on mobile devices by leveraging cloud infrastructure. Using cloud services, developers create and update feature-rich mobile applications, which are then deployed for remote access on any device. These cloud-based mobile applications utilize cloud technology to store and process data, making them compatible with both older and newer mobile devices.

The primary advantage of Mobile Cloud Computing (MCC) is that it does not require expensive hardware and has a longer battery life. Besides the following advantages:

Wider reach; MCC's platform independence lets mobile app developers access a huge market. Serverless cloud-based mobile applications work on any device and Operating System (OS). Developers can manage them centrally and update all platforms easily.

Live analytics; Cloud applications centrally store data. Backend cloud services may swiftly combine various data points and interface with multiple apps to give precise real-time analytics. Data may be collected and integrated securely. IoT allows cloud-connected, real-time mobile app experiences and communications.

Better usability; Mobile cloud application users may have a smooth experience across Personal Computers (PCs), mobiles, and tablets with a robust internet connection. They may use sophisticated computing resources not on their device. Cloud data storage lets them swiftly retrieve lost or stolen devices.

Cost reduction; You only pay for the cloud resources you utilize using a pay-as-you-go strategy. It's cheaper than buying and maintaining servers. If the cloud applications are for internal use, your company may let workers install them on their phones. They don't need employee-specific device setups.

The only drawbacks are its limited bandwidth and heterogeneity.

As two prevalent technologies, ***Big Data*** and Cloud Computing are at the forefront of concern in the IT industry. Every day, a vast quantity of data is generated from various sources. These data are so large that conventional processing tools cannot handle them. In addition to its size and velocity, this data has a great deal of variety. ***Big Data*** refers to the concept of preserving, processing, and analyzing massive quantities of data. Cloud computing, on the other hand, entails providing the infrastructure to facilitate such cost-effective and adequate processes. Many industries, including small and large enterprises, healthcare, education, etc., are attempting to harness the potential of Big Data.

Big data refers to the technology that denotes the enormous quantity of data. This data is classified as structured (organized data), semi-structured and unstructured (unorganized) data.

Big data is characterized by the following three main Vs:

- Volume – It refers to the quantity of data that technologies such as Hadoop manage.
- Variety – This refers to the current data format.
- Velocity – This refers to the rate at which data is generated and transmitted.

This can be used for research purposes and by businesses to identify failures, costs, and problems. Big data and Hadoop are among the most important research topics.

Regarding ***Cloud Deployment Model***, there are models such as:

- *Public Cloud* - It is administered by a third party. It has a pay-as-you-go benefit.
- *Private Cloud* – It is under the control of a single organization and thus has fewer limitations. We can only use it for a specific individual or group within the organization.
- *Hybrid cloud* – It is comprised of two or more distinct model types. The architecture is difficult to deploy.
- *Community cloud computing*- It is a collaborative endeavor in which multiple organizations share infrastructure.

Cloud Security is one of the most important technological shifts. This innovation revolutionizes the present business model. Cloud computing has an open gate, as cloud security is becoming a new popular topic.

To construct a robust secure cloud storage model and manage cloud issues, one can hypothesize that cloud groups can identify the issues, develop a context-specific access model that limits data and protects privacy.

There are three distinct areas in security research, including trusted computing, information-centric security, and privacy-preserving models.

Cloud Security safeguards information against loss, theft, accident, and deletion. With tokenization, VPNs, and firewalls, our data can be protected. Cloud Security is an extensive topic that can be utilized for additional research.

The number of businesses utilizing cloud services is rising. There are a number of security measures that will aid in implementing cloud security, including Accessibility, Integrity, and Confidentiality.

Besides, ***real cases*** involving the implementation of new cloud computing technologies within organizations must be discussed and studied.

Thus, Cloud Computing can be used for remote application processing, outsourcing, and data acceleration. The aforementioned Cloud Computing research topics can greatly assist in providing various customer benefits and enhancing the cloud.

This book, titled *Emerging Trends in Cloud Computing Analytics, Scalability, and Service Models* focuses on the aforementioned research topics, beginning with the fundamental concepts of cloud computing and moving on to explain green cloud computing, Edge Computing, Cloud Cryptography, Load Balancing, Cloud Analytics, Cloud Scalability, Cloud Service Models, Cloud Computing Platforms, Mobile Cloud Computing, Big Data and cloud computing, Cloud Deployment Models, and Cloud Security, as well as real world implementation of cloud computing new technologies in organizations.

This book covers a variety of topics pertaining to Cloud computing and how it is utilized within organizations to improve resource utilization. This book is also intended for industry experts, researchers, students, practitioners, and institutions of higher education interested in Cloud computing's new technologies and techniques.

Dina Darwish
Ahram Canadian University, Egypt

Chapter 1
Fundamental Concepts of Cloud Computing

Dina Darwish
Ahram Canadian University, Egypt

ABSTRACT

Cloud computing has transformed corporate and consumer lives. Cloud computing may save startups and businesses money and improve services. Independent developers may build global apps and services, share, and analyze data at scales formerly reserved for well-funded projects. Internet users may quickly create, share, and preserve digital content beyond their devices' computing capabilities. The cloud provider owns and maintains computer resources in cloud computing. Browser-based apps like Netflix, third-party data storage for images and other digital files like iCloud or Dropbox, and third-party servers used to support a company, research, or personal project's computer architecture are examples of such resources. This chapter discusses many topics related to cloud computing, such as: Cloud computing term, entities, technologies, delivery models, environments, and platforms, advantages and disadvantages of cloud computing, benefits of cloud computing, using cloud computing, risks and security concerns, cloud computing ethics, challenges, and costs, and research directions.

INTRODUCTION

The impact of cloud computing on industries and end users is of significant magnitude, as the extensive utilization of cloud-based applications has resulted in the transformation of various aspects of everyday life. Cloud computing offers startups and companies the opportunity to reduce costs and enhance their service offerings by eliminating the need to procure and manage hardware and software internally. Individual developers possess the autonomy to create internet services and software applications that are universally accessible. The advancements in data sharing and analysis have facilitated the ability to conduct research on a larger scale, which was previously limited to projects with substantial funding. Furthermore, individuals utilizing the internet have the convenient ability to access software applications and storage systems, enabling them to create, disseminate, and store digital content in quantities that surpass the limitations of their personal computer devices.

DOI: 10.4018/979-8-3693-0900-1.ch001

Cloud computing refers to the allocation of computer resources as a service, wherein the responsibility for ownership and management of these resources lies with the cloud provider, rather than the end user. These resources encompass a wide range of options, including web-based software programs such as TikTok or Netflix, as well as third-party data storage solutions like iCloud or Dropbox. Additionally, third-party servers are utilized to provide support for the computing infrastructure of various entities, including companies, research projects, or personal endeavors.

To cultivate innovation, the National Institute of Standards and Technology (NIST), an independent agency under the jurisdiction of the United States Department of Commerce, provides the following definition of cloud computing (Mell & Grance, 2011):

This statement describes a conceptual framework that facilitates widespread and easily accessible network connectivity, allowing users to access a shared collection of adaptable computing resources. These resources may include networks, servers, storage, applications, and services. The provisioning and release of these resources can be done quickly and with minimal involvement from the user or service provider.

- ***On-demand self-service***: Cloud resources can be accessed or provisioned without the need for human intervention. Customers have the option to enroll in this particular model, which grants them immediate access to cloud services. Furthermore, organizations have the capability to establish operational frameworks that facilitate the seamless utilization of internal cloud services by employees, customers, or collaborators, in alignment with predetermined protocols, thereby eliminating the need for IT support.
- ***Broad network access*** enables users to securely access cloud services and resources from any networked location and any authorized device.
- ***Resource pooling*** refers to the practice of maintaining the privacy of individual customers' data from other clients, while simultaneously allowing multiple tenants to utilize resources provided by the cloud provider.
- ***Quick elasticity:*** In contrast to hardware and software deployed on-site, cloud computing resources possess the ability to swiftly and flexibly increase, decrease, or modify in accordance with the evolving requirements of the cloud user.
- ***Metered service***: The utilization of cloud resources is measured, enabling companies and other cloud customers to solely incur charges for the specific resources they actively utilize within a designated billing cycle.

These characteristics offer both organizations and individuals a wide range of transformative possibilities. Before the ubiquitous adoption of cloud computing, organizations and individual computer users frequently had to procure and uphold the software and hardware they intended to employ. Due to the increasing prevalence of cloud-based applications, storage, services, and devices, both businesses and individuals now have the opportunity to utilize a diverse range of on-demand computing resources that are accessible through internet-based platforms. The adoption of cloud services has relieved users from the need to invest significant time, financial resources, and expertise in procuring and overseeing computing resources. This transition has occurred as organizations have moved away from on-premise software and hardware towards utilizing networked resources that are geographically distant. The advent of widespread access to computing resources has given rise to a novel cohort of cloud-based enterprises. This development has not only brought about significant changes in IT practices across various industries but has also disrupted conventional computer-aided routines. The utilization of cloud technology has enabled individuals to engage in collaborative activities with colleagues through video conferences and various online tools. Additionally, it has facilitated access to on-demand entertainment and instructional resources, as well as the ability to communicate with household appliances and arrange transportation services through mobile devices. Furthermore, individuals can conveniently make hotel reservations while on vacation.

This chapter examines the importance of cloud computing for organizations and end users. It specifically concentrates on fundamental cloud computing concepts, various cloud computing delivery models, different cloud computing environments, as well as the advantages and applications of cloud computing. Additionally, it explores the most widely used cloud computing platforms, among other related topics. The chapter will encompass the following main topics:

- Cloud Computing Term
- Cloud Computing Entities
- Cloud Computing Technologies
- Cloud Delivery Models
- Cloud Environments
- Advantages and disadvantages of Cloud computing
- Benefits of Cloud computing
- Uses of cloud computing
- Popular cloud computing platforms
- Cloud computing real life implementation examples
- Challenges and costs in Cloud Computing
- Risks and security concerns in Cloud Computing
- Security and privacy of data in Cloud Computing
- Controls for Cloud Security
- Ethics in cloud computing
- Research directions in cloud computing
- Future scopes in cloud computing

Also, this chapter is organized as follows; the first section contains the background, then, the second section includes the main focus of the chapter, including the main topics mentioned in the previous section, then finally, comes the conclusion section.

BACKGROUND

The origins of various aspects of cloud computing can be attributed to the 1950s, during which academic institutions and enterprises would lease computational resources on mainframe computers. During that period, the act of renting was among the limited approaches available for individuals to gain access to computing resources, primarily due to the substantial size and cost associated with owning or managing computing technology. During the 1960s, notable computer scientists including John McCarthy from Stanford University and J.C.R Licklider from The U.S. Department of Defense Advanced Research Projects Agency (ARPA) put forth visionary concepts that anticipated several key aspects of contemporary cloud computing. These ideas encompassed the notion of computing as a public utility and the potential establishment of a computer network enabling users to remotely access data and programs from any location worldwide.

Cloud computing did not become a widely adopted reality and a commonly used term until the initial decade of the twenty-first century. The past ten years have seen the emergence of various cloud services, including Amazon's Elastic Compute (EC2) and Simple Storage Service (S3) in 2006, Heroku in 2007, Google Cloud Platform in 2008, Alibaba Cloud in 2009, Windows Azure (now known as Microsoft Azure) in 2010, IBM's SmartCloud in 2011, and DigitalOcean in 2011. These services facilitated cost optimization for established businesses by facilitating the transition of their internal IT infrastructure to cloud-based resources. Additionally, they offered independent developers and small developer teams with the necessary tools for application development and deployment. During this time period, there was a notable increase in the popularity of cloud-based applications that fall under the category of Software as a Service (SaaS). In contrast to on-premise software, which necessitates physical installation and maintenance on individual workstations, the advent of Software as a Service (SaaS) has significantly enhanced application accessibility. SaaS allows users to conveniently access applications from a diverse range of devices whenever needed.

Certain cloud-based applications, such as Google's suite of productivity apps (Gmail, Drive, and Docs), as well as Microsoft 365 (a cloud-based iteration of the Microsoft Office Suite), were developed by the companies that introduced cloud infrastructure services. Conversely, applications like Adobe Creative Cloud were introduced as cloud-based offerings, utilizing the services provided by cloud providers. Emerging from the novel opportunities offered by cloud providers, various Software-as-a-Service (SaaS) products and enterprises have surfaced. Notable examples include Netflix's streaming services in 2007, Spotify's music platform in 2008, Dropbox's file-hosting service in 2009, Zoom's video conferencing service in 2012, and Slack's communication tool in 2013. Currently, there is a growing preference for cloud-based IT infrastructure and cloud-based applications among enterprises and individual consumers, with an expected rise in their market share.

According to this definition (Ray, 2018), cloud computing refers to the provision of computer system resources, such as data storage (commonly known as cloud storage) and computing capacity, without requiring direct active management by the user (Montazerolghaem et al., 2020). It is common for expansive cloud infrastructures to have their functionalities dispersed among numerous data centers. Cloud computing is a paradigm that leverages the sharing of resources to achieve coherence and commonly adopts a pay-as-you-go framework. This approach can effectively mitigate capital expenditures, although it may also give rise to unforeseen operating expenses for users (Wray, 2014).

The concept of "Everything as a service" (EaaS or XaaS) is promoted by service-oriented architecture. However, cloud-computing providers offer their services in various models, as defined by the National Institute of Standards and Technology (NIST). These models include Infrastructure as a Service (IaaS), Platform as a Service (PaaS), and Software as a Service (SaaS) (Mell & Grance, 2011). These models exhibit progressive levels of abstraction and are often represented as hierarchical layers: infrastructure-as-a-service, platform-as-a-service, and software-as-a-service. However, it is important to note that these layers are not inherently interdependent. For example, it is possible to deploy Software as a Service (SaaS) on physical machines (bare metal) without utilizing the underlying Platform as a Service (PaaS) or Infrastructure as a Service (IaaS) layers. Similarly, one can run a program on IaaS and directly access it without encapsulating it as a Software as a Service (SaaS) offering.

Cloud computing has gained significant attention in recent years as a subject of academic inquiry. A considerable volume of scholarly articles has been published in this particular domain. The subsequent discourse presents an overview of contemporary endeavors in the field of cloud computing. In recent years, there have been various endeavors to replicate task performance in datacenters with the aim of facilitating the achievement of Service Level Objectives (SLOs) or deadlines. The techniques known as Jockey (Ferguson et al., 2012) and ARIA (Novakovi et al., 2013) employ historical traces and adaptively modify resource allocations in order to fulfil time constraints. In the context of our study, we aim to reduce the amount of training data needed by developing a model that does not rely on historical data. In their study, Jalaparti and his colleagues (Jalaparti et al., 2012) put forth methodologies aimed at modelling the network utilization of MapReduce tasks through the utilization of small data subsets. The framework-independent, high-level features are utilized to capture the computation and communication characteristics in Ernest. The MRTuner framework, developed by Shi and his colleagues (Shi et al., 2014), provides a detailed modelling of MapReduce tasks, allowing for precise optimization of various parameters including memory buffer sizes. Ernest primarily utilizes a limited set of fundamental features, and places a high priority on collecting training data to maximize their utilization.

Lastly, scheduling frameworks such as Quasar (Delimitrou & Kozyrakis, 2014) attempt to estimate the scale out and scale up factor for projects based on the development rate of the initial few tasks. Ernest, on the other hand, performs the entire job on tiny datasets and is able to capture how various phases of a task interact along a lengthy pipeline. Query Optimization: Database query progress predictors (Morton et al., 2010) resolve a performance prognosis issue comparable to Ernest. Typically, database systems use summary statistics such as cardinality counts to direct this procedure. Moreover, these techniques are typically applied to a known collection of relational operators. A research (Huang et al., 2015) have also adapted similar concepts to linear algebra operators. In Ernest, we utilize sophisticated analytics tasks for which we have limited knowledge of the data or computation being performed. Recent research has also examined providing SLAs for OLTP and OLAP operations in the cloud, and it is known that some of the observations made in a study (Alipourfard et al., 2017) regarding variation across instance categories in EC2 also impact database queries. Tuning and Benchmarking are concepts related to experiment design in which we investigate a space of potential inputs and select the optimal inputs. These concepts have been applied to other applications, such as server benchmarking (Tang et al., 2011). Similar methods, such as Latin Hypercube Sampling, have been utilized to efficiently investigate the file system design space (Damblin et al., 2013). Autotuning BLAS libraries such as ATLAS (Whaley et al., 2001) also address the issue of investigating a state space efficiently. Choosing the optimal cloud configuration offered by the service provider is difficult. Various approaches have been proposed for determining the optimal cloud configuration (Novakovi et al., 2013; Alipourfard et al., 2017; Tang et al., 2011; Venkataraman et al., 2016; Yadwadkar et al., 2017; Hsu et al., 2017). These methods can be broadly categorized into (1) prediction, which uses extensive offline evaluation to generate a machine learning (ML) model that predicts the performance of workloads, and (2) search-based techniques, which iteratively evaluate configurations in search of a near-optimal one (Ferdman et al., 2012; Shi et al., 2014).

Several articles have investigated the efficacy of big data applications on scale-out platforms and clouds (Makrani et al., 2014; Makrani et al., 2018; Sayadi et al., 2017; Malik et al., 2017; Malik et al., 2019; Sayadi et al., 2018). All of the aforementioned works utilize performance counters to monitor the efficacy and behavior of applications. In papers (Makrani & Homayoun, 2017), the authors conduct a series of exhaustive experiments to examine the effect of memory subsystem on the efficacy of data-intensive applications operating in a cloud environment. After identifying the performance impediment with performance counters, the author of a paper (Namazi et al., 2019) employs compress sensing to enhance data mobility. Performance counters can also be utilized to track the behavior of an application in order to identify nefarious behavior (Sayadi et al., 2018; Dinakarrao et al., 2019; Sayadi et al., 2019). In addition, there are new ways to enhance the efficacy of modern computing systems, such as hardware acceleration (Neshatpour et al., 2018; Makrani et al., 2019) and cloud computing.

MAIN FOCUS OF THE CHAPTER

Cloud Computing Term

Cloud computing refers to the provisioning of various computing resources, including servers, storage, databases, networking, software, analytics, intelligence, and other related components, through the utilization of the Internet, commonly referred to as the Cloud.

Cloud computing presents itself as a feasible substitute for on-premises data centers. The management of all aspects related to an on-premises data center is imperative, encompassing tasks such as procuring and deploying hardware, implementing virtualization, installing the operating system and requisite software, establishing network infrastructure, configuring firewall settings, and setting up data storage systems. Once all necessary setup tasks have been accomplished, it becomes our responsibility to ensure the ongoing maintenance of the system throughout its entire lifespan. Nevertheless, in the case of opting for Cloud Computing, the responsibility of hardware procurement and maintenance will be assumed by a cloud provider. In addition, they offer a wide array of software and platform as a service options. It is permissible to engage the services of any necessary service providers. Cloud computing services will be charged based on usage. The cloud environment provides a user-friendly web interface through which individuals can manage various resources such as compute, storage, network, and applications. Figure 1 depicts the various components of Cloud computing.

Cloud Computing Entities

In the business market, there are two primary entities: cloud providers and consumers. However, service brokers and resellers are two increasingly prominent entities in the realm of Cloud computing.

Cloud providers are companies that offer computing resources and services over the internet. These providers enable individuals and organizations to store their data. This category encompasses entities such as Internet service providers, telecommunications corporations, and major enterprises process outsourcers, which offer either media, such as Internet connections, or infrastructure, such as hosted data centers, to facilitate consumer access to cloud services. Service providers may also encompass systems integrators who construct and maintain data centers that house private clouds. These providers offer a range of services, such as Software as a Service (SaaS), Platform as a Service (PaaS), and Infrastructure as a Service (IaaS), to consumers, service brokers, or resellers (Pring et al., 2009).

Cloud Service Brokers encompass various entities such as technology consultants, business professional service organizations, registered brokers and agents, and influencers. These entities play a crucial role in assisting consumers in the process of choosing appropriate cloud computing solutions. Service brokers focus on facilitating the negotiation and establishment of relationships between consumers and providers, without assuming ownership or management responsibilities over the entire Cloud infrastruc-

Figure 1. Cloud computing components

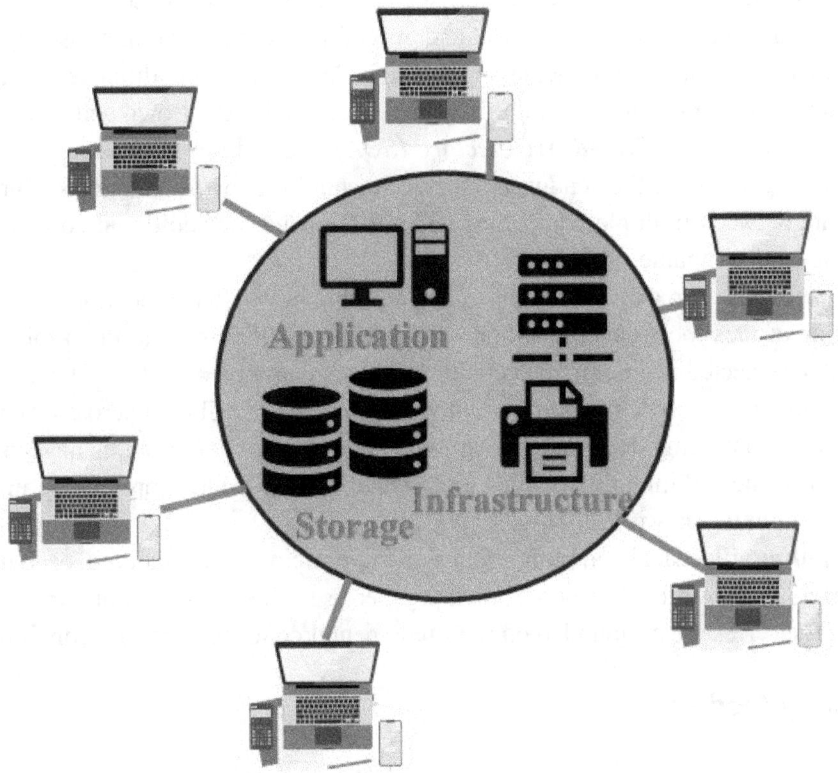

ture. Additionally, supplementary services are incorporated onto the existing infrastructure of a Cloud provider in order to constitute the user's Cloud environment.

Cloud resellers play a significant role in the global cloud market as cloud providers expand their operations to different continents. Cloud providers have the option to select local IT consultancy firms or resellers of their current products to serve as "resellers" for their Cloud-based products within a specific geographical area.

Cloud consumers refer to the end users who fall under the category of individuals utilizing cloud services. However, Cloud service brokers and resellers can also be classified within this category if they function as customers of another Cloud provider, broker, or reseller.

Cloud Computing Technologies

There exist certain contemporary advancements that are driving the development of cloud computing systems, rendering them adaptable, reliable, and efficient. ***Virtualization*** is a technology that allows for the creation of virtual versions of physical resources, such as servers, storage devices, or networks. It enables the efficient utilization of hardware resources by running multiple virtual instances on a single physical machine. ***Grid computing*** and ***utility computing*** are two important concepts in the field of computer science. Grid computing refers to the use of a network of computers to solve complex computational problems. It involves the sharing and coordination of resources across multiple machines.

Virtualization: Virtualization is a method that enables the sharing of a single physical instance of an application or resource among multiple entities, such as organizations or individuals. This is achieved by assigning a suitable label to a tangible asset and providing a reference to that asset upon request. The Multitenant style provides a means of achieving digital isolation among multiple lessees, allowing firms to benefit from and customize their operations as if they each have their own dedicated environment.

The concept of ***Service-Oriented Architecture (SOA)*** enables the utilization of services to fulfil various requests, regardless of the vendor, product, or technology involved. Consequently, it is feasible to exchange data between multiple companies without the need for additional computer programs or modifications to said companies.

Grid Computing refers to a form of organized computing in which a collection of computer entities, originating from various locations, collaborate to solve complex computational problems. Numerous websites are interconnected in order to collectively achieve a common objective. The available resources for personal computer units exhibit significant diversity and are distributed across different geographical locations. Grid Computing decomposes complex tasks into smaller, more manageable components. The distribution of these diminutive entities is directed towards central processing units that remain interconnected within the network.

Utility computing: Electrical computing relies on the principle of investing in each utilization style. The service offers computational resources on a pay-per-use basis. Cloud computing, grid computing, and managed IT services are all founded on the fundamental concept of energy computing.

Cloud Delivery Models

Cloud resources can be accessed through different delivery methods, each offering clients different levels of support and flexibility.

Infrastructure as a Service (IaaS)

Infrastructure as a Service (IaaS) is a term used to describe the provision of computer infrastructure on a demand basis. This includes various components such as operating systems, networking, storage, and other infrastructure elements. Infrastructure as a Service (IaaS) operates in a manner akin to virtual representations of physical servers, thereby liberating cloud users from the obligation of procuring and upkeeping tangible servers. Additionally, IaaS empowers users to scale their resources as needed. Infrastructure as a Service (IaaS) is a widely adopted option among enterprises seeking to leverage the advantages of cloud computing while also maintaining the presence of system administrators responsible for overseeing the installation, configuration, and management of operating systems, development tools, and underlying infrastructure components. Nevertheless, individuals such as developers, researchers, and other professionals who seek to personalize the fundamental structure of their computational ecosystem opt for Infrastructure as a Service (IaaS). Infrastructure as a Service (IaaS) possesses a high degree of adaptability, enabling it to effectively manage a wide range of tasks, including the administration of a company's computer infrastructure, provision of web hosting services, and facilitation of extensive big data research endeavors.

The most fundamental illustration of Infrastructure as a Service (IaaS) cloud computing is exemplified by conventional web hosting. In order to have a firm store your data on their servers, you are required to make monthly payments or pay based on the amount of data consumed, typically measured in megabytes or gigabytes. Infrastructure as a Service (IaaS) is a highly adaptable solution as it provides users with the ability to customize the architecture of the computing environment to their specific requirements. Infrastructure as a Service (IaaS) encompasses a comprehensive spectrum of services, spanning from web hosting to the processing and analysis of large-scale datasets.

Platform as a Service (PaaS)

Platform as a Service (PaaS) refers to a computing platform wherein the provider is responsible for the installation, configuration, and maintenance of the underlying infrastructure, including the operating system and other software components. This allows users to focus on the development and delivery of programs within a reliable and standardized environment. Platform as a Service (PaaS) is widely utilized by software developers and development teams due to its ability to alleviate the challenges associated with the establishment and upkeep of computer infrastructure. Additionally, PaaS facilitates remote collaboration among geographically dispersed teams. Platform as a Service (PaaS) is an appropriate choice for developers who do not require extensive customization of their underlying infrastructure or who prioritize their focus on development activities rather than DevOps and system management responsibilities.

Platform as a Service (PaaS) mitigates the challenges associated with the establishment and upkeep of an infrastructure, while concurrently enabling streamlined collaboration among teams. For instance, consider the scenario where an individual establishes their own e-commerce platform but carries out the entire operational procedure on a distinct server. Similar to Software as a Service (SaaS), users are solely exposed to the interface through which they engage.

Software as a Service (SaaS)

Software as a Service (SaaS) refers to a cloud computing model where software applications are provided to users over the internet on a subscription basis. In this model, the software is hosted and maintained by a third-party provider.

Software as a Service (SaaS) providers furnish customers with cloud-based applications that can be accessed on demand via the internet, eliminating the need for program installation or updates. Several examples of commonly used software platforms include GitHub, Google Docs, Slack, and Adobe Creative Cloud. Software-as-a-Service (SaaS) applications have gained significant popularity among both corporate entities and everyday consumers due to their user-friendly nature, ability to be accessed from various devices, and the provision of free, premium, and enterprise editions of their software offerings. Software as a Service (SaaS), similar to Platform as a Service (PaaS), provides a level of abstraction that conceals the underlying infrastructure of a software application, thereby consumer exposure is limited to the interface through which they interact.

A web-based mail service can be considered as an exemplification of a Software-as-a-Service (SaaS) application. Google's additional offerings, namely Google Docs and Google Sheets, can also be classified as Software as a Service (SaaS) applications. Adobe Creative Cloud services serve as another illustrative example of Software as a Service (SaaS) in practice. The user's exposure is limited to the interface they select for engagement within this paradigm. Figure 2 depicts the architecture of cloud computing, while Figure 3 presents the arrangement of cloud computing service models arranged as layers in a stack.

Figure 2. Cloud computing architecture

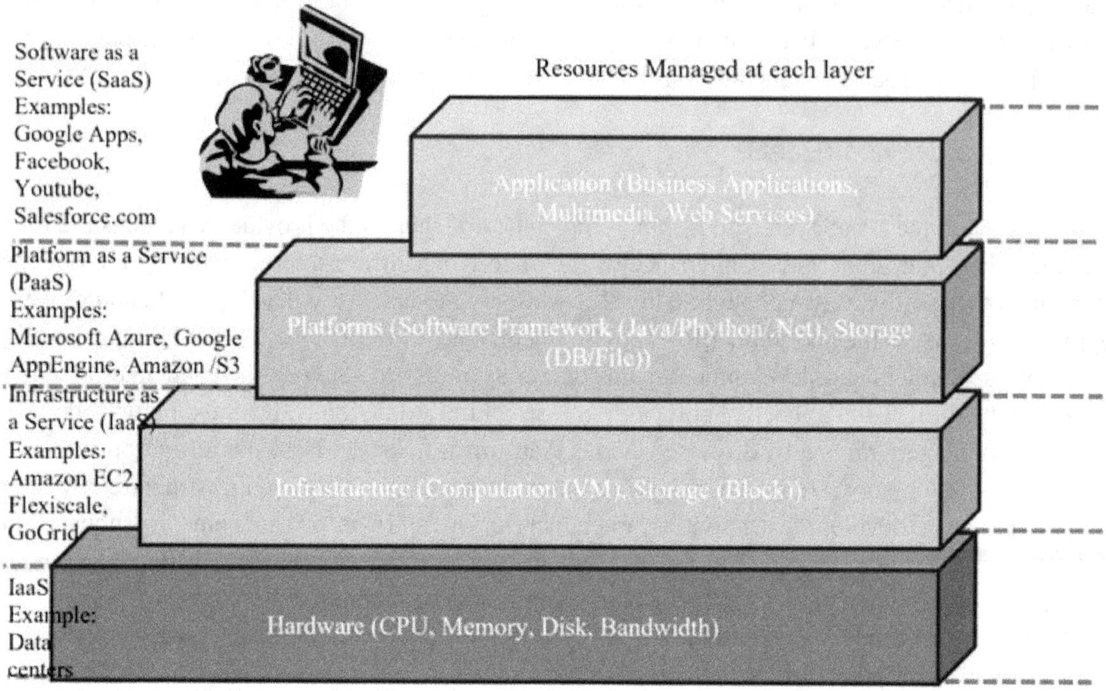

Cloud Environments

Cloud services are available as public or private resources, each of which serves different needs.

Public Cloud

The term "public cloud" refers to cloud services (such as virtual machines, storage, or apps) made available to organizations and consumers by a commercial provider. The commercial provider's hardware hosts public cloud resources, which consumers access over the internet. They are not necessarily appropriate for organizations in highly regulated areas, such as healthcare or finance, since public cloud environments may not adhere to industry laws governing consumer data. Microsoft Azure is one of the largest public cloud servers, owning and managing massive hardware and software infrastructure that you, as a user, may use online.

Private Cloud

The private cloud refers to cloud services that are owned and controlled by the organization that utilizes them and are only accessible to workers and customers of that organization. Private clouds enable organizations to exercise more control over their computing environment and stored data, which is especially important for organizations in highly regulated sectors. Private clouds are often seen to be

Figure 3. Cloud computing service models arranged as layers in a stack

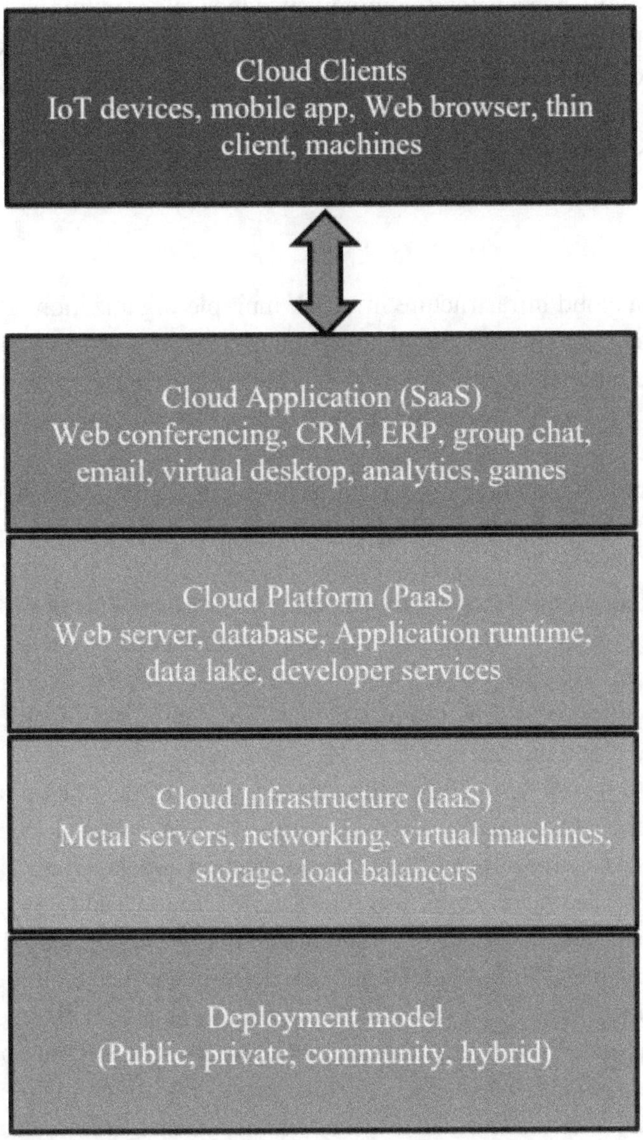

Cloud computing service models arranged as layers in a stack

more secure than public clouds since they are accessible over private networks and allow organizations to personally supervise cloud security. Public cloud providers may provide their services as apps that can be deployed on private clouds, enabling organizations to maintain their infrastructure and data on-premise while benefiting from the newest public cloud advancements. Private clouds are often housed in an organization's office building, however third-party services are sometimes used. They are much safer than public clouds.

Multicloud and Hybrid Cloud

Many organizations employ a hybrid cloud environment, which mixes public and private cloud resources to meet the computing demands of the organization while remaining in compliance with industry regulations. Multicloud deployments, which include more than one public cloud provider (for example, Amazon Web Services and DigitalOcean), are also widespread. Amazon Web Services, or AWS, is one of the largest providers of hybrid cloud solutions.

Community Cloud

A community cloud is a cloud infrastructure in which multiple organizations share resources and services based on common operational and regulatory requirements. The concept of a community cloud is akin to a community garden, where different individuals grow produce on a single piece of shared land. Community clouds are a recent phenomenon compared to other cloud models such as public, private, and hybrid clouds.

Members of a community cloud are organizations that have common business requirements. These requirements are usually driven by the need for shared data, shared services, or shared industry regulations. This means they're typically organizations in the same industry or departments of the same organizational body. In other words, a community cloud is an integrated setup that combines the features and benefits of multiple clouds to address the needs of a specific industry. To set up a community cloud, organizations can choose to host their own data centers and split the cost and responsibilities. This may be on-premise in the existing infrastructure of a member or even at peer facilities. Alternatively, they can also consider hybrid cloud providers.

It is common to come across 'cloud for government' or 'government cloud' among the offerings of most cloud vendors. These are community clouds that are specifically meant for government bodies. Government processes and services require constant communication and data transactions between multiple departments. They all operate on similar infrastructure, with resources and services shared across them.

COVID-19 has thrown the education sector into uncharted waters, essentially making face-to-face education close to impossible. The fast-spreading virus effectively moved all forms of learning online. This meant that universities and schools had to technologically catch up with other industries. A barrage of new services was required to connect administrators, teachers, students, and parents. This came with costs, licensing management, and hardware & software procurement and maintenance. Since not every university can afford this, community cloud is a solution that's being explored across various countries.

Besides regulatory compliance of daily transactions, the healthcare industry is also moving into the artificial intelligence (AI) space, processing huge volumes of sensitive data for predicting new trends in disease management and personalized patient care and determining the risk factors of various diseases. A community cloud would enable storage and accessibility of data from multiple sources. Figure 4 illustrates the different types of cloud environments, and Figure 5 illustrates the structure of the community cloud.

Advantages and Disadvantages of Cloud Computing

This section is going to examine the many benefits that may be gained by using cloud computing, and to look at a few of the drawbacks that might occur as a result of using this technology. There are excellent

Figure 4. The different types of cloud environments

Figure 5. The structure of the community cloud

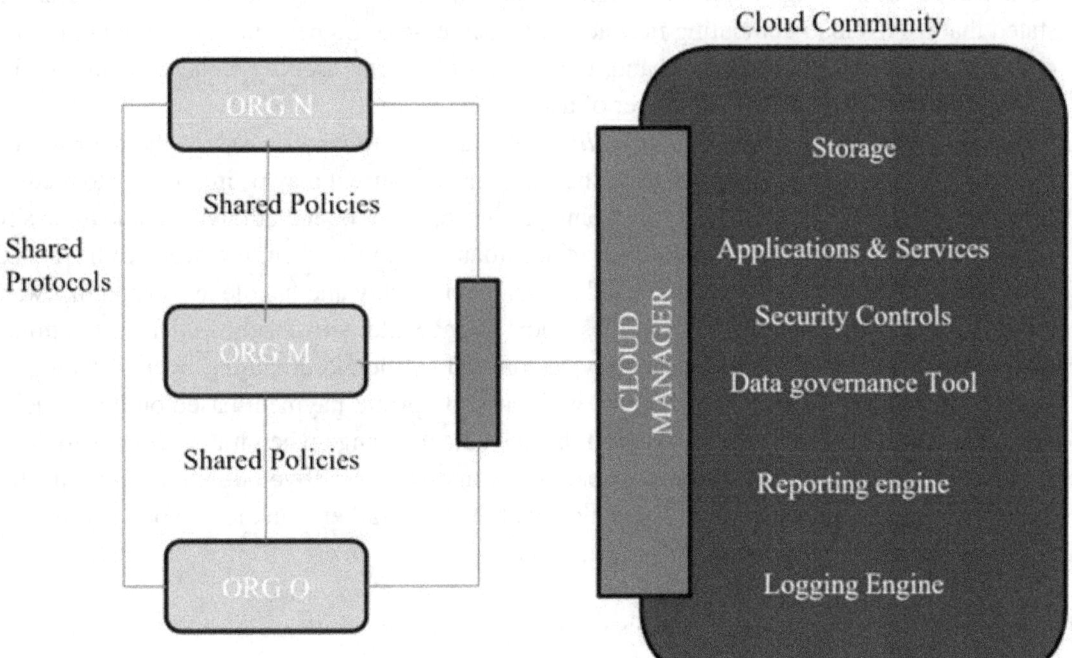

pieces and poor bits, just as there are with everything else in the digital arena. We are still learning the ins and outs of cloud computing since it is still a relatively new concept.

The following is a list of advantages of cloud computing:

- ***Rapidity:*** Users may get the resources they need in a matter of minutes, often with just a few mouse clicks.
- ***Increased Productivity:*** By using cloud computing, we are able to reduce the amount of work that is spent on day-to-day operations. We have no need for upgrades, and we also have no need to maintain our gear and software. In this way, the IT staff will be able to increase their productivity and concentrate on the accomplishment of business goals.
- ***Reliability:*** When it comes to maintaining the continuity of a company, backing up and recovering data is both more efficient and less expensive.
- Security: A great number of cloud service providers provide a complete suite of rules, technologies, and controls that improve the safety of our data.
- ***Lower Initial Costs and Lower Expenditures for Infrastructure***: Operating and maintaining a mainframe storage system may be quite costly. You will be able to save money, especially on the first expenditure, if you choose to hand over responsibility for this task to a third party that already has all of the relevant resources and the required level of experience. You will not have to be responsible for the maintenance of your own infrastructure, which will save you both time and money.
- ***Decrease carbon emissions***: Companies all around the globe are looking for ways to lessen the carbon footprint that their operations leave. When compared to the scenario in which each user had their own system, making use of a centralized cloud computing system that is expertly managed will result in a significant reduction in the amount of energy that is used. AWS has even stated that using cloud computing may achieve a decrease of 88 percent in the amount of carbon emissions produced. On the other hand, the amount of energy used by cloud computing will increase proportionately with the number of users.
- ***It is simple to scale up or down (Scalability)***: We are able to raise or reduce the demand for resources according to the requirements of the company. Because it may be impossible to predict the growth and success of apps as they are being produced, it can be incredibly valuable to be able to adjust your cloud computing capabilities in accordance with the changing needs of the business. Cloud computing was developed to be able to scale up quickly and handle expansion that was not foreseen. It also makes it possible to access more storage alternatives at the click of a button.
- ***Paying for use:*** The majority of the services offered by cloud computing operate on a pay-as-you-go approach. This indicates that you will have an upfront payment based on how much you believe you will consume, which you will then be able to change when it is necessary to do so. It is quite simple to reduce your storage capacity if you discover that you do not need as much of it as you had anticipated you would. The majority of the time, rather than the exception, your service provider will also notify you of this information.

The following are some of the drawbacks of cloud computing:

- ***Ongoing running costs***; despite the fact that you will have access to computing services for a fraction of the cost that it would cost to have your own, these charges may add up over the course of time. Your service provider may assess an additional fee if you have experienced unplanned growth and your storage consumption has exceeded the capacity of the system you are using.

- ***Security***: The usage of application programming interfaces (APIs) and credentials stored in the cloud results in an increase in the number of security vulnerabilities. These risks may come about due to the fact that you are entrusting a third party at an unknown area with potentially sensitive and confidential information, in addition to the fact that prospective attackers may be there. Find out why it is so important to have strong cyber security, and make sure you are acquainted with the basics of cyber security.
- ***Access to the cloud requires a connection to the internet***; without an internet connection, cloud storage cannot be accessed. This characteristic, by itself, may be rather restrictive, especially if you do not have the chance to connect with other people. If the connection to your cloud system is lost, your whole organization will be rendered unable to function. And mayhem is likely to break out in the event that there is no reliable backup mechanism in place.
- ***Vendor lock-in; It*** is when it becomes difficult or impossible to switch cloud computing service providers owing to the closed and proprietary nature of your existing computer systems. This may make switching providers difficult or impossible. Moving to a new cloud server is challenging in and of itself, but if your existing system has an excessive amount of structure, it may be considerably more challenging to make the switch.

Benefits of Cloud Computing

Cloud computing offers a multitude of advantages for individuals, businesses, developers, and various other organizations. The benefits of an activity or objective may vary depending on the user's specific goals and actions.

For Independent Developers

For independent developers, the accessibility of computing resources that were previously limited to large corporations and organizations has significantly improved. These resources can now be readily accessed through an internet connection, at a significantly reduced cost compared to their previous rates. Independent developers possess the capability to promptly deploy and engage in experimentation with cloud-based applications. Cloud-based applications, such as GitHub, have facilitated the process of code sharing, thereby simplifying the expansion and collaboration of developers on open source software projects. Furthermore, the advent of cloud-based educational platforms and interactive coding tutorials has significantly expanded the availability of developer education, enabling individuals without formal technical training to acquire coding skills autonomously.

The utilization of cloud-based computing and educational resources has effectively mitigated the obstacles associated with obtaining developer skills and implementing cloud-based applications. The necessity of formal training, company support, and substantial startup capital for individuals to engage in app creation and deployment has diminished a lot, thereby facilitating increased participation in cloud development. This development allows a broader range of individuals to enter the market, compete with established industry players, and engage in the creation and dissemination of apps as supplementary endeavors.

For Researchers

The significance of machine learning methodologies in scientific research has grown substantially, necessitating the integration of cloud computing in various scientific domains including astronomy, physics, genomics, and artificial intelligence. In many instances, the volume of data amassed and processed in machine learning and other research endeavors that heavily rely on data surpasses the computational capabilities of an individual researcher or the hardware resources available through the university. Cloud computing provides researchers with the ability to access and utilize computing resources in a flexible and cost-effective manner, based on their specific needs. Additionally, it facilitates seamless and instantaneous collaboration with research partners across the globe. The absence of commercial cloud service providers would impose limitations on the majority of academic machine learning research, confining it to individuals who have access to university-provided, high-performance computing resources.

For Industry and Business

Before the emergence of cloud computing, a significant number of businesses and organizations were obligated to acquire and uphold the necessary software and hardware infrastructure to facilitate their computing operations. With the increasing availability of cloud computing resources, numerous businesses have started to leverage them for purposes such as data storage, provisioning of enterprise software, and deployment of online products and services. Certain cloud-based innovations and adoptions exhibit specificity to particular industries. Within the healthcare sector, numerous clinicians utilize cloud services that have been specifically developed for the purpose of storing and exchanging patient information, as well as facilitating communication with patients. Educators and researchers in academia make use of cloud-based teaching and research applications. Furthermore, various cloud-based tools with broad applicability have been widely embraced across diverse industries. These tools encompass a range of functionalities, including productivity applications, messaging platforms, expense management systems, video conferencing solutions, project management software, newsletter platforms, survey tools, customer relations management systems, identity management platforms, and scheduling applications. The exponential growth of cloud-based business applications and infrastructure serves as evidence that the cloud is not solely revolutionizing business IT strategy, but is also a flourishing industry in its own regard.

There are numerous advantages associated with the utilization of cloud-based technologies in enterprises. Firstly, they have the potential to mitigate IT expenditures. In the process of adopting computational resource licensing, businesses allocate reduced investments towards the acquisition and maintenance of on-premises IT infrastructure. Cloud computing is highly flexible, enabling businesses to rapidly adjust the scale of computing resources they employ and incur costs only for the resources utilized. Nevertheless, the cost factor does not singularly dictate the adoption of cloud technology within the enterprise. The utilization of cloud-based technologies allows employees to conveniently access resources without the requirement of obtaining IT approval, resulting in improved efficiency within internal IT operations. Cloud-based applications have the potential to enhance collaboration within an organization by facilitating real-time communication and data sharing.

For Educators and Students

Cloud computing has additionally furnished students with tools to complement their educational pursuits and avenues to apply their technical proficiencies while acquiring knowledge. Cloud-based applications, such as GitHub and Jupyter Notebooks, provide students with the opportunity to develop technical skills through practical engagement with code and data. These platforms facilitate the study, deployment, and contribution to open source software and research projects that are relevant to their academic discipline and professional aspirations. Moreover, akin to autonomous developers, students have the opportunity to leverage cloud computing resources for the purpose of disseminating their code and applications to the general public, thereby attaining a sense of fulfilment through the practical manifestation of their acquired proficiencies.

Furthermore, cloud computing resources can be employed by students, researchers, and educators to enhance personalized academic infrastructure and exert increased authority over their computing environments. Certain scholars favor this methodology due to its capacity to allow them to select the applications they wish to utilize, tailor the functionality and design of these tools, and impose limitations or prohibitions on data collection. Furthermore, there has been a notable rise in the availability of cloud-based applications that are specifically tailored for academic use, serving as supplementary resources or alternative options to conventional academic information technology solutions. Voyant Tools offers a user-friendly approach for students and researchers to perform textual analysis on selected documents, without requiring coding skills. On the other hand, the HathiTrust grants users access to a vast digital library containing millions of volumes. Reclaim Hosting, Commons in a Box, the Modern Language Humanities Commons, and Manifold offer a range of specialized tools tailored for academic communities, encompassing educational resources, publishing platforms, and networking capabilities.

For Community Infrastructure

Certain individuals and communities choose to independently install and manage cloud-based software as a means to fulfil community needs and principles, tailor functionality, safeguard user data, and exert enhanced authority over their computing ecosystem. Open source software, exemplified by social media tools like Mastodon, video conferencing software like Jitsi, collaborative text editors like Etherpad, and web chat tools like Rocket Chat, present viable alternatives to Software-as-a-Service (SaaS) platforms. These alternatives address the common issues of restricted user control, compromised privacy, and limited oversight over the computing environment that are often associated with SaaS platforms. Although SaaS applications and social media platforms typically involve less administrative work, certain communities exhibit a preference for these alternatives due to ethical concerns surrounding the utilization of personal data and business practices associated with widely-used platforms and SaaS applications.

Uses of Cloud Computing

What you may not realize is that you're probably using a form of cloud computing right now. If you have been using an online email server, or you use Google docs, or if you even watch TV and listen to music on the internet, you have inadvertently been using forms of cloud computing. This fact is made all the more remarkable because even the earliest cloud computing systems are barely 10 years old. Cloud Computing may be applied to solve problems in many domains of Information Technology like GIS

(Geographical Information Systems), Scientific Research (Oliveira & Ogasawara, 2010), e-Governance Systems (Mukherjee & Sahoo, 2010), Decision Support Systems (Chan et al., 2009), Enterprise Resource Planning (ERP) (Foster et al., 2004), Web Application Development (Liladhar et al., 2010), Mobile Technology (Anand et al., 2010), etc. Yet already, organizations big and small have been migrating to the cloud owing to the many different things that cloud computing offers the user. Let's take a look at the different ways people use cloud computing.

Audio and Video Streaming

The process of transmitting and receiving audio and video content over a network, commonly referred to as audio and video streaming, has become increasingly prevalent in contemporary digital communication. The utilization of cloud computing has greatly simplified the process of engaging with an audience. There are individuals who may recall the time when Netflix's delivery method involved physical shipment of DVDs to their mailboxes. However, with the advent of cloud computing, the preferred movie of an individual can now be streamed to them on a wide range of electronic devices. Similarly, Spotify eliminates the need to visit libraries in order to borrow CDs.

Data Analysis

Is the process of examining and interpreting data in order to uncover meaningful patterns, relationships, and insights. Cloud computing enables the consolidation of dispersed teams and their respective datasets, regardless of their geographical locations. One can employ machine learning or artificial intelligence techniques to analyze the aforementioned data utilizing the Python programming language. This analytical process facilitates the discovery of various insights, thereby enhancing decision-making and problem-solving capabilities.

App Development

The field of application development encompasses the process of creating software applications for various platforms and devices. The utilization of pre-existing cloud computing infrastructures enables developers to significantly diminish both the duration and expenses associated with application development. Cloud-native technologies and methodologies enable the rapid development, deployment, and scalability of applications across web, mobile, and API platforms. Additionally, Python serves as a versatile programming language for these purposes.

Data Storage

The concept of data storage refers to the process of storing and preserving digital information for future use. The utilization described can be considered as one of the most prevalent applications of cloud computing. Large corporations inevitably accumulate vast amounts of data that necessitate appropriate storage solutions. The procurement of the necessary mainframe infrastructure for incorporating this voluminous dataset would entail significant financial costs. Cloud computing provides a storage solution that is characterized by increased cost efficiency.

Smart Cities

Cloud computing represents a contemporary advancement in the realm of smart cities, facilitated by the escalating abundance of diverse data generated by various applications. To effectively handle this magnitude of data, it is imperative to have increased storage capacity and enhanced processing power, and at the same time, keeping the data secured. The study (Kumar et al., 2023) introduced two classifiers, namely Support Vector Machine (SVM) and Novel K-Nearest Neighbors (KNN), which were employed for the analysis of data derived from a benchmark database sourced from the UCI repository. The SVM classification method was initially employed for the detection of intrusions. The study presented herein showcases the superior performance of the novel K-nearest neighbors (KNN) algorithm in terms of distance capacity, surpassing the outcomes of previous investigations. The evaluation of the accuracy of the results of both approaches is conducted. The findings indicate that the utilization of the suggested system yields the most favorable outcomes, as evidenced by the intrusion detection system (IDS) achieving a 98.98% accuracy rate.

Learning Systems

Cloud computing technology plays a significant role in academic activities, particularly in the realm of learning. The application of cloud computing in the context of learning offers various advantages, with one notable benefit being enhanced accessibility. Specifically, learners can access data at any time and from any location, provided they have an internet connection. Another notable advantage of cloud computing is its scalability, which enables the expansion of data storage capacity without the need for additional hardware investments, such as hard drives or similar equipment. Regarding security; Cloud computing service providers ensure the security of stored data. A research (Singh & Hemalatha, 2012) assert that in the event of a natural disaster, the data stored in cloud computing remains secure, even in cases where the hard drive or hardware sustains damage. The utilization of cloud computing in the realm of education offers numerous advantages. Cloud computing offers numerous benefits to all stakeholders involved, encompassing students, lecturers, IT personnel, administrative staff, and even the university board of directors. The perceived advantages of cloud computing vary significantly, encompassing benefits related to enhancing the quality of educational media, economic advantages such as resource conservation, and the ease of application and infrastructure maintenance (Ashari & Setiawan, 2011).

Cloud Based Design and Manufacturing

A Cloud-based design and manufacturing (CBDM) system can be classified as a knowledge management system (KMS) that facilitates the creation of knowledge repositories through the utilization of data and knowledge bases. The Knowledge Management System (KMS) facilitates the exchange of knowledge and resources between service providers and consumers. With the utilization of intelligent search engines and negotiation mechanisms through the cloud to serve global consumers (Wu et al., 2014).

Popular Cloud Computing Platforms

This section will provide an overview of several prominent cloud computing products.

A. Amazon Web Services (AWS)

Amazon Web Services (AWS) is a cloud computing platform provided by Amazon. Amazon Web Services (AWS) is a comprehensive suite of cloud services that facilitates the deployment of applications and services at affordable rates. It offers cloud-based computing, storage, and various other functionalities, empowering both organizations and individuals to access these resources as needed (AWS, 2023). The accessibility of Amazon Web Services offerings is facilitated through the utilization of HTTP, REST, and SOAP protocols. Amazon Elastic Compute Cloud (Amazon EC2) allows users to deploy and manage server instances within data centers through a variety of accessible APIs, tools, and utilities.

EC2 instances are virtual machines that function atop the Xen virtualization engine. Individuals have the ability to upload software and implement alterations to an instance subsequent to its creation and initiation. Once the necessary modifications have been carried out, it is possible to generate a novel machine image. Subsequently, it is possible to initiate an indistinguishable duplicate at any given moment. Users are granted extensive control over the entire software system on EC2 instances, which are perceived by them as physical hardware. However, this particular characteristic poses inherent challenges for Amazon in providing autonomous resource scaling. The EC2 service provides the capability to deploy instances in various geographical locations. Availability Regions consist of one or more Availability Zones and are distributed geographically. The geographical distribution of EC2 instances is structured into two components: Regions and Availability Zones. Availability Zones are discrete geographical areas that are intentionally separated from one another to minimize the impact of failures occurring in other Availability Zones. They are also strategically positioned to facilitate cost-effective and efficient network connectivity with other Availability Zones within the same Region.

The storage and retrieval of EC2 machine images is facilitated by Amazon's Simple Storage Service (Amazon S3). The S3 storage system organizes data into containers, with each container containing categorized objects. Every individual entity is composed of a range of data, spanning from 1 byte to 5 gigabytes. URI pathnames are the predominant form of object names. Prior to their utilization, buckets must be explicitly created. The container has the ability to be stored in any of the Regions that are currently available. Individuals have the ability to select a specific geographical area in order to enhance the speed of data transmission, reduce expenses, or adhere to legal obligations. The Amazon Virtual Private Cloud (VPC) facilitates a secure and efficient integration between an organization's pre-existing IT infrastructure and the AWS cloud. The Amazon Virtual Private Cloud (VPC) allows organizations to establish a connection between their current infrastructure and a collection of segregated AWS computing resources through a Virtual Private Network (VPN) connection. This connection enables organizations to expand their existing management capabilities, such as security services, firewalls, and intrusion detection systems, to encompass their AWS resources. Amazon CloudWatch is a valuable management tool for individuals utilizing cloud services. It effectively collects raw data from various AWS services, including Amazon EC2, and subsequently converts this data into easily understandable metrics that are updated in near real-time. The EC2 metrics encompass various measurements such as CPU utilization, network input/output bytes, disc read/write operations, and others.

B. ***Microsoft Windows Azure platform***

The Windows Azure platform, developed by Microsoft, consists of three distinct components, each offering a unique set of cloud-based services to users (Azure, 2023). Windows Azure provides a

Windows-oriented platform for the operation of applications and storage of data on servers located in data centers. SQL Azure offers cloud-based data services that are built upon SQL Server technology. Additionally, .NET Services offers distributed infrastructure services to both cloud-based and local applications. Applications running in the cloud as well as those operating on local systems can make use of the Windows Azure platform.

Windows Azure also provides support for applications developed using the.NET Framework and various other programming languages that are compatible with the Windows platform, such as C, Visual Basic, and C++, among others. Windows Azure has the capability to support a wide range of applications, encompassing various categories of computation. Web applications can be created by developers through the utilization of technologies such as ASP.NET and Windows Communication Foundation (WCF). These applications can function as independent background processes or can integrate both ASP.NET and WCF. Windows Azure facilitates the storage of data in various entities such as containers, tables, and queues. These entities can be accessed using the HTTP or HTTPS protocols, adhering to the principles of Representational State Transfer (REST). Both SQL Azure Database and Huron Data Sync are integral components of the SQL Azure platform. SQL Azure Database is a cloud-based database management system (DBMS) that operates on the Microsoft SQL Server platform. ADO.NET and other data access interfaces designed for Windows can be utilized to retrieve data. The information stored in the cloud can also be accessed using software installed on local servers. The Huron Data Sync software facilitates the synchronization of relational data across multiple on-premise database management systems (DBMSs).

C. IBM Cloud

The intricacy surrounding IBM's public cloud computing capabilities is attributed to the extensive utilization of diverse brand names by the company to represent its various cloud services (IBM Cloud, 2023). The term "IBM Cloud" serves as a comprehensive classification that encompasses IBM's hardware, software, and services aimed at assisting enterprises in constructing private clouds, in addition to its offerings of public cloud services. Ensuring the security of a company's data is of utmost importance. Cloud storage with automated backup offers scalability, flexibility, and a sense of security. IBM offers a range of Cloud Services, such as:

Compute Infrastructure — The compute infrastructure encompasses various components, such as metal servers, virtual servers, GPU computing, POWER servers based on IBM's POWER architecture, and server software. Metal servers are single-tenant servers that offer a high level of customization. Virtual servers provide a virtualized environment for running applications. GPU computing utilizes graphics processing units for enhanced computational capabilities. POWER servers are built on IBM's POWER architecture, offering specific advantages. Additionally, server software plays a crucial role in managing and optimizing the performance of these infrastructure components.

Compute Services — The Compute Services category encompasses various technologies such as OpenWhisk serverless computing, containers, and Cloud Foundry runtimes.

Storage —Storage encompasses various types, namely object, block, and file storage, along with the added functionality of server-backup capabilities.

Network —The network infrastructure encompasses various components such as load balancing, Direct Link private secure connections, network appliances, content delivery network, and domain services.

Mobile —The mobile offerings provided by IBM encompass various tools and packages aimed at facilitating the creation and deployment of iOS applications. These include the incorporation of IBM's

Swift tools, which enable the development of iOS apps, as well as the MobileFirst Starter package, designed to expedite the initial setup and launch of mobile applications. Additionally, IBM offers Mobile Foundation, a suite of back-end services specifically tailored for mobile applications.

Watson —Watson encompasses IBM's suite of artificial intelligence and machine learning offerings, collectively referred to as "cognitive computing." These include Discovery search and content analytics, Conversation natural language services, and speech-to-text capabilities.

Data and analytics — The domain of data and analytics encompasses a range of services, such as data services, analytics services, big data hosting, Cloudera hosting, MongoDB hosting, and Riak hosting.

Internet of Things — The Internet of Things (IoT) encompasses IBM's IoT platform along with its IoT starter packages.

Security — concept of security encompasses a range of tools that are designed to ensure the protection of cloud environments. These tools include a firewall, hardware security modules (which are physical devices equipped with key management capabilities), Intel Trusted Execution Technology, security software, and SSL certificates.

DevOps —The DevOps framework encompasses various components, such as the Eclipse Integrated Development Environment (IDE), tools for continuous delivery, and mechanisms for monitoring system availability. The application services encompass various components such as Blockchain, Message hub, and business rules, among other functionalities. Integration encompasses a range of tools designed to construct virtual bridges within hybrid cloud and multi-cloud environments. Notable examples of such tools include API Connect and Secure Gateway.

D. **Google Cloud**

Google Cloud is a cloud computing platform offered by Google. It provides a range of services and products that enable individuals and organizations to build, deploy, and manage applications and data. According to Google Cloud (Google Cloud, 2023), their platform is designed to support conventional web applications and is hosted in data centers managed by Google. At present, the programming languages that are endorsed are Python and Java. The Google App Engine supports various web frameworks, including Django, CherryPy, Pylons, web2py, and a proprietary web application framework developed by Google, which bears similarities to JSP or ASP.NET. Google is responsible for managing the deployment of code to a cluster, monitoring system performance, implementing failover mechanisms, and initiating the launch of application instances as required. The existing application programming interfaces (APIs) provide functionality for tasks such as storing and retrieving data from a non-relational database known as BigTable, performing HTTP requests, and implementing caching mechanisms. On App Engine, developers are granted read-only access to the filesystem.

E. ***Alibaba Cloud***

Alibaba Cloud, also known as Aliyun, is a prominent cloud computing service provider that offers a wide range of services and solutions to businesses and individuals. Alibaba Cloud, commonly known as Aliyun in Chinese, is a cloud computing enterprise functioning as a subsidiary of the prominent Alibaba Group (Alibaba, 2023). Alibaba Cloud provides cloud computing services to both external online enterprises and Alibaba's internal e-commerce ecosystem. The company's international operations are formally registered and have established their headquarters in Singapore. Alibaba Cloud offers

Figure 6. The cloud platform giant companies

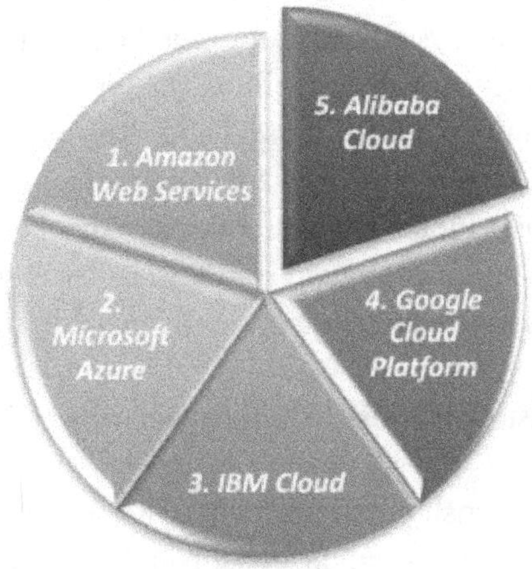

cloud services that can be accessed using a pay-as-you-go pricing model. The aforementioned services include elastic compute, data storage, relational databases, big-data processing, anti-DDoS protection, and content delivery networks (CDN). Based on Gartner's analysis, this particular company is recognized as the foremost cloud computing organization in China, as well as across the Asia Pacific area. Alibaba Cloud presently operates data centers across 24 regions and 74 availability zones on a global scale. Alibaba Cloud has been placed in the Visionaries' quadrant of Gartner's Magic Quadrant for cloud infrastructure as a service, worldwide, as of June 2017. Figure 6 depicts the cloud platforms utilized by prominent corporations.

Cloud Computing Real Life Implementation Examples

Cloud computing has emerged as a significant facet of contemporary society, exerting its influence ubiquitously, often without our conscious awareness. Cloud computing is the underlying technology that supports a wide range of services and apps that are commonly utilised in our daily lives, including messaging, streaming music, and video.

Presented below are several practical illustrations of cloud computing in real-world scenarios.

Netflix is a popular streaming service that offers a wide range of films, TV shows.

Netflix utilises cloud computing infrastructure to deliver streaming services to a vast global customer base. By utilising cloud servers to house its content, the organisation can guarantee dependable and adaptable distribution to a worldwide demographic.

Netflix employs a diverse range of cloud computing services and technologies, such as Amazon Web Services (AWS) and content delivery networks (CDNs). Netflix relies on Amazon Web Services (AWS) to fulfil the majority of its cloud computing needs, encompassing various aspects such as storage, processing capabilities, and data administration. Netflix utilises Content Delivery Networks (CDNs) in order to provide efficient and reliable distribution of its content to its user base. Content Delivery Networks (CDNs) store multiple copies of content in several global locations to facilitate user access from the nearest proximity.

The communication platform known as Slack.

Slack is a cloud-based messaging and collaboration tool that facilitates real-time communication and collaboration among teams. The system employs cloud computing technology to offer customers with enhanced scalability, reliability, and accessibility. The cloud infrastructure of Slack enables it to effectively accommodate a substantial volume of users and messages, while also facilitating convenient accessibility to its platform across various devices and geographical locations.

The Slack platform operates on a cloud-based architecture that has been specifically built to exhibit high availability and fault tolerance. The company employs a distributed system of data centres to provide continuous availability of its services, mitigating the impact of potential failures in any individual data centre.

Salesforce is a cloud-based customer relationship management (CRM) platform that enables organisations to manage services.

Salesforce offers customer relationship management (CRM) services via cloud computing technology. This enables enterprises to effectively handle consumer data, automate operational procedures, and optimise sales procedures.

Salesforce cloud computing encompasses the utilisation of diverse cloud services and technologies, which encompass:

Salesforce utilises Infrastructure as a Service (IaaS) providers like as Microsoft Azure and AWS to procure the foundational infrastructure necessary for its cloud-based platform.

Salesforce provides its software products in the form of Software as a Service (SaaS), which differs from conventional software installations on local devices.

Platform as a Service (PaaS) is utilised by Salesforce to facilitate the development and dissemination of distinct applications on their platform. This is achieved through the utilisation of PaaS technologies such as Force.com and Heroku.

Salesforce offers mobile applications to its users, enabling them to access their customer and sales data at any time and location.

The Google Cloud Platform (GCP) is a comprehensive suite of cloud computing services provided by Google. GCP offers a wide range of infrastructure and platform services, including computing.

The Google Cloud Platform (GCP) is a cloud computing platform offered by Google, which facilitates the development, deployment, and expansion of applications and services by leveraging a diverse array of computer resources. This particular instance can be classified as an illustration of cloud computing due to its provision of readily available access to a diverse array of computing resources, encompassing virtual machines, storage, networking, databases, and several other services. These resources are given through the medium of the internet.

An illustration of the utilisation of Google Cloud involves the construction and implementation of web apps. Software developers have the opportunity to utilise the computing resources provided by Google Cloud in order to host their application code and data. Additionally, they may take advantage of other services offered by Google Cloud, including as load balancing, autoscaling, and container orchestration, to effectively manage and optimise the performance and availability of their applications. In addition, users have the option to leverage Google Cloud's machine learning capabilities for the purpose of incorporating intelligent functionalities into their applications, such as the ability to recognise images or parse natural language.

The topic of discussion in this section pertains to applications used for the purpose of editing images.

Numerous cloud platforms provide consumers complimentary editing services for images. This cloud-based service provides a comprehensive range of image manipulation functionalities, including resizing, editing, cropping, and application of special effects, all accessible through a unified graphical user interface. In addition to the aforementioned services, cloud services include programmes that allow for the adjustment of contrast and brightness.

The cloud service application provides advanced and intricate functionalities for the payment of membership fees. The products are tailored to enhance user-friendliness for end-users.

Two well-known cloud-based picture editing tools are Fotor and Adobe Creative Cloud.

In the present era, the cloud computing paradigm provides a multitude of data storage applications. The cloud storage service allows customers to store information in a remote server. These types of clouds have the potential to be categorised as either a public cloud or a private cloud.

Data, files, and photos can be stored on cloud-based platforms. Cloud computing facilitates the exchange of information and enables collaborative efforts. The data stored in cloud computing systems can be effectively safeguarded and promptly backed up. Cloud storage services offer data format conversion capabilities.

Several data storage applications include DropBox, OneDrive, Box, Mozy, and Google suites.

The antivirus application is a software programme designed to detect, prevent, and remove malicious software from computer systems.

In addition to their primary functions, cloud services also offer supplementary features such as antivirus protection and support services. It facilitates the enhancement of the efficient operation of the system. Cloud-based antivirus software assists customers in periodically cleaning their systems.

These tools enable the detection, identification, and remediation of security risks arising from malware and various types of viruses. The presence of these qualities provides various advantages to the end-users. These applications are provided at no charge. The threat is detected and a report is transmitted to the cloud's data centre, thereby facilitating the resolution of the issue for the end-users.

Prominent instances of Cloud antivirus software encompass Kaspersky endpoint protection and Sophos endpoint protection.

Cloud service companies offer a multi-cloud strategy. The facilitation of interaction between entertainment applications and their intended audience is beneficial. The term "comprises" refers to the inclusion or incorporation of online gaming and entertainment services.

Google Stadia is a cloud-based gaming service that offers users the opportunity to engage in video gaming activities at a resolution of 4K, accompanied by a smooth gameplay experience of up to 60 frames per second. Project Atlas represents a prominent illustration of cloud-based entertainment applications.

These applications facilitate the establishment of immediate and seamless connectivity for online gamers, enabling them to immerse themselves in a fluid virtual gaming environment.

Challenges and Costs in Cloud Computing

Despite the numerous advantages offered by cloud computing, it is imperative to acknowledge the associated risks, costs, and ethical concerns that necessitate careful consideration. Certain issues in this context possess relevance for all users of cloud services, whereas others primarily pertain to businesses and organizations that utilize the cloud as a means of storing customer data:

Security: The utilization of cloud resources introduces potential security vulnerabilities that surpass those found in traditional on-premise data centers. This is primarily due to the reliance on application programming interfaces (APIs), cloud-based credentials, and on-demand services, which inadvertently facilitate unauthorized access for malicious actors. There is a need to determine the security measures employed by the cloud service provider to protect customer data against theft and other forms of attacks, as well as identify the practices or supplementary services that customers can adopt to enhance the security of their data.

Data loss: can occur in cloud services, similar to physically-owned or managed devices, as a result of various factors such as physical disasters, software bugs, unintended synchronization, user-generated errors, or other unforeseen complications. When deploying cloud services, it is imperative to ascertain the backup services offered by the provider and to acknowledge that these services may not be provided automatically or without cost. Alternatively, users have the option to personally execute backup procedures.

Data persistence: refers to the ability of cloud users to ensure the complete removal of personal data that has been provided to cloud service providers. Nevertheless, the procedures involved in eradicating data on cloud resources and ensuring its complete removal can prove to be time-consuming, intricate, or potentially unattainable. Prior to granting cloud service providers access to your data, it is imperative to ascertain their policies regarding data deletion, particularly in the event that you may desire to remove the data at a later stage.

Costs: While the utilization of cloud computing services offers significant cost advantages compared to owning and maintaining such services, it is important to note that expenses associated with cloud services can escalate rapidly as usage increases. When enrolling in a cloud service, it is advisable to review the billing particulars in order to ascertain the manner in which services are measured and to determine whether it is possible to establish limits or receive notifications when usage exceeds predetermined thresholds. It is also worthwhile to investigate the manner in which billing information is conveyed, as the billing practices employed by certain service providers may not always be readily comprehensible.

Vendor lock-in: is a concern that users of proprietary cloud services may face, as it entails the difficulty or even impossibility of transitioning to alternative providers once computing operations are tailored to a closed, proprietary system. The utilization of open source cloud solutions can mitigate this risk, as the adoption of open standards facilitates the seamless transition of computing operations between different providers. Nevertheless, it is imperative for cloud users to acknowledge that the process of migration necessitates considerable effort, careful planning, and specialized knowledge.

The utilization of data by companies: Cloud service providers have the ability to analyze customer usage patterns of their product, employ data for advertising purposes, customize advertisements to individual users, enhance machine learning algorithms through data training, and potentially engage in the sale of customer data to external entities. If one possesses concerns regarding the utilization of their personal or organizational data, it is imperative to ascertain the policies of the service provider in relation to its usage.

Loss of user control and visibility: The utilization of third-party computing resources in cloud computing introduces challenges regarding user control and visibility. This situation hinders cloud users from attaining comprehensive oversight and authority over their computing environments, thereby giving rise to a range of technical and trust-related issues. Monitoring and analytics tools can assist in addressing certain technical concerns by enabling cloud users to remain informed about the performance of their infrastructure. This enables users to promptly respond to any issues that may arise. Trust concerns, specifically those pertaining to a company's utilization of personal data, can be effectively mitigated through a comprehensive evaluation of the company's customer data policies and publicly available analyses regarding its data handling practices.

Complexity: The process of transitioning an organization's computing resources to the cloud is a highly intricate undertaking that necessitates thorough planning, the establishment of governance structures, and ongoing supervision to mitigate the risks of incompatibilities, data loss, and suboptimal cost management. While the utilization of cloud technology can indeed result in cost reductions for organizations in terms of computing infrastructure, it remains imperative for them to retain the expertise of IT professionals who can effectively oversee and administer infrastructure.

Regulatory standards and compliance: There are some limitations and requirements imposed by regulatory bodies and compliance standards. In several European nations, governmental regulations prohibit the physical relocation of customer's personal information and other sensitive data outside the jurisdiction of the state or country. To fulfil these stipulations, cloud service providers must establish a dedicated data center or storage facility within the nation to adhere to regulatory standards. The establishment of such infrastructure may not always be feasible and poses a significant challenge for cloud service providers.

Capabilities in Management. Despite the existence of various cloud providers, the administration of platform and the development of infrastructure is still in its early stages. Features such as "Auto-scaling" are considered essential for numerous enterprises. There exists significant potential for enhancing the scalability and load balancing capabilities currently available.

Risks and Security Concerns in Cloud Computing

Cloud computing and the data it generates are subject to a number of hazards and security issues. However, this section covers the topics of virtualization, cloud storage, and multitenancy, which are connected to cloud computing's data security.

A. Virtualization

Virtualization is a technique that involves the encapsulation of a fully functional operating system image within another operating system, thereby enabling the optimal utilization of the underlying system resources. The execution of a guest operating system in the form of a virtual machine within a host operating system requires the utilization of a dedicated component known as a hypervisor.

Virtualization plays an essential part in the realm of cloud computing, serving as a critical element that facilitates the realization of its fundamental principles. Nevertheless, virtualization for cloud computing data raises inherent concerns. One potential concern is the compromise of a hypervisor. If a hypervisor is exploited, it has the potential to compromise the entire system, including the data it contains. One potential concern associated with virtualization is the allocation and reallocation of resources. There is a potential risk of data exposure to subsequent Virtual Machines (VMs) if the operational data of a VM is written to memory and not erased prior to the reallocation of memory to the subsequent VM. An improved approach to utilizing virtualization represents a viable resolution to the previously mentioned challenges. Before allocating additional resources, it is imperative to exercise care and rigorously verify the authenticity of all data.

B. ***Public cloud storage***

Table 1. Cloud security categories

Category	*Description*
Network	The network encompassed various forms of attacks, including denial of service (DoS), distributed denial of service (DDoS), and others
Security Standards	Pertains to the prescribed measures necessary for safeguarding cloud computing systems against potential attacks.
Access Control	Encompasses various types of attacks, namely identification, authentication, and authorization attacks.
Cloud Infrastructure	Encompasses attacks that target each layer of the cloud, namely Software as a Service (SaaS), Platform as a Service (PaaS), and Infrastructure as a Service (IaaS). These attacks are specifically focused on the virtualization environment.
Data	Encompasses a comprehensive examination of security concerns pertaining to data, specifically focusing on topics such as data migration, data integrity, data confidentiality, and data warehousing.

Another security concern pertaining to cloud computing involves the storage of data on a publicly accessible cloud platform. Cloud computing frequently employs centralized storage, which may present an attractive opportunity for malicious actors seeking unauthorized access. Storage resources encompass intricate systems comprising both hardware and software components. In the event of a security breach occurring within the public cloud infrastructure, there is a potential risk of data exposure. It is commonly recommended to implement a private cloud infrastructure, if feasible, for the purpose of safeguarding highly sensitive data and mitigating potential risks associated with its storage and management.

C. Multiple Tenancy

Another significant danger to data in cloud computing is shared access or multitenancy. Multiple users are at risk since they are utilizing the same shared computer resources, such as the central processing unit (CPU), storage, and memory, among others. In such circumstances, there is always a chance that sensitive information may unintentionally reach other users. Due to the possibility that a single system flaw might provide another user or hacker access to all other data, multitenancy attacks can be particularly dangerous. These kinds of problems may be avoided by judiciously verifying people before granting them access to the data. In order to prevent problems with multitenancy in cloud computing, many authentication approaches can be utilized.

The attacks and security issues pertaining to cloud computing are categorized into five distinct groups, as outlined in Table I (Khalil et al., 2014):

Table II provides a comprehensive overview of attack names and their corresponding attack categories, as documented by researches (Khalil et al.,2014; Gruschka & Jensen, 2010; Singh & Shrivastava, 2012).

Security and Privacy of Data in Cloud Computing

Data encryption is just one aspect of cloud computing data security. The SaaS, PaaS, and IaaS service models, all have different requirements for data protection. Data at Rest, or data that is held in the cloud, and Data in Transit, or data that is flowing into and out of the cloud, are the two stages of data that are often at risk for security in clouds. The type of data protection techniques, procedures, and processes

Table 2. Known attacks on clouds

Attack name	*Category*
Denial of service	Network, cloud infrastructure
Flooding assault	Cloud infrastructure
Port scanning	Network
Malware injection attack in the cloud	Cloud infrastructure, Access
Virtual machine (VM) and hypervisor (HV) assaults	Cloud infrastructure
Man-in-the-middle cryptographic attack	Network, access management, data
Phishing	Cloud infrastructure, network, access
Cross VM side channels	Cloud infrastructure

determines the confidentiality and integrity of a given data set. One of the most important components of any information system is data integrity. Protecting data against unauthorized erasure, alteration, or fabrication is the general definition of data integrity.

The admission and rights of the managing entity to certain corporate resources guarantee that priceless information and services are not misused, misappropriated, or stolen. In a standalone system with a single database, data integrity is simply attained.

Through database constraints and transactions, which are typically handled by a database management system (DBMS), data integrity is ensured in the standalone system. To guarantee data integrity, transactions should adhere to the ACID (Atomicity, Consistency, Isolation, and Durability) criteria. Most databases can maintain data integrity and handle ACID transactions.

The usage of authorization is used to regulate data access. It is the process through which a system chooses the degree of access that an authorized user should have to resources that are under its control.

In a cloud system, maintaining data integrity involves protecting information integrity. Unauthorized users shouldn't be able to alter or lose the data. The foundation for offering cloud computing services like SaaS, PaaS, and IaaS is data integrity.

For consumers to save their private or sensitive data in the cloud, data confidentiality is crucial. Strategies for access control and authentication are used to guarantee data confidentiality. By enhancing cloud dependability and trustworthiness, the concerns with data confidentiality, authentication, and access control in cloud computing may be resolved. Customers should avoid directly storing their sensitive data in cloud storage since customers do not trust cloud providers and internal threats are almost difficult to eradicate for cloud storage service providers. The non-disclosure of data in the two states listed above is the most important issue.

A. *Data Resting*

Data that is stored in the cloud or that can be accessed over the Internet is referred to as data at rest. This applies to both live and backup data. As was previously known, because organizations do not have physical control of the data while using a private cloud, it may be quite challenging for them to safeguard data at rest. But by keeping a private cloud with strictly limited access, this problem may be overcome.

B. ***Transferring Data***

Data that is travelling into and out of the cloud is often referred to as being in transit. This information may be requested for usage at another location in the form of a file or database that is kept in the cloud. Data in transit refers to information that is present at the moment of upload to the cloud. Sensitive data in transit, such as usernames and passwords, may sometimes be encrypted. Data in transit also includes information that isn't encrypted. Because it must move from one place to another, data in transit is sometimes more vulnerable to danger than data at rest. There are several ways that intermediate software might intercept the data and, sometimes, modify the data as it travels to its destination. Encryption is one of the finest methods for securing data while it is being sent.

Controls for Cloud Security

There is a need for controls and measures to be taken to keep the data safe and secured inside the cloud. This section illustrates the measures and controls that can be used in the cloud. A collection of rules known as cloud security controls enables cloud architecture to protect users from vulnerabilities and to lessen the impact of harmful attacks. It is a general phrase that refers to all the procedures, standards, and laws that must be followed in order to safeguard a cloud computing system.

To measure and manage cloud security, there are five fundamental assumptions, which are:

1) *Network segmentation*, first

   When it is feasible, think about using a strong zone strategy to keep instances, containers, applications, and whole systems separated from one another. This will prevent any threat actor from lateral attack movement or improper system access.

2) *Access controls* based on the cloud

   Access control lists should be used in all elements of cloud computing. It is more crucial to develop and implement appropriate access controls for several premises than it is for one since services like databases might be created independently. Any virtual infrastructure, operating systems, programs, and even environment monitoring tools fall under this category. It is best to use the totally closed, or least privilege, security paradigm. Furthermore, just because something is on the cloud does not automatically indicate that it has to be publicly accessible. If any, just make the resources you really need accessible through the Internet; otherwise, secure them.

3) *Cloud computing with several tenants*

   Although segmentation and scalability are advantages of multi-tenancy, there is a risk of data leakage and erroneous boundaries (such reporting or data export) that may not be regulated in the cloud. In a multi-tenant system, take into consideration access restrictions and policy limits for any accounts that could have access to several tenants.

4) *Cloud Access Administration*

   Do not forget that these are not your machines. The idea of a crash cart is not always relevant. Therefore, you must control privileged access to all cloud resources while taking disaster recovery and any faults in your privileged access scope into account. Today, administrator accounts and password management software are used to control rights locally. The cloud requires the same ideas, but we don't want cloud administrator powers to be granted everywhere. The ideas of zones and access control lists from before would be invalidated by this. To make sure the access is acceptable, privileges must be role-based, properly allocated, and monitored for use.

5) *Threats and Vulnerabilities* in Cloud Computing

To discover the premise of vulnerabilities, this notion translates one for one from one premise implementations, although it may employ agents and other integration technologies. Once discovered, they must be given a high priority utilizing threat intelligence, then promptly remedied. No matter the computer environment, it is essential to complete this low-hanging fruit in a timely manner in order to maintain excellent cyber security hygiene.

Despite the fact that the architecture for cloud security has a wide variety of controls, most of them fall into one of the following groups:

A. ***Protective measures***

Attacks on a cloud system are to be decreased by means of these measures. Provide a notice to a possible attacker rather than protecting the cloud architecture or infrastructure.

B. ***Preventative measures***

These Controls are used to manage, fortify, and safeguard a cloud's vulnerabilities. Strong authentication of cloud users, for instance, increases the likelihood that cloud users are positively recognized and decreases the likelihood that unauthorized users may access cloud services.

C. ***Detective measures***

Internal controls used to identify issues with a company's procedures are referred to as "detective controls" in accounting. In order to achieve a variety of objectives, including quality control, fraud prevention, and legal compliance, detective control may be used.

D. ***Remedial measures***

These safeguards are intended to address dangers or faults and stop them from happening again. They start when unfavorable consequences are seen and maintain the "spotlight" on the issue until management can address it or fix the flaw.

Ethics in Cloud Computing

In the context of running a company, the factors and considerations that follow are ones that need to be taken into account.

Ethics in the Workplace: Users of cloud services would have to evaluate the ethical concerns connected with the firm they choose to support for their business requirements in view of the enormous effect that some cloud service providers have on global issues. This is because selecting cloud service providers have a major influence on these issues. Consumers of cloud services can select a provider that is in the most congruent alignment with their own personal ethical principles by investigating the operational procedures of companies in areas such as data acquisition, promotional activities, expressions of hostility, politics, the dissemination of inaccurate information, concerns regarding the environment, and labor practices.

Regulation: When it comes to the storage and use of client data, some businesses, such as healthcare, banking, and education, enforce rigorous laws, which may expressly prohibit the storage of such data in public cloud environments. Users of the cloud in a variety of different sectors commonly discover that it is required to adopt a hybrid cloud approach and utilize customized IT solutions in order to guarantee compliance with legislation relating to client data. Organizations are expected to conform to data protection and privacy laws relevant to the country in which their services are accessed, in addition to complying with industry rules. These laws may vary from jurisdiction to jurisdiction. An illustration of this may be seen in the situation of cloud service providers who cater to consumers located inside the European Union. These providers are required to conform to the restrictions that are defined in the General Data Protection legislation (GDPR), which is an example of a legislation that protects personal data.

Research Directions in Cloud Computing

Many concerns remain unresolved, while new ones arise coming from industry. Cloud computing research directions are listed below (Pradhy et al., 2011; Reddy et al., 2011).

- Service Level Agreements (SLA's)
- Cloud Data Management & Security
- Data Encryption
- Migration of virtual Machines
- Interoperability
- Access Controls
- Energy Management
- Multi-tenancy
- Server Consolidation
- Reliability & Availability of Service
- Common Cloud Standards
- Platform Management
- Mobile Cloud computing
- Quantum computing
- Hybrid cloud solutions
- Automation

Service Level Agreements (SLAs): SLAs let the cloud shut down or replicate a lower-priority application on numerous servers. Cloud customers struggle to evaluate SLAs. SLAs safeguard unwarranted consumers. Before signing SLAs, clients should evaluate data protection, downtime, and cost (Lin et al., 2009). Customers appreciate fast SLAs.

Cloud Data Management & Security: Cloud research encompasses data management. Infrastructure vendors safeguard data because service providers lack data center physical security. Service providers can only remotely setup virtual private cloud security. Infrastructure suppliers need privacy and auditability to safeguard data. Cryptography provides anonymity and remote auditability. Cloud VMs move, making remote attestation unreliable. Every cloud architecture layer needs trust mechanisms. Hadoop and MapReduce use GFS and HDFS. Since they don't support POSIX, older file systems and programs are incompatible. Several research addressed this (Zhang et al., 2010).

Data Encryption: Remember that security ranges from simple, cheap, and insecure to complex, costly, and restricted. Cloud providers and customers have several options. Cloud providers can be allowed to upload encrypted files to protect your cloud.

Migration of virtual Machines: Virtualization enables several computers to execute one program. Cloud computing may balance data center load with virtual machine migration. Virtual machine migration delivers reliable and fast data center provisioning. Xen-VMware "live" VM migration takes tens of milliseconds to a second. Complex VM movement prevents hotspots. Hotspot detection and migration are workload-insensitive. One solution is to convey in-memory state reliably (Wang et al., 2009).

Interoperability: Locked public clouds cannot connect. These networks cannot use cloud IT to save money and time. Cloud providers require industry standards for data portability and interoperability. One solution must automatically construct services, maintain VM instances, and connect with cloud-based and enterprise-based applications across programs and cloud providers.

Access Controls: Identity verification matters. Provider verifies password strength and frequency as well as Access logs. Strong, updated passwords and IT security safeguards are needed in internal systems and data.

Energy Management: Cloud data centers save energy without affecting SLA. Datacenters spend 53% on electricity and cooling. Data centers must reduce energy costs and meet environmental and regulatory requirements. Energy-efficient data centers are popular. Energy-efficient CPU and component shutdowns are common. Server consolidation and energy-aware task scheduling turn off superfluous workstations. Dynamic cloud performance and power management are understudied. The Global Energy Management Centre (GEMC) helps businesses track energy usage from several sources. These trends may lower energy usage, cost, and emissions. Cloud-based Remote Control Units serve global consumers (Wu et al., 2010)...

Multi-tenancy: Internet users may access cloud services from little widgets to large commercial apps with greater security requirements depending on the software vendor's infrastructure data. Multi-tenancy solves cost and other difficulties. Similar hardware, application servers, and databases impede answers. Application-layer multi-tenancy degrades infrastructure security and performance. Wait times rise while CPU time does not. The service must wait or cancel if HTTP server connections are exhausted (Subashini & Kavitha, 2011).

Server Consolidation: Cloud consolidation maximizes resource use and minimizes electricity and cooling. Cloud server consolidation saves energy and resources. Live VM migration may save energy by consolidating VMs from underutilized hosts. NP-hard vector bin packing is used in server consolidation models. Server consolidation shouldn't effect application performance. VMs may choke bandwidth, memory cache, and disc I/O. VM footprint modifications may aid server consolidation. Finally, resource congestion requires prompt response.

Reliability & Availability of Service: On-demand clouds can fail. Slow networks require reliable software, and on-demand software instability caused issues. Cloud-based programming avoids Gears, AIR, and Curl issues. These technologies link cloud applications to desktop storage and computation. 3D gaming and videoconferencing make cloud-based IT unstable.

Common Cloud Standards: Security certification encompasses technology, personnel, and operations. Jericho Forum promotes technical standards before ISO2 ratifies them. IISP certifies security experts. SAS 704 may use ISO 27001. Cloud accreditation is disorganized and hard.

Platform Management: Multi-tenant, elastic, scalable middleware concerns are addressed in a study (Lin et al., 2009). Cloud platforms enable app development and use. On-demand systems are PaaS. An on-premises software team uses pre-existing components. Operating systems control programs and storage, whereas other devices store remotely.

Mobile Cloud-Computing: Mobile cloud computing must support apps and compute power due to smartphone availability and advancements. Mobile cloud computing combines mobile and cloud computing. Khan and his colleagues (Khan et al.,2013) described mobile computing as cloud computing integrated with mobile devices to offer processing power, memory, and storage. Mobicloud computing was coined by Huang (Huang, 2011). Mobile cloud computing concerns apps, security, and uniform standards were discussed in a research (Khan et al., 2014). Smartphones may last longer with mobile cloud computing.

Performance, resources, and methods are mobile cloud computing problems (Akherfi et al., 2018). Standard design would boost mobile devices' cloud processing and storage power (Akherfi et al., 2018). Mobile cloud computing is crucial for online social network services including gaming, image processing, video processing, and e-business. Mobile cloud computing was important in many general polls. Fan et al. (Fan et al., 2011) stressed intelligent access techniques. Researches (Klein et al., 2010; Dinh et al.,2013; Guan et al.,2011) examined general mobile cloud concerns. Kovachev et al. (Kovachev et al., 2011) contrasted application models.

Quantum computing: Quantum has emerged as a prominent subject within the cloud industry, presenting a significant challenge to the current state of cloud computing and the potential to bring about a complete transformation. Service providers are engaged in fierce competition, and in this context, it is anticipated that Quantum Computing will emerge as a dominant force in the realm of cloud computing in the foreseeable future.

Hybrid cloud solutions: Hybrid cloud solutions are projected to emerge as a prominent trend in the field of cloud computing, alongside other anticipated developments. Furthermore, Hybrid Cloud Solutions are recognized for their dynamic nature, cost-effectiveness, and ability to adapt to the ever-changing demands of the market. Hybrid cloud solutions have emerged as a viable means to address the market demands that have been intensified by the increasing competition from large-scale enterprises.

Automation: The rapid and imperative rise in cloud adoption necessitates increased computational capacity for organizations, consequently leading to a surge in data and application resources. This would necessitate an increase in administrative positions and the undertaking of time-intensive responsibilities. The implementation of automation in task execution has the potential to decrease the occurrence of repetitive tasks, minimize errors, and enhance overall productivity. Hence, it is imperative for companies of varying scales to strive towards the automation of diverse operational procedures. The implementation of automation in cloud administration has the potential to streamline and optimize various tasks, resulting in cost and time savings for administrators.

Future Scopes in Cloud Computing

The subsequent subjects delineate the prospective areas of development within the field of cloud computing:

1. Advanced Security Measures

Cloud security incorporates the utilization of artificial intelligence (AI) and machine learning (ML) techniques to automate the processes of identifying and mitigating potential threats. The utilization of machine learning techniques facilitates the examination of global cloud transaction data. Artificial intelligence (AI) has an effect on the accuracy of temporal and functional indications. It is anticipated that forthcoming cloud formations will exhibit heightened intensity. Customers have the potential to cause cloud security breaches on certain occasions. The future of cloud security is envisioned to possess intelligent, automated, and reliable characteristics. Artificial intelligence (AI), machine learning (ML), and quantum computing are expected to be the driving forces behind its development.

2. The Internet of Things (IoT)

The Internet of Things (IoT) refers to the network of interconnected physical devices, vehicles, buildings, and other objects. One of the prevailing trends in the field of cloud computing is the integration of Internet of Things (IoT) platforms. Cloud computing plays a pivotal role in facilitating the success of the Internet of Things (IoT). It is anticipated that there will be a continual annual growth in the quantity of interconnected devices. Cloud IoT facilitates, as well as designs and implements applications. The Internet of Things (IoT) enables autonomous management of smart devices by remotely capturing data and providing real-time notifications for troubleshooting purposes. The Internet of Things (IoT) facilitates the implementation of monitoring protocols that can be utilized for intelligent predictions. The trend of cloud computing in the Internet of Things (IoT) is characterized by a significant emphasis on high levels of interaction and performance in terms of connectivity.

3. Multi-Cloud

The concept of multi-cloud refers to the practice of utilizing multiple cloud computing services from different providers simultaneously. The term "multi-cloud" refers to the utilization of multiple public or private cloud services simultaneously. Cloud service providers offer the aforementioned service. The utilization of multi-cloud architecture facilitates the distribution of workloads across multiple cloud platforms. Private clouds have the potential to store data that is of a sensitive nature. It is advisable to also allocate less critical tasks to the public cloud infrastructure. According to recent data, a significant majority of companies, specifically 93%, have adopted multi-cloud strategies. The utilization of multi-cloud architecture enhances security measures by emphasizing the prioritization of features, risk mitigation, and functionality, while concurrently minimizing the risk of vendor lock-in. The utilization of multi-cloud infrastructure offers a multitude of cloud options, owing to its inherent flexibility and ability to enhance the returns on cloud investments.

4. Edge Computing

The utilization of edge computing can be in lieu of traditional datacenter infrastructure. It is imperative for companies to establish data centers in close proximity to the source. The demand is effectively addressed by the implementation of edge computing. IBM, Dell, and Intel are intensifying their focus on edge solutions. There is an anticipated rise in the quantity of Internet of Things (IoT) devices that will employ edge computing as a means to manage data. The implementation of edge computing is necessary for the facilitation of distribution. The system stores data within its local storage. The data is stored in close proximity to the user rather than being stored on a centralized server. Edge computing has been shown to enhance performance and optimize bandwidth utilization. The advantages of fast insights and efficiency are evident in its ability to effectively manage and process large volumes of data generated by the Internet of Things (IoT). The implementation of 5G technology significantly enhances data transmission speeds.

5. Artificial Intelligence (AI)

Artificial Intelligence (AI) is a field of computer science that focuses on the development of intelligent machines capable of performing tasks that typically require human intelligence. Artificial intelligence (AI) is currently a prominent and widely discussed trend in the field of cloud computing. It is projected that the annual value of AI will reach 89 billion USD by the year 2025. This suggests that organizations that disregard this trend will lag behind. Artificial intelligence (AI) experiences growth and advancement through the utilization of cloud computing, resulting in the optimization and efficiency of various operational procedures. Artificial intelligence (AI) is responsible for the management and provision of insights in the field of cloud computing. Business enterprises strive to optimize their utilization of artificial intelligence (AI) and cloud computing services. Investing in AI necessitates a high level of technical proficiency, substantial computational capabilities, and substantial financial resources. Cloud-based solutions have the potential to enhance the accessibility of AI technology by rendering it more cost-effective.

6. Serverless Computing

Serverless computing is a paradigm in which cloud providers manage the infrastructure and automatically allocate resources for executing code, eliminating the need for developers to provision and manage servers. Serverless technology emerged as one of the top five rapidly expanding Platform as a Service (PaaS) solutions. The future is anticipated to witness a significant growth in the adoption and utilization of serverless computing. The utilization of serverless architecture enables enterprises to develop and deploy applications without the need for traditional server infrastructure. Cloud providers are responsible for the scalability, maintenance, and upgrading of their services. Amazon Web Services (AWS) offers a serverless architecture that encompasses the management of servers on which applications are executed. Serverless systems will experience rapid growth. Cloud services are procured on a demand basis, with pricing determined by the extent of utilization. Organizations may opt to utilize serverless hybrid cloud architectures. Serverless computing offers advantages to developers of all backgrounds by streamlining the process of system and application development.

7. The Expansion of Data Storage

The popularity of cloud data storage is expected to increase. The future of cloud computing is expected to enhance the capacity for data storage. The defining characteristics of cloud storage are its price and speed, which contribute to the provision of faster cloud storage solutions. Datacenters are expected to accommodate larger volumes of data, while Cloud companies are anticipated to enhance data security measures. The removal of storage levels will facilitate expedited retrieval. The integration of cloud storage with edge computing is anticipated. The presence of competition in the data center industry is expected to result in a reduction in prices, while the availability of affordable data storage solutions is anticipated to stimulate innovation.

CONCLUSION

In recent times, cloud computing has emerged as a compelling paradigm for the management and delivery of services via the Internet. The rapid emergence of cloud computing is significantly transforming the information technology sector, effectively transforming the longstanding concept of utility computing. Nevertheless, despite the considerable advantages presented by cloud computing, the existing technologies have not yet reached a level of maturity that allows for the complete realization of its potential. The research community has recently begun to address several significant challenges in this field, such as automatic resource provisioning, power management, and security management. Cloud technologies provide a diverse range of prospects for businesses, individual developers, researchers, educators, and students. Through an extensive understanding of the diverse array of services, models, advantages, and potential drawbacks provided by cloud computing, individuals can make judicious choices regarding the optimal utilization of its offerings.

Thus, there stays a substantial scope for researchers to generate pioneering contributions in this domain, thereby exerting a substantial influence on its advancement within the industry. This chapter encompasses various subjects pertaining to cloud computing, covering fundamental concepts, architectural designs, notable characteristics, key technologies, as well as security and ethical considerations, along with research directions. Given the recent development of cloud computing technology, this chapter offers a comprehensive examination of the challenges associated with cloud computing. Moreover, it serves as a foundation for future investigations in this domain.

REFERENCES

Akherfi, K., Gerndt, M., & Harroud, H. (2018). Mobile cloud computing for computation offloading: Issues and challenges. *Applied Computing and Informatics*, *14*(1), 1–16. doi:10.1016/j.aci.2016.11.002

Alipourfard, O. (2017). Cherrypick: Adaptively unearthing the best cloud configurations for big data analytics. *14th {USENIX} Symposium on Networked Systems Design and Implementation ({NSDI} 17)*. Usenix.

Anand, S., Gupta, S., Fatnani, S., Sharma, V., & Jain, D. (2010). Article: Semantic Cloud for Mobile Technology. *International Journal of Computer Applications*, *8*(12), 1–4. doi:10.5120/1260-1795

Armbrust, M., Fox, A., Griffith, R., Joseph, A. D., Katz, R., Konwinski, A., Lee, G., Patterson, D., Rabkin, A., Stoica, I., & Zaharia, M., (2010). A view of cloud computing, Communications. *ACM Magazine, 53*, 50-58.

Ashari, A., & Setiawan, H. (2011). Cloud Computing: Solusi ICT? *Jurnal Sitem Informasi, JSI.*, *3*(2), 336–345.

Chan, W. K., Mei, L., & Zhang, Z. (2009). Modeling and testing of cloud applications. *Proceedings of 2009 IEEE Asia-Pacific Services Computing Conference (APSCC 2009)*, (Singapore, December 7-11, 2009), IEEE Computer Society Press. 10.1109/APSCC.2009.5394131

Damblin, G., Couplet, M., & Iooss, B. (2013). Numerical studies of space filling designs: Optimization of Latin Hypercube Samples and subprojection properties. *Journal of Simulation*, *7*(4), 276–289. doi:10.1057/jos.2013.16

Delimitrou, C., & Kozyrakis, C. (2014). Quasar: Resource-efficient and qos-aware cluster management. In ACM SIGARCH [ACM.]. *Computer Architecture News*, *42*(1), 127–144. doi:10.1145/2654822.2541941

Dinakarrao, S. M. P. (2019). Lightweight Node-level Malware Detection and Network-level Malware Confinement in IoT Networks. 2019 Design, Automation & Test in Europe Conference & Exhibition (DATE). IEEE.

Dinh, H. T., Lee, C., Niyato, D., & Wang, P. (2013). A survey of mobile cloud computing: Architecture, applications, and approaches. *Wireless Communications and Mobile Computing*, *13*(18), 1587–1611. doi:10.1002/wcm.1203

Duan, Y., Fu, G., Zhou, N., Sun, X., Narendra, N., & Hu, B. (2015). Everything as a Service (XaaS) on the Cloud: Origins, Current and Future Trends. *2015 IEEE 8th International Conference on Cloud Computing*. IEEE. 10.1109/CLOUD.2015.88

Fan, X., Cao, J., & Mao, H. (2011). A survey of mobile cloud computing. *ZTE Communications*, *9*(1), 4–8.

Ferdman, M., Adileh, A., Kocberber, O., Volos, S., Alisafaee, M., Jevdjic, D., Kaynak, C., Popescu, A. D., Ailamaki, A., & Falsafi, B. (2012). Clearing the clouds: a study of emerging scale-out workloads on modern hardware. In ACM SIGPLAN Notices, 47, 37–48. ACM. doi:10.1145/2150976.2150982

Ferguson, A. D., Bodik, P., Kandula, S., Boutin, E., & Fonseca, R. (2012). Jockey: guaranteed job latency in data parallel clusters. In *Proceedings of the 7th ACM European conference on Computer Systems*, (pp. 99–112). ACM. 10.1145/2168836.2168847

Foster, S., Hawking, P., & Stein, A. (2004). Change Management: The Forgotten Critical Success Factor in Enterprise Wide System Implementations. *Proc. Of the 15th Australasian Conference on Information Systems (ACIS)*. IEEE.

Google cloud, (2023), Available: https://cloud.google.com/appengine/docs/the-appengine-environments

Gruschka, N., & Jensen, M. (2010). Attack surfaces: A taxonomy for attacks on cloud services. *Proc. 2010 IEEE 3rd Int. Conf. Cloud Comput. CLOUD 2010*, (pp. 276–279). IEEE. 10.1109/CLOUD.2010.23

Guan, L., Ke, X., Song, M., & Song, J. (2011). A survey of research on mobile cloud computing. In S. Xu, W. Du, & R. Lee (Eds.), *2011 10th IEEE/ACIS International Conference on Computer and Information Science* (pp. 387–392). Washington, DC: IEEE. 10.1109/ICIS.2011.67

Hsu, C.-J., Nair, V., Freeh, V.W., & Menzies, T. (2017). *Low level augmented Bayesian optimization for finding the best cloud VM.*

Huang, B., Boehm, M., Tian, Y., Reinwald, B., Tatikonda, S., & Frederick, R. R. (2015). Resource elasticity for largescale machine learning. In *Proceedings of the 2015 ACM SIGMOD International Conference on Management of Data*, (pp. 137–152). ACM. 10.1145/2723372.2749432

Huang, D. (2011). Mobile cloud computing. IEEE ComSoc Multimedia Communications Technical Committee (MMTC). *E-Letter*, *6*(10), 27–31.

Jalaparti, V., Ballani, H., Costa, P., Karagiannis, T., & Rowstron, A. (2012). Bridging the tenant-provider gap in cloud services. In *Proceedings of the Third ACM Symposium on Cloud Computing*. ACM. 10.1145/2391229.2391239

Khalil, I., Khreishah, A., & Azeem, M. (2014). Cloud Computing Security: A Survey. *Computers*, *3*(1), 1–35. doi:10.3390/computers3010001

Khan, A. R., Othman, M., Madani, S. A., & Khan, S. U. (2013). A survey of mobile cloud computing application models. *IEEE Communications Surveys and Tutorials*, *16*(1), 393–413. doi:10.1109/SURV.2013.062613.00160

Klein, A., Mannweiler, C., Schneider, J., & Schotten, H. D. (2010). Access schemes for mobile cloud computing. In *2010 Eleventh International Conference on Mobile Data Management* (pp. 387–392). IEEE. 10.1109/MDM.2010.79

Kovachev, D., Cao, Y., & Klamma, R. (2011). *Mobile cloud computing: A comparison of application models*. arXiv preprint.

Kumar, A., Kan, S. B., Pandey, S. K., Shankar, A., Maple, C., Mashat, A., & Malibari, A. A. (2023). Development of a cloud-assisted classification technique for the preservation of secure data storage in smart cities. *Journal of Cloud Computing (Heidelberg, Germany)*, *12*(1), 92. doi:10.1186/s13677-023-00469-9

Liladhar, R. R., & Ujwal, A. L. (2010). Article: Implementation of Cloud Computing on Web Application. [Published By Foundation of Computer Science.]. *International Journal of Computer Applications*, *2*(8), 28–32. doi:10.5120/685-964

Lin, H. C., ShivnathBabu, J. S. C., & Parekh, S.S. (2009). *Automated Control in Cloud Computing: Opportunities and Challenges*. Proc. of the 1st Workshop on Automated control for data centers and clouds, New York, NY, USA.

Makrani, H. M. (2014). Evaluation of software-based fault tolerant techniques on embedded OS's components. *Proceedings of the International Conference on Dependability (DEPEND'14)*. IEEE.

Makrani, H. M. (2018). Compressive Sensing on Storage Data: An Effective Solution to Alleviate I/0 Bottleneck in Data-Intensive Workloads. *2018 IEEE 29th International Conference on Applicationspecific Systems, Architectures and Processors (ASAP)*. IEEE. 10.1109/ASAP.2018.8445131

Makrani, H. M. (2019). XPPE: cross-platform performance estimation of hardware accelerators using machine learning. *Proceedings of the 24th Asia and South Pacific Design Automation Conference*. ACM. 10.1145/3287624.3288756

Makrani, H. M., & Homayoun, H. (2017). Memory requirements of hadoop, spark, and MPI based big data applications on commodity server class architectures. *2017 IEEE International Symposium on Workload Characterization (IISWC)*. IEEE. 10.1109/IISWC.2017.8167763

Malik, M. (2019). ECoST: Energy-Efficient Co-Locating and Self Tuning MapReduce Applications. *Proceedings of the 48th International Conference on Parallel Processing*. ACM. 10.1145/3337821.3337834

Malik, M., Tullsen, D. M., & Homayoun, H. (2017). Co-Locating and concurrent fine-tuning MapReduce applications on micro servers for energy efficiency. *2017 IEEE International Symposium on Workload Characterization (IISWC).* IEEE. 10.1109/IISWC.2017.8167753

Mell, P., & Grance, T. (2011). *The NIST Definition of Cloud Computing (Technical report).* National Institute of Standards and Technology: U.S. Department of Commerce. Special publication 800-145.

Montazerolghaem, A., Yaghmaee, M. H., & Leon-Garcia, A. (2020). Green Cloud Multimedia Networking: NFV/SDN Based Energy-Efficient Resource Allocation". *IEEE Transactions on Green Communications and Networking*, *4*(3), 873–889. doi:10.1109/TGCN.2020.2982821

Morton, K., Balazinska, M., & Grossman, D. (2010). Paratimer: a progress indicator for mapreduce dags. In *Proceedings of the 2010 ACM SIGMOD International Conference on Management of data*, (pp. 507–518). ACM. 10.1145/1807167.1807223

Mukherjee, K., & Sahoo, G. (2010). Article: Cloud Computing: Future Framework for e-Governance. *International Journal of Computer Applications*, *7*(7), 31–34. doi:10.5120/1262-1613

Namazi, M. (2019). Mitigating the Performance and Quality of Parallelized Compressive Sensing Reconstruction Using Image Stitching. *Proceedings of the 2019 on Great Lakes Symposium on VLSI.* ACM. 10.1145/3299874.3317991

Neeraja, J., Yadwadkar, B. H., Gonzalez, J. E., Smith, B., & Katz, R. H. (2017). Selecting the best VM across multiple public clouds: a data-driven performance modeling approach. In *Proceedings of the 2017 Symposium on Cloud Computing*, (pp. 452–465). ACM.

Neshatpour, K. (2018). Design Space Exploration for Hardware Acceleration of Machine Learning Applications in MapReduce. *2018 IEEE 26th Annual International Symposium on Field-Programmable Custom Computing Machines (FCCM).* IEEE. 10.1109/FCCM.2018.00055

Novakovi, D., Vasic, N., Novakovic, S., Kostic, D., & Bianchini, R. (2013). Deepdive: Transparently identifying and man- aging performance interference in virtualized environments. In *Presented as part of the 2013 USENIX Annual Technical Conference (USENIX ATC 13).* USENIX.

Oliveira, D., & Ogasawara, E. (2010). Article: Is Cloud Computing the Solution for Brazilian Researchers? *International Journal of Computer Applications*, *6*(8), 19–23. doi:10.5120/1096-1432

Padhy, R.P., Patra, M., & Satapathy, S.C., (2011). Cloud Computing: Security Issues & Research Challenges. *IJCSITS, 1*(2), 136-146.

Pring. (2009). *Forecast: Sizing the cloud; understanding the opportunities in cloud services, Gartner Inc*. Tech.

Ray, P. P. (2018). An Introduction to Dew Computing: Definition, Concept and Implications. *IEEE Access : Practical Innovations, Open Solutions*, *6*, 723–737. doi:10.1109/ACCESS.2017.2775042

Reddy, K.V., Thirumal-Rao, B., Reddy, L.R.R., & SaiKiran, P., (2011). Research Issues in Cloud Computing. *Global Journal of Computer Science and Technology, 11*(11).

Sayadi, H. (2017). Machine learning-based approaches for energy efficiency prediction and scheduling in composite cores architectures. *2017 IEEE International Conference on Computer Design (ICCD)*. IEEE. 10.1109/ICCD.2017.28

Sayadi, H. (2018). Customized machine learning-based hardware assisted malware detection in embedded devices. *2018 17th IEEE International Conference On Trust, Security And Privacy In Computing And Communications/12th IEEE International Conference On Big Data Science And Engineering (TrustCom/BigDataSE)*. IEEE. 10.1109/TrustCom/BigDataSE.2018.00251

Sayadi, H., Makrani, H. M., Dinakarrao, S. M. P., Mohsenin, T., Sasan, A., Rafatirad, S., & Homayoun, H. (2019). *2SMaRT: A Two-Stage Machine Learning-Based Approach for Run-Time Specialized Hardware-Assisted Malware Detection. 2019 Design, Automation & Test in Europe Conference & Exhibition (DATE)*. IEEE.

Sayadi, H., Manoj, S. P. D., Amir Houmansadr, A., Rafatirad, S., & Homayoun, H. (2018). Comprehensive assessment of run-time hardware-supported malware detection using general and ensemble learning. *CF '18: Proceedings of the 15th ACM International Conference on Computing Frontiers,* (pp. 212–215). ACM. 10.1145/3203217.3203264

Shi, J., Zou, J., Lu, J., Cao, Z., Li, S., & Wang, C. (2014). MRTuner: A toolkit to enable holistic optimization for MapReduce jobs. *Proceedings of the VLDB Endowment International Conference on Very Large Data Bases*, *7*(13), 1319–1330. doi:10.14778/2733004.2733005

Singh, A., & Hemalatha, M. (2012). Cloud Computing for Academic Environment. *International Journal of Information and Communication Technology Research*, *2*(2), 98–101.

Singh, A., & Shrivastava, M. (2012). Overview of Attacks on Cloud Computing. *Int. J. Eng. Innov. Technol.*, *1*(4), 321–323.

ADDITIONAL READING

Subashini, S., & Kavitha, V. (2011). A survey on security issues in service delivery models of cloud computing|| [Academic Press Ltd., UK.]. *Journal of Network and Computer Applications*, *34*(1), 1–11. doi:10.1016/j.jnca.2010.07.006

Tang, L., Mars, J., Vachharajani, N., Hundt, R., & Soffa, M. L. (2011). The impact of memory subsystem resource sharing on datacenter applications. In ACM SIGARCH [ACM.]. *Computer Architecture News*, *39*(3), 283–294. doi:10.1145/2024723.2000099

Venkataraman, S., Yang, Z., Franklin, M., Recht, B., & Stoica, I. (2016). Ernest: efficient performance prediction for largescale advanced analytics. In *13th USENIX Symposium on Networked Systems Design and Implementation (NSDI 16),* (pp. 363–378). IEEE.

Wang, C., Wang, Q., Ren, K., & Lou, W. (2009). Ensuring Data Storage Security in Cloud Computing. *17th International workshop on Quality of Service.*

Whaley, R. C., Petitet, A., & Dongarra, J.J., (2001). Automated empirical optimizations of software and the atlas project. *Parallel computing, 27*(1- 2):3–35.

Wray, J. (2014). Where's The Rub: Cloud Computing's Hidden Costs". *Forbes*.

Wu, D., Rosen, D. W., & Schaefer, D. (2014). *Cloud-Based Design and Manufacturing: Status and Promise, Cloud-Based Design and Manufacturing*. Springer.

Wu, H., Ding, Y., Winer, C., & Yao, L. (2010). *Network Security for Virtual Machines in Cloud Computing*. 5th Int'l Conference on Computer Sciences and Convergence Information Technology, Seoul.

Zhang, X., Wuwong, N., Li, H., & Zhang, X. J. (2010). Information Security Risk Management Framework for the Cloud Computing Environments. In *Proceedings of 10th IEEE International Conference on Computer and Information Technology*, (pp. 1328- 1334). IEEE.

KEY TERMS AND DEFINITIONS

Atomicity, Consistency, Isolation, and Durability (ACID): This is a set of properties of database transactions. It is a term from database theory and describes rules and procedures for data transactions.

Chartered Institute of Information Security: Formerly the Institute of Information Security Professionals IISP), this is an independent, not-for-profit body governed by its members.

Content Delivery Network (CDN): This it is a network of servers that are geographically distributed to speed up the delivery of web content by caching copies of files or facilitating dynamic content in servers closer to users than the host server, which is where the website originates.

Distributed Denial of Service (DDOS): This is a malicious attempt to make a server or a network resource unavailable to users, usually by temporarily interrupting or suspending the services of a host connected to the internet.

Enterprise Resource Planning (ERP): It is a type of software system that helps organizations automate and manage core business prosses for optimal performance.

Google File System (GFS): It is designed by Google, while HDFS is an open source version of distributed file system that referenced GFS.

Hadoop Distributed File System (HDFS): This is an open source implementation of the GFS architecture that is also available on the Amazon EC2 cloud platform.

Hypertext Transfer Protocol (HTTP): This is an application layer protocol in the internet protocol suite model for distributed, collaborative, hypermedia information systems. Also, it is the foundation of data communication for the world wide web.

IBM Power Architecture: This is a reduced instruction set computer (RISC) instruction set architecture (ISA) developed by IBM. The name is an acronym for performance optimization with enhanced RISC.

Jericho Forum: This promotes technical standards before ISO2 ratifies them. The Jericho Forum was an international group working to define and promote de-parameterization.

Online Analytical Processing (OLAP): This is one type of data processing systems, uses data to gain valuable insights, which is used to solve data problems.

Online Transaction Processing (OLTP): This is one type of data processing systems, is purely operational, and is used to solve data problems.

Representational State Transfer (REST): This is a web service communication protocol.

Service Level Agreement (SLA): It is an agreement between a service provider and a customer.

Service Level Objectives (SLOs): These are used to quantifiably measure customer experience and happiness, which directly impacts the business.

Simple Object Access Protocol (SOAP): This is a web service communication protocol. It was long the standard approach to web service interfaces, but it was dominated by REST in recent years, with REST now representing more than 70% of public APIs (Application Programming Interfaces).

Structured Query Language (SQL): This is a standardized programming language that is used to create, manage, and retrieve data stored in a relational database management system (RDBMS). A RDBMS is a type of database management system (DBMS) that stores inter-related data in tables and allows SQL queries to access and manipulate the data.

Virtual Machine (VM): This is the virtualization or emulation of a computer system. Virtual machines are based on computer architectures and provide the functionality of a physical computer. Their implementations may involve specialized hardware, software, or a combination of the two.

Windows Communication Foundation (WCF): This is a framework for building service oriented applications. Using WCF, you can send data as asynchronous messages from one service endpoint to another.

Chapter 2
Paving the Path to a Sustainable Digital Future With Green Cloud Computing

Kassim Kalinaki
https://orcid.org/0000-0001-8630-9110
Islamic University in Uganda, Uganda

Musau Abdullatif
https://orcid.org/0000-0002-2654-3885
Uganda Revenue Authority, Uganda

Sempala Abdul-Karim Nasser
Uganda Revenue Authority, Uganda

Ronald Nsubuga
Pride Data Solutions, Uganda

Julius Kugonza
Pride Data Solutions, Uganda

ABSTRACT

Amidst an era marked by a relentless surge in digital data and computational demands, the imperative for eco-conscious and sustainable computing solutions has reached unprecedented significance. This study delves into the emerging realm of green cloud computing (GCC), a pivotal catalyst in cultivating a greener digital tomorrow. To nurture a sustainable digital frontier, this research investigates various GCC strategies encompassing efficient data center designs, resource optimization techniques, and innovative virtualization practices. Additionally, the authors scrutinize real-world instances of industry leaders embracing sustainable energy sources. Furthermore, they shed light on the obstacles within eco-friendly cloud computing while illuminating forthcoming trends for the triumphant integration of sustainable and eco-friendly technologies. This study offers profound insights for researchers, students, and stakeholders alike.

DOI: 10.4018/979-8-3693-0900-1.ch002

INTRODUCTION

The dawn of the 21st century ushered in an unprecedented digital transformation era. The Internet seamlessly integrated into our daily lives, business operations, and scientific endeavors, resulting in an insatiable demand for data storage, computational power, and connectivity (Alouffi et al., 2021; Kalinaki, Thilakarathne, et al., 2023; Katal et al., 2023; Shafik & Kalinaki, 2023). Traditional computing infrastructures struggled to keep pace with this ever-escalating demand, leading to a paradigm shift in the provisioning and utilization of computing resources. From this upheaval emerged cloud computing, a technological revolution that would reshape the IT industry by offering scalable, on-demand access to computational resources via the World Wide Web (Golightly et al., 2022; Kalinaki, Namuwaya, et al., 2023). Cloud computing, characterized by its ability to deliver a diverse array of services, including infrastructure as a service (IaaS), platform as a service (PaaS), and software as a service (SaaS), hosts these services in colossal data centers housing thousands of servers and networking equipment (Ullah Khan et al., 2022). This transformative approach enables users and organizations to access these services remotely, obviating the necessity for extensive on-premises infrastructure.

As the embrace of cloud computing surged, data centers multiplied to support the burgeoning demand for computational resources. These data centers are the linchpin of cloud infrastructure, serving as the tangible facilities that house servers, storage devices, and networking equipment (Tiwari et al., 2022). They are indispensable for the seamless delivery of cloud services, enabling the storage and processing of vast volumes of data and applications. However, this proliferation of data centers has precipitated profound environmental concerns. The exponential growth in the number and size of data centers has correspondingly driven up energy consumption. For instance, Google commands a legion of servers exceeding a million in number, while Microsoft's Chicago data center boasts over three hundred thousand servers. These digital juggernauts consume a staggering 23.5% of the electrical energy grid, drawing its power from the depths of American coal-fired generators (Bharany et al., 2022). Moreover, according to the International Energy Agency (IEA), in 2022, data centers accounted for approximately 1% of global electricity consumption, with projections indicating a significant increase in the years to come (International Energy Agency, 2022). This upsurge in energy usage contributes to escalating operational costs for cloud service providers and leaves a substantial carbon footprint, further compounding the challenges of climate change.

The energy consumption of data centers is a weighty concern from both environmental sustainability and economic viability perspectives. These facilities demand prodigious amounts of electricity to power servers, cooling systems, and other infrastructure components (Ahmad et al., 2023). Notably, cooling systems constitute a substantial portion of the total energy consumption, as maintaining optimal operating temperatures is crucial to prevent hardware failures and preserve data integrity (Shao et al., 2022). The ramifications of this energy usage are multifaceted. First and foremost, it places an onerous burden on power grids, which may struggle to meet the surging demands from data centers, potentially leading to energy shortages and grid instability. Second, the carbon emissions from electricity generation for data centers are substantial, contributing to greenhouse gas emissions and the broader issue of climate change (Ortar et al., 2023). These concerns have garnered the attention of policymakers, environmental advocates, and the general public.

In this context, the necessity for sustainability within cloud computing becomes abundantly clear. While cloud computing offers unparalleled flexibility, scalability, and cost-effectiveness, it is imperative to address the environmental consequences it poses. The imperative lies in finding innovative and sustainable solutions that reconcile the burgeoning demand for digital services with the need to curtail the carbon footprint of data centers. Sustainability in cloud computing transcends mere energy efficiency; it encompasses resource optimization, responsible data management, and adherence to the best environmental practices. As data centers continue to expand and increase, the industry must embrace GCC practices to mitigate its environmental impact (Katal et al., 2023).

GCC embodies a resolute response to the environmental challenges precipitated by the digital era by envisioning a landscape where the remarkable computational prowess of data centers is harnessed while meticulously curbing the ecological footprint they leave behind (Patel et al., 2015; Radu, 2017). To realize this, GCC strives to optimize the design and operation of data centers to reduce energy consumption without compromising performance or reliability (Mandal et al., 2023). Moreover, it seeks to integrate renewable energy sources like solar and wind power into data centers, reducing reliance on fossil fuels and reducing carbon emissions (Ghazanfari-Rad & Ebneyousef, 2023). Furthermore, GCC advocates for developing and using energy-efficient algorithms for resource allocation and load balancing, leading to significant energy savings (Mandal et al., 2023). Furthermore, GCC seeks to monitor and measure the environmental impact of cloud services through metrics like Power Usage Effectiveness (PUE) and Carbon Usage Effectiveness (CUE) to ensure accountability and continuous improvement (Cao et al., 2023; Fatima & Ehsan, 2023; Murino et al., 2023). All the above goals will be achieved while complying with environmental certifications and standards, like Leadership in Energy and Environmental Designs (LEED) and ENERGY STAR, as well as adhering to government regulations concerning energy efficiency and environmental responsibility, which are vital for long-term sustainability (Fatima & Ehsan, 2023; Rai & Rawat, 2023).

In summary, the convergence of the digital revolution and the proliferation of data centers has thrust us into a pivotal moment where the environmental sustainability of cloud computing assumes paramount importance. This study serves as a guiding light through this critical domain, underscoring the urgency of sustainable practices and innovative solutions to confront the challenges presented by the exponential growth of cloud computing in an environmentally responsible manner. More specifically, this study makes the following contributions.

1. A comprehensive introduction to GCC and its role in ensuring a sustainable digital frontier.
2. A detailed discussion of the different energy-efficient data center designs for a sustainable digital era.
3. An exploration of the various resource optimization and virtualization approaches for fostering sustainability in the digital age.
4. An elaborate discussion on the GCC resource management techniques, strategies, and algorithms.
5. Presentation of real-world case studies from leading companies spearheading the green computing transition.
6. A detailed discussion of the challenges of GCC and
7. A highlight of the future trends of GCC for a sustainable digital frontier.

Chapter Organization

After the introduction, the rest of this study is organized as follows: Section 2 explores energy-efficient data center designs, innovative cooling technologies, and the seamless integration of renewable energy sources for a sustainable digital age. Section 3 delves into the resource optimization and virtualization techniques for fostering a sustainable digital age. Section 4 sheds light on the real-world cases of leading organizations integrating sustainable technologies and renewable energy. Section 5 discusses the challenges involved in integrating GCC into the existing infrastructure. Future trends in GCC are presented in section 6, and the conclusion is depicted in section 7.

ENERGY EFFICIENCY AND DATA CENTERS FOR A SUSTAINABLE DIGITAL AGE

The digital revolution has ushered in an era of unprecedented data generation and consumption, transforming every facet of human endeavor. Data centers, the engines powering this digital transformation, have multiplied to meet the insatiable demand for computational resources. However, their rapid proliferation has brought profound concerns regarding energy consumption and environmental impacts. This section explores energy-efficient data center designs, innovative cooling technologies, and the seamless integration of renewable energy sources for a sustainable digital age.

Energy-Efficient Data Center Designs

Data centers, the backbone of the digital age, facilitate the storage, processing, and dissemination of immense volumes of data. Nonetheless, their voracious appetite for energy has long been a cause for concern. Visionary leaders in the data center industry have taken the lead in pioneering innovative and energy-efficient designs to address these concerns (Ahmad et al., 2023). At the heart of energy-efficient data center designs lies the optimization of server infrastructure. Industry behemoths like Google and Facebook have blazed a trail by embracing high-efficiency servers with energy-saving features. These servers incorporate cutting-edge low-power processors, advanced power management systems, and hardware configurations meticulously optimized for energy efficiency (Bharany et al., 2022). Consequently, they deliver outstanding performance while making significant strides in reducing energy consumption, thereby setting a gold standard for energy-conscious design. Moreover, modular data centers have emerged as a paragon of energy-efficient design. These compact, self-contained units are distinguished by their modular, scalable architecture, which enables meticulous cooling management and precise server placement (Manganelli et al., 2021). Furthermore, modular data centers offer rapid deployment capabilities, ensuring that computational resources are efficiently allocated and minimizing energy waste in underutilized areas (Ran et al., 2019). This starkly contrasts traditional data centers' inefficiencies, making them a beacon of sustainability in the digital landscape.

Advanced Cooling Technologies

The quest for energy efficiency in data centers extends to cooling technologies, where traditional approaches have been found wanting. A transformative innovation in data center cooling is adopting liquid cooling solutions. These systems replace conventional air cooling with dielectric fluids to transfer heat away from servers. Immersion cooling, a notable technique in this category, submerges servers directly in a non-conductive liquid, resulting in remarkable energy savings (Huang et al., 2020; Wang et al., 2022; Y. Zhang et al., 2022). Companies like BitFury have embraced this technology wholeheartedly, achieving substantial reductions in energy consumption and exceptional gains in server density (Haghshenas et al.,

2023). Moreover, the concept of free cooling has gained prominence as an energy-efficient alternative to traditional cooling methods. These systems capitalize on fluctuations in ambient air temperature to reduce the dependence on energy-intensive mechanical cooling systems. Data centers can significantly diminish their energy consumption by harnessing outside air during favorable environmental conditions. The National Renewable Energy Laboratory (NREL) in the United States serves as an exemplary case, demonstrating the practicality and benefits of free cooling systems (Mayyas et al., 2019).

Renewable Energy Integration

Achieving true sustainability in data centers hinges on seamlessly integrating renewable energy sources. Industry leaders recognize the urgency of transitioning from fossil fuels to clean, renewable energy to power their data centers (Peng et al., 2022). For instance, solar power installations have emerged as symbolic of the commitment to sustainability within the data center industry. Prominent technology companies like Apple have substantially invested in large-scale solar farms to meet their energy needs (Apple, 2018; X. Zhang & Huang, 2023). These installations provide renewable energy and yield significant reductions in greenhouse gas emissions, exemplifying the dual benefits of such initiatives. Additionally, wind farms and geothermal energy sources have been prominent in pursuing green data centers. Tech giants such as Google have harnessed the natural energy potential of wind and geothermal heat to power their data centers (Guo et al., 2014; Oman & Stearns, 2022). These sources offer reliable, clean energy while substantially diminishing the carbon footprint associated with data center operations.

Resource Optimization and Virtualization for Fostering Sustainability in the Digital Age

Data centers are at the heart of this technological transformation, the powerhouses underpinning the digital ecosystem. Yet, this rapid growth in computational demands has raised concerns about resource utilization, electronic waste, and environmental consequences. This section delves into resource optimization and virtualization, shedding light on virtualization's critical role in maximizing resource efficiency, reducing hardware requirements, and mitigating electronic waste.

Maximizing Resource Efficiency Through Virtualization

As the digital age advances, utilizing computing resources poses technical and environmental challenges. Traditional computing models often lead to inefficient use of hardware, underutilized servers, and rapid obsolescence, resulting in substantial electronic waste. Virtualization stands as a promising solution to address these concerns. Virtualization is the concept of creating virtual instances of computing resources, including servers, storage, and networks, abstracted from the underlying physical hardware (Sneha et al., 2023). It allows multiple virtual machines (VMs) to run independently on a single physical server, enabling more efficient utilization of resources. This transformative approach has profound implications for resource optimization and sustainability.

Server Consolidation

Server consolidation stands as a cornerstone of virtualization's resource efficiency. By implementing this technique, organizations transcend the conventional approach of dedicating a single physical server to a specific task. Instead, multiple VMs coexist on a single physical server (Singh & Walia, 2023). This consolidation eliminates the need for an array of standalone servers operating at suboptimal utilization levels, drastically diminishing hardware requirements and energy consumption. Industry pioneers like VMware and Microsoft Hyper-V have spearheaded server consolidation technologies, offering organizations the means to substantially reduce their hardware footprint and energy consumption (VMware, 2023).

Dynamic Resource Allocation

Dynamic resource allocation is another breakthrough attribute of virtualization (Godhrawala & Sridaran, 2023; Wu et al., 2023). This technique endows virtualized environments with the capacity to allocate computing resources in real time, dynamically responding to the fluctuating demands of applications and services. This adaptability ensures that resources are allocated with surgical precision, thus curtailing the energy overhead associated with operating underutilized servers. Notable exemplars of dynamic resource allocation include cloud giants such as Amazon Web Services (AWS) and Microsoft Azure, which employ this strategy to optimize resource utilization on a monumental scale. By adapting to demand, these providers successfully curtail waste and energy consumption on an impressive scale.

Fault Isolation

Virtualization extends its resource efficiency prowess through robust fault isolation. The virtualization environment is adept at insulating individual VMs from one another, thwarting the propagation of failures across the system (Tian & Gao, 2023). This preventive measure significantly reduces the need for redundant infrastructure, culminating in further energy conservation. In essence, fault isolation minimizes an IT ecosystem's physical and energy footprints, promoting sustainability and resilience.

Live Migration

The technique of live migration allows VMs to traverse physical server boundaries seamlessly. This dynamic capability empowers data centers to allocate workloads judiciously, ensuring that no single server is overburdened while others remain underutilized (Elsaid et al., 2022; Gupta & Namasudra, 2022). Live migration optimizes server usage and minimizes the imperative for excess hardware, ultimately fostering an environment where resources are harnessed to their fullest potential. This bolsters resource efficiency and reduces the energy in managing hardware (Soma & Rukmini, 2023).

Extending Hardware Lifespans

By abstracting the underlying hardware, virtualization emerges as a custodian of hardware sustainability. Accordingly, it enables organizations to maximize the utility of their servers by extending their lifespans. Rather than embarking on the frequent and often wasteful replacement of entire physical servers, virtualization permits the strategic upgrading and replacement of individual hardware components as needed

(Basu et al., 2020; Semenkov et al., 2019). This approach, advocated for by proponents of sustainability, significantly reduces electronic waste, aligning businesses with eco-conscious practices and promoting the longevity of IT infrastructure.

Minimizing Electronic Waste Through Thin Clients

The concept of thin client computing assumes a pivotal role in the mission to minimize electronic waste. Thin clients and streamlined terminals reliant on a central server to perform computing tasks epitomize the concept of centralized computing power (Awasthi & Awasthi, 2023; Salles et al., 2022). By consolidating computational functions at the server level, organizations can prolong the lifespan of thin clients, mitigating the frequency of hardware replacements and the resultant generation of electronic waste. This

Figure 1. Resource optimization and virtualization for fostering sustainability in the Digital Age

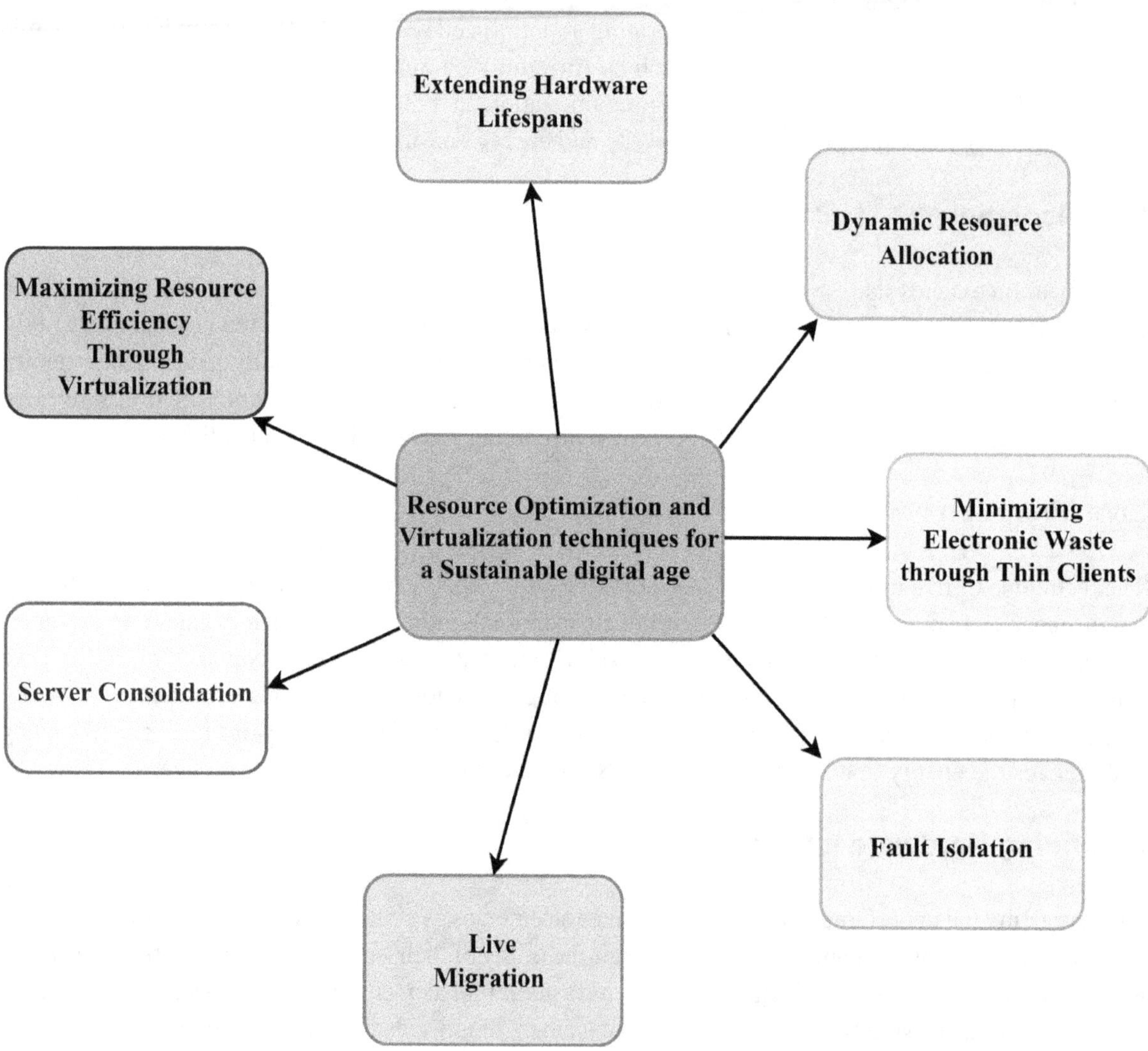

sustainable approach resonates with the principles of eco-friendliness and efficiency, epitomizing the essence of resource conservation. Figure 1 summarizes the above.

GREEN CLOUD COMPUTING RESOURCE MANAGEMENT TECHNIQUES, STRATEGIES, AND ALGORITHMS

Resource management in the context of GCC is a critical aspect that focuses on optimizing the allocation and utilization of computing resources to enhance efficiency while minimizing energy consumption. This optimization is essential for achieving sustainability and reducing the environmental impact of data centers and cloud services. Several technologies and strategies are employed to facilitate resource management in GCC:

Dynamic Scaling

One of the cornerstone techniques in GCC is dynamic scaling. Cloud platforms employ this approach to automatically adjust the allocation of computing resources in response to fluctuating workloads. When the demand for computing resources is low, the system can scale down, releasing excess resources to conserve energy. Conversely, during periods of high demand, resources are scaled up to ensure that the required computing power is readily available. This dynamic adaptation enhances resource utilization and reduces energy consumption during idle periods. Techniques such as Elastic Tree (Bharany et al., 2022), Dynamic Voltage Frequency Scaling (DVFS) (S. Kumar et al., 2023; Sohaib Ajmal et al., 2021), power-aware DVFS-based schemes (Beloglazov & Buyya, 2012), Particle Swarm Optimization (PSO)-based algorithm (W. Zhang et al., 2014) and Q-learning based algorithms (Ding et al., 2020) has been deployed with varying efficiency in power adjustment for different computing resources.

Load Balancing

Load balancing is another essential component of green resource management. Load balancers distribute incoming network traffic across multiple servers or VMs to ensure even and efficient resource utilization. This technology prevents any single server or VM from becoming overloaded, which can lead to energy waste and reduced performance. Strategies such as Round Robin (Ghosh & Banerjee, 2018), Max-Min Algorithm (Hung et al., 2019), Throttled Load Balancing Algorithm (Mulat et al., 2022), Equally Spread Current Execution Algorithm (Alankar et al., 2020) and Min-Min Algorithm among others have been deployed. Other studies have deployed machine learning (ML) (Begam et al., 2022), deep learning (Talaat et al., 2022), Shuffled Frog Leaping Algorithm (Karpagam et al., 2020), Q-learning (Ziyath & Subramaniyan, 2022), PSO (Pradhan et al., 2022), Artificial Bee Colony (ABC) (Kruekaew & Kimpan, 2022), Honey Bee behavior and Crow-inspired metaheuristic algorithm among others. In a nutshell, load balancing contributes to resource efficiency and minimizes energy consumption by distributing workloads effectively.

Dynamic Resource Scheduling

Advanced resource scheduling algorithms play a crucial role in GCC. These algorithms allocate workloads to servers based on various factors, including energy efficiency and server utilization. Different resource scheduling types exist that include task, VM, and storage (Belgacem, 2022) Several algorithms for dynamic resource scheduling have been proposed, including multi-objective nested Particle Swarm Optimization (TSPSO) (Jena, 2015), Heuristic-based PSO algorithm (Alsaidy et al., 2022), Hybridized Whale Optimization algorithm (Strumberger et al., 2019), and Deep-Learning-Based algorithms (Jiang et al., 2020) among others. By ensuring that the most energy-efficient resources are utilized first, resource scheduling helps reduce the overall energy footprint of data centers and cloud services.

Energy-Aware Software

The design of software applications and platforms has also evolved to consider energy efficiency (Choudhary et al., 2022). Developers increasingly focus on creating software that can adapt to varying power demands. For example, applications can be programmed to reduce their power consumption during inactivity (Medara & Singh, 2022). This conserves energy and extends the lifespan of hardware components, reducing electronic waste (Zolfaghari et al., 2022).

Resource Monitoring and Reporting

Real-time monitoring tools are essential for tracking resource utilization in GCC environments (Kakati et al., 2022). These tools provide data center administrators with insights into the performance and efficiency of the infrastructure. They enable prompt identification of underutilized or overburdened resources, allowing administrators to take corrective actions, such as reallocating workloads or adjusting resource settings, to optimize energy consumption.

REAL-WORLD GREEN COMPUTING CASES FROM LEADING ORGANIZATIONS

Various initiatives have been launched across the technology industry, from the sustainable sourcing of energy to energy-efficient data centers and eco-conscious hardware design. This section explores real-world case studies where companies and organizations have taken significant steps towards a sustainable digital future by harnessing renewable energy sources and optimizing their computing operations for minimal environmental impact.

Google's Green Data Centers Powered by the Wind and Sun

Google, the tech behemoth with a sprawling network of global data centers, stands at the forefront of eco-friendly computing (Oman & Stearns, 2022). They've made a monumental commitment to power 100% of their worldwide electricity consumption with renewable energy. This includes sizable investments in wind and solar power, achieved through direct partnerships with wind and solar farms. The result is a constant flow of clean, green energy. But that's not all. For instance, their data center in Hamina, Finland, employs an ingenious seawater cooling system (Huang et al., 2020). This reduces energy usage and eases the burden on traditional power grids. Google also utilizes innovative cooling techniques like free cooling and AI-driven temperature optimization. These strategies not only slash energy consumption but also meet the performance requirements. In a nutshell, Google's reliance on renewable energy and eco-conscious data center designs has had a substantial impact, including carbon neutrality and 100% renewable energy usage. Their commitment sets a gold standard for the industry and showcases the transformative potential of green computing.

Facebook's Eco-Smart Data Centers and the Open Compute Project

Facebook is leading the charge for sustainability through its Open Compute Project (OCP), focusing on hardware and energy. Facebook's data centers are designed for maximum energy efficiency with creative solutions like evaporative cooling, power management systems, and airside economization (Lee & Rowe, 2020). These energy-efficient data centers are powered by renewable energy sources, making them even more eco-friendly. Additionally, Facebook shares designs for energy-efficient servers, storage solutions, and data center facilities through the OCP, encouraging other organizations to adopt these green computing technologies and improve energy efficiency (Roenigk et al., 2021). Furthermore, Facebook is committed to powering its operations entirely with renewable energy. They've invested in wind and solar projects to ensure a significant portion of their energy needs are met through sustainable sources. The Open Compute Project and Facebook's unwavering commitment to renewable energy have significantly impacted the sustainability of the data center industry, setting the stage for a greener digital future.

Apple's Renewable Energy Commitment and Sustainable Supply Chain

Apple is on a mission to power all its data centers with 100% renewable energy. They've invested in solar and wind projects to ensure that their iCloud and online services run on clean energy (Apple, 2018). For example, they've built a massive solar farm in Maiden, North Carolina, to support their data center operations. Beyond that, Apple's corporate offices and retail stores also operate on renewable energy, thanks to on-site solar panels, wind turbines, and power purchase agreements. Their commitment extends globally, as they're pushing their suppliers to adopt renewable energy and sustainable practices. This effort ensures that the manufacturing of Apple's products has a reduced environmental impact. Apple's dedication to renewable energy and supply chain sustainability underscores its commitment to the environment. By powering their operations with clean energy and encouraging their suppliers to do the same, they significantly reduce their overall carbon footprint.

Microsoft's Sustainable Energy Vision for Data Centers

Microsoft is fully engaged in securing renewable energy for its data centers and operations. They aim to be carbon-negative by 2025, powering 100% of their data centers and offices with renewable energy (Welsch, 2022). They enter long-term power purchase agreements with wind and solar farms to ensure a stable, clean energy supply. Microsoft also employs innovative data center designs for enhanced energy efficiency. Project Natick, their underwater submerged data center, utilizes seawater for cooling, reducing the energy needed for temperature control (Microsoft, 2022; Miller, 2020). Additionally, they're harnessing artificial intelligence (AI) to optimize energy consumption in their data centers. AI systems predict cooling needs, adjust power usage, and identify areas for improving energy efficiency. Microsoft's commitment to renewable energy and data center sustainability has global implications. Their carbon-negative pledge, use of submerged data centers, and integration of AI demonstrate a holistic approach to green computing, setting a high industry standard. They inspire other organizations to embrace sustainability as the core of digital growth to pursue a more environmentally conscious, responsible, and sustainable digital future.

In summary, the above case studies spotlight the admirable efforts of tech giants like Google, Facebook, Apple, and Microsoft in integrating sustainable practices into the heart of the digital world. These cases showcase their initiatives and emphasize the tangible impact of reducing carbon emissions and driving the transition to green computing, all in pursuing a more sustainable, responsible, and environmentally conscious digital future.

CHALLENGES OF GREEN CLOUD COMPUTING

In the digital transformation era, where the advantages of enhanced efficiency and unprecedented data and application accessibility are evident, we are also confronted with substantial sustainability concerns. This section delves deeper into the multifaceted challenges of GCC within the broader context of the sustainable digital age:

Energy Consumption and Escalating Demand

The relentless energy consumption in data centers remains a pressing concern. For instance, in 2020, the global data center industry consumed 200 terawatt-hours of electricity, equivalent to the entire energy consumption of the United Kingdom. Meeting the soaring demand for cloud services while reducing this astronomical energy consumption is a formidable challenge. The solution necessitates optimizing efficiency without compromising accessibility and reliability (Malla & Sheikh, 2023).

Carbon Footprint and Transitioning to Clean Energy

Data centers primarily rely on fossil fuels, significantly contributing to carbon emissions. For instance, a typical data center's annual emission can rival a small town's(Kilgore, 2023). Transitioning to cleaner energy sources and enhancing energy efficiency is paramount. However, executing this entails addressing technical, financial, and infrastructural challenges. Successful examples, like Apple's commitment to making all data centers carbon-neutral, demonstrate the potential for change in this realm (Apple Environmental Progress, 2020).

E-Waste Management

The rapid pace of technological advancement leads to a staggering volume of e-waste. For instance, it is estimated that over 50 million metric tons of e-waste were generated globally in 2020 (UNITAR, 2020). Managing this influx while integrating sustainable practices into the cloud computing lifecycle presents complex challenges. Organizations like Dell have implemented e-waste recycling programs to mitigate these environmental concerns, but scalability and adherence remain problematic (DELL ESG Report, 2023).

Strategic Data Center Location

The strategic location of data centers is pivotal for energy efficiency. For example, Google's data centers, situated in regions with abundant renewable energy, have demonstrated substantial reductions in environmental impact (Oman & Stearns, 2022). Nonetheless, the challenge lies in addressing financial constraints, infrastructure availability, and the complexities of reevaluating data center locations on a broader scale (Google Sustainability, 2023).

Supply Chain Sustainability

Upholding sustainability across the supply chain is a complex orchestration. Ensuring every phase adheres to eco-friendly practices, from material sourcing to end-of-life considerations, is daunting(R. Kumar, 2020). Companies like Tesla, in its electric vehicle supply chain, navigate issues of conflict minerals and ethical sourcing. However, achieving comprehensive sustainability in supply chains remains an intricate challenge (Tesla, 2021).

Regulation and Standards Implementation

The absence of consistent, globally accepted environmental standards and regulations for data centers and cloud services poses a substantial challenge. Harmonizing and incentivizing these standards across diverse jurisdictions and stakeholders is imperative. The European Union's ambitious Green Data Centre Framework aims to set a precedent, but its enforcement and global adoption remain uncertain (European Commission, 2022).

Balancing Technological Advancements and Sustainability

Rapid technological progress in cloud computing accelerates hardware and software obsolescence, contributing to resource inefficiency. Companies like IBM, balancing innovation and sustainability, are developing novel, energy-efficient server designs. Nevertheless, striking the equilibrium between technological advancement and environmental responsibility remains a nuanced and delicate challenge (IBM, 2022). Table 1 summarizes the challenges of green cloud computing

In summary, the challenges of GCC, as exemplified by the issues presented above, are intricate and multifaceted. Addressing these challenges requires a combination of technological innovation, policy development, collective action, and a commitment to sustainable practices. These examples underscore the urgency of these challenges in our rapidly evolving digital age.

FUTURE TRENDS OF GREEN CLOUD COMPUTING

We highlight GCC's future trends in the following section.

Table 1. Summary of the challenges of GCC

Challenge	Reference
Energy Consumption and Escalating Demand	(Malla & Sheikh, 2023)
Carbon Footprint and Transitioning to Clean Energy	(Kilgore, 2023)
E-Waste Management	(UNITAR, 2020)
Strategic Data Center Location	(Oman & Stearns, 2022)
Supply Chain Sustainability	(R. Kumar, 2020)
Regulation and Standards Implementation	(European Commission, 2022)
Balancing Technological Advancements and Sustainability	(IBM, 2022)

Edge Computing and Fog Computing

Edge and fog computing models will reduce the need to transfer data over long distances, reducing network and data center energy usage (Ahmed & Haskell-Dowland, 2021; Alli et al., 2021; Hazra et al., 2023). These distributed computing paradigms will become more prevalent, particularly for latency-sensitive applications like IoT and autonomous vehicles.

AI for Data Center Management

AI and ML will be increasingly used for optimizing data center operations. AI can predict and manage workloads, allocate resources efficiently, and optimize cooling and power usage, ultimately reducing energy consumption (Dharaniya et al., 2023; Yi et al., 2023).

Circular Economy and E-Waste Reduction

A circular economy approach will be adopted, emphasizing the refurbishing, recycling, and responsible disposal of hardware to reduce e-waste (Acaru et al., 2022; Ali & Shirazi, 2023; Srivastav et al., 2023). Cloud providers will develop take-back programs and sustainable procurement practices.

Quantum Computing for Energy-Efficient Computing

Quantum computing has the potential to perform specific tasks much more efficiently, reducing the computational energy required for particular applications. While quantum computing is still in its infancy, it holds promise for green computing in the long term (Liu, 2023; Reddy et al., 2023).

Hybrid and Multi-Cloud Strategies

Hybrid and multi-cloud strategies will become more prevalent, allowing organizations to choose cloud providers with green data center initiatives or regions powered by renewable energy sources (Krishnasamy et al., 2023). This flexibility can help reduce the carbon footprint of cloud services.

Blockchain for Transparency and Sustainability

Blockchain technology can track and verify the sustainability of data center operations, supply chains, and energy sources (Radmanesh et al., 2023; Rahman et al., 2023). This can provide greater transparency and accountability in GCC initiatives.

Regulatory and Policy Initiatives

Governments and international bodies will introduce more stringent regulations and incentives for GCC practices (Kineber et al., 2022; Salles et al., 2022). Compliance with environmental standards will become a competitive advantage for cloud providers.

In a nutshell, the future of GCC is promising, focusing on reducing energy consumption, minimizing carbon emissions, and optimizing resource utilization. These developments are critical for the sustainability of the digital age and the responsible management of the growing amount of data in our increasingly connected world.

CONCLUSION

In summation, the chapter has delivered a thorough examination of GCC's pivotal role in shaping a sustainable digital landscape. We have undertaken an in-depth exploration of various facets within this transformative domain, elucidating the concept of GCC and its salience in ameliorating the ecological repercussions of the digital era. Throughout the chapter, we have scrutinized avant-garde methodologies designed to architect energy-efficient data centers, encompassing the implementation of Advanced Cooling Technologies and the seamless integration of renewable energy sources. These pioneering initiatives symbolize the industry's unwavering commitment to curtailing the carbon footprint associated with data center operations, a substantial contributor to global energy consumption. Moreover, the chapter has delved into the intricacies of virtualization techniques intended to optimize resource efficiency. These include server consolidation, dynamic resource allocation, fault isolation, live migration, the extension of hardware lifespans, and the propagation of thin client infrastructures. These strategies underscore the vast potential for resource optimization, leading to diminished energy consumption and a marked reduction in electronic waste generation within cloud computing environments. Resource management techniques, strategies, and algorithms have also been subject to rigorous examination. Key focal points include dynamic scaling, load balancing, dynamic resource scheduling, energy-aware software, and the continuous monitoring and reporting of resources. These instrumental tools and methodologies empower cloud service providers with the capacity to make prudent, data-driven decisions that advance energy efficiency and sustainability. The chapter has accentuated tangible real-world illustrations of green computing undertakings by industry forerunners. Google's Green Data Centers, bolstered by renewable energy sources, and Facebook's Eco-Smart Data Centers exemplify large-scale endeavors to make significant strides toward sustainability. Concurrently, the Open Compute Project, Apple's unwavering commitment to renewable energy, and Microsoft's visionary Sustainable Energy outlook for data centers typify a wide array of sustainability initiatives that fundamentally reshape the industry's prevailing landscape. Despite the notable advancements, the chapter has also shed light on the persisting challenges in pursuing GCC and future trends.

In closing, this chapter offers a comprehensive examination of the current state, avenues for advancement, and attendant challenges within the sphere of GCC. By adopting the principles and practices espoused in this chapter, we are poised to advance resolutely toward a digital future distinguished by technological prowess and ecological accountability. This trajectory will ensure a sustainable, eco-sensitive digital frontier that is emblematic of technological progress and a conscientious commitment to environmental stewardship, thereby bequeathing a legacy of sustainable digital innovation to posterity.

REFERENCES

Acaru, S. F., Abdullah, R., Lai, D. T. C., & Lim, R. C. (2022). Hydrothermal biomass processing for green energy transition: Insights derived from principal component analysis of international patents. *Heliyon*, *8*(9), e10738. doi:10.1016/j.heliyon.2022.e10738 PMID:36177226

Ahmad, S., Mishra, S., & Sharma, V. (2023). Green computing for sustainable future technologies and its applications. *Contemporary Studies of Risks in Emerging Technology, Part A*, 241–256. Emerald. doi:10.1108/978-1-80455-562-020231016

Ahmed, M., & Haskell-Dowland, P. (2021). *Secure Edge Computing: Applications, Techniques and Challenges*. CRC Press. doi:10.1201/9781003028635

Alankar, B., Sharma, G., Kaur, H., Valverde, R., & Chang, V. (2020). Experimental Setup for Investigating the Efficient Load Balancing Algorithms on Virtual Cloud. *Sensors, 20*(24), 7342. doi:10.3390/s20247342

Ali, S., & Shirazi, F. (2023). The Paradigm of Circular Economy and an Effective Electronic Waste Management. *Sustainability, 15*(3), 1998. doi:10.3390/su15031998

Alli, A. A., Kassim, K., Mutwalibi, N., Hamid, H., & Ibrahim, L. (2021). Secure Fog-Cloud of Things: Architectures, Opportunities and Challenges. In M. Ahmed & P. Haskell-Dowland (Eds.), *Secure Edge Computing* (1st ed., pp. 3–20). CRC Press. doi:10.1201/9781003028635-2

Alouffi, B., Hasnain, M., Alharbi, A., Alosaimi, W., Alyami, H., & Ayaz, M. (2021). A Systematic Literature Review on Cloud Computing Security: Threats and Mitigation Strategies. *IEEE Access : Practical Innovations, Open Solutions*, *9*, 57792–57807. doi:10.1109/ACCESS.2021.3073203

Alsaidy, S. A., Abbood, A. D., & Sahib, M. A. (2022). Heuristic initialization of PSO task scheduling algorithm in cloud computing. *Journal of King Saud University. Computer and Information Sciences*, *34*(6), 2370–2382. doi:10.1016/j.jksuci.2020.11.002

Apple. (2018). *Apple now globally powered by 100 percent renewable energy*. Apple. https://www.apple.com/newsroom/2018/04/apple-now-globally-powered-by-100-percent-renewable-energy/

Apple Environmental Progress. (2020). *Apple's Environmental Progress Report*. Apple. https://www.apple.com/environment/pdf/Apple_Environmental_Progress_Report_2021.pdf

Awasthi, K., & Awasthi, S. (2023). Green Computing: A Sustainable and Eco-friendly Approach for Conservation of Energy (A Contribution to Save Environment). *Sustainable Computing: Transforming Industry 4.0 to Society 5.0*, 319–333. Springer. doi:10.1007/978-3-031-13577-4_20

Basu, K., Maqousi, A., & Ball, F. (2020). Architecture of an end-to-end energy consumption model for a Cloud Data Center. *2020 12th International Symposium on Communication Systems, Networks and Digital Signal Processing, CSNDSP 2020*. IEEE. 10.1109/CSNDSP49049.2020.9249479

Begam, G. S., Sangeetha, M., & Shanker, N. R. (2022). Load Balancing in DCN Servers through SDN Machine Learning Algorithm. *Arabian Journal for Science and Engineering*, *47*(2), 1423–1434. doi:10.1007/s13369-021-05911-1

Belgacem, A. (2022). Dynamic resource allocation in cloud computing: Analysis and taxonomies. *Computing*, *104*(3), 681–710. doi:10.1007/s00607-021-01045-2

Beloglazov, A., & Buyya, R. (2012). Optimal online deterministic algorithms and adaptive heuristics for energy and performance efficient dynamic consolidation of virtual machines in Cloud data centers. *Concurrency and Computation*, *24*(13), 1397–1420. doi:10.1002/cpe.1867

Bharany, S., Sharma, S., Khalaf, O. I., Abdulsahib, G. M., Al Humaimeedy, A. S., Aldhyani, T. H. H., Maashi, M., & Alkahtani, H. (2022). A Systematic Survey on Energy-Efficient Techniques in Sustainable Cloud Computing. *Sustainability*, *14*(10), 6256. doi:10.3390/su14106256

Cao, Z., Zhou, X., Wu, X., Zhu, Z., Liu, T., Neng, J., & Wen, Y. (2023). Data Center Sustainability: Revisits and Outlooks. *IEEE Transactions on Sustainable Computing*, 1–13. doi:10.1109/TSUSC.2023.3281583

Choudhary, A., Govil, M. C., Singh, G., Awasthi, L. K., & Pilli, E. S. (2022). Energy-aware scientific workflow scheduling in cloud environment. *Cluster Computing*, *25*(6), 3845–3874. doi:10.1007/s10586-022-03613-3

DELL ESG Report. (2023). *Dell ESG Report FY23*. DELL. https://www.dell.com/en-us/dt/corporate/social-impact/esg-resources/reports/fy23-esg-report.htm#scroll=off

Dharaniya, R., Saranya, V. S., Sarath Babu, N., & Zaid, S. A. (2023). AI Agents at Different Data Centers to Minimize the Energy Spending. *2023 9th International Conference on Advanced Computing and Communication Systems, ICACCS 2023*, (pp. 813–818). IEEE. 10.1109/ICACCS57279.2023.10113130

Ding, D., Fan, X., Zhao, Y., Kang, K., Yin, Q., & Zeng, J. (2020). Q-learning based dynamic task scheduling for energy-efficient cloud computing. *Future Generation Computer Systems*, *108*, 361–371. doi:10.1016/j.future.2020.02.018

Elsaid, M. E., Abbas, H. M., & Meinel, C. (2022). Virtual machines pre-copy live migration cost modeling and prediction: A survey. *Distributed and Parallel Databases*, *40*(2–3), 441–474. doi:10.1007/s10619-021-07387-2

European Commission. (2022). *Green cloud and green data centres - Shaping Europe's digital future*. EC. https://digital-strategy.ec.europa.eu/en/policies/green-cloud

Fatima, E., & Ehsan, S. (2023). Data Centers Sustainability: Approaches to Green Data Centers. *4th International Conference on Communication Technologies, ComTech 2023*, (pp. 105–110). IEEE. 10.1109/ComTech57708.2023.10165494

Ghazanfari-Rad, S., & Ebneyousef, S. (2023). A Survey of Renewable Energy Approaches in Cloud Data Centers. *2023 8th International Conference on Technology and Energy Management, ICTEM 2023*. IEEE. 10.1109/ICTEM56862.2023.10083820

Ghosh, S., & Banerjee, C. (2018). Dynamic time quantum priority based round robin for load balancing in cloud environment. *Proceedings - 2018 4th IEEE International Conference on Research in Computational Intelligence and Communication Networks, ICRCICN 2018*, (pp. 33–37). IEEE. 10.1109/ICRCICN.2018.8718694

Godhrawala, H., & Sridaran, R. (2023). A dynamic Stackelberg game based multi-objective approach for effective resource allocation in cloud computing. *International Journal of Information Technology : an Official Journal of Bharati Vidyapeeth's Institute of Computer Applications and Management*, *15*(2), 803–818. doi:10.1007/s41870-022-00926-9

Golightly, L., Chang, V., Xu, Q. A., Gao, X., & Liu, B. S. C. (2022). Adoption of cloud computing as innovation in the organization. *International Journal of Engineering Business Management*, *14*. doi:10.1177/18479790221093992

Guo, Y., Gong, Y., Fang, Y., Khargonekar, P. P., & Geng, X. (2014). Energy and network aware workload management for sustainable data centers with thermal storage. *IEEE Transactions on Parallel and Distributed Systems*, *25*(8), 2030–2042. doi:10.1109/TPDS.2013.278

Gupta, A., & Namasudra, S. (2022). A Novel Technique for Accelerating Live Migration in Cloud Computing. *Automated Software Engineering*, *29*(1), 1–21. doi:10.1007/s10515-022-00332-2

Haghshenas, K., Setz, B., Blosch, Y., & Aiello, M. (2023). Enough hot air: The role of immersion cooling. *Energy Informatics*, *6*(1), 1–18. doi:10.1186/s42162-023-00257-4

Hazra, A., Rana, P., Adhikari, M., & Amgoth, T. (2023). Fog computing for next-generation Internet of Things: Fundamental, state-of-the-art and research challenges. *Computer Science Review*, *48*, 100549. doi:10.1016/j.cosrev.2023.100549

Huang, P., Copertaro, B., Zhang, X., Shen, J., Löfgren, I., Rönnelid, M., Fahlen, J., Andersson, D., & Svanfeldt, M. (2020). A review of data centers as prosumers in district energy systems: Renewable energy integration and waste heat reuse for district heating. *Applied Energy*, *258*, 114109. doi:10.1016/j.apenergy.2019.114109

Hung, T. C., Hy, P. T., Hieu, L. N., & Phi, N. X. (2019). MMSIA: Improved max-min scheduling algorithm for load balancing on cloud computing. *ACM International Conference Proceeding Series*, (pp. 60–64). ACM. 10.1145/3310986.3311017

IBM. (2022). *IBM 2022 ESG Report and Addendum*. IBM. https://www.ibm.com/impact/files/reports-policies/2022/IBM_2022_ESG_Report_and_Addendum.pdf

International Energy Agency. (2022). *Data Centres and Data Transmission Networks*. IEA. https://www.iea.org/energy-system/buildings/data-centres-and-data-transmission-networks

Jena, R. K. (2015). Multi Objective Task Scheduling in Cloud Environment Using Nested PSO Framework. *Procedia Computer Science*, *57*, 1219–1227. doi:10.1016/j.procs.2015.07.419

Jiang, F., Wang, K., Dong, L., Pan, C., Xu, W., & Yang, K. (2020). Deep-Learning-Based Joint Resource Scheduling Algorithms for Hybrid MEC Networks. *IEEE Internet of Things Journal*, *7*(7), 6252–6265. doi:10.1109/JIOT.2019.2954503

Kakati, S., Mazumdar, N., & Nag, A. (2022). Green Cloud Computing for IoT Based Smart Applications. In *Green Mobile Cloud Computing* (pp. 201–212). Springer International Publishing. doi:10.1007/978-3-031-08038-8_10

Kalinaki, K., Namuwaya, S., Mwamini, A., & Namuwaya, S. (2023). Scaling Up Customer Support Using Artificial Intelligence and Machine Learning Techniques. In *Contemporary Approaches of Digital Marketing and the Role of Machine Intelligence* (pp. 23–45). IGI Global. doi:10.4018/978-1-6684-7735-9.ch002

Kalinaki, K., Thilakarathne, N. N., Mubarak, H. R., Malik, O. A., & Abdullatif, M. (2023). Cybersafe Capabilities and Utilities for Smart Cities. In *Cybersecurity for Smart Cities* (pp. 71–86). Springer. doi:10.1007/978-3-031-24946-4_6

Karpagam, M., Geetha, K., & Rajan, C. (2020). A modified shuffled frog leaping algorithm for scientific workflow scheduling using clustering techniques. *Soft Computing*, *24*(1), 637–646. doi:10.1007/s00500-019-04484-4

Katal, A., Dahiya, S., & Choudhury, T. (2023). Energy efficiency in cloud computing data centers: A survey on software technologies. *Cluster Computing*, *26*(3), 1845–1875. doi:10.1007/s10586-022-03713-0 PMID:36060618

Kilgore, G. (2023). *Carbon Footprint of Data Centers & Data Storage Per Country*. Eight Billion Trees. https://8billiontrees.com/carbon-offsets-credits/carbon-ecological-footprint-calculators/carbon-footprint-of-data-centers/

Kineber, A. F., Oke, A. E., Alyanbaawi, A., Abubakar, A. S., & Hamed, M. M. (2022). Exploring the Cloud Computing Implementation Drivers for Sustainable Construction Projects—A Structural Equation Modeling Approach. *Sustainability, 14*(22), 14789. doi:10.3390/su142214789

Krishnasamy, K. G., Periasamy, S., Periasamy, K., Prasanna Moorthy, V., Thangavel, G., Lamba, R., & Muthusamy, S. (2023). A Pair-Task Heuristic for Scheduling Tasks in Heterogeneous Multi-cloud Environment. *Wireless Personal Communications*, *131*(2), 773–804. doi:10.1007/s11277-023-10454-9

Kruekaew, B., & Kimpan, W. (2022). Multi-Objective Task Scheduling Optimization for Load Balancing in Cloud Computing Environment Using Hybrid Artificial Bee Colony Algorithm with Reinforcement Learning. *IEEE Access : Practical Innovations, Open Solutions*, *10*, 17803–17818. doi:10.1109/ACCESS.2022.3149955

Kumar, R. (2020). Sustainable Supply Chain Management in the Era of Digitialization. In Handbook of Research on Social and Organizational Dynamics in the Digital Era (pp. 446–460). IGI Global. doi:10.4018/978-1-5225-8933-4.ch021

Kumar, S., Pal, S., Singh, S., Singh, V. P., Singh, D., Saha, T. K., Gupta, H., & Jaiswal, P. (2023). Energy Efficient Model for Balancing Energy in Cloud Datacenters Using Dynamic Voltage Frequency Scaling (DVFS) Technique. *Lecture Notes in Networks and Systems*, *479*, 533–540. doi:10.1007/978-981-19-3148-2_45

Lee, D., & Rowe, J. (2020). *Software, servers, systems, sensors, and science: Facebook's recipe for hyperefficient data centers*. Facebook. https://tech.facebook.com/engineering/2020/1/hyperefficient-data-centers/

Liu, Y. (2023). *Leveraging Emerging Technologies towards Energy-Efficient and High-Performance Computing*. Handle. https://hdl.handle.net/10657/15006

Malla, P. A., & Sheikh, S. (2023). Analysis of QoS aware energy-efficient resource provisioning techniques in cloud computing. *International Journal of Communication Systems*, *36*(1), e5359. doi:10.1002/dac.5359

Mandal, R., Mondal, M. K., Banerjee, S., Srivastava, G., Alnumay, W., Ghosh, U., & Biswas, U. (2023). MECpVmS: An SLA aware energy-efficient virtual machine selection policy for green cloud computing. *Cluster Computing*, *26*(1), 651–665. doi:10.1007/s10586-022-03684-2

Manganelli, M., Soldati, A., Martirano, L., & Ramakrishna, S. (2021). Strategies for Improving the Sustainability of Data Centers via Energy Mix, Energy Conservation, and Circular Energy. *Sustainability, 13*(11), 6114. doi:10.3390/su13116114

Mayyas, A. T., Ruth, M. F., Pivovar, B. S., Bender, G., & Wipke, K. B. (2019). *Manufacturing Cost Analysis for Proton Exchange Membrane Water Electrolyzers*. OSTI. doi:10.2172/1557965

Medara, R., & Singh, R. S. (2022). A Review on Energy-Aware Scheduling Techniques for Workflows in IaaS Clouds. *Wireless Personal Communications, 125*(2), 1545–1584. doi:10.1007/s11277-022-09621-1

Microsoft. (2022). *Microsoft Project Natick Phase 2*. Microsoft. https://natick.research.microsoft.com/

Miller, R. (2020). *Microsoft: Servers in Our Underwater Data Center Are Super-Reliable*. Data Center Frontier. https://www.datacenterfrontier.com/design/article/11428732/microsoft-servers-in-our-underwater-data-center-are-super-reliable

Mulat, W. W., Mohapatra, S. K., Sathpathy, R., & Dhal, S. K. (2022). *Improving Throttled Load Balancing Algorithm in Cloud Computing*, (pp. 369–377). Springer. doi:10.1007/978-981-19-0332-8_27

Murino, T., Monaco, R., Nielsen, P. S., Liu, X., Esposito, G., & Scognamiglio, C. (2023). Sustainable Energy Data Centres: A Holistic Conceptual Framework for Design and Operations. *Energies, 16*(15), 5764. doi:10.3390/en16155764

Oman, M., & Stearns, I. F. (2022). *Clean energy projects begin to power Google data centers*. Google Cloud. https://cloud.google.com/blog/topics/sustainability/clean-energy-projects-begin-to-power-google-data-centers

Ortar, N., Taylor, A. R. E., Velkova, J., Brodie, P., Johnson, A., Marquet, C., Pollio, A., & Cirolia, L. (2023). *Powering "smart" futures: data centres and the energy politics of digitalisation. 10*, 125–168. https://shs.hal.science/halshs-03907750

Patel, Y. S., Mehrotra, N., & Soner, S. (2015). Green cloud computing: A review on Green IT areas for cloud computing environment. *2015 1st International Conference on Futuristic Trends in Computational Analysis and Knowledge Management, ABLAZE 2015*, (pp. 327–332). IEEE. 10.1109/ABLAZE.2015.7155006

Peng, X., Bhattacharya, T., Cao, T., Mao, J., Tekreeti, T., & Qin, X. (2022). Exploiting Renewable Energy and UPS Systems to Reduce Power Consumption in Data Centers. *Big Data Research, 27*, 100306. doi:10.1016/j.bdr.2021.100306

Pradhan, A., Bisoy, S. K., Kautish, S., Jasser, M. B., & Mohamed, A. W. (2022). Intelligent Decision-Making of Load Balancing Using Deep Reinforcement Learning and Parallel PSO in Cloud Environment. *IEEE Access : Practical Innovations, Open Solutions, 10*, 76939–76952. doi:10.1109/ACCESS.2022.3192628

Radmanesh, S. A., Haji, A., & Fatahi Valilai, O. (2023). Blockchain-Based Architecture for a Sustainable Supply Chain in Cloud Architecture. *Sustainability, 15*(11), 9072. doi:10.3390/su15119072

Radu, L. D. (2017). Green Cloud Computing: A Literature Survey. *Symmetry, 9*(12), 295. doi:10.3390/sym9120295

Rahman, A., Islam, M. J., Band, S. S., Muhammad, G., Hasan, K., & Tiwari, P. (2023). Towards a blockchain-SDN-based secure architecture for cloud computing in smart industrial IoT. *Digital Communications and Networks, 9*(2), 411–421. doi:10.1016/j.dcan.2022.11.003

Rai, P., & Rawat, Y. (2023). Trends and Challenges in Green Computing. *Sustainable Digital Technologies*, 109–134. Taylor & Francis. doi:10.1201/9781003348313-6

Ran, Y., Hu, H., Zhou, X., & Wen, Y. (2019). DeepEE: Joint optimization of job scheduling and cooling control for data center energy efficiency using deep reinforcement learning. *Proceedings - International Conference on Distributed Computing Systems, 2019-July*, (pp. 645–655). IEEE. 10.1109/ICDCS.2019.00070

Reddy, M. I., Rao, P. V., Kumar, T. S., & K, S. R. (2023). Encryption with access policy and cloud data selection for secure and energy-efficient cloud computing. *Multimedia Tools and Applications*, 1–27. doi:10.1007/s11042-023-16082-6

Roenigk, M., Baldonado, O., & Jani, D. (2021). *How OCP revolutionized the open hardware community - Tech at Meta*. Facebook. https://tech.facebook.com/engineering/2021/11/open-compute-project/

Salles, A. C., Lunardi, G. L., & Thompson, F. (2022). A Framework Proposal to Assess the Maturity of Green IT in Organizations. *Sustainability, 14*(19), 12348. doi:10.3390/su141912348

Semenkov, K., Mengazetdinov, N., & Poletykin, A. (2019). Extending Operation Lifespan of Instrumentation and Control Systems with Virtualization Technologies. *Proceedings - 2019 International Russian Automation Conference, RusAutoCon 2019*. IEEE. 10.1109/RUSAUTOCON.2019.8867595

Shafik, W., & Kalinaki, K. (2023). Smart City Ecosystem: An Exploration of Requirements, Architecture, Applications, Security, and Emerging Motivations. In Handbook of Research on Network-Enabled IoT Applications for Smart City Services (pp. 75–98). IGI Global. doi:10.4018/979-8-3693-0744-1.ch005

Shao, X., Zhang, Z., Song, P., Feng, Y., & Wang, X. (2022). A review of energy efficiency evaluation metrics for data centers. *Energy and Building, 271*, 112308. doi:10.1016/j.enbuild.2022.112308

Singh, J., & Walia, N. K. (2023). A Comprehensive Review of Cloud Computing Virtual Machine Consolidation. *IEEE Access : Practical Innovations, Open Solutions, 11*, 1–1. doi:10.1109/ACCESS.2023.3314613

Sneha, T., V., Singh, P., & Pandey, P. (2023). Green Cloud Computing: Goals, Techniques, Architectures, and Research Challenges. *2023 International Conference on Advancement in Computation and Computer Technologies, InCACCT 2023*, (pp. 438–443). IEEE. 10.1109/InCACCT57535.2023.10141845

Sohaib Ajmal, M., Iqbal, Z., Zeeshan Khan, F., Bilal, M., & Majid Mehmood, R. (2021). Cost-based Energy Efficient Scheduling Technique for Dynamic Voltage and Frequency Scaling System in cloud computing. *Sustainable Energy Technologies and Assessments*, *45*, 101210. doi:10.1016/j.seta.2021.101210

Soma, S., & Rukmini, S. (2023). Virtual Machine and Container Live Migration Algorithms for Energy Optimization of Data Centre in Cloud Environment: A Research Review. *Lecture Notes in Networks and Systems*, *528*, 637–647. doi:10.1007/978-981-19-5845-8_45

Srivastav, A. L., Markandeya, Patel, N., Pandey, M., Pandey, A. K., Dubey, A. K., Kumar, A., Bhardwaj, A. K., & Chaudhary, V. K. (2023). Concepts of circular economy for sustainable management of electronic wastes: challenges and management options. *Environmental Science and Pollution Research*, *30*(17), 48654–48675. doi:10.1007/s11356-023-26052-y

Strumberger, I., Bacanin, N., Tuba, M., & Tuba, E. (2019). Resource Scheduling in Cloud Computing Based on a Hybridized Whale Optimization Algorithm. *Applied Sciences (Basel, Switzerland)*, *9*(22), 4893. doi:10.3390/app9224893

Sustainability, G. (2023). *Sustainable Innovation & Technology - Google Sustainability*. Google. https://sustainability.google/reports/google-2023-environmental-report

Talaat, F. M., Ali, H. A., Saraya, M. S., & Saleh, A. I. (2022). Effective scheduling algorithm for load balancing in fog environment using CNN and MPSO. *Knowledge and Information Systems*, *64*(3), 773–797. doi:10.1007/s10115-021-01649-2

Tesla. (2021). *Tesla Impact Report*. Tesla. https://www.tesla.com/ns_videos/2021-tesla-impact-report.pdf

Tian, Y.-C., & Gao, J. (2023). *Virtualization and Cloud*, 447–499. Springer. doi:10.1007/978-981-99-5648-7_12

Tiwari, R., Sille, R., Salankar, N., & Singh, P. (2022). Utilization and Energy Consumption Optimization for Cloud Computing Environment. *Lecture Notes on Data Engineering and Communications Technologies*, *73*, 609–619. doi:10.1007/978-981-16-3961-6_50

Ullah Khan, H., Ali, F., & Nazir, S. (2022). Systematic analysis of software development in cloud computing perceptions. *Journal of Software (Malden, MA)*, *2485*, e2485. doi:10.1002/smr.2485

UNITAR. (2020). *GEM 2020 - E-Waste Monitor*. UNITAR. https://ewastemonitor.info/gem-2020/

VMware. (2023). *Server Virtualization and Consolidation*. VMware, Inc. https://www.vmware.com/solutions/consolidation.html

Wang, X., Wen, Q., Yang, J., Xiang, J., Wang, Z., Weng, C., Chen, F., & Zheng, S. (2022). A review on data centre cooling system using heat pipe technology. *Sustainable Computing : Informatics and Systems*, *35*, 100774. doi:10.1016/j.suscom.2022.100774

Welsch, C. (2022). *As the world goes digital, datacenters that make the cloud work look to renewable energy sources*. Microsoft. https://news.microsoft.com/europe/features/as-the-world-goes-digital-datacenters-that-make-the-cloud-work-look-to-renewable-energy-sources/

Wu, Y., Cai, C., Bi, X., Xia, J., Gao, C., Tang, Y., & Lai, S. (2023). Intelligent resource allocation scheme for cloud-edge-end framework aided multi-source data stream. *EURASIP Journal on Advances in Signal Processing*, *2023*(1), 1–20. doi:10.1186/s13634-023-01018-x

Yi, Z., Zilin, Z., & Yuhe, Z. (2023). *Application status and development of artificial intelligence technology in large data center.* Spie. doi:10.1117/12.2683016

Zhang, W., Xie, H., Cao, B., & Cheng, A. M. K. (2014). Energy-Aware Real-Time Task Scheduling for Heterogeneous Multiprocessors with Particle Swarm Optimization Algorithm. *Mathematical Problems in Engineering*, *2014*, 1–9. doi:10.1155/2014/287475

Zhang, X., & Huang, P. (2023). *Data Centers as Prosumers in Urban Energy Systems*. Springer., doi:10.1007/978-981-99-1222-3_4

Zhang, Y., Zhao, Y., Dai, S., Nie, B., Ma, H., Li, J., Miao, Q., Jin, Y., Tan, L., & Ding, Y. (2022). Cooling technologies for data centres and telecommunication base stations – A comprehensive review. *Journal of Cleaner Production*, *334*, 130280. doi:10.1016/j.jclepro.2021.130280

Ziyath, S. P. M., & Subramaniyan, S. (2022). An Improved Q-Learning-Based Scheduling Strategy with Load Balancing for Infrastructure-Based Cloud Services. *Arabian Journal for Science and Engineering*, *47*(8), 9547–9555. doi:10.1007/s13369-021-06279-y

Zolfaghari, R., Sahafi, A., Rahmani, A. M., & Rezaei, R. (2022). An energy-aware virtual machines consolidation method for cloud computing: Simulation and verification. *Software, Practice & Experience*, *52*(1), 194–235. doi:10.1002/spe.3010

KEY TERMS AND DEFINITIONS

Energy Efficient Data Centers: Energy Efficient Data Centers are facilities designed and operated to minimize energy consumption and maximize the efficient use of resources for storing, processing, and managing digital information. Strategies include advanced cooling systems, efficient hardware, and optimized server virtualization.

Environmental Responsibility: Environmental Responsibility refers to the ethical obligation of individuals, organizations, or communities to make choices and take actions that consider the environmental impact of their activities. In the context of computing, it involves adopting practices that minimize negative effects on the environment, such as reducing energy consumption and promoting sustainability.

Green Cloud Computing: Green Cloud Computing refers to the practice of designing, implementing, and utilizing cloud computing resources in an environmentally responsible and energy-efficient manner. It involves minimizing the environmental impact of data centers, reducing energy consumption, and optimizing resource utilization.

Renewable Energy: Renewable Energy refers to energy derived from natural resources that are continually replenished, such as sunlight, wind, rain, tides, waves, and geothermal heat. The use of renewable energy sources is a key component of sustainable practices to reduce dependence on non-renewable fossil fuels.

Sustainable Computing: Sustainable Computing is an approach that focuses on developing and using computing technologies in ways that promote long-term environmental and social sustainability. This involves considering the ecological impact of hardware and software, as well as addressing social and economic aspects related to technology.

Virtualization: Virtualization is a technology that enables the creation of virtual instances or representations of computer resources, such as servers, storage, or networks. This allows multiple virtual environments to run on a single physical hardware, leading to better resource utilization, improved scalability, and energy efficiency.

Chapter 3
Edge Computing Empowering Distributed Computing at the Edge

Yogita Yashveer Raghav
https://orcid.org/0000-0003-0478-8619
K.R. Mangalam University, India

Ramesh Kait
https://orcid.org/0000-0002-3084-7646
Kurukshetra University, India

ABSTRACT

Edge computing is a revolutionary approach that enables processing and decision-making in close proximity to data sources, reducing latency and optimizing bandwidth usage. This paradigm involves various components such as edge devices, servers, and networks, integrating sensors, actuators, and IoT devices with real-time analysis enabled by edge processing units and containerization technologies. Edge networks, facilitated by edge routers and gateways and diverse communication protocols, ensure seamless data flow. Network edge computing (NEC) further minimizes latency and supports critical network functions. In conclusion, edge computing is reshaping the computing landscape, fostering innovation across industries. The chapter also addresses challenges, potential solutions, and promising trends for future research.

INTRODUCTION

Edge computing represents a decentralized computing approach that facilitates data processing and computation in close proximity to the data origin, or the network's "edge," instead of depending exclusively on centralized cloud servers. This approach is a direct reaction to the growing necessity for rapid response times and instantaneous data processing in the contemporary digital environment.. Edge computing is not just a buzzword but a transformative technology with profound implications for data processing and

DOI: 10.4018/979-8-3693-0900-1.ch003

storage. Its ability to reduce latency, enhance reliability, optimize bandwidth, and improve data privacy and security positions it as a key enabler of the digital future. By unlocking real-time insights and enabling highly responsive applications, edge computing is poised to revolutionize how we interact with and leverage data in our increasingly connected world (Cao et al., 2019; Meneguette et al., 2021; Ren et al., 2019). In today's digital landscape, where data is generated at an unprecedented rate and applications require real-time responsiveness, edge computing plays a vital role. It enables businesses to harness the full potential of emerging technologies like IoT, AI, and 5G, allowing them to make faster and more informed decisions, enhance user experiences, and improve overall operational efficiency. As a result, edge computing is becoming increasingly important for organizations looking to stay competitive in the digital age (Satishkumar et al., 2023).

Significance of Edge Computing

• Proximity to Data Origins: Within traditional cloud computing, data is transmitted to centralized data centers for processing, leading to potential delays and constraints in bandwidth, especially when dealing with substantial data volumes. Edge computing situates computational resources in closer proximity to where the data originates, diminishing latency and ensuring immediate or near-immediate responses (Chakraborty et al., 2023).

- Reduced Latency: Edge computing substantially lessens the time required for data to travel from the source to the processing unit and back. This is critical for applications necessitating minimal latency, such as autonomous vehicles, industrial automation, and augmented reality.
- Enhanced Bandwidth Efficiency: Processing data at the edge results in less data transmission over the network to centralized data centers, helping to decrease network congestion and conserve bandwidth costs.
- Improved Reliability: Edge computing can bolster system reliability by enabling operations even when connectivity to the cloud is disrupted. This is particularly vital for crucial applications like healthcare, where downtime could lead to severe consequences (Raghav & Vyas, 2019).
- Privacy and Security: Data processed at the edge frequently remains on local devices or within a particular network, lowering the risk of data breaches and ensuring better compliance with data privacy regulations.
- Scalability: Edge computing can be readily expanded by incorporating more edge devices or nodes as necessary, rendering it a flexible solution for managing varying workloads.
- Real-time Data Analysis: For applications such as IoT (Internet of Things), edge computing facilitates immediate data analysis, enabling businesses to make instant decisions based on sensor data.
- Cost-Effective Optimization: By processing data locally and transmitting only pertinent information to the cloud, businesses can streamline cloud computing expenses, potentially requiring fewer resources in the cloud.
- Application Scenarios: Edge computing discovers applications across diverse industries, including healthcare (patient monitoring), manufacturing (predictive maintenance), retail (customer analytics), agriculture (precision farming), and smart cities (traffic management) (Tarnanidis et al., 2023).
- Hybrid Cloud Integration: Edge computing complements cloud computing within a hybrid architecture, where specific processing tasks are executed locally (at the edge) while others are man-

aged in the cloud. This adaptability empowers organizations to effectively balance performance, cost, and scalability (Raghav & Vyas, 2023).

Components of Edge Computing

Efficient data processing and analysis at the edge of a network involve the seamless collaboration of various components, each playing a crucial role in optimizing resource utilization and enhancing responsiveness. Here's how edge devices, edge servers, networks, edge processing units, and containerization technologies work together:

Edge Devices (Sensors, IoT Devices):

Data Collection: Edge devices, such as sensors and IoT devices, are responsible for collecting data from the environment. These devices are deployed in the field, often in remote or distributed locations, to capture real-time information about the ecosystem, wildlife, or environmental conditions (Tarnanidis et al., 2023).

Edge Servers:

Local Processing: Edge servers are positioned close to the edge devices, acting as local hubs for processing and managing data. These servers enable preliminary data analysis and filtering, reducing the volume of information that needs to be transmitted to centralized servers or the cloud. This local processing helps alleviate latency and bandwidth constraints.

Networks:

Connectivity: Networks, including wired and wireless communication channels, facilitate the seamless transfer of data between edge devices, edge servers, and other components. Reliable and high-speed connectivity is crucial for real-time data transmission and maintaining a responsive edge computing environment.

Edge Processing Units:

Data Processing and Analysis: Edge processing units, such as GPUs or specialized accelerators, handle more intensive computational tasks. They contribute to the local processing capabilities of edge servers, allowing for advanced data analytics, machine learning inference, and decision-making directly at the edge. This reduces the need for transmitting raw data to centralized servers.

Containerization Technologies:

Resource Optimization: Containerization technologies, like Docker or Kubernetes, enable the encapsulation of applications and their dependencies into lightweight, portable containers. These containers can run consistently across different environments, ensuring that edge processing units and edge servers efficiently allocate resources for specific tasks without compatibility issues (Tarnanidis et al., 2023).

How They Collaborate

Data Flow: Edge devices collect raw data, which is then preprocessed locally on edge servers to filter, aggregate, or transform it into a more manageable form. The processed data is transferred over networks to edge processing units for more complex analyses, often involving machine learning algorithms.

Real-Time Decision-Making: Edge processing units, with the support of containerization technologies, facilitate real-time decision-making at the edge. This is particularly crucial in time-sensitive applications, such as wildlife monitoring or habitat assessment, where rapid responses are necessary (Raghav & Vyas, 2023).

Reduced Latency: By distributing processing tasks across edge devices, servers, and processing units, the overall system reduces latency. Critical decisions can be made locally without relying on round-trip communication to a centralized server, enhancing responsiveness (Raghav et al., 2022).

Bandwidth Optimization: The combination of edge devices, local processing on servers, and edge processing units minimizes the amount of raw data that needs to be transmitted over networks. This optimizes bandwidth usage, reducing the load on network infrastructure.

Literature Survey

In this article (Cao et al., 2019), author commence by presenting the fundamental concept of Mobile Edge Computing (MEC) and its primary applications. Subsequently, a comprehensive examination of existing foundational research that employs a variety of machine learning (ML) based approaches within the realm of MEC has been done. Additionally, a discourse on potential challenges and concerns associated with the utilization of artificial intelligence (AI) in MEC, providing insights into directions for future research.

This article (Ren et al., 2019) offers an in-depth examination of the emerging computing paradigms, observed within the framework. At the outset, the authors compare the architectures and traits of various computing paradigms. Following that, they perform a comprehensive examination, discussing the most recent research in computation offloading, caching, security, and privacy.The authors conclude by envisioning potential paths for research, aiming to foster ongoing efforts in this field.

The survey (Meneguette et al., 2021) explores the concepts and technologies of VEC (Vehicular Edge Computing), along with an overview of existing VEC architectures, illustrated through layered designs. Additionally, the survey outlines the fundamental vehicular communication mechanisms that facilitate resource allocation. To address security concerns, the authors review relevant security approaches and methods within the VEC context.

This research (Siriwardhana et al., 2021) conducts a comprehensive exploration of the landscape of Mobile Augmented Reality (MAR), delving into its historical evolution and future prospects, particularly in the context of 5G systems and the complementary technology MEC (Multi-access Edge Computing). The analysis in the study focuses on the network structures of both existing and upcoming MAR systems, encompassing various architectural options such as cloud, edge, localized, and hybrid approaches. Furthermore, the research delves into the significant application areas for MAR, considering their development in tandem with the emergence of 5G technologies.

In this article (Mansouri & Babar, 2021), the authors conduct a detailed exploration of cloud and edge computing paradigms, carefully examining their characteristics and fundamental principles to identify the driving forces behind the transitions between these virtualized computing paradigms. They then shift their focus towards computing and network virtualization methods, emphasizing the pivotal roles played by virtualization attributes, resource abundance, and application requirements in selecting virtualization approaches within IoT frameworks. Leveraging these attributes, the authors proceed to compare various state-of-the-art research studies within the IoT domain. Furthermore, they analyze the implementation of virtualized computing and networking resources, evaluating performance considerations within an edge-cloud environment. This analysis is followed by aligning existing research with the provided taxonomy in the field. The key insight gleaned from this review underscores that the selection of virtualization techniques, as well as the placement and migration of virtualized resources, relies on the specific demands of IoT services. In this survey paper (Pan & McElhannon, 2017), the authors undertake an investigation into the primary motivations, current state-of-the-art initiatives, essential enabling technologies, and research focal points, along with typical IoT applications that derive advantages from edge cloud computing. Their objective is to provide a holistic overview of both existing research endeavors and prospective directions for future research, achieved through thorough and extensive discussions.

This article (Zeyu et al., 2020) presents an extensive evaluation of the current state of research on security in edge computing. It examines the security challenges in the realm of edge computing, taking into account the impact of new models, emerging application scenarios, and evolving technological landscapes. It identifies security concerns in edge computing along five key dimensions: controlling access, managing keys, protecting privacy, mitigating attacks, and detecting anomalies. Additionally, it provides separate discussions on research progress in these five areas within the academic community, offering a critical assessment of their respective strengths and weaknesses. Finally, the article delves into the exploration and projection of the future trajectory of edge computing security, incorporating elements of collaboration between edge cloud and edge intelligence.

In this scholarly paper (Qiu et al., 2020), the authors outline the advancements in edge computing within the context of the Industrial Internet of Things (IIoT). The paper initiates by examining the fundamental principles of IIoT and edge computing. It subsequently provides a thorough analysis and synopsis of the progress made in edge computing research. The authors put forward a prospective architectural viewpoint for edge computing in IIoT, evaluating its technological advancements in routing, task scheduling, data storage and analysis, security, and standardization.

In this paper (Hartmann et al., 2022), the main goal of the authors is to conduct a survey of current and emerging edge Exploring computing frameworks and methodologies within the context of healthcare applications, the authors seek to comprehend the specific demands and obstacles linked to devices tailored for diverse healthcare scenarios. The primary focus of edge computing applications revolves around the categorization of health data, particularly in tasks such as monitoring vital signs and detecting falls. Moreover, it emphasizes swift response applications that monitor specific disease symptoms, such as identifying irregularities in the walking patterns of patients with Parkinson's disease. The paper thoroughly assesses the operations of edge computing data, encompassing procedures like transmission, encryption, authentication, classification, reduction, and prediction. Despite the benefits offered by edge computing, the authors acknowledge particular associated challenges, including the necessity for sophisticated privacy measures and data condensation techniques to attain performance comparable to cloud-based solutions while sustaining reduced computational intricacies. Lastly, the paper identifies future pathways for research in the realm of edge computing for healthcare, which could notably enhance the well-being of users if adequately addressed.

This article (Carvalho et al., 2021) commences with an exploration of Edge Computing (EC), followed by a concise overview of the definitions and fundamental characteristics of different EC architectures as documented in current literature. These architectures encompass Multi-access Edge Computing, Fog Computing, Cloudlet Computing, and Mobile Cloud Computing. The article proceeds to analyze notable use cases linked with each of these EC architectures. Additionally, it engages in a discourse concerning promising directions for future research in this field.

In their work (Cao et al., 2018), the authors provide a condensed overview of the issues associated with Edge Computing and put forward potential solutions and research avenues that require deeper investigation. These areas of focus include aspects such as programmability, naming, data abstraction, service management, privacy and security, and optimization metrics.

In this paper (Hamdan et al., 2020), the authors conduct a comprehensive examination of edge computing architectures for the Internet of Things (IoT), referred to as ECAs-IoT. They categorize these architectures based on various factors, including data placement, orchestration services, security, and big data handling. The paper thoroughly investigates each architecture and provides comparisons across multiple features. Additionally, the authors map ECAs-IoT within the framework of two established IoT layered models, facilitating the identification of capabilities, features, and gaps within each architecture. The paper highlights significant limitations observed in existing ECAs-IoT and offers recommendations for potential solutions. Moreover, this survey extensively explores IoT applications within the domain of edge computing. Finally, the paper proposes four distinct usage scenarios for the application of ECAs-IoT in conjunction with IoT applications.

In this analysis (Kong et al., 2022), the authors initially explore the influence of edge computing on the evolution of the Internet of Things (IoT) and explain the reasons why edge computing represents a more suitable computing paradigm for IoT when compared to other alternatives. They subsequently undertake an investigation into the essential requirement for a systematic exploration of edge-computing-driven IoT (ECDriven-IoT) and outline the new challenges that arise within this context. The survey classifies recent progress, encompassing six aspects of ECDriven-IoT, ranging from foundational components to more advanced layers. Finally, the authors summarize the insights gained from their research and suggest a series of complex areas that warrant further examination and study in this field.

In this article (Khan et al., 2020), the authors emphasize the significance of edge computing in the realization of smart cities. Initially, they analyze the historical development of edge computing paradigms. They then provide a critical review of the existing literature, focusing on applications of edge computing within smart cities. The paper categorizes and classifies the reviewed literature, employing a comprehensive and detailed taxonomy. Additionally, the authors identify and discuss key prerequisites, as well as highlight recent findings related to the synergies achieved through the implementation of edge computing in smart cities. Finally, the article addresses a series of crucial open challenges, explaining their underlying causes and offering guidelines for potential solutions. These discussions serve as valuable pointers for future research directions in this field.

In this paper (Yu, 2016), the authors provide an architectural description of the Multi-Access Edge Computing (MEC) platform, elucidating its key functionalities that facilitate the mentioned features. The paper then surveys relevant state-of-the-art research endeavors in the MEC domain. Furthermore, the paper engages in discussions that focus on identifying and exploring open research challenges within the realm of MEC.

Edge Computing vs. Cloud Computing vs. Fog Computing: A Comparison

Edge computing, cloud computing, and fog computing are all paradigms for processing data and running applications in the digital age. They share some similarities but also have key differences. These computing paradigms offer varying trade-offs in terms of latency, scalability, and reliability, making them suitable for different use cases. Edge computing excels in low-latency, real-time applications, while cloud computing offers vast scalability and resources. Fog computing bridges the gap between the two, catering to applications that require a balance between responsiveness and scalability (Ansari

Table 1. Edge computing vs. cloud computing vs. fog computing: A comparison

Edge Computing:	Cloud Computing:	Fog Computing:
Proximity to Data Sources: Edge computing focuses on processing data as close as possible to the data source, typically on devices or local servers at the "edge" of the network (Liao et al., 2019).	**Centralized Processing**: Cloud computing centralizes data processing and storage in remote data centers, providing on-demand resources over the internet.	**Intermediate Layer:** Fog computing is positioned between edge and cloud computing. It extends cloud capabilities closer to the edge, often within a local network.
Latency: It offers extremely low-latency processing, making it suitable for real-time applications like autonomous vehicles and IoT devices	**Latency**: It may introduce latency due to data traveling to and from centralized data centers, making it less suitable for applications requiring real-time responsiveness.	**Latency**: While offering lower latency than cloud computing, fog computing may still introduce some latency compared to pure edge computing.
Scalability: Edge computing can be easily scaled by adding more edge devices or nodes, but it's often limited by the computational resources available at the edge.	**Scalability:** Cloud computing is highly scalable, allowing organizations to provision resources on-demand and scale as needed (Raghav & Vyas, 2023).	**Scalability:** It provides a balance between edge and cloud scalability by distributing computing resources across the network (Ateya et al., 2022; Dai et al., 2019; Yang et al., 2018; Zhang et al., 2019).
Privacy and Security: Data processed at the edge often remains on local devices, enhancing data privacy and security.	**Privacy and Security**: Data security and privacy can be a concern as data is stored and processed off-site.	**Privacy and Security**: Data can be processed locally or in a more controlled environment, enhancing privacy and security compared to pure cloud computing
Reliability: Edge computing can function independently, even if connectivity to the cloud is lost	**Reliability:** It relies on continuous internet connectivity, and downtime can impact services and applications	**Reliability:** Fog computing is designed to be more resilient than pure cloud computing but may still depend on network connectivity (Duan, Wang, Ren, Lyu, Zhang, Wu, & Shen, 2022; Duan, Wang, Ren, Lyu, Zhang, Wu, & Shen, 2022; Fan & Ansari, 2018; Syu et al., 2023; Zhou et al., 2022).

& Sun, 2018; Baresi et al., 2017; Gai et al., 2019; Garg et al., 2018; Raghav et al., 2022). The choice among these paradigms depends on the specific needs and constraints of a given application or system. In Table1 comparison of these three computing models has been shown:

Key Similarities

- Data Processing: All three paradigms involve data processing, albeit at different locations along the network continuum.
- Scalability: Edge, fog, and cloud computing can all be scaled to accommodate changing workloads.
- Privacy and Security: Edge and fog computing prioritize data privacy and security by keeping data closer to its source (Vallati et al., 2016).

Key Differences

- Location: Edge computing is the closest to data sources, cloud computing is centralized, and fog computing is an intermediate layer.

- Latency: Edge computing offers the lowest latency, followed by fog computing, with cloud computing introducing the most latency.
- Scalability: Cloud computing typically offers the highest scalability, followed by fog and edge computing.
- Reliability: Edge computing is the most resilient in terms of operating independently, while cloud computing is the most dependent on continuous connectivity (Xu et al., 2021).

GENERAL ARCHITECTURE OF EDGE COMPUTING

Edge computing architecture comprises sensors, actuators, and IoT devices at the edge, edge servers for data processing and decision-making, and edge networks that facilitate seamless connectivity. It's a decentralized approach that optimizes data processing for applications requiring low latency, real-time responses, and reduced network bandwidth. Edge computing is particularly valuable in applications like industrial automation, autonomous vehicles, remote monitoring, and augmented reality, where instantaneous data processing is crucial. In Fig. 1general architecture of edge computing has been illustrated.

- **Edge Devices:**
  Sensors serve as the crucial gateways for data entry into the intricate realm of edge computing. These devices meticulously collect an array of data from the physical world, encompassing variables like temperature, humidity, motion, and beyond (Kohli et al., 2022). Sensors are versatile and find their place in a broad spectrum of devices, ranging from environmental monitoring systems that track climate conditions to the inner workings of industrial machinery. In tandem with sensors, actuators step into the spotlight, functioning as the dynamic executors of actions precipitated by data and decisions emanating from the edge. This real-time influence over physical processes is made possible through devices such as motors, valves, and switches, cementing the fundamental role of actuators in the realm of edge computing. IoT Devices, in turn, form a specialized subset of edge devices, encapsulating a diverse array of sensors and actuators. They are often equipped with connectivity features like Wi-Fi or cellular capabilities, which facilitate the swift transmission of data to edge servers, making them integral components in the data-driven architecture of the Internet of Things (Baresi & Mendonça, 2019).
- **Edge Servers:**
  At the heart of edge computing infrastructure, you'll find Edge Processing Units, strategically situated at the edge's proximity, in close quarters with the devices generating data. These units shoulder the critical responsibility of real-time data processing, analysis, and instantaneous decision-making. Notably, edge servers are often equipped with specialized hardware accelerators tailored for demanding AI and machine learning tasks, enhancing their capacity for complex computations. To ensure data availability and resilience, local storage is a common feature of edge servers, serving as a temporary repository for data awaiting processing or as a buffer against potential network disruptions. Containerization technologies like Docker and Kubernetes play a pivotal role in the world of edge computing by facilitating the deployment and management of software workloads on these servers. This adoption ensures scalability and flexibility, vital attributes in dynamic edge environments. Finally, a myriad of Edge Ap-

plications, encompassing specific software applications and services, run on edge servers, actively processing data and executing tasks that draw from real-time insights. These applications can take on various forms, from predictive maintenance algorithms that optimize machinery performance to intricate video analytics that bolster security systems. Together, these elements constitute a robust and responsive edge computing ecosystem (Fan et al., 2019) (Xiang et al., 2023).

- **Edge Networks:**

The backbone of the edge computing landscape lies within its Communication Infrastructure. Edge networks play a pivotal role by providing the essential connectivity necessary for seamless data exchange between the multitude of edge devices and their respective edge servers. These networks can take diverse forms, with options ranging from traditional wired solutions like Ethernet to the dynamic realm of wireless connectivity, encompassing technologies such as Wi-Fi, 5G, and LoRaWAN, all chosen according to the specific demands of each deployment scenario. Managing the intricate flow of data between edge devices and edge servers, Edge Routers and Gateways come into play, executing vital functions like data aggregation, protocol translation, and routing. Moreover, the complex world of Edge Protocols emerges, with a multitude of communication protocols tailored to the nuanced requirements of various use cases and connectivity needs. Notably, MQTT, CoAP, and HTTP/HTTPS stand out as common choices, particularly in the realm of IoT and sensor data transmission. Additionally, the concept of Network Edge Computing (NEC) pushes the edge further by embedding computational resources within or in close proximity to the network infrastructure itself, resulting in even lower latency and support for critical network functions, enhancing the responsiveness of the edge computing ecosystem (Wang & Cai, 2023).

Figure 1. General architecture of edge computing

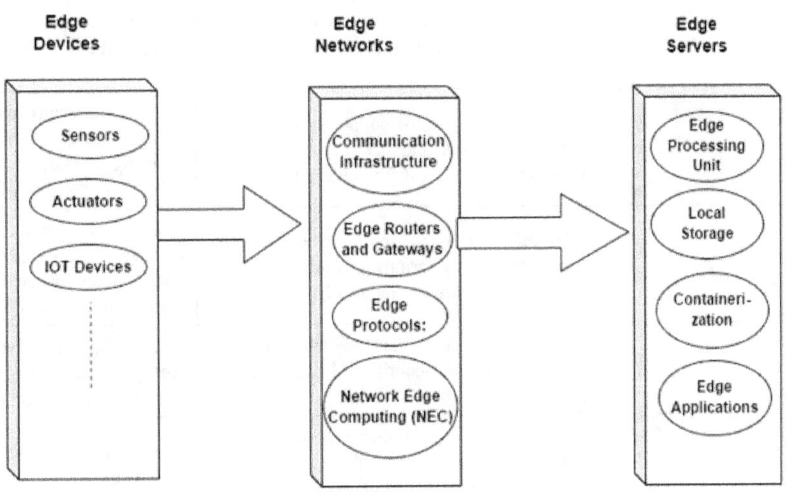

CHALLENGES OF EDGE COMPUTING AND ITS POTENTIAL SOLUTIONS

Edge computing offers numerous benefits but also presents challenges related to network bandwidth, latency, security, maintenance, data handling, mobility, and architecture. Addressing these challenges requires a combination of innovative technologies, robust security measures, and thoughtful design considerations to fully harness the potential of edge computing. Edge computing faces several challenges, along with potential solutions to address them has shown in table 2.(Hassan et al., 2019).

USE CASES WHERE EDGE COMPUTING HAS MADE A SIGNIFICANT IMPACT

1. Manufacturing:
   Use Case: Predictive Maintenance
   Example: In manufacturing plants, edge computing is deployed to perform real-time analysis of equipment sensor data. By utilizing edge devices, such as sensors and local processing units, manufacturers can predict equipment failures before they occur. This approach reduces downtime, extends the lifespan of machinery, and improves overall operational efficiency ().
2. Healthcare:
   Use Case: Remote Patient Monitoring

Table 2. Challenges and its potential solutions of Edge computing

Matrices	Challenge	Solution
Network Bandwidth	Shifting compute and data to the edge demands higher network bandwidth, which may not have been traditionally allocated.	Allocate increased bandwidth to edge computing endpoints, ensuring data can flow smoothly from edge devices.
Latency	Edge computing aims to reduce latency, but it can introduce latency issues due to distributed computing and bidirectional data flow.	Optimize edge server configurations to minimize latency. This includes placing computational resources closer to data sources.
Security	Edge devices and IoT endpoints are often vulnerable and lack robust security measures (Raghav & Vyas, 2023).	Enhance security by implementing stringent measures on edge devices and ensuring regular updates. Employ robust encryption and authentication protocols.
Maintenance Costs:	Troubleshooting and repairing edge servers distributed over various locations can be logistically complex and costly.	Implement remote monitoring and management tools to reduce the need for on-site maintenance. Employ predictive maintenance techniques.
Data Handling	Collecting large volumes of data at edge servers can pose security and accessibility challenges.	Develop innovative data handling techniques, including encryption, secure storage, and efficient data transfer protocols
Mobility	Many edge devices, such as mobile devices and wearables, are in constant motion, posing connectivity and data exchange challenges (Gai et al., 2019).	Develop mobile-friendly edge architectures, ensuring seamless data exchange even with moving endpoints.
Architecture	Existing architectures may not fully exploit edge computing features.	Design and implement better architectures tailored for edge computing, optimizing bandwidth usage and logistics.

Example: Edge computing in healthcare facilitates remote monitoring of patients by processing and analyzing health data at the edge. Wearable devices equipped with edge processing capabilities can monitor vital signs, detect anomalies, and alert healthcare providers in real-time. This has improved patient care, especially for individuals with chronic conditions, while reducing the burden on centralized healthcare systems ().

3. Autonomous Vehicles:
   Use Case: Real-Time Decision-Making
   Example: Edge computing is integral to the functioning of autonomous vehicles. The vehicles process sensor data locally to make split-second decisions, such as detecting obstacles, pedestrians, or changing road conditions. This reduces dependence on centralized cloud processing, ensuring faster response times and enhancing the safety and reliability of autonomous driving systems ().
4. Retail:
   Use Case: In-Store Customer Analytics
   Example: Edge computing is leveraged in retail for in-store customer analytics. Cameras and sensors at the edge analyze customer behavior, track foot traffic, and provide insights into purchasing patterns. This information aids retailers in optimizing store layouts, improving product placements, and enhancing the overall shopping experience ().
5. Agriculture:
   Use Case: Precision Farming
   Example: Edge computing is transforming agriculture through precision farming. Sensors in the field collect data on soil conditions, crop health, and weather. Edge devices process this data locally to make real-time decisions, such as adjusting irrigation or applying fertilizers. This leads to more efficient resource utilization, increased crop yield, and sustainable farming practices ().
6. Energy:
   Use Case: Smart Grids
   Example: Edge computing plays a crucial role in smart grids for energy distribution. Localized processing of data from smart meters and sensors allows utilities to monitor and manage the grid in real-time. This leads to improved energy efficiency, faster response to faults, and the integration of renewable energy sources into the grid ().
7. Logistics and Supply Chain:
   Use Case: Warehouse Automation
   Example: Edge computing is utilized in warehouse automation for real-time tracking and management of inventory. Edge devices, including RFID tags and sensors, enable accurate and efficient inventory management, reducing errors, minimizing delays, and optimizing overall supply chain operations ().
8. Telecommunications:
   Use Case: Edge Computing in 5G Networks
   Example: In the telecommunications industry, edge computing is integral to the implementation of 5G networks. Edge servers process data closer to the end-users, reducing latency and enabling high-bandwidth applications. This has paved the way for new applications like augmented reality (AR), virtual reality (VR), and low-latency services ().

These examples demonstrate that edge computing has a profound impact across diverse industries, fostering innovation, improving efficiency, and enabling new applications. The localized processing power at the edge empowers organizations to harness real-time insights, enhance decision-making, and unlock the full potential of emerging technologies.

FUTURE TRENDS AND RESEARCH DIRECTIONS

The convergence of edge computing with the power of 5G, the proliferation of AI at the edge, heightened security measures, and the adoption of decentralized cloud models herald a transformative era for industries and the emergence of groundbreaking applications. This evolution necessitates interdisciplinary collaboration, involving industry leaders, academia, and standardization bodies. As the landscape of edge computing unfolds, several promising trends emerge. First, the integration with 5G networks promises ultra-low latency, enabling real-time applications like autonomous vehicles and remote surgery (Yu, 2016) (Lei, 2023). Second, Edge AI and machine learning will thrive, driven by on-device AI and privacy-preserving federated learning. Autonomous edge computing, with self-healing networks and dynamic resource orchestration, will become prevalent. Enhanced edge security will employ zero-trust architecture and AI-powered threat detection. Decentralized clouds such as Multi-Access Edge Computing (MEC) and Fog Computing will optimize resource utilization and reduce latency. Improved edge data management, catering to intelligent data analytics and distributed data stores, will enhance efficiency. Industries like healthcare, manufacturing, and smart cities will harness edge computing for various applications, from remote patient monitoring to optimizing manufacturing processes. Establishing open edge standards and fostering cross-industry collaboration will be instrumental in maximizing the potential of edge computing (Gai et al., 2019) (Lei, 2023).

CONCLUSION

The emergence of edge computing represents a pivotal shift in the realm of distributed computing, offering unprecedented opportunities to redefine the capabilities of networked systems. Throughout this chapter, we have delved into the transformative potential of edge computing, exploring its capacity to enhance data processing, reduce latency, and optimize bandwidth utilization. By bringing computation closer to the data source, edge computing empowers a new wave of applications that demand real-time processing, responsiveness, and enhanced security. As we have elucidated, the deployment of edge computing is not without challenges. From addressing security concerns to managing the complexities of diverse edge devices, a holistic approach is essential to harness the full potential of this technology. Nonetheless, the benefits it offers in terms of improved scalability, efficiency, and performance are undeniable. Looking ahead, the trajectory of edge computing appears poised for exponential growth, heralding a future where interconnected devices seamlessly interact to create a dynamic and responsive digital ecosystem. Embracing this evolution will necessitate a collaborative effort from various stakeholders, including industry leaders, researchers, and policymakers, to establish standardized protocols, robust security measures, and a comprehensive framework for seamless integration. In essence, the narrative of edge computing is not merely about augmenting the capabilities of computing systems but rather fostering a paradigm shift in how we conceive, deploy, and interact with technology. It holds the promise of reshaping industries, driving innovation, and revolutionizing the digital landscape, ultimately paving the way for a more interconnected, intelligent, and efficient world. As we embark on this transformative journey, it is imperative to remain vigilant, adaptable, and innovative to fully harness the potential of edge computing in the era of distributed computing at the edge.

REFERENCES

Ansari, N., & Sun, X. (2018). Mobile edge computing empowers internet of things. *IEICE Transactions on Communications*, *101*(3), 604–619. doi:10.1587/transcom.2017NRI0001

Ateya, A. A., Mahmoud, M., Zaghloul, A., Soliman, N. F., & Muthanna, A. (2022). Empowering the internet of things using light communication and distributed edge computing. *Electronics (Basel)*, *11*(9), 1511. doi:10.3390/electronics11091511

Baresi, L., Filgueira Mendonça, D., & Garriga, M. (2017). Empowering low-latency applications through a serverless edge computing architecture. In Service-Oriented and Cloud Computing: 6th IFIP WG 2.14 European Conference, ESOCC 2017, Oslo, Norway, September 27-29, 2017 [Springer International Publishing.]. *Proceedings*, *6*, 196–210.

Baresi, L., & Mendonça, D. F. (2019, June). Towards a serverless platform for edge computing. In *2019 IEEE International Conference on Fog Computing (ICFC)* (pp. 1-10). IEEE. 10.1109/ICFC.2019.00008

Cao, B., Zhang, L., Li, Y., Feng, D., & Cao, W. (2019). Intelligent offloading in multi-access edge computing: A state-of-the-art review and framework. *IEEE Communications Magazine*, *57*(3), 56–62. doi:10.1109/MCOM.2019.1800608

Cao, J., Zhang, Q., Shi, W., Cao, J., Zhang, Q., & Shi, W. (2018). Challenges and opportunities in edge computing. Edge Computing. *PRiMER: Peer-Reviewed Reports in Medical Education Research*, 59–70.

Carvalho, G., Cabral, B., Pereira, V., & Bernardino, J. (2021). Edge computing: Current trends, research challenges and future directions. *Computing*, *103*(5), 993–1023. doi:10.1007/s00607-020-00896-5

Dai, Y., Xu, D., Maharjan, S., Qiao, G., & Zhang, Y. (2019). Artificial intelligence empowered edge computing and caching for internet of vehicles. *IEEE Wireless Communications*, *26*(3), 12–18. doi:10.1109/MWC.2019.1800411

Dewan, M., Mudgal, A., Pandey, P., Raghav, Y. Y., & Gupta, T. (2023). Predicting Pregnancy Complications Using Machine Learning. In D. Satishkumar & P. Maniiarasan (Eds.), *Technological Tools for Predicting Pregnancy Complications* (pp. 141–160). IGI Global. doi:10.4018/979-8-3693-1718-1.ch008

Duan, S., Wang, D., Ren, J., Lyu, F., Zhang, Y., Wu, H., & Shen, X. (2022). Distributed artificial intelligence empowered by end-edge-cloud computing: A survey. *IEEE Communications Surveys and Tutorials*.

Earney, S. (2023a). *How edge computing is transforming enterprises.* Xailient. https://xailient.com/blog/how-edge-computing-is-transforming-enterprises/

Earney, S. (2023b). *What are the top seven edge computing use cases?* Xailient. https://xailient.com/blog/what-are-the-top-7-edge-computing-use-cases/

Fan, Q., & Ansari, N. (2018). Application aware workload allocation for edge computing-based IoT. *IEEE Internet of Things Journal, 5*(3), 2146–2153. doi:10.1109/JIOT.2018.2826006

Fan, X., Xiang, C., Gong, L., He, X., Chen, C., & Huang, X. (2019, May). UrbanEdge: Deep learning empowered edge computing for urban IoT time series prediction. In *Proceedings of the ACM Turing Celebration Conference* (pp. 1-6). ACM. 10.1145/3321408.3323089

Gai, K., Wu, Y., Zhu, L., Xu, L., & Zhang, Y. (2019). Permissioned blockchain and edge computing empowered privacy-preserving smart grid networks. *IEEE Internet of Things Journal, 6*(5), 7992–8004. doi:10.1109/JIOT.2019.2904303

Garg, S., Singh, A., Batra, S., Kumar, N., & Yang, L. T. (2018). UAV-empowered edge computing environment for cyber-threat detection in smart vehicles. *IEEE Network, 32*(3), 42–51. doi:10.1109/MNET.2018.1700286

Gupta, T., Pandey, P., & Raghav, Y. Y. (2023). Impact of Social Media Platforms on the Consumer Decision-Making Process in the Food and Grocery Industry. In T. Tarnanidis, M. Vlachopoulou, & J. Papathanasiou (Eds.), *Influences of Social Media on Consumer Decision-Making Processes in the Food and Grocery Industry* (pp. 119–139). IGI Global. doi:10.4018/978-1-6684-8868-3.ch006

Hamdan, S., Ayyash, M., & Almajali, S. (2020). Edge-computing architectures for internet of things applications: A survey. *Sensors (Basel), 20*(22), 6441. doi:10.3390/s20226441 PMID:33187267

Hartmann, M., Hashmi, U. S., & Imran, A. (2022). Edge computing in smart health care systems: Review, challenges, and research directions. *Transactions on Emerging Telecommunications Technologies, 33*(3), e3710. doi:10.1002/ett.3710

Hassan, N., Yau, K. L. A., & Wu, C. (2019). Edge computing in 5G: A review. *IEEE Access : Practical Innovations, Open Solutions, 7*, 127276–127289. doi:10.1109/ACCESS.2019.2938534

Khan, L. U., Yaqoob, I., Tran, N. H., Kazmi, S. A., Dang, T. N., & Hong, C. S. (2020). Edge-computing-enabled smart cities: A comprehensive survey. *IEEE Internet of Things Journal, 7*(10), 10200–10232. doi:10.1109/JIOT.2020.2987070

Kohli, V., Chougule, A., Chamola, V., & Yu, F. R. (2022, May). MbRE IDS: an AI and edge computing empowered framework for securing intelligent transportation systems. In *IEEE INFOCOM 2022-IEEE Conference on Computer Communications Workshops (INFOCOM WKSHPS)* (pp. 1-6). IEEE. 10.1109/INFOCOMWKSHPS54753.2022.9798390

Kong, L., Tan, J., Huang, J., Chen, G., Wang, S., Jin, X., Zeng, P., Khan, M., & Das, S. K. (2022). Edge-computing-driven internet of things: A survey. *ACM Computing Surveys, 55*(8), 1–41. doi:10.1145/3555308

Lei, Q. (2023). Artificial Intelligence Empowered Traffic Control for Internet of Things with Mobile Edge Computing. *Journal of Circuits, Systems, and Computers, 32*(08), 2350048. doi:10.1142/S0218126623500482

Liao, H., Zhou, Z., Zhao, X., Zhang, L., Mumtaz, S., Jolfaei, A., Ahmed, S. H., & Bashir, A. K. (2019). Learning-based context-aware resource allocation for edge-computing-empowered industrial IoT. *IEEE Internet of Things Journal, 7*(5), 4260–4277. doi:10.1109/JIOT.2019.2963371

Mansouri, Y., & Babar, M. A. (2021). A review of edge computing: Features and resource virtualization. *Journal of Parallel and Distributed Computing*, *150*, 155–183. doi:10.1016/j.jpdc.2020.12.015

Meneguette, R., De Grande, R., Ueyama, J., Filho, G. P. R., & Madeira, E. (2021). Vehicular edge computing: Architecture, resource management, security, and challenges. *ACM Computing Surveys*, *55*(1), 1–46. doi:10.1145/3485129

Pan, J., & McElhannon, J. (2017). Future edge cloud and edge computing for internet of things applications. *IEEE Internet of Things Journal*, *5*(1), 439–449. doi:10.1109/JIOT.2017.2767608

Pratt, M. (2021). Top Ten edge computing use cases and examples. *TechTarget.* https://www.techtarget.com/searchcio/feature/4-edge-computing-use-cases-delivering-value-in-the-enterprise

Qiu, T., Chi, J., Zhou, X., Ning, Z., Atiquzzaman, M., & Wu, D. O. (2020). Edge computing in industrial internet of things: Architecture, advances and challenges. *IEEE Communications Surveys and Tutorials*, *22*(4), 2462–2488. doi:10.1109/COMST.2020.3009103

Raghav, Y. Y., & Gulia, S. (2023). The Rise of Artificial Intelligence and Its Implications on Spirituality. In S. Chakraborty (Ed.), *Investigating the Impact of AI on Ethics and Spirituality* (pp. 165–178). IGI Global. doi:10.4018/978-1-6684-9196-6.ch011

Raghav, Y. Y., & Vyas, V. (2019). *A comparative analysis of different load balancing algorithms on different parameters in cloud computing*. 2019 3rd International Conference on Recent Developments in Control, Automation & Power Engineering (RDCAPE), Noida, India. 10.1109/RDCAPE47089.2019.8979122

Raghav, Y. Y., & Vyas, V. (2023a). ACBSO: A hybrid solution for load balancing using ant colony and bird swarm optimization algorithms. *International Journal of Information Technology : an Official Journal of Bharati Vidyapeeth's Institute of Computer Applications and Management*, *15*(5), 1–11. doi:10.1007/s41870-023-01340-5

Raghav, Y. Y., & Vyas, V. (2023b). A Comparative Analysis Report of Nature-Inspired Algorithms for Load Balancing in Cloud Environment. In *Women in Soft Computing* (pp. 47–63). Springer Nature Switzerland.

Raghav, Y. Y., Vyas, V., & Rani, H. (2022). Load balancing using dynamic algorithms for cloud environment: A survey. *Materials Today: Proceedings*, *69*, 349–353. doi:10.1016/j.matpr.2022.09.048

Ren, J., Zhang, D., He, S., Zhang, Y., & Li, T. (2019). A survey on end-edge-cloud orchestrated network computing paradigms: Transparent computing, mobile edge computing, fog computing, and cloudlet. *ACM Computing Surveys*, *52*(6), 1–36. doi:10.1145/3362031

Shurpali, S. (2020). *Role of Edge Computing in Connected and Autonomous Vehicles.* eInfo Chips. https://www.einfochips.com/blog/role-of-edge-computing-in-connected-and-autonomous-vehicles/

Siriwardhana, Y., Porambage, P., Liyanage, M., & Ylianttila, M. (2021). A survey on mobile augmented reality with 5G mobile edge computing: Architectures, applications, and technical aspects. *IEEE Communications Surveys and Tutorials*, *23*(2), 1160–1192. doi:10.1109/COMST.2021.3061981

Syu, J. H., Lin, J. C. W., Srivastava, G., & Yu, K. (2023). A Comprehensive Survey on Artificial Intelligence Empowered Edge Computing on Consumer Electronics. *IEEE Transactions on Consumer Electronics*, 1. doi:10.1109/TCE.2023.3318150

Vallati, C., Virdis, A., Mingozzi, E., & Stea, G. (2016). Mobile-edge computing come home connecting things in future smart homes using LTE device-to-device communications. *IEEE Consumer Electronics Magazine*, *5*(4), 77–83. doi:10.1109/MCE.2016.2590100

Wang, Z., & Cai, X. (2023). Teaching mechanism empowered by virtual simulation: Edge computing–driven approach. *Digital Communications and Networks*, *9*(2), 483–491. doi:10.1016/j.dcan.2022.03.016

Xiang, H., Wu, K., Chen, J., Yi, C., Cai, J., & Niyato, D. (2023). Edge Computing Empowered Tactile Internet for Human Digital Twin: Visions and Case Study. arXiv preprint arXiv:2304.07454.

Xu, D., Li, T., Li, Y., Su, X., Tarkoma, S., Jiang, T., Crowcroft, J., & Hui, P. (2021). Edge intelligence: Empowering intelligence to the edge of network. *Proceedings of the IEEE*, *109*(11), 1778–1837. doi:10.1109/JPROC.2021.3119950

Yang, L., Zhang, H., Li, M., Guo, J., & Ji, H. (2018). Mobile edge computing empowered energy efficient task offloading in 5G. *IEEE Transactions on Vehicular Technology*, *67*(7), 6398–6409. doi:10.1109/TVT.2018.2799620

Yu, Y. (2016). Mobile edge computing towards 5G: Vision, recent progress, and open challenges. *China Communications*, *13*(2, Supplement2), 89–99. doi:10.1109/CC.2016.7405725

Zeyu, H., Geming, X., Zhaohang, W., & Sen, Y. (2020, June). Survey on edge computing security. In *2020 International Conference on Big Data, Artificial Intelligence and Internet of Things Engineering (ICBAIE)* (pp. 96-105). IEEE.

Zhang, K., Zhu, Y., Leng, S., He, Y., Maharjan, S., & Zhang, Y. (2019). Deep learning empowered task offloading for mobile edge computing in urban informatics. *IEEE Internet of Things Journal*, *6*(5), 7635–7647. doi:10.1109/JIOT.2019.2903191

Zhou, A., Li, S., Ma, X., & Wang, S. (2022). Service-Oriented Resource Allocation for Blockchain-Empowered Mobile Edge Computing. *IEEE Journal on Selected Areas in Communications*, *40*(12), 3391–3404. doi:10.1109/JSAC.2022.3213343

KEY TERMS AND DEFINITIONS

Bandwidth: Bandwidth refers to the maximum rate of data transfer across a network, typically measured in bits per second (bps), kilobits per second (kbps), megabits per second (Mbps), or gigabits per second (Gbps). It represents the capacity or throughput of a communication channel and is a critical factor in determining how much data can be transmitted within a given timeframe. In the context of edge computing, bandwidth is a crucial consideration as it influences the speed and efficiency of data transmission between edge devices and the central processing resources, impacting overall system performance. Efficient bandwidth management is essential for optimizing communication and ensuring timely data processing in distributed computing environments.

Decentralized Architecture: A decentralized architecture in edge computing involves distributing computing resources across a network of edge devices rather than relying on a central data center. This approach enhances scalability, reliability, and resilience, as tasks can be processed locally without a single point of failure. Decentralized architectures are well-suited for edge computing environments.

Distributed Computing: Distributed computing involves the use of multiple interconnected computers or devices to work together on a task. In the context of edge computing, distributed computing is fundamental as it enables the decentralization of computational resources, allowing tasks to be executed across various edge devices rather than relying solely on a centralized server.

Edge Computing: Edge computing refers to the paradigm of processing data near the source of data generation, often at the periphery of the network or close to the devices producing the data. This approach reduces latency, bandwidth usage, and dependence on centralized cloud resources, enabling faster and more efficient data processing.

Fog Computing: Fog computing extends the principles of edge computing by introducing an additional layer of computing resources between edge devices and the cloud. This intermediate layer, known as the "fog" layer, facilitates processing tasks closer to the edge while still leveraging the benefits of cloud services. Fog computing is particularly valuable in scenarios where a hybrid approach combining edge and cloud resources is optimal.

Latency Reduction: Latency reduction in edge computing refers to the minimization of the time delay between data generation and its processing. By bringing computing resources closer to the data source, edge computing significantly reduces the time it takes for data to travel to a distant data center and back. This reduction in latency is critical for applications requiring real-time or near-real-time responses.

Chapter 4
Cloud Cryptography

Renuka Devi Saravanan
Vellore Institute of Technology, Chennai, India

Shyamala Loganathan
Vellore Institute of Technology, Chennai, India

Saraswathi Shunmuganathan
Sri Sivasubramaniya Nadar College of Engineering, Chennai, India

ABSTRACT

Cloud computing is a recent technology that facilitates wide access and storage on the internet. Cloud computing faces few challenges like data loss, quality issues, and data security. Data security became a major concern in the cloud domain as the demand for cloud services is increasing drastically due to its scalability and allowance of concurrent access to users for using various cloud resources. As a consequence, malicious attacks and data breaches happen which also affect other cloud users. Cloud security is made possible with cryptography, which protects from malware and unauthorized users. Traditional cryptographic algorithms are often used to provide data privacy, integrity, and confidentiality. Most recently, a new data encryption scheme was proposed for cloud computing that uses quantum cryptography to improve security. The proposed chapter will provide the complete details about need of data security in cloud computing, significance of cryptography in cloud, existing cryptographic solutions, and proposes a generic model for cloud data security.

INTRODUCTION

National Institute of Standards and Technology (NIST) proposed and described cloud computing, a new century-old technology, in 2006. The rise and development of cloud technology is unexpected in many ways, including cost, stability, performance, and storage capacity. The cloud computing environment allows storing and sharing a huge volume of digital data like text, image, audio, video, etc. through the Internet (Sahinoglu and Cueva-Parra, 2011). It has become an exclusive technology due to its flexibility to access the data at any time as per user convenience. Cloud computing capabilities are now necessary for practically all business types. Taking into account aspects like vast storage and cost-effectiveness,

DOI: 10.4018/979-8-3693-0900-1.ch004

the adoption of cloud-based environments and IaaS, PaaS, or SaaS computing models has increased in contemporary organizations((Mell and Grance, 2011). They provide data storage, facilitate real-time communication and collaboration, and connect new gadgets to business networks. Crucially, cloud installations may scale up fast, which has aided numerous businesses in creating new relationships and working environments with external teams, partners, clients, and remote workers.

However, due to its centralized storage, Cloud computing faces few challenges like data loss, quality issues, and data security. Data security became a major concern in the cloud domain as the demand for cloud services is increasing drastically due to its scalability and allowance of concurrent access to users for using various cloud resources. As a consequence, malicious attacks and data breaches happen which also affect other cloud users using the same resources within the organizations that use cloud services. A study found that 85% of business executives cited security as the biggest obstacle when it comes to cloud computing (IBM Data Breach Report, 2022). One issue is that a lot of businesses just haven't evaluated the risks involved with cloud deployments or figured out what security aspects are under their purview. It can be difficult to ascertain which components of these systems need to be maintained because the majority of businesses rely on cloud service providers, or CSPs. Cloud security should follow a "cover the basics" approach that includes fundamentals, such as: A thorough understanding of the data gathered, powerful identity and authentication tools, Access controls based on the principle of least access, Correct configuration of the deployment, encryption of data in motion, in use, at rest, network activity monitoring limited privileged access to cloud settings, proper training of IT, security and individual users(Chitturi and Swarnalatha, 2020).

A CSP may offer continuous monitoring solutions to help detect suspicious user activity and assess an organization's threat status in real time. The process of storing the data in the cloud securely is made possible with cryptography in the cloud which protects from malware and unauthorized users. Encryption technique is used for the security of the data hosted by cloud providers and limited users can access the services that were shared by cloud providers comfortably and securely. Cryptography provides integrity, confidentiality, and authentication and it mainly secures the information from unauthorised/third-party access.

Rest of the chapter discusses the need of cloud security and the challenges involved in it, elaborates the different security techniques exist at present with their advantage and disadvantage, reviews the security services required in CSP and suitability of the existing techniques, proposes a model for cloud data security.

NEED FOR CLOUD SECURITY

Organizations can outsource many of the time-consuming IT-related duties thanks to these as-a-service models(Xiao et al., 2016). Technology and numerous other technology-related aspects have evolved over time with regard to how businesses operate digitally. Most businesses today take liberty of the advantages of digital data sharing and storage, which greatly facilitate and accelerate their work. Organizations of all sizes typically benefit from this form of data computing. It can significantly assist these firms in managing IT-related infrastructure while also assisting them in lowering their capital expenditures. It should also be noted that as technology has advanced, most businesses have switched to online forms and are creating larger, more effective digital infrastructure. It is crucial that businesses use strategies that other businesses use in platforms that are compatible with their own. The majority of businesses choose Cloud computing because the data center doesn't meet their clients' needs. People then begin to contemplate. There are a variety of benefits to dynamic infrastructure management, particularly when increasing applications and services (Senyo, Effah,, Addae, 2016). When organizations use cloud for effectively resource their departments, the dynamic nature of infrastructure management, particularly in scaling applications and services, can present a number of issues. As businesses adopt these ideas and work to improve their operational strategy, new difficulties in balancing security and productivity levels occur. While moving largely to cloud-based settings can have various ramifications if done insecurely, more contemporary technologies do enable firms develop capabilities outside the boundaries of on-premise infrastructure.

Understanding the security standards for keeping data safe has become essential as businesses continue to shift to the cloud. Although third-party cloud computing service providers might take over the management of this infrastructure, the accountability and security of data assets may not necessarily move with it(Cole et al, 2019).

Cloud security is a set of practices and tools created to address both internal and external security threats to businesses. As they implement their digital transformation strategy and integrate cloud-based tools and services into their infrastructure, organizations need cloud security. With the continued development of the digital environment, security concerns have advanced. Due to an organization's general lack of visibility in data access and movement, these risks specifically target suppliers of cloud computing. Organizations may encounter serious governance and compliance issues when handling client information, regardless of where it is housed, if they don't take proactive measures to increase their cloud security.

In this case, the cloud service provider (CSP) is crucial to the administration of the user's data. As a result, CSP distinguishes between data ownership and management, and the user cannot manage the data solely through CSP (Xiao et al., 2016).. The result is, the CSP has simple access to the data, and hackers have access to the CSP server via which they can steal user data and associated files. These are the two scenarios that can result in data loss or leakage, where security is a concern. These issues exist with cloud computing and storage. However, despite using a number of encryption mechanisms, the inside attack continued. The major goal of the fog idea in the cloud and IoT is to increase reliability and efficiency while lowering the volume of data transferred to the cloud for storage, processing, and analysis (Qing-hail et al., 2012). Deduplication technology is generally used to eliminate redundant data and decrease the amount of space and bandwidth required whenever multiple users save their data.

Hence the CSP should concern about,

- Controls designed to prevent data leakage
- Strong authentication
- Data encryption
- Visibility and threat detection
- Continuous compliance
- Integrated security

However, putting in place sufficient defences against contemporary cyber-attacks is essential for a successful cloud adoption. To ensure business continuity, organization needs to use cloud security solutions and best practices regardless of whether it operates in a public, private, or hybrid cloud.. The challenges involved in cloud security are,

Lack of Visibility:

Businesses may now access and keep their data online more easily thanks to cloud computing, but there are risks involved. Companies must therefore safeguard their data against theft and unwanted access. However, because cloud computing relies on other servers, it also presents security risks. Businesses must put security mechanisms like robust authentication, data loss prevention (DLP), data breach detection, and data breach response into place to make sure that only authorized sources can access their systems. Businesses must routinely audit security processes and procedures to find vulnerabilities and threats before they materialize as a serious issue. Visibility is essential when using cloud computing. Organizations may make sure that by adopting security best practices and taking the required steps.

Multitenancy:

Multiple client infrastructures are housed under one roof in public cloud settings, therefore it's feasible that your hosted services could be penetrated by hostile attackers as collateral damage when they target other companies.

Access control and dark IT:

While businesses may be able to control and limit access points across on-premises systems, enforcing the same sorts of limitations in cloud settings can be difficult. Businesses that don't have bring your own device (BYOD) regulations and permit unrestricted access to cloud services from any device or location may find this to be risky.

Compliance:

Regulatory compliance management can present a challenge for companies using public or hybrid cloud deployments. Data security and privacy are still ultimately the company's responsibility, so if it relies too much on outside solutions to handle this aspect, it could lead to costly compliance issues.

Inappropriate Access:

One of the biggest problems businesses have with cloud security is unauthorized access to data. Businesses may easily store and access data in the cloud, but this makes the data more susceptible to cyber threats. Malware attacks, data theft, and unauthorized access to user data are a few examples of cloud security flaws. Businesses must make sure that only authorized individuals have access to their data in order to safeguard it from risks of this nature.Encrypting sensitive data in the cloud is another security measure that businesses can use. It's beneficial.

Abuse of Accounts:

One of the most common breaches in cloud security involves user account theft. Utilizing cloud-based software and services will raise your risk of account theft. Users must therefore be careful to safeguard their passwords and other private information if they want to maintain their security in the cloud.Strong passwords, security questions, and two-factor authentication are ways that users can safeguard themselves when logging into their accounts. Additionally, they can keep an eye on account activity and take precautions against unauthorized access or use. This will make it more difficult for hackers to access user data or take over their accounts. In general, maintaining security awareness and updating your security protocols are essential to cloud computing security.

Data Confidentiality and Privacy:

Concerns about data security and privacy are crucial when it comes to cloud computing. Security issues arise because cloud computing allows organizations to access their data from anywhere in the world. Companies must make sure that only authorized users may access their data because they have no control over who has access to it. When hackers access corporate data, data breaches may occur.

Due to the growth of big data and the expanding usage of cloud computing in business, there will be even more concerns regarding data privacy and confidentiality in the upcoming years.As the use of data-intensive applications continue to rise, concerns over data privacy and confidentiality will remain a top priority for enterprises. But according to managed IT specialists

External Data Sharing:

One of the biggest problems firms have with cloud security is external data sharing. When data is sent to outside suppliers, who must be investigated and approved by the organization, this problem occurs. External data sharing might consequently result in the loss of crucial corporate data as well as theft and fraud. Companies must use strong security measures, such encryption, and data management procedures to reduce these threats. Additionally, it will support maintaining the confidentiality and security of sensitive data. Companies may safeguard their data from illegal access and assure its dependability and integrity by putting in place the proper security measures. In general, enterprises must consider external data sharing as a serious cloud security risk to stay ahead of the competition.

Legal and Regulatory Compliance:

A cloud is an effective instrument that can lower expenses and increase operational efficiency for businesses. To protect data and guarantee compliance with legal and regulatory obligations, cloud computing poses new security concerns that must be handled. To guarantee the security and integrity of their cloud-based systems, businesses must assure data security and adhere to legal and regulatory standards. Malware, data breaches, and phishing are just a handful of the problems businesses have while embracing cloud computing.It's crucial to carry out routine security audits, maintain current security configurations, establish robust authentication procedures, use strong passwords, employ multi-factor authentication techniques, and routinely upgrade software and operating systems to combat these cybersecurity risks.

Unsafe Resources from Third Parties:

Applications, websites, and services provided by third parties are not under the cloud provider's control. These tools could contain security flaws, making it possible for someone else to access your information. Furthermore, unprotected third-party resources could provide hackers access to your cloud data. These flaws could jeopardize your security. As a result, it is crucial to guarantee that only reliable and secure resources are used for cloud computing. Additionally, it will lessen the chance of unauthorized data loss or breach and assist ensure that only authorized users have access to data. When engaging with sensitive data stored in cloud storage accounts, unsecure third-party resources can be a cybersecurity risk. These resources are accessible by hackers, who can use them to access your cloud systems and data. Strong security measures like multi-factor authentication and tight password regulations can be used to reduce this danger. Additionally, you may guarantee that only authorized users have access to data and lower the possibility of illegal data loss or breach by limiting access to only trustworthy resources.

Hence, Cloud security refers to the set of policies, technologies, applications, and controls that protect data, applications, and infrastructure associated with cloud computing (Butt et al, 2023). As businesses increasingly adopt cloud services for their operations, the need for robust security measures to safeguard sensitive information has become paramount. Cloud security aims to mitigate risks associated with data breaches, unauthorized access, data loss, and other cyber threats that can compromise the confidentiality, integrity, and availability of data stored or processed in the cloud.

SIGNIFICANCE OF CRYPTOGRAPHY IN CLOUD

Key aspects of cloud security include encryption, access management, identity and access management (IAM), network security, and compliance with regulatory standards. Encryption ensures that data remains secure both at rest and in transit, while access management and IAM systems control user access and permissions, reducing the risk of unauthorized data exposure. Network security protocols are essential for protecting the communication channels between cloud servers and client devices, preventing unauthorized interception and data manipulation.

Furthermore, maintaining compliance with industry regulations and standards, such as GDPR, HIPAA, and PCI DSS, is crucial for businesses handling sensitive data in the cloud. Failure to adhere to these requirements can result in legal ramifications and reputational damage. Overall, a comprehensive cloud security strategy combines various tools and practices to create a secure and resilient cloud environment, enabling businesses to leverage the benefits of cloud computing while safeguarding their digital assets from potential threats.

The process of storing the data in the cloud securely is made possible with cryptography which protects from malware and unauthorized users. Encryption technique is used for the security of the data hosted by cloud providers and limited users can access the services that were shared by cloud providers comfortably and securely. Cloud cryptography mainly depends on encryption where the algorithms are used to convert the plain text into cipher text. Encryption is the process of encoding information to prevent unauthorized access. Nowadays, it is desirable to secure the information that is either stored in the cloud or in transit against various attacks. The most-suitable cryptographic techniques for each of the cases are identified based on the factors like expected response time, confidentiality level, bandwidth, and integrity. Furthermore, security is a significant factor in cloud computing for ensuring the confidentiality of the client data in the cloud. Cryptography provides integrity, confidentiality, and authentication and it mainly secures the information from unauthorised/third-party access.

Traditional cryptographic algorithms are often used to provide data privacy, integrity, and confidentiality. In particular, Symmetric key cryptographic algorithms which uses single shared key provides authentication and authorization to the data stored in the Cloud. Most popularly used algorithms are Data Encryption Standard (DES), Triple Data Encryption Standard (3DES) and Advanced Encryption Standard (AES). Asymmetric key cryptographic algorithms make use of two different but related keys for the encryption and decryption process in order to protect the data on the cloud. These algorithms are used for encryption and secure key management. Digital Signature Algorithm (DSA), RSA and Diffie-Helman Algorithm are common among them. In addition, cryptographic hashing techniques are used to validate the authenticity and integrity of data. It is a cryptographic process that converts any form of data into a unique string of text.

Figure 1. Symmetric key cryptography (K-Secret key)

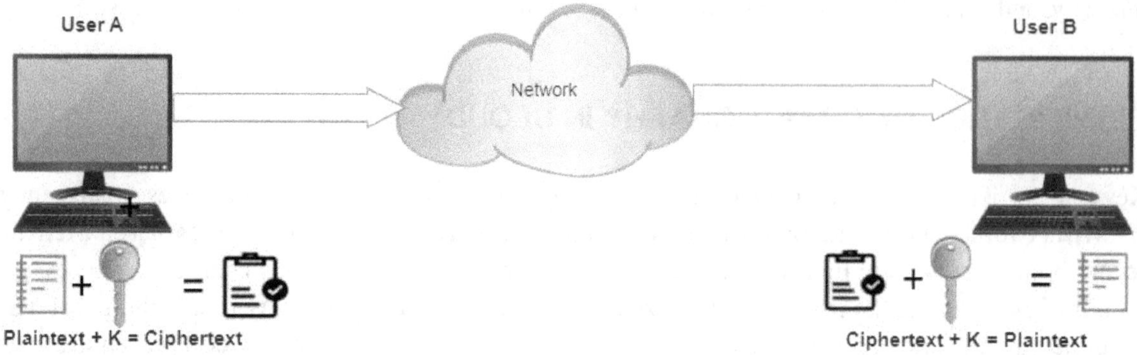

CRYPTOGRAPHY: AN OVERVIEW

Cryptography, process of hiding information, is necessary for secure communication and secure storage of data. It is made possible through a collection of methods and algorithms known as traditional cryptographic solutions Traditional cryptographic solutions provide a broad spectrum of approaches and strategies for protecting data during transit and storing. The most common cryptographic solutions are symmetric cryptography, asymmetric cryptography and Hash Algorithms (Stallings William 2017).

Traditional Cryptography

Symmetric Key Cryptography

Symmetric Key Cryptography is a process of encrypting and decrypting data using a single shared secret key. This secret key based cryptography is a quick and effective method. The two parties that want to communicate with each other must securely share and agree on a secret key prior to communication. The safe distribution and management of the shared secret key is very important for the security of the system. The sender uses the secret key and an encryption algorithm to convert plaintext into ciphertext. The receiver uses the same key and the same algorithm in the reverse to decrypt the ciphertext, given in figure 1. The decrypted plaintext will be same as the original message only if the same secret key is used for decryption.

Symmetric key cryptography can guarantee speedy encryption and decryption while comparing asymmetric cryptography. It provides data integrity in addition to being incredibly effective at protecting data confidentiality. It is suitable for securing closed systems and trusted networks. But because of the key management requirement like secure key sharing and identifying whether the key is compromised or not makes symmetric key cryptography less appropriate for open systems with many users. Common symmetric encryption algorithms include the Advanced Encryption Standard (AES), Data Encryption Standard (DES), Triple DES (3DES), and the Rivest Cipher (RC4) (Hercigonja, Zoran, 2016).

Data Encryption Standard, (DES) was developed in the 1970s by IBM. It is a symmetric key block cipher which uses a key size of 56-bit and block size 64-bit. It uses 16 rounds of series of mathematical operations like expansion, permutation, substitution and transform. It provides data integrity and authentication. Due to the increase in computing power the key size used is vulnerable to brute force attack.

Advanced Encryption Standard (AES) is a symmetric key encryption established during 2001. It uses 128-bit block and 128, 192, or 256-bit keys correspondingly the number of round varies as 10, 12 and14. It is a block cipher based on Rijndael algorithm. It uses series of mathematical operations like subbytes, shiftrows, mixcolumns, key expansion and add round keys. It is a complex cipher but well secured one.

Rivest Cipher 4, RC4 is a symmetric stream cipher algorithm designed in 1987. Stream ciphers encrypt one bit or byte at a time and more suitable for realtime streaming data. Key Length vary from 40 to 2,048 bits but 128 bits and 256 bits are commonly used.

Triple DES, 3DES, is a symmetric key encryption algorithm that more secures than DES. In Triple DES, three different keys K1, K2, K3 are used. The data is first encrypted with K1, then decrypted with K2, and finally re-encrypted with K3. This increases the security. Key Length may be 112-bit or 168-bit.

Asymmetric Key Cryptography

Asymmetric key cryptography is a process of encrypting and decrypting using a pair of keys, a public key and a private key. These keys are different but mathematically they are related. Every entity or user has a distinct key pair. While the private key is kept private and the public key is shared freely. The way how the key pairs are used contributes to provide secrecy, authentication or both.

Secrecy can be provided by using the receiver's public key for encryption and receiver's private key for decryption, given in figure 2. The sender encrypts a message using the receiver's public key and generates the cipher text. At the receiver side the receiver uses his private key to convert the received cipher text to plaintext. In this system anyone can send message secretly to the receiver but only the receiver can extract the original message using his private key. This system maintains the secrecy of the data but the authenticity of the sender cannot be verified.

Asymmetric cryptography can be used to verify the authenticity of the sender by using the same public private key pair. For authenticated message transmission the sender uses his private key to encrypt the plaintext and at the receiver side the sender's public key is used to decrypt the received cipher text, given in figure 3. Here the authenticity of the sender can be verified but the since the public key is open anyone can extract the data from the cipher text.

Figure 2. Asymmetric key cryptography: Secrecy (KUM-Public key, KRM private key of user M)

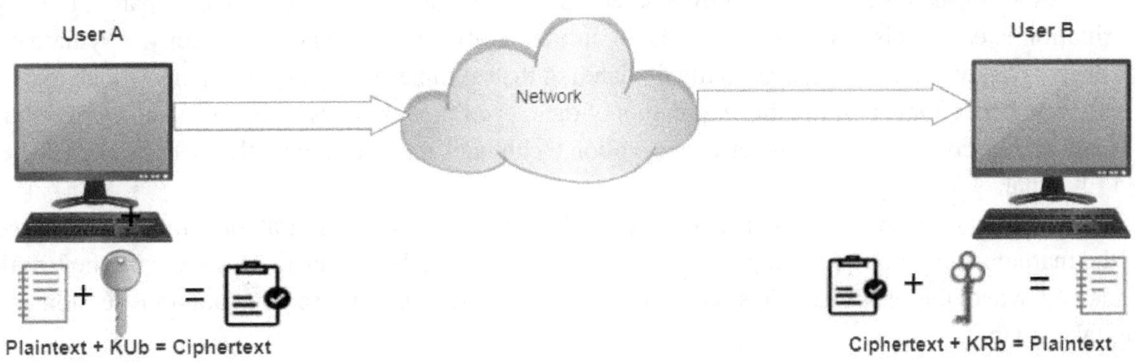

Figure 3. Asymmetric key cryptography: Authenticity (KUM-Public key, KRM private key of user M)

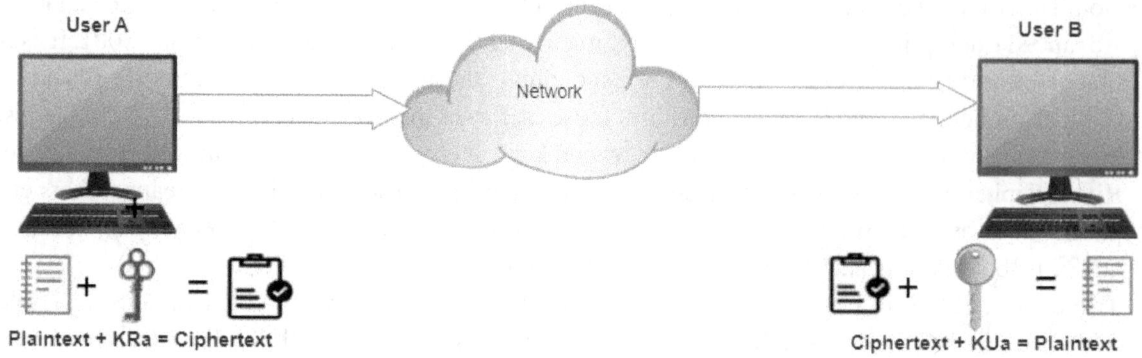

Figure 4. Asymmetric key cryptography: Secrecy and authenticity (KUM-Public Key, KRM Private Key of user M)

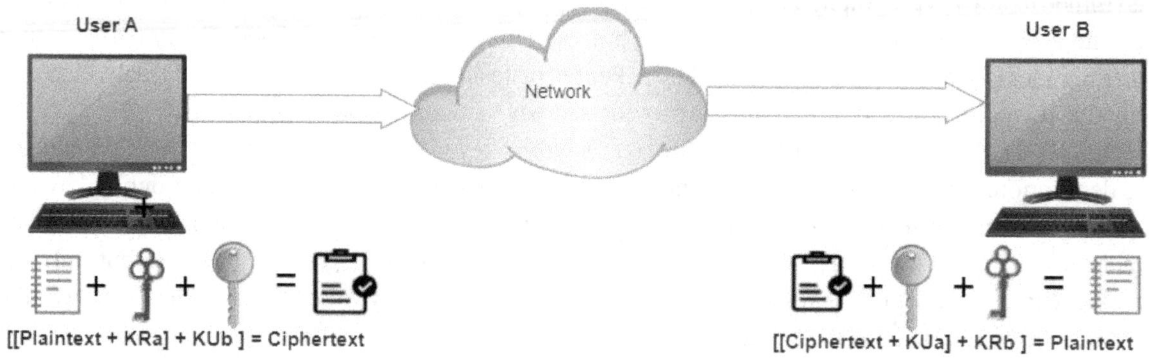

Asymmetric cryptography can be used to provide both secrecy and authenticity by using the senders and receivers key pair. The plaintext is first encrypted using sender's private key and then by using the receiver's public key. On the other end the cipher text will be decrypted using the receiver's private key and then by senders public key, given in figure 4. This, form of applying the keys will provide both secrecy and authenticity.

Asymmetric key pairs are related mathematically, but it is not possible to compute the derivation of one key from the other which improves safety. Since the public key can be freely shared, the key distribution is easy. This system provides data confidentiality, integrity and authenticity. Asymmetric key cryptography is more computationally demanding than symmetric key cryptography, which makes it less appropriate for encrypting huge amounts of data, even though it has advantages in key distribution and increased security. Asymmetric encryption techniques that are frequently used are RSA, ECC and ElGamal.

Rivest-Shamir-Adleman (RSA) is a widely used asymmetric encryption algorithm. RSA is based on the mathematical properties on prime numbers and factoring. The security of RSA is on the length of the key, where the secure length is 2048-bit or 3072- bits. It is used for secure data transmission and Digital Signature.

Elliptic Curve Cryptography (ECC), is a public-key cryptography. It depends on the algebraic structure of elliptic curves over finite fields. Varying key lengths are used, 256-bit, 384-bit, and 521-bit. Its security is based on the difficulty of the discrete logarithm. ElGamal is a public-key encryption and digital signature used for secure communication and digital signatures. It depends on discrete logarithm and modular arithmetic.

Hashing

Hashing is a cryptographic technique that is used to convert variable length data values into unique identifiers called hashes for quick and secure access. This mapping is done using a hash table. The output data is then saved in the digest (Stallings William 2017). In the context of security, reconstructing the input data from the output is practically impossible even with knowledge of the hash function. As a result, since the one-way process stops anyone from accessing or changing the source data, it can be used to secure data.

Passwords are processed through a hash function and its hash stored in the digest whenever you create an account that needs one. On the next login attempt, the password that is input runs through the hash again and the computed digest is compared with the stored one to verify an exact match thereby providing authentication (Bauspiess and Damm, 1992). Data integrity and authenticity are verified using hashing techniques. A site's security can be significantly improved by combining hashing and encryption.

Applications of hashing include

- Password storage - Hashes of password are stored rather than the plaintext to provide more security to an organization's cyber system so that hackers cannot recover the original password
- Digital Signatures – Digital signature can be obtained by encrypting the hash of the sender's message.
- Document Management: Hashing algorithms can be used to confirm the veracity of data.
- File management: Hashing is a technique used by businesses to identify files, index data, and remove duplicate files. When managing a cyber system with thousands of files, an organization can save a lot of time by using hashes.

Some of the most widely used hashing techniques are MD5(Message Digest method 5) which produces a 128-bit hash, SHA-1(Secure Hash Algorithm-1) which generates a160-bit hash. It is the one of the most popular and widely used algorithms. There are different variants of SHA like SHA-224, SHA-256, SHA-384, and SHA-512. The numbers associated with the name denoted the hash length (in bits) that it produces.

Limitations of Traditional Cryptography

Cryptography is very much essential for data security (Salami etal.,2023, Alabdulrazzaq et al., 2022, Sharma et al.2022). A strong cryptographic algorithm must reduce the chances of attack and increase the data security, but the poor design and implementation may cause problem. Even the cryptographic algorithm implementing hardware and software may have flaws that contribute to vulnerabilities. The improvement in technology has increased the processing power of the computing system, this also makes the cryptographic algorithm vulnerable to attack. Increase in computation power has made the brute force attack comfortable where systematically each possible key is tried on a known plaintext/ciphertext pair.

The key management is a difficult task in cryptography because the secret key that is to be used for encryption and decryption has to be generated, distributed, stored and frequently updated. In symmetric cryptography it is necessary for the key to be larger in size and it should be securely shared. Also it is needed to frequently update the key at least for each session establishment. It is necessary for a strong key management practice to provide good security. Asymmetric key cryptography needs a Public key infrastructure to maintain the key. A determined attacker may use social engineering attack to disclose the key and gain access. Human may knowingly or unknowingly leak the key or use a very week key or may not update the key. These may cause the key to be compromised. Cryptography is unable to stop insider threats, which occur when authorized people involves in unlawful activity and exploit their access privileges. Only cryptography will not help in providing complete security, in addition to encryption hashing, access control and physical security is essential.

Quantum Cryptography

Quantum cryptography is an encryption method that allows two entities to communicate in a more confidential way. It is considered to be more secure than the security guaranteed by traditional cryptographic techniques. Traditional cryptographic techniques relied mainly on Number theory concepts. Attempts to factorize extremely large prime numbers may compromise an encrypted code in most of the traditional methods. Unlike traditional cryptography, Quantum cryptography relies on Physics. It uses the properties of quantum mechanics to provide data confidentiality. (Fatima et al., 2021). It is completely secure and cannot be compromised without the knowledge of the communicating entities. In other words, it is practically impossible to eavesdrop the data enciphered in a quantum state without the knowledge of the sender or receiver. Quantum cryptography relies on the laws of quantum physics and uses photons to transmit data over fibre optic cables (Gisin, 2002). The photons are represented as binary bits. Quantum Cryptography works as follows:

The model is for two communicating entities—a sender and a receiver who wish to safely exchange a secret key or a short message. By providing the recipient with a key, the sender starts the communication. The unidirectional photon stream holds the secret. Every photon is a binary bit, denoting either a 1 or a 0. Photons typically vibrate or oscillate in a specific way during transmission. Consequently, the photons are designed to pass through a polarizer, a filter that allows some photons to pass through it with the same vibrations and allows others to pass through with a different vibration. In polarization, there are four possible states: 45 degrees to the right (1 bit), 45 degrees to the left (0 bit), vertical (1 bit), and horizontal (0 bit).

After leaving the polarizer, the photons proceed via optical fiber to the receiver. A beam splitter is used to detect the polarization of each photon. On reception, the receiver is unaware of the correct polarization of each photon, so it chooses one at random. Subsequently, the recipient gets in touch with the sender and openly shares the polarization method used for every bit. Which types were correct is confirmed by the sender.. The photons read with the wrong polarization are then discarded, and the remaining sequence constitutes the short message/key.

Let's assume that there is an eavesdropper who attempts to read the message and possess the same tools as the receiver. But the receiver has an advantage of confirming the polarizer type used for each photon with the sender. eavesdropper doesn't. Even if eavesdropper reads the signal in between then the polarization of photons will change. The attempt made is noticeable for both sender and receiver. The ease of identifying eavesdroppers and mitigating the harm they cause is what makes quantum cryptography so secure.

Quantum entanglement is a process that makes use of entangled photons. Entangled photons, are produced by splitting a single photon into two by passing a laser through a crystal. The most intriguing thing about entangled photon is that, regardless of how far apart they are, changing the state of one will immediately change the other according to the laws of physics. This is very helpful in identifying the eavesdroppers.

Although quantum cryptography cannot transfer large amounts of data, it can transfer short messages (Keys) in a very secure way. Quantum coding allows the secret key to be sent with the highest possible speed, size, and security, but conventional techniques and algorithms are needed to encode and transmit the data (payload). By ensuring that their key is as secure as current technology allows it to be, users can increase their level of privacy while still transferring data as fast as possible.

Quantum Cloning

Quantum cryptography systems do not protect against the "bucket brigade," or "man-in-the-middle," attack, in which an attacker can intercept, read, copy, and replay data instantly and with perfect accuracy. However, the laws of physics will prevent such an attacker from ever existing. The impossibility of perfectly copying (or cloning) an arbitrary quantum state is one of the basic rules governing the physics of quantum systems (Scaran, 2005). Entangled photons are still regarded as totally safe despite this. But Antia Lama-Linares(2007) and her team of Oxford scholars investigated the possibility of listening in on regular photon transfer, and they came up with some amazing findings to overcome those attacks.

Advantages of Quantum Cryptography

- Detects eavesdropping: The quantum state changes if an attacker tries to decipher the encoded data, changing what the users would expect to happen.
- Facilitates safe communication: Quantum cryptography is a more advanced and secure form of encryption that is based on the principles of physics rather than hard-to-crack numbers.
- Provides several ways to increase security: Many protocols are used in quantum cryptography. Certain techniques, such as QKD, can be used in conjunction with traditional encryption techniques to boost security.

Limitations of Quantum Cryptography

The following are some potential drawbacks and restrictions associated with quantum cryptography:

- Changes in polarization and error rates: Error rates may rise as a result of photons' tendency to alter polarization while in transit.
- Scope: With the exception of Terra Quantum, the maximum coverage of quantum cryptography has often been between 400 and 500 km.
- Cost: Usually, quantum cryptography needs its own fiber optic line and repeater equipment.
- Limited destination: Keys cannot be sent to more than two locations in a quantum channel.

- Implementation of Quantum cryptography is not always perfect.

LITERATURE REVIEW ON VARIOUS CRYPTOGRAPHIC SOLUTIONS IN CLOUD

Authentication

Yadav et al. (2023) proposed a symmetric key- based authentication mechanism to fog and dew computing. They use this for long and short authentication process and claim that the level of security provided by the symmetric key-base authentication is same as asymmetric key cryptosystem. Halak et al. (2022) claim that numerous digital applications rely on public key techniques and most of them are susceptible to quantum attacks. In addition they claim that symmetric key systems might be a preferable option in situations that need to be more energy-efficient and resistant to quantum attacks. Also symmetric key systems can reduce energy expenses by 58%. In order to facilitate authentication and non-repudiation across nodes without the requirement for a group key, the study (Vandervelden et al. 2022) suggests a symmetric-key-based authentication technique for wireless sensor and actuator networks (WSANs). The suggested technique, which works even in the presence of hostile nodes, achieves effective authentication and non-repudiation by using a hash chain with numerous outputs.

Yadav et al. ((2023) suggest a unique authentication and key agreement (AKA) methodology that makes use of blockchain technology to improve security and privacy for 5G roaming services. The authors suggest to use the combination of both asymmetric key and symmetric key for security. They use authentication and key agreement protocol that depends on ECC and hash function. The generated asymmetric key is used for session key generation. On the other hand, the symmetric key algorithm is used for the handover phase for secure communication. Their suggested protocol is more effective and scalable since it does not require a secure link to operate between the home network and the serving network.

A Secure Multifactor Cloud Authentication Scheme was proposed by Kaur et al. (2022) to prevent unauthorized access to the Service Provider. In addition to standard user IDs, passwords, and OTP verification procedures, this scheme incorporates a one-way hash and nonce-based two-factor secure authentication scheme that is resistant to brute force attacks, Man in the middle attacks, session hijacking attacks and replay attacks. This authentication scheme comprises of two phases: registration phase and login phase.

In Registration phase, with the aid of an OTP, cloud users register with the cloud server and provide the required information to access the services offered by the cloud server. After confirming the received OTP, the server creates an EC-keypair and sends the public key to the client. The client then selects its password, type of service and expected service time and communicates all information to the server using shared secret key. Subsequently, the server securely stores all user provided information in the server database and creates a cloud certificate which includes the details of user ID, subscription details and lifetime. The user will receive the encrypted cloud certificate back from the Server using its private key. Using the client nonce that was received, the server encrypts the encrypted subscription certificate once more. The server then notifies the client of the success and provides a double-encrypted subscription certificate.

Login(Authentication) phase has two-factor authentication for verifying the identity of the client (user). In First Factor Cloud Authentication, the user requests the first factor of authentication in the first phase. The cloud platform receives and handles the request. A web server and a database server make up the cloud platform. The database server verifies the credentials against records that have already been registered, and once this is done, it sends a confirmation back to the cloud server so that it can successfully notify the user of the authentication. Here, the cloud user sends the encrypted hash of their password and user ID to the cloud server. The cloud server authenticates the client, sends an OTP to the registered email address and mobile device, and then waits for the second authentication step.

When a request for two factor authentication is received, the cloud server verifies the first factor and returns the confirmation or rejection for processing to the cloud. Following a successful verification of first phase, the cloud requests a second factor verification and sends the user an OTP request to validate their device. The user gains access to the cloud upon successful authentication. The multifactor authentication process that a cloud user must go through starts by verifying their login information, such as their user ID and strong salted password, and continues by verifying the certificate that the cloud server has already issued.

Multi-Owner Authentication

To improve the security of the cloud data, an improved Merkle hash tree method of effective authentication model is proposed in the multi-owner cloud (Jayaprakash et a., 2022). To encrypt the large data, the Merkle Hash Tree uses leaf nodes with hash tags and non-leaf nodes with a table of child hash information. Because of its appropriate structure, the Merkle Hash tree facilitates effective data mapping and makes it simple to identify modifications made to the data. The developed model offers a secure cloud storage system that supports public auditing while protecting privacy. The data owners use the private key to edit the data after uploading it to the cloud. The data is split into batches and stored on the cloud server using an improved Merkle hash tree method. A third-party auditor audits the data files that the data owner has requested, and the multiowner authentication method is used to authenticate the user during the modification process. This method is used for providing data integrity, load balancing, and multi-owner authentication in the cloud environment.

The data owner first uploads the data in an encrypted format using an improved Merkle hash tree technique to the cloud server. For the purpose of viewing and downloading the data, the user is given a public key. The data owner uses the public key to confirm whether the user is authorized or not. The data owner gives the user a decryption key. If they are authorized, they can decrypt the data. The idea of implementing load balancing is to process the job request from the user. Ultimately, the cloud server receives the user request. The cloud server responds to the user's query if the user has successfully authenticated.

Confidentiality

Elkana et al. (2021) proposed an enhanced symmetric key encryption algorithm (ESKEA) for secure data storage in cloud networks with data deduplication. The proposed algorithm is based on the AES algorithm and is designed to improve the security and efficiency of data storage in cloud networks. The paper presents the results of a performance analysis of ESKEA and compares it to other widely used symmetric key algorithms.

Asymmetric key cryptography can also be applied. Fouzar et al. (2023) use Elliptic Curve Cryptography (ECC) based asymmetric cryptosystem for video communication. Using ECC they generate several dynamic keys for encrypting and decrypting tiny video data chunks. Compared to more conventional techniques, this strategy lowers essential management overhead while enhancing security. Sundararajan et al. (2022) suggests that for devices with limited resources a lightweight asymmetric key cryptography algorithm will provide the necessary security characteristics along with the other characteristics like low energy usage, computational overhead, and implementation complexity. Odeh et al. (2022) specifically focus on the use of asymmetric algorithms, such as public-key cryptography, to secure blockchain-based healthcare applications. The use of asymmetric algorithms can help to improve patient data security, ensure the integrity of medical records, and prevent fraud and abuse. Public-key cryptography can also be used to track the movement of drugs and medical devices, and to prevent counterfeiting and theft.

Chen et al. (2023) proposed a hybrid cryptographic algorithm, called HAE, to improve security and efficiency for blockchain-based medical applications. They have used the combination of symmetric and asymmetric algorithm by combining the best features of AES and ECC. HAE makes managing vast volumes of sensitive medical data on the blockchain safer and more scalable by encrypting medical data with AES and encrypting the AES key using ECC.

In order to help secure patient data in e-health cloud environments, Dhanalakshmi and George (2022) proposed a secure hash-based cryptographic algorithm (SHA-512) with a Password-Based Key Derivation Function (PBKDF2). Hospital administrators refer to the computerized tracking of health-related data as “E-Health”. To stop data manipulation, patient-sensitive data must always be protected. This system is built on smart devices, including wireless sensor networks, laptops, desktop computers, and mobile phones, enabling real-time analysis of various patient characteristics (victo, 2021, Rajeswari and Gobinath, 2021). It seeks to develop a number of modules that, by tracking patient data online, will assist physicians in diagnosing their patients. It also enables attendants and caregivers to keep an eye out for any emergencies with the patient. Using the data gathered from the server, physicians and other caregivers can monitor the patient in real time. Every patient’s medical record is updated on cloud servers for convenient processing in the event of any logistical problems. This method combines SHA-512 with a Password-Based-KDF2 which accepts as input parameters the SHA-512 input message, password, salt, and counter (number of iterations).The number of iterations and the salt value are either saved with the hashed password or delivered as plain text with an encrypted message.

In order to ensure security when sharing data, the data must be encrypted and secured with a key and key must be kept confidential in order to prevent malicious access. With that concern, Quantum Cryptography based Cloud Security Model (QC-CSM), which shares the secret key between parties via the Quantum Key Distribution Protocol (QKDP) is developed. Attribute Based Encryption (ABE) is used to guarantee the data owner about the security of their shared data over the cloud. Additionally, authenticated user who has access to the decryption key from a secure quantum channel can only access the data(Sundar et al., 2023).

A reliable cloud user and a cutting-edge quantum cryptography service (QCaaS) are required for Cryptographic Cloud Computing Environment (CCCE)(Jasim et al., 2014, Mohamad et al., 2015). A new security service called QCaaS is responsible of resolving issues with key distribution, generation, and administration that arose through negotiations between the cloud provider and cloud customer. One such service is the quantum advanced encryption standard (QAES), which is a proposed symmetric quantum encryption technique. QAES is created by fusing an improved version of AES with two distinct modes—online and offline—with a quantum key distribution (QKD). Furthermore, by installing and configuring bare-metal Hyper-V with System Center Manager 2012-SPI, CCCE built more secure data communication routes (Mohammad et al., 2019).

The two most popular and well-liked quantum cryptography applications in the context of mobile cloud computing were thoroughly examined by Abidin et al (2022). They are the DARPA Network and IPSEC, which include quantum elements, key distribution, and protocols. The DARPA Quantum Network has two transmitters and two receivers connected directly through the fibre with quantum channels via a two-stage optical switch. One or both senders may set up a shared key for the other collector. The switch appears visually remote, which means that no photon passing through it is enhanced or distinguished, maintaining the same quantum condition of the photons encoding the fundamental pieces unaltered. (Lo et al., 2007). With respect to IPSec, both the sender and receiver are able to alter the keys used in their cryptographic computations fairly and consistently (Nguyen et al, 2006). The IKE convention need agreement from two endpoints regarding the cryptographic computations and conventions that they may wish to apply and the keys they use to encode and validate the message traffic that goes along with it in this affiliation with security (Niemiec, Marcin, 2019).

Quick Search through Indexing

Andola et al. (2022) proposed a hash based indexing for secure searchable encryption. It includes Elliptic curve based ElGamal additive homomorphic encryption.. Indexing eases the users' and cloud server's computational burden. The scheme eliminates the need for binary query schemes and complicated trapdoor systems. The security of this system completely relies on the concept of discrete logarithm.

At the beginning, files are encrypted using a symmetric encryption technique. For quick and efficient searching of user request, hash of keyword identity (ID) is used as a search index. There is also the corresponding tf-idf. The EC-based ElGamal cryptosystem, which supports multi-keyword requests and offers additive homomorphism, is used to encrypt the tf-idf. Since the EC-ElGamal Encryption requires a pre-shared key between the Data Owner and the Data User, it also makes sure that the hackers or even the server cannot recover the tf-idf weight of a file. On receipt of any search request, the server computes the total weight by summing up the encrypted tf-idf weights of all the keywords mentioned in the request. This provides a ranked multi keyword search over encrypted data.

For effective and secure searching, Binary Search Tree (BST) and hash table linked list are used. In this work, it is assumed that the entities authenticates with each other prior to communication. This scheme is more suitable for large data sets and it is efficient in handling the frequently changing updates and effective ranking of files with respect to the requested multi keywords.

PREFERRED MODEL

As already mentioned in section 4, quantum cryptography is not preferred for transferring large amounts of data. So, it is better to use Quantum Cryptography for key sharing(distribution) among the communicating entities and conventional techniques for securing the data (payload). For the proposed model, it is assumed that the users (sender and receiver) already possess a certificate issued by the trusted Cloud / third-party Certifying Authority to authenticate themselves with other users.

The flow diagram of the preferred model is shown in figure 5. Initially, the communicating entities, both sender and receiver, share the secret key through Quantum Cryptography in a separate secure channel. This secret key is used for providing data confidentiality during transit and storage as well. The Sending entity encrypts the data to be stored in cloud using the shared secret key. Then the client approaches the

Figure 5. Flow diagram of the proposed model

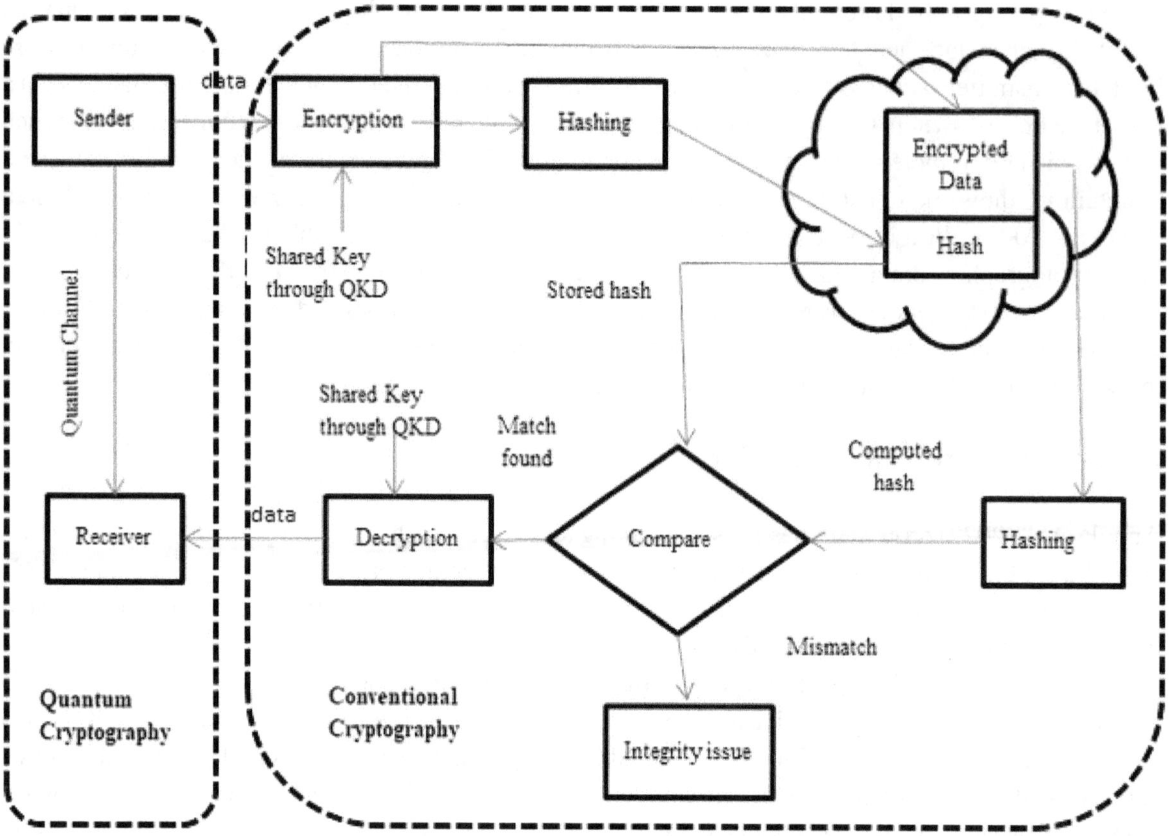

Cloud Service Provider (CSP) with its certificate to authenticate itself and makes a request to store the data. On successful verification, an agreed upon hashing technique is applied on the enciphered message to get the message digest/hash. The enciphered message along with the hash is stored on the cloud.

On the receiving end, the receiver authenticates itself to the CSP with its certificate and requests the cloud data. Cloud service provider checks the authenticity of the receiver. On successful verification, CSP computes the hash and checks it with the original hash which is appended with the message during storage. If there is a match, the requested data is sent to the receiver. The receiver then decrypts the data with the shared secret key. In this model, only one level of encryption is shown. Instead, double encryption can also be applied in order to provide one more layer of security. Moreover, asymmetric key encryption can also be used instead of single shared key.

CONCLUSION

The cloud computing environment allows storing and sharing a huge volume of digital data like text, image, audio, video, etc. through the Internet. It has become an exclusive technology due to its flexibility to access the data at any time as per user convenience. However, due to its centralized storage, Cloud computing faces few challenges like data loss, quality issues, and data security. Data security became a major concern in the cloud domain as the demand for cloud services is increasing drastically due to its scalability and allowance of concurrent access to users for using various cloud resources. As a consequence, malicious attacks and data breaches happen which also affect other cloud users using the same resources within the organizations that use cloud services. This chapter highlights the need of cryptography in securing cloud data, provides a detailed study of various traditional cryptographic techniques and modern quantum cryptography and its role in cloud computing. Moreover, a generic model incorporating quantum and traditional cryptographic techniques is proposed for securing the cloud data.

REFERENCES

Abidin, S., Swami, A., Ramirez-Asís, E., Alvarado-Tolentino, J., Maurya, R. K., & Hussain, N. (2022). Quantum cryptography technique: A way to improve security challenges in mobile cloud computing (MCC). *Materials Today: Proceedings*, *51*, 508–514. doi:10.1016/j.matpr.2021.05.593

Alabdulrazzaq, H., & Alenezi, M. N. (2022). Performance evaluation of cryptographic algorithms: DES, 3DES, blowfish, twofish, and threefish. *International Journal of Communication Networks and Information Security*, *14*(1), 51–61. doi:10.17762/ijcnis.v14i1.5262

Andola, N., Prakash, S., Yadav, V. K., Raghav, Venkatesan, S., & Verma, S. (2022). A secure searchable encryption scheme for cloud using hash-based indexing. *Journal of Computer and System Sciences*, *126*, 119–137. doi:10.1016/j.jcss.2021.12.004

Bauspiess, F., & Damm, F. (1992). Requirements for Cryptographic Hash Functions. *Computers & Security*, *11*(5), 427–437. doi:10.1016/0167-4048(92)90007-E

Bijapure, S., & Borse, Y. (2023). Cloud security threats and solutions: A survey. *Wireless Personal Communications*, *128*(1), 387–413. doi:10.1007/s11277-022-09960-z

Chen, Z., Gu, J., & Yan, H. (2023). HAE: A Hybrid Cryptographic Algorithm for Blockchain Medical Scenario Applications. *Applied Sciences (Basel, Switzerland)*, *13*(22), 12163. doi:10.3390/app132212163

Chitturi, A. K., & Swarnalatha, P. (2020). Exploration of various cloud security challenges and threats. In *Soft Computing for Problem Solving: SocProS 2018* (Vol. 2, pp. 891–899). Springer Singapore. doi:10.1007/978-981-15-0184-5_76

Cole, T., Bhardwaj, A. K., Garg, L., & Shrivastava, D. P. (2019). Investigation into cloud computing adoption within the hedge fund industry. [JCIT]. *Journal of Cases on Information Technology*, *21*(3), 1–25. doi:10.4018/JCIT.2019070101

Dhanalakshmii, G., & George, G. V. (2022). An Enhanced Data Integrity for the E-Health Cloud System using a Secure Hashing Cryptographic Algorithm with a Password Based Key Derivation Function2 (KDF2). *Int J Eng Trends Technol*, *70*(9), 290–297. doi:10.14445/22315381/IJETT-V70I9P229

Ebinazer, E., Silambarasan, N. S., & Mary Saira Bhanu, S. (2021). ESKEA: Enhanced symmetric key encryption algorithm based secure data storage in cloud networks with data deduplication. *Wireless Personal Communications*, *117*(4), 3309–3325. doi:10.1007/s11277-020-07989-6

Fatima, S., & Ahmad, S. (2021). Quantum key distribution approach for secure authentication of cloud servers. [IJCAC]. *International Journal of Cloud Applications and Computing, 11*(3), 19–32. doi:10.4018/IJCAC.2021070102

Fouzar, Y., Lakhssassi, A., & Ramakrishna, M. (2023). A Novel Hybrid Multikey Cryptography Technique for Video Communication. *IEEE Access : Practical Innovations, Open Solutions, 11*, 15693–15700. doi:10.1109/ACCESS.2023.3242616

Gisin, N., Ribordy, G., Tittel, W., & Zbinden, H. (2002). Quantum cryptography. *Reviews of Modern Physics, 74*(1), 145–195. doi:10.1103/RevModPhys.74.145

Halak, B., Yilmaz, Y., & Shiu, D. (2022). Comparative analysis of energy costs of asymmetric vs symmetric encryption-based security applications. *IEEE Access : Practical Innovations, Open Solutions, 10*, 76707–76719. doi:10.1109/ACCESS.2022.3192970

Hercigonja, Z. (2016). Comparative analysis of cryptographic algorithms. *International Journal of Digital Technology & Economy, 1*(2), 127–134.

IBM Data Breach Report. (2022). IBM. https://www.ibm.com/reports/data-breach

Jasim, O. K., Abbas, S., El-Horbaty, E.-S. M., & Salem, A.-B. M. (2014). Cryptographic cloud computing environment as a more trusted communication environment. [IJGHPC]. *International Journal of Grid and High Performance Computing, 6*(2), 38–51. doi:10.4018/ijghpc.2014040103

Jayaprakash, J. (2022). Cloud Data Encryption and Authentication Based on Enhanced Merkle Hash Tree Method. *Computers, Materials & Continua, 72*(1). doi:10.32604/cmc.2022.021269

Kaur, S., Kaur, G., & Shabaz, M. (2022). A secure two-factor authentication framework in cloud computing. *Security and Communication Networks, 2022*, 1–9. doi:10.1155/2022/7540891

Lamas-Linares, A., & Kurtsiefer, C. (2007). Breaking a quantum key distribution system through a timing side channel. *Optics Express, 15*(15), 9388–9393. doi:10.1364/OE.15.009388 PMID:19547285

Lo, H.-K., & Lütkenhaus, N. (2007). Quantum cryptography: from theory to practice. arXiv preprint quant-ph/0702202 (2007).

Mell, P., & Grance, T. (2011). The NIST definition of cloud computing. *National Institute of Standards and Technology, NIST Special Publication USA, 53*(6), 50–50.

Mohammad, O. K. (2015). Securing cloud computing environment using a new trend of cryptography. In *2015 International Conference on Cloud Computing (ICCC),* (pp. 1-8). IEEE.

Mohammad, O. K. (2019). Detailed quantum cryptographic service and data security in cloud computing. *Advances in Data Science, Cyber Security and IT Applications: First International Conference on Computing*. Springer.

Nguyen, T. M. T., Sfaxi, M. A., & Ghernaouti-Hélie, S. (2006). Integration of quantum cryptography in 802.11 networks. In *First International Conference on Availability, Reliability and Security (ARES'06),* (pp. 8). IEEE. 10.1109/ARES.2006.75

Niemiec, M. (2019). Error correction in quantum cryptography based on artificial neural networks. *Quantum Information Processing*, *18*(6), 174. doi:10.1007/s11128-019-2296-4

Odeh, A., Keshta, I., & Abu Al-Haija, Q. (2022). Analysis of Blockchain in the Healthcare Sector: Application and Issues. *Symmetry*, *14*(9), 1760. doi:10.3390/sym14091760

Qing-hail, B., Wen, Z., Peng, J., & Xul, L. (2012). Research on design principles of elliptic curve public key cryptography and its implementation. *Int. Conf. on Computer Science and Service System*, Nanjing, China.

Rajeswari, V., & Gobinath, G. S. R. A. R. (2021). Securing an E-Health Care Information Systems on Cloud Environments with Big Data Approach. *Design Engineering (London)*, 6986–6994.

Sahinoglu, M., & Cueva-Parra, L. (2011). Cloud computing. Wiley interdisciplinary reviews: Computational statistics, 3(1), 47-68. Wiley.

Salami, Y., Khajevand, V., & Zeinali, E. (2023). Cryptographic Algorithms: A Review of the Literature, Weaknesses and Open Challenges. *J. Comput. Robot*, *16*(2), 46–56.

Scarani, V., Iblisdir, S., Gisin, N., & Acin, A. (2005). Quantum cloning. *Reviews of Modern Physics*, *77*(4), 1225–1256. doi:10.1103/RevModPhys.77.1225

Senyo, P. K., Effah, J., & Addae, E. (2016). Preliminary insight into cloud computing adoption in a developing country. *Journal of Enterprise Information Management*, *29*(4), 505–524. doi:10.1108/JEIM-09-2014-0094

Sharma, D. K., Singh, N. C., Noola, D. A., Doss, A. N., & Sivakumar, J. (2022). A review on various cryptographic techniques & algorithms. *Materials Today: Proceedings*, *51*, 104–109. doi:10.1016/j.matpr.2021.04.583

Sundar, K., Sasikumar, S., Jayakumar, C., Nagarajan, D., & karthick, S. (2023). Quantum cryptography based cloud security model (QC-CSM) for ensuring cloud data security in storage and accessing. *Multimedia Tools and Applications*, *82*(27), 1–16. doi:10.1007/s11042-023-15463-1

Sundararajan, A. D. D., & Rajashree, R. (2022). A Comprehensive Survey on Lightweight Asymmetric Key Cryptographic Algorithm for Resource Constrained Devices. *ECS Transactions*, *107*(1), 7457–7468. doi:10.1149/10701.7457ecst

Vandervelden, T., De Smet, R., Steenhaut, K., & Braeken, A. (2022). Symmetric-key-based authentication among the nodes in a wireless sensor and actuator network. *Sensors (Basel)*, *22*(4), 1403. doi:10.3390/s22041403 PMID:35214305

Victo Sudha George, G. (2021). A Review of Classifying and Securing Sensitive Customer Data on Cloud Environments using Cryptographic Algorithms. *Design Engineering (London)*, 12424–12444.

Xiao, L., Li, Q., & Liu, J. (2016). Survey on secure cloud storage. *Journal of Data Acquis Process*, *31*(3), 464–472.

Yadav, A. K., Braeken, A., & Misra, M. (2023). Symmetric key-based authentication and key agreement scheme resistant against semi-trusted third party for fog and dew computing. *The Journal of Supercomputing*, *79*(10), 1–39. doi:10.1007/s11227-023-05064-y

Yadav, A. K., Misra, M., Braeken, A., & Liyanage, M. (2023), A Secure Blockchain-based Authentication and Key Agreement Protocol for 5G Roaming. *IEEE Consumer Communications and Networking Conference (CCNC) 2023*. IEEE. 10.1109/CCNC51644.2023.10059918

KEY TERMS AND DEFINITIONS

Asymmetric Encryption: A type of encryption which uses a key pair (public key, private key). If one key is used for encryption then only its pair key is used for decryption.

Authentication: This is process of verifying the identity of user or entity.

Confidentiality: This is protecting information from unauthorised access.

Cryptography: The study of techniques for secure communication using mathematical concepts.

Encryption: The process of converting the original text into an alternate form (code) to prevent unauthorised access.

Hashing: This is a technique to convert the variable length data into a fixed length identifier called hash.

Symmetric Encryption: A type of encryption with a single shared secret key which is used for both encryption and decryption of data.

Chapter 5
Load Balancing Techniques in Cloud Computing

Veera Talukdar
https://orcid.org/0000-0002-9204-5825
D.Y. Patil International University, India

Ardhariksa Zukhruf Kurniullah
Institut Tazkia, Indonesia

Palak Keshwani
The ICFAI University, India

Huma Khan
https://orcid.org/0000-0003-1653-8676
Rungta College of Engineering and Technology, India

Sabyasachi Pramanik
https://orcid.org/0000-0002-9431-8751
Haldia Institute of Technology, India

Ankur Gupta
https://orcid.org/0000-0002-4651-5830
Vaish College of Engineering, Rohtak, India

Digvijay Pandey
https://orcid.org/0000-0003-0353-174X
Department of Technical Education, IET Lucknow, Government of Uttar Pradesh, India

ABSTRACT

In a cloud framework, conveyed figuring is a flexible and modest area. It permits the development of a strong environment that supports pay-per-view while taking client demands into account. The cloud is a grouping of replicated approaches that collaborate as one computing system with constrained scope. Spread management's main goal is to make it simple to provide consent to distant and geographically distributed resources. Cloud is taking little steps in the direction of a turn while dealing with a massive array of issues, among them organizing. There are many methods for determining how to correspond with the volume of work that a PC structure is expected to complete. According to the evolving scenario and such an effort, the scheduler modifies the occupations' coordinating situation. The suggestion for thinking Improvements to the assignment movement combination planning estimate have been made for assessment with FCFS and least fulfillment time booking and expert execution of initiatives.

DOI: 10.4018/979-8-3693-0900-1.ch005

INTRODUCTION

The most recent advancement that is perhaps widely recognized nowadays in IT adventures, just like in research and development, is appropriate managing. This improvement in dispersed figures serves as a paradigm of advancement after the introduction of streaming dealing with. There is a paralyzed virtualization in contrast to the dispersed handling and the distributed signing up for this. The all of the labor that is related to sporadic figuring takes place in a virtual environment. Clients just need to communicate with the web in order to get the anticipated increases from the cloud, after which they may easily use the unexpected figures and cutoff limits. Client basics demonstrate the dispersed handling associations provided by CSP (cloud master relationship). They provide grouped character of organizations to satiate the interests of diverse clientele. To sum up, the stretch cloud is an executable environment with a dynamic lead of resources as well as customers providing different forms of assistance. One of the more unquestionably successful actions that take place in the delivered figuring state is booking. Sorting things out is one of the efforts made to get the most impressive advantage in order to increase the benefit of the labor store of distributed figuring. The main goal of the cloud booking reminders is to effectively employ the resources while managing the store between them to get the quickest execution time.

Appropriate enrollment has recently attracted a lot of attention as a potentially effective method of disseminating the advantages of Data and Correspondence Innovations (ICT) as a utility. The use of datacenter resources, which are operating in most astonishing quantity and have worked waiting to be done conditions, must be reduced in order to provide these affiliations. The main components of conveyed handling are datacenters. A single datacenter often has hundreds of thousands of virtual employees working at any one time.

Time passes while carrying out various chores and the cloud infrastructure keeps receiving groups of project needs.

LITERATURE SURVEY

There have been earlier studies on workload pattern analysis for cloud computing systems (Dogani, J. et al., 2023). This section delineates the most pertinent methodologies, while also addressing their constraints and deficiencies.

Figure 1. Scheduling methods

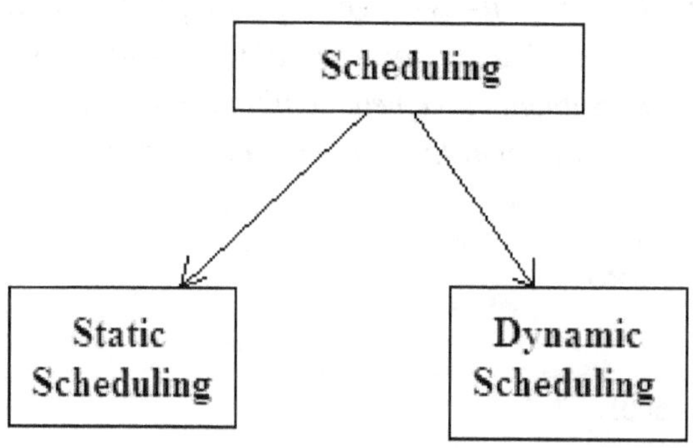

(Zhao, S. et al, 2023) to characterizing cloud computing Hadoop ecosystems' workloads is based on an examination of the Google tracelog's first version. This work's primary goal is to gather coarse-grained statistical information on jobs and activities in order to categorize them according to length. This feature restricts the work's applicability to the research of timing difficulties and renders it inappropriate for the analysis of other Cloud computing challenges involving resource utilization patterns. Furthermore, as previously noted, the study overlooks the interaction with users in favor of tasks, despite the fact that this relationship is a critical component of cloud workload.

(Wadhwa, H. et al, 2023) assesses whether the task waiting time, CPU, memory, and disk consumption means are appropriate for correctly capturing the real-world performance characteristics. The research used data that is not publicly accessible and included the historical traces of six Google compute clusters over a period of five days. According to the assessment that was done, mean values of runtime task resource consumption show promise as a means of characterizing the total utilization of task resources. It does not, however, address how members act or how the limits for task categorization were established.

A method for creating workload classifications for cloud computing based on task resource consumption patterns is described by (Katal, A. et al, 2023). The records from five Google clusters during a four-day period make up the studied data. The suggested method defines the features of the workload, creates a task categorization, determines the qualitative borders of each cluster, and then merges neighboring clusters to decrease the number of clusters. This method works well for classifying jobs, but it doesn't analyze the properties of the resulting clusters to provide a comprehensive workload model. Finally, user patterns are completely ignored in favor of task modeling.

MapReduce traces are statistically analyzed by (Aarthee, S. et al, 2023). Ten months' worth of MapReduce logs from the M45 supercomputing cluster served as the basis for the investigation. Here, the authors provide a collection of coarse-grained statistical features of the data pertaining to work patterns, failure causes, and resource use. This study only offers extremely generic information regarding resource consumption and user activity patterns, but it gives a full description of the distributions followed by the task completion times.

(Shehloo, A.A. et al, 2023) provide a method for Hadoop task characterization. 11,686 tasks from a 24-hour data set from one of Yahoo!'s production clusters are used in the research. The measurements in this data collection are produced by the Hadoop framework. The primary goal of this effort is to use clustering to group tasks with comparable attributes and then examine the centroids that are produced. This study ignores other vital resources like CPU and Memory in favor of concentrating only on how the storage system is used.

Our earlier work (Chen, L. et al, 2023) presents coarse-grain statistical properties of the Google tracelog and uses statistical mechanisms to select the number of clusters for classifying tasks and users. It offers a method for characterizing Cloud workload based on user and task patterns using the second version of the tracelog. The best suited distributions for each cluster are determined after a brief examination of the clusters. In order to validate the computed analytical parameters, they are then simulated and contrasted with the empirical data. There are some drawbacks with this study. First, the analysis was limited to a two-day period instead of the whole tracelog, which might leave out important activity in the system environment. Furthermore, the high-level data provided by the cluster and intra-cluster analyses lack the specificity necessary to measure the variety of workload. Moreover, not enough information is provided on the parameter distributions that were employed; additional information is required so that other researchers can replicate the workload that was achieved. Last but not least, the simulated model's validation against the empirical data is based only on a visual match of the patterns from a single run and ignores more exacting statistical methods.

It is evident from the review of relevant work that there aren't many production tracelogs available for examining workload trends in cloud settings. It is necessary to fill in the gaps found in earlier assessments in order to obtain more realistic workload patterns. Large data samples must be analyzed, as done by (Wang, J. et al. 2023). Models with small operating time periods, such those in (Mandal, R. et al., 2023) may be erroneous. Secondly, investigations should go beyond cluster centroids and coarse-grain statistics. It's also essential to do parameter analysis and look at the trends for each cluster feature in order to identify the patterns of grouped people. While earlier methods give some insights on the nature of the workload, they don't provide a structured model that can be utilized to run simulations. Ultimately, because users are the ones who drive the burden, realistic workload models need to include user behavior patterns that are connected to specific activities. The methods previously discussed only concentrate on tasks, ignoring the influence of user behavior on the total burden of the environment.

CLOUD COMPUTING

In the middle of this specific situation, there should be less turned-on employees than objective specialists who can do certain pushing-ahead jobs. Therefore, undertaking coordination is a challenging problem that significantly affects how the cloud authority center is presented. Common approaches that are employed in progress are predictable, quick, and excellent in their recommendations, but they consistently log problems on nearby optimums. The most well-known method for including generally clearing interest space with a correspondingly large number of anticipated systems, Non Polynomial, fits the multifaceted arrangement of the task coordination problem and avoids taking additional time to find the best solution. Under these circumstances, there is no pre-made, widely used approach to address the problems. Finding the closest, best method, ideally quickly, is acceptable regardless of the cloud cover. IT professionals are concentrating on heuristic methods in this strategy. It is one of the most often used pronunciations at the moment. The idea of communicated handling is pervasive regardless of whether we open an IT magazine or any website. A crisis might occur when the number of customers for the same information's portion increases. Different aid models are offered through appropriate reasoning. It very well may be making another attempt as an affiliate portrayal, presenting content on a single stage. It may very well be a stage where an affiliation provides a location from which things and data may be obtained, but ultimately it will be a system where an affiliation provides security and fortress affiliations. The client uses a portable device, a computer, or a PDA to access the web-based dimness advantages.

The client relationship is provided via the authority link. Framework as an affiliation (IaaS) proposes the sharing of physical resources for carrying out affiliations, often leveraging advancements in virtualization. The alternative way is called "Stage as a Support" (PaaS), and it combines a thing's execution condition, like an application worker. In the Software as a Service (SaaS) model, all applications are made available on the Web. As an example, your statement orchestrating developing PC programs isn't shown locally on your PC but rather is accessed via a web program and is instead running on a specialist in the organization.

Conveyed enrollment is a conceptual framework in which a vast array of plans is linked in private or public frameworks to provide an adaptable foundation for application, data, and record collecting. The cost of figuring, application engagement, content accumulating, and advancement is fundamentally re-

Figure 2. A scenario for cloud computing

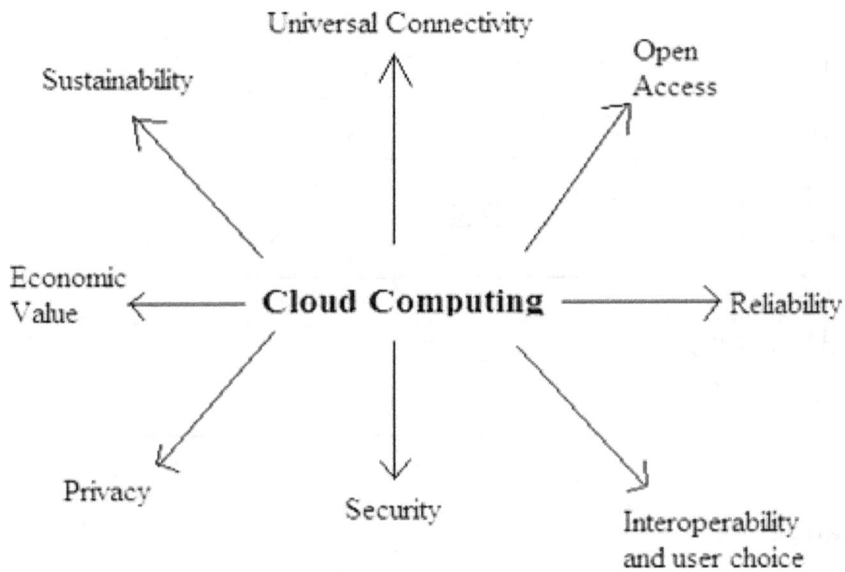

duced by the existence of this movement. It may transform a professional ranch from a capital-raised set up to a changeable overviewed condition. Given dealing with is a gigantic technique to direct experience coordinate cash conserving focal concentrations. The "reusability of IT limits" is a crucial first for cloud computing. The separation that flowing figuring brings meandering from conventional considerations of "network arranging", "scattered choosing", "utility figuring", or "autonomic signing up" is to broaden horizons spanning over modest cutoff points.

The affiliations that cloud suppliers provide may be combined into three orders.

1. Software as a Service (SaaS): In this approach, the customer is offered the use of a whole program on demand. While other end users are updated, a single affiliation event runs on the fog. Customers' direct interest in employees or programming licenses is eliminated, but provider expenses are reduced since just one application has to be supported and maintained. Today, SaaS is presented via partnerships with companies like Google, Deals Power, Microsoft, and Zoho, among others.
2. Thing as a Help (PaaS): In this case, a programming layer or improvement condition is shown and presented as a partnership, after which further, more significant levels of partnership may be communicated. The customer gets the chance to support his own apps while they are still active on the supplier's system. PaaS suppliers provide a predetermined combination of operating system and application workers, such as Light stage (Linux, Apache, MySql, and PHP), bound J2EE, Ruby, and so on, to satisfy the basic sensitivity and adaptability requirements of the entry. Google's Application Motor, Force.com, and other well-known PaaS examples are included.
3. IaaS, or Infrastructure as a Service, provides significant assembling and recruiting restrictions as an ordered connection over the design. Worker pools and open access to expert homestead space, collection systems, collecting materials, and other resources are used to divert surplus loads. Typically, the customer would supply his own customized programming on the plan. A few common examples are Amazon, GoGrid, Tera, and so on.

Figure 3. Cloud computing services offered

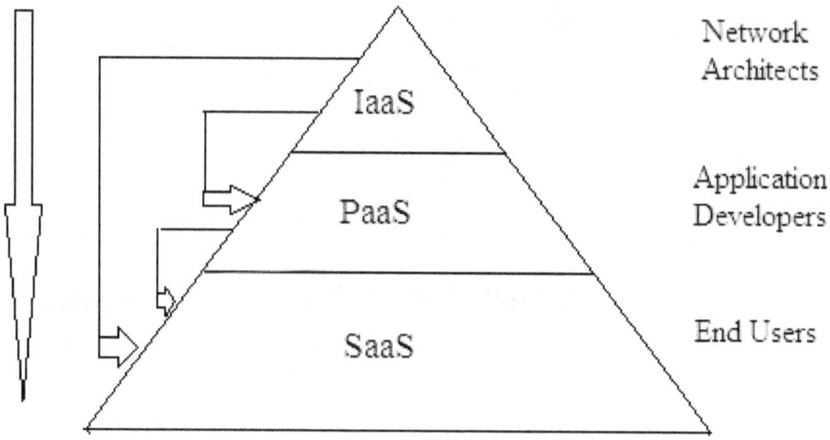

CLOUD Arrangement

Surrounded dealing with is only beginning to get traction as a business reality in the realm of reality enhancement. In any case, progress has not yet been accomplished in full. Currently, there are a few zones that ought to have been developed.

1. Executives' assets
2. Planning an errand

The main problem areas in both the Framework and in dispersed care are undertaking booking and resource mapping. Conveyed figuring is advancing in the IT industry. The cash-saving inclination of these hiring standards is impacted by how professional firms set up their cloudiness relationships with their customers. Booking is the process of allocating jobs to available resources after determining the merits and requirements of an activity. Extended resource consumption without affecting the cloud-provided connectivity is the typical purpose of booking. There are two types of setup, such as scheduling work and arranging resources. The following are some prerequisites for making reservations and handling spreads.

1. Fair resource fragment - Booking is done similarly with the specific goal that tasking of resources is done in a reasonable amount of time.
2. QoS - Resources and vocations are common in such a course as a result, creating the character of connections.
3. Asset use: This measures how well the plan's resources are being used. A reasonable holding estimate results in the best resource utilization.
4. Energy consumption - This measures how quickly resources for development are depleted. A good holding assessment reduces need usage.

Unambiguously, the booking measure in fog is divided into three phases:

1. Asset locating and filtering Datacenter Merchant locates the items currently present in the affiliation structure and compiles location data on the items.
2. Asset confirmation - The target asset is chosen in accordance with the explicit requirements of the assignment and asset. Picking stage is now.
3. Task - Assignment is given to selected asset.

There are so many reviews for reservations in distributed dealing with. Getting an unparalleled is the main motivation for the point of view of coordinating count. FCFS, Cooperative effort, Min computation, Max-Min figuring, and meta-heuristic assessments (ACO, GA, Recreated fortification, PSO, Forbidden seek after, and others) are important examples of coordinating counts.

FCFS: The initial beginning of things serve concept suggests that the first work be carried out initially.

Supportive Calculation (RRA): In this Planning, time is being allocated to resources in a time-efficient manner.

Calculated with the minimum possible value, the most menial activities are completed first.

Max-Min counting: Max-Min count chooses to perform the more observable activities first.

Three phases may be identified when anticipating dispersed enlistment.

1. Identifying and isolating a resource.
2. Selecting an impartial resource (the choice kinds).
3. The concept of a specific attempt to an impartial resource

Figure 4. Scheduling stages
Datacenter Counselor, DB

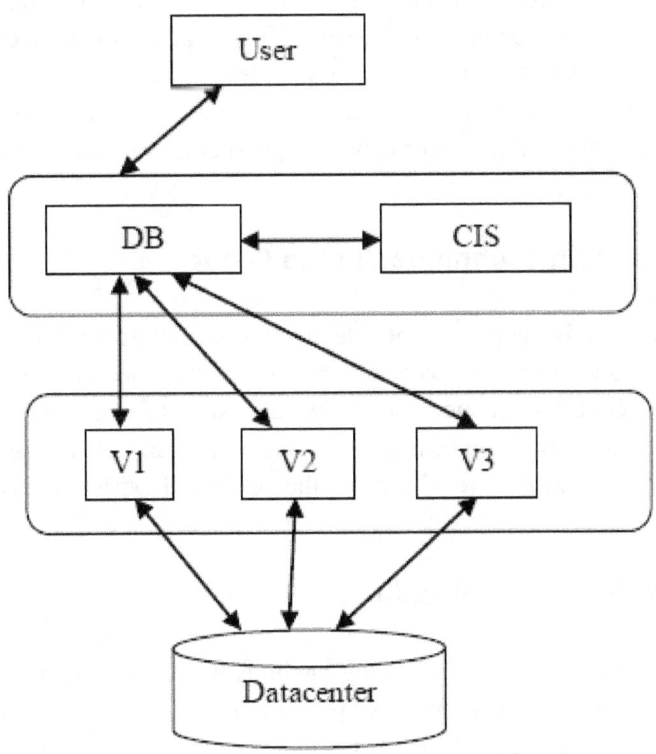

CIS: The robotic machines V1, V2, and V3 belong to the Cloud Material organizations.

FEATURES AND ADVANTAGES

They have attractive qualities that help both Cloud Arrangement Buyers (CSCs) (Pramanik, S. et al. 2021) and Cloud Master Centers (CSPs) (Chellam, V. V. et al. 2023) due to their dispersed handling. Those are

1. There are no honest pledges
2. Access when requested
3. Beautiful evaluation
4. Altered application flexibility and acceleration
5. Competent task asset
6. Energy potential
7. Development and use of untouchable associations on a regular basis.

The somewhat lengthy beneficial advantage from record of the decreased maintenance charges and utility prices linked with IT programming and setup is the most obvious astonishing case from the act of Cloud managing plans and improvements. This is a broad way of thinking about how IT resources—clearly programming and foundation—are converted into utility charges, which are paid however extensively and slowly they are used. Capital expenditures are inexorably related with resources that must be paid for up front in order to launch a company improvement. Prior to cloud computing, IT foundation and programming were considered capital costs since they had to be paid in accordance with the price of a support design that enabled a connection's commercial operations. Following some time, these costs are reimbursed from the expert's remuneration. Since affiliations are often linked to depreciable assets, they consistently restrict capital costs. This is how equipment works: a worker bought today for $1,000 will be valued by the market at little more than half of its exceptional cost when it is guaranteed to be moved by machinery. Affiliations must also pay back the harm that various systems have caused in order to get advantage.

Existing Load Balancing Techniques in the Cloud

In a nutshell, load balancing is the process of effectively distributing workloads (data) across several computer services to enhance network speed, redundancy, and reliability. Comparable to traffic cops are load balancers. They control communication between business servers. In order to handle changing traffic patterns and prevent overload on business servers, load balancers are essential nowadays. Enterprise IT teams may add or remove servers based on the needs and expectations of the company thanks to load balancers.

Techniques for Load Balancing Algorithms

IT teams choose from a variety of load balancing methods based on the distribution of the load, i.e., whether the demand is on the network layer or the application layer. Based on the load balancing methods in use, the choice of backend servers to route the traffic is made. The two components of the server that the algorithms analyze are: (i) server health; and (ii) predefined condition. A few popular load balancing algorithms that IT teams often use include

1. Algorithm of Round Robin: The circular distribution of requests to corporate servers in a sequential fashion is known as the round robin (RR) algorithm. Weighted round robin and dynamic round robin are the two varieties of round robin. In a weighted round robin, which is mostly used for a cluster of distinct servers, each server is given a weight based on its makeup. In a cyclical process, the load is distributed based on the pre-assigned efficiency. Requests are sent to related servers using dynamic round robin, which is based on the real-time assignment of server weights.
2. Fewest relationships: The "Least Connections" load balancing technique selects the server with the fewest active transactions (connections) in order to disperse the load between application instances based on the number of connections that are currently active.
3. Connections with the least weight: The load distribution in weighted least connections takes into account the relative capacity of each server as well as the number of active and current connections to each server.
4. Source IP hash: A distinct hash key is used to pick a server for load balancing in a source IP hash. The request's source and destination are used to construct the hash key. Clients are given servers based on the hash key that is created.
5. Hash URL: In order to deliver requests for URLs—that is, to offer material that is unique to each server—load balanced servers employ URL hashing as a load balancing approach. By preventing cache duplication, it increases the capacity of backend caches.
6. The quickest reaction time: The backend server with the fewest active connections and the lowest average response time is chosen in the least response time algorithm. With this approach, IT guarantees end users will get a fast response.
7. The least amount of bandwidth: Backend servers are chosen using the least bandwidth approach according to their bandwidth usage, or more specifically, the server with the lowest bandwidth consumption (measured in Mbps). The least packets approach is comparable to the least bandwidth method. Here, the load balancer chooses the server that transmits the fewest packets.
8. The unique loading technique: The backend servers are selected using the custom load approach in accordance with the load. The server load is determined by factoring in the CPU, memory, and response time of the server. IT teams often utilize this technique in organizations to effectively determine resource use. This algorithm works best in situations when traffic is steady and predictable; it is less effective in situations where traffic fluctuates abruptly and unevenly.

Different Development Methodologies

The suitable hiring viewpoint guarantees a financially prudent solution for executing company applications using virtualization advancements, really flexible distributed figuring, and data affiliation frameworks, as well as a pay-as-you-go assessment model. Recently, it has also provided the highest enrollment cap for apps to manage difficult challenges. Restructuring resource utilization is crucial to attaining cost sufficiency. Low utilization has been a problem in professional ranches for a very long time. In a typical expert ranch, employees are only used 10 to 50 percent of their maximum capacity. In seasoned ranches, 10% to 20% usage is typical. For a professional ranch, or a group of employees inside

Table 1. Methods for cloud load balancing found in the literature

Reference	Algorithm Utilized	Characteristic utilized	Category of load balancing	Method involved	Pros	Cons
(Saidi, K. et al, 2023)	Traditional	VM scheduling	VM LB	Optimization (classical, LP)	Capable of completing challenging tasks by the deadline. Reduce the task rejection percentage. Carry out resource scaling automatically.	Tasks that take longer to complete than the allotted time are refused. Merely space sharing policy, rather than time shared policy, is used in the Cloudsim experiments.
(Xiong, S. et al, 2023)	Algorithms for creating columns and whole sets	Task scheduling	Task LB	Heuristic	Load balancing is done over the bare minimum of virtual machines. enhanced use of resources	An approach simply assesses one objective function.
(Saif, M.A.N. et al. 2023)	Load balancing utilizing constraint measures and dragonfly optimization	VM scheduling	Task LB	Optimization (swarm dependent)	Load balancing is carried out through reduced power use.	Unable to do activities that exceed the barrier. The task rejection rate is large.
(Xu, H. et al, 2023)	Fairness Aware Algorithm	Task scheduling	Task LB	Optimization (game theory dependent)	Achieving optimal LB occurs at the Nash equilibrium point. Limit the anticipated time of responding	lengthy job completion time
(Sangaiah, A.K., et al, 2023)	Honey Bee Conduct	Resource scheduling	CPU LB	Optimization (swarm dependent)	Quick reaction time. small makespan	Limited scalability
(Bashir, S. et al, 2023)	Nature-inspired Algorithmic driven by Agents	Resource scheduling	Resource LB	Heuristic	Very scalable Low reaction time is not taken into account enhanced use of resources	Don't take execution costs into account Violators of service levels are not regarded Task refusal rate is not taken into account
(Adewojo, A.A. et al, 2023)	Weighted Round Robin	Task scheduling	Task LB	Heuristic	good use of available resources Increasing throughput	response time was not selected quantity of equilibrium not selected

a professional ranch, that primarily manages applications with exceptional preparation requirements and manages similar jobs, problem might be problematic. We describe our cloud calculating booking evaluations in this area. We initially have a discussion about the fundamental orchestrating computations and then provide our solidifying strategies in accordance with these evaluations.

Scheduling of Cloud Services

The organizational benefits of the cloud are seen at the client and developer levels. Organizing addresses difficulties brought up by advantage outline between customers and providers at the client level. The resource affiliation special datacenter coordination is handled at the development level. A datacenter includes several actual machines. Clients provide many tasks, which are then assigned to real machines in the datacenter. This project or assembly often affects how the datacenter is presented. Despite the usage of the structure, a variety of requirements such as QoS (Praveenkumar, S. et al. 2023), SLA, resource sharing, assortment to minor discontent, dependability, reliable satisfaction, and other factors should be taken into consideration.

Glassy User Scheduling

Market-based and closeout-based schedulers are suitable for managing the unrestricted economic expansion of cloud resource. When resources are virtualized and provided to clients as an affiliation, a market-based resource package might be helpful. According to (Larsen, M.L. 2023), a set-up of market coordinated task organizing assessments to a bartering network is planned for varied appropriated settings. The development of a fog assessment model that uses processor sharing is suggested in (Khurana, D., et al. 2023), as is the use of this in connection to an old-style composite relationship with certainty thought and the update of two schemes for advantage-driven booking figuring. Assistance Equivalent Arrangements (SLA) is used for affiliation supply in Mists. If a situation of clarification encroachment should arise, SLA keeps an eye out for a strategy that is set aside between the client and the professional relationship, providing the focal points of the understanding along with non-practical affiliation essentials depicted as Nature of Office (QoS), commitments, and disciplines. In order to implement this plan, processes that take into account varied SLA restrictions and robust resource development must be put together. For passing on applications in the dark, a remarkable booking heuristic taking into account different SLA constraints is provided in (Wadhwa, H., et al. 2023). The scheduler calculation that permits resource re-provisioning on the premise that faulty assumptions could occur is presented in (Dutta, P., et al. 2023). The social event of modeling is to provide customers and clients with reasonable plans, further build the nature of affiliation, and in addition produce the perfect compensation season. An approach for sorting out narrative clouds makes advantage of a nearby trust screen SLA to provide faster booking of the overflowing client interest while still protecting the interest. (Hesaraki, A.F., et al. 2023) proposes an amazing way of heuristic-based interest booking at each trained professional, throughout all of the geographically encircling worker ranches, very remote from the focus assigned to the dispersed selection frame. This framework looks at two heuristic combinations, one significantly contemplating gi-FIFO booking and the other the mimicked empowering concept for neighborhood looks for. (Canbaloğlu, G., et al. 2023) proposes a computation to obtain the gathered certain assessment of relationship for each occupation in the separating no-preplanned need M/G/1 covering model, taking into consideration the dealing with model and structure expense work, taking into translation the complaints of the appropriated dealing with affiliation clients and providers. This system ensures that the customers' QoS requirements are met, and it also provides the finest assistance for the transmitted figuring authority affiliations. Pitch driven resource fragment has been developed and used by open Framework as-a-Administration (IaaS) providers like Amazon EC2 to manage constantly shifting resource needs. In this scenario, certain types of virtual machines (VMs) are supplied as cloud resources, and the cloud provider operates a closeout-based market for each VM type with the aim of eventually obtaining the most above absurd pay. (Fusaro, D., et al. 2023) makes a suggestion for a predictable assessment of a single cloud provider and how to best satisfy client demand while helping the providers via payment and customer successes while enforcing cost imperatives. It is suggested in (Rezakhani, M., et al. 2023) to use another closeout-based tool for dynamic VM provisioning and job that takes the client's interest in VMs into account.

Static and Active Scheduling

Static sorting takes into account gathering necessary information in advance and scheduling certain times for job completion. Runtime above is decreased by static booking. Assuming a dynamic booking event should occur and no prior knowledge of the job elements or task exists. As a result, the project's execution season may not be known, and tasks are carried out as they arise while the program runs.

In order to provide the customer with a flexible assessment model while in the meanwhile, Flextic attempts a variety of static booking frameworks sorting for the cloud service provider has been shown in (Mahajan, H.B., et al. 2023). The three-level cloud structure's affiliation request arranging systems, which include resource suppliers, ace affiliations, and buyers, should appease the rivalries between the power affiliations and customers. To overcome the aforementioned problems, a strong need coordination count (DPSA) is anticipated in (Nakamura, V.A., et al. 2023). A second, more forgiving booking assessment MaxRe is suggested in (Dai, P., et al. 2023). This estimate combines the unwavering quality assessment for the robust replication architecture with a remarkable quantity of mimes for various tasks. A task coordinating paradigm based on a trust instrument is shown in (Szameitat, A.J., et al. 2023). By employing the Bayesian scholarly framework, trust relationships are built amongst enrolling centers, and center centers' bravery is focused. In (Wei, B., et al. 2023) a dynamic assessment calculation for a graspable job booking structure is presented. When resource examinations are brutal, a proper, competent booking improves the practice of placing resources in clouds and information thinking in above evaluations. Because the jobs on cloud structures are all quite baffling in relation to one another, dispersed figuring prevents typical methods for project coordination from checking the cost of cloud resources unambiguously. Researches provides a recalculated count for undertaking booking that takes ABC (headway based costing) into account in the authorized figure and its execution. In accordance it acts as an introduction to several improvement strategies for cost regions of strength for optimum for cross collecting cloud situations. A common trim calculation is employed in a changing winding (BS) approach to achieve QOS in cloudy conditions. This study compared three distinct business planning estimations: Simple, Moderate, and CBA. Getting organized calculation is proposed that evaluates resource cost and estimation performance, as well as upgrades the count/correspondence degree by grouping client endeavors in accordance with a given cloud resource's orchestration limit and sending the assembled endeavors to the power. The correspondence of coarse-grained jobs and resources smooth out computation/correspondence degree in light of work collection. Continuous figure-makers squander a tremendous amount of resources and emit a lot of carbon dioxide. Green task (Ngọc, T. H. et al. 2023) organization is effective in cutting tainting and centrality usage on a very fundamental level. In

(Nye, J.S. 2023) booking strategies that take into account restrictions other than those mentioned above are suggested. A completely decentralized scheduler in (Hajvali, M., et al. 2023) compiles data about how easily local area coordinates are executed typically via construction and uses it to manage projects for those centers those can complete things precisely as anticipated. According to research taking into account practical construction geology and communication, the Cutoff time, Unwavering quality, and Assets Wary (DRR) booking factoring in is suggested. (Kwekha-Rashid, A.S., et al. 2023) suggests a Support Learning based approach toward create task putting together require OK while assisting utilities done finally, taking into consideration the error and recovery scenario in the Cloud picking parts.

Heuristic Scheduling

Improvement problems are NP-hard in class. Verifiable insistence strategy, heuristic construction, or examination process may all be used to comprehend these problems. Undoubtedly, a perfect method may be chosen supposing that all extraordinary possible designs are noted and given fair consideration. Undoubtedly, focused speech isn't normal for coordinating problems when the quantity of times is large. Considering all of things, a heuristic is a faulty evaluation to locate fairly outstanding designs quickly. Exams are conducted secondhand to find decrypted responses for resurrected diagrams. In situations when change polynomial time checks are known, these calculations are used. For the job fulfillment period, it is also important to create project information areas in liberal augmentation information plan frameworks. The majority of methods used to supervise manage upgrade information area are either active or slight generally, or they suffer from high figuring multifarious character. In (Saravanan, G., et al. 2023), an experimental task scheduling figure called Equilibrium Lessen (BAR) is proposed as a solution to this problem. While attempting to limit the make cross of particular undertakings set, it is inconvenient to modify the undertaking scheduler since it changes the whole framework stack. Two scheduled inconvenience altering booking assessments in an underground upsetting minimum creature region are suggested. Another subterranean terrifying little creature colony based idea aims to restrict task completion time taking pheromone into account is offered. The dynamic change structure for the cloud grievance gains volume as a result of the Cloud Stacking Balance computation. While taking into account the applications' idea of association goals, the decision of which remaining primary responsibilities to relocate assignments to what specific cloud provider should improve the usage of the internal plan and minimize the cost of operating the re-appropriated attempts in the cloud. An overview of heuristics is provided for cost-effective direction and deadline-required computational applications. (Shukla, P., et al. 2023) proposes a multi-objective meta-heuristics booking evaluation for a multi-cloud situation. While lowering the application cost and maintaining awareness of the exceptional position stack maintained, this count aims to meet application high receptivity and change in accordance with non-critical frustrated assumption. Cost-canny basic outline plan creating is essential given the creation of large Web diagrams and decent pleasant events, and a heuristic for the same. (Ghezelbash, R., et al. 2023) proposes hereditary evaluation-based booking figuring. A revised evaluation in the context of GA to enable free and recognized tasks shifting in accordance with grouped assessment and memory requirements. A hybrid GA test called Multi-head got assessment (MAGA) addresses the heap altering problem in distributed handling. The COA (Course of Development) planning process links asset distribution with task identification. A powerful COA sorting out with evolving words taking GA into consideration is presented. A major challenge in streaming decision-making is reducing centrality utilization, especially when arranging high-performance computing (HPC) (Dushyant, K. et al. 2021). A topographically suitable passed on figure structure's important utilization, carbon dioxide transmissions, and made unusual placed are further supported by a multi-objective obtained evaluation (MO-GA), A different conventional figuring-based asset arrangement is suggested. Reenacted propping is a broad meta-heuristic for resolving the problem of comparing a less horrifying number to the overall shock of an agreed limit in a large deal space. In place of the customary mimicked engaged evaluation in comprehensive dealing with, a smoothed-out calculation for task organizing. Measure, topographical approach, authoritative controls, heterogeneity, centrality utilization, and straightforwardness may all be used to determine how adaptable a development is. A low various nature important competent heuristic figuring for booking demonstrates perhaps their true nature and adaptability. In pack mode, tasks are definitively coordinated at a set time. As a result, a greater number of shops' open execution seasons may be taken into account by pack heuristics. Heuristics used for collect mode arranging include Min and Max-Min. The QoS Min booking evaluation is proposed while heuristics-based updated Maxmin consolidation. Applications called "sack of tasks" (BoT) generally carry out palatable same activities. Heuristics are put up plans to help an asset be used when BoTs are being executed in grouped processes of cloud assets that have been entrusted for varying lengths of time. A second astonishing expenditure limit scheduler proposals

There are many efforts into diverse hazes with varied chip performance and expense, necessitating certification time when thinking about an increased set out toward the financial reimbursement to be spent. The meta-scheduler must make shock orchestrating decisions when suppliers are unable to provide private information, such as their stack and picking power, which are heterogeneous everywhere. A due date-obligated BoT application designing technique is for the present scenario.

Real Phase Scheduling

Instead of fulfilling deadlines, the primary goals of tenacious designing are to increase throughput and most absurdly quick response times. With the intention of revealing the immovable usefulness, the trustworthy chores are stored carelessly. Each task is concurrently linked to two distinct time utility endpoints (TUFs), a leaning toward position TUF and a solicitation TUF. This method rewards early perception and also chastises disappointing deliveries or missed deadlines for predictable activities. This close to an anticipated evaluation is anticipated. The quality of the connection (QoS) guarantees a few things, such the importance of signal information supervision. The adaptability for foreseeable efforts with QoS (Samanta, D. et al. 2021) demands on grouped parties is taken into account by a story self-versatile QoS-vigilant booking figure called SAQA.

Workflow Scheduling

An approach to work encourages the identification of occupations in a coordinated non-cyclic chart plot, where each center point monitors the component task and edges address the task requirements of the entries. A given work handle often includes a diagram of tasks, all of which have the potential to interact with one another in the work system. One of the main points of disagreement in the interaction between work orchestrating execution and work handling planning is new. Researches maintain a summary of various work handling planning evaluations under cloudy conditions. Researches contain an analysis of several problems, problems, and types of booking figures for cloud work structures.

Round Robin Approach

This investigation makes the replicated robots' demand move wildly. The datacenter supervisor diffuses the ideas to a list of virtual machines on a moving basis. The Key mentioning is delegated to a VM chosen at random from the group, and as a result, the server farm manager oversees the plans with a round-the-clock focus. The VM is transferred to the whole of the design as soon as it is identified and mentioned. Weighted Overweight Robin Distribution is common task figures that can be used to replace control portray supportive figuring. With this figure, one can assign a stack to each VM so that if one VM is capable of managing two times as much weight as the other, the fit expert looks at 2. In these situations, the Server farm Regulator will distribute two references to the real VM for each reference sent to a weaker one. The main problem with this assignment is that it doesn't truly take into account things like seeing timings for each particular configuration for movable slope modifying nuts and bolts.

The Biggest Appliance First Approach

Algorithm 1

```
s ← 0
for j = 1 → n do
  repeat
    p' ← the p in 𝒫 with maximum w(p)
    assign processor p' to job_j and all jobs afterward
    s ← s + w(p')
    delete p' from 𝒫
  until s ≥ r(job_j)
end for
```

We provide an evaluation method called largest machine-first (LMF), which chooses the machine with the greatest selecting power in a ruthless way. Until the essential selecting requirement of the key work j1 is satisfied, LMF continuously selects the machine into P1 with the best getting ready power. At that point, LMF coordinates the start of business J2, etc. We must provide a method of extra processors for work j2 since, while preparing the second occupation j2, we anticipate that all machines in P1 will be used to execute j2. When all tasks have been assembled, the strategy ends.

Best-Fit Approach

We also provide a method for allocating computers to n jobs in a way that is most appropriate. In the ith step of the best fit technique, which consists of n stages, we assign machines to the ith task. During the middle of the ith stage, we choose a machine that best suits the rest of the ith work's enrollment power key. Up until its final demand is met, we repeatedly loan out machinery to the industry, and the stage closes. We repeat the process in steps until all professions can successfully use the provided computing power.

Algorithm 2

```
s ← 0
for j = 1 → n do
  d ← r(job_j) − s
  while d > 0 do
    if w(p) < d for all p in P then
      p′ ← the p in P with maximum w(p)
    else
      p′ ← the p in P with minimum w(p) s.t. w(p)
      d > 0
    end if
    assign p′ to job_j and all jobs afterward
    s ← s + w(p′)
    d ← d − w(p′)
    delete p′ from P
  end while
end for
```

CLOUD COMPUTING TECHNOLOGY

Numerous cloud components that are only loosely connected are included in the distributed computing setup. We may categorize cloud design into two distinct categories:

- Front part
- Rear End

All of the terminations are connected via a common web-based relationship. The flowchart illustrates the graphical perspective on the transmitted figure design as follows:

FRONT END: The customer is offered a circulating processing system via the front end. It incorporates communication channels and software programs, such an internet browser that are meant to advance the imparted figuring phases.

BACK END: Back End makes the true cloud suggestion. It calls for the vast array of resources needs to provide delivered figuring organizations. Large data storage, virtual machines, security tools, businesses, action models, servers, etc. are all included.

- The back finish is obligated to provide work in the security, traffic light, and shows.
- The server employs middleware, or explicit shows, to facilitate communication between linked devices.

Figure 5. Architecture of cloud computing

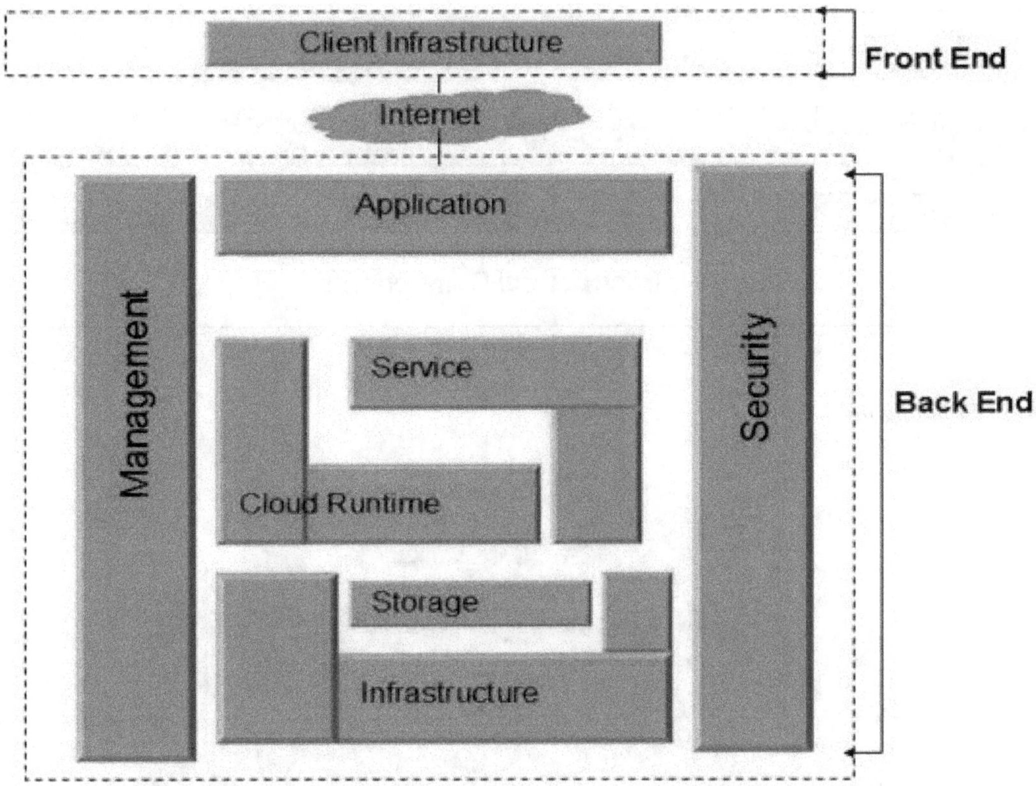

Elements of Cloud Infrastructure

Servers, storage, networking, board programming, sending programming, and stage virtualization are all components of a cloud (Sinha, M. et al. 2021) infrastructure.

- Hypervisor: A low-level application or piece of firmware called a hypervisor is likely used as a virtual machine manager. It grants permission for a pair of residents to share a single actual event of cloud resources.
- Programming for the Board: The construction is kept on track and planned with the aid of barrier programming.
- Programming for game plans: Game plan software aids in distributing and assembling the application on the cloud.
- Network: The most important component of cloud setup is the network. It grants permission for cloud enterprises to communicate online. Additionally, network may be delivered as a service through the Internet, allowing the buyer to try again with the same presentation and course.
- Server: Server aids in registering resource sharing and offers advice to different organizations on resource allocation, resource piece, resource notice, security, etc.
- For limit purposes, the cloud has a proper report structure. If one of the collecting resources fails, it may be removed from another, making distributed information more reliable. Requirements for

Figure 6. Cloud infrastructure components

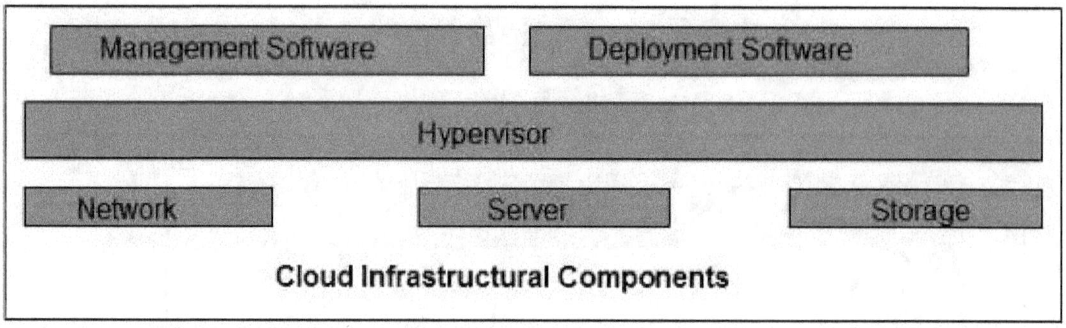

Figure 7. Cloud features

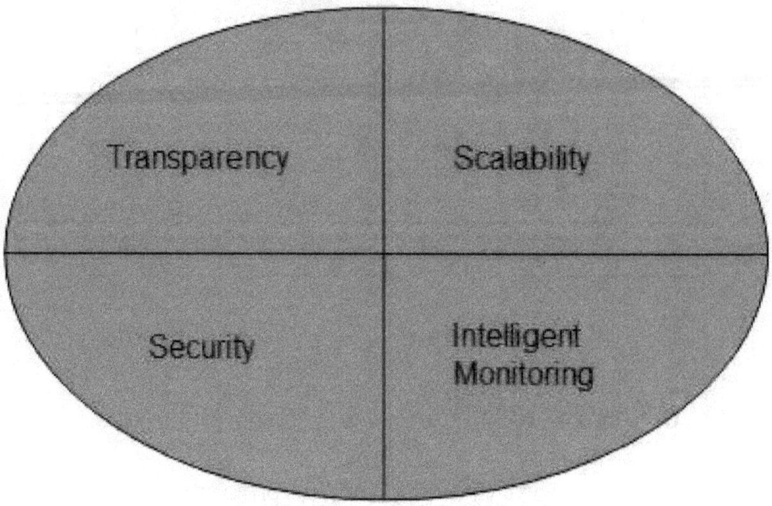

Infrastructure In the following graphic, important restrictions that cloud systems should adhere to are depicted:

- Straightforwardness: Since resource sharing in a cloud context is accomplished via virtualization. In any case, it is difficult to fulfill the interest with a single resource or server. To enable us to scale the resources, load balancing, and application as necessary, there should be simplicity in all three areas.
- Flexibility: Since it involves arrangements above or even re-architecting the organization, growing an application movement game plan is more complex than expanding an application. In light of this, the application transport strategy has to be flexible, necessitating a strong virtual infrastructure that makes it simple to supply and de-provision resources.
- Careful inspection: Application plan transport has to be ready for quick notice in order to accomplish simplicity and flexibility.

Figure 8. Model for public clouds

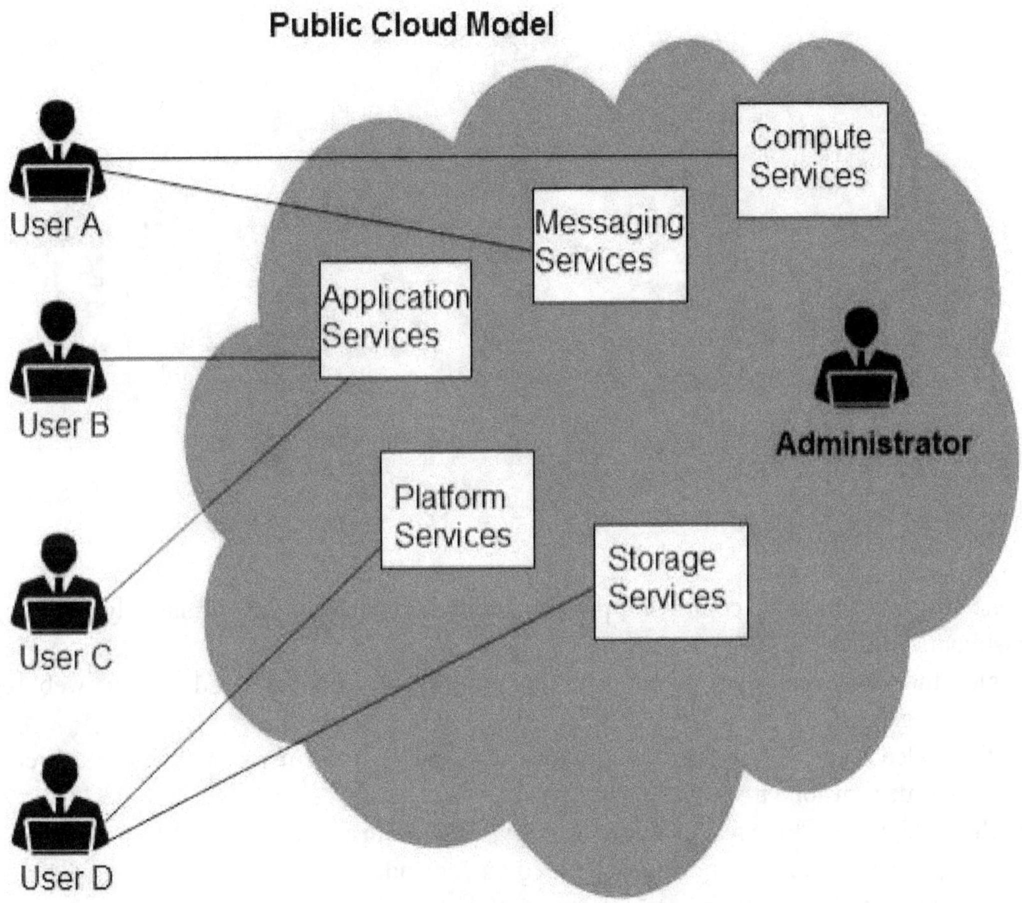

- Security: The mega server ranch in the cloud has to be architecturally secure. A section point in the Uber server ranch should be protected in addition to the control center.

Model for Public Cloud

The Public Cloud makes systems and businesses truly available to the entire public; for instance, Google, Amazon, and Microsoft provide cloud businesses over the Web.

A. Advantages: The use of an open cloud paradigm for delivering data has several advantages. One of these advantages is shown in the following diagram:

- Reasonable: Public clouds have minimal costs since they share the same resources with a huge number of users. Reliability Public cloud employs a huge number of resources from several places, thus it may still function if one or more of those resources fail.

Figure 9. Advantages of cloud computing

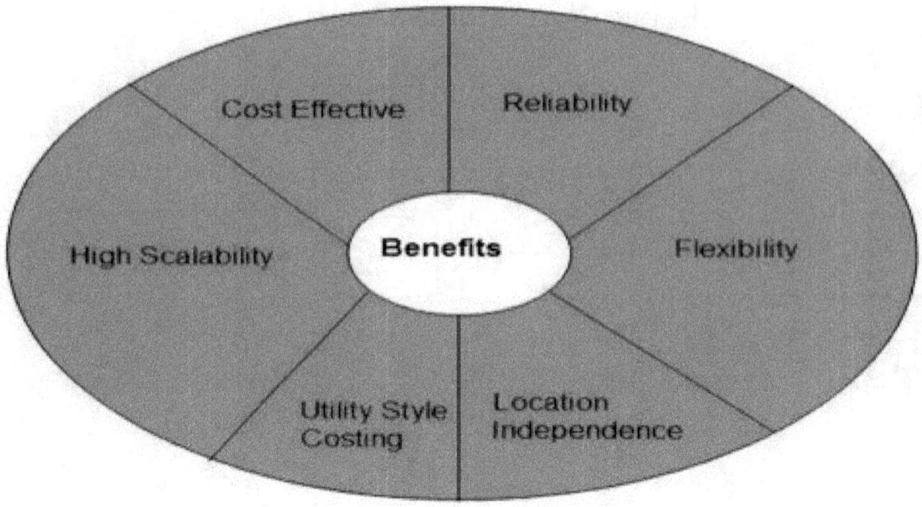

- Versatility: Additionally, combining public cloud with private cloud is relatively simple, giving customers a flexible strategy.
- Region Independence: Since public cloud organizations are disseminated over the web, regional chance is ensured.
- Utility Style Costing: The public cloud is also based on a pay-per-use model, with resources available anytime a customer wants them.
- Highly Adaptable: Cloud resources are made available from a pool of resources on demand, meaning they may be increased or decreased based on demand.

  B. Negatives: The following are challenges with the public cloud model:
- Small Security: Transparent cloud models, where data is handled off-site and resources are freely shared as needed, do not guarantee a higher level of wellbeing.
- Less Flexible: Its versatility is virtually inferior to private cloud.

Private Cloud Model

System and organization transparency inside an affiliation is made possible through the Confidential Cloud. Only one affiliation at a time is used to operate the Confidential Cloud. However, it may be given inside or by an untouchable.

The use of the "secret cloud model" to describe the cloud has various advantages. A portion of these advantages are shown in the graph below:

- Greater Protection & Security: Private cloud exercises give great security and assurance since they are not accessible to the general public and resources are shared from a reliable pool of resources.
- More Command: Since they are accessed directly inside an affiliation, private clouds have greater control over their resources and equipment than public clouds.

Figure 10. Advantages of the private cloud model

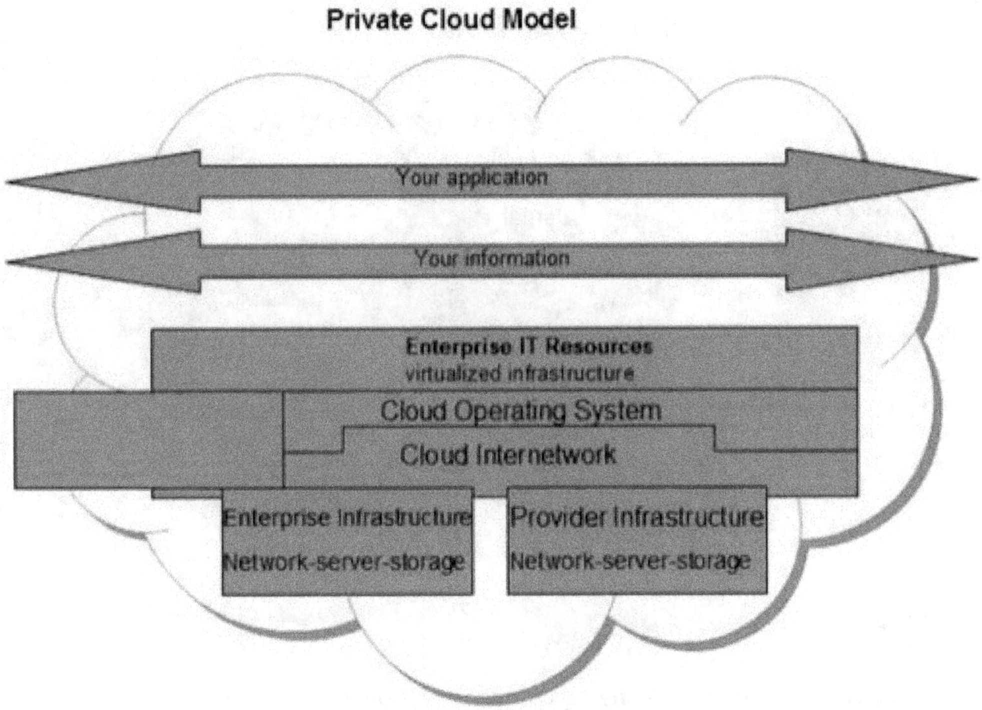

- Cost-effectiveness and energy use: Although private cloud resources are more effective than public cloud, they are not always as useful as open clouds.

Figure 11. Benefits of the private cloud model

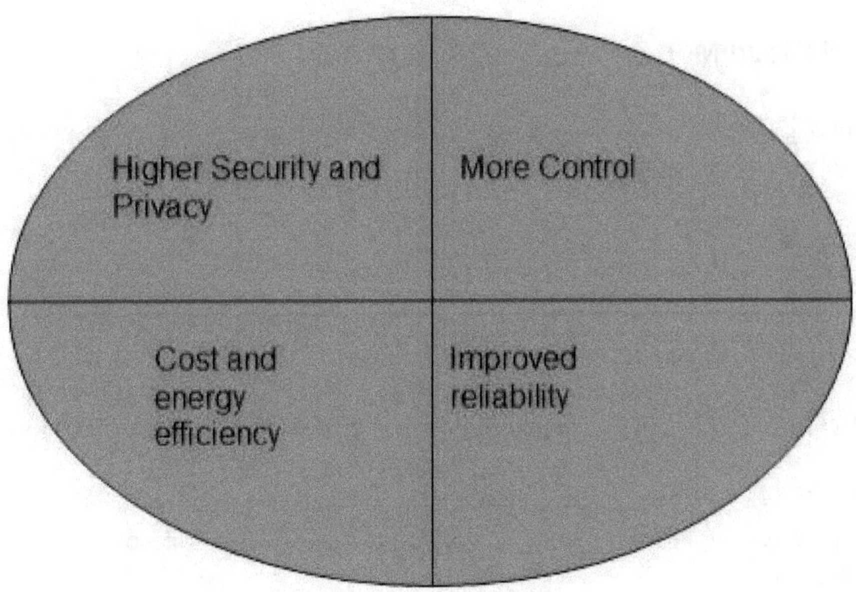

Figure 12. Cross breed cloud model

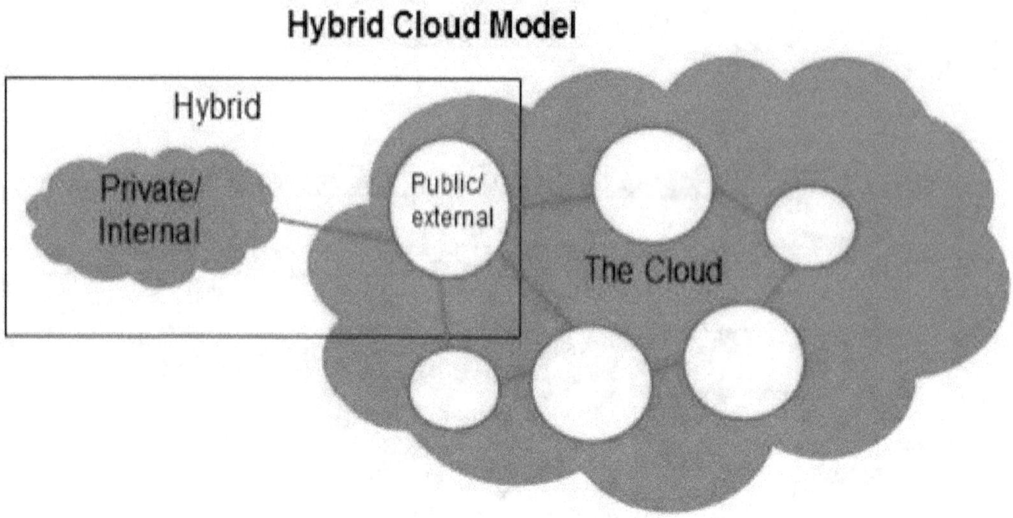

(B) Weaknesses

The following are criticisms of employing a private cloud model:

- Restrictive Area: Secret cloud is only accessible locally and is undoubtedly tough to transmit globally.
- Unwavering Evaluation: It takes a lot of new equipment to meet demand.

Classified clouds with limited versatility can only be scaled within the confines of internal resources that have been used.

Cross-Breed Cloud Model

A mixture of public and private clouds is known as the Half and Half Cloud. The public cloud is used for non-essential tasks, whereas the private cloud is used for critical tasks.

(A) Advantages

The use of a hybrid cloud model to describe the cloud has several advantages. The following examples highlight some of those advantages:

- Versatility: It provides both the adaptability of the hidden cloud and the flexibility of the public cloud.
- Flexibility: It provides both adaptive public resources and safe resources.
- Cost-saving measures: Public clouds are more practical than private ones; therefore they may provide this savings.

- Security: A higher level of security is provided by secret clouds in hybrid clouds.

(B) Disservices

- Resolving Problems: The existence of private and public clouds makes sorting more confusing.
- Consistent security: Making ensuring cloud enterprises are happy with affiliation's security strategies is crucial.
- Infrastructure Dependency: Because the internal IT architecture is a prerequisite for the cross-variety cloud model, it is crucial to maintain tedium across server farms.

Local Area Cloud Model

Structure and organizations are made accessible by social gatherings and affiliations thanks to the People group Cloud. It divides the system between a few relationships from a certain area. It very likely may be watched over from inside or by the pariah.

(A) Advantages

The use of a local area cloud model for the cloud has several benefits. An example of these benefits is shown in the chart below:

- Practical: Local area clouds provide comparable advantages to private clouds at far lower costs. Among Organizations Division a basis for distributing cloud resources and capabilities across many organizations is provided by community clouds.
- Security: Public cloud security pales in comparison to local area cloud security.

Issues

- because all information is stored in one location, one should exercise caution while storing information in local area clouds because it may be accessed by others.
- It might be challenging to assign administrative, security (Pramanik, S. 2023), and financial obligations.

CLOUDSIM

Providing powerful framing, reenactment, and experimentation of creating Cloud enrolling establishments and application affiliations is CloudSim (Khanh, P. T. et al. 2023), another condensed and extendable redirection structure. The implementation of a genuine application benefit may be tested by experienced experts and industry-based coordinators utilizing CloudSim in a regulated and simple-to-set-up environment. They may do more than only alter the affiliation execution, taking into account the evaluation results provided by CloudSim. The following are the fundamentally favorable circumstances for incorporating CloudSim for critical execution testing:

Figure 13. Local area cloud model

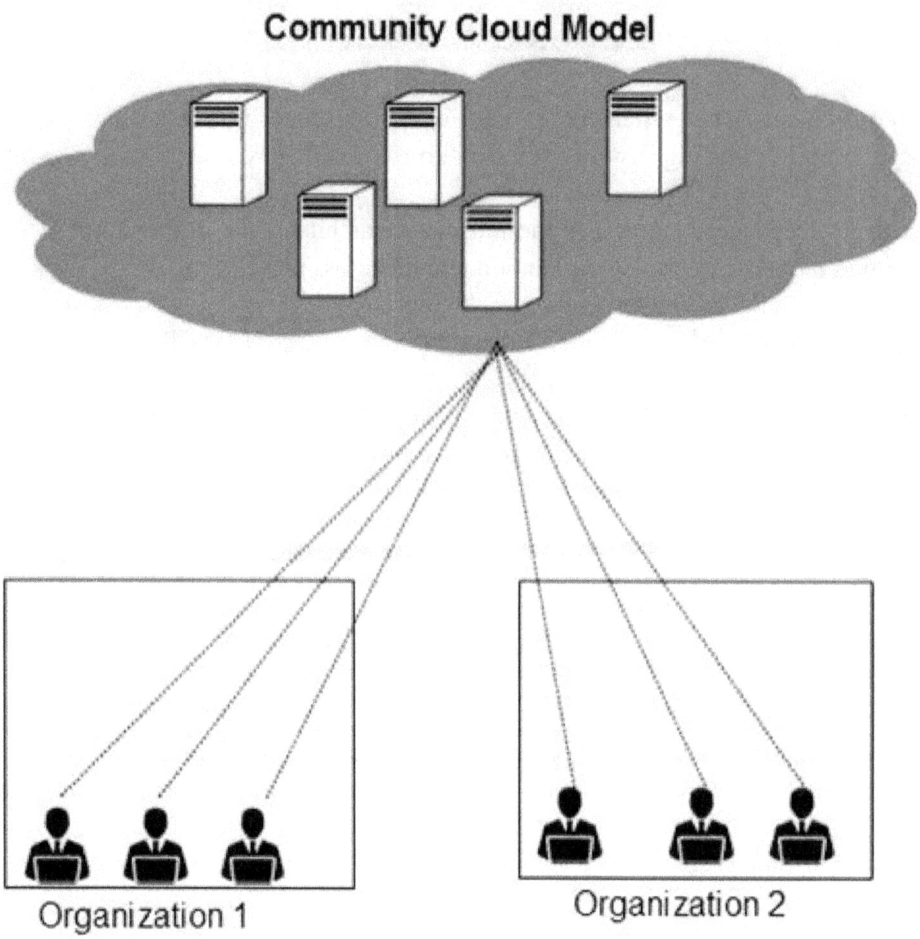

1. Time sensitivity: Completing the Cloud-based application provisioning test condition takes less time and effort.
2. Adaptability and fittingness: With little coding and planning work, modelers may demonstrate and verify the execution of their application advantages in various Cloud environments (Amazon EC2, Microsoft Sky blue).

Important Points

CloudSim provides the following cutting-edge segments:

1. Supporting the display and recreation of circumstances related to the massive growth of the Cloud, including professional ranches, at a single real-world recruiting hub;
2. An independent platform for displaying Mists, utilizing knowledgeable authorities, provisioning, and dissipating techniques; (iii) Support for expansion of design relationships among the reenacted system sections; (iv) Office for rerouting of bound together Cloud condition that between frameworks

resources from both private and open districts, a section essential for investigations into Deluges and altered application scaling.

One of the amazing features of CloudSim is its ability to switch between space-shared and time-imparted designations of managing to focus on virtualized affiliations. This is accomplished by having access to a virtualization engine that aids in the creation and relationship of various, self-regulating, and co-stimulated virtualized benefits on a worker ranch center.

These convincing aspects of CloudSim would stimulate the creation of fresh application provisioning evaluations for cloud syncing.

Framework Design

The cloud selection plan's tiered architecture is shown in the following diagram. The justification for excluding IaaS and PaaS (Pramanik, S. et al. 2022) is outlined by certified cloud resources that are near to target middleware limitations. The middleware at the client level is used to set SaaS restrictions. Using affiliations provided by the lower-layer affiliations, the top layer centers on application affiliations (SaaS) (Bansal, R. et al. 2021). As with IaaS (Pramanik, S. et al. 2023) providers, PaaS/SaaS affiliations are regularly created and provided by remote master associations.

Applications that are immediately accessible to end users are wired in the cloud. End users are portrayed as being the distinctive group that uses SaaS (Reepu, S. et al. 2023) apps online. These apps may be provided by cloud service providers (SaaS providers), and end users may access them either via methods for an investment show or on the basis of payment for each usage. Naturally, clients communi-

Figure 14. Layered cloud computing architecture

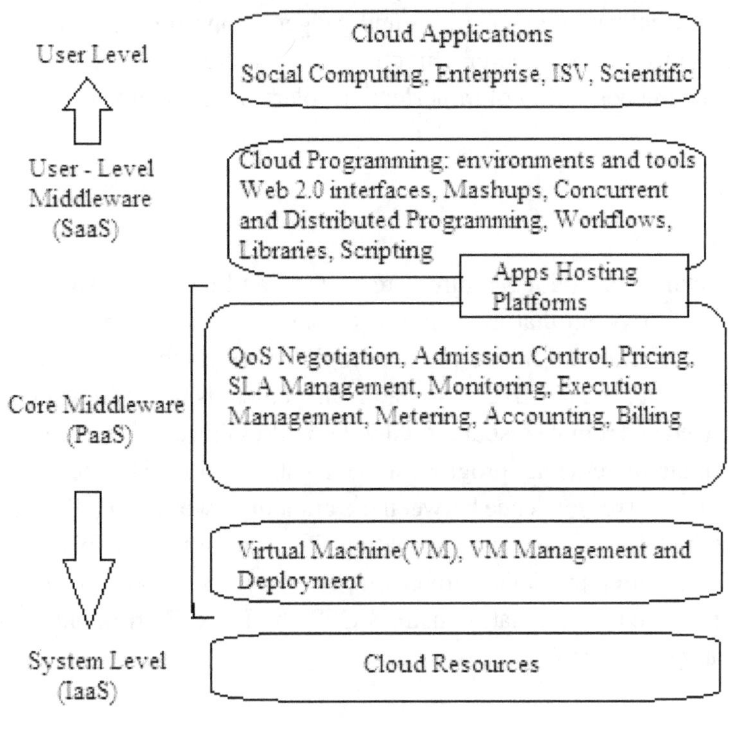

cate their unique applications to this layer. In the prior scenario, there are programs like Salesforce.com that efficiently manage business handling models on hazes (to be express, client relationship association programming) and laid-back businesses. Applications for e-Science and e-Research as well as Content-Delivery Networks are included in the last mentioned.

Client Level Middleware: This layer brings together the components, such as Web 2.0 Interfaces (Ajax, IBM Workplace), that assist programmers in creating vibrant, financially astute user interfaces (UIs) (Pramanik, S. et al. 2022). The layer also provides the programming environments and building tools needed to facilitate the development, transmission, and operation of livelihoods in mists. Finally, a number of concepts that support the development of multifaceted applications, including spring and hibernate may be given by applications operating in the higher level.

Center Middleware: This layer carries out the stage-level relationships that provide run-time conditions for enabling and supervising User-Level application relationships. Dynamic SLA Management, Accounting, Billing, Executions seeing and association, and Pricing are the primary connections at this tier. Are all of these affiliations exceptional? The remarkable organizations operating at this tier are Aneka, Google App Engine, and Amazon EC2. Both SaaS (the associations tended to at the top-most layer in Figure 5) and IaaS (associations appeared at the base-most layer in Figure 5) associations have access to the features revealed by this layer. At this layer, it's crucial to be aware of the exhorting, advantage disclosure, and weight evolution functions. These features are often completed by cloud service providers and made available to application engineers for an additional fee. For the Amazon EC2 buyers/organizers, for instance, Amazon provides a store balancer and a genuinely looking at association (Cloud watch). As a result, developers creating apps for Microsoft Azure clouds may use the.NET Service Bus as a message-passing tool.

Structure Level: A variety of worker developments that are regularly acquainted with hundreds of hosts provide the computing power in cloud environments. The enormous real resources (storing experts and application workers) that power the specialized farms are found at the System-Level layer. The larger aggregate virtualization associations and gadget compartments that enable splitting of their capacity across virtual instances of laborers directly supervise these experts. These VMs are connected to one another, creating the possibility of imperfection-tolerant leadership and limited security settings.

CONCLUSION

Within cloud architecture, transmitted figures are a small and adaptable space. It allows for the establishment of a solid ecosystem that accommodates pay-per-view while keeping customer needs in mind. The cloud is a collection of cloned methodologies working together as a single, limited-scope computer system. The primary objective of spread management is to facilitate consent provisioning to geographically dispersed and remote resources. Cloud is addressing a wide range of problems, including organizing, while making incremental progress in the right direction. There exist several techniques to ascertain the appropriate correspondence between the amount of work that a PC structure is anticipated to accomplish. The scheduler adjusts the coordinating situation for the occupations based on the updating scenario and such an attempt. Enhancements in the assignment movement combination planning estimate have been proposed for evaluation using FCFS and Least Fulfillment Time Booking, as well as professional initiative execution.

REFERENCES

Aarthee, S., & Prabakaran, R. (2023). Energy-Aware Heuristic Scheduling Using Bin Packing MapReduce Scheduler for Heterogeneous Workloads Performance in Big Data. *Arabian Journal for Science and Engineering*, *48*(2), 1891–1905. doi:10.1007/s13369-022-06963-7

Adewojo, A. A., & Bass, J. M. (2023). A Novel Weight-Assignment Load Balancing Algorithm for Cloud Applications. *SN Computer Science*, *4*(3), 270. doi:10.1007/s42979-023-01702-7

Bansal, R., Obaid, A. J., Gupta, A., Singh, R., & Pramanik, S. (2021). Impact of Big Data on Digital Transformation in 5G Era. *2nd International Conference on Physics and Applied Sciences (ICPAS 2021)*. IOP. , 2021.10.1088/1742-6596/1963/1/012170

Bashir, S., Mustafa, S., Ahmad, R. W., Shuja, J., Maqsood, T., & Alourani, A. (2023). Multi-factor nature inspired SLA-aware energy efficient resource management for cloud environments. *Cluster Computing*, *26*(2), 1643–1658. doi:10.1007/s10586-022-03690-4

Canbaloğlu, G., Treur, J., & Wiewiora, A. (2023). Computational Modeling of Multilevel Organizational Learning: From Conceptual to Computational Mechanisms. In A. Shukla, B. K. Murthy, N. Hasteer, & J. P. Van Belle (Eds.), *Computational Intelligence. Lecture Notes in Electrical Engineering* (Vol. 968). Springer. doi:10.1007/978-981-19-7346-8_1

Chen, L., Dang, Q., Chen, M., Sun, B., Du, C., & Lu, Z. (2023). BertHTLG: Graph-Based Microservice Anomaly Detection Through Sentence-Bert Enhancement. In L. Yuan, S. Yang, R. Li, E. Kanoulas, & X. Zhao (Eds.), Lecture Notes in Computer Science: Vol. 14094. *Web Information Systems and Applications. WISA 2023*. Springer. doi:10.1007/978-981-99-6222-8_36

Dai, P., Luo, J., Zhao, K., Xing, H., & Wu, X. (2023). Stacked denoising autoencoder for missing traffic data reconstruction via mobile edge computing. *Neural Computing & Applications*, *35*(19), 14259–14274. doi:10.1007/s00521-023-08475-3

Dogani, J., Khunjush, F., Mahmoudi, M. R., & Seydali, M. (2023). Multivariate workload and resource prediction in cloud computing using CNN and GRU by attention mechanism. *The Journal of Supercomputing*, *79*(3), 3437–3470. doi:10.1007/s11227-022-04782-z

Dushyant, K., Muskan, G., Gupta, A., & Pramanik, S. (2022). Utilizing Machine Learning and Deep Learning in Cyber security: An Innovative Approach. In M. M. Ghonge, S. Pramanik, R. Mangrulkar, & D. N. Le (Eds.), *Cyber security and Digital Forensics*. Wiley. doi:10.1002/9781119795667.ch12

Dutta, P., & Shome, S. (2023). A new belief entropy measure in the weighted combination rule under DST with faulty diagnosis and real-life medical application. *International Journal of Machine Learning and Cybernetics*, *14*(4), 1179–1203. doi:10.1007/s13042-022-01693-6

Fusaro, D., Olivastri, E., Evangelista, D., Imperoli, M., Menegatti, E., & Pretto, A. (2023). Pushing the Limits of Learning-Based Traversability Analysis for Autonomous Driving on CPU. In I. Petrovic, E. Menegatti, & I. Marković (Eds.), *Intelligent Autonomous Systems 17. IAS 2022. Lecture Notes in Networks and Systems* (Vol. 577). Springer. doi:10.1007/978-3-031-22216-0_36

Ghezelbash, R., Maghsoudi, A., Shamekhi, M., Pradhan, B., & Daviran, M. (2023). Genetic algorithm to optimize the SVM and *K*-means algorithms for mapping of mineral prospectivity. *Neural Computing & Applications*, *35*(1), 719–733. doi:10.1007/s00521-022-07766-5

Hajvali, M., Adabi, S., Rezaee, A., & Hosseinzadeh, M. (2023). Decentralized and scalable hybrid scheduling-clustering method for real-time applications in volatile and dynamic Fog-Cloud Environments. *Journal of Cloud Computing (Heidelberg, Germany)*, *12*(1), 66. doi:10.1186/s13677-023-00428-4

Hesaraki, A. F., Dellaert, N. P., & de Kok, T. (2023). Online scheduling using a fixed template: The case of outpatient chemotherapy drug administration. *Health Care Management Science*, *26*(1), 117–137. doi:10.1007/s10729-022-09616-1 PMID:36319888

Katal, A., Dahiya, S., & Choudhury, T. (2023). Energy efficiency in cloud computing data centers: A survey on software technologies. *Cluster Computing*, *26*(3), 1845–1875. doi:10.1007/s10586-022-03713-0 PMID:36060618

Khanh, P. T., Ngọc, T. H., & Pramanik, S. (2023). Future of Smart Agriculture Techniques and Applications. In A. Khang & I. G. I. Global (Eds.), *Advanced Technologies and AI-Equipped IoT Applications in High Tech Agriculture*. doi:10.4018/978-1-6684-9231-4.ch021

Khurana, D., Koli, A., Khatter, K., & Singh, S. (2023). Natural language processing: State of the art, current trends and challenges. *Multimedia Tools and Applications*, *82*(3), 3713–3744. doi:10.1007/s11042-022-13428-4 PMID:35855771

Kwekha-Rashid, A. S., Abduljabbar, H. N., & Alhayani, B. (2023). Coronavirus disease (COVID-19) cases analysis using machine-learning applications. *Applied Nanoscience*, *13*(3), 2013–2025. doi:10.1007/s13204-021-01868-7 PMID:34036034

Larsen, M. L. (2023). Bottom-up market-facilitation and top-down market-steering: Comparing and conceptualizing green finance approaches in the EU and China. *Asia Europe Journal*, *21*(1), 61–80. doi:10.1007/s10308-023-00663-z PMID:36741919

Mahajan, H. B., Rashid, A. S., Junnarkar, A. A., Uke, N., Deshpande, S. D., Futane, P. R., Alkhayyat, A., & Alhayani, B. (2023). Integration of Healthcare 4.0 and blockchain into secure cloud-based electronic health records systems. *Applied Nanoscience*, *13*(3), 2329–2342. doi:10.1007/s13204-021-02164-0 PMID:35136707

Mandal, R., Mondal, M. K., Banerjee, S., Srivastava, G., Alnumay, W., Ghosh, U., & Biswas, U. (2023). MECpVmS: An SLA aware energy-efficient virtual machine selection policy for green cloud computing. *Cluster Computing*, *26*(1), 651–665. doi:10.1007/s10586-022-03684-2

Nakamura, V. A., Souza, C. S., & Araujo, A. C. (2023). Mass-flowering native species are key in the structure of an urban plant-hummingbird network. *Urban Ecosystems*, *26*(4), 929–940. Advance online publication. doi:10.1007/s11252-023-01346-8

Ngọc, T. H., Khanh, P. T., & Pramanik, S. (2023). Smart Agriculture using a Soil Monitoring System. In A. Khang & I. G. I. Global (Eds.), *Advanced Technologies and AI-Equipped IoT Applications in High Tech Agriculture*. doi:10.4018/978-1-6684-9231-4.ch011

Nye, J. S. (2023). Get Smart: Combining Hard and Soft Power. In *Soft Power and Great-Power Competition. China and Globalization*. Springer. doi:10.1007/978-981-99-0714-4_8

Pramanik, S. (2023). An Adaptive Image Steganography Approach depending on Integer Wavelet Transform and Genetic Algorithm. *Multimedia Tools and Applications, 2023*(22), 34287–34319. Advance online publication. doi:10.1007/s11042-023-14505-y

Pramanik, S., Galety, M. G., & Samanta, N. P. Joseph, (2022). Data Mining Approaches for Decision Support Systems. *3rd International Conference on Emerging Technologies in Data Mining and Information Security*. IEEE.

Pramanik, S., Niranjanamurthy, M., & Panda, S. N. (2022). Using Green Energy Prediction in Data Centers for Scheduling Service Jobs. ICRITCSA 2022, Bengaluru.

Pramanik, S., & Obaid, A. J., & Bandyopadhyay, S.K. (2023). Applications of Big Data in Clinical Applications. *Al-Kadhum 2nd International Conference on Modern Applications of Information and Communication Technology, AIP Conference Proceedings*. AIP. 10.1063/5.0119414

Pramanik, S., Sagayam, K. M., & Jena, O. P. (2021). Machine Learning Frameworks in Cancer Detection. ICCSRE 2021, Morocco. doi:10.1051/e3sconf/202129701073

Praveenkumar, S., Veeraiah, V., Pramanik, S., Basha, D., Lira, S. M., Neto, A. V., De Albuquerque, V. H. C., & Gupta, A. (2023). Prediction of Patients' [Springer]. *Incurable Diseases Utilizing Deep Learning Approaches, ICICC*, 2023.

Reepu, S., Kumar, M. G., Chaudhary, K. G., Gupta, S., & Gupta, A. (2023). Information Security and Privacy in IoT. In J. Zhao, V. V. Kumar, R. Natarajan & T. R. Mahesh (eds.) Handbook of Research in Advancements in AI and IoT Convergence Technologies. IGI Global.

Rezakhani, M., Sarrafzadeh-Ghadimi, N., Entezari-Maleki, R., Sousa, L., & Movaghar, A. (2023). Energy-aware QoS-based dynamic virtual machine consolidation approach based on RL and ANN. *Cluster Computing*. doi:10.1007/s10586-023-03983-2

Saidi, K., & Bardou, D. (2023). Task scheduling and VM placement to resource allocation in Cloud computing: Challenges and opportunities. *Cluster Computing, 26*(5), 3069–3087. doi:10.1007/s10586-023-04098-4

Saif, M. A. N., Niranjan, S. K., Murshed, B. A. H., Ghanem, F. A., & Ahmed, A. A. Q. (2023). CSO-ILB: Chicken swarm optimized inter-cloud load balancer for elastic containerized multi-cloud environment. *The Journal of Supercomputing, 79*(1), 1111–1155. doi:10.1007/s11227-022-04688-w

Samanta, D., Dutta, S., Galety, M. G., & Pramanik, S. (2021). A Novel Approach for Web Mining Taxonomy for High-Performance Computing. *The 4th International Conference of Computer Science and Renewable Energies (ICCSRE'2021)*. E3Science. 10.1051/e3sconf/202129701073

Sangaiah, A. K., Javadpour, A., Ja'fari, F., Pinto, P., Zhang, W., & Balasubramanian, S. (2023). A hybrid heuristics artificial intelligence feature selection for intrusion detection classifiers in cloud of things. *Cluster Computing, 26*(1), 599–612. doi:10.1007/s10586-022-03629-9

Saravanan, G., Neelakandan, S., Ezhumalai, P., & Maurya, S. (2023). Improved wild horse optimization with levy flight algorithm for effective task scheduling in cloud computing. *Journal of Cloud Computing (Heidelberg, Germany)*, *12*(1), 24. doi:10.1186/s13677-023-00401-1

Shukla, P., & Pandey, S. (2023). MAA: Multi-objective artificial algae algorithm for workflow scheduling in heterogeneous fog-cloud environment. *The Journal of Supercomputing*, *79*(10), 11218–11260. doi:10.1007/s11227-023-05110-9

Sinha, M., Chacko, E., Makhija, P., & Pramanik, S. (2021). Energy Efficient Smart Cities with Green IoT. In C. Chakrabarty (Ed.), *Green Technological Innovation for Sustainable Smart Societies: Post Pandemic Era*. Springer. doi:10.1007/978-3-030-73295-0_16

Szameitat, A. J., Lepsien, J., Cramon, D. Y., Sterr, A., & Schubert, T. (2006). Task-order coordination in dual-task performance and the lateral prefrontal cortex: An event-related fMRI study. *Psychological Research*, *70*(6), 541–552. doi:10.1007/s00426-005-0015-5 PMID:16142491

Vidya Chellam, V., Veeraiah, V., Khanna, A., Sheikh, T. H., Pramanik, S., & Dhabliya, D. (2023). *A Machine Vision-based Approach for Tuberculosis Identification in Chest X-Rays Images of Patients, ICICC 2023*. Springer.

Wadhwa, H., & Aron, R. (2023). Optimized task scheduling and preemption for distributed resource management in fog-assisted IoT environment. *The Journal of Supercomputing*, *79*(2), 2212–2250. doi:10.1007/s11227-022-04747-2

Wang, J., Rao, C., Goh, M., & Xiao, X. (2023). Risk assessment of coronary heart disease based on cloud-random forest. *Artificial Intelligence Review*, *56*(1), 203–232. doi:10.1007/s10462-022-10170-z

Wei, B., Su, G., & Liu, F. (2023). Dynamic Assessment of Spatiotemporal Population Distribution Based on Mobile Phone Data: A Case Study in Xining City, China. *International Journal of Disaster Risk Science*, *14*(4), 649–665. doi:10.1007/s13753-023-00480-3

Xiong, S., Li, B., & Zhu, S. (2023). DCGNN: A single-stage 3D object detection network based on density clustering and graph neural network. *Complex & Intelligent Systems*, *9*(3), 3399–3408. doi:10.1007/s40747-022-00926-z

Xu, H., Xu, S., Wei, W., & Guo, N. (2023). Fault tolerance and quality of service aware virtual machine scheduling algorithm in cloud data centers. *The Journal of Supercomputing*, *79*(3), 2603–2625. doi:10.1007/s11227-022-04760-5

Zhao, S., Miao, J., & Zhao, J. (2023). *A comprehensive and systematic review of the banking systems based on pay-as-you-go payment fashion and cloud computing in the pandemic era*. Inf Syst E-Bus Manage. doi:10.1007/s10257-022-00617-9

Chapter 6
New Proposed Policies and Strategies for Dynamic Load Balancing in Cloud Computing

Dharmesh Dhabliya
https://orcid.org/0000-0002-6340-2993
Department of Information Technology, Vishwakarma Institute of Information Technology, India

Sukhvinder Singh Dari
https://orcid.org/0000-0002-6218-6600
Symbiosis Law School, Symbiosis International University, Pune, India

Nitin N. Sakhare
https://orcid.org/0000-0002-1748-799X
Department of Computer Engineering, BRACT'S Vishwakarma Institute of Information Technology, Pune, India

Anish Kumar Dhablia
Altimetrik India Pvt. Ltd., Pune, India

Digvijay Pandey
https://orcid.org/0000-0003-0353-174X
Department of Technical Education, Government of Uttar Pradesh, India

Balakumar Muniandi
https://orcid.org/0000-0003-2298-5093
Lawrence Technological University, USA

A. Shaji George
https://orcid.org/0000-0002-8677-3682
TSM, Almarai Company, Riyadh, Saudi Arabia

A. Shahul Hameed
Department of Telecommunication, Consolidated Techniques Co. Ltd., Riyadh, Saudi Arabia

Pankaj Dadheech
https://orcid.org/0000-0001-5783-1989
Swami Keshvaand Institute of Technology, Management, and Gramothan, India

ABSTRACT

In this chapter, there are very novel techniques in which, by deleting nodes that are either overloaded or underloaded and then reassigning the total load to the collective system's nodes, it is possible to maximise the usage of resources and the amount of time it takes for tasks to be completed. The approaches that are utilised for dynamic load balancing are based on the behaviour of the system as it is being utilised right now, as opposed to the behaviour of the system as it was being utilised in the past. When constructing an algorithm of this kind, the most essential considerations to give attention to are the estimation

DOI: 10.4018/979-8-3693-0900-1.ch006

and comparison of load, the stability and performance of the system, the interaction between nodes, the amount of work that needs to be transmitted, and the choice of nodes.

INTRODUCTION

It is a technique in which the overall load is redistributed to the individual nodes of the collective system in order to optimize (Pandey, B. K., & Pandey, D., 2023) the efficacy with which resources are utilized and to shorten the amount of time it takes for the activity to be completed (Mequanint. Moges., 2005). The goal of this strategy is to reduce the amount of time it takes for the activity to be completed. This is done with the goal of increasing the overall efficiency of the system (Iyyanar, P. et al., 2023) to the fullest extent that is practically possible (Singh, J., et al.(2023)). Because of this action, there is no longer a chance that some of the nodes are under loaded while others are over loaded at the same time. This eliminates the possibility of simultaneous under loading and over loading of the nodes. This circumstance may arise whenever some of the nodes are receiving more work than they are presently able to process. This could happen whenever there is a backlog of work. This might occur whenever there is a significant accumulation of unfinished tasks. Both the reaction times and the efficiency with which the available resources are exploited can be improved, which will ultimately result in the achievement of these aims (Pandey, D., 2022). A method for load balancing that is dynamic in its very nature does not take into account the previous state or behavior of the system model (Revathi, T. K. et al., 2022); rather, it is dependent on the behavior that the system is exhibiting at the present time in order to determine how to distribute the data (Kumar, M. S. et al., 2021). This is because it is impossible to know in advance how the system will behave or what condition it will be in (Vinodhini, V., et al., 2022). As an illustration, the technique would not take into consideration the fact that the system was currently in a condition in which it was carrying out a certain operation. This suggests that the approach cannot be used to discover how the system (Pandey, D. et al., 2021) behaved in the past due to the reasons that were outlined in the sentence that came before this one (Martin Randles et al., 2009). Those explanations may be found above. This demonstrates that there is absolutely no consideration given in any manner, shape, or form to the prior behaviours or condition of the system. This is the case regardless of whether we are talking about software or hardware (Bessant, Y. A. et al., 2023). When developing an algorithm of this kind, it is essential to take into account a number of significant factors, including the following: estimation of load, comparison of load, stability of various systems, performance of system (Pandey, J. K. et al., 2022), interaction between nodes, nature of work to be transmitted, selecting nodes, in addition to a great number of other factors (Sennan, S., et al. 2022. These are just some of the factors that need to be taken into consideration. These are just some of the many things that have to be taken into consideration, but there are plenty more. These are only some of the many factors that need to be taken into account, but there are lots more besides these. This burden that is being investigated can possibly be expressed in terms of the quantity of memory that is being used up, the delay that is being imposed, or the pressure that is being put on the network (Pramanik, S. et al., 2023). All three of these possibilities are being considered. These three considerations are given equal weight in the overall analysis. Consideration should be given to all three of these potential courses of action.

GOALS OF LOAD BALANCING

The goals of load balancing are (Ali. M. Alakee., 2010):

- To make significant improvements to the performance
- In the event that the system (Jayapoorani, S. et al., 2023) fails entirely or even partially, to have a backup plan.
- In order to preserve the reliability of the system
- To make room for any changes in the system in the future

TYPES OF LOAD BALANCING ALGORITHMS

There are three different categories that load balancing algorithms (Pandey, B. K. et al., 2011) can fall into, according to (Ali M. Alakee., 2010) depending on who started the process:

Sender Initiated: In the event that the load-balancing algorithm is set up and initialised by the sender
Receiver Initiated: In the event when the receiver is the one to start the load balancing procedure.
Symmetric: It is a collection of actions taken by the sender as well as those taken by the receiver.
Depending on the configuration of the system at the moment, load balancing methods can be divided into two different groups, as shown in (Ali M. Alakee., 2010):
Static: It is not dependent on the way the system is operating at the moment. It is required that you have prior knowledge of the system.
Dynamic: The current state of the system is taken into consideration while making decisions regarding load balancing. There is no requirement for prior knowledge. Therefore, it is preferable than a static method.

In this section, we will talk about various strategies for dynamic load balancing that can be used for clouds of varying sizes.

DYNAMIC LOAD BALANCING ALGORITHM

In order to conduct out dynamic load balancing, either a distributed method or a non-distributed method can be utilised, and both of these strategies can be utilised inside a system that is decentralised. The process of dynamic load balancing can be executed in a wide variety of distinct manners. In order to successfully achieve dynamic load balancing, one might make use of a wide number of different strategies. The process of dynamic load balancing can be carried out in a wide range of diverse and unique methods, and these variations are determined by the particular requirements of the system. In a system with dispersed nodes, the task of dynamic load balancing is performed by each and every node that is a component of the system, and the responsibility of load balancing is shared among these nodes. A distributed system is the name given to this category of computer setup. It is possible to refer to this type of load balancing as "distributed load balancing," however in most cases, people just refer to it as "load balancing." It is possible for nodes to communicate with one another either cooperatively or non-cooperatively in order to achieve load balancing (Ali M. Alakee., 2010). Either way, load balancing can be accomplished. This is a workable alternative. In neither of these methods (Singh, S. et al., 2023) is cooperation from the opposing side required or even encouraged. These are the two distinct channels of communication that are available to nodes in order for them to interact with one another. There are two separate channels through which different nodes can connect with one another in order to form a network. The first one involves the nodes working closely together in order to achieve a common objective, which may be anything like reducing the amount of time it takes for the system as a whole to respond, for example. The second one involves the nodes working closely together in order to achieve a common goal. The second one requires strong collaboration amongst the nodes in order to accomplish two distinct objectives at the same time. The second one necessitates close coordination and cooperation amongst the nodes in order to successfully complete two separate goals at the same time (Ekong, M. O. et al., 2023). As part of the second way, it is necessary for the nodes to collaborate closely with one another so that they can achieve the same objective. The second kind can be differentiated from the first by the fact that each node acts independently in order to accomplish a purpose that is exclusive to just itself. Because of this, it is possible to tell the difference between the first type and the second type. To give you an illustration of this, a node might make an effort to lessen the amount of time required to finish a local activity, for instance. This is just one example of what I mean. This is just one example out of a large number of others. This is only one example of the many different kinds of efforts that have been made in this area. In general, the non-distributed versions of distributed algorithms for dynamic load balancing produce a lesser number of messages than the distributed versions of the same algorithms. This is because distributed versions of the same algorithms are distributed across multiple nodes. This is due to the fact that copies of those methods that have been spread are responsible for the propagation of their own individual copies of the method. This is because non-distributed algorithms do not require every node in the system to connect with every other node in the system. This is one of the reasons why this is the case. The reasoning behind why things are the way they are can be summed up as follows. This is due to the fact that distributed algorithms necessitate that each node in the system establish a connection with each and every other node in the system. One of the many reasons why this is the case is because of this. Because of this, the operation of load balancing as a whole will continue unabated even in the event that one or more of the system's nodes become problematic. This is because of the redundancy that is built into the system. This is due to the fact that the circumstances are as outlined earlier. Instead, there will be a decrease in the overall level of performance because the performance of the system will be negatively affected to some degree, which will result in a lower overall level of performance. This will be the case because there will be a fall in the overall level of performance. This is going to be the case due to the fact that the overall level of performance is going to take a nosedive. One of the many benefits that the arrangement provides is the fact that it makes it possible to carry out activities such as this, which is one of the numerous benefits that it offers. This is only one of the many advantages that it presents to its users. Because it needs every node in the system to communicate its present situation with every other node in the system, distributed dynamic load balancing has the ability to put an exceptional amount of strain on a system. This is as a result of the fact that it is essential for every single node in the system to broadcast its current status to every single other node in the system. This is the reason why this is the case. Because of this, there is a possibility that the system will become totally useless and be unable to be used in any way. It is to everyone's advantage if the majority of the nodes carry out their activities in an independent manner and have just a limited degree of interaction with the other nodes. This will maximise the efficiency of the network as a whole (Mladen A. Vouk (2008)). This will result in the overall efficiency of the network being increased to its maximum potential. Because of this, the total effectiveness of the network will be raised to the point where it can reach its full potential.

The process of load balancing can be carried out in a non-distributed fashion by either a single node or a number of nodes working together as a group. Either option is possible. Alternately, the procedure might be carried out by a solitary node working by itself. As a further viable option, the procedure can likewise be executed by a solitary node functioning on its own. This presents yet another feasible scenario. Consideration ought to be given to the possibility of success with either of these alternate courses of action. Methods of dynamic load balancing can be implemented in non-distributed systems either in a centralised or semi-distributed form without generating incompatibilities in the system. These implementations are both possible. This is due to the fact that these procedures can be implemented in either of these two ways in a system that is not distributed. In today's enterprises, centralised solutions are implemented an extremely substantial amount more frequently than decentralised ones do. When the algorithm is utilised in its most fundamental form, load balancing is handled by a single node across the entire system. This node is responsible for determining how the load is distributed. This node is ultimately responsible for the operation of the entire system. This is due to the fact that the strategy is only implemented by a single node in the network at any one point in time. Because this particular node is the only one that takes the process to a successful finish, it is referred to as the central node due to the fact that it is the only one that satisfies the requirements of its job. Consequently, it is the only one that fulfils the responsibilities associated with its role. This specific node is wholly accountable for ensuring that the system as a whole maintains an appropriate load distribution, and this is the only need that falls within its remit in order for it to be able to accomplish this objective. Because it is the only node that serves as a connecting point, the central node is the only point through which the other nodes can communicate with one another. This is because it is the only node that works as a connecting point (Martin. Randles. et al., 2010). This is due to the fact that it is the sole node that performs the function of a connecting point. Although the nodes of the system are arranged into clusters inside the framework of the system, load balancing in a semi-distributed system is performed through the use of a centralized approach. In contrast to this, a completely distributed system does not make use of a centralized technique in any of its operations. A hybrid distributed and non-distributed system is the name given to the particular configuration of a computer that has been described here. The fact that it mixes characteristics of different sorts of systems is where the name derives from. Elections are held inside each cluster in order to select a central node for each cluster. The voting mechanism that is regarded to be the most appropriate is utilised during the elections for each cluster. It is the job of this central node to guarantee that the workload in that cluster is distributed among all of the other nodes that are contained within that cluster in a manner that is both just and equitable. This is the responsibility that this central node has taken on for itself. This requirement falls under the heading of the obligations that are associated with the central node. Because of this, the process of load balancing the entire system is performed by utilizing the core nodes that are a component of each cluster (Ali. M. Alakee., 2010). This is because core nodes are distributed evenly throughout each cluster. This is because the core nodes are in a better position to spread the load evenly throughout the clusters than the other nodes are.

When compared to the scenario of semi-distributed load balancing, the process of arriving at a conclusion with centralized dynamic load balancing requires a significantly smaller number of messages. This is the case because the number of nodes participating in the load balancing process is significantly reduced. This is the situation as a result of the increased number of nodes that are taking part in the process of load balancing. This is because there are currently a greater number of nodes participating

Figure 1. Interaction between a dynamic load balancing algorithm's components

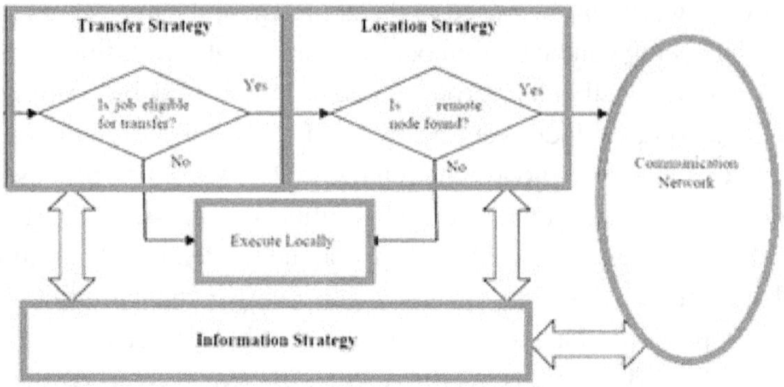

in the process of load balancing. This is the reason for this change. This is the outcome of an increasing number of nodes that are participating in the process of load balancing, which has led to this result. As a consequence of this, this result has occurred. This is the result of a significant decrease in the total number of interactions that are carried out inside of the system. On the other side, centralised solutions can result in a bottleneck in the system at the central node, and the process of load balancing will be rendered ineffective in the case that the central node is unable to function properly. Because of the nature of the scenario, the system will not be able to adequately disperse the load. Due to the fact that it possesses this quality, this strategy is capable of achieving the best possible level of efficiency (David, S et al., 2023) when used to networks that have a restricted number of nodes. This is a direct consequence of the fact that it possesses this characteristic.

POLICIES OR STRATEGIES IN DYNAMIC LOAD BALANCING

There are 4 policies:

Transfer Policy: Transfer policy, also known as transfer strategy, is the part of the algorithm for dynamic load balancing that determines which workloads should be moved from a local node to a remote node. It can also be called transfer strategy. This component decides which jobs should be transferred to the new location.

Selection Policy: It provides information (Babu, S. Z. D. et al., 2022, July) on the processors that are participating in the load swap, which is sometimes referred to as processor matching.

Location Policy: The term "location policy" or "location strategy" refers to the section of the load-balancing algorithm that is responsible for selecting a destination node for a transferred job.

Information Policy: In the context of the dynamic load balancing algorithm, the term "information policy" or "information (Pandey, B. K. et al., 2022) strategy" refers to the component of the algorithm that is in charge of acquiring information about the nodes that are present in the system in Figure 1.

CONCLUSION

In the following chapter, we will examine load balancing from a high-level perspective by focusing on the fundamentals that are involved in the process. These basics include the many load balancing algorithms, the idea of a dynamic load balancing algorithm in its most general sense, and the rules that can be included into it in a variety of different guises. In addition, the aforementioned three categories are a good way to categories these foundational components (Anthony. T. et al., 2010).

FUTURE WORK

When working with clouds, load balancing is an extremely essential element that needs to be taken into account. Since the idea of computing in the cloud refers to a very broad category of services, this is not surprising. In this specific industry, there is a massive amount of unrealized potential that is just waiting to be found and utilised. We have only gone over two of the many different methods for scheduling divisible loads that can be utilised in clouds. There are a wide variety of other methods. In spite of this, there is a wide variety of strategies that can be implemented in order to accomplish load balance in cloud environments. You can experiment with the various setting choices to determine what works best for you in order to better improve the functionality of the algorithms that have been provided.

REFERENCES

Ali, M. (2010). A Guide to Dynamic Load Balancing in Distributed Computer Systems. *IJCSNS International Journal of Computer Science and Network Security, 10*(6).

Anthony, T. (2010). Cloud Computing A Practical Approach. McGraw-Hill.

Babu, S. Z. D., Pandey, D., Naidu, G. T., Sumathi, S., Gupta, A., Bader Alazzam, M., & Pandey, B. K. (2022, July). Analysation of Big Data in Smart Healthcare. In *Artificial Intelligence on Medical Data: Proceedings of International Symposium, ISCMM 2021* (pp. 243-251). Singapore: Springer Nature Singapore.

Bessant, Y. A., Jency, J. G., Sagayam, K. M., Jone, A. A. A., Pandey, D., & Pandey, B. K. (2023). Improved parallel matrix multiplication using Strassen and Urdhvatiryagbhyam method. *CCF Transactions on High Performance Computing*, *5*(2), 1–14. doi:10.1007/s42514-023-00149-9

David, S., Duraipandian, K., Chandrasekaran, D., Pandey, D., Sindhwani, N., & Pandey, B. K. (2023). Impact of blockchain in healthcare system. In *Unleashing the Potentials of Blockchain Technology for Healthcare Industries* (pp. 37–57). Academic Press. doi:10.1016/B978-0-323-99481-1.00004-3

Ekong, M. O., George, W. K., Pandey, B. K., & Pandey, D. (2023). Enhancing the Fundamentals of Industrial Safety Management in TVET for Metaverse Realities. In *Applications of Neuromarketing in the Metaverse* (pp. 19–41). IGI Global. doi:10.4018/978-1-6684-8150-9.ch002

Iyyanar, P., Anand, R., Shanthi, T., Nassa, V. K., Pandey, B. K., George, A. S., & Pandey, D. (2023). A Real-Time Smart Sewage Cleaning UAV Assistance System Using IoT. In *Handbook of Research on Data-Driven Mathematical Modeling in Smart Cities* (pp. 24–39). IGI Global.

Jayapoorani, S., Pandey, D., Sasirekha, N. S., Anand, R., & Pandey, B. K. (2023). Systolic optimized adaptive filter architecture designs for ECG noise cancellation by Vertex-5. *Aerospace Systems*, *6*(1), 163–173. doi:10.1007/s42401-022-00177-3

Kumar, M. S., Sankar, S., Nassa, V. K., Pandey, D., Pandey, B. K., & Enbeyle, W. (2021). Innovation and creativity for data mining using computational statistics. In *Methodologies and Applications of Computational Statistics for Machine Intelligence* (pp. 223–240). IGI Global. doi:10.4018/978-1-7998-7701-1.ch012

Mladen, A. (2008). Cloud Computing Issues, Research and Implementations. *Proceedings of the ITI 2008 30th Int. Conf. on Information Technology Interfaces*. IEEE.

Pandey, B. K., & Pandey, D. (2023). Parametric optimization and prediction of enhanced thermoelectric performance in co-doped CaMnO3 using response surface methodology and neural network. *Journal of Materials Science Materials in Electronics*, *34*(21), 1589. doi:10.1007/s10854-023-10954-1

Pandey, B. K., Pandey, D., Nassa, V. K., George, S., Aremu, B., Dadeech, P., & Gupta, A. (2022, July). Effective and secure transmission of health information using advanced morphological component analysis and image hiding. In *Artificial Intelligence on Medical Data: Proceedings of International Symposium, ISCMM 2021* (pp. 223-230). Singapore: Springer Nature Singapore.

Pandey, B. K., Pandey, S. K., & Pandey, D. (2011). A survey of bioinformatics applications on parallel architectures. *International Journal of Computer Applications*, *23*(4), 21–25. doi:10.5120/2877-3744

Pandey, D., Pandey, B. K., & Wairya, S. (2021). Hybrid deep neural network with adaptive galactic swarm optimization for text extraction from scene images. *Soft Computing*, *25*(2), 1563–1580. doi:10.1007/s00500-020-05245-4

Pandey, D., Wairya, S., Pradhan, B., & Wangmo. (2022). Understanding COVID-19 response by twitter users: A text analysis approach. *Heliyon*, *8*(8), e09994. doi:10.1016/j.heliyon.2022.e09994 PMID:35873536

Pandey, J. K., Jain, R., Dilip, R., Kumbhkar, M., Jaiswal, S., Pandey, B. K., & Pandey, D. (2022). Investigating Role of IoT in the Development of Smart Application for Security Enhancement. In *IoT Based Smart Applications* (pp. 219–243). Springer International Publishing.

Pramanik, S., Pandey, D., Joardar, S., Niranjanamurthy, M., Pandey, B. K., & Kaur, J. (2023, October). An overview of IoT privacy and security in smart cities. In AIP Conference Proceedings (Vol. 2495, No. 1). AIP Publishing. doi:10.1063/5.0123511

Randles, M. (2009). A Comparative Experiment in Distributed Load Balancing. *Second International Conference on Developments in eSystems Engineering*. Semantic Scholar.

Randles, M., & Lamb, D. A. (2010). A Comparative Study into Distributed Load Balancing Algorithms for Cloud Computing. *IEEE 24th International Conference on Advanced Information Networking and Applications Workshops*. IEEE.

Revathi, T. K., Sathiyabhama, B., Sankar, S., Pandey, D., Pandey, B. K., & Dadeech, P. (2022). An intelligent model for coronary heart disease diagnosis. *Networking Technologies in Smart Healthcare: Innovations and Analytical Approaches*, 234. Taylor & Francis.

Sennan, S., Kirubasri, Alotaibi, Y., Pandey, D., & Alghamdi, S. (2022). EACR-LEACH: Energy-Aware Cluster-based Routing Protocol for WSN Based IoT. *CMC-COMPUTERS MATERIALS & CONTINUA, 72*(2), 2159-2174

Singh, J., Pandey, D., & Singh, A. K. (2023). *Event detection from real-time twitter streaming data using community detection algorithm*. Multimed Tools Appl. doi:10.1007/s11042-023-16263-3

Singh, S., Madaan, G., Kaur, J., Swapna, H. R., Pandey, D., Singh, A., & Pandey, B. K. (2023). Bibliometric Review on Healthcare Sustainability. Handbook of Research on Safe Disposal Methods of Municipal Solid Wastes for a Sustainable Environment, 142-161. Research Gate.

Vinodhini, V., Kumar, M. S., Sankar, S., Pandey, D., Pandey, B. K., & Nassa, V. K. (2022). IoT-based early forest fire detection using MLP and AROC method. *International Journal of Global Warming, 27*(1), 55–70. doi:10.1504/IJGW.2022.122794

Chapter 7
Mutation-Based Glow Worm Swarm Optimization for Efficient Load Balancing in Cloud Computing

Avtar Singh
https://orcid.org/0000-0001-7526-6813
National Institute of Technology, Jalandhar, India

Shobhana Kashyap
National Institute of Technology, Jalandhar, India

ABSTRACT

Cloud computing has evolved as an innovation that facilitates tasks by dynamically distributing virtual machines. User has to pay for the resources as per the demand. This is a challenging task for cloud service providers. The problems caused in load balancing are selecting random solutions, low speed convergence and picking up the original optima. To attain the best result, a mutation-based glow worm swarm optimization (MGWSO) technique is proposed. With this method, the makespan is reduced for a single work set across multiple datacentres. The work is motivated to decrease the consumption of resources in dynamic contexts while simultaneously increasing their availability. The simulated result shows that the suggested load balancing method dramatically reduces makespan in comparison to mutation-based particle swarm optimization.

INTRODUCTION

The cloud is the next computer paradigm and the next step in the evolution of information technology. It provides access to vast amounts of online storage and processing power on a pay-as-you-go basis. Problems like finding what you need; handling failures, spreading the load evenly, and keeping your data secure are magnified in the cloud (Dave et al., 2016). Distributing the burden or job evenly among the

DOI: 10.4018/979-8-3693-0900-1.ch007

nodes or servers is a significantly difficult and crucial function, for which load balancing is essential. It is the key difficulty with cloud computing.

The word "load balancing" refers to distributing the workload among multiple processors. It helps to utilize computing resources efficiently. It evenly distributes the workload, preventing any server from being overloaded while others are idle. This maximizes resource utilization and reduces costs (Kumar & Kumar, 2019). Its additional goals include prioritizing activities that need immediate execution above those that can wait and enabling scalability & flexibility for growing-in-size applications over time and so need more resources. In order to adjust load balancing, it must be able to reduce energy consumption, prevent bottlenecks, provide assistance, and fulfil quality of service (QoS) standards (Chen et al., 2017). The load balancer divides client demands into many servers. Virtual machine management (VMM) and hypervisors are used to implement the virtualization concept.

The three cloud computing deployment options are SaaS, PaaS, and IaaS. In SaaS, users rent software or applications from a cloud service provider. Users can utilize the provider's platform to build and launch their own applications using Paas model. IaaS provides computing resources over the internet, allowing users to acquire processing power, data storage, and other infrastructure components. Load balancing can be performed in static or dynamic cloud environments. Static load balancing maintains constant inputs and outputs throughout execution, while dynamic load balancing adapts to changing resource availability and workload demands. Static load balancing methods may not be suitable for dynamic environments, which require load changes during execution (Kaur, 2017).

Glow Worm Swarm Optimization (GWSO) is a Particle Swarm Optimization (PSO) variant that is utilized for optimization issues in a variety of disciplines, including cloud computing. It is more scalable because the control decentralised at various nodes. GWSO is based on how glow worms behave. GWSO is based on the behaviour of glow-worms. A glow worm with a high amount of light production (high luciferin) is better positioned and has a higher objective function value. Each glow worm chooses a neighbour with a higher luciferin value than its own and moves in that direction, according to probabilistic estimation. These movements are entirely based on local knowledge. As a result, the glow worms can form smaller groups, making it possible to discover various optima for the stated goal function. The GWSO algorithm starts by randomly distributing glow worms over the workspace, each with an equal amount of luciferin. A GWSO algorithm includes four phases: initialization, luciferin updating, movement, and local radial range updating. The algorithm is population-based. GSO is a metaheuristic method inspired by glow worm activity.

The proposed approach tackles the cloud computing load balancing issue by lowering the makespan time with the MGWSO technique. The result of this work shows that MGWSO has a lower makespan than the MPSO method. The fitness feature is also enhanced further it eliminates dummy jobs.

1. The chapter identifies and addresses the challenges faced by cloud service providers in load balancing, including the issues of selecting random solutions, low convergence speed, and the difficulty in identifying the original optima. By highlighting these challenges, the chapter establishes the necessity for innovative load balancing techniques in dynamic cloud environments.
2. The chapter introduces a mutation-based technique for load balancing, leveraging the GWSO metaheuristic. This approach represents a novel contribution to the field, as it enhances traditional load balancing methods by incorporating mutation strategies inspired by natural processes. The integration of GWSO introduces adaptability and self-learning capabilities, enabling the system to explore and exploit the solution space effectively.

3. The proposed mutation-based technique, based on GWSO, demonstrates its effectiveness by reducing the makespan for a single work set across multiple datacenters. This reduction in makespan signifies improved task completion times and enhanced system efficiency, crucial metrics in evaluating the performance of load balancing algorithms. The ability to optimize makespan across distributed datacenters is a noteworthy contribution, emphasizing the applicability of the proposed technique in real-world cloud scenarios.
4. The chapter conducts a comparative analysis between the proposed MGWSO-based load balancing method and the mutation-based particle swarm optimization. Through simulations, the chapter demonstrates the superiority of the suggested approach by dramatically reducing makespan in comparison to the existing techniques. This comparative analysis provides empirical evidence of the effectiveness of the proposed method, establishing its competitiveness in the domain of cloud computing load balancing.

The work is structured into distinct sections, each serving a specific purpose. Literature Survey provides a comprehensive overview of existing research, including methodologies, findings, and limitations in the field. Proposed Algorithm section explains the novel algorithm developed for the research study is detailed, explaining its underlying principles and design. Experimental Outcomes section explains the results of experiments and research activities are presented, offering insights into the study's findings and their implications. The conclusion section summarizes the main discoveries, discusses their significance, and addresses the limitations of the study. Also, it outlines potential areas for future research, identifying gaps in the current study and suggesting directions for further exploration and improvement.

LITERATURE SURVEY

In recent years, cloud computing has emerged as a revolutionary innovation, enabling the dynamic distribution of virtual machines to facilitate various tasks (Kashyap & Singh, 2023). This model, where users pay for resources based on their demand, presents a significant challenge for cloud service providers (Singh et al., 2014). The details of load balancing further exacerbate this challenge, encompassing issues such as the selection of solutions, achieving rapid convergence, and identifying the original optima (Agarwal et al., 2020),(Singh et al., 2014).

An overview of load balancing in cloud computing was suggested by (Kansal & Chana, 2012). This overview included a classification of load balancing methods based upon system load and system topology, as well as examples of load balancing and several research issues related to load balancing. While in (Menasce & Ngo, 2009) the authors examined the majority of the available strategies, most of them are geared at decreasing the related overhead as well as enhancing the performance of the methodology. The study (Wang et al., 2010) discussed the concept of cloud computing, its pros, cons and described several existing cloud computing platforms. The study (Braun et al., 2001) presented a scheduling algorithm as their contribution. Their algorithm combined the capabilities of both OLB (Opportunistic Load Balancing) (Anandharajan & Bhagyaveni, 2011) and LBMM (Load Balance Min-Min) (Galloway et al., 2011) scheduling algorithms, and is comparatively more efficient. The objective of (Alonso-Calvo et al., 2010) is to locate the most suitable cloud resource while taking into account Co-operative Power aware Scheduled Load Balancing as a potential solution to the problem of Cloud load balancing. The

Table 1. Comparison analysis of different work

Ref.	Technique	Finding	Limitation
(Hlaing & Yee, 2019)	• Tasks are initially categorized based on the length of their instructions before being assigned to the appropriate VM depending on the availability of each resource in terms of processing power, cost, and the number of accessible processing elements.	• Simulations show that the proposed method is better than both the Shortest Job First (SJF) algorithm and the First Come First Serve (FCFS) algorithm in terms of Makespan and cost of execution when using Amazon EC2 instances.	• The research is only concerned with static work scheduling, ignoring the dynamic nature of cloud computing settings. • Dynamic factors such as changing workload demands, resource availability, and network circumstances can all have a substantial impact on the performance of task scheduling algorithms. Ignoring these aspects may limit the suggested approach's scalability and adaptability.
(Pradeep & Pravakar, 2022)	• The suggested paper examined several methods used to schedule various tasks in the cloud.	• The research investigates how alternative scheduling algorithms affect the quality of service (QoS) delivered to cloud clients. It assesses the success of the algorithms in achieving customer needs by evaluating parameters such as response time, execution time, and cost.	• The report does not go into detail about the algorithms that were evaluated, the criteria utilised for comparison, or the selection procedure. • This lack of comparative analysis may make it difficult to reach significant conclusions about the relative strengths and shortcomings of various scheduling algorithms.
(Aref et al., 2022)	• This paper describes a hybrid task scheduling system that combines three methods to reduce Makespan and get the best load distribution among resources. • Min-Min scheduling, the genetic algorithm, and Max-Min scheduling.	• Max-Min, Min-Min, and the suggested work Makespan and resource consumption are estimated and compared in the experimental outcome. • The proposed work outperforms the Max-Min and Min-Min results.	• The scheduling approach (Max-Min or Min-Min) is chosen using a genetic algorithm in the study; it takes longer to choose the scheduling technique. • A boost can be used to speed up specific scheduling procedures.
(Agarwal et al., 2020)	• The goal of the proposed method is to decrease makespan time while enhancing fitness function. • The suggested approach employs mutation-based particle swarm optimization.	• By adding mutation to the best solution obtained by the prior PSO method, the Makespan and fitness function were enhanced. • In comparison to PSO, the MPSO algorithm yields superior outcomes.	• There is a possibility that the study does not handle load balancing in dynamic cloud computing systems with changing workloads and resource availability in an adequate manner.
(Swarnakar et al., 2020)	• An efficient dynamic load balancing technique has been suggested that efficiently manages coming jobs for distribution across different virtual servers across many datacenters.	• The proposed method results in Makespan time better than existing Dynamic load management algorithm (DLMA) and Optimal Load Balancing in Cloud Computing (OLBCCA).	• Three dynamic Tables are used in the paper. • To plan a task, the load balancer needs to check all three tables, which takes more time, and these tables needs to be updated simultaneously
(Patel & Bhalodia, 2019)	• The proposed algorithm includes two methods for sharing workload among the cloud system. • For priority-based tasks, a modified algorithm that is inspired by honeybee behavior was used, while for non-priority-based tasks, an enhanced weighted round-robin technique was applied.	• This proposed work is designed to optimize resource utilization, reduce completion time, and increase system performance.	• If the incoming tasks are all high priority, high priority tasks may be kept waiting and scheduled using a round-robin method.
(Agarwal & Srivastava, 2021)	• To handle the task scheduling problem, the suggested approach employs the PSO algorithm. • To avoid premature convergence, the proposed approach employs an opposition-based learning technique.	• The suggested algorithm's results reveal that it has better Makespan time which outperforms PSO, the genetic algorithm (G.A), and the Max-Min algorithm.	• The parameters of stability and load balance are not considered in the preceding paper. • As the number of jobs and resources in the cloud environment grows, it is critical to evaluate how the method operates.

research (Singh & Dutta, 2013) focuses on boosting the efficiency of a standard Genetic Algorithm (GA) for work scheduling in cloud computing utilizing Fuzzy Logic (FL).

Table 1 provides a comprehensive summary of techniques employed, findings obtained, and limitations identified by various researchers in the field. The table serves as a condensed overview of the existing literature, offering valuable insights into the methodologies used by previous researchers, the outcomes of their studies, and the challenges they encountered.

In this chapter to address these challenges, a novel approach known as MGWSO has been proposed. This technique aims to optimize load balancing by reducing the makespan for a single work set distributed across multiple data centers. The primary objective is to minimize resource consumption in dynamic contexts while enhancing their availability.

PROPOSED ALGORITHM (MGWSO)

This section explains the new algorithm designed for the research work, illustrating its fundamental concepts and design.

In GWSO glow worms, by nature, gravitate towards neighbors with higher levels of luciferin than their own. However, VM is drawn to its neighbor with the lowest Makespan, which is the inverse of the glowworm's properties. The proposed algorithm is the enhanced version of GWSO. To improve cloud computing load balancing, the suggested method uses MGWSO to lower Makespan time and increase fitness function. Figure 1 depicts the suggested MGWSO algorithm's flowchart, where each glow worm is initialized for the first time and has the same quantity of Luciferin l_o. There are four phases occur in each iteration of the algorithm: the Luciferin update, mutation performed on luciferin, update of the movement, and update of the Local Radial Range.

During the glow worm phase, which is expressed by the luciferin modification stage, the function is assessed. Each glow worm revises its previous Luciferin reading using equation 1.

$$l_i\left(t+1\right)=\left(1-\rho\right)l_i\left(t\right)+\gamma J\left(x_i\left(t+1\right)\right) \tag{1}$$

Figure 1. MGWSO algorithm

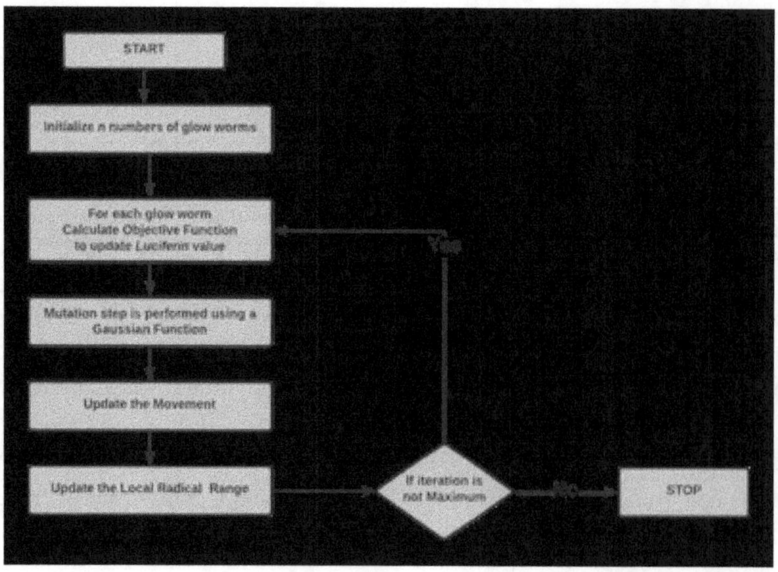

where, $l_i(t)$ is the level of Luciferin in the ith glowworm at time t, ρ is the Luciferin degeneration variable (0, 1), γ is the Luciferin enhancement variable, and $J(x_i(t))$ denotes the cost of the objective function. Next, we apply the mutation on the optimal Luciferin value and determine the new optimal luciferin value using equation 2.

$$Luciferin\ g1(d) = Luciferin\ g(d) - (Xmax(d) - Xmin(d)).\ Gaussian \quad (2)$$

where, Luciferin g1(d) shows the updated or next iteration value *pf* luciferin at a particular location or position "*d*" within the optimization problem. Luciferin *g*(*d*) is the current value of luciferin at position "*d*" in the optimization problem. *X*max(*d*) – *X*min(*d*) denotes the gap in a variable's minimum and maximum values "Luciferin" at position "*d*". It represents the range or spread of the variable within the optimization problem. Gaussian refers to a Gaussian function, which is commonly used to model probability distributions and has a characteristic bell-shaped curve.

"*(Xmax(d) – Xmin(d))· Gaussian*" represents the product of the range of the variable "Luciferin" at position "*d*" and a Gaussian function. It indicates the influence or impact of the range on the update of luciferin.

There are four further steps in the movement phase:

Step 1: Locate Neighbors:

The collection of VMs' neighbors is computed using equation 3.

$$N_j(t) = \{n : x_n(t) - x_j(t) \| \le \gamma_d^j(t); l_j(t) \ge l_n(t)\} \quad (3)$$

Here, *n* is the nearest VM index, $x_n(t)$ and $x_j(t)$ are the completion timings of VM_n and VM_j and $l_j(t)$ and $l_n(t)$ are the luciferin values of VM_n and VM_j respectively.

Step 2: Calculate Probabilities:

The likelihood of predicting movement direction towards a neighbor with a greater luciferin value is determined for each VM_j using equation 4.

$$p_{jn}(t) = \frac{l_n(t) - l_j(t)}{\sum_{k \in N_j(t)} \{l_k(t) - l_j(t)\}} \quad (4)$$

where, $p_{jn}(t)$ is the likelihood of a task in VM_j moving to VM_n.

Step 3: Selection:

The task in VM_j selects the VM_n from the neighbor set having greatest likelihood of being chosen from the neighbor set.

Step 4: Movement:

Using equation 5 VM's completion time is updated.

$$x_j(t+1) = x_j(t) + s\left(\frac{x_n(t) - x_j(t)}{x_n(t) - x_j(t)}\right) \tag{5}$$

where, $x_j(t + 1)$, $x_j(t)$ denote the new and current completion times of VM_j and s is the magnitude of the moving step.

Using equation 6, the local radial range is calculated to create the neighbor set.

$$\gamma_d^j(t+1) = \min\left\{\gamma_s, max\left\{0, \gamma_d^j(t) + \beta\left(n_t - \left|N_j(t)\right|\right)\right\}\right\} \tag{6}$$

where, β is the rate of change in the immediate region, γ is the enhancement coefficient of luciferin, $\gamma_d^j(t)$ is the VM_j's local radial range, γs is the maximum sensor range of $\gamma_d^j(t)$,$N_j(t)$ is VM_j Neighbors Set, n_t is number of expected neighbors and $|N_j(t)|$ is number of true neighbors.

EXPERIMENTAL OUTCOMES

This chapter evaluates the MGWSO proposed algorithm by comparing it to establish practices. To perform this experiment, the required configuration is the Eclipse Java Development Environment and the CloudSim toolkit. It is implemented on a system having an Intel(R) Core (TM) i5-9300H CPU @ 2.40GHz, 8 GB of RAM and 64-bit Windows 11 operating system. The reason for the study is the need to reduce resource use while making more resources available in changing situations. In this part, we compared the performance of MGWSO algorithm to that of MPSO algorithm. The Figure 2 and 3 show the Makespan results, Table 2 shows the average Makespan results, and this section discusses the comparative evaluation between the proposed MGWSO and the MPSO algorithm. The makespan value is evaluated for 10 data centers DCs (shown in Fig2) and 20 DCs (shown in Fig.3). The comparison results used 50 to 200 cloudlets and 10 to 20 datacenters.

Figure 3 depicts Makespan value for 20 datacenters with 50, 100, 150, and 200 cloudlets for both MPSO and MGWSO techniques.

In Table 2, we can see how the suggested model for Average Makespan with 50-200 cloudlets over 10-20 datacenters compares to MPSO. On 10 datacenters, the proposed MGWSO achieves better results than the MPSO algorithm, with an average Makespan time of 3367.42 seconds instead of the

MPSO algorithm's 3749.52 seconds; this indicates that the proposed MGWSO improves upon the MPSO algorithm. On 15 datacenters, the proposed MGWSO achieves better results than the MPSO algorithm, with an average Makespan time of 2129.55 seconds instead of the MPSO algorithm's 2506.34 seconds.

The following figure 4 shows the comparison between MPSO and proposed model for Total CPU time using 50 to 200 cloudlets on 20 datacentres. The proposed MGWSO obtain better results on 50 cloudlets that get 12642.68 Total CPU time in seconds while MPSO algorithm shows 14072.33 Total CPU time on 50 cloudlets. For 100 cloudlets MPSO total CPU time is 27340.17 sec and proposed MGWSO total CPU time is 25533.47 sec. Similarly, for 150 cloudlets MPSO total CPU time is46050.04 and proposed MGWSO total CPU time is 38951.87 and for 200 cloudlets MPSO total CPU time is 59200.217 and proposed MGWSO total CPU time is 50778.70 .The results shows that total CPU time is also improved, the proposed algorithm takes less time than MPSO algorithm.

Figure 2. MPSO and MGWSO Makespan time with ten Datacenters

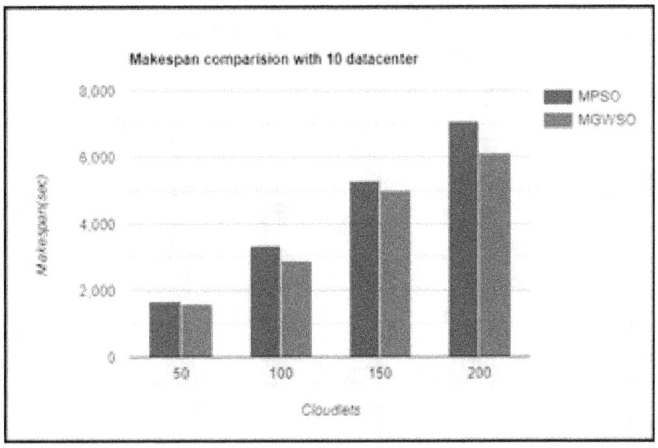

The successful implementation of MGWSO could significantly enhance resource utilization in cloud environments, reducing costs and improving overall efficiency. If proven effective in real-world scenarios, MGWSO could lead to decreased makespan and improved performance for workload distribution across multiple datacenters. Cloud service providers adopting MGWSO could gain a competitive edge by offering more efficient and cost-effective services, attracting more users and businesses. The research and

Figure 3. MPSO and MGWSO Makespan time for 20 Datacenters

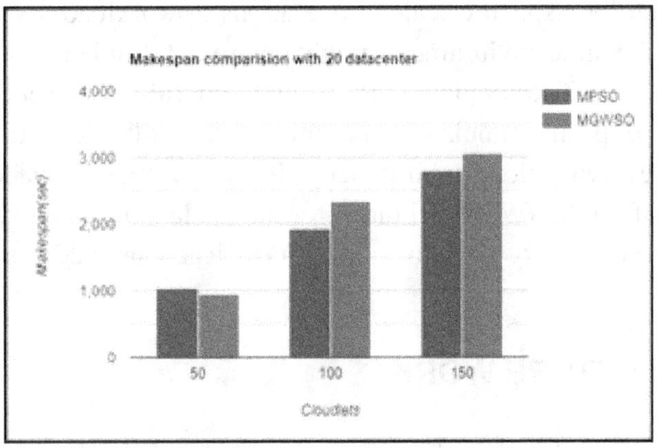

Table 2. Comparing average Makespan time for MGWSO and MPSO

Datacenter	Avg Makespan time of MPSO (In sec)	Avg Makespan time of MGWSO (In sec)	Reduced Makespan time by (In sec)
10	3749.52	3367.42	382.10
15	2506.34	2129.55	376.79
20	1840.29	1648.83	191.46

Figure 4. Bar graph of MPSO and propose model comparison with total CPU time using 20 datacenters

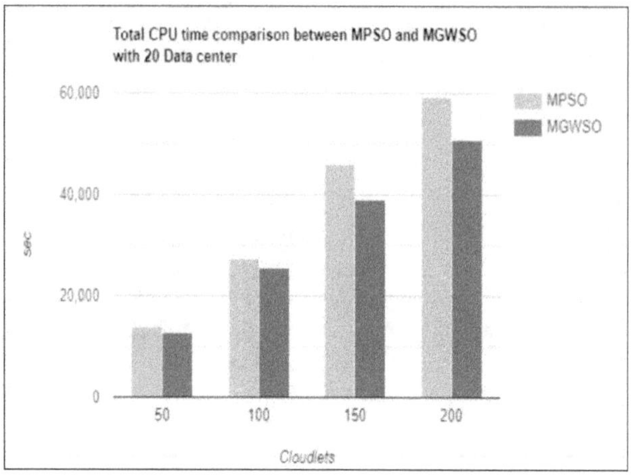

development of optimization techniques like MGWSO contribute to the advancement of cloud computing technologies, paving the way for more sophisticated and efficient systems.

Limitations of the Work

The MGWSO technique sounds promising for improving load balancing in cloud computing. However, like any research or technique, it's likely to have limitations. The effectiveness of optimization techniques often varies with different workload patterns, system configurations, and network conditions. The MGWSO technique might excel in certain scenarios but could perform less optimally in others. While the technique might work well for a specific scale of operations or workload, its scalability to larger cloud infrastructures or highly dynamic environments might be limited. Implementing it across massive datacenters might pose challenges. The simulated results might not fully represent the real-world scenarios. Overfitting the technique to specific simulated conditions could result in less effectiveness when deployed in practical, diverse, and evolving cloud environments. It's important to consider these limitations while evaluating the potential of the MGWSO technique for load balancing in cloud computing. Real-world testing and refinement are necessary steps to validate its efficacy and address any shortcomings.

CONCLUSION AND FUTURE WORK

The major issue in cloud computing has always been load balancing. The algorithm's goal is to reduce makespan while improving fitness function. In this case a Mutation-Based Glow Worm Swarm Optimization is applied. The suggested method uses a Mutation operator into this naturalistic optimization strategy. By adding mutation to the best solution found by the existing GSO method, the makespan and fitness functions have been made better. When compared to MPSO, the outcomes from the MGWSO algorithm are superior. The proposed method for load balancing takes advantage of preemptive virtual machine scheduling. Other parameters such as average time, throughput, waiting time, resource utilization, and so on may be examined in future study to improve dynamic load balancing even further.

REFERENCES

Agarwal, M., & Srivastava, G. M. S. (2021). Opposition-based learning inspired particle swarm optimization (OPSO) scheme for task scheduling problem in cloud computing. *Journal of Ambient Intelligence and Humanized Computing*, *12*(10), 9855–9875. doi:10.1007/s12652-020-02730-4

Agarwal, R., Baghel, N., & Khan, M. A. (2020). *Load Balancing in Cloud Computing using Mutation Based Particle Swarm Optimization*. 2020 International Conference on Contemporary Computing and Applications (IC3A), Lucknow, India. 10.1109/IC3A48958.2020.233295

Akhtar, T., Haider, N. G., & Khan, S. M. (2022). *A Comparative Study of the Application of Glowworm Swarm Optimization Algorithm with other Nature-Inspired Algorithms in the Network Load Balancing Problem*. Engineering, Technology & Applied Science Research. doi:10.48084/etasr.4999

Aldossary, M. (2021). A Review of Dynamic Resource Management in Cloud Computing Environments. *Computer Systems Science and Engineering*, *36*(3), 461–476. doi:10.32604/csse.2021.014975

Alguliyev, R., Imamverdiyev, Y., & Abdullayeva, F. (2019). PSO-based Load Balancing Method in Cloud Computing. *Automatic Control and Computer Sciences*, *53*(1), 45–55. doi:10.3103/S0146411619010024

Alonso-Calvo, R., Crespo, J., Garcia-Remesal, M., Anguita, A., & Maojo, V. (2010). On distributing load incloud computing: A real application for very-large image datasets. *Procedia Computer Science*, *1*(1), 2669–2677. doi:10.1016/j.procs.2010.04.300

Anandharajan, T., & Bhagyaveni, M. (2011). Co-operative scheduled energy aware load-balancing technique for an efficient computational cloud. *International Journal of Computational Science*, *8*(2).

Aref, S., Kadum, J., & Kadum, A. (2022). Optimization of Max-Min and Min-Min Task Scheduling Algorithms Using G.A in Cloud Computing. *2022 5th International Conference on Engineering Technology and its Applications (IICETA)*, Al-Najaf, Iraq. 10.1109/IICETA54559.2022.9888542

Braun, T. D., Siegel, H. J., Beck, N., Boloni, L. L., Maheswaran, M., Reuther, A. I., Robertson, J. P., Theys, M. D., Yao, B., Hensgen, D., & Freund, R. F. (2001). A comparison of eleven static heuristics for mapping a class of independent tasks onto heterogeneous distributed computing systems. *Journal of Parallel and Distributed Computing*, *61*(6), 2669–2677. doi:10.1006/jpdc.2000.1714

Chen, S. L., Chen, Y. Y., & Kuo, S. H. (2017). CLB: A novel load balancing architecture and algorithm for cloud services. *Computers & Electrical Engineering*, *58*, 154–160. doi:10.1016/j.compeleceng.2016.01.029

Dave, A., Patel, B., & Bhatt, G. (2016). Load balancing in cloud computing using optimization techniques: A study. *Proceedings of the International Conference on Communication and Electronics Systems, ICCES 2016*. IEEE. 10.1109/CESYS.2016.7889883

Elmagzoub, M. A., Syed, D., Shaikh, A., Islam, N., Alghamdi, A., & Rizwan, S. (2021). A survey of swarm intelligence based load balancing techniques in cloud computing environment. In Electronics (Switzerland). doi:10.3390/electronics10212718

Galloway, J. M., Smith, K. L., & Vrbsky, S. S. (2011). Power aware load balancing for cloud computing. *Proceedings of the World Congress on Engineering and Computer Science*, (vol. 1, pp. 19–21).

Hlaing, Y. T. H., & Yee, T. T. (2019). Static independent task scheduling on virtualized servers in cloud computing environment. *2019 International Conference on Advanced Information Technologies (ICAIT)*. IEEE. 10.1109/AITC.2019.8920865

Kansal, N. J., & Chana, I. (2012). Existing load balancing techniques in cloud computing: A systematic review. *Journal of Information Systems & Communication*, *3*(1), 87–91.

Kashyap, S., & Singh, A. (2023). Prediction-based scheduling techniques for cloud data center's workload: A systematic review. *Cluster Computing*, *26*(5), 1–27. doi:10.1007/s10586-023-04024-8

Kaur, A. (2017). Particle Swarm Optimization based Dynamic Load Balancing in Cloud Environment. *International Journal on Computer Science and Engineering*.

Kokilavani, T., & Amalarethinam, D. (2011). Load balanced min-min algorithm for static metatask scheduling in grid computing. *International Journal of Computer Applications*, *20*(2), 24–31. doi:10.5120/2403-3197

Kumar, P., & Kumar, R. (2019). Issues and challenges of load balancing techniques in cloud computing: A survey. *ACM Computing Surveys*, *51*(6), 1–35. doi:10.1145/3281010

Menasce, D. A., & Ngo, P. (2009). Understanding cloud computing: Experimentation and capacity planning. *Computer Measurement Group Conference*. George Mason University.

Patel, K. D., & Bhalodia, T. M. (2019). An Efficient Dynamic Load Balancing Algorithm for Virtual Machine in Cloud Computing. *2019 International Conference on Intelligent Computing and Control Systems (ICCS)*, Madurai, India. 10.1109/ICCS45141.2019.9065292

Pradeep, K., & Pravakar, D. (2022). *Exploration on Task Scheduling using Optimization Algorithm in Cloud computing*. 2022 6th International Conference on Trends in Electronics and Informatics (ICOEI), Tirunelveli, India. 10.1109/ICOEI53556.2022.9777120

Singh, A., & Dutta, K. (2013). A genetic algorithm based task scheduling for cloud computing with fuzzy logic. *Ieie Transactions on Smart Processing & Computing*, *2*(6), 367–372.

Singh, A., Dutta, K., & Gupta, H. (2014). A survey on load balancing algorithms for cloud computing. *Int. J. Comput. Appl*, *6*(4), 66–72.

Swarnakar, S., Kumar, R., Krishn, S., & Banerjee, C. (2020). Improved Dynamic Load Balancing Approach in Cloud Computing. *2020 IEEE 1st International Conference for Convergence in Engineering (ICCE)*, (pp. 195-199). IEEE. 10.1109/ICCE50343.2020.9290602

Wang, S. C., Yan, K.-Q., Liao, W.-P., & Wang, S.-S. (2010). *Towards a load balancing in a three-level cloud computing network* (Vol. 1). IEEE.

Chapter 8
Mastering Cloud Scalability:
Strategies, Challenges, and Future Directions: Navigating Complexities of Scaling in Digital Era

Kaushikkumar Patel
https://orcid.org/0009-0005-9197-2765
TransUnion LLC, USA

ABSTRACT

This chapter takes the reader on a journey through the world of cloud scalability, showing how crucial it is in today's digital world. It starts with the basics and then dives deep into understanding scalability, from how we measure it to new ways of building scalable systems. It also explores the balance between scalability, security, and following the rules. When it comes to real-world problems, the chapter offers practical solutions based on industry knowledge. Finally, it looks to the future, suggesting exciting new areas for research in the ever-changing digital landscape. Whether you're an IT pro, a business leader, or a researcher, this chapter offers valuable insights into the world of cloud scalability.

INTRODUCTION

The modern digital landscape is evolving unprecedentedly, with businesses increasingly relying on cloud computing to meet their IT needs. Within this transformative shift, one concept stands out as paramount: cloud scalability. It has become a linchpin for organizations of all sizes, enabling them to flexibly adapt to fluctuating workloads, optimize resource utilization, and ensure seamless service delivery.

The Significance of Cloud Scalability: Cloud scalability, in its essence, represents the ability of a cloud computing infrastructure to adjust resources to meet changing demands dynamically. Whether it's a surge in website traffic, a sudden uptick in data processing requirements, or an expanding user base, scalability allows businesses to scale up or down swiftly without costly hardware upgrades or infrastructure overhauls. This capability is a game-changer, empowering organizations to meet customer expectations, enhance operational efficiency, and ultimately drive growth.

DOI: 10.4018/979-8-3693-0900-1.ch008

Navigating the Complexity of Cloud Environments: To understand cloud scalability fully, it's crucial to grasp the intricacies of modern cloud environments. These environments are marked by their distributed nature, comprising vast networks of servers, data centers, and virtualized resources. Managing these complex infrastructures demands a strategic approach, and scalability emerges as a foundational pillar in this endeavor.

Scope of This Chapter: In this chapter, we embark on an in-depth exploration of cloud scalability. Our journey encompasses various facets, from the quantitative aspects measured through scalability metrics to the architectural patterns that facilitate scalability. This chapter also delves into the interplay of scalability with security and compliance, examining the challenges and offering pragmatic solutions. Furthermore, this chapter looks into the future, envisioning the research directions that promise to reshape the landscape of cloud scalability.

Guiding the Cloud-Driven Transformation: As we navigate these dimensions of cloud scalability, it's essential to recognize that this chapter serves as a guiding compass for businesses and IT professionals embarking on their cloud-driven transformation. It offers insights, best practices, and a roadmap for mastering cloud scalability to harness its full potential.

To underpin our exploration, this chapter draws from a wealth of research and expertise. References such as "Database Scalability, Elasticity, and Autonomy in the Cloud" (D. Agrawal, 2011) provide foundational insights into the scalability paradigms that underpin cloud computing. Meanwhile, "A Study on Scalability of Services and Privacy Issues in Cloud Computing" (R. L. Patibandla, 2012) addresses the critical issue of privacy in the context of scalability.

In the ensuing sections, this chapter delves deeper into the nuances of cloud scalability, unveiling the metrics that quantify it, the architectural blueprints that enable it, and the security considerations that safeguard it. Additionally, this chapter scrutinizes the challenges encountered on the scalability journey and proposes pragmatic solutions. The final section will explore the future of cloud scalability and the emerging trends set to redefine it.

As we embark on this comprehensive journey through the realm of cloud scalability, it's our hope that this chapter equips you with the knowledge, insights, and strategic guidance needed to master cloud scalability in an era where adaptability and efficiency are the cornerstones of success.

LITERATURE REVIEW

In cloud computing, understanding the roots of cloud scalability is essential for harnessing its transformative potential. A critical analysis of existing scholarly articles, papers, and other sources sheds light on the historical evolution and foundational concepts underpinning cloud scalability.

a. **Historical Perspectives:** The journey of cloud scalability began with the seminal work (D. Agrawal, 2011), titled "Database Scalability, Elasticity, and Autonomy in the Cloud." This pioneering research laid the groundwork for comprehending the principles of scalability, elasticity, and autonomy in cloud environments. It underscored the need for dynamic resource adjustments to handle varying workloads efficiently.
b. **Comparative Analyses:** In the pursuit of scalability, a pivotal study (Al-Said Ahmad, 2019), titled "Scalability Analysis Comparisons of Cloud-Based Software Services," engaged in comprehensive comparisons of cloud-based software services. By evaluating scalability metrics and performance

across different cloud platforms, services, and auto-scaling policies, this research unveiled significant insights. It emphasized the importance of tailoring scalability strategies based on platform and demand characteristics.

c. **Metric Pioneers:** The role of auto-scaling in enhancing cloud scalability is a notable point of discussion in the literature. The research (S. Lehrig, 2015), delves into "Scalability, Elasticity, and Efficiency in Cloud Computing: A Systematic Literature Review of Definitions and Metrics." This systematic review scrutinized diverse scalability metrics and efficiency indicators, providing a foundational understanding of how to gauge and optimize cloud scalability.
d. **Challenges and Solutions:** Cloud scalability is not without its challenges. The paper (S. Verma, 2021), titled "Auto-Scaling Techniques for IoT-Based Cloud Applications: A Review," explores the intricacies of auto-scaling techniques for IoT-based cloud applications. It highlights the complexities involved in handling diverse data streams and computing demands in IoT scenarios and proposes solutions to ensure seamless scalability.
e. **Scalability and Security Nexus:** A significant dimension of cloud scalability lies in its interplay with security and compliance. The work (J. Cáceres, 2010), titled "Service Scalability Over the Cloud," discussed the inherent challenges in maintaining security while achieving scalability. This chapter underscores the importance of balancing scalability with stringent security measures, a critical consideration in contemporary cloud environments.
f. **Future Research Horizons:** Scalability in cloud computing is an ever-evolving field. As we gaze into the future, the study (M. D. Assunção, 2015), titled "Big Data Computing and Clouds: Trends and Future Directions," offers valuable insights into emerging trends. It anticipates the convergence of big data and cloud computing, presenting opportunities and challenges that will shape the scalability landscape.

In this literature review, we have delved into the foundational works that have paved the way for understanding and mastering cloud scalability. The references cited here represent a fraction of the vast body of knowledge on this subject, highlighting the interdisciplinary nature of cloud scalability and its far-reaching implications. The subsequent sections of this chapter will explore scalability metrics, architectural patterns, security considerations, and future research directions, weaving together a comprehensive narrative on mastering cloud scalability.

SCALABILITY METRICS AND MEASUREMENT

A fundamental aspect of mastering cloud scalability lies in the ability to measure and quantify it accurately. Scalability metrics provide the quantitative foundation upon which effective scalability strategies are built. In this section, we explore various scalability metrics and measurement methods, drawing insights from the existing body of literature. This section delves into various quantitative aspects of cloud scalability, accompanied by illustrative data presented in Table 1 named 'Scalability Metrics and Measurement' for reference.

a. **Volume and Quality Metrics:** Two key dimensions that underpin scalability measurement are volume and quality. The paper (G. Brataas, 2017), titled "Scalability Analysis Comparisons of Cloud-Based Software Services," introduces technical volume and quality scalability metrics. These metrics quantify how actual scaling behavior differs from ideal linear scaling. The volume metric assesses service instance growth compared to ideal proportional growth, while the quality metric quantifies service response time relative to ideal constant time (G. Brataas, 2017). These metrics, which focus on technical aspects, provide a robust framework for assessing scalability.

b. **Auto-Scaling Efficiency:** Auto-scaling is a pivotal technique for achieving scalability in cloud environments. The research (S. Verma, 2021), "Auto-Scaling Techniques for IoT-Based Cloud Applications: A Review," explores auto-scaling techniques in the context of IoT-based cloud applications. While this study primarily addresses IoT scenarios, it elucidates the critical role of auto-scaling in ensuring resource efficiency and service availability during demand spikes (S. Verma, 2021). The insights derived from this work are applicable to a broader range of cloud applications.
c. **Variable Demand Challenges:** Scalability becomes particularly challenging when dealing with variable demand patterns. The research (M. M. Falatah, 2014), titled "Cloud Scalability Considerations," emphasizes the importance of considering scalability in cloud environments under variable demand conditions. It highlights that over-provisioning of instances can occur when attempting to accommodate variable demand, necessitating the refinement of scalability metric equations. This study offers valuable insights into addressing one of the most pressing challenges of cloud scalability.
d. **Cost-Efficiency Metrics:** While scalability metrics primarily focus on technical aspects, cost considerations are equally crucial. Cloud scalability should align with cost-efficient practices. The article published (Spot, 2021), "Horizontal vs. Vertical Scaling in the Cloud," provides insights into cost-effective scaling strategies. It discusses the differences between horizontal and vertical scaling and their implications for cost management in the cloud. The article is a practical guide for organizations seeking to strike the right balance between scalability and cost efficiency.
e. **Combined Metrics for Holistic View:** Scalability metrics are most effective when combined with utility-oriented metrics based on cost. The paper, "CloudScale: Scalability Management for Cloud Systems," introduces the concept of scalability management in cloud systems. This work emphasizes the importance of combining technical scalability metrics with economic scalability views to make informed decisions regarding scaling operations (G. Brataas, 2013). By integrating these two perspectives, organizations can achieve a holistic understanding of scalability.

Table 1. Scalability metrics and measurement

Metric/Aspect	Description
Volume and Quality Metrics	Metrics quantifying scaling behavior, focusing on volume (service instance growth) and quality (service response time)
Auto-Scaling Efficiency	Techniques for efficient auto-scaling to ensure resource efficiency and service availability during demand spikes
Variable Demand Challenges	Considerations for scalability in the presence of variable demand patterns, addressing over-provisioning issues
Cost-Efficiency Metrics	Insights into cost-effective scaling strategies, including horizontal and vertical scaling implications
Combined Metrics for Holistic View	Integration of technical scalability metrics with economic scalability views for informed scaling decisions

In this section, we have delved into the diverse landscape of scalability metrics and measurement methods. These quantitative tools enable organizations to assess, optimize, and monitor their cloud scalability effectively. The subsequent sections of this chapter will explore architectural patterns for scalability, the interplay of scalability with security and compliance, challenges and solutions, and future research directions, providing a comprehensive roadmap for mastering cloud scalability.

ARCHITECTURAL PATTERNS FOR SCALABILITY

Architectural patterns play a pivotal role in shaping the scalability of applications and services in the cloud. Choosing an architectural pattern can significantly impact how well a system can handle increased loads and changing demands. In this section, this chapter explores several architectural patterns that have gained prominence in the context of cloud scalability. This section explores Architectural Patterns for Scalability and different design strategies, with Table 2, named 'Architectural Patterns for Scalability' providing visual insights into the diverse architectural approaches.

a. **Microservices Architecture:** Microservices have emerged as a leading architectural pattern for building highly scalable applications. By decomposing an application into small, independent services that can be developed, deployed, and scaled independently, microservices enable fine-grained scalability (T. C. Chieu, 2011). This decoupling of services allows organizations to allocate resources precisely where they are needed, ensuring optimal resource utilization.
b. **Serverless Computing:** Serverless computing takes scalability to the next level by abstracting infrastructure management. In this model, cloud providers handle the provisioning and scaling of resources automatically, based on the application's actual demand (HP, 2023). This event-driven approach to computing optimizes resource utilization and eliminates the need for capacity planning.
c. **Containerization with Kubernetes:** Containers and orchestration tools like Kubernetes have revolutionized scalability in the cloud (VMWare, 2023). Containers provide a lightweight and consistent environment for applications, making it easier to scale services up or down rapidly. Kubernetes orchestrates containerized workloads, automatically distributing them across clusters of machines, ensuring high availability and scalability.
d. **Service Mesh Architectures:** As applications grow in complexity, service mesh architectures have emerged to address challenges related to scalability and network communication (M. D. Assunção, 2015). A service mesh provides a dedicated infrastructure layer for handling service-to-service communication, allowing for features like load balancing, traffic management, and secure communication. This architecture enhances scalability by optimizing how services interact.
e. **Event-Driven Architectures:** Event-driven architectures promote scalability by decoupling components through the use of events (S. Verma, 2021). When a service produces an event, others can react accordingly. This approach allows for asynchronous processing, which is vital for handling bursts of traffic or varying workloads effectively.
f. **Caching Strategies:** Caching frequently accessed data or computations can significantly improve system scalability (S. Maheshwari, 2018). By storing data in a cache, applications can reduce the load on databases and backend services, resulting in faster response times and better resource utilization.

g. **Sharding Databases:** When dealing with large volumes of data, sharding databases can enhance scalability (G. Brataas, 2017). In this approach, data is distributed across multiple database instances or servers, allowing for parallel processing of queries. Sharding prevents any single database from becoming a bottleneck as the dataset grows.
h. **Content Delivery Networks (CDNs):** CDNs are an essential architectural component for scalability, especially for content-heavy applications (R. L. Patibandla, 2012). CDNs distribute content to edge servers closer to end-users, reducing latency and server load. This results in improved scalability and a better user experience.
i. **Hybrid Architectures:** Hybrid cloud architectures combine on-premises infrastructure with public or private cloud resources (Al-Said Ahmad, 2019). This approach offers scalability options that extend beyond the confines of a single cloud provider. Organizations can leverage cloud and on-premises resources based on their specific scalability requirements.
j. **State Management Strategies:** Managing state in a scalable manner is a critical consideration. Architectural patterns like the Statelessness pattern promote scalability by avoiding the storage of session or state data on servers (H. Duisters, 2023). Instead, session data is stored externally, allowing any server to handle requests.

Incorporating these architectural patterns into cloud-based systems can significantly enhance scalability, enabling applications and services to adapt seamlessly to changing demands. However, choosing the most appropriate pattern requires a thorough understanding of the specific scalability requirements and constraints of a given system. As cloud technologies evolve, architectural patterns will be crucial in achieving scalable and efficient solutions.

Table 2. Architectural patterns for scalability

Pattern	Description	Key Benefits
Microservices Architecture	Decomposing applications into independent services for fine-grained scalability.	Independence, Resource Allocation
Serverless Computing	Automatic provisioning and scaling of resources based on demand, eliminating infrastructure management.	Event-Driven, Resource Efficiency
Containerization with Kubernetes	Utilizing lightweight containers and orchestration for efficient scaling.	Consistency, High Availability
Service Mesh Architectures	Dedicated infrastructure for service-to-service communication, optimizing interactions and scalability.	Load Balancing, Security
Event-Driven Architectures	Decoupling components through events, enabling asynchronous processing and scalability.	Asynchronous, Scalability
Caching Strategies	Storing frequently accessed data or computations in a cache to reduce load on backend services.	Performance, Reduced Latency
Sharding Databases	Distributing data across multiple database instances for parallel processing and scalability.	Parallel Queries, Data Distribution
Content Delivery Networks (CDNs)	Distributing content to edge servers for reduced latency and server load.	Low Latency, Scalable Content Delivery
Hybrid Architectures	Combining on-premises and cloud resources to extend scalability options.	Flexibility, Resource Diversity
State Management Strategies	Managing state externally to achieve statelessness and scalability.	Stateless Architecture, Improved Resource Utilization

THE INTERPLAY OF SCALABILITY, SECURITY, AND COMPLIANCE IN THE CLOUD

Cloud computing has revolutionized how businesses operate by providing scalability that allows organizations to expand or contract their computing resources based on demand. However, this scalability introduces complex challenges related to security and compliance that organizations must navigate. In this section, we delve into the intricate interplay between cloud scalability, security measures, and regulatory compliance, highlighting the importance of addressing these aspects collectively.

a. **Understanding the Dynamics:** The ability to scale resources dynamically in response to changing workloads is a hallmark of cloud computing. Scalability enhances operational efficiency and cost-effectiveness, allowing businesses to stay competitive in rapidly evolving markets. However, as organizations scale their cloud infrastructure, they often grapple with heightened security concerns and the need to adhere to industry-specific compliance requirements.
b. **Security in Scalability:** Scalability and security are intrinsically linked. While scaling offers operational agility, it can inadvertently expose vulnerabilities if not managed correctly. Unauthorized access, data breaches, and other security threats have become more pronounced in larger cloud environments. Thus, organizations must implement robust security measures to safeguard their expanding cloud resources.

Several references, such as (G. Brataas, 2013) and (M. D. Assunção, 2015), provide valuable insights into the evolving landscape of cloud security. These sources delve into the challenges organizations face in maintaining security while scaling their operations and provide perspectives on future directions in this complex interplay.

c. **Compliance Considerations:** Besides security, regulatory compliance is a significant concern, particularly for industries that handle sensitive data. Healthcare organizations must adhere to regulations like HIPAA, while financial institutions must comply with GDPR and other data protection laws. This complicates scalability efforts, as any expansion must align with these stringent requirements.

Real-world examples, as presented by (S. Maheshwari, 2018) and (J. Cáceres, 2010), showcase how scalability can affect security and compliance in edge cloud systems and service scalability. These case studies underscore the practical implications of scalability decisions and the need to maintain compliance throughout the scaling process.

d. **Balancing Act - DevSecOps:** Balancing scalability, security, and compliance necessitates adopting robust security measures. DevSecOps, as outlined by the paper (S. Verma, 2021), provides a methodology for integrating security into the scalability process. It emphasizes the importance of considering security from the outset, rather than treating it as an afterthought.

This section aims to deepen the understanding of how scalability, security, and compliance interact in the cloud. It offers valuable insights for organizations seeking to harness the power of scalable cloud solutions while maintaining data security and regulatory compliance. By comprehending the delicate balance required to manage these three facets effectively, organizations can leverage cloud scalability to its fullest potential without compromising on security or compliance.

CHALLENGES AND SOLUTIONS IN CLOUD SCALABILITY

Achieving effective cloud scalability is a complex endeavor with various challenges that organizations must navigate. In this section, we delve into the multifaceted challenges associated with scalability in cloud computing and present comprehensive solutions to overcome these obstacles. Refer to Table 3, named 'Challenges and Solutions in Cloud Scalability' for an organized summary of key challenges and corresponding solutions.

Cost Optimization Challenges:

i. Challenge: Scaling resources in the cloud can lead to increased costs if not managed effectively. Organizations may struggle to forecast usage accurately and align it with budgets.
ii. Solution: Implementing robust cost management strategies is crucial. Employ tools like nOps (nOps, 2023) for real-time insights into cloud spending. Additionally, take advantage of cloud provider cost optimization features and reserved instances to reduce expenses.

Performance and Bottlenecks

i. Challenge: As applications and services scale, performance bottlenecks can emerge, hindering user experiences and productivity.
ii. Solution: Employ performance monitoring tools and practices. Implement load balancing, as discussed in the article (T. C. Chieu, 2011), to distribute workloads evenly and ensure consistent performance. Utilize content delivery networks (CDNs) to reduce latency.

Security Complexity

i. Challenge: Scaling cloud resources introduces new security complexities. Managing access controls, encryption, and compliance across a larger infrastructure can be daunting.
ii. Solution: Emphasize security best practices. Implement identity and access management (IAM) policies. Regularly conduct security audits and penetration testing. Follow the guidance provided by the paper (G. Brataas, 2013) and (M. D. Assunção, 2015) to fortify your cloud security.

Compliance and Regulatory Requirements

i. Challenge: Industries such as healthcare and finance must adhere to stringent compliance regulations. Scaling while maintaining compliance can be intricate.
ii. Solution: Conduct thorough compliance assessments. Choose cloud solutions that align with industry-specific regulations. Implement encryption, data masking, and access controls to safeguard sensitive data, as recommended by the paper (S. Maheshwari, 2018) and (M. D. Assunção, 2015).

Infrastructure Management

i. Challenge: As cloud environments expand, infrastructure management becomes more complex and resource intensive.
ii. Solution: Adopt Infrastructure as Code (IaC) principles and automation tools. Leverage cloud orchestration platforms like AWS CloudFormation and Terraform to manage infrastructure efficiently. Follow the insights provided by the paper (G. Brataas, 2013) and (S. Verma, 2021).

Data Management and Governance

i. Challenge: Scaling can lead to data sprawl, making data management and governance a daunting task.
ii. Solution: Implement data governance frameworks. Classify data based on sensitivity and importance. Use data lakes and warehouses for structured and unstructured data. Implement data lifecycle management strategies, as recommended by the article (M. D. Assunção, 2015).

Network Scalability

i. Challenge: Networking challenges can arise when scaling cloud resources. Ensuring efficient data transfer and low latency is essential.
ii. Solution: Opt for Virtual Private Cloud (VPC) solutions and use Content Delivery Networks (CDNs) to optimize data transfer. Implement efficient network protocols and ensure proper subnetting.

Vendor Lock-In Concerns

Challenge: Organizations may face vendor lock-in challenges when scaling on a specific cloud platform.

Solution: Adopt multi-cloud or hybrid cloud strategies to avoid vendor lock-in. Containerize applications using technologies like Docker and Kubernetes for portability.

i. Resource Synchronization
   i. Challenge: Scaling resources horizontally can introduce synchronization issues, impacting data consistency.
   ii. Solution: Implement distributed databases and caching solutions to maintain data consistency across resources. Use tools like Redis and Apache Kafka to handle data synchronization.
j. Elasticity and Auto-Scaling
   i. Challenge: Configuring auto-scaling policies correctly to ensure timely resource allocation can be challenging.
   ii. Solution: Thoroughly analyze historical usage patterns and set up auto-scaling policies accordingly. Use predictive scaling based on machine learning models to anticipate demand.

In this extended section, we have explored a range of challenges that organizations encounter when pursuing cloud scalability. By implementing the suggested solutions and best practices, businesses can navigate these challenges effectively and harness the full potential of scalable cloud solutions. Successful scalability will empower organizations to stay competitive and agile in the ever-evolving digital landscape.

FUTURE RESEARCH DIRECTIONS

Cloud scalability is an ever-evolving field, and as technology advances, new challenges and opportunities emerge. In this section, we explore future research directions that can further enhance our understanding and implementation of cloud scalability. These research areas are essential for staying ahead in the rapidly changing landscape of cloud computing. For a visual summary of these directions, refer to Table 4, named 'Future Research Directions in Cloud Scalability' to guide your exploration of future possibilities.

Table 3. Challenges and solutions in cloud scalability

Challenge	Solution
Cost Optimization Challenges	Implement cost management strategies, utilize cloud provider cost optimization features.
Performance and Bottlenecks	Employ performance monitoring tools, implement load balancing, utilize CDNs.
Security Complexity	Implement IAM policies, conduct security audits, follow security best practices.
Compliance and Regulatory Requirements	Conduct compliance assessments, implement encryption, data masking, access controls.
Infrastructure Management	Adopt Infrastructure as Code (IaC) principles, leverage cloud orchestration platforms.
Data Management and Governance	Implement data governance frameworks, use data lakes, and warehouses, apply data lifecycle management.
Network Scalability	Opt for VPC solutions, use CDNs, implement efficient network protocols.
Vendor Lock-In Concerns	Adopt multi-cloud or hybrid cloud strategies, containerize applications.
Resource Synchronization	Implement distributed databases, caching solutions, use Redis, Apache Kafka.
Elasticity and Auto-Scaling	Analyze usage patterns, set up auto-scaling policies, use predictive scaling.

a. **Edge Computing and Scalability:** Edge computing is gaining prominence for applications that require low-latency processing, such as autonomous vehicles and IoT devices. Future research should investigate how edge computing can leverage cloud scalability principles. Topics to explore include optimizing edge resource allocation, dynamic load balancing among edge nodes, and efficient data synchronization strategies in edge environments. Research could result in novel algorithms and frameworks that enable seamless scaling of edge computing applications, ensuring they can handle varying workloads effectively.

b. **Quantum Computing Integration:** Quantum computing has the potential to revolutionize various computational tasks, including those related to cloud scalability. Research should focus on how quantum computing can be integrated into cloud infrastructure for tasks like optimizing scaling algorithms, cryptographic key management, and complex simulations. Developments in this area could lead to faster, more efficient, and quantum-resistant scalability solutions.

c. **Energy-Efficient Scalability:** Sustainability is a growing concern in cloud computing. Future research should explore methods to make cloud scalability more energy efficient. This research could encompass the development of algorithms and strategies for dynamically allocating resources based on energy consumption and environmental impact. The goal is to create scalable solutions that not only meet performance demands but also minimize energy usage, contributing to a greener cloud.

d. **Blockchain and Scalability:** Scalability remains a challenge for blockchain networks. Future research should investigate innovative consensus algorithms and architectural designs. Topics of interest include sharding, off-chain solutions, and hybrid approaches to improve the scalability of blockchain-based applications hosted in the cloud. Research in this area could lead to more scalable and efficient blockchain platforms that can handle a broader range of applications.

e. **AI and Machine Learning for Scalability:** Artificial intelligence and machine learning can enhance the scalability of cloud resources. Future research should focus on AI-driven solutions for predictive scaling and resource optimization. This includes developing algorithms that can analyze historical usage patterns and predict future resource demands accurately. AI-driven scalability could result in cloud environments that automatically adapt to changing workloads, improving resource efficiency.

f. **Serverless and Event-Driven Architectures:** Serverless computing and event-driven architectures offer scalability advantages. Research should explore how these paradigms impact scalability and provide best practices. Topics for investigation include designing serverless functions for optimal scaling, event-driven triggers, and efficient resource provisioning. The goal is to offer guidelines for organizations leveraging serverless and event-driven approaches for scalable cloud applications.
g. **Multi-Cloud and Interoperability:** Multi-cloud environments introduce interoperability challenges. Future research should address these challenges by developing standards and tools. Research could lead to the creation of interoperable management and orchestration frameworks that enable seamless scalability across diverse cloud providers. The result would be greater flexibility for organizations that wish to leverage multiple clouds for scalability and redundancy.
h. **Hybrid Cloud Scalability:** Hybrid cloud environments combine on-premises infrastructure with public and private clouds. Research should investigate strategies for scaling applications in these complex setups. Topics include workload distribution between on-premises and cloud resources, data synchronization, and hybrid cloud management tools. Research outcomes could provide organizations with a blueprint for effectively scaling applications in hybrid cloud configurations.
i. **Security-Scalability Tradeoffs:** Balancing security and scalability is critical. Future research should delve into the tradeoffs involved and provide insights into striking the right balance. Research areas include scalable encryption methods, threat detection at scale, and secure identity and access management for large cloud environments. Findings in this area could guide organizations in implementing robust security measures while ensuring their cloud systems remain highly scalable.
j. **Serverless Containerization:** Combining serverless and containerization has the potential to improve scalability. Research should explore how these two paradigms can synergize. Topics include containerized serverless functions, container orchestration, and resource allocation for containerized serverless applications. The result could be a scalable architecture that benefits from both serverless and containerization advantages.
k. **Real-time Scalability:** Applications requiring real-time data processing pose unique scalability challenges. Research should delve into optimizing real-time scalability for use cases like IoT and streaming analytics. Topics include stream processing frameworks, distributed data processing, and resource allocation for real-time applications. Research outcomes could lead to highly responsive and scalable real-time systems.
l. **Resilience and Fault Tolerance:** Scalable systems must also be resilient. Future research should focus on enhancing fault tolerance mechanisms within scalable architectures. Areas of interest include automated failover, disaster recovery strategies, and redundancy planning for highly scalable cloud deployments. Research outcomes would ensure that scalable systems remain available and reliable even in the face of failures.
m. **Ethical Considerations:** As cloud scalability impacts various aspects of society, ethical considerations arise. Future research should explore the ethical implications of scalable cloud deployments. Topics include data privacy in large-scale cloud environments, fairness in resource allocation, and ethical guidelines for using scalable cloud systems. Ethical research in this context aims to create frameworks that ensure cloud scalability is employed responsibly and ethically.

Table 4. Future research directions in cloud scalability

Research Direction	Description
Edge Computing and Scalability	Investigating scalability challenges and solutions in edge computing environments.
Quantum Computing Integration	Exploring the integration of quantum computing for optimizing scalability-related tasks.
Energy-Efficient Scalability	Researching methods to make cloud scalability more energy-efficient and environmentally friendly.
Blockchain and Scalability	Developing scalable solutions for blockchain-based applications hosted in cloud environments.
AI and Machine Learning for Scalability	Leveraging AI and ML for predictive scaling and resource optimization in the cloud.
Serverless and Event-Driven Architecture	Investigating the impact of serverless and event-driven paradigms on scalability.
Multi-Cloud and Interoperability	Addressing interoperability challenges in multi-cloud environments for seamless scalability.
Hybrid Cloud Scalability	Strategies for scaling applications in hybrid cloud configurations, combining on-premises and cloud resources.
Security-Scalability Tradeoffs	Balancing security and scalability considerations, exploring tradeoffs and best practices.
Serverless Containerization	Synergizing serverless and containerization to improve scalability in cloud architectures.
Real-time Scalability	Optimizing scalability for real-time data processing applications, such as IoT and streaming analytics.
Resilience and Fault Tolerance	Enhancing fault tolerance mechanisms within scalable cloud architectures for reliability.
Ethical Considerations	Exploring the ethical implications of scalable cloud deployments and establishing ethical guidelines.

In conclusion, these future research directions aim to push the boundaries of cloud scalability, making it more efficient, sustainable, and adaptable to emerging technologies and challenges. By addressing these areas, we can ensure that cloud scalability continues to meet the evolving needs of businesses and society.

CONCLUSION

In an era of digital transformation and the increasing reliance on cloud technologies, mastering cloud scalability has become paramount for organizations seeking to thrive in this dynamic landscape. This chapter delved into the multifaceted domain of cloud scalability, exploring its significance, challenges, measurement metrics, architectural patterns, and the interplay with security and compliance. We have also examined the prevailing challenges and provided pragmatic solutions, ensuring that scalability is approached holistically.

Cloud scalability is not merely an operational feature; it is a strategic asset that impacts an organization's flexibility, cost-effectiveness, performance, and overall competitiveness. As cloud ecosystems continue to evolve, the need for scalable architectures and resource management practices will persist.

Drawing insights from a comprehensive literature review and real-world experiences, this chapter has shed light on the key dimensions of cloud scalability. Whether it's horizontal or vertical scaling, the choice of architectural patterns, or the intricacies of maintaining security and compliance during scaling operations, organizations must make informed decisions aligned with their specific goals and constraints.

The challenges of scaling in the cloud are as diverse as the solutions themselves. Scalability requires a nuanced understanding of infrastructure, application design, and the intricacies of cloud service providers. However, with the right strategies, tools, and mindset, organizations can harness the full potential of cloud scalability to fuel their growth and innovation.

As we gaze into the future, it is evident that cloud scalability will continue to evolve in response to emerging technologies and business requirements. Researchers and practitioners must collaborate to explore uncharted territories, investigating how scalability intersects with areas like edge computing, serverless architectures, and the integration of Artificial Intelligence and Machine Learning. Furthermore, the ethical dimensions of scalability, including its environmental impact, deserve greater scrutiny.

In closing, mastering cloud scalability is not a destination but a journey. It involves continuous learning, adaptation, and innovation. Organizations that embrace scalability as a core element of their cloud strategy will be better equipped to navigate the ever-changing digital landscape, ensuring that they remain agile, cost-effective, and competitive in the years to come.

REFERENCES

Admin. (2023). A Comprehensive Guide to Digital Scalability with Cloud Computing. *Best Urdu Poetry for U.* https://www.besturdupoetryforu.com/2023/06/a-comprehensive-guide-to-digital.html

Agrawal, D., El Abbadi, A., Das, S., & Elmore, A. J. (2011). Database Scalability, Elasticity, and Autonomy in the Cloud. International conference on database systems for advanced applications, (pp. 2-15), Springer. 10.1007/978-3-642-20149-3_2

Ahmad, A.-S., & Andras, P. (2019). Scalability analysis comparisons of cloud-based software services. *Journal of Cloud Computing (Heidelberg, Germany)*, *8*(1), 1–17.

Ahmad, A.-S., & Andras, P. (2019). Scalability analysis comparisons of cloud-based software services. *Journal of Cloud Computing (Heidelberg, Germany)*, *8*(1), 1–17.

Assunção, M. D., Calheiros, R. N., Bianchi, S., Netto, M. A. S., & Buyya, R. (2015). Big Data Computing and Clouds: Trends and Future Directions. *Journal of Parallel and Distributed Computing*, *79–80*, 3–15. doi:10.1016/j.jpdc.2014.08.003

Brataas, G., Herbst, N., Ivansek, S., & Polutnik, J. (2017). Scalability Analysis of Cloud Software Services. *2017 IEEE International Conference on Autonomic Computing (ICAC),* (pp. 285-292). IEEE. 10.1109/ICAC.2017.34

Brataas, G., Stav, E., Lehrig, S., Becker, S., Kopčak, G., & Huljenic, D. (2013). CloudScale: scalability management for cloud systems. *Proceedings of the 4th ACM/SPEC International Conference on Performance Engineering*, (pp. 335-338). ACM. 10.1145/2479871.2479920

Cáceres, J., Vaquero, L. M., Rodero-Merino, L., Polo, A., & Hierro, J. J. (2010). Service scalability over the cloud. Handbook of Cloud Computing, (pp. 357-377). Springer. doi:10.1007/978-1-4419-6524-0_15

Cebula, D. (2022). *How to Build Scalable Cloud Architecture?* Net Guru. https://www.netguru.com/blog/how-to-build-scalable-cloud-architecture

Chieu, T. C., Mohindra, A., & Karve, A. A. (2011). Scalability and Performance of Web Applications in a Compute Cloud. *2011 IEEE 8th International Conference on e-Business Engineering*, (pp. 317-323). IEEE. 10.1109/ICEBE.2011.63

Deft. (2014). Scalability in cloud computing: using virtualization to save money. *Deft*. https://deft.com/blog/scalability-in-cloud-computing/

Duisters, H. (2023). *Scaling Startups In The Cloud: Ways To Make That Journey*. ProShore. https://proshore.eu/ways-to-scale-startups-in-the-cloud/

Falatah, M. M., & Batarfi, O. A. (2014). Cloud scalability considerations. *International Journal of Computer Science and Engineering Survey*, *5*(4), 37–47. doi:10.5121/ijcses.2014.5403

Flower, Z. (2020). Top 6 complexity challenges of operating a cloud at scale. *Tech Target*. https://www.techtarget.com/searchcloudcomputing/tip/Top-6-complexity-challenges-of-operating-a-cloud-at-scale

Horizontal vs. Vertical Scaling in the Cloud. (2021). Cloud Checkr. https://cloudcheckr.com/cloud-automation/horizontal-vertical-cloud-scaling/

HP. (2023). *What is Cloud Scalability?* HP. https://tinyurl.com/3yt9w9xa

Kirvan, P. (2021). How to effectively plan cloud storage scalability. *Tech Target*. https://www.techtarget.com/searchstorage/tip/How-to-effectively-plan-cloud-storage-scalability

Maheshwari, S., Raychaudhuri, D., Seskar, I., & Bronzino, F. (2018). Scalability and Performance Evaluation of Edge Cloud Systems for Latency Constrained Applications. *IEEE/ACM Symposium on Edge Computing (SEC)*, (pp. 286-299). ACM. 10.1109/SEC.2018.00028

nOps (2023). *What is Scalability in Cloud Computing? Types, Benefits, and Practical Advice*. nOps. https://www.nops.io/blog/cloud-scalability/

Patibandla, R. L., Kurra, S. S., & Mundukur, N. B. (2012). *An Overview of Environmental Scalability and Security in Hybrid Cloud Infrastructure Designs*. Distributed Computing and Internet Technology: 8th International Conference, ICDCIT 2012, Bhubaneswar, India.

Scalability: What every business using the cloud needs to know. (2023). Hack Mamba. https://dev.to/hackmamba/scalability-what-every-business-using-the-cloud-needs-to-know-54ci

Verma, S., & Bala, A. (2021). Auto-scaling techniques for IoT-based cloud applications: A review. *Cluster Computing*, *24*(3), 2425–2459. doi:10.1007/s10586-021-03265-9

VMware. (2023). *How do you determine optimal cloud scalability?* VMware. https://www.vmware.com/topics/glossary/content/cloud-scalability.html

Vyshnova, J. (2023). *How to Ensure Cloud Scalability in 2023*. Dinarys. https://dinarys.com/blog/how-to-ensure-cloud-scalability

KEY TERMS AND DEFINITIONS

Auto-Scaling: Auto-scaling is a cloud computing feature that allows resources, such as virtual machines, to automatically adjust based on demand, ensuring optimal performance and cost-efficiency.

Cloud-Native: Cloud-native applications are designed to run on cloud infrastructure, taking full advantage of cloud scalability, resilience, and agility.

Containerization: Containerization is a lightweight form of virtualization that enables the packaging and running of applications and their dependencies in isolated containers, enhancing scalability and portability.

Content Delivery Network (CDN): CDNs are distributed networks of servers that deliver web content, including images and videos, to users from locations closer to them, reducing latency.

Cost Optimization: Cost optimization in the cloud focuses on minimizing expenses by right-sizing resources, optimizing workloads, and taking advantage of cost-effective cloud services.

DevOps: DevOps is a set of practices that combine software development and IT operations to enable faster development, testing, and deployment of applications, contributing to scalability.

Elasticity: Elasticity is the ability of a cloud system to quickly and efficiently allocate or deallocate resources in response to changing workloads.

High Availability: High availability refers to a system's ability to remain operational and accessible, even in the face of hardware or software failures.

Horizontal Scaling: Horizontal scaling, also known as scaling out, involves adding more identical resources, such as servers, to distribute the load and enhance performance.

Infrastructure as Code (IaC): IaC is a practice of managing and provisioning infrastructure using code and automation, enhancing scalability and reproducibility.

Latency: Latency is the delay in data transmission between a source and a destination, and minimizing it is crucial for real-time applications and gaming.

Load Balancing: Load balancing involves distributing incoming network traffic across multiple servers to ensure efficient resource utilization and prevent overload.

Microservices Architecture: Microservices architecture is an approach to software development where an application is divided into small, independently deployable services, enhancing scalability and flexibility.

Multi-Cloud Strategy: A multi-cloud strategy involves using multiple cloud service providers to avoid vendor lock-in and enhance scalability and redundancy.

Resource Efficiency: Resource efficiency is the ability to use computing resources, such as CPU and memory, optimally to minimize waste and cost.

Resource Pooling: Resource pooling in cloud computing refers to the practice of aggregating computing resources to serve multiple users, optimizing resource utilization.

Scalability Metrics: Scalability metrics are quantitative measurements used to assess the performance and efficiency of scalable systems, such as response time, throughput, and resource utilization.

Security Compliance: Security compliance in the cloud involves adhering to regulatory standards and best practices to ensure data security and privacy.

Serverless Computing: Serverless computing is a cloud computing model where developers can run code without managing servers, allowing for automatic scaling and reduced operational overhead.

Vertical Scaling: Vertical scaling, or scaling up, involves increasing the capacity of existing resources, typically by adding more CPU, memory, or storage to a single server.

Chapter 9
Mobile Cloud Computing

Ranjan Mondal
Department of CSE, School of Engineering, Swami Vivekananda University, West Bengal, India

ABSTRACT

A wide range of applications, many of which need ever-increasing processing capability, may now be supported by smartphones. Smartphones are resource-constrained devices with limited computation power, memory, storage, and battery; therefore, this presents a hurdle. Fortunately, dynamic resources for processing, storage, and service supply are nearly endless thanks to cloud computing technologies. In order to get beyond the limitations of smartphones, experts foresee expanding cloud computing services to mobile devices. Cloud computing, software as a service, community networks, online stores, and other application models have grown rapidly over the past several years as a result of developments in network -based computing and applications on demand. Since 2007, the scientific and business sectors have turned to studying cloud computing, an important application model in the Internet era. Since mobile cloud computing is still in its infancy, it is essential to have a complete understanding of the technology in order to identify the course of future research.

INTRODUCTION

Cloud computing on the go Mobile Cloud Computing (Cisco, n.d.) is a novel approach to developing mobile apps in which the majority of processing and data storage tasks are transferred from the mobile device to robust, centralized cloud computing infrastructure. Then, a thin native client or web browser on the device is used to access these centralized apps through the mobile Internet. This mobile cloud computing approach, meanwhile, still falls short of fully using the mobile network's potent contextual, marketing, and communications capabilities. Mobile Cloud Computing expands on the fundamentals of cloud computing by bringing attributes like on-demand access, no on-premise software, and "XaaS" (Everything as a Service) to the mobile domain. It also adds Network as a Service (NaaS) and Payment as a Service to the highest degree of on-demand capabilities and enables applications to fully utilize mobile networking and billing without the need for specialized application servers. After the "Cloud Computing" idea was presented in the middle of 2007, the term "Mobile Cloud Computing" was coined (Mell, n.d.).

DOI: 10.4018/979-8-3693-0900-1.ch009

Figure 1. Mobile cloud computing

It has been grabbing the interest of researchers as a promising solution for green core IT as well as entrepreneurs as a lucrative business option that lowers the development and operating cost of mobile applications and mobile users as a new technology to achieve rich experience of a variety of mobile services at low cost.

As opposed to local computers or servers, mobile cloud computing uses virtualized resources that are dispersed across a large group of multiple distributed systems. Many mobile cloud computing-based applications have been created and made available to consumers, including Google's Gmail, mobile maps and navigation apps, voice search, certain apps for the Android platform, MobileMe from Apple, LiveMesh from Microsoft, and Motoblur from Motorola. The general architecture is depicted in Fig 1 below.

There are several difficulties and difficulties while delivering cloud services in a mobile context. Complex apps cannot be run on mobile devices owing to their inherent characteristics. Additionally, since a mobile device cannot constantly be connected to the internet, the offline functionality of the device must also be taken into account. The growth of mobile cloud computing may be hampered by the lack of standards, security and privacy requirements, and elastic mobile application requirements. Recognizing this unique method is crucial for providing more room for study and for recognizing the obstacles (Marston et al., 2011).

Fig.2 displays the general design of the MCC as presented by (Kosta et al., 2012). Base stations, such as base transceiver stations (BTS), access points, or satellites, are used to connect mobile devices to mobile networks by establishing and managing connections (air links) and functional interfaces between the networks and mobile devices. Requests and data from mobile users, such as their ID and location, are sent to central processors that are linked to servers that offer mobile network services (Qi & Gani, 2012).

Here, mobile network operators can offer AAA (Authentication, Authorization, and Accounting) services to mobile customers based on the subscriber's data kept in databases and the house agent (HA). Following that, the subscriber's requests are transmitted through the Internet to a cloud. In the cloud, the cloud controllers handle the requests and deliver the related cloud services to mobile users. These

Figure 2. Mobile cloud computing (MCC) architecture

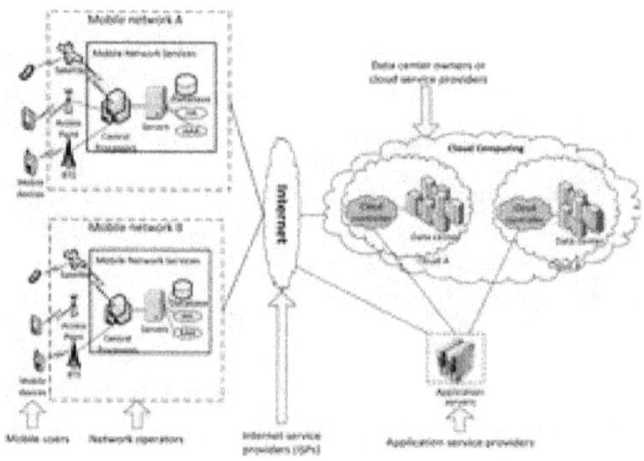

services were created using service-oriented architecture, virtualization, and utility computing ideas (such as web applications and database servers).

KEY REQUIREMENTS FOR MOBILE CLOUD COMPUTING

It is feasible to achieve seamless service delivery in a network environment thanks to a few essential characteristics of mobile cloud computing. The goals of the Mobile Cloud Computing platform are, from the viewpoint of the enterprise solution provider or web/mobile application developer (Fan et al.,):

- Simple APIs provide transparent access to mobile services and don't call for any special knowledge understanding of the technology underpinning networks.
- The capacity to deploy applications across many carrier networks while utilizing a single commercial agreement.
- Seamless implementation of each carrier's unique network policies, such as selected mobile subscriber standards for privacy management and proven opt-in/opt-out.

IMPORTANCE OF MOBILE CLOUD APPLICATIONS

One of the upcoming developments in mobile technology is mobile cloud computing, which combines the benefits of both mobile and cloud computing integration to offer mobile consumers the best services possible. Mobile cloud computing supports a variety of applications, including those in mobile education, mobile healthcare, and mobile commerce. The following problems and solutions for mobile cloud computing (i.e., from the computing and communication fields) have been identified. Future work has been investigated for the problems that are now present and their fixes. A sizable portion of the global mobile market is now occupied by mobile applications. The benefits of mobile cloud computing have been utilised by several mobile applications. The following are a few implications (Dinh et al., 2011):

m-Commerce

A business concept for employing mobile devices for commerce is called mobile commerce (m-commerce). Some tasks that call for mobility are typically completed via m-commerce apps (such as mobile transactions and payments, mobile messaging, and mobile ticketing). The m-commerce apps must overcome a number of obstacles, such as security, complicated mobile device setups, and limited network capacity. To solve these problems, m-commerce apps are incorporated into cloud computing environments (Buyya et al., 2008). Introduces a cloud-based 3G e-commerce platform (Foster et al., 2009).

m-Learning

Electronic learning (e-learning) and mobility serve as the foundation for mobile learning (m-learning). Traditional mobile learning apps, however, have drawbacks such as expensive network and device costs, slow network transmission rates, and a lack of extensive instructional materials. To address these issues, cloud-based mobile learning applications have been developed. For instance, by utilising a cloud with significant storage and processing power, the applications offer learners much richer services in terms of data (information) size, processing speed, and battery life (Youseff et al., 2008).

m-Health Care

MCC is being used in medical applications to reduce the drawbacks of conventional technology. medical care (such as limited physical storage, lack of confidentiality and privacy, and mistakes in medical care). Mobile Healthcare (m-healthcare) offers mobile users easy access to resources (such as patients) swiftly and efficiently (health records). In addition, m-Healthcare provides healthcare facilities with a range of cloud-based on-demand services as opposed to owning independent apps on local servers (Buyya et al., 2008).

m-Banking

The phrase "mobile banking" refers to using a mobile device, such as a mobile phone or Personal Digital Assistant (PDA), to conduct account transactions, payments, and other tasks. It is also referred to as "m-Banking," "SMS Banking," etc. Today, mobile banking is often carried out by SMS or mobile Internet, but it is also possible to employ specialized applications, known as clients, that are downloaded to the mobile device (Buyya et al., 2009).

m-Game

The mobile game (m-game) sector has the potential to bring in money for service providers. M-game shows how offloading (multimedia code) can save energy for mobile devices, extending the amount of time that users can play games on their devices. M-game can completely offload game engines requiring large computing resources (e.g., graphic rendering) to the server in the cloud (Forman & Zahorjan, 1994).

KEY BENEFITS OF MOBILE CLOUD COMPUTING APPLICATIONS

MCC offers the software engine that powers the integration of open mobile networks, mobile cloud computing, on-demand corporate solutions, and online and mobile apps, creating new low-friction commercial channels between a variety of different sectors and vertical market segments. Our solution makes it simple for enterprise solution providers and web or mobile application developers to turbo-charge a wide range of applications and services, enhancing them with powerful mobile network features and intelligence available on demand via the mobile cloud when deployed either by mobile operators or cross-network mobile cloud providers. A variety of businesses, including Mobile Cloud Providers, Network Operators, Enterprise Solution Providers, and Web or Mobile Application Developers, gain significantly from the solutions. The following sections provide an overview of these advantages (Paulson, 2003).

- Mobile Cloud Providers - By including mobile network enablers and intelligent commerce into their portfolio of on-demand cloud-based services, Mobile Cloud Providers are now able to create brand-new, industry-specific B2B solutions.
- Network Operators - By offering a complete commercial Network as a Service solution, it enables operators to make money out of their mobile network and billing assets.
- Enterprise Solution Providers - The system enables businesses and organisations to streamline business procedures, boost employee cooperation, and increase productivity.
- Web and Mobile Application Developers - It gives web and mobile application developers the ability to distinguish their apps with mobile network capabilities and enables them to connect with and charge their largest possible consumer base.

The solution offers a new direct-to-billing route for developers' apps and makes it simple for them to enhance their programs with useful mobile network features and analytics.

BACKGROUND

Mobile cloud computing, which has been coined as a new term since 2009, is an inheritance and emergence of cloud computing and mobile computing. From a basic perspective, mobile cloud computing can be thought of as infrastructure where data and processing could happen outside of the mobile device, enabling new types of applications like context-aware mobile social networks. Laptops, PDAs, cellphones, and other mobile devices are examples of mobile devices that connect to a base station or hotspot over a radio link, such as 3G, Wi-Fi, or GPRS. Cloud computing is still the basic idea, even though the client has evolved from PCs or stationary equipment to mobile devices. Mobile users utilize a web browser or desktop application to submit service requests to the cloud. The mobile cloud computing monitoring and calculation features are then applied to guarantee the QoS up until the connection is complete. The management component of the cloud subsequently distributes resources to the request to create a connection (Rudenko et al., 1998).

The NIST definition of the cloud model includes three service models, four deployment models, and five fundamental features, and encourages availability.

Essential Characteristics

On-demand self-service: When necessary, a customer can unilaterally provide computer resources like server time and network storage automatically without interacting with each service provider personally.

Broad network access: The availability of capabilities across the network and the usage of common access methods encourage their adoption by a variety of thin or thick client platforms, such as mobile phones, laptops, PDAs, and other devices.

Resource pooling: Using a multi-tenant approach, the provider pools its computing resources to serve a number of customers, with various physical and virtual resources being dynamically assigned and reassigned in response to customer demand. The precise location of the materials that are delivered is not under the customer's control or awareness. Storage, computation, memory, network bandwidth, and virtual machines are a few examples of resources.

Rapid elasticity: For quick scale out and quick scale in, capabilities can be swiftly and elastically supplied, sometimes automatically. *Measured Service*: By utilizing a metering capability at an abstraction level relevant to the kind of service, cloud systems automatically manage and optimize resource utilisation.

The NIST definition of the cloud model includes three service models, four deployment models, and five fundamental features, and encourages availability (e.g. storage, processing, bandwidth and active user accounts).

Service Models

Software as a Service (SaaS): The capacity to utilize the provider's applications that are operating on a cloud architecture is made available to the customer. Through a thin client interface like a web browser, the apps may be accessed from a variety of client devices (for example, web-based email). With the possible exception of a small number of user-specific application configuration parameters, the customer does not manage or otherwise have influence over the underlying cloud infrastructure.

Platform as a Service (PaaS): The user is given the option to upload programs they have developed themselves or bought using the provider's supported programming languages and tools to the cloud infrastructure. The customer has control over the installed programs and perhaps the parameters of the application hosting environment but does not manage or control the underlying cloud infrastructure, including the network, servers, operating systems, or storage.

Infrastructure as a Service (IaaS): The customer is given the power to set up processing, storage, networks, and other basic computer resources so that they may deploy and execute any software, such as operating systems and apps. Although the user has no management or control over the underlying cloud infrastructure, they do have some limited influence over some networking components, operating systems, storage, and installed applications (e.g. host firewalls). Fig 3 below shows a typical Cloud Service Model.

Deployment Models

Private Cloud: The only entity using the cloud infrastructure is the organisation. It might exist on or off premises and be controlled by the company or a third party.

Figure 3. Cloud service model

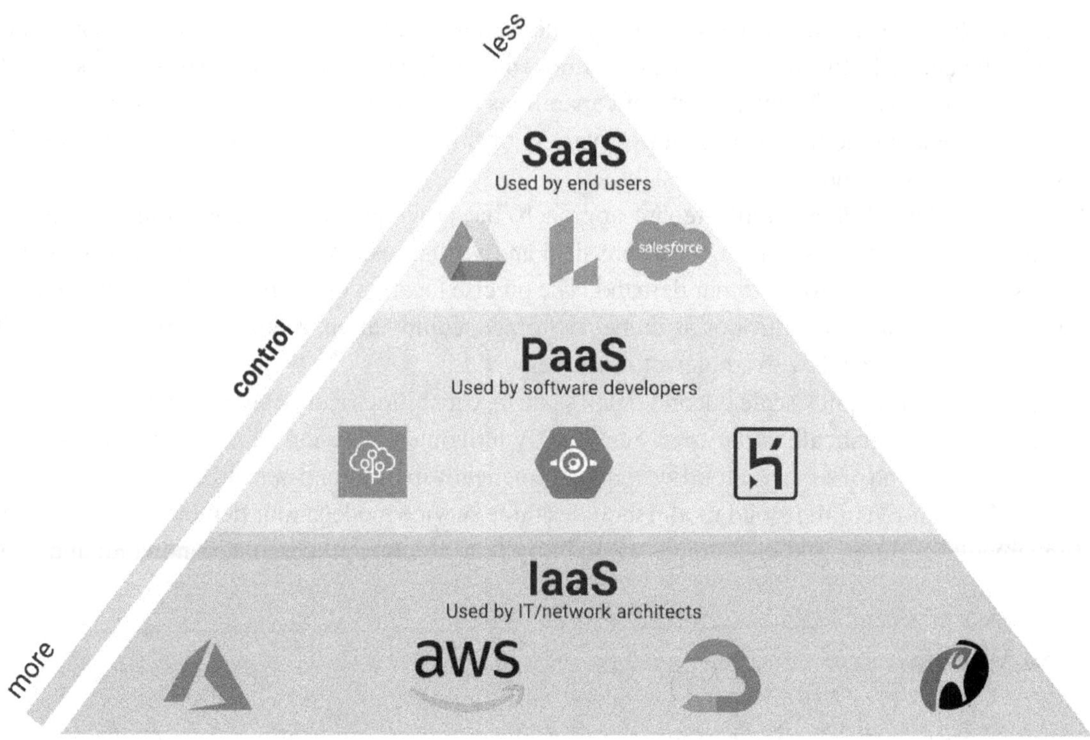

Community Cloud: A particular community with common concerns (such as purpose, security needs, policy, and compliance issues) is supported by the cloud infrastructure, which is shared by a number of organisations. It might exist on or off premises and be controlled by the organisations or a third party.

Public Cloud: A company offering cloud services owns the cloud infrastructure, which is made available to the general public or a sizable industry group.

Hybrid Cloud: The cloud infrastructure is made up of two or more clouds (private, communal, or public), each of which is distinct but connected by standardized or proprietary technologies to allow for the mobility of data and applications. (e.g., cloud bursting for load-balancing between clouds). Fig 4 below illustrates Public, Private and Hybrid cloud deployment examples.

ARCHITECTURE

An overview of basic Mobile Cloud Computing was presented in the previous section. A general architecture in a broader sense is depicted in Fig 2. A more detailed representation will be presented in this section.

The base stations that build and manage the connections (air interface) and functional interfaces between the networks and mobile devices are what connect the mobile devices to the mobile networks. The central processors attached to the servers offering mobile network services receive the requests and data from mobile users. On the basis of Home Agent (HA) and subscriber data kept in databases, services

Figure 4. Public, private and hybrid cloud deployment

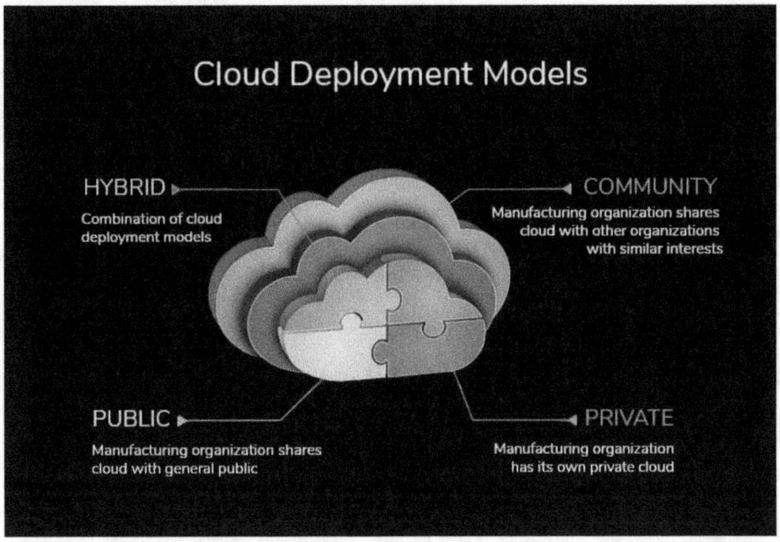

like AAA (Authentication, Authorization, and Accounting) may be offered to consumers in this situation. The queries from the subscribers are subsequently transmitted via the Internet to a cloud. The cloud's controllers handle the requests and deliver the related cloud services to mobile users. These services were created using the principles of virtualization, utility computing, and service-oriented architecture. The major function of a cloud computing system is storing data on the cloud and using client-side technology to access that data. Some authors mentioned that Cloud Computing is not entirely a new concept. Lamia Youseff et al. have stated in their paper (Buyya et al., 2009) that Cloud Computing has manifested itself as a descendent of several other computing areas such as service-oriented architecture, grid, and disaggregated computing. By offering software applications, programming platforms, data storage, computer infrastructure, and hardware as services, several business models quickly developed to make use of this technology. A market-oriented architecture was introduced by R. Buyya et al. in (Forman & Zahorjan, 1994) and (Paulson, 2003). They defined the cloud as a form of parallel and distributed system made up of a network of linked, virtualized computers that deliver computing resources from service providers to consumers in accordance with their established SLA (Service Level Agreement).

We concentrate on a layered design that frequently exemplifies how well the cloud computing paradigm meets user needs. This section's prior discussion of the service model. A summary of the cloud stack's layered architecture and users is shown in Figure 5 below.

CHALLENGES AND SOLUTIONS

There have been several improvements in the way we view computing and mobility during the past ten years. After water, electricity, gas and telephone, computing will be the fifth utility and will offer the entry-level computer service that is deemed necessary to satisfy the daily demands of the general public. The most recent paradigm put out to realize this ambition is cloud computing. For a variety of factors

Figure 5. Cloud stack

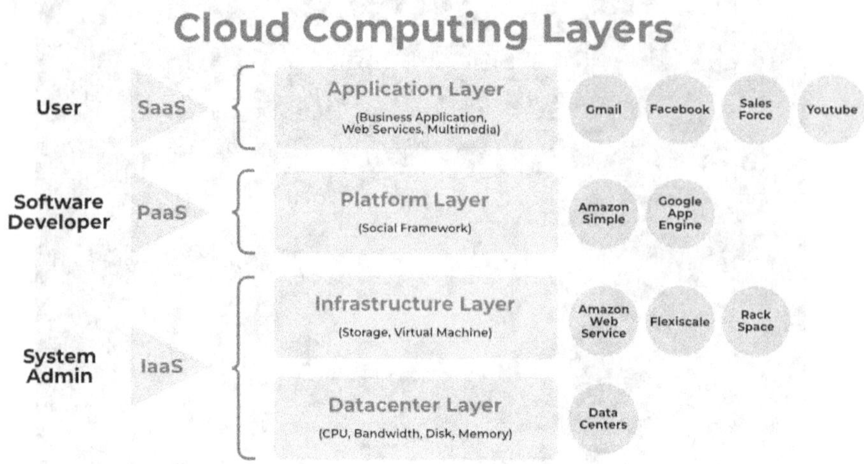

(including mobility, communication, and portability), it has shown to be a potential option for mobile computing.

Resource poverty: A smartphone's capacity to use energy greatly exceeds that of the battery as processors become quicker, displays become crisper, and devices are outfitted with additional sensors. Thus, the design of mobile applications continues to be significantly constrained by the battery life of mobile devices. Limited battery capacity and a rise in user demand for energy-intensive apps are the two primary causes. User demand for resource-intensive apps, such as video games, streaming video, and sensors installed on mobile devices that continuously provide streams of data about the user's environment, is rising every day. Numerous approaches have been suggested to improve CPU performance and use the existing resources efficiently to cut down on power usage. These solutions, however, call for modifications to the design of mobile devices or new hardware, which necessitates more engineering and raises the price compared to regular devices. By moving massive calculations and sophisticated processing from resource-constrained devices to resourceful machines, computation offloading techniques prevent mobile devices from requiring a long execution time. The efficiency of offloading strategies has been assessed through a number of trials.

Data storage capacity and processing power: Another significant issue with mobile devices is storage. MCC was created to give mobile users access to and storage for substantial volumes of cloud-based data. One such instance is Amazon Simple Storage Service (S3). It offers a straightforward web services interface that can be utilized to store and retrieve any volume of data, whenever needed, from any location on the internet. The most effective MCC-based photo-sharing programme is probably Flickr. Users may post and share photographs via mobile and web-based platforms. The most popular social network programme today, Facebook, is a perfect illustration of how to share photographs utilizing the cloud. MCC also lowers the ongoing expenses for applications that require a lot of computing power. Data warehousing, management, and online document synchronization duties are all effectively supported by cloud computing. Because their data is now saved on the cloud, mobile devices are no longer limited by storage space. Microsoft will create new office applications that seamlessly interact with all sorts of mobile devices and embrace cloud computing. Users will be able to store, publish, and share their work on desktop computers, mobile devices, and with other users.

Division of application services: The mobile devices have inherently limited resources. Thus the applications have to be divided in order to achieve a particular performance target (low latency, minimization of data transfer, fast response time etc.)

Considering the demands of MCC, the essential factors for delivering 'good' cloud services have been enumerated below:

- The best possible division of application services between cloud and mobile platforms.
- High network capacity for quicker data transfer between the cloud and mobile devices; • Low network latency to meet application and code offload interaction
- Adaptive network status monitoring to balance network and device expenses with user perceptions of the Cloud application's performance.
  Service providers might employ the following tactics to deal with the aforementioned problems:
- Network bandwidth strategy: bringing content closer to mobile broadband through the use of local data centres or other techniques.
- Application processor nodes will be pushed to the edge of mobile broadband as part of the network latency plan.
- Battery-saving technique: cloning the device in the network for computational and power-intensive management chores like automated mobile device virus detection.
- Mobile cloud application elasticity: Dynamic optimization of application delivery and execution between the device and the network.

Task-Oriented Mobile Services

The provision of mobile devices with adaptable task-oriented services for offloading apps to the cloud is the second design challenge. Mobile devices' processing, memory, and display capabilities are severely constrained. The wireless network environment is frequently unstable and offers erratic communication. Smartphone use is also common among mobile users, albeit not for all tasks. Therefore, task-oriented mobile services are necessary for mobile devices.

SaaS, PaaS, and IaaS services are available through cloud computing, but MCC must explicitly design task-oriented mobile services for mobile users.

Mobile-Data-as-a-Service

One of the main reasons why mobile data transmission has increased since 2008 is due in large part to cloud computing applications. The data may be high dimensional and diverse. Furthermore, as they are dynamically gathered with location and temporal information, mobile data are transferred to the cloud. Mobile-data-as-a-service adapts to user needs to give customized data analytics services, utilizing indexing techniques for spatio-temporal data storage and retrieval such as B-Tree, R-Tree, and TPR-tree. Scalable computation and storage are supplied by MCC. GPAC was proposed for continuously verifying mobile queries for querying on mobile data. Due to the long sequence of mobile data, segmenting part of them is helpful to understand the entire sequence.

Mobile-Computing-as-a-Service

Reduce the transmission time between the cloud server and the mobile device as one method of raising the QoS while serving a mobile device. A common solution is to utilize a server that is physically close to the mobile device to instantly fulfil the request and then to move the virtual machine (VM) from the server to a server that has greater power, such as a data centre, for additional processing. Moving VMs around can enhance cloud performance. The same virtual machine (VM) can be contacted from several places when a mobile device requests a service.

In order to reduce the access latency and data delivery delay, a VM might be moved to a cloud server close to the user location. Additionally, VM migration can distribute heavy traffic to distant places while distributing the load among several cloud servers or data centres.

Ongoing research is being done on VM migration and routing in the cloud. By connecting several devices to one virtual router's virtual ports. There are several areas where forwarding routers, also known as forwarding elements (FE), are dispersed. FEs are coordinated by a central controller, who also keeps track of where VMs are right now. Outside networks will receive any outgoing traffic from virtual machines (VMs).

Mobile Multimedia-as-a-Service

MCC is especially well-suited for multimedia data storage and dissemination because it offers scalable processing and flexible network service delivery. A multimedia request immediately starts a number of cloud-based processes, such as data storage, retrieval, and distribution for load balancing, all of which must be managed at runtime; (b) MCC must provide QoS provisioning for multimedia applications and adapt to dynamically changing network and workload conditions with parallel processing and dynamic offloading support. When implementing the mobile multimedia service using IaaS, a virtual machine is established and moved along with the mobile client to serve as a proxy between the cloud and the mobile client. Resource distribution in a multimedia cloud based on Queueing network analysis was addressed for scheduling, calculation, and data transmission of multimedia services, they took into account three queues in the multimedia cloud.

Location-Based Mobile Cloud Services

Applications that operate on mobile devices frequently include location-based services. Location-based services have already been built by several companies, including Intel and AT&T. The majority of mobile devices include GPS, which may identify the user's position. The cloud server can start pushing adverts once a mobile device connects to the nearby cloud, or the user can ask the cloud server questions. In addition to location-based services, the cloud may be used to access friends' and family's information.

METHODOLOGY

S.S Qureshi *et al.* have categorized MCC into two broad categories viz. General Purpose Mobile Cloud Computing (GPMCC) and Application Specific Mobile Cloud Computing (ASMCC) in ().

A. GPMCC

1. Approach

Cloud Computing has a broad perspective and finds feasible applications in varied applications. This necessitates a mobile device to utilize the internet to use a resource in an on-demand manner. Thus computation-hungry tasks that are usually executed on a resource-constrained mobile device can now be outsourced to the cloud.

2. Augmented Execution

B. Chun *et al.* have proposed an architecture (Chun & Maniatis, 2009) that addresses the challenges of executing potential applications on mobile devices via seamless but partially off-loading execution from the smartphone to a computational infrastructure hosting a cloud of smartphone *clones*.

In (Chun et al., 2011), the CloneCloud idea was made a reality. By offloading the proper amount of an application's execution onto device clones running in a computing cloud, CloneCloud improves unmodified mobile apps. The main justification was that it would be worthwhile to pay the cost of transmitting the pertinent data and code from the device to the cloud and back as long as cloud execution is much quicker than execution on mobile devices. Removing the programmer from application partitioning was the second driving force. Applications are automatically partitioned at a fine granularity by CloneCloud, which also optimises execution time and energy consumption for a target computing and communication environment. In (Chun et al., 2011), the CloneCloud idea was made a reality. By offloading the proper amount of an application's execution onto device clones running in a computing cloud, CloneCloud improves unmodified mobile apps. As long as the plan was executed, that was the main driving force.

The partitioning of the programme happens at runtime by migrating a thread from the mobile device to the cloud clone at a predetermined point, running for the duration of the partition there, and then re-integrating the migrated thread to the mobile device. This prototype can adjust application partitioning to varied circumstances, according to the assessment, and can enable some programs to run 20 times faster and use 20 times less energy on mobile devices. This however suffers from limitations because only a fixed computation scheduling in the mobile device is considered.

The goal was to reduce the amount of energy that the mobile device used overall. By carefully planning the clock frequency of the mobile device, the computing energy used to run the programs on the device may be kept to a minimum. By carefully planning the transmission data rate using a stochastic wireless channel, the transmission energy may be reduced when the apps are running in the cloud clone. The numerical findings show that the wireless transmission mechanism and application profile—specifically, the quantity of the input data and the deadline—are key determinants of the best policy.

B. ASMCC

1. Approach

Application Particular Creating customised apps for mobile devices is a component of mobile cloud computing. ASMCC has an advantage over GPMCC in that it offers more than just compute power, even though both may offload the calculation from and increase the mobile device's efficiency. Email and chat, for instance, require ASMCC because they use the internet as a resource for communication rather than just storage (Wen et al., 2012).

2. Mobile Service Clouds

Samimi *et al.* (Farshad, 2006) have introduced service clouds for MCC and named them Mobile Service Clouds. With the help of this paradigm, services may be dynamically instantiated, composed, configured, and reconfigured on an overlay network to allow mobile computing.

3. Elastic Application Weblets

X.Zhang *et al.* (2010) have proposed a model that enables the seamless and transparent use of cloud resources to augment the capability of resource-constrained mobile devices. The division of a single programme into numerous components known as weblets and a dynamic adaption of weblet execution configuration are the key components of this paradigm. A weblet can operate on a mobile device or be moved to the cloud, that is, run on one or more nodes provided by a CCSP, even if it can be platform agnostic (e.g., Java or.Net bytecode or Python script) or platform dependent (native code). In light of dynamic execution configuration in accordance with device status, including CPU load, memory, battery level, network connection quality, and user preferences, an elastic application can therefore enhance the capabilities of a mobile device, including computation power, storage, and network bandwidth.

4. Thinkair

Sokol Kosta *et al.* have proposed *Thinkair* in (2012) which takes the best of MAUI (Chun et al., 2011) and CloneCloud projects. By building Virtual Machines (VMs) of an entire smartphone system in the cloud, it overcomes MAUI's lack of scalability and eliminates the limitations on apps that CloneCloud imposes by implementing an online method-level offloading. Additionally, it offers a useful method for on-demand resource allocation and makes use of parallelism by dynamically generating, resuming, and deleting virtual machines in the cloud as necessary. These two facets of movable clouds are the first ones it addresses.

5. Partitioning and Execution of Applications

A system for splitting and running data stream applications in mobile cloud computing was developed by Lei Yang et al. (2012). It seeks to maximize the throughput of an application that processes streaming data by dividing it across a mobile and cloud environment. In contrast to prior studies, the framework provides the sharing of computing instances among several users in the cloud to promote effective utilisation of the underlying cloud resources in addition to allowing dynamic partitioning for a single user.

Open Research Issues

Energy Efficiency

Owing to the limited resources such as battery life, available network bandwidth, storage capacity and processor performance, on mobile devices, researchers are always on the lookout for solutions that result in optimal utilization of available resources.

Security

The absence of standards poses a serious issue specifically with respect to the security and privacy of data being delivered to and from mobile devices to the cloud.

Better Service

The original motivation behind MCC was to provide PC-like services to mobile devices. However, owing to the varied differences in features between fixed and mobile devices, a transformation of services from one to the other may not be as direct.

Task Division

Researchers are always on the lookout for strategies and algorithms to offload computation tasks from mobile devices to the cloud. However, due to differences in the computational requirements of numerous applications available to the users and the variety of handsets available in the market, an optimal strategy is an area to be explored.

CONCLUSION

The most recent and widely embraced technology with rapid growth is mobile cloud computing, which a development and extension of cloud computing and mobile is computing. The basis for the innovative computing model has been set by the integration of cloud computing, wireless communication infrastructure, portable computing devices, location-based services, mobile Web, etc. We have provided an overview of mobile cloud computing in this paper, including its architecture, advantages, major difficulties, ongoing research, and outstanding problems.

High-end hardware production is a costly, time-consuming, and energy-intensive process that calls for current technology. Smartphones are not inherently secure data storage devices. Because of the possibility of device failure, theft, and loss, data security and privacy are at risk. Cloud computing, however, has expanded into the mobile space in an effort to lessen the need for expensive hardware, cut ownership and maintenance costs over time, and improve data security and privacy.

To reduce the execution of demanding already-developed apps and adaptive programs on mobile devices, fidelity adaptation and cyber foraging are practical and generally accepted ways. However, a number of issues confront the development, including user and service provider security, accurate resource consumption prediction, the accessibility of remote resources, maintenance costs, and network slowness.

The key method for reducing resource needs is a new programming design that makes use of cloud computing and mash up technologies. Applications such as cloud-mobile and mashups might request the remote execution of resource-demanding portions of their code.

REFERENCES

Buyya, R., Yeo, C., & Venugopal, S. (2008). Market-oriented cloud computing: Vision, hype, and reality for delivering IT services as computing utilities. *10th IEEE International Conference on High Performance Computing and Communications, (HPCC '08).* IEEE. 10.1109/HPCC.2008.172

Buyya, R., Yeo, C. S., Venugopal, S., Broberg, J., & Brandic, I. (2009). Cloud computing and emerging IT platforms: Vision, hype, and reality for delivering computing as the 5th utility. *Future Generation Computer Systems, 25*(6), 599–616. doi:10.1016/j.future.2008.12.001

Chun, B., Ihm, S., Maniatis, P., Naik, M., & Patti, A. (2011). Clonecloud: Elastic execution between mobile device and cloud. *Proceedings of the sixth conference on Computer systems.* ACM. 10.1145/1966445.1966473

Chun, B. G., & Maniatis, P. (2009). Augmented smartphone applications through clone cloud execution. *Proceedings of the 12th conference on Hot topics in operating systems*, Berkeley, CA, USA.

Cisco. (n.d.). *Mobile Consumers reach for the Cloud.* IBSG Cisco.

Cuervo, E., & Balasubramanian, A. (2010). MAUI: Making Smartphones Last Longer with Code offload. *Proceedings of the 8th International Conference on Mobile systems, applications, and services*, (pp. 49-62). ACM. 10.1145/1814433.1814441

Dinh, H. T., Lee, C., Niyato, D., & Wang, P. (2011). A survey of Mobile Cloud Computing: Architecture, Applications and Approaches. *Wireless Communications and Mobile Computing.*

Fan, X., Cao, J., & Mao, H. (2012). *A Survey on Mobile Cloud Computing*. ZTE Corporation.

Farshad, A. (2006). *Mobile Service Clouds: A Self-Managing Infrastructure for Autonomic Mobile Computing Services*. Self-Managed Networks, Systems, and Services.

Forman, G. H., & Zahorjan, J. (1994). The Challenges of Mobile Computing. *Computer, 27*(4), 38–47. doi:10.1109/2.274999

Foster, I., Zhao, Y., Raicu, I., & Lu, S. (2009). Cloud Computing and Grid Computing 360-Degree Compared. *Proceedings of Workshop on Grid Computing Environments (GCE)*, (pp. 1-10). ACM.

Kosta, Aucinas, Hui, Mortier, & Zhang. (2012). Thinkair: Dynamic resource allocation and parallel execution in cloud for mobile code offloading. *INFOCOM IEEE Proceedings*, 945-953.

Marston, S., Li, Z., Bandyopadhyay, S., Zhang, J., & Ghalsasi, A. (2011). Cloud Computing – The business perspective. *Decision Support Systems, 51*(1), 176–189. doi:10.1016/j.dss.2010.12.006

Mell, P. & Grance, T. (2011). *The NIST definition of Cloud Computing. v15.3.* NIST.

Paulson, L. D. (2003). Low-Power Chips for High-Powered Handhelds. *Computer*, *36*(1), 21–23. doi:10.1109/MC.2003.1160049

Qi, H., & Gani, A. (2012). Research on Mobile Cloud Computing: Review,Trend and Perspectives. *Proceedings of the Second International Conference on Digital Information and Communication Technology and its Applications (DICTAP)*. IEEE. 10.1109/DICTAP.2012.6215350

Rudenko, A., Reiher, P., Popek, G. J., & Kuenning, G. H. (1998). Saving portable computer battery power through remote process execution. *Journal of ACM SIGMOBILE on Mobile Computing and Communications Review*, *2*(1), 19–26. doi:10.1145/584007.584008

Wen; Y., Zhang; W., & Luo, H. (2012). Energy-Optimal Mobile Application Execution: Taming Resource-Poor Mobile Devices with Cloud Clones. *INFOCOM IEEE Proceedings*, (pp. 2716-2720). IEEE.

Yang, L., Cao, J., Tang, S., Li, T., & Chan, A. T. S. (2012). A Framework for Partitioning and Execution of Data Stream Applications in Mobile Cloud Computing. *5th International Conference on Cloud Computing (CLOUD)*. IEEE. 10.1109/CLOUD.2012.97

Youseff, L., Butrico, M., & Da Silva, D. (2008). Toward a unified ontology of cloud computing. *Grid Computing Environments Workshop*. IEEE. 10.1109/GCE.2008.4738443

Zhang, X. (2010). *Towards an elastic application model for augmenting computing capabilities of mobile platforms*. Mobile Wireless Middleware, Operating Systems, and Applications.

Chapter 10
Cloud Computing Platforms

Kiran Peddireddy
Central Connecticut State University, USA

ABSTRACT

The advent of cloud computing has dramatically transformed our perceptions of IT infrastructure, software rollouts, and the scaling of services. As the cloud's prominence has risen, organizations can now sidestep hefty investments in tangible hardware and sideline extensive capacity planning concerns. This chapter embarks on a journey through the predominant platforms of cloud computing, exploring their distinct features, and guiding on the selection process tailored to individual requirements. The emergence of cloud technology has ushered in a new era in how we approach IT infrastructures, software implementations, and the expansion of services. With cloud computing taking center stage, companies are relieved from sinking large sums into on-premises hardware and are granted more flexibility in their resource allocation strategies. This chapter sheds light on the leading cloud computing ecosystems, their characteristic advantages, and offers insights into making an informed choice that aligns with specific needs.

INTRODUCTION

The advent of cloud computing has dramatically transformed our perceptions of IT infrastructure, software rollouts, and the scaling of services. As the cloud's prominence has risen, organizations can now sidestep hefty investments in tangible hardware and sideline extensive capacity planning concerns. This chapter embarks on a journey through the predominant platforms of cloud computing, exploring their distinct features, and guiding on the selection process tailored to individual requirements. The emergence of cloud technology has ushered in a new era in how we approach IT infrastructures, software implementations, and the expansion of services. With cloud computing taking center stage, companies are relieved from sinking large sums into on-premises hardware and are granted more flexibility in their resource allocation strategies. This chapter sheds light on the leading cloud computing ecosystems, their characteristic advantages, and offers insights into making an informed choice that aligns with specific needs.

In today's digital age, cloud computing has become a cornerstone, reshaping our viewpoints on IT infrastructure management, software distribution, and the versatility of service growth. The ascent of the cloud paradigm means organizations can bypass substantial capital expenditures in traditional

DOI: 10.4018/979-8-3693-0900-1.ch010

hardware and streamline their operational planning. In this chapter, we navigate the vast expanse of cloud computing platforms, highlighting their singular strengths, and furnishing guidelines for picking the most fitting solution for diverse needs. The dawn of cloud computing has signaled a sea change in our conceptualization of IT frameworks, the deployment of software solutions, and the adaptability of service enhancement. As the cloud's influence permeates, corporate entities find themselves freed from the constraints of heavy hardware investments and exhaustive capacity forecasting. This chapter ventures into the heart of cloud computing's dominant platforms, accentuating their individual offerings, and bestowing wisdom on the decision-making process to best match distinct demands (Braun et al., 2001; Kratzke & Quint, 2017; Wang et al., 2010).

Cloud computing's emergence has marked a significant pivot in the landscape of IT architecture, software introduction, and service scalability tactics. The cloud's ascent means that businesses have a reprieve from pouring vast resources into hardware and can adopt a nimbler approach to resource planning. This chapter dives deep into the major players in the cloud computing arena, elucidating their standout features, and offering a compass to navigate the selection process based on unique prerequisites.

UNDERSTANDING CLOUD COMPUTING

At its essence, cloud computing embodies the provision of a spectrum of services via the internet. This vast array encompasses aspects like data storage, database management, server access, network functionalities, software tools, data analytics, smart algorithms, among other offerings. Instead of sinking funds into setting up and maintaining their dedicated IT frameworks and data facilities, businesses have the option to lease a range of resources, from software solutions to storage capacities, courtesy of cloud service vendors.

Advantages

a. There are various types of KPIs metrics that organizations can utilize to measure different aspects of their performance. Some common types of KPIs include:
b. Economic Viability: Sidesteps the upfront financial commitment associated with hardware and software acquisition.
c. Adaptability: One of the standout perks of cloud-based services is their inherent ability to dynamically adjust to load demands.
d. Operational Excellence: Preeminent cloud platforms operate atop an expansive, fortified global data center network.
e. Swift Execution & Flexibility: Owing to the vast computational power at their disposal, cloud infrastructures offer nimble responses.
f. Robust Defense Mechanisms: A substantial number of cloud vendors proactively furnish a suite of protocols and innovative tools designed to enhance overall data safety and integrity.

Demystifying Cloud Computing: At a foundational level, cloud computing is the modern approach of offering a diverse set of digital services via online channels. This service spectrum is broad, covering storage solutions, database operations, server utilities, interconnected networking, diverse software applications, insightful analytics, and advanced intelligence processes. Rather than bear the burden and expenditure of crafting and managing in-house IT structures and data repositories, businesses are empowered to lease a gamut of resources, from bespoke software to expansive storage provisions, through dedicated cloud facilitators (Arockiam et al., 2017; Bastiaanssen et al., 1998; Braun et al., 2001; Pons & Ninyerola, 2008).:

a. Budget-friendly Approach: Bypasses the initial financial outlay typically associated with tangible IT assets and software suites.
b. Responsive Scaling: A hallmark of cloud offerings is their innate propensity to flexibly accommodate varying operational loads.
c. Consistent High-Caliber Output: Leading-edge cloud systems are grounded on a meticulously curated and secure global data center lattice.
d. Rapid Turnaround & Nimbleness: Leveraging the vast computational reservoir of the cloud ensures both speed and adaptability in operations.
e. Fortified Protective Layers: Numerous cloud specialists put forth a comprehensive array of protective norms and avant-garde tools to amplify the overarching safety landscape of users.

CLOUD SERVICE PROVIDERS

In the expansive realm of cloud services, several entities have carved a niche for themselves. However, a few stand out due to their extensive offerings and technological superiority:

1. **Amazon Web Services (AWS):** This giant in the cloud domain boasts an array of services, encompassing everything from sophisticated machine learning tools to robust storage frameworks.
2. **Microsoft Azure:** Azure offers a diverse suite of services. Noteworthy among these are their cutting-edge solutions tailored for the Internet of Things (IoT) and their prowess in Artificial Intelligence.
3. **Google Cloud Platform (GCP):** GCP has earned accolades primarily for its potent computational services and its adeptness at handling vast data analytics projects.
4. **Oracle Cloud (OCI):** Oracle, a veteran in the IT landscape, has pivoted emphatically into the cloud sector. Its cloud arm is especially revered for delivering top-tier database services on-demand.
5. **IBM Cloud:** A distinguished player in the cloud arena, IBM Cloud is celebrated for its blended cloud offerings that synergize both public and private cloud functionalities. Moreover, its services are accentuated with AI-enhancements, giving it a distinct edge.
6. **VMware vCloud Air:** Pioneering in virtualization, VMware extends its expertise into the cloud sphere with vCloud Air, serving as a hybrid cloud solution integrating on-premises datacenters with cloud-based infrastructure.

Amazon Web Services (AWS): AWS is the vast universe of cloud services, one name has consistently stood out: Amazon Web Services, commonly referred to as AWS. Born from the tech-savvy foundations of Amazon, AWS has reshaped how enterprises and users perceive IT utilities and cloud tech. AWS's story began in 2006, as Amazon, primarily known for e-commerce, saw an opportunity to leverage its advanced IT capabilities to present a range of cloud services to a broader audience. Thus, AWS was introduced, providing a dependable, adaptable, and cost-effective cloud platform for both developers

Figure 1. AWS services

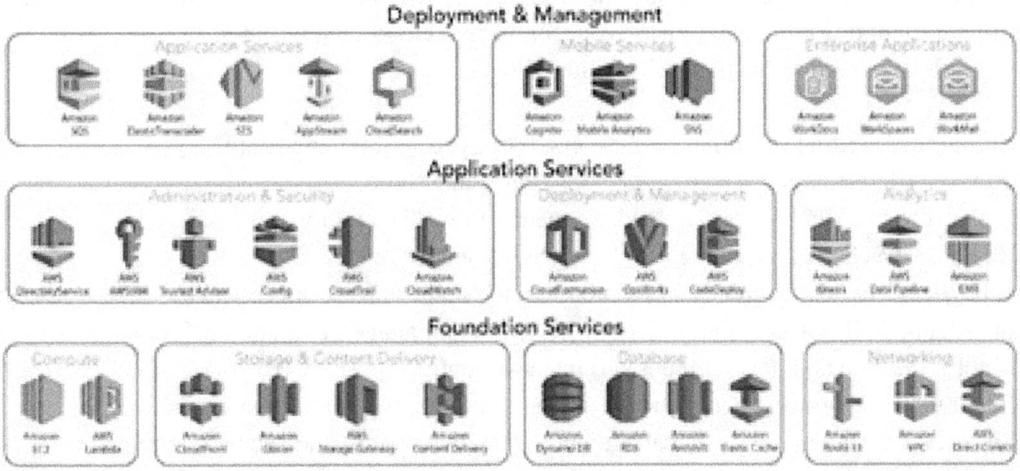

and businesses. While it commenced with simple storage options, AWS quickly diversified its offerings, broadening its service spectrum().

a. Compute Power (EC2): The Elastic Compute Cloud, or EC2, allows users to run virtual servers and scale computing capacity based on their needs.
b. Storage (S3): Simple Storage Service, popularly known as S3, offers scalable object storage for data backup, archival, and analytics.
c. Databases: RDS (Relational Database Service) and DynamoDB (NoSQL database service) cater to diverse database needs, whether relational or non-relational.
d. Machine Learning with Sage Maker: AWS's Sage Maker provides developers and data scientists the tools to build, train, and deploy machine learning models.
e. Networking: Virtual Private Cloud (VPC) enables users to create isolated networks within the AWS cloud, ensuring robust security.
f. Developer Tools: AWS offers a suite of developer tools like Code Build and Code Deploy to streamline the development lifecycle.

Discovering an expansive array of services is just a sign-up away at the AWS portal: https://aws.amazon.com/ . By navigating to the AWS website, users are introduced to a diverse landscape of cloud-based solutions and tools tailored to meet varied business and individual needs. This platform, hosted by Amazon Web Services, has continually evolved to remain at the forefront of cloud technology. Whether you're a developer, an entrepreneur, or an individual curious about cloud capabilities, the AWS site is your gateway to a realm of limitless possibilities. Joining the AWS community not only provides access to cutting-edge tools but also connects you to a global network of innovators and thinkers.

Microsoft Azure: Microsoft Azure, commonly known simply as Azure, represents Microsoft's foray into the cloud computing arena. This platform provides a comprehensive suite of tools that allow users to create, manage, and deploy applications and services across a network of global data hubs. Azure extends the promise of scalability, agility, and a vast array of solutions, transcending geographical boundaries by leveraging its widespread data centers around the world. This initiative by Microsoft underscores its commitment to innovation and its vision of a connected, cloud-first world.

Azure offers a broad range of services, including:

- Computing: Virtual machines, containers, batch processing, and more.
- Storage: Blob storage, file storage, disk storage, and more.
- Networking: Virtual networks, load balancers, firewalls, and more.
- Databases: SQL Server, PostgreSQL, MySQL, and more.
- Analytics: Big data analytics, machine learning, and artificial intelligence.
- Internet of Things (IoT): Device connectivity, data management, and analytics.
- Mobile: Mobile app development and management.
- Integration: Integration with other cloud services and on-premises systems.
- Security: Identity and access management, data encryption, and security monitoring.
- Azure is a popular choice for businesses of all sizes, from startups to Fortune 500 companies. It is used to run a wide variety of applications, including websites, web applications, mobile apps, enterprise applications, and IoT applications.
- Scalability: Azure can scale to meet the needs of any business, regardless of size.
- Reliability: Azure is a highly reliable platform, with a 99.9% uptime guarantee.
- Security: Azure is a secure platform, with multiple layers of security to protect your data.
- Global reach: Azure is available in over 140 countries, so you can deploy your applications anywhere in the world.
- Cost-effectiveness: Azure is a cost-effective platform, with a variety of pricing options to choose from.

Venturing into the realm of cloud computing, Microsoft's Azure platform stands as a beacon for those seeking diverse and powerful cloud-based solutions. By heading to the Azure website, users are granted a gateway into a vast ecosystem of services designed to cater to a multitude of business and technological needs. Azure, with its continually evolving suite of tools and services, exemplifies Microsoft's dedication to innovation in the cloud sector. A simple sign-up on the Azure portal: https://azure.microsoft.com/e unlocks a treasure trove of potential. The platform is meticulously crafted, catering to everyone from individual developers to multinational corporations. Once inside, users are presented with a plethora of options, ranging from data management and AI tools to more complex enterprise solutions. Moreover, Azure boasts a global infrastructure. This means that regardless of where you are located, there's a good chance an Azure data center isn't too far away. This extensive network ensures reliability, speed, and robustness for its users. It's not just about the physical infrastructure, though. Microsoft's commitment to excellence is reflected in the user experience, with an intuitive interface and abundant resources to help newcomers navigate the platform.

As technology keeps advancing, the need for platforms that can adapt and evolve is paramount. Azure understands this, continuously updating its service offerings and tools to stay ahead of the curve. This dynamism ensures that users always have access to the best and latest in cloud computing. But it's not just about the services. Joining the Azure community also means being part of a global conversation. With forums, webinars, and a vast array of educational resources, Azure fosters a culture of learning

Figure 2. Azure services

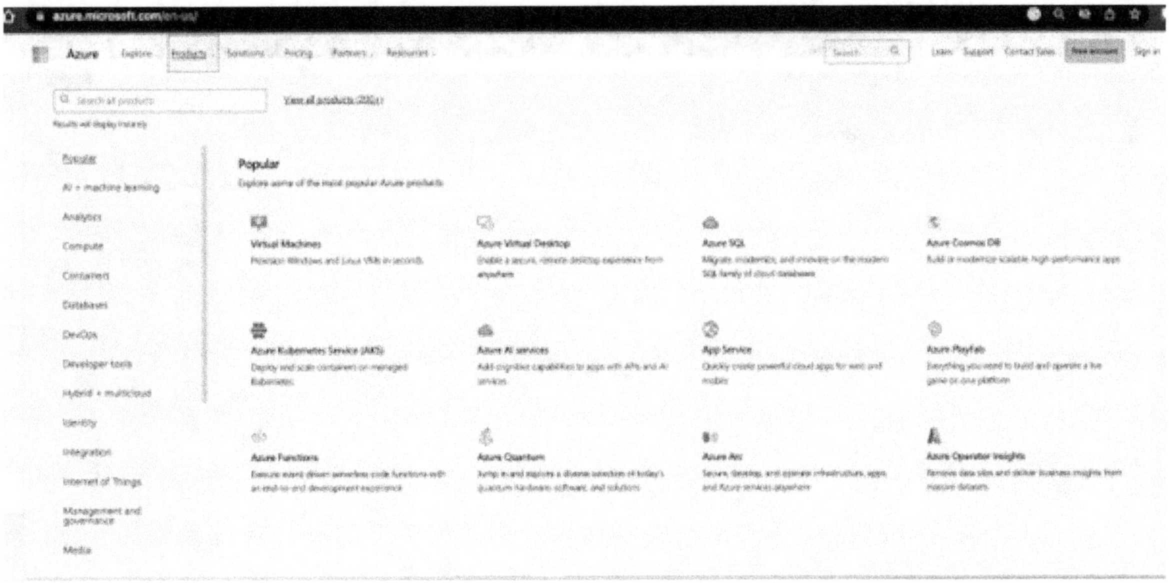

and collaboration. It's a platform where beginners can find guidance, and experts can share insights, ensuring a continuous cycle of growth and innovation.

Google Cloud Platform (GCP): Google Cloud Platform (GCP) stands as a testament to Google's expertise and innovation in the world of cloud computing. Leveraging the same robust infrastructure that powers widely used products like Google Search and YouTube, GCP provides a comprehensive range of cloud services tailored for diverse needs. At its core, GCP is designed to bring Google's scale and efficiency to businesses, developers, and institutions globally. This unique positioning allows users to benefit from the same reliability and speed that they associate with Google's consumer products. Among its offerings, GCP's computing solutions stand out, providing users with powerful computational capabilities, ideal for running applications at scale. Whether it's for a startup launching its first app or a multinational corporation looking for seamless global operations, GCP's computing services are up to the task.

Some of the most popular GCP services include:

- Compute Engine: Virtual machines for running your workloads.
- App Engine: A managed platform for running web applications.
- Kubernetes Engine: A managed, production-ready environment for deploying containerized applications.
- Cloud Storage: Durable, highly scalable object storage.
- Cloud SQL: Fully managed relational database service.
- Cloud Bigtable: NoSQL database for large-scale analytical and operational workloads.
- Cloud Dataproc: Managed Hadoop and Spark service for big data processing.
- Cloud Dataflow: Managed streaming data processing service.
- Cloud AI Platform: A unified platform for developing, training, and deploying machine learning models.

Figure 3. Google cloud services

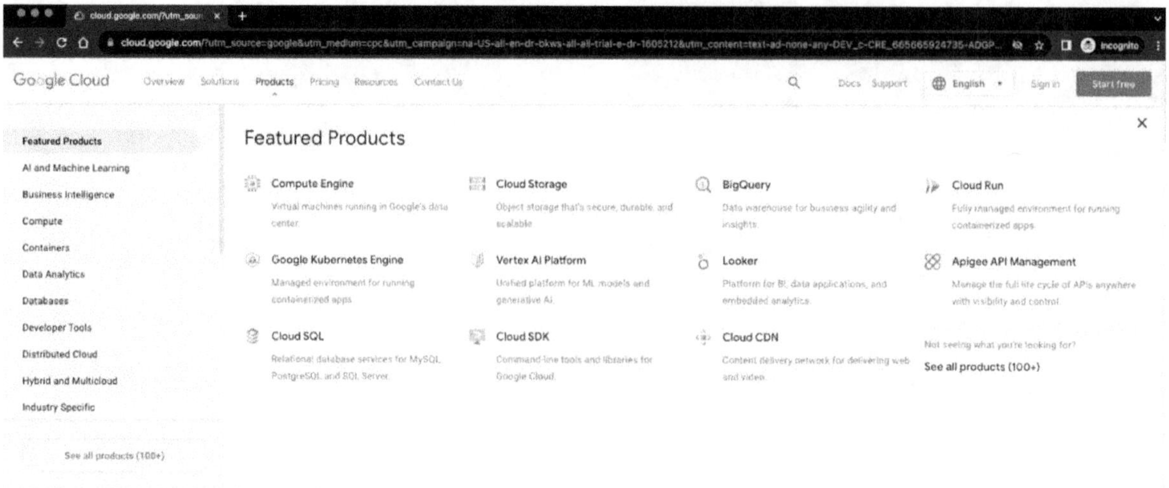

Exploring the expansive digital world often leads us to dynamic platforms that promise a range of services. One such prominent platform is Google's cloud offering, accessible through its dedicated portal. By navigating to and registering on https://cloud.google.com/, users unlock a treasure trove of features and solutions designed for varied needs. From individual developers to large-scale enterprises, this platform caters to a wide audience. Once signed up, the user is introduced to a universe of tools and services, each meticulously crafted to optimize performance, enhance scalability, and ensure robust security. These offerings are not just limited to storage solutions but span across computing, machine learning, data analytics, and more.

The beauty of such a platform lies not just in its diverse range of services but also in its user-friendly interface, making cloud computing accessible to both novices and experts alike. Moreover, Google's commitment to innovation ensures that the platform is continually evolving, introducing newer tools and refining existing ones to keep pace with the rapid advancements in technology.

GCP is a popular choice for businesses of all sizes, from startups to large enterprises. It offers several advantages, including:

- Scalability: GCP is designed to scale to meet the needs of any business, no matter how large or small.
- Reliability: GCP is built on the same infrastructure that Google uses for its own products, so it is highly reliable.
- Security: GCP offers a wide range of security features to protect your data and applications.
- Innovation: GCP is constantly innovating and adding new services.
- Open source: GCP is committed to open source and offers a number of open-source services.

GCP is a powerful and versatile cloud platform that can be used to build and deploy a wide range of applications and services. If you are looking for a cloud platform that is reliable, scalable, and secure, then GCP is a great option to consider.

Figure 4. Oracle cloud infrastructure services

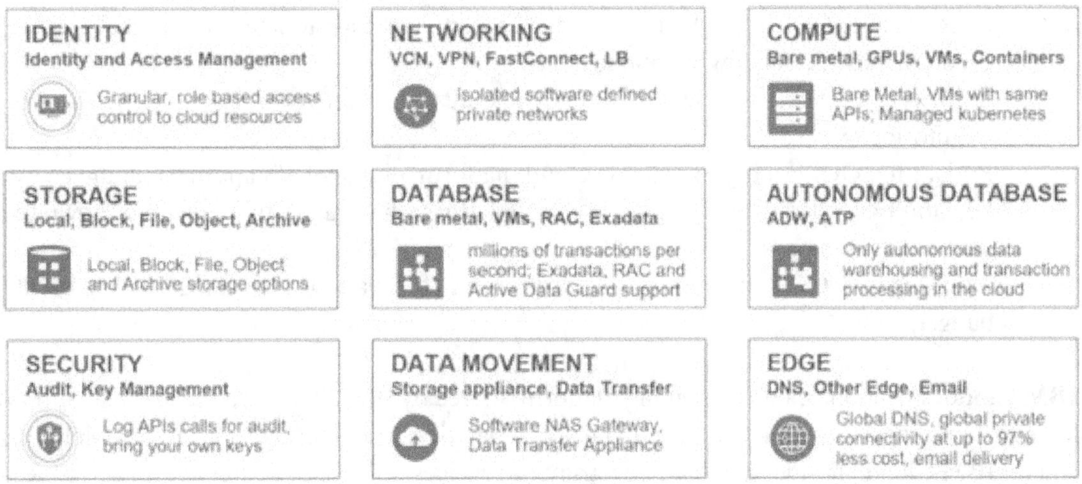

Oracle Cloud Infrastructure (OCI): is a cloud computing service offered by Oracle Corporation. It provides a broad set of infrastructure as a service (IaaS), platform as a service (PaaS), and software as a service (SaaS) offering. OCI is available in more than 30 data centers worldwide, including regions in the United States, Europe, Asia Pacific, and Latin America().

OCI offers a wide range of services, including:

- Compute: OCI offers a variety of compute options, including bare metal, virtual machines, and containers.
- Storage: OCI offers a variety of storage options, including block storage, object storage, and file storage.
- Networking: OCI offers a variety of networking options, including virtual private clouds (VPCs), load balancers, and VPNs.
- Databases: OCI offers a variety of database services, including Oracle Database, MySQL, and PostgreSQL.
- Analytics: OCI offers a variety of analytics services, including Oracle Big Data Service and Oracle Data Warehouse.
- Applications: OCI offers a variety of application services, including Oracle Fusion Cloud ERP and Oracle Fusion Cloud HCM.

By registering on their official website: https://www.oracle.com/cloud/, users gain access to a diverse range of tools designed to meet various IT and business needs. Oracle, renowned for its technological prowess, ensures that those who venture onto their platform are greeted with cutting-edge cloud services. From infrastructure to software applications, every facet of the cloud ecosystem is meticulously curated on this platform. By taking the step to sign up, individuals and organizations unlock a world of potential, optimized for performance, scalability, and security. Delving deeper into Oracle's cloud landscape offers insights into the future of digital transformation.

Here are some of the benefits of using OCI:

- Performance: OCI offers high-performance compute and storage options that can support even the most demanding workloads.
- Security: OCI offers a variety of security features, including encryption, access control, and monitoring.
- Reliability: OCI is a highly reliable cloud platform with a 99.9% uptime guarantee.
- Scalability: OCI is a highly scalable cloud platform that can easily scale up or down to meet your changing needs.
- Affordability: OCI offers competitive pricing and a variety of pricing models to fit your budget.

IBM Cloud: is a public cloud computing platform offered by IBM. It offers a broad range of services, including computing, storage, networking, databases, analytics, machine learning, artificial intelligence, and more. IBM Cloud provides a diverse spectrum of services tailored to address various business and technological needs. Some of the notable offerings include:

- Computing Services: Whether you're seeking virtual servers, containers, or cloud functions, IBM provides choices like Virtual Private Cloud, Bare Metal Servers, and Kubernetes Service.
- Storage Solutions: Options such as Block Storage, Object Storage, and File Storage ensure data is kept safely and can be accessed swiftly.
- Networking: Features like Virtual Private Network (VPN), Content Delivery Network (CDN), and Load Balancers ensure optimal data flow and connectivity.
- Databases: From SQL-based databases like Db2 to NoSQL solutions like CouchDB, there's a broad range of managed database services.
- Analytics: Tools like IBM Watson Studio and Cloud Pak for Data facilitate deep data analysis, allowing businesses to derive actionable insights.
- AI & Machine Learning: With IBM Watson services, users can integrate AI capabilities into their applications, ranging from chatbots to complex machine learning models.
- Security: Comprehensive security solutions including Identity and Access Management, Activity Tracker, and Key Protect safeguard data and applications.
- IoT (Internet of Things): IBM's IoT platform helps in connecting devices, collecting data, and deriving insights.
- Integration: Services like API Connect and App Connect assist in seamlessly integrating apps and data across different environments.
- Management Tools: To simplify cloud management, services like Monitoring, Logging, and Resource Controller are available.
- Hybrid Deployments: With tools like IBM Cloud Satellite, businesses can deploy applications in any environment - on-premises, on public clouds, or at the edge.
- Quantum Computing: IBM Q Experience provides users with access to experimental quantum systems.

Exploring the digital world often leads us to discover a plethora of services that can revolutionize the way we approach technology and business. One such destination for cloud-based solutions is the IBM

Figure 5. IBM cloud services

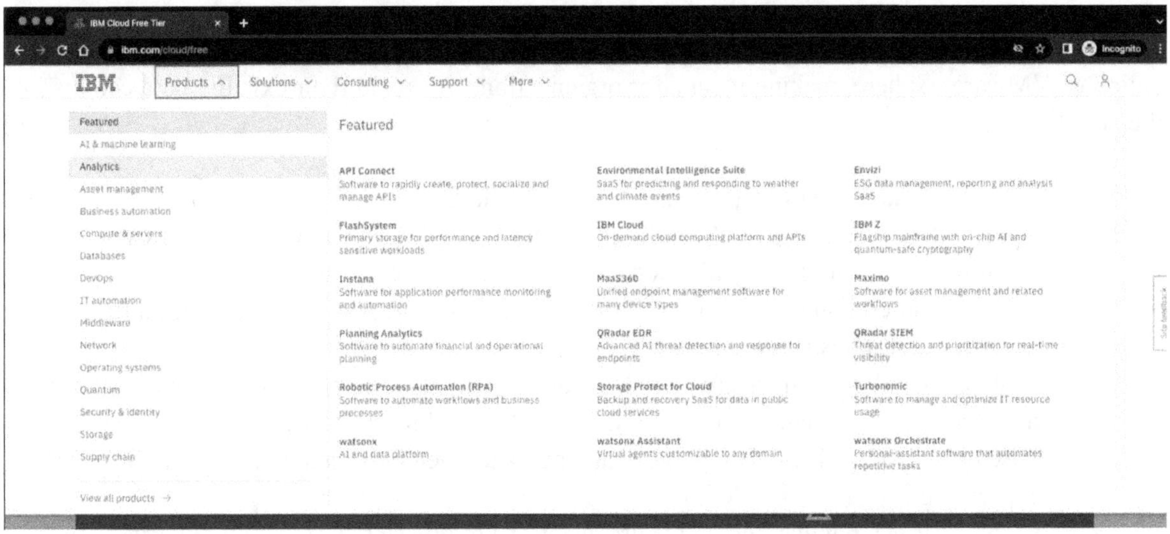

Cloud platform. By navigating to IBM's official cloud website: https://www.ibm.com/cloud/, users are introduced to a myriad of cutting-edge tools and services designed to elevate their digital experience.

IBM, a name synonymous with technological innovation for decades, has curated a platform that caters to various needs - from data analytics to artificial intelligence, from blockchain to cybersecurity. By simply registering on their cloud website, individuals and businesses alike gain access to these resources, offering opportunities to streamline operations, optimize performance, and harness the power of the cloud.

Some of the key benefits of using IBM Cloud include:

- Reliability: IBM Cloud is built on a global infrastructure of data centers, with a focus on reliability and uptime.
- Security: IBM Cloud offers a wide range of security features to help protect your data and applications.
- Performance: IBM Cloud is designed for performance, with a focus on scalability and low latency.
- Innovation: IBM Cloud is constantly innovating, with new services and features being added regularly.

IBM Cloud also offers a number of unique features, such as:

- Confidential computing: IBM Cloud offers a confidential computing platform that helps you protect your data at rest, in transit, and in use.
- Hybrid and multicloud: IBM Cloud supports hybrid and multicloud deployments, so you can run your workloads wherever it makes the most sense.
- AI and machine learning: IBM Cloud offers a wide range of AI and machine learning services, so you can build and deploy AI-powered applications.

IBM Cloud is a powerful and versatile cloud computing platform that can help you meet your business needs. It is a good choice for businesses of all sizes and industries.

VMware vCloud: Air is a public cloud service operated by VMware. It is built on the trusted foundation of VMware vSphere, making it easy for organizations to extend their existing data centers into the cloud().

vCloud Air offers a wide range of features and benefits, including:

- Hybrid cloud capabilities: vCloud Air can be easily integrated with on-premises vSphere environments, enabling organizations to create a seamless hybrid cloud.
- Security and compliance: vCloud Air is built on a secure platform and is compliant with a wide range of industry standards.
- Scalability and performance: vCloud Air offers a highly scalable and performant infrastructure that can meet the needs of even the most demanding applications.
- Ease of use: vCloud Air is easy to use and manage, even for organizations with limited cloud experience.
- vCloud Air is a popular choice for organizations of all sizes, from small businesses to large enterprises. It is a versatile and reliable cloud platform that can be used for a wide range of workloads, including production applications, development and testing, and disaster recovery.

Here are some examples of how vCloud Air can be used:

- Extend your on-premises data center: vCloud Air can be used to extend your on-premises data center, giving you access to additional computing resources, storage, and networking.
- Run production applications: vCloud Air is a reliable and secure platform for running production applications. It offers a variety of features that can help you meet your performance and compliance requirements.
- Develop and test new applications: vCloud Air is a great platform for developing and testing new applications. It provides you with a sandbox environment where you can experiment with new technologies and configurations without affecting your production environment.
- Implement disaster recovery: vCloud Air can be used to implement a disaster recovery solution for your on-premises data center. In the event of a disaster, you can quickly and easily restore your applications and data to vCloud Air.

CHOOSING THE OPTIMAL CLOUD SOLUTION

As you navigate the landscape of cloud service providers, several factors merit careful consideration.

g. Technical Specifications: Evaluate if the platform aligns with the programming languages, utilities, and structural designs central to your operations.
h. Cost Structures: Familiarize yourself with their financial model. It could range from on-the-spot payment structures, pre-booked capacities, to other pricing schemas.
i. Commitment and Service Guarantees (SLA): Scrutinize the provider's service promises to ascertain they dovetail with your operational prerequisites.

j. Data Jurisdiction: Investigate the geographical location of your data repositories. Do they conform to locational legal mandates and guidelines?
k. Platform Compatibility & External Synchronization: Determine whether the provider's digital landscape is conducive to integrations with external tools or services, whether already in use or envisioned for future adoption.

By utilizing KPI dashboards in decision-making processes, organizations can enhance agility, increase efficiency, and improve outcomes. They can respond quickly to emerging trends, identify strategic opportunities, and address performance gaps promptly.

INITIAL PRINCIPLES FOR CLOUD ONBOARDING

a. Evaluation: Comprehensively analyze the digital assets in question, determining what's primed for the cloud and the driving factors for such decisions.
b. Framework Development: Handpick the cloud solutions that align with your strategic vision and draft an intricate plan for the ensuing migration.
c. Experimentation: Before committing fully, it's astute to conduct experimental phases, placing certain application sections under the cloud's lens.
d. Shift: Gradually usher your digital resources, data reservoirs, and application architecture into the cloud realm.
e. Calibration: After successfully migrating, maintain an active oversight, finessing operations to accentuate performance and remain cost-efficient.

CONCLUSION

Transitioning into the cloud domain is a transformative maneuver that calls for a systematic approach. Steering through this metamorphosis with the above tenets can not only smoothen the journey but also position an organization to harness the full potential of cloud innovations. Adopting cloud technology transcends mere technological choices; it epitomizes a calculated business strategy targeting expansive growth, adaptability, and streamlined operations. The optimal cloud solution hinges on individualized requirements, fiscal considerations, and overarching objectives. With a comprehensive grasp of the cloud terrain, businesses can fully leverage the extensive capabilities of cloud solutions, propelling their corporate ambitions (Arockiam et al., 2017; Bastiaanssen et al., 1998; Braun et al., 2001; Kratzke & Quint, 2017; Kumar & Goudar, 2012; Wang et al., 2010).

Integrating cloud functionalities is not solely about tech advancement; it reflects a pivotal business trajectory aimed at fostering growth, nimbleness, and operational prowess. The most suitable cloud infrastructure is influenced by distinct prerequisites, financial planning, and aspirational milestones. By immersing oneself in the nuances of the cloud ecosystem, enterprises can tap into the vast potentialities of the cloud, bolstering their market position. Transitioning to the cloud isn't merely a shift in technology; it's emblematic of a holistic business vision emphasizing enhanced scale, agility, and operational efficacy. The choice of an apt cloud system is determined by tailored needs, monetary allocations, and visionary targets. With an in-depth understanding of the expansive cloud canvas, organizations can effectively channel the immense capacities of cloud computing, amplifying their organizational impact.

The journey to the cloud is not just a tech-centric leap; it signifies a comprehensive business evolution that seeks augmented scalability, adaptative capacity, and peak operational effectiveness. The selection of an ideal cloud environment is governed by unique operational demands, budgetary frameworks, and future-focused strategies. By demystifying the multifaceted world of cloud computing, companies stand poised to exploit the myriad benefits of the cloud, reinforcing their competitive edge. Migrating to cloud infrastructures is more than an IT-centric initiative; it embodies a profound business transformation underscored by aspirations of growth dimensions, operational dexterity, and optimized outcomes. The quintessential cloud model resonates with specific operational desires, financial contours, and strategic horizons. By delving deep into the cloud domain, businesses can unlock the expansive reservoir of cloud-driven advantages, fortifying their market trajectory (Arockiam et al., 2017; Pons & Ninyerola, 2008).

REFERENCES

Arockiam, L., Monikandan, S., & Parthasarathy, G. (2017). Cloud Computing: A Survey. *International Journal of Computer and Communication Technology*, 21–28. doi:10.47893/IJCCT.2017.1393

AWS. (n.d.). *Home.* Amazon. https://aws.amazon.com/

Bastiaanssen, W. G. M., Menenti, M., Feddes, R. A., & Holtslag, A. A. M. (1998). A remote sensing surface energy balance algorithm for land (SEBAL). 1. Formulation. *Journal of Hydrology (Amsterdam), 212-213*, 198–212. doi:10.1016/S0022-1694(98)00253-4

Braun, T. D., Siegel, H. J., Beck, N., Bölöni, L. L., Maheswaran, M., Reuther, A. I., Robertson, J. P., Theys, M. D., Yao, B., Hensgen, D., & Freund, R. F. (2001). A Comparison of Eleven Static Heuristics for Mapping a Class of Independent Tasks onto Heterogeneous Distributed Computing Systems. *Journal of Parallel and Distributed Computing*, *61*(6), 810–837. doi:10.1006/jpdc.2000.1714

Google. (n.d.). *About OS Images.* Google. https://cloud.google.com/compute/docs/images

IBM. (n.d.). *Home.* IBM. https://cloud.ibm.com/

Kratzke, N., & Quint, P.-C. (2017). Understanding cloud-native applications after 10 years of cloud computing - A systematic mapping study. *Journal of Systems and Software*, *126*, 1–16. doi:10.1016/j.jss.2017.01.001

Kumar, S., & Goudar, R. H. (2012). Cloud Computing – Research Issues, Challenges, Architecture, Platforms and Applications: A Survey. *International Journal of Future Computer and Communication*, *356–360*, 356–360. doi:10.7763/IJFCC.2012.V1.95

Microsoft. (n.d.). *Azure.* Microsoft. https://azure.microsoft.com/

OCI. (n.d.). *Home. OCI.* https://www.oracle.com/cloud/

Pons, X., & Ninyerola, M. (2008). Mapping a topographic global solar radiation model implemented in a GIS and refined with ground data. *International Journal of Climatology*, *28*(13), 1821–1834. doi:10.1002/joc.1676

VM Ware. (n.d.). *Home.* VM Ware. https://www.vmware.com/

Wang, L., von Laszewski, G., Younge, A., He, X., Kunze, M., Tao, J., & Fu, C. (2010). Cloud Computing: A Perspective Study. *New Generation Computing*, *28*(2), 137–146. doi:10.1007/s00354-008-0081-5

Chapter 11
Cloud Security:
Challenges, Solutions, and Future Directions: Navigating the Complexities of securing Cloud

Kaushikkumar Patel
https://orcid.org/0009-0005-9197-2765
TransUnion LLC, USA

ABSTRACT

This chapter delves into the multifaceted aspects of cloud security, highlighting unique challenges posed by the cloud environment, such as multi-tenancy and virtualization, and the critical need for robust data privacy measures. It explores advanced security protocols and measures, emphasizing the importance of encryption and threat mitigation strategies. The discourse extends to the dynamics of mobile cloud computing security, underscoring pertinent considerations. The chapter culminates with insights into future research directions, advocating for continuous innovation in cybersecurity mechanisms to pace with evolving threats.

INTRODUCTION

In recent years, the technological landscape has undergone a significant transformation, with cloud computing emerging as a cornerstone of global digital infrastructure. This innovative approach to computing has fundamentally altered how businesses, governments, and individuals access and interact with digital resources. Cloud computing offers unprecedented efficiency, agility, and scalability, enabling users to access a vast array of resources and services seamlessly over the internet. However, as with any revolutionary technology, this digital metamorphosis ushers in a host of security challenges and considerations that demand meticulous analysis and strategic planning to protect sensitive data, ensure privacy, and maintain compliance with an increasingly complex regulatory environment.

Cloud computing represents a paradigm shift from traditional IT hardware and software management to a more flexible and cost-effective model where resources are provided as services over the Internet.

DOI: 10.4018/979-8-3693-0900-1.ch011

This model allows organizations to avoid the substantial capital expenditure and operational costs associated with maintaining their own IT infrastructure. Instead, they can leverage cloud service providers' capabilities, utilizing advanced computing power, storage, and various applications on a pay-per-use basis. This evolution has facilitated a more collaborative, decentralized, and, in many ways, more resilient approach to computing, where resources can be rapidly provisioned and scaled according to demand.

However, the features that make cloud computing attractive also introduce significant security concerns. The shared nature of the cloud environment, where resources such as networks, servers, and storage systems are pooled among multiple users, presents unique vulnerabilities. Threat vectors such as data breaches, account hijacking, insecure interfaces, malicious insiders, and the ephemeral aspects of a virtual infrastructure are magnified in a cloud setting. The division of security responsibilities between the provider and the customer is often a point of confusion and can lead to gaps in security postures.

The security landscape becomes even more complex when considering the different service models of cloud computing: Infrastructure as a Service (IaaS), Platform as a Service (PaaS), and Software as a Service (SaaS). Each of these models requires different levels of security considerations. For example, IaaS customers have control over their infrastructure, making them responsible for securing everything from the operating system up to the applications they deploy. In contrast, SaaS customers, who use software applications over the internet, depend almost entirely on their providers for security, as they have control over very few, if any, application-level security features.

Adding to these technical challenges are the legal and regulatory hurdles. With regulations like the General Data Protection Regulation (GDPR) in Europe and various data sovereignty laws worldwide, cloud users often find themselves navigating a minefield of compliance obligations. These laws impose strict rules on personal data processing, and failure to comply can lead to severe penalties. Consequently, cloud security is no longer just an IT concern; it's a high-stakes legal matter.

This chapter aims to provide a comprehensive exploration of the multifaceted cloud security ecosystem. We will dissect the various challenges that organizations face in this realm, delve into strategic solutions that encompass technological tools, procedural adaptations, and human oversight, and project future trends and evolutions in cloud security protocols. By offering a panoramic view of the current state of cloud security and its complexities, this chapter seeks to equip readers with the knowledge and insights necessary to forge robust, proactive strategies for risk mitigation, regulatory compliance, and data protection in the cloud.

As we proceed, it is imperative to acknowledge that cloud security is not a static discipline. It is a dynamic, ever-evolving field, responding to new threats and vulnerabilities that arise with technological advancements. It demands continuous vigilance, adaptability, and foresight from stakeholders to safeguard digital assets in an environment characterized by constant change and uncertainty. The journey through this intricate terrain requires a balance of technical acumen, strategic thinking, and a deep understanding of the risks and rewards that cloud computing entails.

LITERATURE REVIEW

This section will delve into various scholarly articles, research papers, and authoritative reports to present a comprehensive overview of the current landscape of cloud security. This review is crucial in understanding the depth of existing research, identifying gaps in current knowledge, and highlighting the significance of ongoing and future studies in this realm.

- **Overview of Cloud Computing Security:**
    i. The advent of cloud computing marked a paradigm shift in how organizations manage and deploy computing resources. While the benefits, such as scalability, cost-efficiency, and flexibility, are evident, the literature extensively discusses the security implications of migrating to the cloud (Tabrizchi, H, 2020). The shared responsibility model, requiring both providers and customers to undertake certain security measures, is a recurrent theme, emphasizing the need for collaboration in securing cloud environments (Farnga, M., 2018).
- **Data Confidentiality and Integrity in Cloud Computing:**
    i. Encryption Techniques for Data Security: Data security is a multifaceted issue in cloud services, with encryption standing out as a critical tool for protecting data confidentiality and integrity (Basan, M., 2023). Advanced encryption methods, such as homomorphic encryption, allow for computations on encrypted data, a revolutionary concept that, however, comes with high computational costs (Shahzad, F., 2014). Other techniques, like multi-layer encryption or searchable encryption, provide alternatives, balancing security and efficiency (Samarati, P., 2016).
    ii. Challenges of Data Deletion: Secure data deletion is a crucial aspect often overlooked in cloud security. Researchers express concerns that cloud providers' data deletion practices may not fully erase data, leaving remnants susceptible to unauthorized recovery (Sharma, S., 2014). This area calls for more robust techniques to guarantee data recoverability after deletion requests (Mell, P., 2012).
- **Trust and Compliance in Cloud Environments:**
    i. The Role of Service Level Agreements (SLAs): Trust between cloud service providers and users hinges significantly on the transparency and enforceability of SLAs (Kumar, R., 2019). These contractual documents are crucial in establishing users' expectations regarding cloud services, especially for security and data protection standards (Coppolino, L., 2017). However, the literature indicates a lack of standardization in SLAs, leading to inconsistencies and potential trust issues (Khan, M. W., 2021).
    ii. Compliance and Third-Party Auditing: Compliance with international data protection regulations is a complex yet indispensable aspect of cloud security (Ugorji, B., 2013). Researchers advocate for regular third-party audits and certifications, ensuring providers' adherence to compliance requirements and enhancing overall trust in cloud services (Khan, N., 2016).
- **Access Control Mechanisms in the Cloud:**
    i. Evolution of Identity and Access Management (IAM): With the cloud's dynamic environment, traditional access control mechanisms fall short. The literature underscores the importance of sophisticated IAM systems, incorporating measures like multi-factor authentication (MFA) and biometric verification (Pfarr, F., 2014). These systems not only prevent unauthorized access but also provide detailed access logs for monitoring and compliance purposes (Kuyoro, S. O., 2011).
    ii. Attribute-Based Access Control (ABAC): ABAC emerges as a more nuanced approach to access control, allowing permissions to be granted based on user attributes and real-time context (Nadeem, M. A., 2016). This granularity enhances security but also introduces complexity in managing user attributes and policies, a challenge that organizations need to navigate (Sridhar, S., 2016).

- **Security Challenges in Mobile Cloud Computing:**
  i. Data Security on Mobile Devices: The integration of cloud computing with mobile devices poses unique challenges, particularly around data security. The literature emphasizes secure data transmission protocols and encryption standards for data at rest on mobile devices, acknowledging the heightened risk of device loss or theft (Samarati, P., 2016).
  ii. Enterprise Mobility Management (EMM) Solutions: EMM solutions, encompassing mobile device management (MDM) and mobile application management (MAM), are gaining traction as mechanisms to secure corporate data on personal devices (Donald, A. C., 2013). These strategies mitigate the risk of data breaches due to compromised mobile devices, though they require careful balancing between security and user privacy (Kandukuri, B. R., 2009).
- **Emerging Threats and Advanced Countermeasures:**
  i. Virtualization and Containerization Security: As cloud computing relies heavily on virtualization, security issues surrounding hypervisors and container environments are prevalent in the literature (Tianfield, H., 2012). Isolation of workloads, secure migration of virtual instances, and vulnerabilities in container orchestrations are discussed as areas needing further advancement (Ermetic Team., 2022).
  ii. AI and Machine Learning in Cloud Security: The application of artificial intelligence (AI) and machine learning (ML) in enhancing cloud security is an emerging topic. These technologies are employed for anomaly detection, automated threat intelligence, and security configuration recommendations, pointing towards a future where cloud security is increasingly proactive and predictive.

The existing literature on cloud security encompasses a broad spectrum of topics, reflecting the field's complexity and the continuous evolution of threats. From advanced encryption techniques to the intricacies of compliance and trust, it's clear that cloud security is a multifaceted domain requiring holistic strategies. The consensus among researchers points towards an integrative approach, combining technological advancements with robust policy frameworks, to navigate the security challenges inherent in cloud computing.

UNIQUE SECURITY CHALLENGES IN CLOUD ENVIRONMENTS

The advent of cloud computing marked a paradigm shift in information technology systems, offering unprecedented flexibility, scalability, and efficiency in data storage and computational capabilities. However, these benefits come with a unique set of security challenges, primarily because the traditional perimeter-based security model does not fit well within the dynamic, distributed nature of cloud services. These challenges are further complicated by the shared responsibility model for security, which requires a clear understanding of security controls maintained by the provider and those that the customer must implement (Mell, P., 2012). To provide a clear overview of the security challenges discussed in this section, refer to Table 1, named 'Overview of Principal Security Challenges in Cloud Computing,' which summarizes the key issues and their implications.

- **Data Breaches and Data Loss:** The cloud model's essence, storing data remotely and accessing it over the internet, inherently increases exposure to potential breaches. The multi-tenancy environment and the massive concentration of resources and data can make cloud computing targets particularly attractive for cybercriminals. Data breaches in cloud services, which can result from vulnerabilities, inadequate security practices, or human error, can lead to unauthorized data disclosure and substantial financial and reputational damages (Basan, M., 2023). Moreover, data loss can occur through malicious actions, such as targeted attacks by cybercriminals, or accidental causes, including user errors or natural disasters. The challenge lies in implementing effective data backup measures and robust security protocols to prevent data loss and facilitate data recovery (Sridhar, S., 2016).

- **Insufficient Identity, Credential, and Access Management:** Robust identity and access management (IAM) systems are crucial in cloud environments to ensure that only authorized individuals can access certain data or applications. Traditional IAM systems may not suffice due to the on-demand, highly scalable nature of cloud services, necessitating more sophisticated solutions. These solutions must manage identification, authentication, and authorization of both users and devices, thereby preventing unauthorized access (Shahzad, F., 2014).
- **Insecure Interfaces and APIs:** Almost every cloud service offers APIs for customers to interact with cloud services. These interfaces must be securely designed to ensure confidentiality and integrity in data transmission. Insecure APIs or GUIs can expose organizations to a range of attacks, including data breaches, data loss, and denial of service (DoS). Developers and cloud providers must both ensure that communications are authenticated and encrypted, and they must regularly update API dependencies to mitigate vulnerabilities (Khan, N., 2016).
- **System Vulnerabilities:** Shared environments in cloud computing mean that system vulnerabilities can have far-reaching impacts. These vulnerabilities, which can exist in any part of a cloud service provider's infrastructure, can be exploited to gain unauthorized access to data. One client's vulnerabilities can potentially lead to breaches across multiple tenants, especially if the underlying hypervisor or containers that segregate customers are not fully secure. Regular vulnerability assessments and prompt patch management strategies are essential in these environments (Kumar, R., 2019).
- **Account Hijacking:** Phishing, exploitation of software vulnerabilities, and credential theft can lead to account hijacking in cloud environments. Attackers gaining control over a user's account can eavesdrop on transactions, manipulate data, and even redirect clients to illegitimate sites. Preventing account hijacking requires multifactor authentication, sophisticated threat intelligence, and monitoring strategies to detect unauthorized access promptly (Samarati, P., 2016).
- **Advanced Persistent Threats (APTs):** These sophisticated, stealthy, and continuous hacking processes or techniques often target specific organizations or nations for business or political reasons. APT attackers pursue their goals repeatedly over an extended period, often adapting to the security measures intended to defend against them. Their persistence means that they can often penetrate well-defended targets, and their techniques can sometimes enable them to remain undetected for years in cloud environments (Tianfield, H., 2012).
- **Legal and Compliance Risks:** The decentralized nature of cloud computing raises complex legal and compliance issues. These challenges include international data privacy regulations, contractual liabilities, intellectual property rights, and regulatory compliance. Navigating this complex legal landscape requires comprehensive knowledge of where data is stored and processed by the cloud service provider and an understanding of the legal implications of data crossing international borders (Khan, M. W., 2021).

- **Shared Technology Vulnerabilities:** The underlying components that cloud service providers use to deliver services—such as CPUs, GPUs, and other hardware—can be vulnerable to attacks. These shared resources can create a potential pathway for vulnerabilities affecting multiple clients. For instance, certain side-channel attacks exploit information leaked from shared physical resources, and other attacks target shared memory in hardware (Nadeem, M. A., 2016).
- **Data Privacy and Sovereignty:** Data privacy is a paramount concern in cloud computing, especially given the global nature of the cloud. With data potentially stored across various jurisdictions, different privacy laws and regulations apply, which can be particularly concerning for sensitive information. This situation often leads to a lack of clarity over data sovereignty, raising questions about which government bodies have jurisdiction over the data (Sharma, S., 2014).
- **Resource Exhaustion (Denial of Service):** DoS attacks are not new, but they take on a new dimension in cloud computing. Attackers can overload a cloud service's infrastructure and computational resources, denying access to legitimate users. The elasticity of cloud environments can help mitigate these attacks, but it also introduces the risk of "economic denial of resources" attacks, where the scaling response to a DoS attack creates significant costs for the customer (Donald, A. C., 2013).

In conclusion, cloud computing introduces a complex array of security challenges that require a multifaceted approach to security. These challenges necessitate not only the adaptation of existing security measures but also the development of new strategies and technologies. As cloud computing continues to evolve, a proactive approach to security, which includes staying abreast of the latest threats and security innovations, is essential for safeguarding data and assets in the cloud environment.

Table 1. Overview of principal security challenges in cloud computing

Challenge	Description	Implications and Considerations
Data Breaches and Data Loss	Increased risk due to remote data storage and multi-tenancy.	Financial and reputational damage; need for robust backup and recovery protocols.
Identity and Access Management	The necessity for advanced systems is due to the dynamic nature of cloud services.	Prevention of unauthorized access; management of user/device credentials.
Insecure Interfaces and APIs	Security of APIs is crucial for safe interaction with cloud services.	Risk of data breaches and loss; necessity for secure communication protocols.
System Vulnerabilities	Shared environments increase impact scope.	Potential for widespread breaches; the importance of regular vulnerability assessments.
Account Hijacking	Risks associated with credential theft and phishing attacks.	Unauthorized access and data manipulation; requirement for multifactor authentication.
Advanced Persistent Threats (APTs)	Prolonged and targeted cyber-attacks.	Penetration of secure targets; undetected presence in cloud environments.
Legal and Compliance Risks	Complexities due to international data privacy regulations and compliance.	Challenges in navigating data sovereignty and privacy laws.
Shared Technology Vulnerabilities	Shared resources among clients create potential attack pathways.	Exploitation of shared hardware; risk of side-channel attacks.
Data Privacy and Sovereignty	Concerns due to data storage across multiple jurisdictions.	Legal implications and jurisdictional complexities; privacy of sensitive information.
Resource Exhaustion (DoS)	Cloud-specific DoS attacks overload infrastructure and resources.	Denial of service to legitimate users; potential for significant operational costs.

ADVANCED SECURITY MEASURES AND PROTOCOLS IN CLOUD COMPUTING

The transformative wave of cloud computing has reshaped how businesses and individuals use computing resources, offering unparalleled scalability, accessibility, and flexibility. However, these advantages also bring unique security challenges, necessitating the evolution of advanced security measures and protocols. These sophisticated strategies are not only reactive but also proactive, addressing potential threats before they materialize and ensuring the three pillars of cybersecurity: confidentiality, integrity, and availability (Tabrizchi, H, 2020). For a concise outline of the various security measures and protocols explored in this section, see Table 2, named 'Overview of Advanced Security Measures in Cloud Computing'.

- **Encryption Techniques:** Data encryption stands as a cornerstone of cloud security, transforming information into unreadable code that cannot be easily deciphered by unauthorized users. Advanced encryption techniques go beyond traditional methods. Homomorphic encryption, for instance, is revolutionary in that it allows computations on encrypted data, providing results that are still encrypted. This method is particularly beneficial for sensitive data, eliminating the need for decryption during processing and thereby reducing exposure to potential breaches (Sridhar, S., 2016). Additionally, the advent of multi-layer encryption, where data is encrypted at several levels, adds redundant security layers, making data breaches exponentially more challenging for attackers (Samarati, P., 2016).
- **Identity and Access Management (IAM):** The principle of least privilege, which is central to IAM, restricts access rights for users to the bare minimum necessary to complete their job functions. This minimization of access rights is crucial in reducing the potential damage of a data breach. IAM solutions in cloud computing have evolved to include multi-factor authentication (MFA), requiring users to present two or more separate credentials for verification, significantly enhancing security by adding an extra layer of defense beyond just a password (Kandukuri, B. R., 2009).
- **Security Assertions Markup Language (SAML):** SAML plays a critical role in implementing Single Sign-On (SSO) services, a user authentication process that permits a user to enter one set of login credentials to access multiple applications. The standard specifies how the authentication information is exchanged between the identity provider and the service provider, ensuring secure traversing of authentication data and automatic sign-in. SAML eliminates the need for passwords for each application, reducing the phishing attack surface and enhancing the user experience (Sharma, S., 2014).
- **Intrusion Detection and Prevention Systems (IDPS):** Cloud-based IDPS solutions represent a significant advancement in threat detection. These systems not only identify potential security breaches by analyzing network traffic for signs of attack but also take corrective actions in real-time. They leverage the cloud's high scalability to analyze vast datasets, using artificial intelligence and machine learning to identify and respond to abnormal activity patterns and potential threats quickly (Tianfield, H., 2012).
- **Tokenization:** In the realm of cloud security, tokenization has emerged as a robust alternative to encryption, especially for financial data. By replacing sensitive data elements with non-sensitive equivalents, referred to as tokens, tokenization ensures that the sensitive data is not accessible to unauthorized users. This method is particularly effective in payment systems, where credit card

information is replaced with tokens, thereby preserving the original data's confidentiality (Mell, P., 2012).

- **Disaster Recovery (DR) and Backup Solutions:** The cloud has revolutionized DR strategies by simplifying the backup and recovery of data and systems. Cloud-based DR solutions, known as Disaster Recovery as a Service (DRaaS), offer fast and flexible recovery of IT infrastructure and data. These solutions replicate and host servers in off-site locations, providing failover in the event of a man-made or natural catastrophe. This approach ensures business continuity and data integrity during critical times (Khan, N., 2016).
- **Virtual Private Networks (VPNs):** With the rise of remote work, VPNs have become integral to cloud security. They extend a private network across a public network, enabling users to send and receive data across shared or public networks as if their computing devices were directly connected to the private network. This setup ensures secure and encrypted connections, safeguarding data in transit from potential eavesdroppers (Kuyoro, S. O., 2011).
- **Compliance and Legal Frameworks:** Compliance standards and legal frameworks, such as GDPR, HIPAA, and SOX, have been instrumental in shaping cloud security protocols. These regulations mandate stringent data protection measures, holding organizations and cloud service providers accountable for breaches. Adherence to these standards not only ensures legal compliance but also fosters customer trust by demonstrating a commitment to data security (Nadeem, M. A., 2016).
- **Advanced Threat Protection (ATP):** ATP solutions in cloud computing are comprehensive and designed to detect and prevent sophisticated malware or hacking-based attacks. These solutions often integrate with existing security systems, providing an additional layer of defense that operates on heuristic principles, allowing them to detect threats that traditional antivirus software may miss. The integration of machine learning allows these systems to evolve continuously, adapting to new threats and attack vectors (Donald, A. C., 2013).
- **Secure Software Development Lifecycle (SSDLC):** Incorporating security into the software development lifecycle has never been more critical. SSDLC ensures that security is a priority from the initial stages of development, significantly reducing vulnerabilities in the final software products. This approach includes regular security audits, code reviews, and penetration testing, ensuring that software vulnerabilities are identified and mitigated early in the development process, thereby safeguarding data and applications in the cloud environment (Pfarr, F., 2014).

In the ever-evolving landscape of cloud computing, maintaining robust security protocols is imperative. The advanced security measures and protocols outlined above underscore the multi-faceted approach required to safeguard digital assets in the cloud environment. From sophisticated encryption techniques to comprehensive legal frameworks, these mechanisms collectively create a secure cloud ecosystem. As cyber threats continue to evolve, so too must the defenses, necessitating ongoing innovation and adaptation in cloud security measures to stay ahead of potential risks (Ugorji, B., 2013).

Balanced Focus on Various Security Issues

In addressing cloud security, it is imperative to maintain a balanced focus across a spectrum of security issues, rather than over-emphasizing certain aspects like data breaches at the expense of others. Identity and Access Management (IAM), for instance, is a critical area that demands attention. IAM in cloud

Table 2. Overview of advanced security measures in cloud computing

Security Measure	Description
Encryption Techniques	Utilizes advanced methods like homomorphic encryption and multi-layer encryption to secure data by transforming it into unreadable code, ensuring it cannot be deciphered without authorized access.
Identity and Access Management (IAM)	Employs the principle of least privilege and multi-factor authentication to ensure secure access controls, minimizing potential breach impacts.
Security Assertions Markup Language (SAML)	Facilitates secure Single Sign-On (SSO) services, allowing secure authentication and authorization information exchange across different services.
Intrusion Detection and Prevention Systems (IDPS)	Monitors network traffic to identify and respond to suspicious activities, leveraging AI and machine learning for real-time threat response.
Tokenization	Replaces sensitive data with non-sensitive tokens, preserving confidentiality, especially in payment systems.
Disaster Recovery (DR) and Backup Solutions	Provides cloud-based solutions for the quick recovery of IT infrastructure and data, ensuring business continuity in the event of disasters.
Virtual Private Networks (VPNs)	Extends private network security across public networks, ensuring safe data transmission by creating secure and encrypted connections.
Compliance and Legal Frameworks	Enforces adherence to international standards and regulations, mandating data protection measures and accountability.
Advanced Threat Protection (ATP)	Offers comprehensive protection against sophisticated malware or hacking attacks, integrating with existing security systems for enhanced defense.
Secure Software Development Lifecycle (SSDLC)	Integrates security protocols throughout the software development process, including regular audits, code reviews, and testing, to reduce vulnerabilities.

computing goes beyond mere user authentication; it encompasses the management of user identities, their authentication, authorization, and the overall security policies governing their access. Effective IAM strategies are essential in mitigating unauthorized access and reducing the risk of insider threats. Similarly, compliance with various regulatory standards is another area that requires equal emphasis. As cloud services often span multiple jurisdictions, understanding and adhering to a range of compliance requirements, such as GDPR for data protection and SOX for financial practices, is crucial in maintaining not just security but also legal and ethical integrity.

Another area that warrants a balanced focus is the management of system vulnerabilities. Cloud environments, with their complex architectures and reliance on shared resources, are susceptible to a variety of vulnerabilities that can be exploited by attackers. Regular vulnerability assessments, coupled with timely patch management and continuous monitoring, are key to identifying and addressing these security gaps. Furthermore, network security in cloud computing, often overshadowed by more sensational security issues, is fundamental to ensuring the safe transmission of data. Implementing robust encryption protocols for data in transit, deploying firewalls and intrusion detection systems, and ensuring secure API connections are vital components of a comprehensive cloud security strategy. By ensuring a balanced focus across these varied security issues, organizations can develop a more holistic and effective approach to cloud security, one that addresses the full range of potential vulnerabilities and threats.

MOBILE CLOUD COMPUTING: SECURITY DYNAMICS AND CONSIDERATIONS

Mobile Cloud Computing (MCC) represents a fusion of cloud computing and mobile applications, extending the benefits of powerful computational capabilities and scalable data storage to mobile devices. While this integration significantly enhances user experience and operational efficiency, it introduces unique security challenges. These challenges stem from the inherent characteristics of mobile devices, such as their diverse operating systems, the nature of mobile applications, and the different network protocols utilized in mobile communications (Donald, A., 2013). Table 3, named 'Key Security Considerations in Mobile Cloud Computing' encapsulates the primary security aspects unique to mobile cloud computing.

- **Security Vulnerabilities in Mobile Cloud Computing:** The integration of mobile devices with cloud services has exposed both platforms to increased security vulnerabilities. One primary concern is the risk of data breaches, as mobile devices can easily be lost or stolen, leading to unauthorized data access (Donald, A., 2013). Additionally, mobile applications often require access to sensitive data, creating potential privacy issues. The diversity in mobile operating systems also introduces complexities in maintaining consistent security protocols, as each system may have unique vulnerabilities (Donald, A., 2013).
- **Network Security Challenges:** Mobile cloud computing relies heavily on network communications, often utilizing public internet access points. This reliance increases the risk of network-based attacks, such as man-in-the-middle attacks, where attackers intercept sensitive data during transmission. The use of public Wi-Fi networks, known for their poor security, exacerbates this risk, making any data transmitted over these networks particularly vulnerable to interception and unauthorized access (Donald, A. C., 2013).
- **Resource Constraints:** Mobile devices are limited by their processing power, battery life, and storage capacity. These constraints can hinder the effectiveness of traditional security measures, such as encryption and regular software updates, as these processes often require substantial computational resources. Consequently, mobile devices are more susceptible to malware and other security threats, necessitating alternative security solutions optimized for resource constraints (Donald, A. C., 2013).
- **Privacy Concerns in MCC:** The nature of mobile devices, often personalized and always-on, raises significant privacy concerns. Location tracking, access to personal contacts, and other sensitive information stored on the device can be exposed to cloud services. This exposure is often exacerbated by the unclear or broad permissions required by mobile applications, leaving users uncertain about the extent of data shared with cloud providers and third-party services (Donald, A. C., 2013).
- **Legal and Compliance Issues:** Mobile cloud services often span multiple jurisdictions, leading to legal and compliance issues. Data stored or processed in different countries may be subject to varying regulations, particularly concerning data protection and privacy. Navigating these regulations is complex and poses challenges in ensuring consistent data protection measures across different regions (Donald, A. C., 2013).

Mobile cloud services often span multiple jurisdictions, leading to legal and compliance issues. Data stored or processed in different countries may be subject to varying regulations, particularly concerning

Table 3. Key security considerations in mobile cloud computing

Security Aspect	Description
Data Breaches	Risks associated with unauthorized data access due to device loss, theft, or application flaws.
Network Security Vulnerabilities	Increased exposure to attacks like man-in-the-middle due to reliance on public internet access.
Resource Constraints	Limitations in processing power, storage, and battery affect security measure effectiveness.
Privacy Risks	Potential exposure of sensitive personal information through device functions and applications.
Legal and Compliance Complexities	Challenges in navigating data protection laws across different jurisdictions and regions.

data protection and privacy. Navigating these regulations is complex and poses challenges in ensuring consistent data protection measures across different regions (Donald, A. C., 2013).

CHALLENGES AND SOLUTIONS

The evolution of cloud computing has continuously presented a range of security challenges. These challenges stem from the cloud's unique characteristics, such as multi-tenancy, resource pooling, and the broad network access it requires. However, with these challenges come innovative solutions that strive to ensure data integrity, confidentiality, and availability within cloud environments. This section delves into the prominent security challenges faced in cloud computing and the corresponding solutions being developed and implemented. This section delves into various cloud security challenges and their solutions, as succinctly captured in Table 4, named 'Overview of Cloud Security Challenges and Solutions.

- **Data Security and Privacy Challenges:**
  - Challenge: One of the foremost concerns in cloud computing is the security and privacy of data. Given that data stored in the cloud can be sensitive and valuable, there is a constant threat of unauthorized access, data breaches, and data leakage. The shared nature of the cloud, coupled with issues related to data residency and control, exacerbates these concerns.
  - Solution: Encryption techniques are paramount in safeguarding data. Advanced methods, such as homomorphic encryption, allow data processing without decrypting, thus maintaining confidentiality even during computations. Furthermore, robust access control policies and identity management solutions ensure that only authorized individuals can access certain data, thereby preserving data privacy.
- **System Vulnerabilities:**
  - Challenge: Cloud environments are often targets for cyber-attacks due to their high value. The systems can be vulnerable to various attacks, including DDoS attacks, which overwhelm the system with traffic, and man-in-the-middle attacks, where unauthorized entities intercept communications.

   - Solution: Regular vulnerability assessments and penetration testing can identify potential security gaps and allow for the fortification of the cloud environment. Implementing security protocols such as intrusion detection and prevention systems (IDPS) can also help monitor the system and thwart attacks before they inflict damage.
- **Compliance and Legal Challenges:**
   - Challenge: With data centers located worldwide, cloud computing often faces challenges in complying with various regional and national regulations concerning data protection, privacy, and cybersecurity. These compliance requirements can be complex and varied, making it difficult for cloud service providers and users to maintain compliance.
   - Solution: Compliance can be managed through a comprehensive understanding of the applicable laws and regulations, followed by the implementation of policies that adhere to these standards. Tools for continuous compliance monitoring and regular audits are essential in ensuring that all data handling and processing activities within the cloud are within legal parameters.
- **Identity and Access Management (IAM):**
   - Challenge: In cloud computing, verifying the identity of users and controlling their access to resources is crucial. The challenge lies in managing numerous users, often with varying levels of permissions and access to different resources.
   - Solution: IAM solutions in cloud computing facilitate the granting of access rights to users based on their identity. Multi-factor authentication (MFA) enhances security by requiring multiple forms of verification before granting access, thereby reducing the risk of unauthorized access.
- **Insecure APIs and Interfaces:**
   - Challenge: Cloud services are accessed and managed through various APIs and interfaces. If these are insecure, they present a significant security risk, potentially leading to the loss of data integrity, confidentiality, and availability.
   - Solution: Regular security assessments of APIs and interfaces can help identify and address security loopholes. Additionally, adopting best practices in API development, such as standard authentication methods and encrypted data transmissions, can mitigate risks associated with insecure APIs.
- **Advanced Persistent Threats (APTs):**
   - Challenge: APTs are prolonged and targeted cyber-attacks in which an unauthorized user gains access to a system and remains undetected for an extended period. These are particularly concerning in cloud computing, where attackers can gain access to vast amounts of data.
   - Solution: A multi-faceted approach is necessary to combat APTs. This includes employing sophisticated threat intelligence systems to detect unusual activity, along with incident response strategies that can quickly address any breaches. Furthermore, user education on security best practices is essential in preventing initial access points for APTs
- **Industry-Specific Considerations in Cloud Security:**
   - In the diverse landscape of cloud computing, industry-specific considerations play a crucial role in shaping security strategies. Different industries face unique challenges and regulatory requirements that significantly influence their approach to cloud security. For instance, in the healthcare sector, the protection of sensitive patient data is paramount, governed by

stringent regulations like HIPAA in the United States. Healthcare organizations leveraging cloud services must ensure that their providers are compliant with these regulations, implementing robust encryption and access controls to safeguard patient information. Similarly, in the financial sector, where data integrity and confidentiality are critical, cloud security measures must align with standards like PCI DSS. Financial institutions must navigate the complexities of protecting financial transactions and customer data while maintaining high availability and resilience against cyber threats.

- The government sector also presents distinct cloud security challenges, often revolving around data sovereignty and national security. Governmental agencies require cloud solutions that not only offer high levels of security but also ensure that data is stored and processed within national boundaries, adhering to country-specific data protection laws. This necessitates cloud providers to have localized data centers and specialized security protocols that align with national regulations. Additionally, industries like retail and manufacturing are increasingly adopting cloud technologies for better scalability and operational efficiency. However, they must address specific security concerns such as protecting customer data, intellectual property, and ensuring secure supply chain management. Each industry's unique requirements underscore the need for tailored cloud security solutions, emphasizing a sector-specific approach rather than a one-size-fits-all strategy.

In conclusion, while cloud computing presents various security challenges, ongoing advancements in cybersecurity are continually providing new solutions. It requires a collaborative effort from businesses, cloud service providers, and security professionals to maintain a secure cloud environment, ensuring that the benefits of cloud computing can be fully realized without compromising security.

Table 4. Overview of cloud security challenges and solutions

Cloud Security Challenges	Proposed Solutions
Data Security and Privacy: Risk of unauthorized access, data breaches, and leakage.	Encryption Techniques: Use of advanced encryption for data security and privacy, including methods like homomorphic encryption. Implementation of strict access control policies.
System Vulnerabilities: Susceptibility to cyber-attacks such as DDoS and man-in-the-middle attacks.	Security Protocols: Regular vulnerability assessments, penetration testing, and the adoption of intrusion detection and prevention systems.
Compliance and Legal Issues: Difficulties in adhering to regional and national regulations concerning data protection and cybersecurity.	Compliance Tools: Comprehensive understanding and implementation of laws and regulations, continuous compliance monitoring, and regular audits.
Identity and Access Management: Challenges in verifying user identity and managing access to resources.	IAM Solutions: Implementation of identity and access management solutions, use of multi-factor authentication.
Insecure APIs and Interfaces: Security risks associated with the use of various APIs and interfaces.	API Security: Regular security assessments of APIs, adoption of best practices in API development, and encrypted data transmissions.
Advanced Persistent Threats: Prolonged and targeted cyber-attacks with significant potential damage.	Threat Management: Employing advanced threat intelligence systems, incident response strategies, and user education on security best practices.

FUTURE RESEARCH DIRECTIONS

The advent of cloud computing has redefined the traditional boundaries of information technology, offering unprecedented levels of flexibility, scalability, and efficiency. However, the transition to cloud-based models comes with intricate security challenges that continue to evolve in tandem with the technology itself. The literature underscores the necessity for continuous research and development efforts to identify and address emerging threats preemptively, ensuring that security measures are not only reactive but also proactive. This necessitates a comprehensive exploration of future research directions, ranging from advanced cryptographic techniques to the human-centric aspects of cybersecurity. To understand the future research directions discussed here, refer to Table 5, named 'Future Research Directions in Cloud Security,' which highlights the main focus areas for upcoming advancements in cloud security.

- **Advanced Cryptographic Solutions in Cloud Security:**
  - Expanding Cryptographic Frontiers: Current cryptographic measures, though robust, face challenges in the cloud environment due to resource constraints and advanced threat vectors. Research dedicated to pioneering agile, resource-efficient, and highly secure cryptographic solutions is essential. This includes exploring post-quantum cryptography, capable of withstanding the computational power of quantum computers, and investigating the practicalities of integrating these futuristic models into existing cloud frameworks.
  - Confidential Computing: The concept of executing computations on encrypted data, or confidential computing, is a promising frontier. However, existing techniques like homomorphic encryption are not yet fully optimized for practical, large-scale applications. Intensive research is needed to enhance the efficiency of these protocols, reducing computational overhead and making them feasible for everyday cloud operations.
- **AI and Machine Learning for Enhanced Security Monitoring:**
  - Intelligent Threat Detection: Leveraging AI and ML for security analytics can transform threat detection and incident response within cloud environments. Future research should aim at evolving these systems to autonomously adapt to new threats, employing predictive analytics to anticipate potential security incidents before they occur. This requires a deep understanding of evolving threat landscapes and integrating that knowledge into machine learning models.
  - Securing AI Systems: As we increasingly rely on AI for security, ensuring the integrity of these AI systems becomes paramount. Research must focus on securing AI against adversarial attacks, ensuring data privacy, and developing robust algorithms that maintain efficacy even when threat actors attempt to corrupt the learning process.
- **Security in Edge Computing and IoT:**
  - Holistic Security Frameworks: The proliferation of IoT devices and the shift towards edge computing present unique security conundrums. There is a dire need for research into holistic security frameworks that encompass the diverse array of devices and communication models inherent in these systems. This includes developing lightweight, scalable security solutions specifically designed for resource-constrained IoT devices.
  - Unified Security Management: With the expanding network peripheries in edge computing, managing security across numerous endpoints becomes a challenge. Research should explore unified security management solutions that offer centralized oversight across cloud

and edge infrastructures, providing seamless security policy enforcement, monitoring, and threat mitigation.

- **Standardization and Security Benchmarking:**
  - Universal Security Metrics: The cloud ecosystem lacks a standardized approach to assessing and comparing security postures, leading to ambiguities in selecting cloud services. Research aimed at developing universal security benchmarks and metrics is crucial. These standards would facilitate objective comparisons among cloud service providers, enhancing transparency and informing better decision-making for consumers.
  - Compliance and Regulatory Evolution: As data protection regulations become more stringent and geographically varied, there is a need for research into adaptive, intelligent compliance tools capable of navigating this complex regulatory landscape. These tools would automatically update controls and processes in response to evolving legal requirements, significantly reducing the administrative burden on organizations.
- **Human Factors and Security Education:**
  - Behavioral Aspects of Cybersecurity: The human element is often the weakest link in security chains. Future research must delve into the psychological and sociological aspects of cybersecurity, aiming to understand why individuals engage in risky cyber behaviors and how best to encourage more secure practices. This research should span various demographics and cultural contexts, considering the global reach of cloud computing.
  - Innovative Education and Training Models: Traditional cybersecurity education methods are often ineffective in instilling lasting, practical security habits. Investigating innovative educational models, leveraging interactive, experiential learning techniques, and utilizing technology-assisted education can revolutionize how individuals learn about cybersecurity. This includes using virtual reality for immersive cybersecurity training scenarios and employing AI to personalize learning experiences.
- **Emerging Technologies in Cloud Security:**
  - The realm of cloud security is rapidly evolving, with emerging technologies such as Artificial Intelligence (AI), Machine Learning (ML), blockchain, and quantum computing playing increasingly pivotal roles. AI and ML, in particular, are revolutionizing how security threats are identified and mitigated in cloud environments. By leveraging vast datasets and learning from patterns of attacks, these technologies enable predictive analytics, offering a proactive approach to security. AI-driven systems can autonomously detect and respond to threats in real-time, significantly reducing the window of vulnerability that human-operated systems might face. Moreover, the integration of AI in cloud security is not just about threat detection; it extends to enhancing security protocols, automating compliance checks, and optimizing resource allocation for better security management.
  - Blockchain technology, known for its robustness in the financial sector, is another emerging technology with significant implications for cloud security. Its decentralized nature and cryptographic foundation offer a new paradigm for securing cloud transactions and data storage. Blockchain can be used to create immutable logs of all activities within the cloud environment, providing a transparent and tamper-proof audit trail. This feature is particularly valuable in sectors where data integrity and traceability are paramount. On the other hand, quantum computing presents both a challenge and an opportunity for cloud security. While its immense processing power poses a threat to current cryptographic standards, it also opens

Table 5. Future research directions in cloud security

Research Area	Description
Advanced Cryptographic Solutions	Exploration of agile, resource-efficient cryptographic methods, including post-quantum cryptography and practical applications of confidential computing.
AI and Machine Learning in Security	Development of autonomous, intelligent systems for predictive threat analytics and securing AI algorithms against adversarial manipulations.
Security Challenges in Edge Computing and IoT	Creation of comprehensive security frameworks for IoT and edge computing, emphasizing lightweight solutions and unified security management.
Standardization and Security Benchmarking	Establishment of universal security metrics for objective assessment and comparison, along with adaptive tools for navigating global regulatory landscapes.
Human Factors in Cybersecurity	Investigation into the behavioral aspects of cybersecurity practices and development of innovative, technology-assisted educational models.

avenues for developing quantum-resistant encryption methods. Research in quantum cryptography is already underway, aiming to develop security protocols that can withstand the potential of quantum computing, ensuring the long-term security of cloud data.

The future of cloud security is a multifaceted arena that demands a concerted effort from academia, industry, and governments worldwide. The outlined research directions emphasize the need for a paradigm shift in our approach to cloud security, advocating for proactive, anticipatory measures that adapt to the ever-evolving digital landscape. By investing in these research areas, we pave the way for a more secure digital future, where trust and confidence in cloud technologies foster continued innovation and growth. The journey ahead, though replete with challenges, holds the promise of groundbreaking discoveries and advancements that will redefine the essence of cybersecurity in the cloud era.

CONCLUSION

As we navigate the digital transformation era, cloud computing has emerged not just as a technological trend, but as an essential fabric of modern IT infrastructure. Its benefits, from scalability and flexibility to cost efficiency, are undeniable. However, as this comprehensive analysis has revealed, the journey to cloud adoption is fraught with security challenges that are unique to the cloud environment.

Throughout this discourse, we have dissected the multifaceted nature of cloud security, highlighting the inherent vulnerabilities introduced by the shared, on-demand nature of cloud services. The issues of data privacy, loss of control over data, and the complexities introduced by multi-tenancy and extensive use of virtualization have been recurrent themes. These challenges are further compounded when cloud services are accessed via mobile devices, introducing another layer of security considerations.

Despite these challenges, the industry's response has been robust. We have explored many advanced security measures and protocols designed to fortify cloud environments. From sophisticated encryption methods to multi-factor authentication and AI-driven security solutions, it is evident that security in the cloud is not a static target but a continuous journey of adaptation and improvement.

Looking ahead, the horizon is rich with opportunities for innovation. The future of cloud security is a tapestry waiting to be woven with threads of advanced cryptography, enhanced user awareness, standardized security benchmarks, and more resilient regulatory frameworks. The integration of AI and machine learning into cloud security presents a particularly promising frontier, with the potential to revolutionize threat detection and response.

However, the path forward is not without its obstacles. This analysis has underscored the need for a collaborative approach to cloud security, one that involves shared responsibility between cloud service providers and consumers. Furthermore, the legal and ethical implications of cloud computing, particularly concerning data sovereignty and privacy, will require concerted global effort and harmonization of laws and regulations.

In conclusion, securing the cloud is an endeavor that calls for a holistic approach, one that encompasses advanced technological tools, proactive regulatory measures, and an informed and vigilant user base. As we stand on the cusp of technological advancements like quantum computing and the proliferation of IoT, the imperative for robust cloud security mechanisms has never been more critical. The collective challenge lies in fostering a security culture that evolves in tandem with the technologies it seeks to safeguard, ensuring that the immense potential of cloud computing can be fully realized without compromising the sanctity of security and trust.

REFERENCES

Basan, M. (2023). 13 Cloud Security Best Practices & [eSecurity Planet. Retrieved from https://www.esecurityplanet.com/cloud/cloud-security-best-practices/]. *Trends in Pharmacological Sciences, 2023.*

Coppolino, L., D'Antonio, S., Mazzeo, G., & Romano, L. (2017). Cloud security: Emerging threats and current solutions. *Computers & Electrical Engineering*, *59*, 126–140. doi:10.1016/j.compeleceng.2016.03.004

Donald, A. C., Oli, S. A., & Arockiam, L. (2013). Mobile cloud security issues and challenges: A perspective. *International Journal of Engineering and Innovative Technology*, *3*(1), 401. https://www.researchgate.net/profile/A-Cecil-Donald/publication/260981217

Ermetic Team. (2022). *Lessons Learned in Cloud Security from Lapsus$ Surfacing*. Ermetic. https://ermetic.com/blog/cloud/lessons-learned-in-cloud-security-from-lapsus-surfacing/

Farnga, M. (2018). Cloud Security Architecture and Implementation-A practical approach. arXiv preprint arXiv:1808.03892. https://doi.org//arXiv.1808.03892 doi:10.48550

Kandukuri, B. R., & Rakshit, A. (2009). Cloud security issues. In *2009 IEEE International Conference on Services Computing* (pp. 517-520). IEEE. https://doi.org/10.1109/SCC.2009.84

Khan, M. W., Khan, S. Y., Altaf, S., & Ali, M. W. (2021). A REVIEW OF THE SECURITY ISSUES IN CLOUD COMPUTING AND ITS REMEDIAL ACTION. *INFORMATION TECHNOLOGY IN INDUSTRY*, *9*(1), 444–455. doi:10.17762/itii.v9i1.150

Khan, N., & Al-Yasiri, A. (2016). Identifying cloud security threats to strengthen cloud computing adoption framework. *Procedia Computer Science*, *94*, 485–490. doi:10.1016/j.procs.2016.08.075

Kumar, R., & Goyal, R. (2019). On cloud security requirements, threats, vulnerabilities and countermeasures: A survey. *Computer Science Review*, *33*, 1–48. doi:10.1016/j.cosrev.2019.05.002

Kuyoro, S. O., Ibikunle, F., & Awodele, O. (2011). Cloud computing security issues and challenges. [IJCN]. *International Journal of Computer Networks, 3*(5), 247–255. http://eprints.lmu.edu.ng/1390/

Mell, P. (2012). What's special about cloud security? *IT Professional, 14*(4), 6–8. doi:10.1109/MITP.2012.84

Nadeem, M. A. (2016). Cloud computing: Security issues and challenges. *Journal of Wireless Communications, 1*(1), 10–15. doi:10.21174/jowc.v1i1.73

Pfarr, F., Buckel, T., & Winkelmann, A. (2014). Cloud Computing Data Protection--A Literature Review and Analysis. In *2014 47th Hawaii International Conference on System Sciences* (pp. 5018-5027). IEEE. 10.1109/HICSS.2014.616

Samarati, P., & De Capitani di Vimercati, S. (2016). Cloud security: Issues and concerns. In *Encyclopedia of cloud computing* (pp. 205–219). Wiley. doi:10.1002/9781118821930.ch17

Shahzad, F. (2014). State-of-the-art survey on cloud computing security challenges, approaches and solutions. *Procedia Computer Science, 37*, 357–362. doi:10.1016/j.procs.2014.08.053

Sharma, S., Gupta, G., & Laxmi, P. R. (2014). *A survey on cloud security issues and techniques.* arXiv preprint arXiv:1403.5627. https://doi.org//arXiv.1403.5627 doi:10.48550

Sridhar, S. D. S. S., & Smys, S. (2016). A survey on cloud security issues and challenges with possible measures. In *International conference on inventive research in engineering and technology* (*Vol. 4*). Research Gate. https://www.researchgate.net/publication/304157460

Tabrizchi, H., & Kuchaki Rafsanjani, M. (2020). A survey on security challenges in cloud computing: Issues, threats, and solutions. *The Journal of Supercomputing, 76*(12), 9493–9532. doi:10.1007/s11227-020-03213-1

Tianfield, H. (2012). Security issues in cloud computing. In *2012 IEEE International Conference on Systems, Man, and Cybernetics (SMC)* (pp. 1082-1089). IEEE. https://doi.org/10.1109/ICSMC.2012.6377874

Ugorji, B., Abouzakhar, N., & Sapsford, J. (2013). Cloud Security: A Review of Recent Threats and Solution Models. In *ICCSM2013-Proceedings of the International Conference on Cloud Security Management: ICCSM 2013* (p. 115). Academic Conferences Limited. https://core.ac.uk/download/pdf/19772349.pdf

KEY TERMS AND DEFINITIONS

Artificial Intelligence (AI): The simulation of human intelligence in machines that are programmed to think like humans and mimic their actions.

Blockchain: A system of recording information in a way that makes it difficult or impossible to change, hack, or cheat the system.

Compliance: The action or fact of complying with a wish or command, especially regarding legal standards and regulations.

Cybersecurity: The practice of protecting systems, networks, and programs from digital attacks.

Data Privacy: The aspect of information technology that deals with the ability an organization or individual has to determine what data in a computer system can be shared with third parties.

Data Sovereignty: The concept that information which has been converted and stored in binary digital form is subject to the laws of the country in which it is located.

Encryption: The process of converting information or data into a code, especially to prevent unauthorized access.

Identity and Access Management (IAM): A framework for business processes that facilitates the management of electronic or digital identities.

Intrusion Detection System (IDS): A system that monitors networks for malicious activities or policy violations, reporting any detected issues for further action.

Machine Learning (ML): A branch of AI and computer science which focuses on the use of data and algorithms to imitate the way that humans learn, gradually improving its accuracy.

Mobile Cloud Computing (MCC): A combination of cloud computing and mobile computing to provide rich computational resources to mobile users, network operators, as well as cloud computing providers.

Multi-Tenancy: A cloud computing architecture where a single instance of software serves multiple customers or tenants.

Network Security: The practice of preventing and protecting against unauthorized intrusion into corporate networks.

Quantum Computing: A type of computing that takes advantage of quantum phenomena like superposition and quantum entanglement.

Resource Exhaustion: A situation where the demands on a system's resources exceed the capacity of that system, leading to degraded performance or system failure.

Security Protocols: Rules and algorithms designed to protect data and manage network traffic securely.

System Vulnerabilities: Weaknesses in a computer system that can be exploited by a threat actor, such as a hacker.

Threat Mitigation: The process of reducing the severity, seriousness, or painfulness of something, especially in the context of cybersecurity threats.

Virtualization: The creation of a virtual version of something, such as a server, a storage device, network resources, or an operating system.

Chapter 12
Big Data and Cloud Computing

Dina Darwish
Ahram Canadian University, Egypt

ABSTRACT

Big data helps organizations of all sizes track performance, detect issues, and find growth opportunities. Big data has advantages, but supporting it with computer resources and software services may cost even the biggest organizations. Sales, IoT sensors, and user feedback give analytics, and clouds can handle big data. Cloud computing changed computer infrastructure, since all services are cloud-based. Cloud computing is great for massive data storage, administration, and analytics due to its flexibility, pay-as-you-go or pay-per-use strategy, and minimal upfront cost. This chapter examines big data and its analytics with cloud computing for businesses and end users and discusses the key concepts of big data and cloud computing; the advantages, benefits, and disadvantages of big data analytics; cloud service types for big data analytics; security challenges; differences between big data and cloud computing; applications of big data analytics; choosing the cloud deployment model; and security and research issues in big data.

INTRODUCTION

Organizations of varying scales acknowledge the significance of data and employ it to assess performance, identify challenges, and uncover novel avenues for expansion. The utilization of big data has become essential in the field of machine learning for the purpose of training intricate models and enabling the advancement of Artificial Intelligence (AI).

Big data offers advantages, however, the substantial amount of computing resources and software services needed to sustain big data projects can impose financial and intellectual strains on even the most sizable enterprises. Cloud computing has made substantial advancements in addressing the need for processing and storing vast amounts of data. The provision of extensive computing resources and services enables the feasibility of big data initiatives for organizations, with the potential for near-limitless capabilities.

This chapter will encompass an analysis of the limitations, an evaluation of the cloud models, and an examination of the current services offered for big data in the cloud. The concepts of big data and

DOI: 10.4018/979-8-3693-0900-1.ch012

cloud computing, although distinct, have become closely interconnected to the point where they are almost synonymous. The definition and interconnection of these two concepts are of utmost importance.

The term "big data" encompasses vast volumes of data that can be categorized as structured, semi-structured, or unstructured. The subject matter pertains to analytics and is commonly obtained from diverse sources, encompassing user input, Internet-of-Things (IoT) sensors, and sales data.

The primary concern associated with big data pertains to the extensive computing and networking infrastructure necessary for the establishment of a large-scale data center. The financial commitment associated with acquiring servers, storage systems, and dedicated networks can be significant, along with the requisite software proficiency needed to establish an effective distributed computing infrastructure. Furthermore, the value of big data to an organization is contingent upon its operational state, rendering it devoid of significance when it is not in use. For an extended period, the technological demands of big data have limited its accessibility to only the most substantial and financially well-endowed organizations. The field of cloud computing has experienced significant advancements in this particular domain.

Cloud computing has revolutionized the utilization and conceptualization of computing infrastructure. The scope of cloud paradigms has been broadened to include any entity that can be classified as a service. Cloud computing has become a highly sought-after solution for big data storage, management, and analytics due to its various benefits. These advantages include its elasticity, pay-as-you-go or pay-per-use pricing model, and minimal initial investment, among others. Amazon, Google, and Microsoft have developed their own cost-effective big data systems, recognizing the growing significance of big data in various organizational and disciplinary contexts. These systems possess the capability to scale in order to meet the needs of businesses across various sizes. The increased adoption of the term Analytics as a Service (AaaS) has been driven by its ability to offer a faster and more efficient approach to integrating, transforming, and visualizing different types of Data Analytics.

This chapter discusses the Significance of implementing Big data and its analytics along with the use of cloud computing for both organizations, and end users, also, this chapter focuses on the main concepts related to Big data and cloud computing, advantages and benefits of Big data analytics, the cloud service types for Big data analytics, and security issues for Big data and cloud clouting, along with other topics in this area. The main topics to be covered in this chapter includes the following;

- Big Data and Cloud Computing Main Concepts
- Types of Big data analytics
- The integration of Big data and Machine learning
- Benefits of Big data analytics
- Difference between Big data and cloud computing
- The cloud service types for Big data analytics
- Applications of Big data analytics
- Trends in applying Big data analytics in the cloud
- Security issues for Big data and cloud computing
- Pros and cons of Big data in the cloud
- Choosing the right cloud deployment model
- Real case studies of applying Big data analytics with cloud computing
- Research issues in Big data
- Future scopes of Big data analytics in the cloud

Also, this chapter is organized as follows; the first section contains the background, then, the second section includes the main focus of the chapter, including the main topics mentioned in the previous section, then finally, comes the conclusion section.

BACKGROUND

The term "big data" also encompasses the process of analyzing vast quantities of data with the aim of addressing a specific inquiry or identifying recurring trends and patterns. The analysis of data involves the application of various mathematical procedures, which are selected based on the nature of the data, the number of sources utilized, and the underlying objective of the analysis for the business. In order to partition and structure intricate analyses, distributed computing software systems such as Apache Hadoop, Databricks, and Cloudera are utilized.

Cloud computing companies frequently adopt a "software as a service" (SaaS) approach in order to facilitate convenient data management for consumers. Frequently, a console that has the capability to accept specialized commands and arguments is provided, although all tasks can also be performed using the user interface of the website. This bundle typically comprises database management systems, cloud-based virtual machines and containers, identity management systems, machine learning capabilities, and various other components.

Massive network-based systems frequently give rise to the generation of Big Data. The format may vary between conventional and non-standard formats. In cases where the data is not in a conventional format, the artificial intelligence capabilities of the Cloud Computing provider may be utilized alongside machine learning techniques to normalize the data. The data can subsequently be retrieved via the Cloud Computing platform and utilized in various manners. It is possible to search, modify, and store the information for future use.

The implemented cloud architecture facilitates the processing of Big Data in real-time. The system has the capability to comprehend substantial volumes of data from high-demanding systems instantaneously. One commonality between Big Data and Cloud Computing is the accelerated processing capability facilitated by the cloud, resulting in significantly reduced time for Big Data analytics compared to previous methods. The study (Mallika and Selvamuthukumaran, 2017) utilized the Hadoop framework for the analysis of workload prediction in cloud computing data. A research (Nodarakis et al., 2016) employed Hadoop for the purpose of conducting large-scale analysis of tweets in the publication. In their study, authors (Meng et al., 2014) introduced an innovative approach to analyze data within service recommender systems by leveraging Hadoop and the MapReduce parallel processing paradigm. The publications' findings suggest that the Hadoop architecture is a highly effective solution for batch processing tasks that do not require real-time processing. Ongoing research endeavors are being undertaken to propose improvements and novel ideas for the Hadoop framework. The research paper (Bhimani et al., 2017) presents a novel approach that integrates the Hadoop framework with the MPI/OpenMP system in order to enhance processing speed. The literature has emphasized the open questions surrounding Hadoop security, specifically regarding the absence of encryption at the storage and network layers.

The authors of this article (Ortiz et al., 2015) propose a new security architecture for G-Hadoop based on public key cryptography and the SSL protocol. In addition to Hadoop, the following articles investigate and propose various additional frameworks. The authors of (Zhaoa et al., 2014) examined the performance of large data applications on Spark using various virtualization frameworks. The infrastructure of another open source framework, Apache Storm, is examined in a review study (Huang et al., 2015). The authors of the study (Miller et al., 2016) explore the development of big data frameworks and present Scalation, a new design framework built using the Scala programming language. Experiments are used to test the Spark, Samza, Kafka, and Scalation frameworks.

The authors of the research (Xhafa et al., 2015) explored the Yahoo!S4 framework for real-time stream processing. The authors of (Baek et al., 2015) describe a novel cloud-based architecture for managing massive data in smart grids. A comprehensive comparison examination of three major frameworks, Apache Hadoop, Project Storm, and Apache Drill, is undertaken in the article (Chandarana & Vijayalakshmi, 2014). The survey article (Singh & Reddy, 2015) also includes a theoretical comparison of the major big data frameworks. (Koliopoulos et al., 2015) investigate Distributed WekaSpark, a distributed Spark framework for the Weka workbench.

The first publication assessed on this subject (Zicari et al., 2016) discusses the necessary technology for big data project implementation. In-memory databases, NoSQL and NewSQL systems, and Hadoop-based solutions are all covered in this article. A article (Sharma et al., 2014) compares the performance of NoSQL databases BigTable, Cassandra, HBase, MongoDB, CouchDB, and CrowdDB. In a research, authors (Matallah & Belalem, 2017) compare the performance of HBase with MongoDB. The authors (Dede et al., 2016) describe a novel approach that blends Cassandra with MapReduce. The paper (Ptiek & Vrdoljak, 2017) provides a review of the research done for integrating a data warehouse with MapReduce for large data processing. A overview of in-memory large data management systems is included in the paper (Zhang et al., 2015). The authors of paper (Oussous et al., 2017) also give a study of contemporary big data technologies for the Data Processing Layer, Data Querying Layer, Data Access Layer, and Management Layer.

The paper (Peng et al., 2017) investigates the solution of different forms of unstructured data storage, analyses all the challenges in the storage system, and summarizes the important concerns to accomplish unstructured data unified storage. The authors of a study (Dehdouh et al., 2015) present novel methods for huge data warehouse deployment using column-oriented NoSQL DBMS. A comprehensive categorization for current big data models is performed in the study (Sharma, 2015). The integration of NoSQL database HBase with enterprise platform is introduced in the paper (Chang et al., 2015). A paper (Venkatraman et al., 2016) compared SQL databases against NoSQL databases and the four NoSQL data architectures (document-oriented, key-value pairs, column-oriented, or graphs). In the study (Santos & Costa, 2016), Hive is used to build a novel architecture that allows for the automated translation of a multidimensional schema into a tabular schema. The last research (Armbrust et al., 2015) assesses the performance of Spark SQL. According to the findings of a study (Canaj & Xhuvani, 2018), the Hadoop framework is best suited for workloads when speed is not crucial. It is an excellent solution for batch processing that is not time-critical. It is an open source solution that is simpler to implement than other options. Storm and S4 are common frameworks for real-time large-scale streaming data processing. These frameworks offer very low processing latency. When used with Kafka, the Samza framework is an excellent option for stream processing. Flink frameworks can handle both stream and batch processing. It has been greatly optimized, yet it remains unstable. Spark is an excellent choice for an interactive environment. Apache drill is also ideal for ad hoc and interactive analysis.

Traditional relational database management solutions are unsuitable for handling large amounts of data. NoSQL database management solutions are intended for use in high-volume, cloud-based applications. MongoDB, Cassandra, CouchDB, CrowdDB, Hypertable, HBASE, Couchbase, and more open source NoSQL databases are available. NoSQL databases are extremely scalable, adaptable, and suitable for large data storage and processing. The present difficulty with NoSQL databases is that they do not provide a declarative query language akin to SQL, and there is no one, unified NoSQL database paradigm. Integrated solutions are being investigated and offered. Applications that use both relational and procedural queries perform better. Numerous studies are still being conducted to improve data storage and processing processes. Data heterogeneity is another issue that is being researched. NoSQL data structures are capable of processing petabytes of data. Exabyte-scale data processing is still an unsolved challenge.

MAIN FOCUS OF THE CHAPTER

Big Data and Cloud Computing Main Concepts

One difficulty that scholars have battled with is what constitutes "big data." As a result, Gartner analyst Doug Laney established the 3V model in 2001, which consists of three elements that must be present in order for data to be termed "big data": volume, velocity, and variety. Volume is a trait or feature that influences the amount of data, which is often measured in Terabytes or Petabytes. For example, social networks such as Facebook keep images of users, among other things. Because of the high number of members, it is believed that Facebook stores over 250 billion photographs and over 2.5 trillion postings. This is a massive quantity of data that must be saved and analyzed. Volume is the most defining characteristic of 'big data' (Gewirtz, 2018). Tera or Peta level data is commonly regarded 'large' in terms of volume, albeit this relies on the capability of individuals analyzing the data and the tools available to them (Gewirtz, 2018).

The second quality or feature is velocity. This refers to the amount of data created or the pace at which it must be processed and analyzed (Gewirtz, 2018). Facebook users, for example, upload around 900 million images every day, which equates to about 104 uploaded photos per second. As a result, Facebook must analyze, store, and retrieve this information in real time for its users. With an increasing trend, social media and the Internet of Things (IoT) are the leading data producers.

The third feature is variety, which refers to various forms of data produced from various sources. "Big Data" is often divided into three categories: structured data (transactional data, spreadsheets, relational databases, and so on), semi-structured data (Extensible Markup Language - XML, web server logs, and so on), and unstructured data (social media postings, audio, photos, and video, among others). In the literature, 'meta-data,' which represents data about data, is suggested as a fourth category. The majority of data nowadays (80%) falls into the category of unstructured data (Akhtar, 2018). The tree aspects of big data have been supplemented throughout time by two new ones: veracity and value.

Veracity is synonymous with quality, which is data that is clean, accurate, and has something to give (WhishWorks, 2019). The idea is also connected to the dependability of extracted data (for example, customer emotions in social media are not very dependable data). The value of data is proportional to the social or economic value that it may produce. The amount of value that data may provide is also determined by the expertise of individuals who utilize it (WhishWorks, 2019). Figure 1 illustrates main characteristics of Big data.

Data processing is classified into two types: batch and stream. ***Batch processing*** occurs in chunks of data that have been stored over time. Because batch data is often large, it takes longer to process. Hadoop MapReduce is widely regarded as the finest framework for batch data processing (Akhtar, 2018). This strategy works effectively in instances when real-time analytics are not required and massive amounts of data must be processed to provide more thorough insights.

Stream processing, on the other hand, is essential for real-time data processing and analysis. Stream processing enables data to be processed as it arrives. This data is quickly put into analytics systems, resulting in instant outcomes. Many situations may benefit from such an approach, such as fraud detection, in which abnormalities that indicate fraud are recognized in real time. Another use case would be online merchants, where real-time processing would allow them to accumulate vast histories of customer interactions in order to propose new purchases to customers in real time (Akhtar, 2018).

Cloud computing is a term used to describe the provision of various computer services, including servers, storage, databases, networking, software, analytics, intelligence, and other related services, through the utilization of the Internet-based Cloud infrastructure. Cloud computing presents itself as a feasible substitute for on-premises data centers. The comprehensive management of all aspects related to an on-premises data center is imperative, encompassing the procurement and installation of hardware, virtualization, operating system and program installation, network establishment, firewall configuration, and data storage configuration. Once all the necessary setup has been completed, it becomes our responsibility to ensure the ongoing maintenance of the system throughout its entire lifespan.

The cloud environment provides a user-friendly web interface through which users can manage various resources such as compute, storage, network, and applications. However, in the case of opting for Cloud Computing, the responsibility of hardware procurement and maintenance will be assumed by a cloud provider. In addition, they offer a wide array of software and platform as a service options. It is permissible to engage the services of any necessary service provider. The payment for cloud computing services will be determined based on usage.

The advent of cloud computing has revolutionized the abstraction and utilization of computer infrastructure. The scope of cloud concepts has been expanded to encompass any entity that can be considered a service (hence denoted as x a service). The numerous benefits of cloud computing, including its flexibility, pay-as-you-go or pay-per-use pricing model, minimal initial investment, and other factors, have established it as a viable and sought-after solution for the purposes of storing, managing, and analyzing large volumes of data (Yadav & Sohal, 2017).

Due to the growing recognition of big data's significance in numerous organizations and industries, prominent service providers like Amazon, Google, and Microsoft have taken the initiative to offer their own economically viable big data platforms. These solutions offer scalability to businesses of different sizes. Consequently, the term Analytics as a Service (AaaS) has acquired significance as a more expedient and efficient method for integrating, modifying, and presenting diverse forms of data.

The processing of large data for analytics differs from the processing of standard transactional data, as stated in a research (Kimball and Ross, 2013). In traditional settings, the initial step involves the examination of data, followed by the development of a model design and the establishment of a database structure. The diagram illustrating the sequence of big data processing is presented in Figure 2 as referenced by a research (Akhtar, 2018). The process commences by gathering data from various sources, including diverse files, systems, sensors, and the Internet. The aforementioned data is subsequently stored on a medium that possesses the capability to effectively process data with regards to its volume, variety, and velocity. This medium is commonly referred to as the "landing zone." In general, this system is classified as a distributed file system. Once data has been stored, it undergoes a series of modifications to ensure its continued efficiency and scalability. According to a research (Kimball and Ross, 2013), these entities are subsequently integrated into distinct analytical tasks, operational reporting, databases, or the extraction of raw data.

The shift from the Extract, Transform, Load (ETL) paradigm to the Extract, Load, Transform (ELT) paradigm. The ETL (Extract, Transform, Load) process involves the extraction of data from a specific data source, followed by the implementation of any required transformations, and ultimately the loading of the transformed data into a data warehouse. This enables the execution of reports and queries against the data warehouse. One drawback of this particular technique or paradigm is its high level of input/output (I/O) operations, string manipulation, variable manipulation, and data parsing (LaprinthX, 2018). The concept of ELT (Extract, Load, Transform) involves transferring the computationally intensive task of data transformation to the cloud, as opposed to relying on an on-premise service that is already overwhelmed with routine transaction processing (LaprinthX, 2018). This suggests that the utilization of data warehousing solutions encompasses a wide range of data types, such as structured, semi-structured, unstructured, and raw data, thereby rendering data staging unnecessary. The strategy employed in this approach utilizes the concept of "data lakes," which differ from OLAP (Online Analytical Processing) data warehouses in that they do not require data transformation prior to loading (LaprinthX, 2018).

The primary differentiation lies in the spatial placement of the transformational procedure. The ELT approach offers numerous advantages in comparison to the traditional ETL paradigm. As previously mentioned, a crucial factor is the timely consumption of data in any given format once it becomes accessible. One additional benefit is the ability to modify only the specific data required for a particular analysis. If the existing framework does not facilitate the incorporation of novel analytical approaches, it may be necessary to make adjustments to the entire data pipeline and structure within the Online Analytical Processing (OLAP) system through the Extract, Transform, Load (ETL) process (Xplenty, 2019).

Figure 1. Big data main characteristics

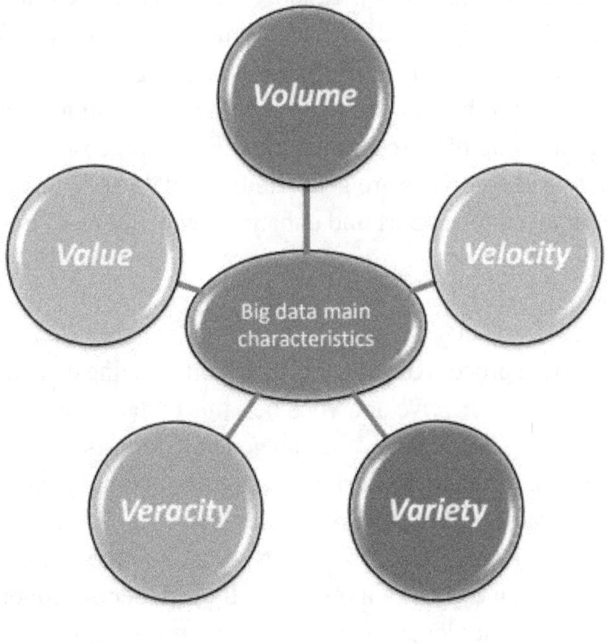

Figure 2. Flow of the processing of Big Data (Akhtar, 2018)

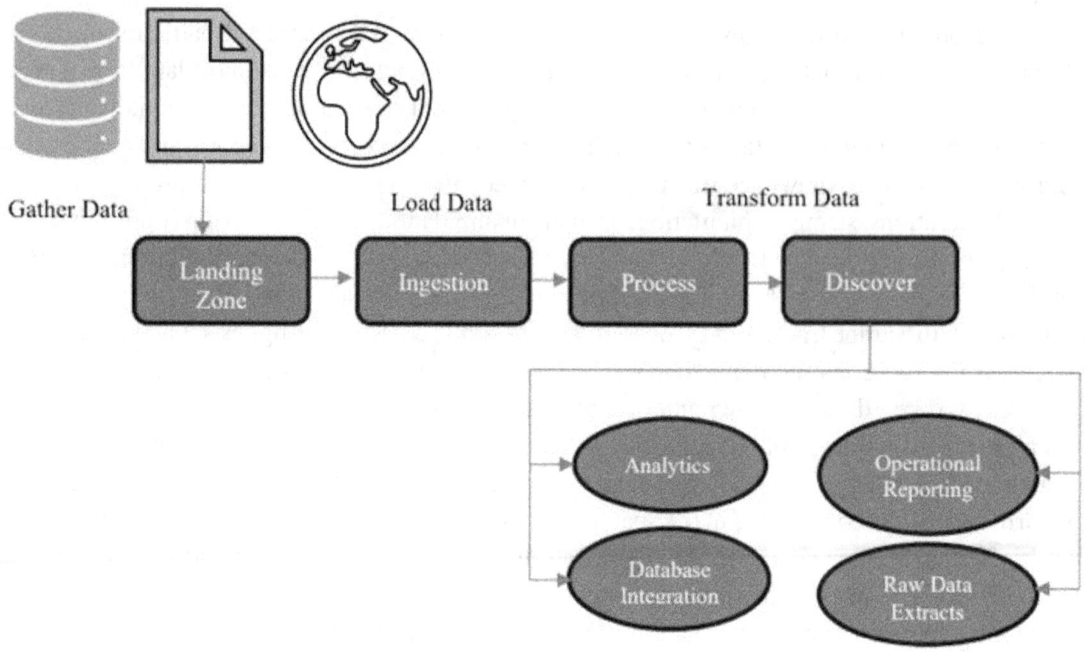

Types of Big Data Analytics

The utilization of big data analytics enables the facilitation of data-driven decision-making processes that are substantiated by scientific evidence, thereby enabling decisions to be grounded in factual data rather than solely relying on past experiences or intuitive judgements. There exist four primary classifications of analytics, namely descriptive analytics, diagnostic analytics, predictive analytics, and prescriptive analytics. Each of these approaches employs distinct methodologies and analysis algorithms in order to attain its outcomes. This implies that varying types of analytical outputs may require distinct quantities of data, storage, and processing resources. The complexity and cost of the analytical environment increase as high-value analytical outcomes are generated. Big data analytics can be classified into four main categories and are employed to support and enhance a wide range of business decisions.

Descriptive Analytics

Descriptive analytics refers to the process of analyzing and summarizing data in order to gain insights and understand patterns and trends. Descriptive analytics pertains to data that is easily comprehensible and amenable to analysis. By utilizing this dataset, one can generate reports and information that effectively depict the sales and profits of a business. Descriptive analytics is employed to furnish insights regarding events that have already transpired. In this particular analytical framework, data is contextualized with the purpose of generating meaningful information. What was the sales volume observed over the preceding 12-month period? This includes an inquiry into the number of support calls made, categorized by geographical location and severity level, as well as the monthly commission received by individual salespersons. Around 80% of the data analytics generated are descriptive in character. Descriptive analytics possess relatively lower value compared to other forms of analytics and require a limited range of expertise. Descriptive analytics is commonly performed through the utilization of ad hoc reporting or dashboards. The reports exhibit a predominantly static characteristic and present historical data through the utilization of visual aids such as graphs or data grids. Operational data repositories are queried within organizational systems, such as Customer Relationship Management (CRM) or Enterprise Resource Planning (ERP) systems. To provide an example, a prominent pharmaceutical corporation analyzed data obtained from its various offices and research facilities during the course of the epidemic. Through the utilization of descriptive analytics, the organization successfully identified and consolidated underutilized areas and divisions, resulting in substantial cost savings amounting to millions of dollars.

Diagnostic Analytics

Diagnostic analytics is a type of data analytics that focuses on examining historical data to identify patterns, trends, and anomalies. Diagnostic analytics can enhance the understanding of issues within business organizations. The utilization of Big data technologies and tools enables users to extract and retrieve data, which facilitates the analysis of issues and their proactive mitigation. Despite the continuous addition of products to customers' shopping carts, the clothing store has experienced a decline in its revenues. The application of diagnostic analytics proved to be valuable in ascertaining the root cause behind the persistent malfunctioning of the payment page over a span of several weeks.

Diagnostic analytics employ queries that focus on the causal factors of an event in order to ascertain the underlying causes of a previous occurrence. This type of analytics is utilized to discern the pertinent data associated with specific phenomena, facilitating the investigation of causative factors behind occurrences. Examples of inquiries that can be addressed include determining the reasons behind a decline in sales during Q2 compared to Q1, understanding the disparity in support calls between the Eastern and Western regions, or examining the factors contributing to an increase in patient re-admission rates over the past three months. Although diagnostic analytics necessitate a more specialized skill set, they hold greater value compared to descriptive analytics. Diagnostic analytics often require the collection of data from multiple sources, which must be stored in a manner that facilitates both drill-down and roll-up analysis. Interactive visualization tools enable users to identify trends and patterns by examining the outcomes of diagnostic analytics. The inquiries are conducted on multidimensional data that is stored in analytical processing systems and are of a greater complexity compared to those of descriptive analytics.

Diagnostic analytics provide more precise and detailed insights compared to descriptive analytics, which is primarily focused on summarizing data. Gaining insight into the factors that contribute to business outcomes is of paramount importance for a company's ability to foster growth and prevent the recurrence of previous mistakes. Diagnostic analytics empower organizations to focus their attention on the underlying factors that contribute to both favorable and unfavorable outcomes, even those that may not be readily discernible. The utilization of diagnostic analytics has the potential to foster the development of a data-centric analytical culture throughout the entire organization. Business executives are inclined to employ diagnostic analytics in their decision-making processes when they possess an awareness of the organization's ability to examine and identify the underlying causes of issues. For example, in the event that an issue pertaining to punctual deliveries is identified, and subsequent examination of the supply chain reveals disruptions and uncertainties in lead times, managers may opt to augment inventory levels in order to fulfil customer demand.

Predictive Analytics

Predictive analytics refers to the practice of utilizing statistical models and algorithms to analyze historical data and make predictions about future events or outcomes. In order to generate predictions, the field of predictive analytics analyses both past and present data. The utilization of data mining, artificial intelligence (AI), and machine learning empowers users to analyze information with the purpose of predicting market trends. An illustrative instance can be observed within the manufacturing sector, wherein enterprises can employ algorithms based on historical data to predict the occurrence and timing of equipment failure or breakdown. Predictive analytics is employed as a means to anticipate and forecast the potential outcomes of forthcoming events. Predictive analytics is employed to assign significance to data, facilitating the acquisition of knowledge that elucidates the interconnections within the data. The construction of models for generating future predictions from past events relies on the robustness and magnitude of the associations. It is imperative to acknowledge that predictive analytics models inherently rely on the contextual factors of past events. If there are changes in the underlying factors, it is necessary to update the models that generate predictions. Typical hypothetical inquiries encompass the likelihood of loan default among customers who have failed to make a monthly payment, the survival rate of patients when substituting drug A with drug B, and the probability of consumer acquisition of Product C subsequent to the purchase of Products A and B.

Prescriptive Analytics

Prescriptive analytics refers to the type of data analytics that utilizes various techniques and algorithms to provide recommendations and actions for optimal decision-making. Prescriptive analytics leverages artificial intelligence (AI) and machine learning techniques to gather data and employ it for the purpose of risk management, thereby providing a resolution to a given problem. In order to manage risk, entities within the energy sector such as utility companies, gas producers, and pipeline owners engage in the identification and analysis of the various factors that exert influence on the pricing dynamics of oil and gas. Prescriptive analytics leverages the insights derived from predictive analytics by delineating the suitable sequence of steps to be taken. The crucial aspect lies not only in selecting the suggested course of action, but also in comprehending the underlying rationale behind it. Prescriptive analytics generate findings that can be justified due to their incorporation of situational information. Consequently, the utilization of such analytics can confer a competitive edge or mitigate potential risks. Illustrative inquiries could include: which among the three aforementioned medications yields optimal outcomes, or at what juncture is it most opportune to engage in trading a particular stock. Prescriptive analytics is widely regarded as the most valuable form of analytics, necessitating a highly advanced skill set as well as specialized software and tools. After conducting calculations for different outcomes, it is advised to determine the most favorable course of actions for each outcome. The strategic approach transitions from an explanatory nature to an advisory one, potentially incorporating the utilization of simulation techniques to explore various scenarios.

The aforementioned data analytics methodology is specifically suitable for addressing transient issues. Therefore, it is recommended that businesses abstain from employing prescriptive analytics in order to make long-lasting decisions. As the duration of time required increases, the reliability of the data tends to decrease. Variability is observed among providers of prescriptive analytics. Enterprises must engage in thorough deliberation when considering the selection of technology and its corresponding provider.

Figure 3. Types of big data analytics

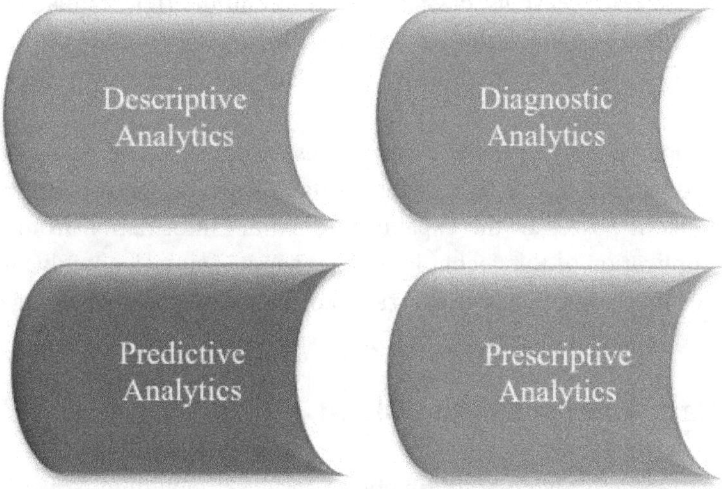

Certain methodologies produce concrete results, while others possess the capacity to leverage extensive datasets but fail to deliver on their promises. Figure 3 depicts a visual representation of the various categories encompassing Big data analytics.

The Integration of Big Data and Machine Learning

The primary objective of employing machine learning techniques is to reveal insights and enhance the process of making informed decisions. Machine learning is widely utilized in various practical domains in the real world, encompassing data mining, recognition systems, recommendation engines, and autonomous control systems, among others. Machine learning is a discipline that can be classified into three primary domains: supervised learning, unsupervised learning, and reinforcement learning (Katal et al., 2013).

Streaming Data Learning

The concept of streaming data learning refers to the process of continuously analyzing and extracting insights from data that is generated in real-time or near real-time. A wide range of modern technologies currently in existence, such as stock management systems, network traffic monitoring tools, and credit card transaction platforms, generate substantial volumes of real-time data. Data mining plays a pivotal role in the detection of meaningful patterns and extraction of valuable insights from hidden streams and datasets.

Deep Learning

Traditional data mining techniques encompass a range of methods, including clustering, association rule mining, accuracy, scalability, and classification. In contrast, big data is commonly linked to dynamic environments (Tsai et al., 2015; Lv et al., 2017).

Deep learning is a subfield of machine learning that focuses on the development and application of artificial neural networks. Deep learning plays a pivotal role in the field of machine learning and pattern recognition. The utilization of technology facilitates the implementation of predictive analysis and encompasses a range of components, including natural language processing, speech recognition, and computer vision.

Deep learning is employed to tackle the complexities associated with data analysis and aid in the extraction of intricate datasets from large volumes of data. Deep learning is often referred to as hierarchical learning because it possesses the capability to extract information from complex datasets at multiple levels. The application of this technology demonstrates significant advantages in the analysis of large datasets, retrieval of information, organization of data, and tasks involving discrimination such as prediction and classification (Jadon et al., 2016).

Benefits of Big Data Analytics in the Cloud

Cloud computing refers to the provision of computing services, including servers, storage, databases, networking, software, and analytics, through the Internet, commonly referred to as "the cloud." The primary objective of cloud computing is to offer flexible resources, facilitate rapid innovation, and achieve economies of scale (Yadav & Sohal, 2017). The advent of cloud computing has brought about a significant transformation in the abstraction and utilization of computing infrastructure. The concept of cloud paradigms has been expanded to encompass a wide range of services, commonly referred to as "X as a service." Cloud computing has become a popular and advantageous option for storing, managing, and analyzing big data due to its numerous benefits, including elasticity, a pay-as-you-go or pay-per-use model, and a low upfront investment (Yadav & Sohal, 2017).

Due to its recognized significance in numerous organizations and domains, big data has become an essential component. Consequently, prominent service providers such as Amazon, Google, and Microsoft have introduced their own cost-effective big data systems. These systems provide the capability to scale operations to accommodate businesses of various sizes. The increased significance of the term ***Analytics as a Service*** (AaaS) has resulted from its ability to offer a more expedient and effective approach to integrating, transforming, and visualizing diverse datasets. The field of data analytics.

Big data analytics offers several benefits, leading companies in diverse industries to utilize this approach to enhance data-driven decision-making processes. In addition to the technology sector, the utilization and prevalence of Big Data have extended to encompass various domains such as healthcare, governance, retail, supply chain management, and education, among others. According to a study conducted by Forbes in 2018 (Forbes, 2018), some of the advantages of Big Data Analytics are:

- The ability to gather data from various sources such as the Internet, online shopping platforms, and social media.
- Databases and external third-party sources are examples of information resources.
- The process of discerning significant elements that are concealed within extensive datasets with the intention of impacting business decision-making. The present study aims to identify the key concerns pertaining to systems and business processes in a real-time context.
- The objective is to effectively facilitate the delivery of services or products in a manner that meets or surpasses the expectations of clients.
- Addressing customer requests, inquiries, and complaints promptly and in a timely manner.

According to Xplenty (Xplenty, 2019), there are additional benefits that are associated with the aforementioned topic.

1) ***Cost optimization*** - A significant benefit of employing Big Data tools such as Hadoop or Spark lies in their capacity to provide cost advantages to enterprises with respect to the storage, processing, and analysis of substantial volumes of data. The logistics industry is cited by authors as an illustrative case to underscore the cost-reduction advantages associated with the utilization of Big Data. Within this particular sector, the expenditure associated with product returns surpasses the actual shipping costs by a factor of 1.5.

By utilizing Big Data Analytics, organizations have the capability to mitigate expenses associated with product returns through the prediction of the probability of such returns occurring. By employing this approach, companies can subsequently make estimations regarding the products that are more prone to being returned. Consequently, this enables them to implement appropriate strategies aimed at minimizing losses incurred from returns.

2) ***Enhancements in Efficiency*** - The utilization of Big Data has the potential to significantly enhance operational efficiency. Big Data tools have the capability to accumulate substantial volumes of valuable customer data through interactive processes and solicitation of feedback. The data can subsequently be analyzed and interpreted in order to uncover significant patterns that may be concealed within, such as customer preferences, tastes, and purchasing behaviors. Consequently, this enables companies to develop individualized or customized products and services.
3) ***Innovation*** - The utilization of Big Data insights enables the refinement of business strategies, the creation of novel products and services, the optimization of service delivery, and the enhancement of productivity, among other potential applications. All of these factors have the potential to foster increased innovation.

Big Data Analytics has predominantly been utilized by commercial enterprises; however, it has also proven advantageous in various other domains. In the healthcare sector, numerous states are currently leveraging the capabilities of Big Data to forecast and proactively mitigate epidemics, treat illnesses, reduce expenses, and achieve other objectives. The utilization of this data has also been employed in the establishment of numerous effective treatment models.

Difference Between Big Data and Cloud Computing

The utilization of Big Data facilitated the generation of more comprehensive reports, which were subsequently transformed into pertinent critical insights in order to enhance the provision of care (Forbes, 2018). Big Data has been widely utilized in the field of education. It has facilitated educators in assessing, tracking, and promptly addressing students' comprehension of the subject matter in real-time. According to report (EDHEC, 2019), educators have developed customized educational resources to cater to the varying levels of knowledge among students, with the aim of enhancing their engagement.

Cloud computing offers on-demand access to computing resources and services. Users have the ability to effortlessly construct the preferred configuration of cloud-based computational units and storage assets, establish connections with cloud services, transfer datasets to the cloud, and conduct analyses within the cloud environment. Individuals have the ability to access a wide range of resources within the public cloud, without any significant limitations. These resources can be utilized for an indefinite period of time and subsequently terminated, with the user being charged solely for the specific resources and services that were effectively utilized.

Prior to delving into the correlation between "Big Data" and "Cloud Computing," it is imperative to establish a precise differentiation between these two concepts. While these terms possess distinct technical definitions, they are frequently encountered in literature due to their synergistic interaction.

- ***Big Data*** is a term used to describe extensive collections of data generated by diverse software applications. The term "it" encompasses a wide range of diverse data types, typically characterized by their extensive size, rendering them impractical to browse or query using conventional computing systems.
- ***Cloud computing*** is a paradigm that encompasses the execution of various computational tasks, such as the analysis of large-scale datasets, within a distributed network infrastructure commonly referred to as the "cloud". The term "cloud" refers to a collection of robust servers offered by various providers. In many instances, individuals have the ability to efficiently access and analyze extensive data sets at a significantly faster rate compared to conventional computing systems.

In essence, the term "Big Data" pertains to extensive collections of data that are amassed, while "Cloud Computing" refers to the mechanism through which this data is remotely accessed and subjected to specified operations.

The Cloud Service Types for Big Data Analytics

The various cloud service types available for Big Data analytics as a service encompass infrastructure as a service (IaaS), platform as a service (PaaS), and software as a service (SaaS).

A. ***Infrastructure as a Service*** (IaaS) refers to the provision of shared server resources, typically virtualized, that enterprises can allocate or purchase in order to meet their computational and storage requirements for Big Data analytics. This can be implemented either on premise or through a cloud provider. The responsibility of managing high-performance network, servers, and storage resources lies with the cloud provider. Organizations engaged in the field of Big Data are not obligated to uphold the hardware and software infrastructure necessary to achieve optimal performance. Hadoop is an open-source solution that utilizes distributed data storage and processing. The technologies employed for Infrastructure as a Service (IaaS) include the Hadoop framework, as well as NoSQL databases like MongoDB, Apache Cassandra, and Couchbase technologies. Some of the Infrastructure as a Service (IaaS) providers include Amazon Web Services, Windows Azure, Citrix CloudPlatform, Microsoft System Centre, OpenStack software, and Rackspace.

B. ***Platform as a Service*** (PaaS) is utilized to offer elevated programming models and database systems. This platform offers a comprehensive suite of tools and libraries that facilitate the development, testing, deployment, and execution of applications within a cloud-based environment. The utilization of Amazon Elastic MapReduce offers a foundational Hadoop framework Platform as a Service (PaaS) ecosystem. The data service HDInsight offered by Windows Azure enables the utilization of Hadoop in a cloud-based setting, alongside additional Microsoft BI tools such as Power Map and Power View. DynamoDB is a widely used Platform-as-a-Service (PaaS) offering for NoSQL database services, while AWS provides Redshift as a PaaS solution for data warehousing. Google also provides Platform-as-a-Service (PaaS) capabilities, including offerings such as Bigtable and Big Query.

C. ***Software as a Service*** (SaaS) refers to the delivery of applications over the internet. Software as a Service (SaaS) provides a cloud-based solution called jKool, which offers business-related services and facilitates real-time analysis of time-sensitive information. Concur is a rapidly expanding software-as-a-service (SaaS) company that operates a singular instance of its software. This instance encompasses the preferences and historical data of countless business travelers worldwide, pertaining to various travel-related services such as airlines, hotels, car rentals, and taxi services. Karmasphere additionally provides a pay-as-you-go application that conducts analysis on data stored within Amazon S3 through the utilization of Amazon Elastic Map Reduce.

Applications of Big Data Analytics in the Cloud

The term "big data application" pertains to distributed applications that operate on extensive data sets. Within the realm of big data, the task of data exploration and analysis has emerged as a formidable challenge across various industries. The management of computation becomes challenging when dealing with large and complex datasets, leading to the emergence of big data applications as a solution. The software systems utilized for big data applications are Google's MapReduce framework and Apache Hadoop. These applications generate a substantial volume of intermediate data. Big data systems are predominantly employed in the domains of manufacturing and bioinformatics.

The utilization of big data in the manufacturing sector provides a transparent framework that enables the sector to effectively tackle various uncertainties, including but not limited to inconsistencies, performance variations in components, and availability issues. The foundational framework of predictive manufacturing commences with the process of data acquisition within the realm of big data applications. In this context, a diverse range of sensory data, encompassing pressure, vibration, acoustics, voltage, current, and controller data, can be procured. The generation of big data in the manufacturing sector involves the amalgamation of sensory data with historical data. The input consists of the large-scale data generated from the aforementioned combination.

Cloud computing integrates parallel distributed computing systems with computer clusters and web interfaces. Software packages designed for Big Data offer a diverse array of tools and options that facilitate the comprehensive mapping of data throughout an organization. This empowers individuals to assess internal risks they encounter. The assurance of data security is widely recognized as one of the foremost advantages associated with big data. This process aids individuals in recognizing potentially vulnerable data that lacks adequate protection and guarantees its handling aligns with regulatory mandates.

The integration of big data with predictive analytics presents a significant challenge for numerous industries. The amalgamation yields an investigation into the aforementioned quartet of domains: the computation of risks pertaining to extensive portfolios. The objectives encompassed in this proposal are the identification, mitigation, and subsequent reassessment of instances of financial fraud, the enhancement of efforts to address delinquent collections, and the implementation of a targeted marketing campaign aimed at maximizing returns. Organizations have the potential to leverage big data in order to develop novel products and services, enhance existing offerings, and potentially create innovative business models.

The utilization of big data analytics has the potential to yield various advantages across multiple domains, encompassing consumer intelligence, supply chain intelligence, performance quality, risk management, and fraud detection. The application of big data analytics in risk management holds potential benefits for various sectors, including investment and retail banking, as well as insurance. The utilization of big data analytics has the potential to enhance the process of investment selection through the examination of the likelihood of positive outcomes in comparison to the likelihood of negative outcomes. This particular aspect holds significant importance within the financial services sector. The comprehensive and dynamic assessment of risk exposures can be facilitated by the evaluation of both internal and external big data.

The application of big data analytics has proven to be effective in the identification and mitigation of fraudulent activities, particularly within the government, banking, and insurance sectors. Although analytics continues to be extensively utilized in automated fraud detection, there is a growing trend among organizations and sectors to leverage big data in order to enhance their systems. Big data can be utilized to correlate electronic data from diverse sources, encompassing both publicly available and privately held information, thereby enabling expedited analytical processes. Big data analytics has the potential to provide significant benefits to various sectors, including manufacturing, retail, central government, healthcare, telecom, and banking.

Trends in Applying Big Data Analytics in the Cloud

Big Data Analytics, as described in research (Searchbusinessanalytics, 2023), refers to the systematic examination of vast quantities of data in order to uncover concealed patterns, unexplored correlations, market trends, customer preferences, and other valuable insights. Data Analytics as a Service (DAaaS) refers to an adaptable analytical platform that is delivered through a cloud-based model. This model offers a range of data analytics tools that can be customized by users to effectively handle and analyze large volumes of diverse data. The integration of Big Data and Cloud technologies has the potential to enhance the utilization of analytical capabilities across diverse and extensive data sources that surpass the capacity of businesses to manage. Organizations greatly reap advantages from the value obtained through the utilization of big data analytics. The intrinsic worth lies within the data itself, rather than the expertise employed in its analysis. Organizations are compelled to avail themselves of advanced big data analytics services in order to effectively navigate the future. In addition, it is imperative for them to cultivate robust infrastructure and make the necessary capital investments. The elasticity property of cloud computing makes it a valuable resource for analytics engineers. Analytics service providers have adopted the Software as a Service (SaaS) model in order to assist cloud computing in addressing significant data challenges. Emcien Corporation offers a software solution for pattern detection, which is delivered as a service and operates on the Amazon Elastic Compute Cloud (EC2) platform. The company serves a diverse range of clients, including major retailers, telecommunications providers, and intelligence agencies. In the Software as a Service (SaaS) model, which was introduced in 2023, users are not obligated to invest in hardware infrastructure. Instead, they only need access to a web browser in order to utilize the service. The utilization of big data entails the implementation of advanced platforms, as consumers seeking cost-effective services from analytics vendors are required to install supplementary software resources, including Hadoop, Cassandra, and other fundamental components, in order to enhance performance.

The rapid evolution of big data and analytics necessitates the adoption of cloud computing by businesses, as cloud technology has supplanted outdated legacy systems. Hadoop (Olavsrud, 2016) and business intelligence (BI) platforms, such as Birst, have introduced a novel framework for conducting analytics within enterprises. Hadoop and Birst provide the necessary capabilities of data accessibility, analytic agility, and application performance that are sought after by large enterprises. Data technologies have gained considerable importance alongside social, mobile, cloud, and analytics as one of the fundamental drivers of change in the digital era. The year 2016 portends significant developments in the realm of data and analytics. Analytics serves as the fundamental basis for the forthcoming business models. The importance of this extends beyond decision makers to encompass customers as well. The diagram presented herein illustrates the prevailing trends in Data Analytic as a Service, accompanied by concise descriptions.

- ***The Internet of Things (IoT)*** refers to the interconnected network of physical devices, vehicles, buildings, and other objects that are embedded with sensors, software, and network connectivity, enabling them to collect and exchange data. According to Gartner's assessment in 2023, the Internet of Things (IoT) has reached the pinnacle of its perceived hype cycle, signifying that it is currently the primary focus of exaggerated expectations. The Statistical Analytical System for Internet of Things (IoT) encompasses the comprehensive analytical process, commencing with the collection, integration, and deployment of data. The Internet of Things (IoT) is widely regarded as the future of data analytics, as it has the potential to revolutionize the way data is collected and analyzed, regardless of whether it is in a stationary or mobile state. By leveraging IoT technologies, organizations can greatly enhance their ability to assess and make informed decisions regarding data storage. A smart city can be defined as an advanced and intelligent system that, through the utilization of sensors, has the capability to transmit real-time data to a cloud-based platform. The utilization of sensors would facilitate intelligent resource allocation as needed. According to an estimation by Gartner, the acceptance of the Internet of Things (IoT) is projected to witness a substantial increase, with the installation of approximately 26 billion Internet-enabled devices by the year 2020.
- ***Real-time analytics*** represents the initial stage of a broader analytical process. Analytic Software provides enterprises with flexible tools for management decision-making and application development, enabling them to make timely real-time decisions more efficiently. The advanced platform tool possesses the capability to effectively manage and evaluate real-time streaming data in close proximity to its source, thereby facilitating the transformation and comprehension of such data. The platform would enable communication in various protocol languages. The emergence of new tools such as the Spark Cassandra Connector enables enterprises to utilize Spark for the analysis of data stored in Cassandra. As a result, companies will have the ability to efficiently gather business intelligence from large volumes of data at a rapid pace.
- ***The future of Big data*** lies in the development and implementation of monitoring integrations and alert systems. In the future, real-time analytics platforms will possess the capability to promptly identify and notify users about potential breaches or vulnerabilities within a network as soon as they transpire. Artificial systems have the potential to serve as the future of Big Data, as they possess the capability to proactively address and resolve issues even before they become apparent to human users. The implementation of artificial system solutions has the potential to transform network management practices from a reactive approach to a proactive one. The demand for Hadoop

deployment in cloud environments is substantial due to its ability to effectively handle and process critical workloads. The Hadoop framework possesses a complex stack due to the intricate process of integrating multiple open source components that lack a unified set of APIs and do not exhibit seamless interoperability. In order to address this challenge, it is necessary to either recruit or cultivate a fresh cohort of analysts who possess advanced technical expertise.

- Currently, there exist ***emerging start-up companies*** that provide innovative solutions aimed at bolstering the functionality and efficacy of SQL. The Analytics market is experiencing growth due to the emergence of new technologies and the entry of prominent industry players who are acquiring start-ups to leverage their technological advancements and expertise. The field of big data has experienced significant growth and rapid development. Hadoop, a prominent platform for big data analytics, has been present in the market for a considerable period of time and has established itself as an integral component of the enterprise IT environment. Furthermore, it is anticipated that there will be increased investment in the domains of security and privacy pertaining to Hadoop in the foreseeable future. Apache Sentry offers a service that enables the implementation of fine-grained, role-based authorization for data and metadata stored on a Hadoop cluster. In the contemporary era, the preservation of security and privacy has emerged as a crucial factor for achieving success in the realm of enterprise. Users seek security measures provided by enterprise-grade relational database management system (RDBMS) platforms, which serve as a hindrance to the adoption of analytics. The demand for Hadoop has risen due to the rapid growth in data volume, leading to an expectation of faster data analysis compared to traditional data warehouses. Cloudera, Actian Vector, AtScale, Impala, and Jethro Data facilitate the implementation of OLAP cubes on the Hadoop platform, effectively bridging the divide between conventional business intelligence practices and the realm of big data.
- ***The convergence of Internet of Things (IoT), cloud computing, and big data*** is observed. Developers have placed significant emphasis on the Internet of Things (IoT), cloud computing, and big data. The Internet of Things (IoT) enables businesses to leverage the rapid influx of Big Data generated within the digital realm for their advantage. Thingalytics, a term derived from the combination of "Things" and "Analytics," provides guidance to organizations on the utilization of real-time analytics and algorithms for the purpose of gathering data from the Internet of Things (IoT), while also mitigating potential risks. The majority of time allocated by big data analytics developers is dedicated to the creation of Internet of Things (IoT) technologies. The technology in question is currently in its early stages of development. However, the data obtained from the various devices utilized within the Internet of Things (IoT) holds significant importance for cloud computing. The proliferation of data generated by the Internet of Things has the potential to contribute significantly to the exponential growth of big data. Cloud and data companies, such as Google, Amazon Web Services, and Microsoft, are actively facilitating the implementation of Internet of Things (IoT) services. These companies enable seamless data transmission to their cloud-based analytics engines, thereby contributing to the realization of IoT capabilities. Figure 4 depicts the trends pertaining to data analytics as a service.

Figure 4. Trends of data analytics as a service

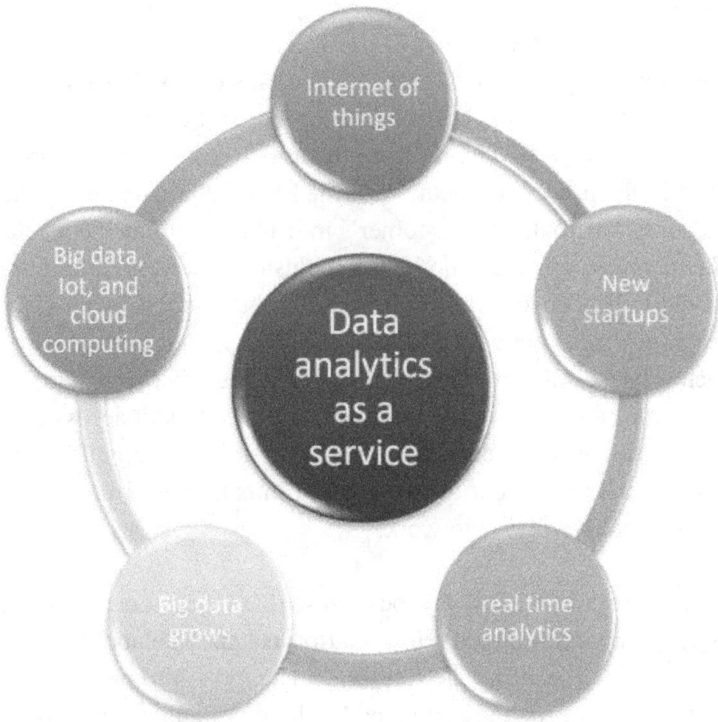

Security Issues for Big Data and Cloud Computing

A. ***Need for security in Big Data***: Too many businesses use Big Data, but they may not have the right setting from a security point of view. If there is a safety problem with big data, it could lead to an even bigger problem. Companies usually use this technology to store data in the zeta-byte range that has to do with the business. This could mean that the classification of information is very important. There is a need to encrypt, log, or set up honeypots to keep the info safe. Attacks and hackers are hard to find, so you need to use big data analysis to find them. Big data analysis and computation: When we look up information in the big data, speed is the most important thing. But the process may be complicated because it takes a long time to go through all the connected data in the whole database. While big data is getting more complicated, its statistics are trying to find the simplest data. The usual series method doesn't work well with this much data.

B. ***Problems with security in the cloud*** – Concerns about safety in cloud computer settings can be put into four groups: network level, user identification level, data level, and general problems.
   1. *Network level*: Network standards and network security problems, like scattered data, Internode communication, and spread nodes, can be put into this category.
   2. *User identification level*: Challenges that can be grouped under the user authentication level have to do with different ways to secure and decrypt data, authentication methods like authenticating applications and nodes, logging, and giving management rights to nodes.
   3. *Data level*: Challenges that can be put into this category have to do with access, like data security and data that is spread out.

4. *General types*: Traditional security tools and the use of different technologies can be put into the general type of problems.

C. ***How to deal with security issues***

1. *Encryption*: Any computer's data is stored in a cluster, so it's easy for someone to steal the data from the system. This could make it hard for any business or organization to keep their very important info safe. We could secure the info to stop this from happening. Different systems can use different ways to secure, and the keys that are made should be kept safe behind fences. By going this route, the customer's information will be kept safe.
2. *Node authentication*: When a node joins the cluster, it must go through authentication. If the node turns out to be a hostile cluster, it shouldn't be verified.
3. *Honeypot nodes*: Honeypot nodes look like regular nodes, but they are actually traps. It instantly catches hackers and prevents them from doing any damage to the system or the data.
4. *Access control*: In a spread setting, the different private and access controls will be a good measure of protection. We use Linux computer system to keep information from getting out. Through the use of Linux Security modules in Linux kernels, Linux is a trait that gives access control security policies a way to work.

Cloud computing lets us store data at a faraway location so that we can get the most out of our resources. Because of this, it is very important that this information is kept safe and that only authorized people can get to it. So, this amounts to securing the release of data by a third party, which is needed for both data sharing and publications outside the company. In cloud computing, the computer acts as a third-party provider and saves private information in the cloud. The data needs to be kept safe, and the above methods must be used to make sure that the data is always accurate and full.

Pros and Cons of Big Data in the Cloud

The public cloud has become the optimal platform for large data sets. A cloud contains the resources and services that a business can utilize on demand, without having to construct, own, or maintain the underlying infrastructure. Thus, the cloud makes big data technologies accessible and affordable for businesses of nearly every size.

Advantages of Cloud-Based Large Data

Cloud computing provides enterprises of all sizes with a number of significant advantages. Some of the most immediate and substantive advantages of big data in the cloud include the following.

- *Scalability*; A typical business data center is limited by physical space, power, ventilation, and budget when it comes to purchasing and deploying the vast volume of hardware required to create a big data infrastructure. In contrast, a public cloud administers tens of thousands of servers dispersed across a global network of data centers. The infrastructure and software services are already in place, and users can construct the infrastructure for a big data undertaking of virtually any scale.

- *Agility*; Not every large data endeavor is identical. One endeavor may necessitate 100 servers, while another may necessitate 2,000 servers. With cloud, users can employ as many resources as necessary to complete a task and then release them when the task is complete.
- *Expense*; A business data center is a substantial investment. In addition to hardware, businesses must pay for facilities, energy, ongoing maintenance, and more. All of these costs are incorporated into a flexible rental model where resources and services are available on demand and follow a pay-per-use model in the cloud.
- *Accessibility*; Numerous clouds offer a global footprint, enabling the deployment of resources and services in the majority of the world's main regions. This enables data and processing activity to occur close to the region where the big data task resides. For instance, if a significant amount of data is stored in a specific region of a cloud provider, it is relatively easy to implement the resources and services for a big data project in that region, as opposed to incurring the expense of transferring the data to another region.
- *Resilience;* Data is the true value of big data initiatives, and the advantage of cloud resilience is the reliability of data storage. Clouds routinely replicate data to ensure the high availability of storage resources, and even more enduring storage options are available in the cloud.

Cloud-Based Large Data's Disadvantages

Public clouds and numerous third-party big data services have demonstrated their worth in big data use cases. Despite the advantages, enterprises must also consider the potential drawbacks. The following are some of the most significant drawbacks of storing large data in the cloud.

- *Dependence on the network;* Cloud use requires comprehensive network connectivity from the Local Area Network (LAN) to the cloud provider's network. Outages along this network path can result in, at best, an increase in latency and, at worst, a complete inability to access the cloud. Despite the fact that an outage may not have the same effect on a big data project as it would on a mission-critical workload, the impact of outages should still be considered when utilizing the cloud for big data projects.
- *Storage costs;* cloud-based data storage can incur significant long-term expenses for big data initiatives. The three principal issues are data storage, data migration and data retention. It takes time to upload massive quantities of data to the cloud, and then those storage instances incur a monthly fee. If the data is relocated a second time, additional fees may apply. Moreover, large data sets are frequently time-sensitive, meaning that some data may be of no use to an analysis of large data sets even if it is performed hours from now. Retaining superfluous data costs money, so businesses must implement comprehensive data retention and deletion policies to control cloud storage costs associated with big data.
- *Security;* The data involved in big data initiatives may contain confidential or personally identifying information that is subject to data protection and other industry- or government-driven regulations. Cloud users must take the necessary precautions to ensure the security of cloud storage and computation, including proper authentication and authorization, encryption for data at rest and in transit, and extensive recording of data access and use.
- *Absence of standardization;* There is no one method to architect, implement, or manage a large data deployment in the cloud. This may result in poor performance and expose the company to

potential security hazards. The architecture of big data should be documented, as well as any applicable policies and procedures. This documentation can serve as a foundation for future optimizations and enhancements.

Choosing the Right Cloud Deployment Model

The primary focus and financial resources of big data initiatives are primarily directed towards the underlying hardware. However, it is the services, specifically the analytical tools, that play a crucial role in enabling big data analytics. Fortunately, organizations aiming to implement big data initiatives are not required to commence their efforts from the beginning.

In addition to providing services and documentation, providers have the capability to facilitate support and consulting services, thereby assisting businesses in optimizing their big data projects. A sampling of available big data services from the top three providers include the following.

AWS
- Amazon Elastic MapReduce
- AWS Deep Learning AMIs
- Amazon SageMaker

Microsoft Azure
- Azure HDInsight
- Azure Analysis Services
- Azure Databricks

Google Cloud
- Google BigQuery
- Google Cloud Dataproc
- Google Cloud AutoML

It is important to consider that there exists a wide range of proficient services offered by external providers. In general, these service providers tend to offer specialized services, while major providers adopt a standardized approach for their services. Several alternative choices from external sources are available, including the following options:

- Cloudera
- Hortonworks Data Platform
- Oracle Big Data Service
- Snowflake Data Cloud

The rising popularity of Software as a Service (SaaS) necessitates a thorough understanding of cloud infrastructure best practices and the appropriate handling of large-scale data. This analysis will examine the distinctions between cloud computing and big data, explore their interconnection, and demonstrate the synergistic relationship that exists between the two. This interconnected alliance has paved the way for the emergence of cutting-edge technologies, including artificial intelligence, thereby fostering innovation in various domains. Figure 5 illustrates applications for cloud service types, and figure 6 shows the management of infrastructure, Operating System and programs at different cloud service types.

Figure 5. Applications for Cloud service types

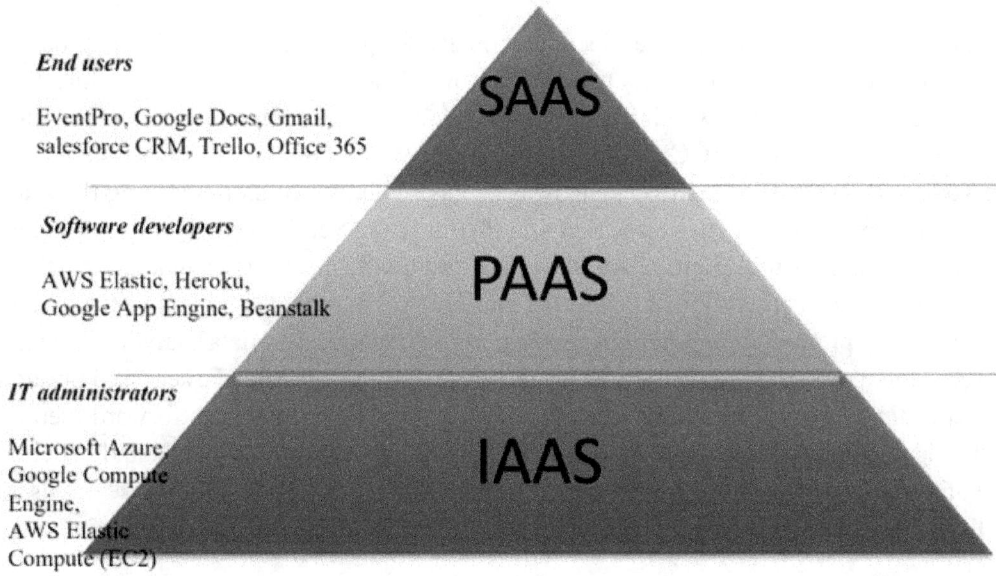

Figure 6. The management of Infrastructure, operating system, and programs at cloud service types

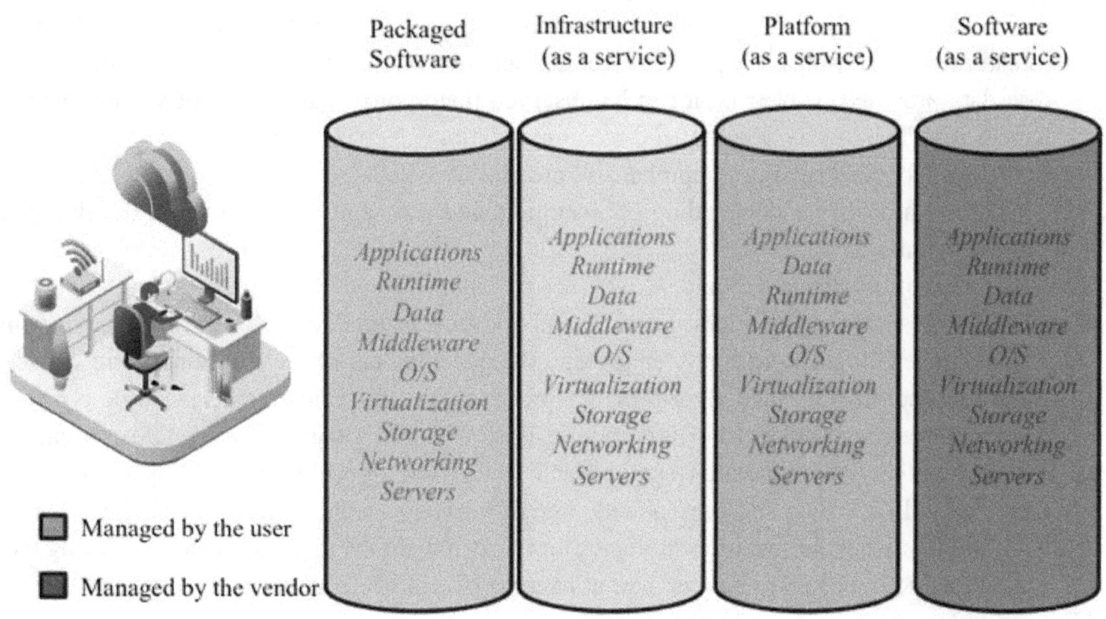

Real Case Studies of Applying Big Data Analytics With Cloud Computing

The Google Cloud Platform offers a range of services specifically designed for the analysis and processing of large-scale data sets. In this section, it is provided an overview and analysis of the architecture and primary components of BigQuery, which is widely recognized as a prominent big data processing tool within the Google Cloud Platform (GCP). BigQuery is a data warehouse that is fully managed and operates in a serverless manner. It facilitates the analysis of large volumes of data, reaching the scale of petabytes. The aforementioned system is classified as a Platform as a Service (PaaS) and is designed to facilitate querying through the utilization of ANSI SQL. Additionally, it possesses inherent machine learning functionalities. Since its inception in 2011, this platform has garnered significant acclaim and has been widely adopted by prominent corporations for the purpose of conducting data analytics (Google, 2020). From a user's standpoint, BigQuery offers an intuitive user interface that can be accessed through various means, depending on the specific requirements of the user. The most straightforward method of engaging with this tool involves utilizing its graphical web interface. More advanced and efficient methods involve utilizing cloud console or BigQuery APIs. The BigQuery web interface provides users with the capability to add or select datasets, schedule and construct queries, transfer data, and display query results.

Case Studies on Big Data

1. The utilization of big data in the context of Netflix

   Netflix utilizes data analytics models to uncover customer behavior and purchasing patterns. Subsequently, based on the aforementioned data, the system proceeds to suggest films and television programs to its clients. This system examines the selection and preferences of the customer and subsequently provides recommendations for television shows and films. Based on data provided by Netflix, it can be observed that approximately 75% of viewer engagement is influenced by personalized recommendations. Netflix typically gathers data that is sufficient for constructing comprehensive profiles of its subscribers or customers. This profile facilitates a deeper understanding of customers and contributes to the overall development of the business.
2. The utilization of big data at Google

   Google leverages Big data in order to enhance and optimize its fundamental search and ad-serving algorithms. Google consistently engages in the development of novel products and services that incorporate advanced algorithms for processing large-scale datasets. Google typically leverages large-scale data from its comprehensive Web index to initially correlate user queries with potentially relevant search results. Machine-learning algorithms are employed to evaluate the credibility of data and subsequently assign rankings to the respective websites. Google has implemented optimization strategies for its search engine to gather user data during web browsing activities. This data is then utilized to provide personalized suggestions based on individual preferences and interests.
3. The utilization of big data within the context of LinkedIn

   LinkedIn primarily serves as a platform for facilitating professional networking. The utilization of Big Data is commonly employed to create product offerings, including features such as suggested connections, profile viewers, recommended job opportunities, and other related functionalities. LinkedIn employs sophisticated algorithms to analyze user profiles and subsequently recommends relevant opportunities based on their qualifications and interests. As the LinkedIn network expands continuously, the abundance of information within it becomes increasingly detailed and comprehensive.

4. The utilization of big data in the context of Wal-Mart.

Walmart is employing the utilization of Big Data in order to analyze the extensive and comprehensive information that is constantly circulating within its various operational processes. The utilization of big data facilitates the acquisition of a contemporaneous perspective on the operational processes spanning the pharmacy, distribution centers, and retail outlets. This section discusses five strategies employed by Walmart to leverage big data in order to enhance, optimize, and personalize the shopping experience.

- To enhance the operational efficiency of Walmart pharmacies.
- To effectively oversee the supply chain.
- To enhance the individualized nature of the shopping experience.
- To enhance the efficiency of the store's checkout process.
- To enhance the efficiency of product assortment.

The utilization of big data enables Walmart to conduct analysis on the transportation route within their supply chain, leading to the optimization of pricing strategies. Consequently, this serves as a pivotal factor in the enhancement of customer experiences.

5. The utilization of big data at eBay

eBay is a multinational e-commerce corporation of American origin, with its headquarters located in San Jose, California. eBay is presently collaborating with various tools such as Apache Spark, Kafka, and Hortonworks HDF. Additionally, it employs a Hadoop-based interactive query engine known as Presto. The eBay website utilizes Big Data for various purposes, including assessing the performance of the site and identifying instances of fraudulent activity. Additionally, Big data was employed to analyze customer data with the objective of increasing their purchasing behavior on the platform. The website eBay boasts a substantial user base of approximately 180 million active buyers and sellers. eBay's auto search engine receives approximately 250 million daily queries, while the platform boasts a staggering 350 million items listed for sale.

6. The utilization of big data within the context of Sprint

Sprint Corporation is a telecommunications holding company based in the United States, specializing in the provision of wireless communication services. The company's headquarters is situated in Overland Park, Kansas. Furthermore, it serves as a prominent international provider of Internet services. The wireless telecommunications company Sprint employs advanced computing technologies. The concept of smarter computing primarily revolves around the utilization of big data analytics to reintroduce real-time intelligence and control into the network, resulting in a significant enhancement of its capacity by approximately 90%. The company provides wireless voice and messaging services, as well as broadband services, through its diverse range of subsidiaries. The Boost Mobile, Virgin Mobile, and Assurance Wireless brands encompass various subsidiaries.

Research Issues in Big Data

With the exponential growth of data, various issues and problems arise during the processing phase. The collection and retention of large volumes of data. There is a limited availability of tools for addressing the various issues and challenges that arise in a cloud computing environment. Various technologies, including PigLatin, Dryad, MongoDB, Cassandra, and MapR, have been found to be insufficient in addressing the challenges associated with big data processing. Despite the assistance provided by Hadoop and MapR, users are limited by low-level infrastructures for data processing and management. Several issues and problems pertaining to big data research can be summarized as follows (Wook et al., 2021):

1) ***A distributed database storage system*** is a type of data storage system that is designed to store and manage data across multiple nodes or servers. A wide array of technologies is employed for the purpose of storing and retrieving vast quantities of data. Cloud computing plays a significant role in the realm of big data. Every day, a vast amount of data is generated by numerous devices. Currently, the primary concern in distributed frameworks pertains to the efficient storage of data and the seamless processing and migration of data across distributed servers.
2) ***Data security*** is a significant concern within the context of cloud computing, as it is susceptible to various security threats. The advent of modern information and communication technologies has significantly impacted cloud computing, leading to various transformations. However, despite these advancements, there are still several unresolved security threats that persist in the realm of big data. The presence of big data exacerbates the risks associated with data security due to the diverse range, rapid pace, and large quantity of data involved. In the context of utilizing cloud computing frameworks, the utilization of big data gives rise to a multitude of concerns and challenges. These include but are not limited to the accessibility of data, the safeguarding of confidential information, the ability to monitor data in real-time, the establishment of identity and access authorization controls, the preservation of data integrity, and the protection of individual privacy. Hence, it is imperative to assess the level of data security when outsourcing data to cloud service providers (Saif & Wazir, 2018).
3) ***Heterogeneity*** is a characteristic of big data as it encompasses data collected from various devices in diverse formats, including images, videos, audio, and text. Prior to being loaded into a warehouse, data must undergo transformation and cleansing procedures, which pose significant challenges in the context of big data (Shamsuddin & Hasan, 2015). The process of aggregating and harmonizing unstructured data for the purpose of generating reports poses significant challenges in real-time scenarios.
4) ***Data processing and cleaning*** encompass the necessary steps of preprocessing and cleaning data for storage and acquisition. These steps involve tasks such as data merging, data filtering, ensuring data consistency, and optimizing data quality. Processing and cleaning data pose challenges due to the diverse range of data sources (Yang & Zhao, 2017). Additionally, it is important to acknowledge that data sources have the potential to be affected by noise, errors, or incompleteness. The primary obstacle lies in effectively managing substantial volumes of data and ascertaining their credibility.
5) ***Data visualization*** is a methodology employed to depict intricate data in a visual format, thereby facilitating enhanced comprehension and clarity. If the data possess a structured format, they can be readily depicted using conventional graphical methods. Visualizing data that is unstructured

or semi structured can be challenging, particularly when there is a wide range of diversity and the need for real-time analysis.

Future Scopes of Big Data Analytics in the Cloud

- ***The field of Machine Learning (ML) and Artificial Intelligence (AI) offers a vast array of potential opportunities and possibilities.***
  The future of Big Data Analytics will primarily revolve around the utilization of Machine Learning (ML) and Artificial Intelligence (AI) to fully exploit their capabilities. Indeed, Artificial Intelligence (AI) and Machine Learning (ML) serve as the fundamental principles underlying Augmented Data Management. It is widely believed that they possess the capability to enhance the efficiency of automating tasks related to metadata management, data integration, data quality, and database management, among other functions. These factors contribute to increased productivity and decreased occurrence of errors. Furthermore, due to the immense size and volume of Big Data, the utilization of Machine Learning algorithms can effectively streamline the task of organizing and managing such vast quantities of data.
- ***The Internet of Things (IoT) is expected to experience significant expansion.***
  The proliferation of Internet of Things (IoT) devices is expected to continue expanding, encompassing a broader range of new devices that will facilitate data exchange within the IoT ecosystem. Consequently, this growth will result in the generation of substantial volumes of data. Through the utilization of sensor data such as health metrics, geographical information, machine data, error messages, and other relevant sources, individuals can harness the capabilities of predictive and diagnostic analytics. For example, individuals can obtain a reasonable estimation of the time it would take for a machine to reach a critical state of failure, enabling them to strategically schedule maintenance and repair activities.
- ***The significance of cloud enterprises***
  When considering the future of Data Analytics, it is imperative to concurrently envision the escalating significance of cloud service providers such as Amazon Web Services, Microsoft Azure, and Google. There is no denying the fact that organizations that utilize analytic tools are increasingly adopting cloud technology to enhance the efficiency of their business performance. The functionalities provided by cloud-native applications are highly valuable in facilitating business innovation and enhancing agility. Additionally, it facilitates the seamless adjustment of all functionalities to meet the requirements of the organization. Another significant benefit of utilizing cloud-based data sources is the ability to enhance internal data by incorporating data from various social media feeds, third-party sources, and Software as a Service (SaaS) tools.
- ***The implementation of automation and DataOps methodologies to enhance data analytics.***
  When contemplating the future of Big Data Analytics, it is imperative to acknowledge the significance of automating the Data Analytics process. The necessity for automation arises due to the extensive volume and unstructured characteristics of Big Data. Furthermore, the automation of Data Analytics proves to be advantageous in a multitude of tasks including Data Preparation, Data Exploration, Data Replication, and Data Warehouse maintenance. The future trajectory of Data Analytics can be comprehended through the conceptual framework of DataOps. The statement asserts the significance of optimizing the procedures involved in the storage, analysis, and interpretation of Big Data. This would necessitate the imperative

to enhance cooperation and collaboration among diverse teams and eliminate the traditional barriers that delineate various departments.

- ***Continuous Intelligence and Real-Time Insights***

  Continuous intelligence refers to the process of collecting, analyzing, and utilizing data in real-time to generate meaningful insights. This approach enables organizations to make informed decisions and take immediate actions based on up-to-date information. By leveraging advanced technologies such as artificial intelligence and machine learning, continuous intelligence empowers businesses.

The future prospects of Data Analytics primarily revolve around the field of Real-Time Data Visualization. The forthcoming trajectory of Big Data Analytics will primarily revolve around the acquisition, examination, investigation, and representation of real-time operational data. Furthermore, the integration of diverse data sources enables the provision of continuous intelligence in real-time. The concept of continuous intelligence and real-time insights is founded on the fundamental principle of data processing, information analysis in relation to past patterns, and the prompt recommendation of actions.

- ***Predictive, Prescriptive and 'X' Analytics***

  This section explores the concepts of predictive, prescriptive, and 'X' analytics in the field of data analytics. The future trajectory of data analytics can be succinctly encapsulated by the concept of 'X' analytics. The year 2020 observed an increasing focus on the utilization of Predictive and Prescriptive Analytics. In light of the escalating circumstances surrounding the Covid-19 pandemic, particularly in the year 2021, organizations have begun seeking more resilient strategies to prevent future crises. Could you please provide a definition of X Analytics? According to Gartner, the concept of 'X' encompasses both structured and unstructured data variables. Video analytics, audio analytics, and text analytics are all viable options for analysis. When integrated with Artificial Intelligence tools, this combination assumes a pivotal role in the anticipation, strategic preparation, and alleviation of forthcoming crises, encompassing both diseases and natural calamities.

- ***Augmented Analytics is the future of Data and Analytics***

  Augmented Analytics is poised to become the predominant approach in the field of Data and Analytics in the future. Gartner has declared Augmented Analytics as the prospective paradigm for Data Analytics. The term "insights automation" utilizing Machine Learning (ML) and Natural Language Processing (NLP) was introduced by The Research Company in 2017. With the increasing magnitude of Big Data, there is a growing imperative to embrace the utilization of "augmented analytics." The substantial volume of data presents a significant challenge in terms of achieving effective interpretation. The data value chain is currently afflicted by biases, as data scientists independently construct their own models and business users independently interpret patterns. This phenomenon leads to the omission of significant discoveries and the formulation of inaccurate interpretations.

As a result, there is a growing consensus that Augmented Analytics represents the future of Data and Analytics. The proposed solution is being regarded as a potential remedy for the bottleneck in the data chain. This is achieved by implementing automation in the data preparation process, employing AutoML techniques to automate ML/AI modelling processes, and automating crucial aspects of Data

Figure 7. AI and ML tasks in big data analytics

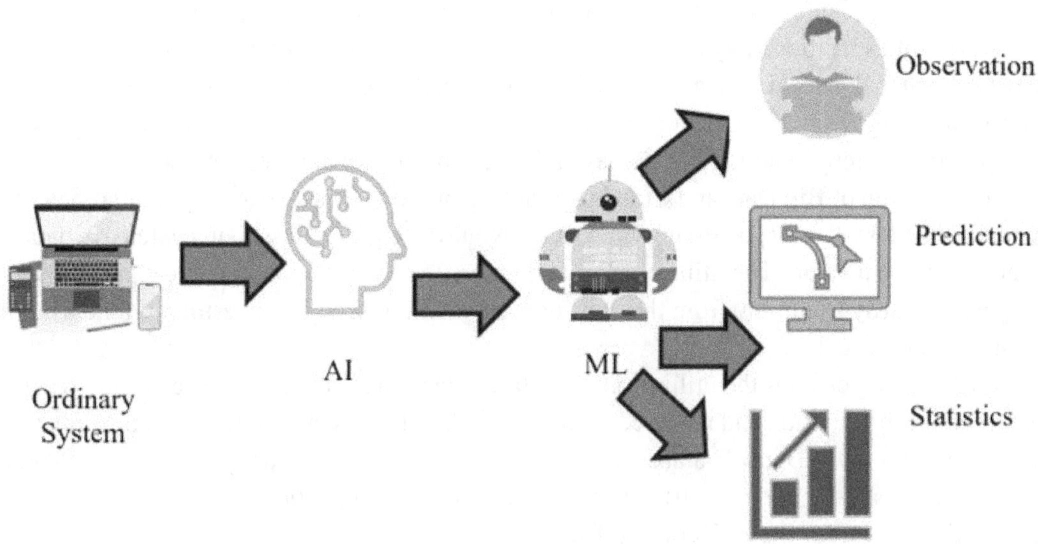

Science. Furthermore, the utilization of conversational analytics and natural language processing aids in the construction of a cohesive narrative consisting of pertinent insights.

Augmented Data Preparation facilitates the expeditious execution of data preparation tasks, encompassing activities such as metadata development, data profiling, data cataloguing, data enrichment, and others. The concept of Augmented Data Science pertains to the mechanization of certain aspects within the field of Data Science, including but not limited to Model Selection, Model Explanation, Model Operationalization, Model Tuning, and Feature Engineering.

Augmented Analytics leverages the integration of artificial intelligence and machine learning techniques with Natural Language Query technologies to automate the tasks of discovering, visualizing, and reporting pertinent insights and discoveries.

Therefore, it is apparent that Augmented Analytics holds significant importance in shaping the future of Data Analytics. The utilization of advanced data analytics techniques has the potential to greatly benefit organizations in effectively managing extensive and intricate datasets. This can facilitate the transformation of organizational processes into a more data-centric approach and promote the widespread adoption of artificial intelligence throughout the data chain, thereby enhancing accessibility to valuable insights. Figure 7 illustrates the various tasks related to Artificial Intelligence (AI) and Machine Learning (ML) within the context of Big Data analytics.

CONCLUSION

The utilization of big data and cloud computing has become increasingly significant in the contemporary digital scenery. The utilization of Big Data within the realm of Cloud Computing appears to possess significant potential in the near future. Big data plays a significant role in providing insights within cloud computing applications when utilizing Software as a Service (SaaS). The utilization of Big Data in the context of cloud computing encompasses a wide range of applications across various domains. Several applications can be observed in relation to big data. One such application involves enhanced analysis capabilities facilitated by the utilization of large data sets. Additionally, the implementation of big data can lead to the development of an efficient infrastructure, resulting in long-term cost reduction. Moreover, the integration of big data can contribute to improved integrity, availability, and security of cloud platforms, thereby enabling businesses and platforms to expand their operations.

The combination of Big Data and Cloud Computing presents a vast array of potential outcomes that are virtually limitless. If only possessing Big Data, it would be equal to possessing extensive datasets with substantial untapped value. The utilization of computers for analysis purposes may present significant challenges, primarily stemming from the considerable time required for investment, rendering it either infeasible or impracticable.

Cloud computing enables the utilization of cutting-edge infrastructure while ensuring that users are only charged for the duration and resources consumed. Cloud application development is further driven by the utilization of Big Data. The absence of Big Data would significantly reduce the prevalence of cloud-based applications, as their existence would lack a compelling rationale. Cloud-based applications are frequently utilized for the collection of Big Data.

Cloud computing services primarily exist as a result of the significant presence of Big data. Similarly, the primary motivation behind the collection of Big Data is the existence of services that possess the capability to process and interpret it, typically within a short timeframe. The compatibility between the two entities is flawless, as the existence of one is contingent upon the existence of the other.

REFERENCES

Akhtar, S. M. F. (2018). *Big Data Architect's Handbook*. Packt.

Armbrust, M., Xin, R. S., Lian, C., Huai, Y., Liu, D., Bradley, J. K., Meng, X., Kaftan, T., Franklin, M. J., Ghodsi, A., & Zaharia, M. (2015). Spark SQL: relational data processing in spark. In: *Proceedings of the 2015 ACM SIGMOD International Conference on Management of Data*, (pp. 1383–1394). ACM. 10.1145/2723372.2742797

Baek, J., Vu, Q., Liu, J., Huang, X., & Xiang, Y. (2015). A secure cloud computing based framework for big data information management of smart grid. *IEEE Transactions on Cloud Computing*, *3*(2), 233–244. doi:10.1109/TCC.2014.2359460

Bhimani, J., Yang, Z., Leeser, M., & Mi, N. (2017). Accelerating big data applications using lightweight virtualization framework on enterprise cloud. In: High Performance Extreme Computing Conference (HPEC), (pp. 1–7). IEEE. doi:10.1109/HPEC.2017.8091086

Canaj, E., & Xhuvani, A. (2018). Big Data in Cloud Computing: A Review of Key Technologies and Open Issues. Springer. doi:10.1007/978-3-319-75928-9_45

Chandarana, P., & Vijayalakshmi, M. (2014). Big data analytics frameworks. In: *Proceedings of the International Conference on Circuits*, (pp. 430–434). IEEE.

Chang, B. R., Tsai, H. F., Chen, C. Y., Huang, C. F., & Hsu, H. T. (2015). Implementation of secondary index on cloud computing NoSQL database in big data environment. *Scientific Programming*, *2015*, 19. doi:10.1155/2015/560714

Dede, E., Sendir, B., Kuzlu, P., Weachock, J., Govindaraju, M., & Ramakrishan, L. (2016). Processing Cassandra datasets with Hadoop-streaming based approaches. *IEEE Transactions on Services Computing*, *9*(1), 46–58. doi:10.1109/TSC.2015.2444838

Dehdouh, K., Bentayeb, F., Boussaid, O., & Kabachi, N. (2015). Using the column oriented NoSQL model for implementing big data warehouses. In: *Proceedings of the International Conference on Parallel and Distributed Processing Techniques and Applications (PDPTA)*. The Steering Committee of the World Congress in Computer Science, Computer Engineering and Applied Computing (WorldComp).

EDHEC. (2019). *Three ways educators are using big data*. EDHEC. https://master.edhec.edu/news/threeways-educators-are-using-bigdata-analytics-improve-learning-process#

Gewirtz, D. (2018). *Volume, velocity, and variety*. ZDNet. https://www.zdnet.com/article/volume-velocity-and-varietyunderstanding-the-three-vs-of-big-data/

Google Cloud. (2020). *BigQuery*. Google. https://cloud.google.com/bigquery

Huang, T., Lan, L., Fang, X., An, P., Min, J., & Wang, F. (2015). Promises and challenges of big data computing in health sciences. *Big Data Res.*, *2*(1), 2–11. doi:10.1016/j.bdr.2015.02.002

Jadon, K. S., Bhadoria, R. S., & Tomar, G. S. (2016). A review on costing issues in big data analytics. *Proc. 2015 International Conference on Computational Intelligence and Communication Networks (CICN)*, Jabalpur, India.

Katal, A., Wazid, M., & Goudar, R. H. (2013). Big data: Issues, challenges, tools and good practices. *Proc. 6th Int. Conf. Contemporary Computing*, Noida, India. 10.1109/IC3.2013.6612229

Kimball, R., & Ross, M. (2013). *The data warehouse toolkit: The definitive guide to dimensional modeling* (3rd ed.). John Wiley & Sons.

Koliopoulos, A., Yiapanis, P., Tekiner, F., Nenadic, G., & Keane, J. (2015). A parallel distributed weka framework for big data mining using spark. In: *2015 IEEE International Congress Big Data (BigData Congress),* (pp. 9–16). IEEE. 10.1109/BigDataCongress.2015.12

Laprinth, X. (2018). *Better, Faster, Stronger.* LaprinthX,. https://laptrinhx.com/better-faster-smarter-elt-vs-etl-2084402419/

Lv, Z., Song, H., Basanta-Val, P., Steed, A., & Jo, M. (2017). Nextgeneration big data analytics: State of the art, challenges, and future research topics. *IEEE Transactions on Industrial Informatics*, *13*(4), 1891–1899. doi:10.1109/TII.2017.2650204

Mallika, C., & Selvamuthukumaran, S. (2017). Hadoop framework: analyzes workload predicition of data from cloud computing. In: *2017 International Conference on IoT and Application (ICIOT),* (pp. 1–6). IEEE. 10.1109/ICIOTA.2017.8073624

Matallah, H., & Belalem, G. (2017). Experimental comparative study of NoSQL databases: HBASE versus MongoDB by YCSB. *Computer Systems Science and Engineering*, *32*(4), 307–317.

Meng, S., Dou, W., Zhang, X., & Chen, J. (2014). KASR: A keyword-aware service recommendation method on MapReduce for big data applications. *IEEE Transactions on Parallel and Distributed Systems*, *25*(12), 3221–3231. doi:10.1109/TPDS.2013.2297117

Miller, J., Bowman, C., Harish, V., & Quinn, S. (2016). Open source big data analytics frameworks written in scala. In: *2016 IEEE International Congress on Big Data (BigData Congress),* (pp. 389–393). IEEE. 10.1109/BigDataCongress.2016.61

Nodarakis, N., Sioutas, S., Tsakalidis, A., & Tzima, G., (2016). *Using Hadoop for Large Scale Analysis on Twitter: A Technical Report.*

Olavsrud, T. (2016). *Data and analytic trends that will dominate 2016.* CIO. https://www.cio.com/article/3023838/analytics/21-data-and-analytics-trends-that-will-dominate-2016.html

Ortiz, J. L. R., Oneto, L., & Anguita, D. (2015). Big data analytics in the cloud: Spark on hadoop vs MPI/OpenMP on Beowulf. *Procedia Computer Science*, *53*, 121–130. doi:10.1016/j.procs.2015.07.286

Oussous, A., Benjelloun, F. Z., Lahcen, A. A., & Belfkih, S. (2017). Big data technologies: A survey. *Journal of King Saud University. Computer and Information Sciences.*

Peng, S., Liu, R., & Wang, F. (2017). *New Research on Key Technologies of Unstructured Data Cloud Storage.* Francis Academic Press.

Ptiček, M., & Vrdoljak, B. (2017). *MapReduce research on warehousing of big data.* Mipro. doi:10.23919/MIPRO.2017.7973634

Saif, S., & Wazir, S. (2018). Performance analysis of big data and cloud computing techniques: A survey. *Procedia Computer Science*, *132*, 118–127. doi:10.1016/j.procs.2018.05.172

Santos, M. Y., & Costa, C. (2016). Data warehousing in big data: from multidimensional to tabular data models. In: *Proceedings of the Ninth International C* Conference on Computer Science and Software Engineering*, (pp. 51–60). ACM. 10.1145/2948992.2949024

SAS. (2023). *SAS: Analytics, Business Intelligence and Data Management.* SAS. https://www.sas.com/en_in/home.html

Searchbusinessanalytics. (2023). *Big data Analytics.* Serious Business Analytics.\: https://searchbusinessanalytics.techtarget.com/definition/big-data-analytics

Shamsuddin, S. M., & Hasan, S. (2015). Data science vs. big data @ UTM big data centre. *Proc. of 2015 IEEE Int. Conf. Science in Information Technology.* IEEE. 10.1109/ICSITech.2015.7407766

Sharma, S., (2015). *An extended classification and comparison of NoSQL big data models.*

Sharma, S., Tim, U. S., Wong, J., Gadia, S., & Sharma, S. (2014). A brief review on leading big data models. *Data Science Journal*, *13*(0), 138–157. doi:10.2481/dsj.14-041

Singh, D., & Reddy, C. K. (2015). A survey on platforms for big data analytics. *Journal of Big Data*, *2*(1), 8. doi:10.1186/s40537-014-0008-6 PMID:26191487

Venkatraman, S.K.F., Kaspi, S., & Venkatraman, R., (2016). *SQL versus NoSQL Movement with Big Data Analytics*.

ADDITIONAL READING

Tsai, W., Lai, C. F., Chao, H. C., & Vasilakos, A. V. (2015). Big data analytics: A survey. *Journal of Big Data*, *2*(1), 1–32. doi:10.1186/s40537-015-0030-3 PMID:26191487

WhishWorks. (2019). "WhishWorks, ", Available: https://www.whishworks.com/blog/data-analytics/understanding-the3-vs-of-big-data-volume-velocity-and-variety/

Wook, M., Hasbullah, N. A., Zainudin, N. M., Jabar, Z. Z. A., Ramli, S., Razali, N. A. M., & Yusop, N. M. M. (2021). Exploring big data traits and data quality dimensions for big data analytics application using partial least squares structural equation modelling. *Journal of Big Data*, *8*(1), 1–15. doi:10.1186/s40537-021-00439-5 PMID:33425651

Xhafa, F., Naranjo, V., & Caballé, S. (2015). Processing and analytics of big data streams with Yahoo!S4. In: *2015 IEEE 29th International Conference on Advanced Information Networking and Applications (AINA),* (pp. 263–270). IEEE.

Xplenty, (2019). "XPlenty ". Available: https://www.xplenty.com/blog/etl-vs-elt/#

Yadav, S., & Sohal, A. (2017). Review Paper on Big Data Analytics in Cloud Computing [IJCTT]. *International Journal of Computer Trends and Technology*, *IX*.

Yang, T. Y., & Zhao, Y. (2017). Application of cloud computing in biomedicine big data analysis cloud computing in big data. *Proc. of the 2017 Int. Conf. Algorithms, Methodology, Models and Applications in Emerging Technologies (ICAMMAET)*, Chennai, India. 10.1109/ICAMMAET.2017.8186626

Zhang, H., Chen, G., Ooi, B. C., Tan, K. L., & Zhang, M. (2015). In-memory big data management and processing: A survey. *IEEE Transactions on Knowledge and Data Engineering*, *27*(7), 1920–1948. doi:10.1109/TKDE.2015.2427795

Zhaoa, J., Wang, L., Tao, J., & Chen, J. (2014). A security framework in G-Hadoop for big data computing across distributed Cloud data centres. *Journal of Computer and System Sciences*, *80*(5), 994–1007. doi:10.1016/j.jcss.2014.02.006

Zicari, R., Rosselli, M., & Korfiatis, N. (2016). Setting up a big data project: Challenges, opportunities, technologies and optimization. [Springer.]. *Studies in Big Data*, *18*, 17–47. doi:10.1007/978-3-319-30265-2_2

KEY TERMS AND DEFINITIONS

Not Only Structured Query Language (SQL) or Non-SQL (NoSQL): An approach to database design that enables the storage and querying of data outside the traditional structures found in relational databases.

Database Management System (DBMS): Essentially nothing more than a computerized data keeping system. Users of the system are given facilities to perform several kinds of operations on such a system for either manipulation of the data in the database or the management of the database structure itself.

Extracting, Loading, and Transforming (ELT): Data streamlines the tasks of modern data warehousing and managing Big data so that businesses can focus on mining their data for actionable insights.

Extract, Transform, Load (ETL): This is the process of combining data from multiple sources into a large central repository called a data warehouse. It uses a set of business rules to clean and organize raw data and prepare it for storage, data analytics, and machine learning.

The Internet of Things (IOT): A system of interrelated computing devices, mechanical and digital machines, objects, animals or people that are provided with unique identifiers and the ability to transfer data over a network without requiring human-to-human or human-to-computer interaction.

Online Analytical Processing (OLAP): Software technology that can be used to analyze business data from different points of view.

Google Cloud AutoML: Scalable, cost efficient VMs integrated with GCP AI/ML & Analytics. Start for free. Customizable VM Instances with sustained-use & committed-use discounts. Start for free. Deploy At ***Google*** Scale. Access From Anywhere. Focus On Your Product. AutoML enables developers with limited machine learning expertise to train high-quality models specific to their business needs. Build your own custom machine learning model in minutes.

AWS Deep Learning AMIs: This provides ML practitioners and researchers with a curated and secure set of frameworks, dependencies, and tools to accelerate deep learning in the cloud. Built for Amazon Linux and Ubuntu, Amazon Machine Images (AMIs) come preconfigured with TensorFlow, PyTorch, Apache MXNet, Chainer, Microsoft Cognitive Toolkit (CNTK), Gluon, Horovod, and Keras, allowing to quickly deploy and run these frameworks and tools at scale.

Chapter 13
Cloud Analytics:
Introduction, Tools, Applications, Challenges, and Future Trends

Hari Kishan Kondaveeti
https://orcid.org/0000-0002-3379-720X
VIT-AP University, India

Biswajit Biswal
https://orcid.org/0000-0002-7287-9419
South Carolina State University, USA

Licia Saikia
VIT-AP University, India

Udithaa Terala
VIT-AP University, India

Sateesh Gorikapudi
VIT-AP University, India

Valli Kumari Vatsavayi
https://orcid.org/0000-0002-7252-8301
Andhra University, India

ABSTRACT

Cloud analytics is the process of using cloud computing resources and technologies to analyze and gain insights from large and complex data. Cloud analytics has become increasingly popular in recent years due to its scalability, cost-efficiency, and accessibility. It enables organizations to process large datasets, perform complex analytics, and make data-driven decisions more effectively and affordably. This book chapter provides a comprehensive overview of cloud analytics, covering its fundamental principles, significance in today's data-driven landscape, benefits and challenges of adoption, critical tools and technologies, data management in cloud environments, and promising future directions and emerging trends. By the end of this chapter, readers will have a deep understanding of cloud analytics and its potential to revolutionize the way organizations analyze and leverage data.

DOI: 10.4018/979-8-3693-0900-1.ch013

Emerging Trends in Cloud Computing Analytics, Scalability, and Service Models

INTRODUCTION

Cloud analytics is a framework for using cloud technologies to store, process and analyze large and complex data (Achar et al., 2015). Cloud analytics provides fast and efficient data processing, enables real-time analysis, and ensures data security. Its popularity is growing due to its many advantages, including significantly enhancing production quality (Ajah, I.A. et al., 2019).

In the present age,_Cloud analytics has many applications, including data warehousing, big data technologies, data visualization, business intelligence, data security, serverless computing, and more. (Ruiz et al., 2021). At the core of cloud analytics are fundamental services that enable organizations to control the full potential of cloud computing resources and advanced analytics tools for efficient data insight extraction. These principles encompass the following critical components.

- Scalability empowers organizations to allocate resources as needed without substantial upfront investments.
- The cost-efficient pay-as-you-go model ensures organizations only pay for actively used resources, enhancing cost-effectiveness.
- Accessibility is another foundation, allowing users to access cloud analytics solutions from anywhere with an internet connection, facilitating remote collaboration
- Cloud providers guarantee speed and performance with robust infrastructure and advanced processing capabilities.
- Streamlined data integration simplifies data collection, which is necessary for applications requiring immediate insights.
- Predictive analytics, data visualization and business intelligence tools improve decision-making.
- Easy maintenance and disaster recovery capabilities enhance the effectiveness of cloud analytics, allowing organizations to excel in their operations and maintain a competitive edge.

Cloud analytics presents a transformative solution in the present data-driven landscape, where data plays a central role in decision-making and gaining a competitive edge. (Henke et al., 2016). It helps to efficiently collect, process, and analyse data, empowering organizations to make real-time, data-driven decisions (Niu, Y, et al., 2021). In addition, the scalability and cost-effectiveness of Cloud Analytics make it accessible to businesses of all sizes, democratizing data analytics. Cloud Analytics enables organizations to adapt to dynamic market conditions, gain deeper insights into their operations, and enhance competitiveness. With data security and easy maintenance, it offers a secure and low-maintenance solution for data analytics (Ranjan et al.,2021). In a world where data is generated at an unprecedented rate, cloud analytics is essential for harnessing data for strategic and operational advantages.

BACKGROUND

In the current environment, there is a dominant trend where individuals and businesses are primarily engaged in a data-driven ecosystem, where data plays an integral role in the vast majority of their professional activities and decision-making problems (Carillo, K. D. A. 2017). To cope with the challenges posed by the exponential growth of data, the adoption of cloud analytics emerges as a pivotal strategy, serving as a means to extract invaluable insights and secure a competitive advantage. Cloud analytics stands as the convergence of cloud computing and data analytics, signifying a transformative shift in the methods employed for data processing, storage, and utilization for informed decision-making (Smith, S. 2022).

In recent years, the digital landscape has witnessed an exponential shift in the way data is generated, collected, and utilized across industries. Traditional on-premises data processing and analysis systems, have proven to be increasingly inadequate in handling the vast and diverse datasets of the present world (Gaffoor et al.,2021). In response to these challenges, cloud computing has emerged as a revolutionary technological breakthrough, providing a scalable and economically efficient infrastructure for the storage and processing of data (Yang, C et al.,2017). Simultaneously, the evolution of cloud analytics has enabled organizations to tap into the capabilities of cloud technology, facilitating the extraction of actionable insights, streamlining decision-making processes, and ultimately achieving a competitive advantage (Barlette, Y. et.al,2022).

Benefits of Cloud Computing

Cloud computing offers a multitude of advantages for organizations and individuals alike, revolutionizing the way we store, access, and process data. A significant advantage of cloud computing is its capacity to reduce the need for investment on individual software or servers (Attaran, M.et,al,2019). Users can access applications and storage from remote locations, thereby eliminating the necessity for physical infrastructure and costly individual installations. By utilizing this feature of the cloud, businesses can reduce ongoing maintenance expenses. Along with this, adoption of Cloud analytics reduces expenses related to licensing fees, as well as cut down on overhead costs, including expenses for data storage, software updates, and management. The cost reduction and expandable quality of hosting data on a non-physical server has proven to be extremely beneficial to the data management and processing practices.

Another key benefit provided by Cloud Analytics is that it brings a significant enhancement to crucial elements like speed and ease of management (Vergilio, T. et al., 2018). For example, Google, a pioneering company in data-centric services, utilizes a framework for executing Big Data Analytics known as Google Cloud Dataproc. This service is a fully adaptable and automated cloud-based solution based on Apache Hadoop and Spark, efficiently streamlining and accelerating cluster management operations while delivering speed, simplicity, and cost efficiency. Being an open-source framework, it presents significant functionalities and advantages, including rapid cluster scaling and economical operations.

Cloud Analytics has demonstrated its efficiency in managing big data on par with traditional analytical tools. Cloud analytics algorithms are applied to massive data sets in the same way that on-premises data analytics algorithms are. This allows the algorithms to find trends, forecast future outcomes, and create other information that is helpful to business decision-makers (Mavridis, I. et al., 2017).

Cloud analytics and cloud services in general also prove to be extremely beneficial in terms of availability for users regardless of their location (Maheshwari et al.,2021). This strategy facilitates convenient information access and caters to the diverse requirements of individuals in various time zones and geographic regions. Additionally, an incidental advantage is the surge in collaborative efforts, as it becomes significantly more straightforward to access, view, and edit shared documents and files. Cloud Analytics has become rapidly growing field due to this feature of accessibility of big data, regardless of its physical location of storage.

Another key feature of Cloud Analytics is its massive Scalability (Bemthuis, R. et.al,2020). This capability enables infrastructure, resources, and services to adjust and grow smoothly, handling changing workloads and diverse data volumes without impacting performance. Scalability is an inherent attribute of cloud environments where cloud instances are provisioned automatically as and when required, enabling us to pay solely for the necessary applications and data storage. It also additionally provides elasticity, as cloud resources can be adjusted to align with your evolving user and system requirements.

Cloud Analytics inherits greater grip over the traditional approach toward data handling and analytics as it is highly resilient. Resilience within a cloud service refers to its ability to swiftly recover from disordering. This depends on the Internet, cloud databases, servers, and the speed at which the network can recover and restart. Ultimately, resilience ensures uninterrupted accessibility.

Analytics has forever aimed to enhance decision-making, a principle unaffected by the advent of big data. Embracing big data analytics using cloud services significantly enhances the decision-making abilities of business managers. Major corporations are actively pursuing faster and superior decision-making use of big data, and they are successfully achieving this goal.

The other benefit offered by cloud analytics is its ability to accommodate and store significantly more data than a personal computer. This feature essentially provides nearly unlimited storage capacity, alleviating concerns about reaching storage limits (Gür, 2018). Additionally, this feature relieves businesses from the necessity of constantly upgrading their computer hardware, thereby reducing overall costs. Businesses now have the capability to adjust computing resources in real-time according to the workload requirements, effectively enhancing performance while ensuring cost efficiency. The decentralized structure of big data processing in the cloud allows for parallel processing, resulting in a substantial reduction in processing time and a significant boost to data processing capabilities.

CHALLENGES ASSOCIATED WITH THE ADOPTION OF CLOUD ANALYTICS

The implementation of cloud analytics presents a host of challenges that organizations must navigate in order to use it to its full potential and derive maximum value from this innovative technology. Relying on an internet connection poses a significant challenge when integrating cloud analytics into the workspace (Hwang et al.,2017). In contrast, conventional computing and analysis tools rely on a physical, hardwired connection to access data stored on servers or storage devices. The reliance on cloud storage and processing on a stable internet connection means that a poor or disrupted connection might impede access to essential information or applications, potentially hindering productivity and access to necessary resources. This reliance on a consistent and robust internet connection is a notable factor to consider when opting for cloud-based services, as interruptions can impact operational continuity and accessibility.

Another issue is the risk of vendor lock-in (Hwang et al.,2017). Vendor lock-in in cloud analytics refers to a situation where a company becomes overly dependent on a particular cloud service provider technology, making it difficult to switch to another vendor without significant challenges or costs. This dependence restricts the ability to migrate data, applications, or processes to an alternative cloud platform or return to an on-premises environment. The risk arises due to the proprietary nature of certain cloud services, unique formats, or specialized tools offered by specific providers, creating a potential barrier to transitioning to other platforms.

A company utilizing a specific cloud service provides unique database or data warehousing technology might find it challenging to easily transfer their data to another platform (Ray, 2016). This is because the data is formatted or optimized specifically for that system, making migration complex and costly. Consequently, businesses could face substantial hurdles and costs in extracting, converting, or reformatting data to be compatible with another technology.

If a company integrates various services or tools from a single cloud provider, migrating away from that provider could be even more complex. For instance, if a business uses a specific cloud provider for analytics, storage, machine learning, and other services, the inter dependencies among these services can create intricate linkages. Shifting these interconnected components to another provider might not be straightforward and could require substantial reconfiguration and redevelopment, thereby posing a significant challenge. The risk of vendor lock-in highlights the importance of strategizing and designing cloud architectures to maintain flexibility and minimize reliance on proprietary features (Harauzek, 2022).

Implementing open standards and ensuring compatibility across multiple platforms can mitigate the risks associated with being locked into eco system of a specific vendor. Integrating the new cloud analytics solution with the existing systems can present various challenges that are mentioned below.

When an organization transitions to cloud-based analytics, several challenges may arise that need to be addressed for a successful integration. One key challenge involves data migration and compatibility, particularly when dealing with a substantial volume of historical data stored in on-premises systems. Transferring this data to the cloud while ensuring compatibility with new analytics tools can be complex due to differences in data formats, structures, or storage methods. Another challenge is interoperability, as integrating cloud analytics with existing systems may encounter compatibility issues. Legacy systems may not readily communicate or sync with the new cloud-based analytics tools, necessitating the development of middleware or connectors to facilitate data exchange between systems.

Ensuring data security and compliance standards, such as GDPR, HIPAA, or industry-specific regulations, across integrated systems is a critical challenge. Maintaining data privacy and security during data movement between on-premises and cloud environments requires careful consideration. Operational adaptation is essential, as employees need to adjust to using the new cloud analytics tools. Training and change management play a crucial role in ensuring that the workforce can effectively utilize the new system without disruptions to ongoing operations.

Finally, aligning the performance of existing systems with the capabilities of the cloud analytics platform is a considerable task. It's essential to ensure that the systems work seamlessly together without performance bottlenecks or downtimes. These challenges should be addressed proactively to maximize the benefits of cloud-based analytics while minimizing potential disruptions.

To address these challenges, companies might employ middleware or integration tools to bridge the gap between on-premises and cloud systems (Zhang, X. et.al,2020).

Cloud analytics could also gradually transition to the cloud by initially moving a subset of data or specific functions to test the integration and address any issues before full-scale adoption. Concerns about security risks, particularly data privacy, represent a significant challenge in the realm of cloud analytics. When organizations entrust their data to cloud service providers for analytics purposes, several potential security issues come to the forefront the most crucial ones are mentioned below (Singh, S. et.al,2016)

Storing sensitive data on cloud servers raises concerns about maintaining the confidentiality and privacy of that information. Instances of unauthorized access, data breaches, or leaks could compromise private and sensitive information.

Various industries and regions have specific data protection regulations (such as GDPR, HIPAA, or CCPA) that mandate strict rules for handling and securing sensitive information. Ensuring compliance with these regulations becomes crucial when data is stored or processed in the cloud.

Cloud systems' broad accessibility may lead to security vulnerabilities. Ensuring robust access controls, strong authentication measures, and encryption techniques are crucial to prevent unauthorized access and protect data.

Cloud data might be stored across various geographic locations. This raises concerns about the physical location of the data and compliance with laws governing data residency and sovereignty in different regions.

Cloud services typically use shared infrastructure, meaning multiple users' data resides on the same servers. While efforts are made to segregate and secure data, the shared nature of the infrastructure poses potential risks if not properly managed.

Trusting a third-party cloud service provider involves understanding their security practices and ensuring transparency regarding how data is handled, stored, and protected.

Addressing all these challenges requires a comprehensive strategy that includes robust security measures, careful planning for data migration and integration, cost management frameworks, and ongoing staff training (Moss, et al.,2003). Organizations need to prioritize data governance, risk assessment, and compliance measures to overcome these obstacles and leverage the full potential of cloud analytics.

CLOUD ANALYTICS TOOLS

Cloud analytics tools revolutionize the way businesses analyse and derive insights from their data, offering advanced solutions and capabilities for efficient processing, storage, and interpretation of information within the cloud environment. The utilization of cloud analytics is gradually gaining traction across organizations of varying sizes. However, the diverse implementation models and customization requirements of various applications pose a challenge for widespread adoption. Despite the challenges, organizations are embracing cloud analytics due to its numerous business advantages.

Cloud-based services within the realm of cloud analytic tools encompass a diverse array of solutions aimed at leveraging the power of the cloud for data analysis. These services offer an innovative approach to managing, processing, and interpreting data, providing businesses with scalable, flexible, and accessible resources to drive insights and decision-making. By utilizing the cloud environment, these tools facilitate seamless data processing, storage, and sharing, empowering organizations to harness the full potential of their data with increased efficiency and agility.

Cloud-based services encompass four primary models: Data as a Service (DaaS), Software as a Service (SaaS), Platform as a Service (PaaS), and Infrastructure as a Service (IaaS). SaaS simplifies user access to pre-built applications running in the cloud, sparing users from the responsibility of managing the underlying infrastructure.

PaaS provides users with developmental environment services, enabling the creation and launch of in-house applications. It includes crucial components like operating systems, programming language environments, databases, and web servers. IaaS offers users virtualized infrastructure, such as servers and storage space, leveraging virtualization to deliver resources on demand from extensive data centre pools.

DaaS, on the other hand, provides readily accessible data through a cloud-based platform, revolutionizing the approach to accessing essential business data within existing data centres. In essence, DaaS is a novel method for tapping into critical data repositories housed within a data centre. (Barroso, L. A. et.al,2019).

Within the cloud analytics, several tools stand out as prevalent and extensively utilized. These tools play an important role in transforming data analysis and interpretation within cloud environments, offering advanced functionalities to meet the diverse needs of businesses across various industries. Several dominant and widely used tools in the realm of cloud analytics are essential for managing and processing extensive datasets efficiently, some of them are mentioned below.

Redshift, a fully managed cloud service, acts as a robust and high-speed data warehouse capable of handling petabyte-scale datasets (Thota, C. et al., 2021). It employs massively parallel processing architecture for intricate analytical queries and offers a Serverless feature, eliminating the need to establish a provisioned data warehouse, streamlining retrieval and scrutiny processes.

BigQuery, an enterprise data warehouse, offers managed solutions for data analysis and integrates advanced features like machine learning and geospatial analysis. Its serverless design enables users to conduct extensive data exploration through SQL queries without managing infrastructure. With a scalable and distributed analysis engine, BigQuery empowers users to process terabytes of data within seconds and petabytes within minutes, making it a potent tool for large-scale data analysis in research environments.

Apache Hadoop, an open-source framework, effectively manages substantial datasets ranging from gigabytes to petabytes (Rao, T. R. et al., 2019). It clusters multiple computers for parallel analysis, leveraging the Hadoop Distributed File System (HDFS) for superior data throughput. The ecosystem includes Yet Another Resource Negotiator (YARN) for resource management, MapReduce for parallel computation, and Hadoop Common, providing shared Java libraries across the Hadoop ecosystem.

Apache Spark, another open-source distributed processing system, handles significant big data workloads (Shaikh, E. et al., 2019). It uses in-memory caching and optimized query execution for rapid analytic queries on datasets of any scale. With development APIs in various languages, Spark allows code reuse across batch processing, interactive queries, real-time analytics, machine learning, and graph processing.

Tableau, a leading data visualization tool, is extensively used in Business Intelligence and Data Science (Sharma, K. et al., 2021). Its primary objective is to aid data comprehension by enabling users to visualize and explore complex datasets, transforming raw data into actionable insights through interactive visual representations.

Power BI, an advanced cloud-based analytics tool developed by Microsoft (Machiraju, S. et al., 2018), enables comprehensive data analysis and visualization from diverse sources. It connects to various data sources, fostering informed decision-making by providing tools for data modelling and tailored data frameworks for meaningful insights extraction.

MANAGING DATA IN CLOUD ENVIRONMENTS

Cloud data management involves practicing, processing, and utilizing technologies for storing, organizing, securing, and optimizing data within cloud computing environments. In cloud data management, various tasks revolve around data storage, retrieval, backup, recovery, and analysis, all of which occur within the

Figure 1. Data elements in cloud storage

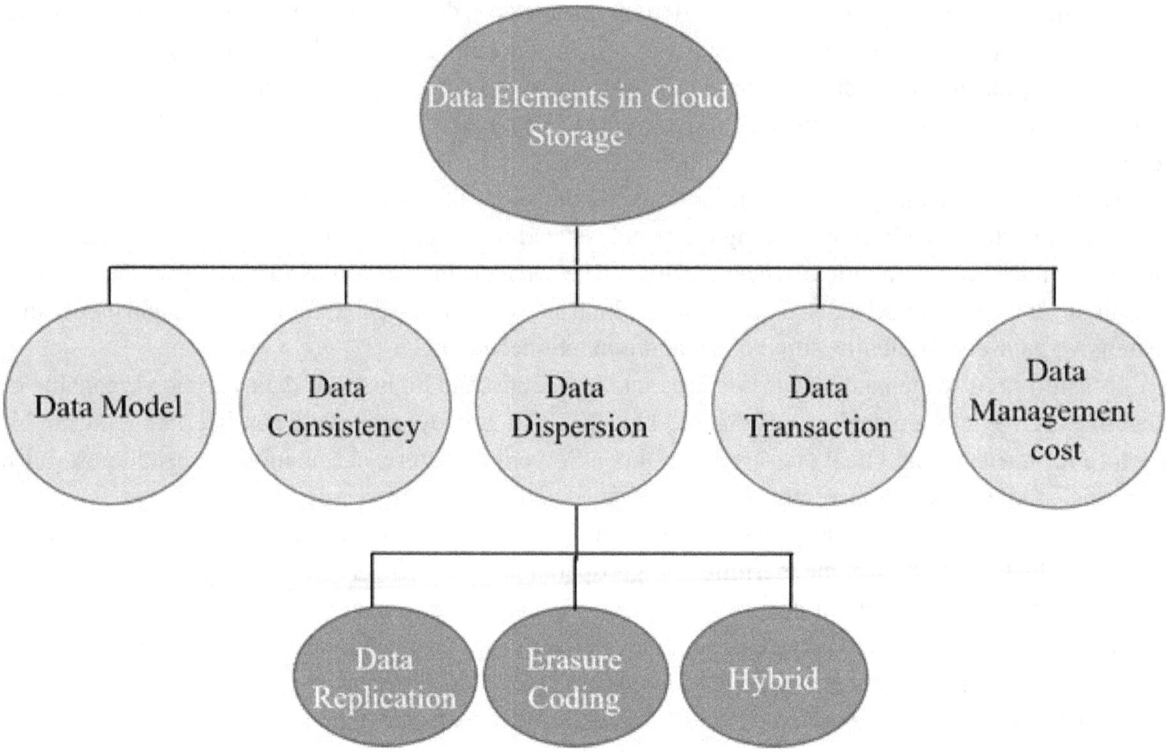

cloud. This aspect of data management holds immense importance for businesses and organizations that use cloud utilities and services. cloud addresses critical aspects like ensuring data availability, accessibility, and security, all while optimizing data resources. In short, cloud data management encompasses data storage, data backup, data security, data integration, data analysis, and data governance. Lately, we have observed major companies such as Amazon, Google, IBM, Microsoft, and Sun Microsystems launching the construction of new data centres worldwide. Cloud data centres are designed to host Cloud computing applications, serving the dual purpose of providing redundancy and ensuring reliability in the event of site failures (Bauer et.al,2012). Cloud computing strategic approach is undertaken to enhance the dependability and resilience of cloud services.

Cloud computing ensures absolute availability in data management by providing uninterrupted access to both read and write data without encountering any blocks or restrictions. This availability guarantees consistently stable response times, regardless of concurrent user counts, database size, or any other system parameter. Additionally, users benefit from seamless backup management, relieving them of the responsibility for backups.

Figure 1 displays the Data Elements within Cloud Storage. The outlined elements cover various aspects crucial to managing data in the cloud environment.

Within the cloud storage context, a data model functions as the fundamental framework that organizes, structures, and represents the stored and processed data. It defines the structural format for organizing data in cloud storage, encompassing diverse models such as relational databases, NoSQL databases, and object storage.

Data transactions are fundamental operations involving the reading and writing of data within the cloud. They ensure the reliability and consistency of these processes, with service levels defining the quality of service provided by cloud storage providers, including metrics like data availability, durability, and response times.

The costs associated with data management encompass expenses related to data storage, processing, and overall management. These costs vary based on factors such as data volume, access patterns, and storage tiers.

Data replication involves strategically creating redundant data copies in different locations to enhance data availability and fault tolerance.

Hybrid cloud storage represents the convergence of on-premises and cloud storage solutions, enabling the combined and cooperative use of both environments (Deb et al., 2021).

Data dispersion techniques distribute data across multiple locations to fortify security and availability while mitigating the risks of data loss. An essential approach, erasure coding, fragments data into smaller units, introduces redundancy, and disperses these units across storage devices to improve data recovery and fault tolerance.

Ensuring data consistency is vital to guarantee the accuracy and uniformity of data across various system segments, ensuring that all users encounter the same data at any given point in time. Cloud storage elements collectively play a pivotal role in nurturing effective data management within cloud storage environments, addressing fundamental aspects of data organization, reliability, cost optimization, and robust data protection. The selection and implementation of cloud storage elements are contingent on the distinct requirements and objectives of individual businesses and organizations, underpinning the versatility and adaptability of cloud data management strategies (Mould-Ul-Huq et al.,2020).

CHALLENGES IN MANAGING DATA IN CLOUD ENVIRONMENTS

Managing data within cloud environments presents a range of complex challenges that organizations must face to effectively harness the full potential of cloud technology. Addressing these challenges is essential in ensuring the seamless and secure management of data, enabling businesses to capitalize on the agility and scalability offered by cloud platforms while upholding data integrity and privacy. Ensuring service availability in a distributed system operating across an extensive network is a fundamental concern, with potential network disruptions posing financial and trust-related risks for organizations.

Data confidentiality is a critical consideration when relocating data off-premises. Transnational databases often contain sensitive information, and data encryption and security measures are essential to prevent unauthorized access. Other challenges include the need for robust security, effective data governance policies, and integration with existing IT systems and applications when deploying cloud analytics solutions. Various cloud analytics platforms and tools are available, each with its own strengths and weaknesses. Data lock-in is another issue, as the lack of standardized cloud computing APIs makes data migration between providers complex, potentially leading to concerns about price hikes, reliability, or provider discontinuation. Efficient data transfer and traffic management, application parallelization, and adherence to a shared-nothing architecture are essential for optimizing cloud resource utilization. Performance unpredictability, debugging large-scale distributed systems, and addressing security issues, including data privacy, data breaches, regulatory compliance, and data residency, are additional challenges that demand attention in cloud data management. These complexities underscore the importance of robust encryption, access controls, and preventive security measures to safeguard sensitive data.

Effectively managing user identities and access to cloud data, including strong authentication and authorization mechanisms is paramount. Data loss and recovery strategies are necessary to maintain data integrity. Protection against malware and phishing attacks is vital, along with mitigating insider threats. Strategies to prevent vendor lock-in and address the vulnerability of denial-of-service attacks are also needed. Regularly applying security patches, data encryption, robust auditing and monitoring, and the adoption of a zero-trust security model are further security measures (Sarkar, et al.,2022). Combining technology, policies, and user awareness is essential to address these challenges effectively and protect cloud-stored data.

Real-Time Analysis

Google: Big-table / App Engine Data store:

Google employs Big table as a system for storing data across multiple locations to manage structured information. Big table engineered for extensive scalability, capable of managing vast amounts of data, often reaching petabytes, across numerous commodity servers. Big table finds applications in over sixty Google products and projects, including the Google search engine, Google Finance, Orkut, Google Docs, and Google Earth. Google utilizes Big table across its services to accommodate various workloads, ranging from high-throughput batch processing to providing responsive data service for end-users (Thota, C. et al.,2021).

Yahoo!: PNUTS/Sherpa:

The PNUTS system, later named Sherpa, serves as a large hosted database system designed for Yahoo!'s web applications. This system divides into regions, each containing a full set of system components and a complete copy of all tables. While regions are generally but not always spread geographically, it's essential to highlight that the PNUTS system doesn't use a standard database log for specifying or archiving data. The system relies on a straightforward relational model where data is structured into tables consisting of records with attributes.

Amazon (Dynamo / S3 / Simple DB / RDS/Redshift):

Amazon provides a suite of data storage and management services that cater to a range of functionalities. One of these services, Dynamo, is a distributed key-value data store designed to support internal Amazon applications. Using a consistent hashing mechanism, Dynamo evenly distributes work among numerous storage hosts. Each data item is replicated across multiple hosts based on a parameter (N) set per instance, with a unique key assigned to a coordinator node. Amazon S3 (Simple Storage Service) is a web-based service for public online data storage provided by Amazon. It enables users to store and retrieve data conveniently over the internet. SimpleDB organizes data into domains, akin to tables, where data can be stored, retrieved, and queried. Each domain comprises items, analogous to records, defined by attribute names and corresponding value pairs. The Relational Database Service (RDS) allows access to the complete functionalities of established databases like MySQL. It offers users a wide range of database management capabilities. Amazon Redshift, a fully managed petabyte-scale data warehouse service in the cloud, is built on massively parallel processing (MPP) architecture. This enables it to handle large datasets and complex analytical queries. Redshift is highly scalable and allows analysis of data from various sources, including operational databases, data lakes, and object storage (Armbrust et al., 2020).

Microsoft: DRYAD / SQL Azure:

Dryad, developed by Microsoft, serves as a distributed execution engine for coarse-grain data-parallel applications. It offers developers detailed control over the communication graph and the routines at its vertices. One of Dryad's key features is its ability to allow graph vertices and computations to use different numbers of inputs and outputs. This differs from Map Reduce, where computations are limited to taking one input set and producing a single output set.

Trade-Offs of Cloud Data Management

Cloud data management presents few trade-offs where organizations must carefully balance various factors to optimize their data storage, accessibility, and security in the cloud. Balancing these competing aspects is essential for businesses aiming to derive maximum value from their cloud-based data while ensuring efficiency, compliance, and robust protection of sensitive information.

Cloud data management involves various components that organizations must carefully balance to optimize data storage, accessibility, and security. Elastic compute clusters dynamically scale based on the application's requirements. Persistent storage, akin to traditional databases and file systems, is structured to be both scalable and reliable. Intra-cloud networks interconnect virtual application instances and cloud-provided services. Wide-area delivery networks (WANs) disseminate application content to end users across multiple global data centres. These elements form a crucial part of optimizing cloud-based data management.

CONCLUSION

Cloud analytics has revolutionized the way organizations process and analyze data. It enabled unprecedented scalability, agility, and accessibility. This book chapter provideds a comprehensive overview of the Cloud Analytics, exploring its potential, applications, challenges associated with its adoption, and limitations. While challenges like data interoperability, integration, and security remain focal points for further development of this domain, hybrid and multi-cloud strategies are gaining traction, optimizing the advantages of different deployment models. Cloud analytics applications are expanding into various sectors, particularly healthcare, finance, and IoT. Real-time analytics will also gain significance, enabling rapid decision-making. The integration of Artificial Intelligence (AI) techniques with Cloud Analytics will transform predictive and prescriptive analytics, providing deeper insights and more accurate forecasts. Augmented analytics will democratize data analysis with intelligent, automated suggestions.

REFERENCES

Ajah, I. A., & Nweke, H. F. (2019). Big data and business analytics: Trends, platforms, success factors and applications. *Big Data and Cognitive Computing*, *3*(2), 32. doi:10.3390/bdcc3020032

Armbrust, M., Das, T., Sun, L., Yavuz, B., Zhu, S., Murthy, M., Torres, J., van Hovell, H., Ionescu, A., Łuszczak, A., Świtakowski, M., Szafrański, M., Li, X., Ueshin, T., Mokhtar, M., Boncz, P., Ghodsi, A., Paranjpye, S., Senster, P., & Zaharia, M. (2020). Delta lake: High-performance ACID table storage over cloud object stores. *Proceedings of the VLDB Endowment International Conference on Very Large Data Bases, 13*(12), 3411–3424. doi:10.14778/3415478.3415560

Attaran, M., & Woods, J. (2019). Cloud computing technology: Improving small business performance using the Internet. *Journal of Small Business and Entrepreneurship, 31*(6), 495–519. doi:10.1080/08276331.2018.1466850

Barlette, Y., & Baillette, P. (2022). Big data analytics in turbulent contexts: Towards organizational change for enhanced agility. *Production Planning and Control, 33*(2-3), 105–122. doi:10.1080/09537287.2020.1810755

Barroso, L. A., Hölzle, U., & Ranganathan, P. (2019). *The datacenter as a computer: Designing warehouse-scale machines*. Springer Nature. doi:10.1007/978-3-031-01761-2

Bemthuis, R., Iacob, M. E., & Havinga, P. (2020). A design of the resilient enterprise: A reference architecture for emergent behaviors control. *Sensors (Basel), 20*(22), 6672. doi:10.3390/s20226672 PMID:33233426

Carillo, K. D. A. (2017). Let's stop trying to be "sexy"–preparing managers for the (big) data-driven business era. *Business Process Management Journal, 23*(3), 598–622. doi:10.1108/BPMJ-09-2016-0188

Deb, M., & Choudhury, A. (2021). Hybrid cloud: A new paradigm in cloud computing. *Machine Learning Techniques and Analytics for Cloud Security*, 1-23.

Gaffoor, Z., Pietersen, K., Bagula, A., Jovanovic, N., Kanyerere, T., & Wanangwa, G. (2021). *Big Data Analytics and Modelling*. Research Gate.

Gür, T. M. (2018). Review of electrical energy storage technologies, materials and systems: Challenges and prospects for large-scale grid storage. *Energy & Environmental Science, 11*(10), 2696–2767. doi:10.1039/C8EE01419A

Harauzek, D. (2022). *Cloud Computing: Challenges of cloud computing from business users perspective-vendor lock-in*. LinkedIn.

Henke, N., & Jacques Bughin, L. (2016). *The age of analytics: Competing in a data-driven world*. McKinsey.

Hwang, K., & Chen, M. (2017). *Big-data analytics for cloud, IoT and cognitive computing*. John Wiley & Sons.

Lu, Y., & Xu, X. (2019). Cloud-based manufacturing equipment and big data analytics to enable on-demand manufacturing services. *Robotics and Computer-integrated Manufacturing, 57*, 92–102. doi:10.1016/j.rcim.2018.11.006

Machiraju, S., & Gaurav, S. (2018). *Power BI Data Analysis and Visualization*. De-G Press. doi:10.1515/9781547400720

Maheshwari, S., Gautam, P., & Jaggi, C. K. (2021). Role of Big Data Analytics in supply chain management: Current trends and future perspectives. *International Journal of Production Research, 59*(6), 1875-1900.

Moudud-Ul-Huq, S., Asaduzzaman, M., & Biswas, T. (2020). Role of cloud computing in global accounting information systems. *The Bottom Line (New York, N.Y.), 33*(3), 231–250. doi:10.1108/BL-01-2020-0010

Niu, Y., Ying, L., Yang, J., Bao, M., & Sivaparthipan, C. B. (2021). Organizational business intelligence and decision making using big data analytics. *Information Processing & Management, 58*(6), 102725. doi:10.1016/j.ipm.2021.102725

Opara-Martins, J., Sahandi, R., & Tian, F. (2016). Critical analysis of vendor lock-in and its impact on cloud computing migration: A business perspective. *Journal of Cloud Computing (Heidelberg, Germany), 5*(1), 1–18. doi:10.1186/s13677-016-0054-z

Ranjan, J., & Foropon, C. (2021). Big data analytics in building the competitive intelligence of organizations. *International Journal of Information Management, 56*, 102231. doi:10.1016/j.ijinfomgt.2020.102231

Rao, T. R., Mitra, P., Bhatt, R., & Goswami, A. (2019). The big data system, components, tools, and technologies: A survey. *Knowledge and Information Systems, 60*(3), 1165–1245. doi:10.1007/s10115-018-1248-0

Ray, P. P. (2016). A survey of IoT cloud platforms. *Future Computing and Informatics Journal, 1*(1-2), 35–46. doi:10.1016/j.fcij.2017.02.001

Ruiz, M. D., Gómez-Romero, J., Fernandez-Basso, C., & Martin-Bautista, M. J. (2021). Big data architecture for building energy management systems. *IEEE Transactions on Industrial Informatics, 18*(9), 5738–5747. doi:10.1109/TII.2021.3130052

Sarkar, S., Choudhary, G., Shandilya, S. K., Hussain, A., & Kim, H. (2022). Security of zero trust networks in cloud computing: A comparative review. *Sustainability (Basel), 14*(18), 11213. doi:10.3390/su141811213

Shaikh, E., Mohiuddin, I., Alufaisan, Y., & Nahvi, I. (2019, November). Apache spark: A big data processing engine. *In 2019 2nd IEEE Middle East and North Africa COMMunications Conference (MENACOMM)* (pp. 1-6). IEEE. 10.1109/MENACOMM46666.2019.8988541

Shakerkhan, K. O., & Abilmazhinov, E. T. (2019). Development of a Method for Choosing Cloud Computing on the Platform of Paas for Servicing the State Agencies. *International Journal of Modern Education & Computer Science, 11*(9), 14–25. doi:10.5815/ijmecs.2019.09.02

Sharma, K., Shetty, A., Jain, A., & Dhanare, R. K. (2021, January). A Comparative Analysis on Various Business Intelligence (BI), Data Science and Data Analytics Tools. In *2021 International Conference on Computer Communication and Informatics (ICCCI)* (pp. 1-11). IEEE. 10.1109/ICCCI50826.2021.9402226

Singh, S., Jeong, Y. S., & Park, J. H. (2016). A survey on cloud computing security: Issues, threats, and solutions. *Journal of Network and Computer Applications, 75*, 200–222. doi:10.1016/j.jnca.2016.09.002

Smith, S. (2022). Maximizing Cloud Computing Benefits in the Age of Big Data. *INTERNATIONAL JOURNAL OF COMPUTER SCIENCE AND TECHNOLOGY, 6*(1), 103–118.

Thota, C., Manogaran, G., Lopez, D., & Sundarasekar, R. (2021). Architecture for big data storage in different cloud deployment models. In Research Anthology on Architectures, Frameworks, and Integration Strategies for Distributed and Cloud Computing (pp. 178-208). IGI Global. doi:10.4018/978-1-7998-5339-8.ch009

Vergilio, T., & Ramachandran, M. (2018, January). PaaS-BDP a multi-cloud architectural pattern for big data processing on a platform-as-a-service model. In *COMPLEXIS 2018-Proceedings of the 3rd International Conference on Complexity, Future Information Systems and Risk* (pp. 45-52). SciTePress. 10.5220/0006632400450052

Wu, C., & Buyya, R. (2015). *Cloud Data Centers and Cost Modeling: A complete guide to planning, designing and building a cloud data center*. Morgan Kaufmann.

Yang, C., Huang, Q., Li, Z., Liu, K., & Hu, F. (2017). Big Data and cloud computing: Innovation opportunities and challenges. *International Journal of Digital Earth*, *10*(1), 13–53. doi:10.1080/17538947.2016.1239771

Zhang, X., & Yue, W. T. (2020). *Integration of on-premises and cloud-based software: the product bundling perspective*. Forthcoming in Journal of the Association for Information Systems.

KEY TERMS AND DEFINITIONS

Artificial Intelligence: Artificial intelligence (AI) is the ability of a machine to think and act like a human, including the ability to learn, reason, solve problems, and make decisions.

Data Governance: Organizations need to establish effective data governance policies and procedures to manage their data in the cloud.

Data Integration: Power BI facilitates connectivity to an extensive array of data sources, encompassing cloud-based platforms like Azure Data Lake, Azure SQL Data Warehouse, and online services such as Excel, SharePoint, and more. This seamless integration process streamlines data aggregation and transformation, laying the groundwork for comprehensive analysis.

Data Modeling: Power BI equips users with a suite of tools for data modelling, encompassing functionalities such as relationship establishment, calculated column creation, and defining measures. This capability enables users to craft data models tailored to their specific business requirements and hierarchies, ensuring a structured data framework conducive to extracting meaningful insights.

Data Privacy: Storing sensitive data on cloud servers raises concerns about maintaining the confidentiality and privacy of that information. Instances of unauthorized access, data breaches, or leaks could compromise private and sensitive information.

Deep Learning (DL): Deep learning is a type of machine learning that uses artificial neural networks to learn from large amounts of data and solve complex problems.

Edge Computing: Edge computing is a distributed computing paradigm that brings computation and data storage closer to the location where it is needed.

Elastic compute clusters: These clusters scale up or down on demand to meet the needs of the application.

Integration: Organizations need to integrate their cloud analytics solutions with their existing IT systems and applications.

Intra-Cloud Networks: These networks connect the virtual instances of an application to each other and cloud-provided services.

Persistent Storage: This storage is similar to traditional databases and file systems, but it is designed to be salable and reliable.

Security: Organizations need to take appropriate measures to ensure the security and privacy of their data in the cloud.

Wide-Area Delivery Networks (WANs): These networks deliver the application's content to end users from multiple data centers around the world.

Chapter 14
Serverless Computing Real-World Applications and Benefits in Cloud Environments

Tarun Kumar Vashishth
https://orcid.org/0000-0001-9916-9575
IIMT University, India

Vikas Sharma
https://orcid.org/0000-0001-8173-4548
IIMT University, India

Kewal Krishan Sharma
https://orcid.org/0009-0001-2504-9607
IIMT University, India

Bhupendra Kumar
IIMT University, India

Sachin Chaudhary
https://orcid.org/0000-0002-8415-0043
IIMT University, India

Rajneesh Panwar
https://orcid.org/0009-0000-5974-191X
IIMT University, India

ABSTRACT

Serverless computing has emerged as a transformative paradigm in cloud environments, revolutionizing the way applications are developed and deployed. In traditional computing models, developers had to manage the underlying infrastructure, server provisioning, and scaling, leading to increased complexity and operational overhead. Serverless computing abstracts away these concerns, allowing developers to focus solely on writing code and delivering business value. This chapter explores the real-world applications and benefits of serverless computing, shedding light on its practical implications for businesses and developers. One of the most significant advantages of serverless computing lies in its ability to dynamically scale resources based on demand, ensuring optimal performance and cost-efficiency. This elasticity enables applications to handle variable workloads effectively, avoiding the underutilization or over provisioning of resources.

DOI: 10.4018/979-8-3693-0900-1.ch014

INTRODUCTION TO SERVERLESS COMPUTING

Serverless computing represents a transformative paradigm in the world of cloud computing. It's a concept that has gained remarkable popularity due to its potential to revolutionize the way applications are developed and managed. In this chapter, we will delve into the core aspects of serverless computing, starting with its definition and concept, followed by an exploration of its historical context and its evolution within the broader landscape of cloud computing.

Definition and Concept of Serverless Computing

Serverless computing is a revolutionary paradigm within cloud computing that shifts the traditional approach to application development and deployment. Serverless Computing is a new form of computing architecture that is becoming increasingly popular due to its advantages of scalability, cost-efficiency, and increased flexibility. Shafiei, Khonsari, and Mousavi (2022) provide a comprehensive overview of serverless computing, exploring its opportunities, challenges, and applications. They found that serverless computing has been adopted for a wide variety of use cases, including web and mobile backend, IoT applications, data processing, machine learning, and DevOps. At its core, serverless computing frees developers from the burdens of managing servers and infrastructure, allowing them to focus solely on writing code and executing tasks. In this model, cloud service providers take on the responsibilities of provisioning, scaling, and maintaining the underlying hardware and software resources. Serverless applications are event-driven, meaning they run in response to specific events or triggers, which can be anything from an HTTP request to changes in a database. This dynamic resource allocation and event-based execution lead to several key benefits, including cost efficiency, scalability, and reduced operational overhead. The concept of serverless computing marks a significant departure from traditional server-based models, and its innovative approach has rapidly gained popularity due to its potential to streamline application development, enhance flexibility, and optimize resource utilization in cloud environments. Eskandani and Salvaneschi (2021) present a new dataset for serverless computing, called the Wonderless Dataset. The dataset consists of real-world serverless workloads, such as Amazon Web Services Lambda and Google Cloud Functions, and provides comprehensive performance metrics to enable better performance analysis and optimization. The authors also discuss the implications for serverless computing and provide a comprehensive evaluation of the dataset. The findings of this study will be of great use to researchers and practitioners exploring serverless computing.

Serverless computing architecture is a revolutionary approach in cloud computing that fundamentally transforms the traditional server-centric model. In a serverless architecture, the primary focus shifts from managing servers to executing individual functions in response to specific events. At the core of this model is Function as a Service (FaaS), where developers deploy discrete functions that are triggered by events such as HTTP requests, database modifications, or file uploads. These functions are executed in ephemeral, stateless containers, eliminating the need for continuous server management. Event-driven programming is a cornerstone of serverless computing, where events, like changes in data or the passage of time, dynamically trigger the execution of functions. Key characteristics include automatic scaling, where cloud providers handle the scaling of resources based on demand, and a pay-as-you-go pricing model, ensuring cost efficiency by charging only for actual function execution time. This architecture enhances agility, scalability, and cost-effectiveness, allowing developers to focus on code logic without

Figure 1. Serverless computing architecture

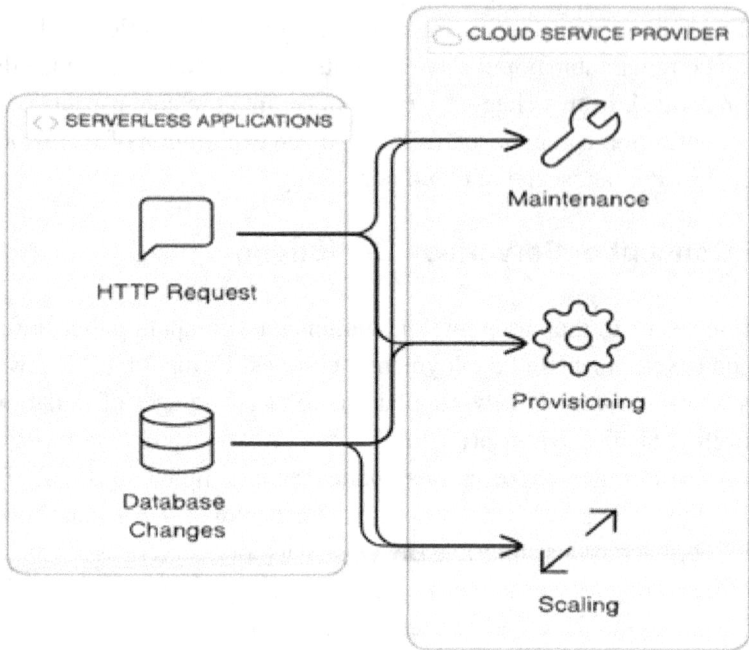

the overhead of infrastructure management. Serverless computing has become a transformative force, facilitating the development of highly scalable and responsive applications.

The Evolution of Serverless in Cloud Computing

Cloud environments have become increasingly important in the world of technology. Serverless computing has played a pivotal role in revolutionizing cloud environments. Serverless computing enables developers to write and deploy applications without managing the underlying infrastructure. This has significantly improved the productivity of developers as they can focus on building applications rather than spending time on managing servers. Cassel et al. (2022) conducted a systematic literature review of serverless computing for IoT and its implications. The authors found that serverless computing could be beneficial for IoT applications in terms of scalability, flexibility, and cost-effectiveness. Additionally, serverless computing has enabled the development of microservices architecture, which promotes scalability, resilience, and ease of deployment for complex applications. The recent increase in cloud computing technologies has led to an evolution of Platform as a Service (PaaS) to Serverless Computing. In their paper, Van Eyk et al. (2018) explore the current landscape of cloud computing and discuss the potential of Serverless Computing for businesses. The authors present case studies of companies that have successfully implemented this new technology and provide insights into the benefits and challenges of using Serverless Computing.

Serverless computing has also paved the way for new innovations in areas such as artificial intelligence (AI) and machine learning (ML). These technologies require massive amounts of data to be processed and analyzed, and serverless computing has provided the necessary computational power and scalability to meet these demands. Machine learning (ML) has become a powerful tool for solving a wide variety of problems. One of the challenges of ML is to efficiently process large datasets. Distributed machine learning is a way to tackle this problem by scaling up the system. Wang, Niu, and Li (2019) proposed a serverless architecture for distributed machine learning. They demonstrated that this architecture can reduce the overhead of re-training and can scale up the system to process large datasets. Additionally, they showed that this architecture is cost-effective and can be easily modified according to the needs of the user. The authors concluded that their serverless architecture is a viable solution for distributed machine learning.In terms of cost savings, serverless computing has become an attractive option for businesses. It offers pay-as-you-go pricing, meaning that businesses only pay for the resources they actually use. This eliminates the need for upfront investments in infrastructure and ensures that businesses only pay for what they need.

Serverless computing has also made it easier for businesses to adopt new technologies and experiment with different application models. The introduction of managed services has further streamlined the development process. Managed services provide pre-configured services and tools that are managed by the cloud provider. This allows developers to leverage the expertise of the cloud provider and focus on building applications. In terms of security, serverless computing offers improved protection through automatic updates and patches, as well as built-in data encryption and security measures. By eliminating the need for traditional servers, businesses can minimize potential vulnerabilities and reduce their attack surface. Serverless computing also provides greater flexibility in terms of capacity management. It automatically scales resources based on demand, reducing the risk of under-utilization or over-utilization. This has made it easier for businesses to adapt to changing demand patterns and maintain optimal resource utilization.

The evolution of serverless computing in cloud environments has led to a wide range of real-world applications and benefits. Dey, Reddy and Lavanya (2023) examines the architectural paradigms, challenges and future directions of serverless computing in cloud technology. The increasing adoption of serverless computing by businesses has led to significant improvements in productivity, convenience, and security. The rise of managed services has further simplified the development process and ensured that businesses can adopt new technologies and experiment with different application models. The future of serverless computing appears promising, as it continues to evolve and redefine the way we interact with cloud environments.

LITERATURE REVIEW

Shafiei, Khonsari, and Mousavi (2022) provide an extensive retrospective on the historical development and contemporary progress in serverless computing research. They categorize serverless applications across eight domains, offering insights into the paradigm's potential and challenges in each domain. Furthermore, the authors identify nine key challenge areas and review existing solutions. The article concludes by highlighting areas demanding more research focus and open issues in serverless computing, pointing to both advancements and gaps in the field. Kounev (2023) provides an account of serverless computing historical evolution, tracing its roots from 1960s mainframe virtualization to contemporary cloud computing. The article examines various cloud service models, critiquing their relevance to the serverless paradigm, shedding light on their interconnections and distinctions. In their paper, Aske and Zhao (2018) introduce MPSC, a framework designed to facilitate Multi-Provider Serverless Computing.

MPSC boasts real-time performance monitoring of serverless providers and application scheduling across them. It also offers user-defined scheduling algorithms through APIs. However, a critical examination reveals that while MPSC delivers a 4X speedup when compared to single-cloud resource scheduling, its performance might vary in different environments and scenarios, warranting further evaluation. Li et al. (2022) provides a comprehensive overview of serverless computing, it could delve deeper into the practical applications of the open-source frameworks discussed. The exploration of how these frameworks address the identified challenges is somewhat lacking in depth and specificity. Wang, Liri & Ramakrishnan (2020) work on supporting IoT applications with serverless edge clouds is insightful, but it could benefit from a more detailed exploration of the security implications. Additionally, the paper's focus on theoretical aspects leaves room for more empirical evidence to support their claims. Shahrad et al. (2020) examined serverless workloads at a large cloud provider. While their study provided valuable insights, critical evaluation is needed to understand the generalizability of their findings to different cloud environments and workloads. Additionally, assessing the real-world impact of their proposed optimizations is essential for practical application. Lloyd et al. (2018) investigated factors influencing microservice performance in the context of serverless computing, a critical examination is required to determine the generalizability of their findings across various cloud platforms and the potential variations in performance based on specific application workloads and architectures. Further research may help validate and expand upon their insights. Mohanty et al. (2018) provide a valuable evaluation of open-source serverless computing frameworks, but a critical analysis is needed to explore the scalability, performance, and compatibility of these frameworks with different cloud providers and applications. This would help in identifying potential limitations and areas for improvement in open-source serverless solutions. McGrath & Brenner (2017) paper on serverless computing provides a solid foundation on the design and implementation aspects, but it falls short in offering a comprehensive analysis of performance metrics. Additionally, the paper could have benefited from a more extensive discussion on the real-world challenges and potential solutions in serverless computing.

Schuler, Jamil & Kühl (2021) paper on AI-based resource allocation in serverless environments provides an interesting approach using reinforcement learning. However, the paper could have benefited from a more thorough evaluation of the model's performance under different scenarios and workloads. Additionally, the discussion on the practical implications and challenges of implementing such a system in real-world serverless environments seems limited. Sampé et al. (2018) paper on serverless data analytics in the IBM cloud provides a focused view, but it lacks a comparative analysis with other cloud platforms. The paper's insights, while valuable, are largely confined to the IBM cloud, limiting its applicability to broader serverless computing contexts. Kaffes, Yadwadkar & Kozyrakis (2021) preprint on practical scheduling for serverless computing provides valuable insights, but it could benefit from peer-review to validate its findings. Additionally, while the focus on scheduling is important, a broader discussion on other aspects of serverless computing, such as security and cost-efficiency, would have added more depth to the paper. Cicconetti et al. (2020) paper on serverless solutions in edge systems provides a valuable perspective on distributed computing environments. However, the paper could have delved deeper into the practical challenges and potential solutions for implementing serverless architectures in edge systems. Additionally, the discussion seems to lack a comprehensive evaluation of the performance and scalability of such systems. Mampage, Karunasekera & Buyya (2022) paper provides a comprehensive taxonomy on resource management in serverless computing, but it could have benefited from more real-world case studies to illustrate the concepts. Additionally, while the paper outlines future directions, a more detailed roadmap for research and development in this area would have been beneficial. Yu et al. (2020) paper provides a valuable characterization of serverless platforms using Serverless Bench. However, the paper could have expanded its scope to include a wider range of serverless platforms for a more comprehensive analysis. Additionally, the methodology and results could have been presented in a more accessible manner for readers not familiar with Serverless Bench. Bebortta et al. (2020) paper on geospatial serverless computing provides a niche perspective, but it could have benefited from a broader discussion on the integration of serverless computing in diverse geospatial applications. Additionally, the paper's focus on architectures and tools leaves room for more exploration of practical implementation challenges and solutions. Kumari et al. (2022) paper on the role of serverless computing in healthcare systems provides interesting case studies, but it could have delved deeper into the specific challenges and solutions of implementing serverless computing in healthcare. Additionally, the paper could have benefited from a broader discussion on the ethical and privacy considerations of using serverless computing in this sensitive field. Patil et al. (2021) paper on serverless computing and Function-as-a-Service provides a good overview, but it lacks a detailed discussion on the practical challenges and potential solutions in implementing these technologies. Additionally, the paper could have benefited from more real-world case studies to illustrate the concepts and their applications. Sarathi et al. (2022) paper on serverless platforms for latency-sensitive applications provides a preliminary study, but it could have benefited from a more comprehensive analysis of different serverless platforms. Additionally, the paper's focus on latency-sensitive applications leaves room for more exploration of serverless computing applicability to a broader range of application types. Kjorveziroski et al. (2021) paper on IoT serverless computing at the edge provides a valuable perspective, but it could have delved deeper into the practical challenges and potential solutions for implementing serverless architectures in edge systems. Additionally, the discussion seems to lack a comprehensive evaluation of the performance and scalability of such systems.

CORE COMPONENTS OF SERVERLESS

Serverless computing represents a paradigm shift in cloud computing architecture, characterized by the absence of traditional server management and a pay-as-you-go model. The core components of serverless computing include Function as a Service (FaaS), which is the fundamental building block where developers deploy individual functions as discrete units of execution. These functions, written in languages like JavaScript or Python, execute in response to specific events triggered by external sources, such as HTTP requests or changes in data. Another key component is Event Sources, which serve as triggers initiating the execution of functions. These sources can range from HTTP endpoints, databases, to message queues. Additionally, serverless computing relies on Stateless Compute Containers, short-lived and stateless environments where functions execute. Cloud providers manage these containers, handling their deployment and scaling automatically. Overall, serverless architecture fosters a highly scalable and cost-efficient model, where developers can focus on writing code without the burden of managing server infrastructure, leading to increased agility and reduced operational complexities.

Understanding Key Components

Serverless computing is composed of several key components that work together to provide a seamless and efficient execution environment. These components include Function as a Service (FaaS), cloud service providers, function execution environments, and the serverless architecture. FaaS is the founda-

Figure 2. Serverless computing components

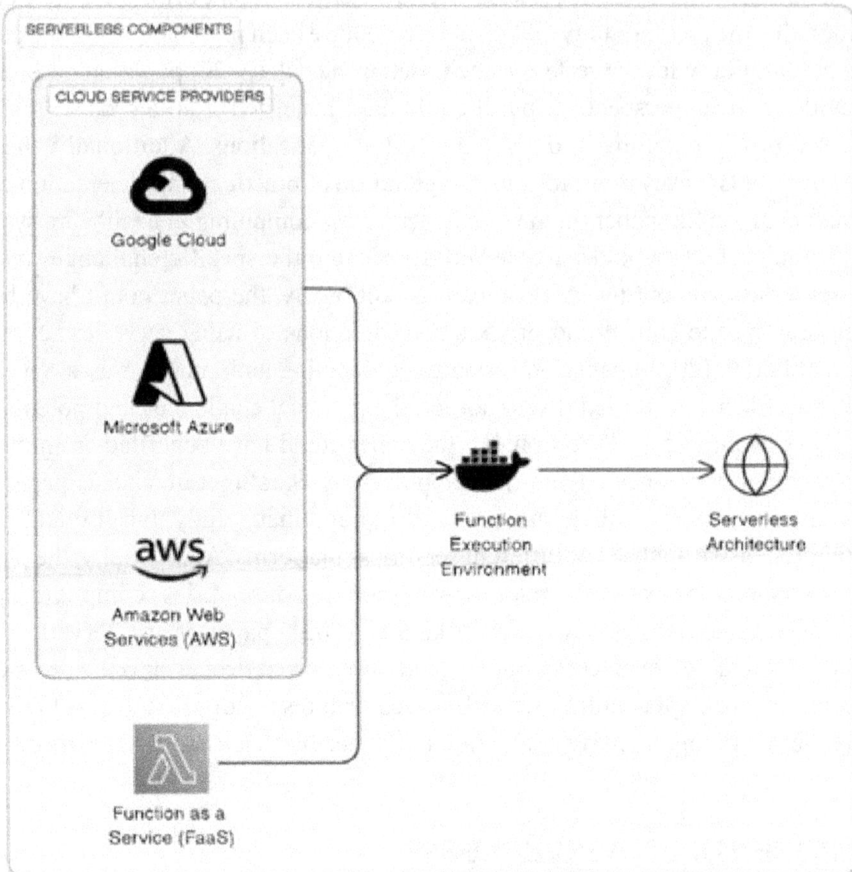

tional component, representing the serverless functions that execute code in response to events. Cloud service providers, such as Amazon Web Services (AWS), Microsoft Azure, and Google Cloud, supply the infrastructure and services for serverless computing. The function execution environment is where the code is run, and the serverless architecture, including event-driven triggers and scalable resource allocation, orchestrates the entire process. A solid understanding of these components is essential for effectively developing and deploying serverless applications.

Event Triggers and Event Sources

Event-driven computing is at the core of serverless architectures. Events, which can be anything from a user request to a database update, trigger the execution of serverless functions. Event triggers define the conditions that initiate the execution of specific functions. These triggers are tied to event sources, which are external entities or services that generate events. Event sources can include databases, message queues, HTTP requests, and more. For example, a serverless function can be triggered by an HTTP request to an API endpoint, a new object uploaded to a storage bucket, or a database update. Understanding how event triggers and sources work is crucial for designing serverless applications that respond effectively to real-world events.

Scalability and Resource Allocation in Serverless

Scalability is one of the defining features of serverless computing. Serverless platforms automatically handle the scaling of resources based on the workload. When an event triggers a function, the serverless platform provisions the necessary resources to execute the code. The allocation of resources is dynamic and depends on the workload's requirements. Resources, such as CPU, memory, and execution time, are allocated as needed to ensure optimal performance. Serverless platforms are designed to handle both individual function scaling and the overall application's scalability. Understanding how resource allocation and automatic scaling work in serverless computing is critical for building applications that can handle varying workloads and deliver consistent performance.

These core components and concepts underpin the functionality and efficiency of serverless computing. To harness the full potential of serverless, developers and architects must have a strong grasp of these elements, allowing them to design and deploy applications that are both responsive to events and highly scalable.

BENEFITS OF SERVERLESS COMPUTING

The Benefits of Serverless Computing are-

Cost Efficiency and Resource Optimization: One of the primary benefits of serverless computing is cost efficiency. With serverless, you only pay for the computing resources used during the execution of functions. This eliminates the need to maintain and provision servers continuously, reducing operational costs. Serverless also optimizes resource utilization by automatically scaling to match the workload, ensuring resources are used efficiently. It's particularly cost-effective for applications with varying workloads, as resources are allocated on-demand.

Scalability and Flexibility: Serverless computing provides exceptional scalability and flexibility. It can automatically scale both up and down in response to incoming traffic or workload demands. This ensures that applications can handle sudden spikes in usage without manual intervention. The ability to scale effortlessly makes serverless well-suited for applications with varying or unpredictable workloads, such as e-commerce websites during holiday sales.

Faster Time to Market: Serverless computing accelerates development and deployment processes, reducing time to market for new applications and features. Developers can focus on writing code for individual functions without worrying about managing servers. This accelerates the development cycle, enabling organizations to respond quickly to changing market dynamics and user needs.

Streamlined Operations and Maintenance: Serverless abstracts much of the infrastructure management, which simplifies operations and maintenance. There is no need to handle server provisioning, patch management, or software updates. Serverless platforms take care of these tasks, allowing operations teams to concentrate on other critical activities, such as security and application performance monitoring. This streamlining of operations contributes to overall system stability and reliability.

Serverless computing offers several key benefits, including cost efficiency through resource optimization, impressive scalability and flexibility, faster development cycles, and streamlined operations and maintenance. These advantages make serverless an attractive choice for businesses looking to build and deploy applications rapidly, efficiently, and cost-effectively.

PERFORMANCE AND OPTIMIZATION IN SERVERLESS

In the realm of serverless computing, performance and optimization are paramount to ensure that applications run smoothly, efficiently, and cost-effectively. The performance and optimization in serverless dedicated to exploring these critical aspects:

Monitoring Serverless Applications: To maintain the health and functionality of serverless applications, monitoring is indispensable. It involves collecting and analyzing data about the application's performance, resource utilization, and user interactions. Real-time metrics enable developers to detect and address issues promptly. Cloud providers offer dedicated monitoring tools like AWS CloudWatch, Azure Monitor, and Google Cloud Monitoring. Additionally, third-party solutions provide advanced insights and integrations for comprehensive application monitoring. Serverless computing is an emerging technology that allows companies to reduce their operating costs while still maintaining a high level of scalability and performance. This technology has seen widespread adoption in recent years due to its cost-saving potential. One of the challenges with serverless computing is designing a file system that can effectively manage data across multiple cloud providers. Schleier-Smith et al. (2020) have proposed a new solution to this problem, the Faas File System (FFS). This system is designed to be an efficient, scalable, and secure file system that can be deployed across multiple cloud providers. Schleier-Smith et al. (2020) discuss the design of FFS, its features, and its performance compared to existing file systems. Furthermore, they provide a detailed evaluation of the system, demonstrating its effectiveness in real-world scenarios. Overall, the Faas File System is a promising solution to the challenge of managing data across multiple cloud providers.

Identifying Performance Metrics: The success of serverless applications hinges on understanding and tracking key performance metrics. These metrics encompass various aspects, such as response times, latency, error rates, and function execution duration. By closely monitoring these indicators, developers can gain insights into how well their applications are performing. Additionally, monitoring resource utilization and distributed tracing can help pinpoint bottlenecks and latency issues, allowing for timely optimization.

Techniques for Optimizing Serverless Functions: Optimizing serverless functions is a multifaceted process. One major concern is mitigating the effects of cold starts, where functions experience delays in start up. Strategies for overcoming this issue are vital for maintaining responsiveness. Proper allocation of memory and CPU resources for functions can significantly impact performance. Efficient coding practices, like minimizing dependencies and maximizing reuse, are also crucial. Furthermore, optimizing concurrency settings, employing caching mechanisms, and managing data storage effectively can contribute to superior function performance.

Cost Management and Scaling Strategies: Efficient performance is not solely about speed; it also involves cost-effectiveness. Therefore, cost management and scaling strategies play a pivotal role. By optimizing performance, applications can also reduce operational costs. Auto-scaling is a key strategy, dynamically adjusting resources to match workload demands. Properly configured resource scaling based on performance metrics further enhances efficiency. Cloud providers offer options like reserved instances and savings plans for economical use of serverless resources.

By exploring these facets, this section provides valuable insights into the world of performance and optimization in serverless computing. It equips readers with the knowledge and tools to not only enhance application performance but also manage costs effectively, resulting in a well-balanced, high-performing, and cost-efficient serverless ecosystem.

PROGRAMMING FOR SERVERLESS

Supported Languages and Frameworks

Serverless computing platforms offer support for a variety of programming languages and frameworks to provide developers with flexibility. Commonly supported languages include JavaScript, Python, Ruby, Java, C#, and more. The choice of language depends on the specific cloud provider and the function as a service (FaaS) offering. In addition to programming languages, serverless platforms often support various open-source frameworks and libraries that can simplify the development process. Understanding the supported languages and frameworks is essential for choosing the right tools for a given serverless project.

Tools and Environments for Serverless Development

Serverless development relies on a set of tools and integrated development environments (IDEs) that streamline the coding, testing, and deployment of serverless functions. These tools often include command-line interfaces (CLIs) provided by cloud service providers, open-source frameworks like the Serverless Framework, and serverless development plug-in for popular IDEs. The primary role of these tools is to simplify the development process, making it easier to create and deploy serverless applications. Having a comprehensive understanding of these tools and their capabilities is crucial for efficient serverless development.

Creating and Deploying Serverless Functions

Serverless applications are built around the concept of functions. Serverless functions are self-contained units of code that are executed in response to specific events. Creating a serverless function involves writing the code that will run when triggered by an event. Developers define the function's logic, configure its event triggers, and specify any required dependencies. Deploying serverless functions typically involves uploading the code to a cloud service provider's environment. This process can be manual or automated, depending on the chosen toolset. Knowing how to create and deploy serverless functions is fundamental to building serverless applications.

Serverless APIs and Endpoints

Serverless applications often expose APIs and endpoints to interact with external systems or provide services to clients. These APIs are built using serverless functions and are designed to handle HTTP requests, database queries, or other types of communication. Developers define the routes, methods, and functionality of these APIs. Serverless platforms offer various options for creating APIs, such as Amazon API Gateway, Azure Functions, or Google Cloud Endpoints. Understanding how to create, manage, and secure serverless APIs is vital for enabling communication with serverless applications.

Programming for serverless computing involves selecting the right programming language, utilizing development tools, creating and deploying serverless functions, and designing serverless APIs and endpoints. A strong grasp of these programming aspects is essential for building effective serverless applications that respond to events and scale dynamically while maintaining optimal performance.

SERVERLESS SECURITY AND COMPLIANCE

Security Considerations in Serverless

Security considerations in serverless computing have emerged as a critical focal point due to the distinct architecture and shared responsibility model. Runtime isolation and function security play a vital role in ensuring the protection of serverless applications. Robust strategies must be implemented to mitigate serverless security risks and address common attack vectors such as injection attacks and privilege escalation. It is imperative to comprehensively identify security threats and vulnerabilities that are specific to the serverless environment to implement effective mitigation strategies and best practices. Organizations need to prioritize threat modeling to proactively address potential security concerns and uphold the integrity of their serverless applications. Additionally, selecting the right security tools and solutions tailored to serverless computing is pivotal in establishing a robust security framework. By fostering a comprehensive understanding of security considerations and advocating proactive security measures, developers and organizations can fortify their serverless architectures and bolster their defenses against potential threats and breaches.

Access Control and Identity Management

Access control and identity management in serverless computing are fundamental components of securing serverless applications. They revolve around defining, managing, and verifying the identities of users, services, and functions interacting with the system and determining their access levels. In a serverless environment, access control and identity management aim to regulate which entities can invoke functions, access data, and perform various actions. One of the key elements of access control in serverless is the use of access policies, which specify what specific actions users or functions are allowed to perform. These policies are typically written in a language like AWS Identity and Access Management (IAM) policies or similar systems in other cloud providers. Policies are attached to roles or identities and grant permissions based on conditions, actions, and resources. Identity management ensures that user and function identities are authenticated and authorized properly. Serverless systems often rely on single sign-on (SSO) or identity federation systems to manage user identities. For functions, roles and permissions dictate their access. It's crucial to apply the principle of least privilege to limit access rights to only what is necessary for each entity.

In addition, many organizations adopt identity federation protocols like OAuth or OpenID Connect for securely managing user identities in a serverless environment. These protocols enable single sign-on across an application, which simplifies access control while enhancing security. However, organizations must

Figure 3. Access control and identity management in serverless computing

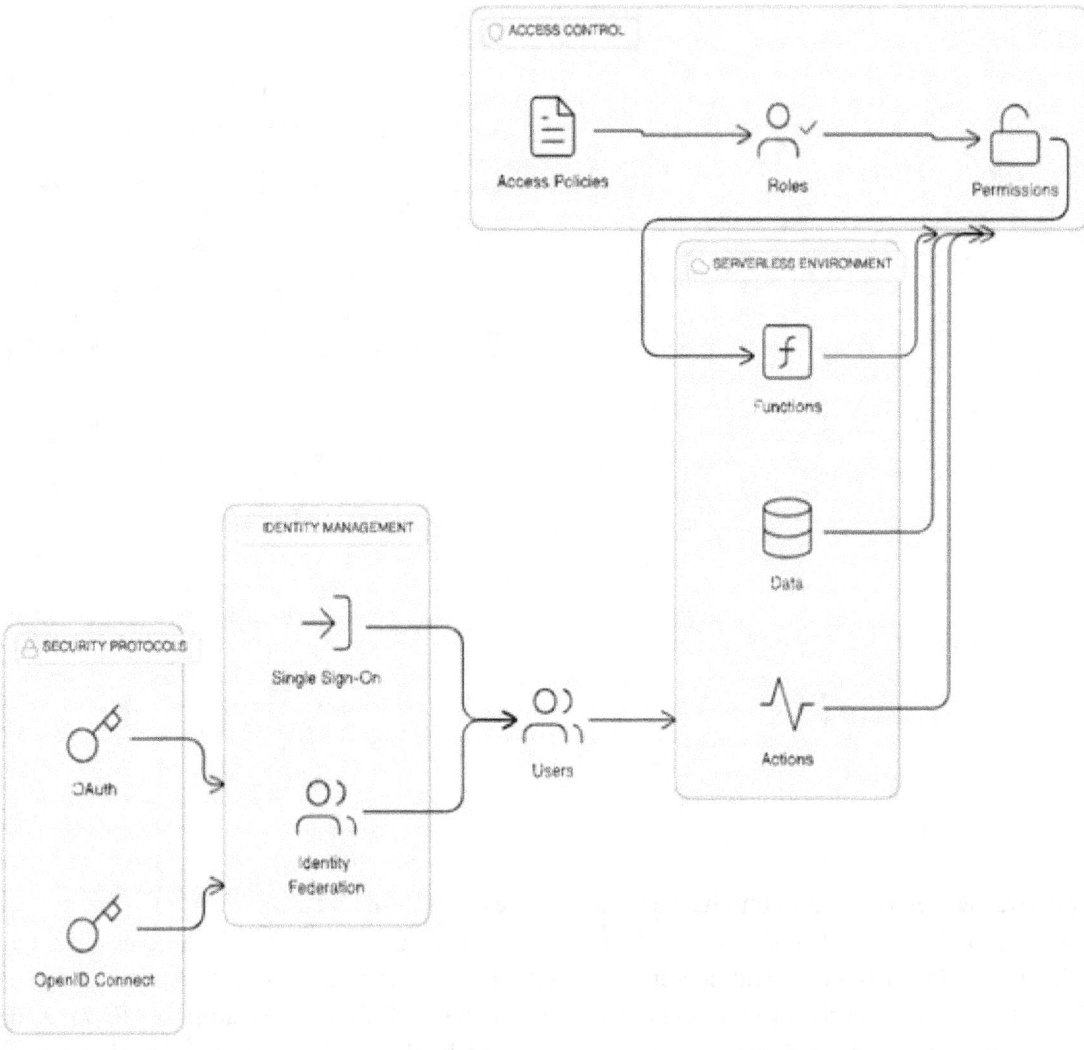

implement these tools correctly to avoid potential vulnerabilities and breaches. Effective access control and identity management are essential to maintaining the security and integrity of serverless applications. By properly configuring and managing access permissions and implementing robust authentication mechanisms, organizations can reduce the risk of unauthorized access and potential security threats.

Compliance, Data Privacy, and GDPR

Compliance, data privacy, and GDPR (General Data Protection Regulation) considerations are critical aspects of serverless computing, especially in an era where data protection and privacy regulations are increasingly stringent. Ensuring compliance with these regulations is essential for organizations to avoid legal and financial consequences and maintain trust with their customers.

Figure 4. Compliance, data privacy, and GDPR in serverless computing

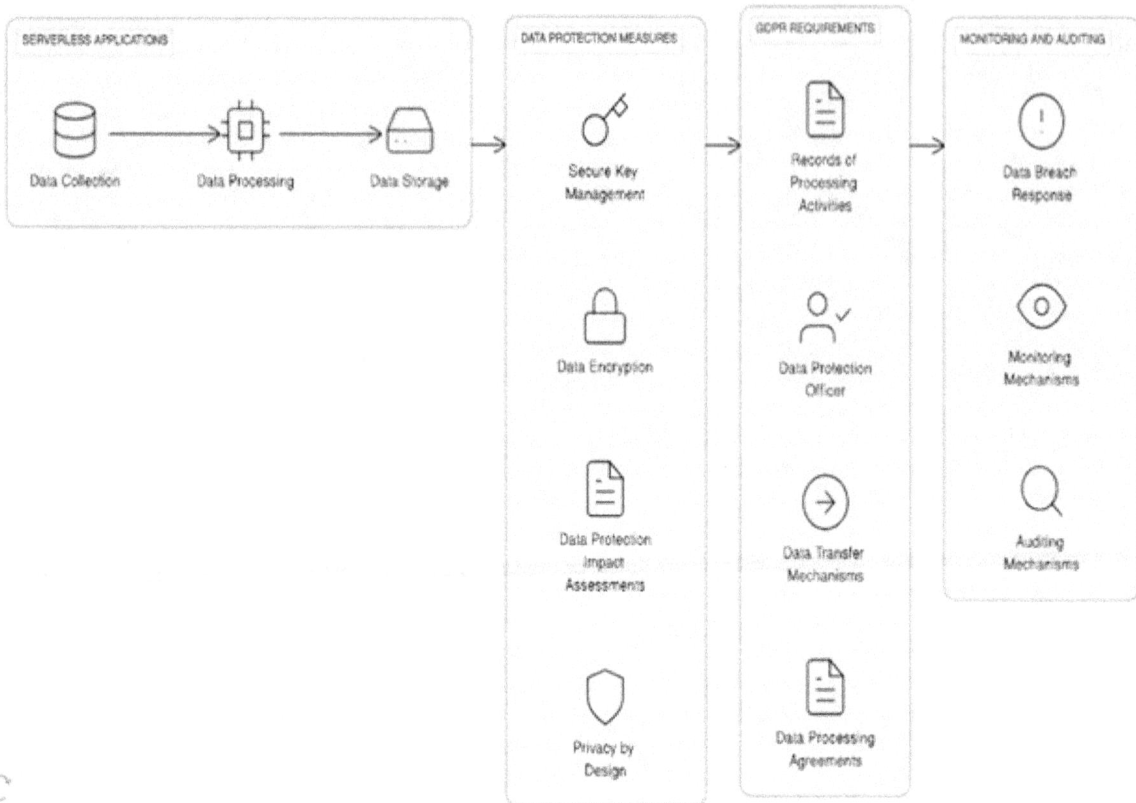

Firstly, data privacy and compliance in a serverless environment revolve around the collection, processing, and storage of sensitive data. Companies must identify and classify the types of data they handle and understand where and how it's used within their serverless applications. In the context of GDPR, which is a data privacy regulation affecting companies dealing with European Union residents' data, organizations must implement privacy by design and by default. This means that privacy and data protection should be integral to the design and operation of serverless applications. Organizations are required to carry out data protection impact assessments to identify and mitigate privacy risks. Data encryption is a fundamental security control to protect data, both at rest and in transit. Data should be encrypted to ensure its confidentiality and integrity, and encryption keys should be managed securely. Compliance may necessitate specific encryption requirements. Regarding GDPR, organizations must have clear data processing agreements and data transfer mechanisms when using serverless services across different regions. They also need to appoint a Data Protection Officer (DPO) and maintain records of processing activities, as required by GDPR.

Compliance may require organizations to implement auditing and monitoring mechanisms to trace data access and usage. They should also be prepared to respond to data breach incidents and report them to relevant authorities within the required timeframes.

Overall, compliance, data privacy, and GDPR in serverless computing demand a thorough understanding of the regulations, robust technical and organizational measures, and a proactive approach to data protection. Organizations must continuously evaluate and update their policies, practices, and technologies to ensure compliance with these evolving regulations. Failure to do so can lead to severe penalties and damage to an organization's reputation.

Best Practices for Securing Serverless Applications

Securing serverless applications requires a proactive and multifaceted approach to protect your resources and data in a shared cloud environment. Here are some best practices for securing serverless applications:

a. Least Privilege Access: Implement the principle of least privilege for all your serverless functions. This means granting only the permissions necessary for the function to perform its task. AWS Identity and Access Management (IAM) roles and policies can help enforce this.
b. Secure Development: Ensure your serverless code is secure. Use well-established coding practices to protect against common vulnerabilities such as SQL injection, cross-site scripting, and others. Regularly update your dependencies to patch vulnerabilities.
c. Data Encryption: Encrypt sensitive data at rest and in transit. Most cloud providers offer encryption services and tools that are easy to integrate with your serverless applications.
d. API Gateway Security: If your serverless functions are exposed through an API Gateway, secure it by implementing authentication and authorization mechanisms. Use OAuth, JWT (JSON Web Tokens), or API keys for access control.
e. Third-Party Security Tools: Consider using third-party security tools that are purpose-built for serverless environments. They can provide an added layer of protection beyond what the cloud provider offers.
f. Runtime Protection: Use runtime protection tools to monitor function execution for anomalies and threats. These tools can help detect and mitigate security risks in real-time.
g. Secure APIs: If your serverless applications communicate with other services or external APIs, ensure these connections are secure. Use HTTPS and API keys, and validate incoming requests.
h. Regular Patching and Updates: Keep your serverless runtime environments up to date with the latest patches and updates. Vulnerabilities can be fixed in newer runtime versions.
i. Disaster Recovery and Backup: Implement disaster recovery and backup mechanisms to ensure data and services can be restored in case of an incident.
j. Employee Training: Train your development and operations teams on security best practices. Security is a shared responsibility, and everyone involved in building and maintaining serverless applications should be aware of potential risks.

By following these best practices, you can help secure your serverless applications and protect your data and resources in the cloud. Remember that security is an ongoing process, and regular audits and updates are essential.

REAL-WORLD SERVERLESS USE CASES

Serverless in Web and Mobile Applications: Serverless computing is highly advantageous in building web and mobile applications. It provides an efficient and cost-effective way to manage the backend of

Figure 5. Real time serverless use cases

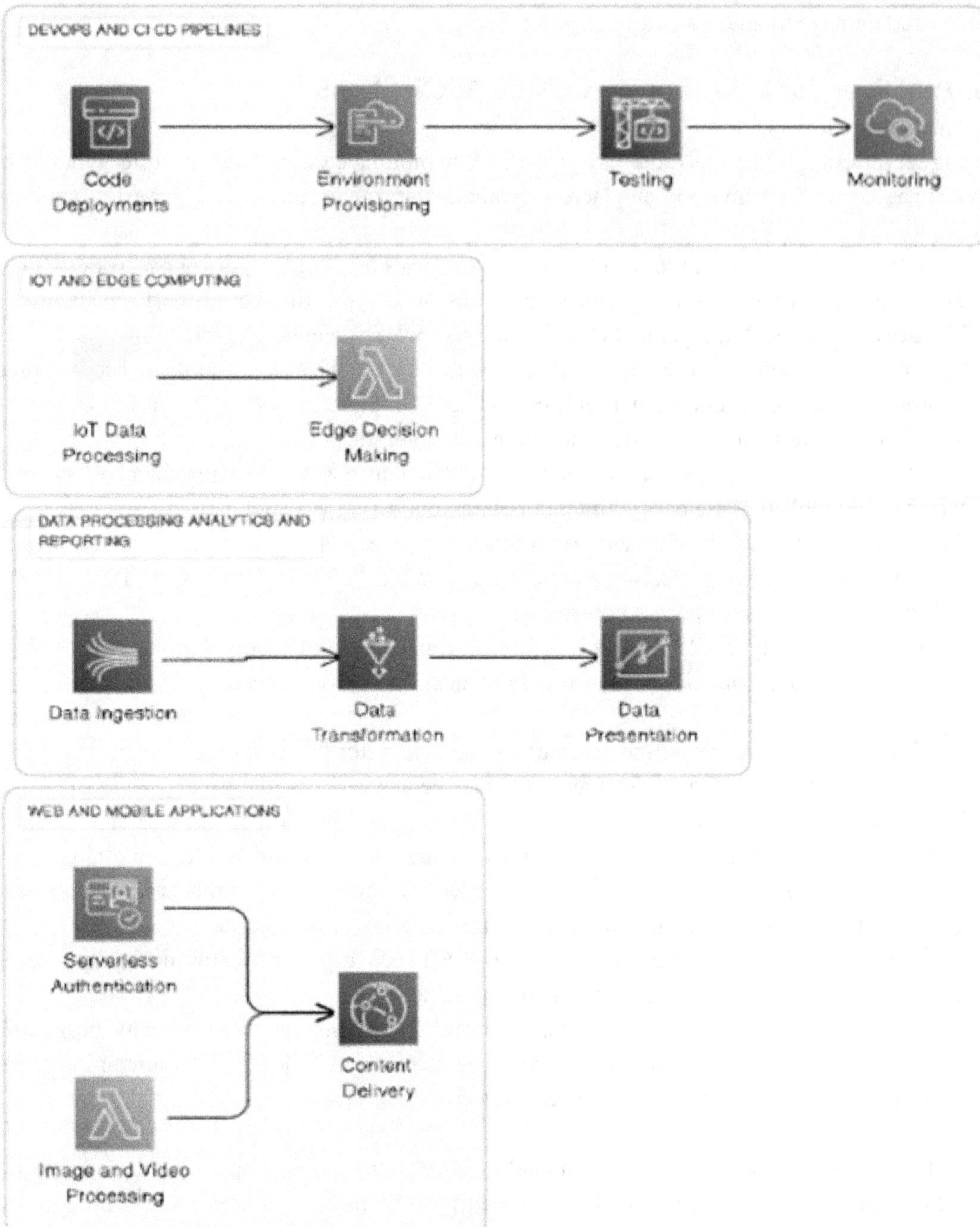

these applications without the need to maintain traditional server infrastructure. Castro et al. (2019) argue that serverless computing is an attractive alternative due to its cost-effectiveness, scalability, and agility. Common use cases include serverless authentication, user management, real-time data processing, and content delivery. For example, you can use serverless functions to handle user authentication, image and video processing, as well as serving content via Content Delivery Networks (CDNs).

Data Processing, Analytics, and Reporting: Serverless computing is well-suited for data processing, analytics, and reporting tasks. By integrating serverless functions into data pipelines, organizations can efficiently process large datasets, generate real-time analytics, and create reports. This is particularly valuable for scenarios involving data ingestion, transformation, and presentation. Serverless computing scales automatically, ensuring that data processing can handle fluctuating workloads efficiently.

IoT and Edge Computing with Serverless: The Internet of Things (IoT) and edge computing benefit from serverless computing. IoT devices often generate massive amounts of data that require real-time processing and analysis. Serverless functions can be deployed at the edge to process this data locally, making quick decisions without the need for extensive server infrastructure. This is critical in applications like smart cities, industrial IoT, and autonomous vehicles. Ivan, Vasile, and Dadarlat (2019), examined the various deployment environments for web APIs in the serverless computing model. In cloud environments, serverless computing offers several real-world applications and benefits. For example, it has facilitated the implementation of IoT (Internet of Things) systems. IoT systems require a massive number of interconnected devices, and serverless computing has provided the necessary scalability and efficiency to manage such systems. Serverless computing has become increasingly popular for implementation of Internet of Things (IoT) solutions.

Serverless in DevOps and CI/CD Pipelines: Serverless plays a pivotal role in DevOps (Development and Operations) practices and Continuous Integration/Continuous Deployment (CI/CD) pipelines. DevOps teams use serverless functions to automate and orchestrate tasks such as code deployments, environment provisioning, testing, and monitoring. By using serverless for these tasks, organizations can significantly enhance their agility and reduce operational overhead.

These real-world use cases demonstrate the versatility and adaptability of serverless computing across various domains. Whether in web and mobile applications, data processing, IoT and edge computing, or DevOps, serverless computing offers a scalable and efficient solution for a multitude of scenarios, making it an increasingly valuable component in the technology stack of modern organizations.

CHALLENGES AND CONSIDERATIONS

Vendor Lock-In and Portability

Vendor lock-in and portability are critical considerations in serverless computing. Vendor lock-in occurs when a company becomes highly dependent on a specific cloud service provider's serverless platform, making it challenging to migrate to another provider or to bring functions in-house. This can lead to several challenges and limitations:

Complexity of Transition: Transitioning from one serverless provider to another is complex, often requiring significant code refactoring and system reconfiguration. This complexity can lead to costly and time-consuming migration processes.

Cost Implications: Vendor lock-in can affect the cost structure. Service providers may change pricing or service terms, leading to increased expenses. Migrating away from a vendor can be expensive due to the need to adapt existing code and infrastructure to the new provider's system.

Limited Flexibility: An organization locked into a single provider may find it difficult to adapt to changing business needs or take advantage of cost-saving opportunities from other providers.

Stifled Innovation: Overreliance on a single vendor may hinder an organization's ability to explore new, innovative technologies or solutions that are not supported by that vendor.

To address these challenges, companies should consider strategies for mitigating vendor lock-in:

Multi-Cloud Strategy: A multi-cloud approach involves using multiple cloud providers simultaneously. This strategy can enhance redundancy, improve performance, and reduce the impact of vendor-specific outages. It also offers flexibility for adopting the services of different cloud providers as needed.

Containerization: Using containers (e.g., Docker) can increase portability. By packaging serverless functions in containers, organizations can run them on different serverless platforms or even on their own infrastructure without being tied to a specific vendor's serverless environment.

Serverless Frameworks: Leveraging serverless frameworks like the Serverless Framework, AWS SAM, or Azure Functions makes it easier to manage and deploy serverless applications across different cloud providers.

It's essential for organizations to carefully evaluate the risks and benefits of vendor lock-in and make strategic decisions regarding their serverless architecture. This evaluation should include considerations of the long-term business strategy, performance, and flexibility, among other factors. By taking a proactive approach to mitigate vendor lock-in, organizations can harness the advantages of serverless computing while preserving their agility and independence.

Architectural Complexity in Serverless

Architectural complexity in serverless computing is a significant concern that arises as applications become more sophisticated and larger in scale. Serverless architecture offers numerous benefits, such as automatic scaling, cost efficiency, and reduced operational overhead, but it also introduces challenges related to complexity. Here are some of the key aspects of architectural complexity in serverless computing:

- Microservices and Distributed Systems: Serverless applications often follow micro services architecture, breaking down complex systems into smaller, independently deployable functions. While this offers flexibility and scalability, it can lead to increased architectural complexity, as managing the interactions and dependencies between micro services becomes crucial.
- Event-Driven Design: Serverless applications are inherently event-driven. Events can be generated from various sources, such as HTTP requests, database changes, and external services. Designing an event-driven system requires a thorough understanding of how events trigger functions, how data flows between functions, and how to maintain consistency in distributed systems.
- State Management: Stateless functions are a fundamental aspect of serverless computing. However, many real-world applications require some form of state management. Handling state within a stateless architecture introduces complexity, as it requires the use of external storage systems, like databases or caching layers.
- Orchestration and Workflow: As serverless applications become more complex, the need for orchestration and workflow management arises. Coordinating the execution of multiple functions

in response to specific events or for long-running processes can be challenging. This complexity often necessitates the use of workflow management tools.
- Third-Party Services: Serverless applications often rely on a variety of third-party services, like databases, authentication services, and external APIs. Integrating these services, handling retries, and managing potential failures can add complexity to the architecture.
- Security and Access Control: Implementing robust security measures and access control becomes increasingly complex in a serverless environment. Properly securing function-to-function and function-to-resource communication is essential to protect against security vulnerabilities.

To address architectural complexity in serverless computing, organizations can consider several strategies:

- Serverless Frameworks: Serverless frameworks like the Serverless Framework or AWS Serverless Application Model (SAM) provide tools and templates for simplifying the development, deployment, and management of serverless applications.
- Serverless Orchestration Services: Services like AWS Step Functions and Azure Durable Functions help manage complex workflows and orchestrate serverless functions.
- API Gateways: API gateways enable the creation of RESTful APIs for serverless applications, simplifying the interaction between clients and serverless functions.
- Centralized Logging and Monitoring: Utilize logging and monitoring services to gain insights into the application's behavior and performance. Services like AWS CloudWatch and Azure Monitor can be invaluable.
- Architecture Reviews: Regular architecture reviews and refactoring can help identify and mitigate unnecessary complexity in serverless applications.

Ultimately, the benefits of serverless computing can outweigh the challenges of architectural complexity. However, it's essential to be mindful of the trade-offs and to apply sound architectural and design principles to keep complexity manageable as applications evolve.

FUTURE TRENDS AND INNOVATIONS

The future trends and innovations in serverless computing, combined with cloud computing, edge computing, and quantum computing, is poised to usher in a new era of unprecedented possibilities and efficiencies in real-world applications. Serverless computing, with its inherent scalability and cost-effectiveness, will play a pivotal role in shaping the future of cloud environments. The integration of serverless functions within cloud platforms will continue to evolve, providing developers with a seamless and serverless-first experience for deploying applications. This trend aligns with the broader adoption of micro services architectures and the growing importance of event-driven, decentralized computing models in the cloud.

In conjunction with edge computing, serverless architectures are set to bridge the gap between centralized cloud resources and the distributed nature of edge devices. Serverless at the edge will enable faster and more responsive applications by executing functions closer to end-users, reducing latency and enhancing user experiences in scenarios such as IoT deployments, real-time analytics, and content delivery. Moreover, the synergy of serverless computing and quantum computing presents a fascinat-

Figure 6. Future trends and innovations in serverless technology

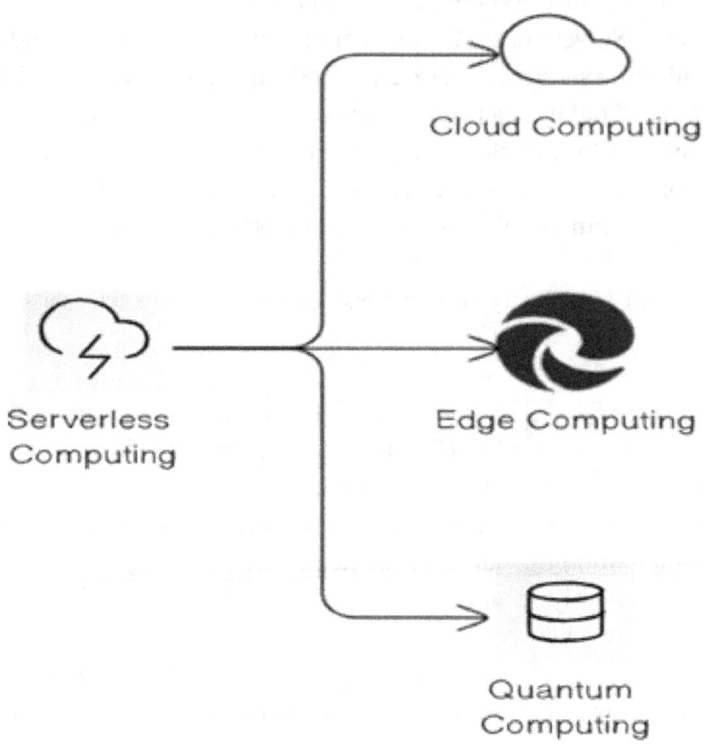

ing avenue for exploration. Quantum computing immense processing power can potentially accelerate complex computations and algorithms, while serverless models offer a scalable and cost-efficient execution environment. This convergence may unlock novel approaches to solving computationally intensive problems in fields like optimization, cryptography, and machine learning.

As these technological threads intertwine, the future of serverless computing holds promise for versatile real-world applications, providing benefits such as enhanced agility, optimized resource utilization, reduced operational complexities, and the ability to harness the power of quantum computing for groundbreaking advancements. The evolution of these technologies within cloud environments signifies a paradigm shift towards a more dynamic, responsive, and efficient computing landscape.

These emerging trends and innovations highlight the dynamic nature of serverless computing. They reflect an ecosystem that continuously adapts to the changing landscape of technology. By exploring these trends, this section provides readers with insights into the future possibilities and applications of serverless computing, offering a glimpse into the groundbreaking developments that lie ahead.

CONCLUSION

In conclusion, this comprehensive exploration of serverless computing has highlighted its growing significance in the cloud computing landscape. We've summarized key takeaways from its definition and core components to real-world use cases, benefits, security considerations, performance optimization, and challenges. The adoption of serverless has the potential to revolutionize how organizations manage their computing resources, delivering cost-efficiency, scalability, and agility. The ongoing evolution of serverless is inevitable, and staying attuned to emerging trends and innovations in this field is essential. As serverless continues to mature, we can anticipate further improvements in performance, security, and integration with other cutting-edge technologies. Looking ahead, there are various exciting areas for future research and development in serverless computing. These include advanced security solutions, enhanced tools for monitoring and optimization, and even novel architectural paradigms for serverless applications. The integration of serverless with edge computing and the exciting possibilities in quantum computing are also intriguing directions for exploration. The role of serverless in the cloud computing landscape is set to expand, with more organizations recognizing its potential to streamline operations and deliver value to their users. As serverless becomes more accessible and developer-friendly, its impact on industries, from e-commerce to healthcare, is likely to grow.

In this rapidly evolving field, embracing serverless computing intelligently, with a keen eye on security, performance, and scalability, will be a key driver of success for businesses and a focal point for future research and innovation. As serverless continues to redefine cloud computing, it offers organizations new ways to meet the demands of modern, digital-first environments while fostering efficiency, flexibility, and innovation.

REFERENCES

Aske, A., & Zhao, X. (2018, August). Supporting multi-provider serverless computing on the edge. In *Workshop Proceedings of the 47th International Conference on Parallel Processing* (pp. 1-6). ACM. 10.1145/3229710.3229742

Bebortta, S., Das, S. K., Kandpal, M., Barik, R. K., & Dubey, H. (2020). Geospatial serverless computing: Architectures, tools and future directions. *ISPRS International Journal of Geo-Information*, *9*(5), 311. doi:10.3390/ijgi9050311

Cassel, G. A. S., Rodrigues, V. F., da Rosa Righi, R., Bez, M. R., Nepomuceno, A. C., & da Costa, C. A. (2022). Serverless computing for Internet of Things: A systematic literature review. *Future Generation Computer Systems*, *128*, 299–316. doi:10.1016/j.future.2021.10.020

Castro, P., Ishakian, V., Muthusamy, V., & Slominski, A. (2019). The rise of serverless computing. *Communications of the ACM*, *62*(12), 44–54. doi:10.1145/3368454

Cicconetti, C., Conti, M., Passarella, A., & Sabella, D. (2020). Toward distributed computing environments with serverless solutions in edge systems. *IEEE Communications Magazine*, *58*(3), 40–46. doi:10.1109/MCOM.001.1900498

Dey, N. S., Reddy, S. P. K., & Lavanya, G. (2023, October). Serverless Computing: Architectural Paradigms, Challenges, and Future Directions in Cloud Technology. In *2023 7th International Conference on I-SMAC (IoT in Social, Mobile, Analytics and Cloud)(I-SMAC)* (pp. 406-414). IEEE. 10.1109/I-SMAC58438.2023.10290253

Eskandani, N., & Salvaneschi, G. (2021, May). The wonderless dataset for serverless computing. In *2021 IEEE/ACM 18th International Conference on Mining Software Repositories (MSR)* (pp. 565-569). IEEE. 10.1109/MSR52588.2021.00075

Ivan, C., Vasile, R., & Dadarlat, V. (2019). Serverless computing: An investigation of deployment environments for web apis. *Computers*, *8*(2), 50. doi:10.3390/computers8020050

Kaffes, K., Yadwadkar, N. J., & Kozyrakis, C. (2021). *Practical scheduling for real-world serverless computing*. arXiv preprint arXiv:2111.07226.

Kjorveziroski, V., Bernad Canto, C., Juan Roig, P., Gilly, K., Mishev, A., Trajkovikj, V., & Filiposka, S. (2021). *IoT serverless computing at the edge: Open issues and research direction*. Transactions on Networks and Communications.

Kounev, S. (2023, April). Serverless Computing Revisited: Evolution, State-of-the-Art, and Performance Challenges. In *Companion of the 2023 ACM/SPEC International Conference on Performance Engineering* (pp. 309-310). ACM. 10.1145/3578245.3584856

Kumari, A., Behera, R. K., Sahoo, B., & Misra, S. (2022, July). Role of serverless computing in healthcare systems: Case studies. In *International Conference on Computational Science and Its Applications* (pp. 123-134). Cham: Springer International Publishing. 10.1007/978-3-031-10542-5_9

Li, Y., Lin, Y., Wang, Y., Ye, K., & Xu, C. (2022). Serverless computing: State-of-the-art, challenges and opportunities. *IEEE Transactions on Services Computing*, *16*(2), 1522–1539. doi:10.1109/TSC.2022.3166553

Lloyd, W., Ramesh, S., Chinthalapati, S., Ly, L., & Pallickara, S. (2018, April). Serverless computing: An investigation of factors influencing microservice performance. In *2018 IEEE international conference on cloud engineering (IC2E)* (pp. 159-169). IEEE. doi:10.1109/IC2E.2018.00039

Mampage, A., Karunasekera, S., & Buyya, R. (2022). A holistic view on resource management in serverless computing environments: Taxonomy and future directions. *ACM Computing Surveys*, *54*(11s), 1–36. doi:10.1145/3510412

McGrath, G., & Brenner, P. R. (2017, June). Serverless computing: Design, implementation, and performance. In *2017 IEEE 37th International Conference on Distributed Computing Systems Workshops (ICDCSW)* (pp. 405-410). IEEE. 10.1109/ICDCSW.2017.36

Mohanty, S. K., Premsankar, G., & Di Francesco, M. (2018). An Evaluation of Open Source Serverless Computing Frameworks. *CloudCom*, *2018*, 115–120. doi:10.1109/CloudCom2018.2018.00033

Patil, R., Chaudhery, T. S., Qureshi, M. A., Sawant, V., & Dalvi, H. (2021, August). Serverless Computing and the Emergence of Function-as-a-Service. In *2021 International Conference on Recent Trends on Electronics, Information, Communication & Technology (RTEICT)* (pp. 764-769). IEEE. 10.1109/RTEICT52294.2021.9573962

Sampé, J., Vernik, G., Sánchez-Artigas, M., & García-López, P. (2018, December). Serverless data analytics in the IBM cloud. In *Proceedings of the 19th International Middleware Conference Industry* (pp. 1-8). ACM. 10.1145/3284028.3284029

Sarathi, T. V., Reddy, J. S. N., Shiva, P., Saha, R., Satpathy, A., & Addya, S. K. (2022, July). A Preliminary Study of Serverless Platforms for Latency Sensitive Applications. In *2022 IEEE International Conference on Electronics, Computing and Communication Technologies (CONECCT)* (pp. 1-6). IEEE. DOI: 10.1109/CONECCT55679.2022.9865790

Schleier-Smith, J., Holz, L., Pemberton, N., & Hellerstein, J. M. (2020). *A faas file system for serverless computing*. arXiv preprint arXiv:2009.09845.

Schuler, L., Jamil, S., & Kühl, N. (2021, May). AI-based resource allocation: Reinforcement learning for adaptive auto-scaling in serverless environments. In *2021 IEEE/ACM 21st International Symposium on Cluster, Cloud and Internet Computing (CCGrid)* (pp. 804-811). IEEE. 10.1109/CCGrid51090.2021.00098

Shafiei, H., Khonsari, A., & Mousavi, P. (2022). Serverless computing: A survey of opportunities, challenges, and applications. *ACM Computing Surveys*, *54*(11s), 1–32. doi:10.1145/3510611

Shahrad, M., Fonseca, R., Goiri, I., Chaudhry, G., Batum, P., Cooke, J., & Bianchini, R. (2020). Serverless in the wild: Characterizing and optimizing the serverless workload at a large cloud provider. In *2020 USENIX annual technical conference (USENIX ATC 20)* (pp. 205-218). ACM.

Van Eyk, E., Toader, L., Talluri, S., Versluis, L., Uță, A., & Iosup, A. (2018). Serverless is more: From paas to present cloud computing. *IEEE Internet Computing*, *22*(5), 8–17. doi:10.1109/MIC.2018.053681358

Wang, H., Niu, D., & Li, B. (2019, April). Distributed machine learning with a serverless architecture. In *IEEE INFOCOM 2019-IEEE Conference on Computer Communications* (pp. 1288-1296). IEEE. 10.1109/INFOCOM.2019.8737391

Wang, I., Liri, E., & Ramakrishnan, K. K. (2020, November). Supporting iot applications with serverless edge clouds. In *2020 IEEE 9th International Conference on Cloud Networking (CloudNet)* (pp. 1-4). IEEE. DOI: 10.1109/CloudNet51028.2020.9335805

Yu, T., Liu, Q., Du, D., Xia, Y., Zang, B., Lu, Z., & Chen, H. (2020, October). Characterizing serverless platforms with serverlessbench. In *Proceedings of the 11th ACM Symposium on Cloud Computing* (pp. 30-44). ACM. 10.1145/3419111.3421280

KEY TERMS AND DEFINITIONS

Cloud Computing: Cloud computing is a technology paradigm that enables on-demand access to a shared pool of computing resources, such as servers, storage, and applications, over the internet, offering flexibility and scalability for users and organizations.

Command-Line Interfaces (CLIs): Command-line interfaces (CLIs) are text-based user interfaces that allow users to interact with a computer program or operating system by typing commands in a text terminal.

Content Delivery Networks (CDNs): Content Delivery Networks (CDNs) are distributed networks of servers designed to efficiently deliver web content, including web pages, videos, and other assets, to users based on their geographic location, reducing latency and improving performance.

Edge Computing: A distributed computing paradigm that brings computational processes closer to the data source or endpoint devices, reducing latency and enhancing real-time data processing. Unlike traditional cloud computing, which centralizes data processing in remote data centers, edge computing shifts computational tasks to the edge of the network, near the data-producing devices. This approach improves response times, bandwidth efficiency, and supports applications requiring low-latency interactions, such as IoT devices, autonomous vehicles, and augmented reality. Edge computing enables faster decision-making and more efficient utilization of network resources by processing data locally or in nearby edge servers, enhancing the overall performance and responsiveness of distributed systems.

General Data Protection Regulation (GDPR): General Data Protection Regulation (GDPR) is a European Union regulation that governs data protection and privacy for all individuals within the EU, emphasizing the control individuals have over their personal data and how organizations handle it.

Internet of Things (IoT): The Internet of Things (IoT) is a concept that refers to the connection of everyday objects to the internet, allowing them to send and receive data. These objects can include devices like smartphones, thermostats, wearables, home appliances, and even vehicles. The idea behind IoT is to create a network where these objects can communicate with each other, collect and share data, and perform tasks more efficiently.

Quantum Computing: is a cutting-edge computing paradigm that leverages the principles of quantum mechanics to process information. Unlike classical computers that use bits to represent information as 0s or 1s, quantum computers use quantum bits or qubits. Qubits can exist in multiple states simultaneously, thanks to a phenomenon called superposition, allowing quantum computers to perform complex computations much more efficiently for certain types of problems.

Chapter 15
Cloud Computing Applications in Biomedicine

Arpit Namdev
University Institute of Technology RGPV, India

Vivek Veeraiah
Adichunchanagiri University, India

S. Dhamodaran
Sathyabama Institute of Science and Technology, India

Shaziya Islam
https://orcid.org/0000-0003-0368-2097
Rungta College of Engineering and Technology, India

Trupti Patil
Bharati Vidyapeeth, India

Sabyasachi Pramanik
https://orcid.org/0000-0002-9431-8751
Haldia Institute of Technology, India

Ankur Gupta
https://orcid.org/0000-0002-4651-5830
Vaish College of Engineering, Rohtak, India

Digvijay Pandey
https://orcid.org/0000-0003-0353-174X
Department of Technical Education, IET Lucknow, Government of Uttar Pradesh, India

ABSTRACT

Today's biology is characterized by a rising requirement for real-time handling of massive quantities of data. New needs for information and communication tools (ICT) result from this. These needs can be satisfied by cloud computing, which also has many benefits like cost reductions, flexibility, and scaling when using ICT. This chapter aims to examine the idea of cloud computing and its associated applications in the field of biomedicine. The researchers provide a thorough examination of the application of the cloud computation method in biological analysis, broken down into framework, infrastructures, and service layers, along with a suggestion in handling huge quantities of data in the field of medicine. The chapter begins by outlining the suitable applications and technical approaches for cloud computing. Second, the cloud computing elements of the high-end computing model are examined. Finally, a discussion of this technology's promise and actual uses in biomedical study is presented.

DOI: 10.4018/979-8-3693-0900-1.ch015

INTRODUCTION

Science has significantly improved our ability to quantify things and collect data in previously unimaginable quantities. This creates new demands for the creation and use of innovative techniques and information and communication technologies (ICT) that can store data and send it for later analysis or possibly use it as input for quantitative modeling. Cloud technologies are being adopted rapidly and abundantly by companies, groups, government entities, and private citizens. Businesses are opening up more to the possibility of expanding their product creation, services, and promotion via information technologies.

Any ICT infrastructure component, including virtual computers, apps, data storage areas, servers, and networking hardware, should be available as an on-demand service thanks to cloud computing. Additionally, it is possible to easily alter the architecture. Cloud tech (Anand, R. et al. 2022) has a lot of benefits like savings on ICT expenses (approximately 2 lakhs per month for a mid-size organization) etc.

Biomedicine, which also requires processing enormous quantities of data, is a major field of ICT use. Real-world scenarios and variable circumstances are frequently depicted in scientific computations based on biological data. The layout and execution of computerized medical labs, supervision services, multipurpose image centers, medical datacenters, remote tracking, bioinstrumentation, etc. are just a few examples of the complicated and comprehensive components that are covered by these issues. The real-time analysis of biological data raises the need for more processing capacity. Because there are 2n stages in one subscription, using a modification like the wavelet is not particularly challenging, but using it on sizable real-world biological datasets that demand completely concurrent processing at high speed is challenging (Pramanik, S. 2023). Cloud computing is the tool that can be used in this situation.

The use of cloud processing in biological research has many benefits, but it also creates new risks and difficulties (Gezimati, M. et al. 2023). In apps that require a lot of processing, cloud computing is regarded as being very effective. (Huang, X., et al. 2022) states that there are numerous considerations that should be made during the implementation process, including the type of business being serviced, the kind of cloud that is needed, nationalized and international quality needs dangers and laws. It is clear out of the preceding sections of the chapter that the incorporation of cloud computation strategy in biology is not only a buy of a single good, yet moreover a difficult technique that is influencing the entire study, organization, and so forth. The end outcome of cloud computing incorporation in biology without a comprehensive strategy can be unclear. The following problems and difficulties are important when using cloud computing in biomedicine.

- Governance of cloud computation
- Privacy and moral considerations
- Service frameworks and
- Grade of cloud computation facilities.

Because data in biological research is frequently extremely delicate, secret, and constrained by law or other policies, security and ethical problems are among the most crucial ones. (Guest, O., et al. 2023) identify three key difficulties in this field. A broad range of data or user-dependent policies, including preservation periods, erasure procedures, restoration schemes, allocation guidelines, access tracking frameworks, user auditing, action recording, etc., are represented by the compliance and responsibility in the first place. The second category is security and privacy, which includes techniques for reducing security risks such as illegal entry, data separation, virtual internetworking and system remoteness, flaw utilization, layered network confidentiality, recovering techniques, or encryption methods. The political procedure is the final difficult problem. The utilization of cloud computation in healthcare (Pramanik, S. et al. 2023) networks is influenced by numerous legal considerations. This is a hot subject right now because researchers frequently overlook these issues when moving biological data to cloud platforms. It is very difficult to move private data to a completely unregulated region of the Internet. This is a very delicate issue that is linked to choosing the best cloud computation facility paradigm for biological frameworks.

EVOLUTION OF CLOUD COMPUTING

Figure 1. Evolution of cloud computing

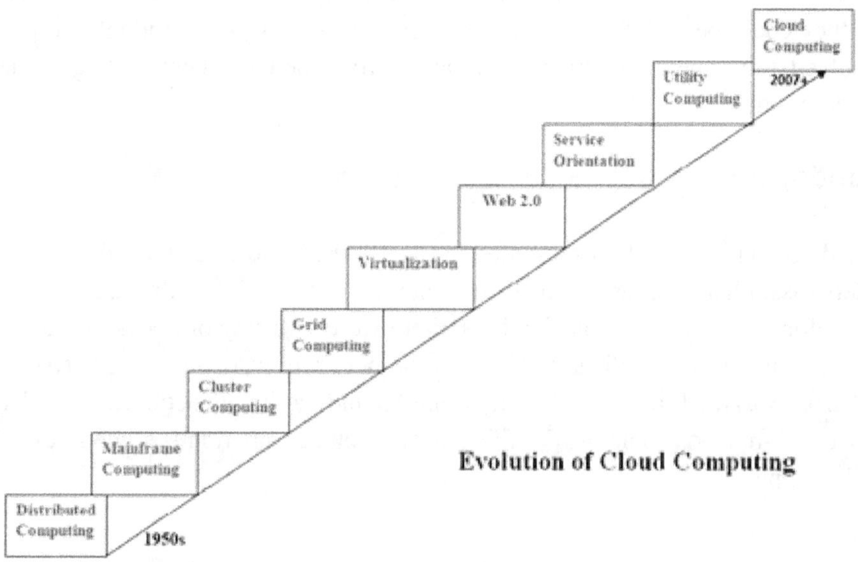

Distributed Computing

Although it is made up of many separate systems, consumers are presented with a unified image of the system. Distributed systems are designed to share resources and make efficient and effective use of them. Scalability, concurrency, continuous availability, heterogeneity, and resilience to errors are some of the characteristics of distributed systems. However, the primary issue with this method was that each system had to be present at the same physical area. Mainframe, cluster, and grid computing are the three additional forms of computing that emerged as a result of distributed computing attempt to address this issue.

Mainframe Computing

Originally developed in 1951, mainframes are very dependable and powerful computer devices. These are in charge of managing huge input-output activities and other data-intensive processes. These are still used today for jobs requiring large processing, like internet transactions, etc. These systems have a high failure tolerance and almost minimal downtime. These improved the system's processing power after distributed computing. However, they were highly priced. Cluster computing emerged as a substitute for mainframe technology to lower this cost.

Cluster Computing

Cluster computing emerged as a mainframe computer substitute in the 1980s. A high bandwidth network linked every computer in the cluster to every other machine. Those mainframe systems were far more expensive than this. These may do complex calculations just as well. Furthermore, if more nodes were needed, they could be added to the cluster with ease. As a result, although the issue of cost was somewhat resolved, the issue of geographic limitations remained. Grid computing is a notion that was presented to address this.

Grid Computing

The idea of grid computing was first presented in the 1990s. It indicates that several systems were installed in widely dissimilar geographic areas and that they were all linked through the internet. Because these systems belonged to various organizations, there were a variety of nodes in the grid. Even while it addressed certain issues, as the distance between the nodes grew, other issues surfaced. The primary difficulty that arose was the limited availability of high bandwidth connection, which also brought with it additional network-related problems. For this reason, cloud computing is sometimes called the "Successor of Grid Computing."

Virtualization

It was first released over forty years ago. It describes the procedure for building a virtual layer on top of the hardware that enables the user to run several instances of the hardware at once. It is a crucial piece of cloud computing technology. It serves as the foundation for several popular cloud computing services, including VMware vCloud, Amazon EC2, and others. One of the most popular forms of virtualization is still hardware virtualization.

Web 2.0

This is the interface that allows customers to communicate with cloud computing services. Our dynamic and interactive web sites are a result of Web 2.0. Additionally, it makes web pages more flexible. Web 2.0 products that are widely used include Facebook, Twitter, Google Maps, and others. Without a doubt, social media is only conceivable because to this technology. It became quite well-known in 2004.

Service Orientation

It serves as a cloud computing reference model. It is compatible with adaptable, affordable, and developing applications. With this computer paradigm, two key ideas were presented. These were Software as a Service (SaaS) and Quality of Service (QoS), which encompasses the SLA (Service Level Agreement).

Utility Computing

A pay-per-use computing paradigm, it describes methods for providing computer services and other important pay-per-use services like storage and infrastructure.

COST ANALYSIS (OR DIFFERENT TYPES OF SUBSCRIPTIONS) FOR DIFFERENT CLOUD COMPUTING

How Much Does Cloud Computing Cost?

The price of cloud computing varies significantly throughout providers and services. Many organizations are unable to correctly estimate the costs of moving their activities to the cloud, even though most can precisely estimate the expenses of putting up and maintaining their own IT infrastructure. Improved productivity and more flexibility are two benefits of cloud computing. Organizations may swiftly scale up and down using cloud-based on-demand resources, while automation features boost productivity. Many organizations, however, have concerns about the accuracy of cost estimations for dynamic (and often transient) cloud resources. Organizations must evaluate their requirements, comprehend the factors influencing costs, create a strategic plan, and regularly analyze and optimize billing and consumption in order to accurately predict, manage, and optimize cloud computing expenses. Cloud suppliers enable cost control for organizations by providing several pricing structures together with solutions for cost management and optimization. Third-party technologies are now available to assist optimize cloud expenses.

Principal Aspects of Cloud Costs

The price of cloud computing services is mostly determined by three factors:

Compute: A variety of compute instance types are available from most cloud providers, each with a certain capacity for CPU, memory, and, sometimes, specialized hardware like graphics acceleration or fast networking. The amount that the consumer pays depends on how many, what kinds, and how long they utilize the instances.

Networking: The majority of cloud services charge their users based on the amount of data that is ingested into the service, ejected from it, or both. Certain virtualized network services, such load balancers, gateways, and static IP addresses, could come with extra fees.

Storage is a service that cloud companies provide. Customers who use elastic storage services pay per gigabyte-month for the storage that is really used. Customers pay for the whole storage volume when using managed storage services, such managed discs connected to compute instances, regardless of how much storage is actually used on the volume.

Comparing the Costs of Traditional and Cloud Infrastructure

The following three major expense categories are often linked to the establishment and upkeep of on-premises infrastructure:

- Capital expenses include network infrastructure, storage settings, backup systems, server hardware, software, and licensing.
- Operational expenses: they include labor costs for system administrators, storage warranties, data centre facilities, server and network infrastructure maintenance, and IT staff training and turnover.
- Indirect business expenses, such as scheduled and unscheduled downtime

Organizations should budget around $2 for managing, maintaining, and safeguarding the expanded infrastructure for every $1 invested on improvements. An organization must first do a thorough audit of all current IT expenditures, including direct and indirect costs, before estimating the total cost of cloud migration and adoption. For instance:

Hardware, software, personnel, administration, upkeep, and any physical facilities are all considered direct expenditures. Direct costs are often simple to calculate and understand.

Indirect costs—such as lost productivity—come from a variety of sources, such as reputational harm, consumer mistrust, and server outages. Generally speaking, indirect expenses are harder to forecast and estimate.

Plan AWS Savings

Savings Plans are a flexible pricing strategy that, like reserved instances, enables organizations to take advantage of reduced pricing than on-demand pricing in return for a defined consumption commitment of one or three years. The commitment is stated as the amount spent on Amazon services each hour.

AWS provides three different kinds of Savings Plans:

The computing Savings Plans are applicable to all uses of Amazon's computing services, such as Fargate, EC2, and AWS Lambda.

Exclusively applicable to Amazon EC2 instance utilization are the EC2 Savings Plans.

Only SageMaker use is eligible for SageMaker Savings Plans.

Web Services on Amazon

Pay-as-you-go pricing is a feature that AWS gives businesses for the majority of its cloud services. Customers only pay for the services they utilize while using AWS. When an organization decides to quit utilizing these cloud services, there are no further fees or termination penalties, and they are not burdened with complicated licensing or long-term contracts.

Elastic Compute Cloud by Amazon

A cloud computation service called Amazon EC2 allows customers to set up virtual machine instances (VM instances) with as much memory, local storage, and CPUs as needed.

For a year, users may obtain 750 hours of Windows and Linux t2.micro instances each month by signing up for a free trial of EC2.

Users may pay for EC2 instances in a variety of methods, such as the following:

Customers may pay for compute capability by the hour or by the second, with a minimum of 60 seconds, thanks to on-demand pricing. No long-term obligations exist.

By requesting spare EC2 computing resources, customers may save up to 90% on on-demand costs using spot instances.

Savings programs prevent customers from buying real instances. Rather, they guarantee on-demand instances for one to three years at a discount of 72% off standard on-demand rates.

Customers that buy on-demand instances in advance for a predetermined period of one to three years may get a discount of up to 75% when they purchase reserved instances.

Lambda on AWS

With AWS Lambda, customers can execute code without worrying about provisioning or managing servers thanks to a server less computing service. It just costs what is used by the user.

AWS Lambda price is determined using the following factors:

- Ask for a quote. One million requests and 400,000 GB-seconds of computation time are included in the AWS Lambda free tier per month. Following that, each request will cost $0.0000002 or $0.20 for every million requests.
- Time-based pricing. A monthly allowance of 400,000 GB-seconds, or up to 3.2 million seconds of compute time, is provided to users. After that, each GB-second used will cost $0.00001667.
- A number of storage services are available via Microsoft Azure, each with a different price structure. The main services are as follows:
- For snapshots, data transactions, and data transfer volume, there are further fees.
- The pricing shown above are an example and may vary for the East U.S. 2 area with locally redundant storage.
- Customers may access a variety of services for free for a full year using Azure's free tier. Every service has a certain amount of money.

Virtual Machine on Azure

Pay as you go, spot instances, and reserved instances are the three ways users may pay for Azure virtual machines.

Six categories—general purpose, compute optimized, memory optimized, storage optimized, GPU, and high performance computer—comprise the different kinds and sizes of virtual machines (VMs) that Microsoft provides. This is an example of East U.S. pricing for Linux virtual machines (VMs) optimized for computation and memory.

- The starting monthly price for pay-as-you-go is $61.7580.

- Memory enhancement offers a high ratio of memory to core.
- Excellent for relational database servers, medium-to-large caches, and in-memory analytics

Google Cloud

The starting monthly price for pay-as-you-go is $82.4900. Google Cloud charges a fee for its storage services according to the amount of data that a client consumes, how long they keep it for, how many operations they execute on it, and if they use any network resources to transport or retrieve the data.

VMs for Google Compute Engine

Virtual machines (VMs) in Google Compute Engine are categorized by workload categories. General purpose, accelerator optimized, compute optimized, and memory optimized are the four primary categories.

METRICS IN COULD COMPUTING IN BIOMEDICAL INDUSTRY

Measures of Performance

Cloud providers that cater to the IT requirements of several businesses provide a variety of unique solutions.

The efficiency of each choice varies greatly in terms of accuracy, service latency, and performance. Institutions needed to assess how well their programs work across several Clouds and whether or not such deployments meet their objectives. Performance has several meanings depending on the situation. It usually has to do with response time (the amount of time it could take to process a request), throughput (the amount of work that can be done on a number of requests in a given amount of time), or even timeliness (the ability to meet deadlines, i.e., to process requests in a settled and appropriate time period).

Numerous elements of the performance traits found in the aforementioned significant studies may be summed up as follows:

BIOMEDICAL CLOUD COMPUTATION TECHNOLOGY OPTIONS

Customers can obtain certain services through a communication network (Pradhan, D. et al. 2022), and the H/W and S/W utilized by data centers that provide the facilities collectively are referred to as "cloud computing". The above-mentioned description was expanded upon by the international research and consulting company Forrester so as to include self-facilitated principles on the user's view as well as the organization of Information and Communication Technology tools on the supplier's side. In reality, cloud computing is a collection of standardized ICT capabilities (facilities, S/W, or hardware) that are accessed online and charged for only as they are used. Hardware uniformity, according to (Kazemzadeh, E., et al. 2023), is an essential condition for the development of cloud computing. The Boston Consulting Group suggests a simpler analysis of the issue. The foundation of the entire idea is the manner in which ICT is used when adaptable and fluid ICT (Wirajing, M.A.K., et al. 2023) tools are made available to third parties as services via internet technologies. The idea as a whole is supported by four unmistakable foundations:

Table 1. Cloud-based service performance characteristics

Features	Description	Metrics
Interaction	Indicated the transmission of data between external customers and the Cloud, or between instances of internal services (or whole distinct Cloud services).	Packet Loss Frequency
		Connection Error Rate
		MPI Transfer bit/Byte Speed
		MPI Transfer Delay
Calculation	Refers to the processing of tasks or data on cloud systems for computing.	CPU Load (%)
		Benchmark OP (FLOP) Rate
		Instance Efficiency (% CPU peak)
Memory	Intended for accessing information that could be retrieved from a hard drive that is difficult to access quickly.	Mean Hit Time (s)
		Memory bit/Byte Speed (MB/s, GB/s)
		Random Memory Update Rate
		Response Time (ms)
Time	Project success greatly depends on timely completion of the project without sacrificing quality.	Computation time
		Communication time

- Scalability– service assigning may be gradually expanded or reduced in accordance with the client requirements
- Allocation by many users – ICT tools is attainable as a facility allocated by many clients
- Calculating by usage – the service usage is calculated by utilizing relevant established levels of measurement, that can be used to calculate the service utilization.
- The use of internet facility, where resources are delivered to the consumer online.

There are three main delivery methods that can be differentiated based on the services that are provided:

- Infrastructure as a Service or IaaS, is when the infrastructure is promised by the service supplier. The primary benefit of this strategy is that the supplier will take care of any technical issues. An organization that possesses software (or a license to it) and doesn't need to maintain hardware, IaaS is a good option. Examples of IaaS include Windows Azure (Choudhary, S. et al. 2022), Rackspace, and Amazon WS.
- Platform as a service, or PaaS, is a business paradigm that provides a sophisticated technology and software infrastructure. Thus, cloudware is another name for it. The PaaS (Sinha, M. et al. 2021) service typically makes it easier to create user interfaces and contains tools and services that make it possible to plan, build, test, execute, and manage applications. Users of the service are not required to engage in or construct the hardware necessary for the creation and ongoing running of their apps. Google App Engine and Force.com are two examples of PaaS companies.
- Saas, or "Software as a Service," refers to the licensing of this program as a utility that the customer rents. Users don't buy the program rather, they buy access to it. SaaS is the best option for people who only need standard program software and need access from anywhere at any moment. The well-known Google Apps suite of programs or the transportation industry's Cargopass System are two examples (Figure 1).

Figure 2. Biomedical study cloud computing spread models

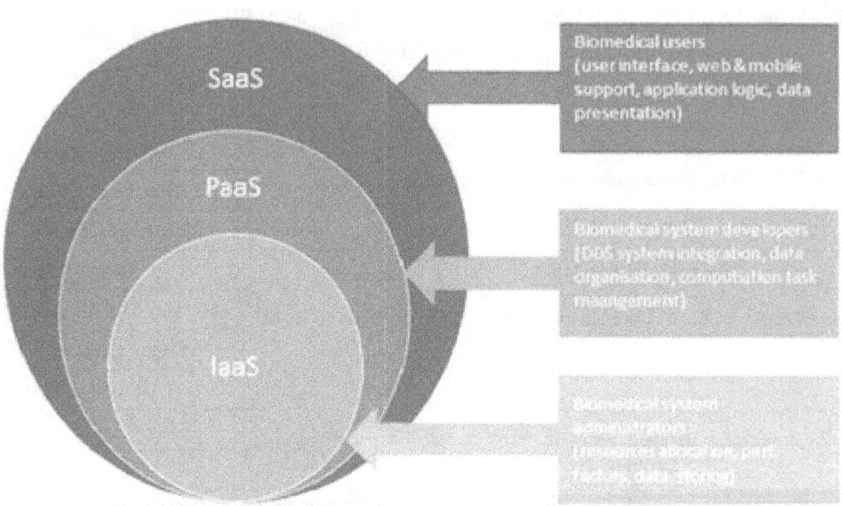

INFRASTRUCTURE SOLUTIONS AS THE FOUNDATION OF CLOUD COMPUTING

The foundation of any ICT (Jayasingh, R. et al. 2022) answer, including healthcare technologies, is infrastructure. Select virtualization systems are tightly linked to the cloud computing design, isolating the physical framework (Ghosh, R. et al. 2020) (CPU, memory, storage, internetworking framework, device connections etc.). Amid the actual H/W and provided S/W explanations, primarily the OS, virtualization (Pramanik, S. et al. 2021) can be seen as an extra layer. The hypervisor is thus the primary software tool in the cloud computing architecture idea. There are various kinds of virtualization methods, including hardware-assisted virtualization, para-virtualization, and complete virtualization. The method used to allocate physical resources is where the primary distinction lies. Unlike para-virtualization, which requires specialist S/W or drivers to connect to the resources, full virtualization entirely separates the H/W assets from the host system.

The entire biological and medical system is significantly influenced by the choice of the cloud computing technology platform (Sarkar, M. et al. 2020). In some instances, the prevalent binary translation methods of the H/W assets can have a detrimental impact on the total separation of full virtualization techniques. As the drivers or instructions were created specifically for this H/W, straight access to virtualization hardware resources through them can be much more effective. The three distinct processing categories that can be differentiated for biomedical study include:

- In memory intensive events: higher memory allocation on computer node, CPU intensive, related I/O allocation;
- CPU intensive jobs: relatively small quantity of data on compute node, complex algorithms;
- I/O intensive jobs: enormous quantity of repository data, storage or database intensive jobs.

Table 2. Scientific standards efficiency for hypervisors

science-based standard (Open source software tools) ↓	ESXi	Xen	Hyper-V	KVM	No-virtualization
DaCapo	5124 (+23%)	6108 (+36%)	6148 (+44%)	6177 (36%)	4251
Pysysbench	1127 (-4%)	1192 (-3%)	578 (-48%)	1183 (-5%)	1260
BulletCache	308 (-39%)	251 (-38%)	159 (-58%)	173 (-47%)	396
SciMark2/C	531 (-3%)	567 (-4%)	512 (-6%)	537 (-5%)	517

The cloud computation infrastructure as a service ought to be tailored for particular biological system tasks in accordance with the various computing kinds used in scientific research that were discussed above. The framework for cloud computing is made up of numerous components that are meant to work together. First off, the decentralized (Mall, P. K. et al. 2023) networking paradigm is used by the processing units and hypervisors, respectively. As a result, it is important to consider networking factors such as jitter, lag, delay, and network performance. This is crucial for network nodes, managers, APIs (Ghosh, R. et al. 2021), and other management components of the cloud computing architecture in addition to processing nodes. Second, science activities typically require a lot of recollection. Different hypervisors manage these resources in different ways, and by sharing parallel binary blocks, virtualization memory methods may save significant amounts of memory while accelerating the entire processing process. Thirdly, because big data operations like analytics, data mining, OLAP (Ghosh, R. et al. 2020), distributed databases, and different ideas related to business intelligence in common are mostly delicate to I/O performance factors, the way that data is distributed in cloud computation framework must admire the biomedical computing categories. On computer systems, data transfer, administration, or duplication can be executed completely, partly, locally or in a decentralized manner. Lastly, the harmony and collaboration between every component are crucial as one component of the framework may affect the others and serve as the system's bottleneck.

The description and evaluation of QoS (Naidu, G. T. et al. 2023) is one of the most difficult aspects of using cloud computing platforms for biological research. In the ICT world, the depiction of infrastructure development and the ultimate specification of needs are done using the QoS - Quality of Systems method. Without understanding the fundamentals of calculation measures, it is impossible to assess the cloud computing infrastructure's level. The topic of cloud computing architecture and speed problems is covered by a number of writers. In order to evaluate the major hypervisors in the chosen scientific study, (Kaur, K., et al. 2023) established the following performance metrics: storage, virtualization, network, administration, security, community, and provider support. Table 1 contains a summary of test outcomes. ESXi, Xen, Hyper-V, KVM are the hypervisors.

Infrastructure for cloud computing includes management frameworks, virtual internetwork hubs, user and application interfaces, as well as a variety of other parts like hypervisors, active and inactive network elements, and repository frameworks. These supporting systems construct the cloud computing architecture and offer the essential services. They are primarily in charge of the installation of virtualized OS, the hypervisors' platform in communication, the definition of data storing and replication, the development of application interface (API) (Mondal, D. et al. 2023) standards, the assurance of

Table 3. Main characteristics of commercial IaaS systems

Business Platforms	Characteristics
AWS (Amazon)	XEN Hypervisor-based, market-tested, improved design with platform interfaces and current healthcare apps that make it suitable as a public cloud option.
GCE (Google)	Short time on the market, designed on Google's system architecture, and based on the KVM virtualization; suitable for public cloud solutions.
Microsoft Azure	In line with public cloud solutions HyperV-based public storage that is similar to Windows-based platforms
VMWarevCD	Built on the ESXi host, improved design, and suitable for private cloud solutions.

user authentication, authorization, and accounting, as well as other infrastructure-related tasks, and the definition of user interface, among other things. A user-adaptive framework interface with online support, mobile, and various technologies for interaction is a feature of contemporary cloud-based systems.

It has recently been very difficult to differentiate between them and choose the best IaaS systems because there are so many cloud computing systems or apps available for biological research. Many writers offer a rudimentary overview of these technologies. These polls can occasionally include a mix of cloud computing systems, hardware, and apps. It is crucial to classify these goods into the proper groups in order to make the poll useful for any biological scholar. According to their specs and test findings, the following sections of this book divide cloud computing systems into two major groups, business companies and open source groups, and connect them with the use of hypervisors (Cinque, M. 2023). Recently, four major commercial suppliers were present on the market, three of which were capable of supporting the implementation of private cloud explanations, and one of which was the private cloud itself. These suppliers all provide infrastructure solutions that serve as the foundation for the implementation of additional biological systems. For their end users, commercial suppliers provide a reliable and backed option. The major business cloud computing infrastructure providers that are mentioned below, however, do not make the code and design available as open source grades for their own assistance. Therefore, these frameworks are perfect for academics and important jobs having adequate funding.

Literally, Amazon's AWS was the first significant competitor on the market (Amazon Web Services). Numerous biological systems are linked to this system's open source public solution, demonstrating how widely used it is (Table 2).

Platforms for open source cloud computing infrastructure reflect a variety of locally created options. Major hypervisors supported by these systems include KVM and Xen. Some systems also enable the integration of Microsoft Hyper-V and VMware ESXi hypervisors for mixed setups. A distinct strategy is used by open source systems, which integrate multiple tools having their own constituents in the cloud interface. Open source cloud computation framework, in contrast to commercial goods, is available for free adoption and is only backed by groups; as a result, it is appropriate in the creation of public cloud results. Typically, managers have all the necessary information and abilities about biological systems. Table 3 lists the fundamental data and virtualization support for the top open source vendors.

Hybrid systems are supported by a toolkit for handling diverse dispersed data centre networks. Platform for automated administration of various data centre networks

Table 4. Key characteristics of open source IaaS systems

Open Source Frameworks	Characteristics
CloudForms	A mixed cloud administration tool with support for other cloud platforms was introduced by Redhat. (AWS, OpenStack etc.)
CloudStack	Large networks of virtual computers can be deployed and managed using the open-source Apache approach.
Eucalyptus	Elastic Computing Architecture supports a variety of hypervisors and is similar to the technological answer of the AWS Clustered Architecture framework.
Ganeti	Google created Ganeti, a solution for managing virtual machine clusters. The virtualization platform in the solution stack is Xen, KVM, or LXC. LVM is used for disk management, and DRBD or shared storage may be used for external replication or disk replication between physical hosts.
Nimbus	Enables the implementation of self-configured virtual groups and provides infrastructure as a service via WSRF or the AMAZON API.
OpenNebula	An open source cloud computing platform called OpenNebula is used to manage infrastructure resources for public clouds, edge computing, and heterogeneous data centers.
OpenQRM	A free and open-source cloud computing management tool called openQRM is used to manage infrastructures with different types of data centers.
OpenStack	robust and adaptable cloud computing framework with plug-in design and assistance from other suppliers
oVirt	Web-based virtualization administration tool with an emphasis on desktop and virtual machine virtualization

HIGH-END PROCESSING MODEL USING THE CLOUD COMPUTING INFRASTRUCTURE

The centre component of the cloud computing idea is typically the cloud computing infrastructure. The infrastructure layer (IaaS), which specifies hardware distribution, virtualization methods, network settings, and administration of processing units, serves as the foundation for this layer. On the other hand, the platform develops a setting for the implementation of biological systems and specifies the API for functions that are implemented. On the contrary, this layer specifies how to reach the networking layer and how the software components should communicate with one another. Due to the high end processing features of this technological domain and the inherent limitations in the popular IaaS frameworks, this comparatively straightforward statement generates the most difficult issue as regards to the use of cloud computation strategy in biological research. Infrastructure for cloud computing is built on hypervisors and virtualization technologies, respectively. Task performance in tandem on the processing processors is not guaranteed by hypervisors or virtualization in and of itself. To question the high-end processing model used in biological research is therefore the primary issue with the cloud computing base layer. Below, this issue is covered in more detail.

The amount of electronic biological information saved in biomedical frameworks has increased in a large extent in the past decade due to the development in biomedical approaches and technologies. Contextualizing data and information produces knowledge and leads to scientific discoveries in a variety of fields, including genetic coding, biological data mining, and various analysis jobs. It is challenging to analyze a large quantity of data. Algorithms for science activities must be run simultaneously using a parallel or dispersed computing method rather than sequentially. This theory is founded on the notion of breaking down difficult jobs into simpler ones. Multi-core CPUs, computer groups, grid computation, utility computation, specialist H/W devices, and S/W systems such as Pthreadsor MPPI are all components of high-performance computing settings.

The next2 major groups of the High-Performance processing kinds may be differentiated, in spite of the ones utilized in the particular instrument or framework.

- Relational form - the relationship is founded on a logical foundation (Set theory and relational theory). The relational computing approach to large data involves the Analytical (EMC, HP Vertica), Traditional SQL databases (Ingress, MySQL), and Data as a utility are among the subcategories that include the goods that are being represented.
- Non-Relational category — built on document-dependent, graph-dependent, object-oriented, and key-value storage frameworks' non-relational data representation traits. The following sub-categories with corresponding products make up the non-relational big data computing type: analytical (Hadoop, Cloudera, MapReduce), document databases (CouchDB, MongoDB), operational (Progress, Versant), and graph databases. (FlocDB, Neo4).

Any of the aforementioned processing platforms must provide a solution for how to gather, arrange, keep, analyze, and exchange data. This issue affects data analysis, segmentation, duplication, and final computation of node consolidation. The non-relational high-performance computing style used in biological research is primarily exemplified by the MapReduce general purpose parallelization paradigm. A cluster can handle big data collections using a dispersed, concurrent method called MapReduce. The processing job is broken up, spread across a large number of calculate processors, and handled in simultaneously. Calculated component findings make up the ultimate score. This is the relevant MapReduce concept, where Map denotes how tasks are distributed and Reduce denotes how the tasks are aggregated

Table 5. Current processing tools and platforms that use MapReduce

Computing resources built on MapReduce Systems	Frameworks
BashReduce	Straightforward MapReduce application utility for Unix-based systems.
Disco	Support for common file systems, flexible and fault-tolerant utility, and MapReduce tasks in Python
GraphLab	Parallel machine learning system with pictorial data specification
tools built on Hadoop	Robust, capable of performing complex concurrent computations, unique HDFS file system. Market leader with a large number of commercial products and communities built on top of Hadoop technologies (OpenSplice, Qlikview, Red Hat Enterprise MRG Grid &JBoss Grid, SAP Real Time Data Platform, ScaleOuthServer, Terracotta BigMemory-Hadoop Connector, SQLstream Connector for Hadoop, Teradata Intelligent Memory, Tervela Turbo, TIBCO ActiveSpaces, Vitria Operational Intelligence (OI);
HPCC Systems	Enterprise Control Language (ECL), a declarative and data-centric strategy, and the use of the networked file system
Windows Dryad	Comparable to the MapReduce principle. Dryad work assignments employ direct sequence computing and the graph theory, enabling the execution of data-parallel program on computer clusters or in data centers.
SciDB	Built for multivariate data administration and analyses is the Array database.
Spark	Eliminates the sophisticated DAG execution engine that allows circular data flow and in-memory processing, combining SQL, streaming, and complicated analytics.
Storm	The distributed computation system, which is primarily written in Clojure, enables bulk and dispersed handling of flowing data.

as a consequence. The Hadoop (Pandey, B. K. et al. 2022) project, which was established by Apache, is the open source application of this paradigm. The categorization above indicates that high-end computing is a reasonably big field. Table 4 lists the findings of a study on the most popular high-end processing devices and platforms in the field of biology.

APPLICATIONS OF CLOUD COMPUTING IN BIOLOGY

A multidisciplinary branch of science is biomedicine. It incorporates both technological and physical scientific understanding. Its goal is to apply this information to issues in biology, clinical medicine, and fundamental medical studies. The tracking of bodily signs, medical imagery, computer analysis of patient data, and therapeutic decision-making are all topics covered in the Biomedical Engineering Handbook (Montesinos, L., et al. 2023). These facts demonstrate how data in distinct number values, physical data, and visual images are used by information systems assisting biological processes.

According to (Khurana, D., et al. 2023), current ICT requirements and biomedical trends are moving in the following directions:

- Access to e-health implementations and clinical information all over
- Patient and individualized tracking
- Location-dependent clinical facilities
- Emergency reactions and management
- Data and image storage and sharing

The implementation of the aforementioned remedies in biology is hampered by a number of issues. The routine is difficult when it comes to e-Health apps for a variety of reasons, including the waste of existing procedures and the reliance on paper for data storage. It is anticipated that in years to come, a doctor will input patient information into a cloud-based computerized appointment system. This information will then be handled by an algorithm to choose the best test instantly, and the patient will be informed immediately of their choices. Other significant difficulties when processing large quantities of data include handling scaling and load sharing, semantically merging various patient medical records, demographic data, and outdoor samples. Utilizing virtualization technology as a solution enables implementations to be moved effortlessly from one physical server to a different server, improving scalability, business durability, load balancing, hardware maintaining and processor and memory usage (Mahajan, H.B. et al. 2023).

The tendency of offering universal healthcare tracking aims to increase access to healthcare. Patients are typically only "treated" in hospitals or clinics, which is anticipated to alter in the future as people use more and more commonplace technology, like mobile phones, to keep track of their grievances. By using the outsourcing system or the code offloading system, mobile cloud computation is anticipated to become a important field, attempting to introduce substantial benefits of the Cloud computing(Kaushik, D. et al. 2022) for resource-constrained cell phones.

Another field that is crucial to the healthcare process is biomedical picture analysis. Imaging is essential for study, medical education, medical dialogue, and health treatment, among other things. It is possible to predict that the quantities of high-resolution and moving imagery data will approach petabytes. This demonstrates how extremely taxing picture restoration and analysis are. Cloud computing is a clear

Table 6. Selected biomedical cloud computing uses

S/W	Usage
CLoVR	Automated genome analysis with cloud processing from a laptop
Crossbow	Software for study of whole genome re-sequencing
CloudAligner	MapReduce-based utility for sequence alignment
Cloud-MAQ	RNA-Seq processing and data quality software
Cloud-Coffee	Method large-scale genome analysis using multiple sequence matching

possible aid in achieving this goal. Image clouds would make it possible to share imagery data across borders and perform sophisticated research on it far from its original location. Numerous researches have demonstrated the effectiveness of MapReducein handling complicated clinical imaging issues in a cloud computation setting. For instance, (Singh, A.K., et al. 2023) used MapReduce in a cloud processing setting to create a rapid and scalable image reconstruction method for 4D cone-beam CT. Utilizing cloud computing, (Hou, M., et al. 2023) suggested a paradigm for clinical colon cancer imaging analysis and study. The goal of the pan-European research infrastructure initiative Euro-Bioimaging (Ghomi, M., et al. 2023) is to implement a dispersed biomedical imaging framework in USA in a planned and synchronized way. It is anticipated to provide tools for mass imagery data storage, distant access, and post-processing.

The findings of a study of pertinent cloud computing uses in biology are shown in Table 6. The collection of well-known uses shows how numerous and diverse cloud computation techniques are in the field of biological analysis. This concept is a natural result of the variety of biomedical analysis, as various technological and biological foundations underlie many of the techniques, tools, and apps used in biomedical research, including virtual screening, patient tracking, genome analysis and parallel processing. The utilization of cloud computation in biomedicine was examined in the preceding volumes, which broke down each application into its component cloud computing layers from various perspectives. From a technical standpoint, it is evident that a specific form of Cloud computing service's prospective use is significantly affected and decided by the relevant biomedical study.

UTILIZING CLOUD TECHNOLOGIES FOR DRUG DEVELOPMENT

The statistical methods used in drug development can also be used with cloud computing. The usage of cloud computation tools in molecular modeling is though in its beginnings, but needs a tremendous possibility to develop as shown in various case studies, according to (Zhao, S., et al. 2023). They assert that cloud computing may have an impact past the services offered by on-demand processing capacity and stimulate creativity and development of innovative methods. They forecast a fast rise as more apps and prices continue to decline. But the security of the app was really the drawback.

The virtual screening (VS) techniques that are presently used to look through molecular databanks for possible novel leads for attaching to molecular targets like receptors, proteins, nucleic acids, and enzymes are a key strategy for the drug development process. In this procedure, cloud software can be very helpful. By adjusting these methods to adjustable cloud facilities and High Performance Computing, the contemporary rapid evolution of computation methods has facilitated this new path and directed to the likelihood of executing ligand-based virtual screening (LBVS).

The typical method of conducting VS studies involves HPC systems with numerous computer processors, whose high number is essential for the process's acceleration. This suggests that the expense of gear, energy, software upgrades, and support staff will be expensive. By essentially virtualizing the cloud setting and the processing time required to complete these computations, cloud computing essentially provides the opportunity to be free of all these obligations (Katal, A. et al. 2023).

A flexible molecular docking (FMD) HPC tool was created by (Nisticò, G. et al. 2023) as an illustration of how cloud computing can be applied to structure-based virtual screening (SBVS). They evaluated the accessibility, scaling, and efficiency of the MPI-HPC improved SBVS/FMD approach with various HPC methods used for unique lead structure finding in clinical chemistry and suggested a remedy for VS utilizing FMD mixing message passing interface (MPI) with multithreading.

AceCloud,an on-demand facility created to make it easier to execute numerous scenarios in a safe manner using a third-party cloud computing service (currently Amazon Web Services). The CycleCloud, created by Cyclecomputing®, is another choice. The availability of new, more complex models has drastically increased, posing a challenge for QSAR studies by requiring the processing of enormous amounts of data and necessitating the use of more effective analytical tools. In this regard, (Warner, B., et al. 2023) work demonstrated the benefits of cloud processing for QSAR research. Using their e-Science Central online infrastructure, they created and deployed an instrument for investigating the model universe. A novel method of conducting QSAR research as well as other kinds of uses was made possible by the increase and pure efficiency obtained, according to the authors.

CONCLUSION

The use of a broad range of testing methods in biomedical research over the past ten years has generated a lot of biological data that must be analyzed instantly. It is impossible to comply with this criterion solely through the use of conventional information tools. With the ability to more effectively handle resources and enable easy access, watching, and sharing of medical pictures across divisions, companies, and suppliers, cloud services offer an alluring option for the biomedical industry. Adopting a cloud computing strategy in biomedical research is not an easy job; rather, it is a complicated procedure that impacts the entire study and presents numerous difficulties in implementing suitable solutions. The fundamental tenets of cloud computing application in biomedicine were presented in this article from the perspectives of IT, high-end processing, biological implementations, and medication technique. The goal to this relevant approach's deployment's success is striking a compromise between the difficult variables, like ethical and security considerations. Once this objective is met, this cutting-edge processing technology will benefit scientific study.

Future Work

Because the data originate from disparate informatics platforms and are stored in various formats (such as numerical values, free text, graphical and imaging material), data sharing across translational bioinformatics subfields is sometimes challenging. The consistent representation of data is mandated by standards due to the enormous dimensionality of various data types. In order to achieve this aim, modern semantic-based models, natural language processing (NLP) methods, and integrated medical/biological terminologies and ontologies must be implemented in order to objectively explain medical and biomolecular discoveries.

In specialized sectors, there have been several efforts to define standards for data integration. For example, a standard designed to describe and communicate microarray data is called minimal information about microarray experiment (MIAME). The basic model of anatomy clinical community and digital imaging and communications in medicine (DICOM) are two current standards in the area of imaging informatics. The worldwide statistical categorization of illnesses and associated health issues (ICD-10), systematized nomenclature of medicine (SNOMED), health level 7 (HL7), and clinical data standards exchange consortium (CDISC) serve as the benchmark for the clinical community.

But intercommunity data exchange cannot be enabled by these community-specific standards alone. The creation of integrated standards will be crucial in this respect. Although a single standard covering all fields is unlikely to be developed, semantic mapping across terminologies seems to be a more workable solution. It is the goal of many innovative medical informatics efforts to establish such intercommunity standards. As an example, the European Union's ACGT project produced a number of methodological strategies, tools, and services for semantic integration of dispersed multilevel datasets.

REFERENCES

Anand, R., Singh, J., Pandey, D., Pandey, B. K., Nassa, V. K., & Pramanik, S. (2022). Modern Technique for Interactive Communication in LEACH-Based Ad Hoc Wireless Sensor Network. In M. M. Ghonge, S. Pramanik, & A. D. Potgantwar (Eds.), *Software Defined Networking for Ad Hoc Networks*. Springer. doi:10.1007/978-3-030-91149-2_3

Choudhary, S., Narayan, V., Faiz, M., & Pramanik, S. (2022). Fuzzy Approach-Based Stable Energy-Efficient AODV Routing Protocol in Mobile Ad hoc Networks. In M. M. Ghonge, S. Pramanik, & A. D. Potgantwar (Eds.), *Software Defined Networking for Ad Hoc Networks*. Springer. doi:10.1007/978-3-030-91149-2_6

Cinque, M. (2023). *Real-Time FaaS: serverless computing for Industry 4.0*. SOCA. doi:10.1007/s11761-023-00360-0

Gezimati, M., & Singh, G. (2023). Advances in terahertz technology for cancer detection applications. *Optical and Quantum Electronics*, *55*(2), 151. doi:10.1007/s11082-022-04340-0 PMID:36588663

Ghomi, M., Zare, E. N., Alidadi, H., Pourreza, N., Sheini, A., Rabiee, N., Mattoli, V., Chen, X., & Makvandi, P. (2023). A multifunctional bioresponsive and fluorescent active nanogel composite for breast cancer therapy and bioimaging. *Advanced Composites and Hybrid Materials*, *6*(1), 51. doi:10.1007/s42114-022-00613-0

Ghosh, R., Mohanty, S., Pattnaik, P., & Pramanik, S. (2020). A Performance Assessment of Power-Efficient Variants of Distributed Energy-Efficient Clustering Protocols in WSN. *International Journal of Interactive Communication Systems and Technologies*, *10*(2), 1–14. doi:10.4018/IJICST.2020070101

Ghosh, R., Mohanty, S., Pattnaik, P. K., & Pramanik, S. (2020). Performance Analysis Based on Probablity of False Alarm and Miss Detection in Cognitive Radio Network. *International Journal of Wireless and Mobile Computing*, *20*(4), 390. doi:10.1504/IJWMC.2021.117530

Ghosh, R., & Pramanik, S. (2021). A Novel Performance Evaluation of Resourceful Energy Saving Protocols of Heterogeneous WSN to Maximize Network Stability and Lifetime. *International Journal of Interdisciplinary Telecommunications and Networking*, *13*(2), 72–88. doi:10.4018/IJITN.2021040106

Guest, O., & Martin, A. E. (2023). On Logical Inference over Brains, Behaviour, and Artificial Neural Networks. *Computational Brain & Behavior*, *6*(2), 213–227. doi:10.1007/s42113-022-00166-x

Hou, M., Zhou, L., & Sun, J. (2023). Deep-learning-based 3D super-resolution MRI radiomics model: Superior predictive performance in preoperative T-staging of rectal cancer. *European Radiology*, *33*(1), 1–10. doi:10.1007/s00330-022-08952-8 PMID:35726100

Huang, X., Lin, Y., Zhang, Z., Guo, X., & Su, S. (2022). A gradient-based optimization approach for task scheduling problem in cloud computing. *Cluster Computing*, *25*(5), 3481–3497. doi:10.1007/s10586-022-03580-9

Jayasingh, R., & Kumar, J. (2022). Speckle noise removal by SORAMA segmentation in Digital Image Processing to facilitate precise robotic surgery. *International Journal of Reliable and Quality E-Healthcare*, *11*(1), 1–19. Advance online publication. doi:10.4018/IJRQEH.295083

Katal, A., Dahiya, S., & Choudhury, T. (2023). Energy efficiency in cloud computing data centers: A survey on software technologies. *Cluster Computing*, *26*(3), 1845–1875. doi:10.1007/s10586-022-03713-0 PMID:36060618

Kaur, K., Bharany, S., Badotra, S., Aggarwal, K., Nayyar, A., & Sharma, S. (2023). Energy-efficient polyglot persistence database live migration among heterogeneous clouds. *The Journal of Supercomputing*, *79*(1), 265–294. doi:10.1007/s11227-022-04662-6

Kaushik, D., Garg, M. Annu, Gupta, A. & Pramanik, S. (2022). Application of Machine Learning and Deep Learning in Cyber security: An Innovative Approach. in M. Ghonge, S. Pramanik, R. Mangrulkar and D. N. Le, (eds.), Cybersecurity and Digital: Challenges and Future Trends, Wiley. doi:10.1002/9781119795667.ch12

Kazemzadeh, E., Fuinhas, J. A., Salehnia, N., & Osmani, F. (2023). The effect of economic complexity, fertility rate, and information and communication technology on ecological footprint in the emerging economies: A two-step stirpat model and panel quantile regression. *Quality & Quantity*, *57*(1), 737–763. doi:10.1007/s11135-022-01373-1

Khurana, D., Koli, A., Khatter, K., & Singh, S. (2023). Natural language processing: State of the art, current trends and challenges. *Multimedia Tools and Applications*, *82*(3), 3713–3744. doi:10.1007/s11042-022-13428-4 PMID:35855771

Mahajan, H. B., Rashid, A. S., Junnarkar, A. A., Uke, N., Deshpande, S. D., Futane, P. R., Alkhayyat, A., & Alhayani, B. (2023). Integration of Healthcare 4.0 and blockchain into secure cloud-based electronic health records systems. *Applied Nanoscience*, *13*(3), 2329–2342. doi:10.1007/s13204-021-02164-0 PMID:35136707

Mall, P. K., Pramanik, S., Srivastava, S., Faiz, M., Sriramulu, S., & Kumar, M. N. (2023). FuzztNet-Based Modelling Smart Traffic System in Smart Cities Using Deep Learning Models. In *Data-Driven Mathematical Modeling in Smart Cities*. IGI Global. doi:10.4018/978-1-6684-6408-3.ch005

Mondal, D., Ratnaparkhi, A., Deshpande, A., Deshpande, V., Kshirsagar, A. P., & Pramanik, S. (2023). Applications, Modern Trends and Challenges of MultiscaleModelling in Smart Cities. In *Data-Driven Mathematical Modeling in Smart Cities*. IGI Global. doi:10.4018/978-1-6684-6408-3.ch001

Montesinos, L., Salinas-Navarro, D. E., & Santos-Diaz, A. (2023). Transdisciplinary experiential learning in biomedical engineering education for healthcare systems improvement. *BMC Medical Education*, *23*(1), 207. doi:10.1186/s12909-023-04171-x PMID:37013525

Nisticò, G. (2023). Three-Dimensional Reconstruction of Coronal Features: A Python Tool for Geometric Triangulation. *Solar Physics*, *298*(3), 36. doi:10.1007/s11207-023-02122-9

Pandey, D. Pandey, Wairya, S., Agarwal, G., Dadeech, P. S. ,Dogiwal, R., & Pramanik, S. (2022). Application of Integrated Steganography and Image Compressing Techniques for Confidential Information Transmission. Cyber Security and Network Security. Wiley. ,. doi:10.1002/9781119812555.ch8

Pradhan, D., Sahu, P. K., Goje, N. S., Myo, H., Ghonge, M. M., Rajeswari, R., & Pramanik, S. (2022). Security, Privacy, Risk, and Safety Toward 5G Green Network (5G-GN)", in Cyber Security and Network Security. Wiley. doi:10.1002/9781119812555.ch9

Pramanik, S. (2023). An Adaptive Image Steganography Approach depending on Integer Wavelet Transform and Genetic Algorithm. *Multimedia Tools and Applications*, *82*(22), 34287–34319. doi:10.1007/s11042-023-14505-y

Pramanik, S., & Bandyopadhyay, S. (2023). Identifying Disease and Diagnosis in Females using Machine Learning. In I. G. I. John Wang (Ed.), *Encyclopedia of Data Science and Machine Learning*. Global. doi:10.4018/978-1-7998-9220-5.ch187

Pramanik, S., Samanta, D., Ghosh, R., Bandyopadhyay, S. K. (2021). A New Combinational Technique in Image Steganography. *International Journal of Information Security and Privacy, 15*(3), IGI Global. doi:10.4018/IJISP.2021070104

Singh, A. K., & Kumar, J. (2023). A privacy-preserving multidimensional data aggregation scheme with secure query processing for smart grid. *The Journal of Supercomputing*, *79*(4), 3750–3770. doi:10.1007/s11227-022-04794-9

Sinha, M., Chacko, E., Makhija, P., & Pramanik, S. (2021). Energy Efficient Smart Cities with Green IoT. In C. Chakrabarty (Ed.), *Green Technological Innovation for Sustainable Smart Societies: Post Pandemic Era*. Springer. doi:10.1007/978-3-030-73295-0_16

Taviti Naidu, G., & Ganesh, K. V. B. (2023). Technological Innovation Driven by Big Data, in In H. Ahmed (ed.) Advanced Bioinspiration Methods for Healthcare Standards, Policies, and Reform. IGI Global. doi:10.4018/978-1-6684-5656-9

Warner, B., Ratner, E., & Lendasse, A. (2023). Edammo's Extreme AutoML Technology – Benchmarks and Analysis. In: Björk, KM. (eds) *Proceedings of ELM 2021. ELM 2021.Proceedings in Adaptation, Learning and Optimization*. Springer, Cham. 10.1007/978-3-031-21678-7_15

Wirajing, M. A. K., & Nchofoung, T. N. (2023). The role of education in modulating the effect of ICT on governance in Africa. *Education and Information Technologies*, *28*(9), 11987–12020. doi:10.1007/s10639-023-11631-w PMID:37361761

Zhao, S., Miao, J., & Zhao, J. (2023). *A comprehensive and systematic review of the banking systems based on pay-as-you-go payment fashion and cloud computing in the pandemic era*. InfSyst E-Bus Manage., doi:10.1007/s10257-022-00617-9

Chapter 16
Harnessing the Power of Geospatial Data:
The Convergence of SDI, Big Data, and Cloud Computing

Munir Ahmad
https://orcid.org/0000-0003-4836-6151
Survey of Pakistan, Pakistan

Aitizaz Ali
Unitar International University, Malaysia

Ting Tin Tin
https://orcid.org/0000-0001-7634-1686
INTI International University, Malaysia

Asmat Ali
https://orcid.org/0000-0002-8804-2285
Survey of Pakistan, Pakistan

ABSTRACT

This chapter explored the transformative impact of cloud computing on geospatial data management, highlighting its scalability, cost-efficiency, and security features. This exploration adopted a qualitative method based on a literature review, systematically analyzing existing works to gain insights into the qualitative dimensions of the evolving intersection between cloud computing and geospatial data management. It detailed the integration of parallel processing, GIS platforms, machine learning, and data visualization within the digital landscape, fostering innovation. The narrative extended to include emerging technologies like edge computing, blockchain, AR/VR, and geospatial data marketplaces, giving rise to a groundbreaking geospatial data as a service (DaaS) model. Emphasizing the cloud's pivotal role in handling geospatial big data, the chapter outlined capabilities in parallel processing, GIS orchestration, machine learning integration, and disaster recovery.

DOI: 10.4018/979-8-3693-0900-1.ch016

Emerging Trends in Cloud Computing Analytics, Scalability, and Service Models

INTRODUCTION

In the modern era, geospatial data has emerged as a cornerstone in addressing a multitude of complex challenges across diverse domains. The convergence of Spatial Data Infrastructure (SDI), Big Data, and Cloud Computing has redefined the way of harnessing and analyzing geospatial information. Big Data, characterized by its sheer volume, velocity, veracity, and variety, has inundated the data landscape. In response, cloud Computing has emerged as a powerful ally, offering utility-based computing services to tackle the complexities posed by big data (Yang et al., 2017). This convergence of technologies is revolutionizing the way of processing geospatial data across various scientific domains.

One of the most notable impacts is within the realm of climate studies, where geospatial data plays a pivotal role. Cloud computing can provide scalable and on-demand computing resources that enable efficient data management and analytics. In the context of geospatial data, this is particularly crucial. It can empower to process vast datasets relevant to climate studies, knowledge mining, land-use analysis, and even the forecasting of phenomena like dust storms (Yang et al., 2017). Data parallelism and automatic provisioning of virtual clusters have significantly enhanced the processing of big data (Yang et al., 2017). This, in turn, has accelerated the analysis and prediction of land use and land-cover changes. Notably, technologies like Google Earth Engine have harnessed cloud computing to process high-resolution global forest cover change maps, exemplifying the transformative potential of these tools. Furthermore, cloud computing is not confined to just processing power. It offers cloud storage and accessibility, which are instrumental in the storage and analysis of large land cover data. Complex algorithms for land cover change modeling can be parallelized and accelerated within Cloud Computing environments, enabling rapid change analysis (Yang et al., 2017).

In parallel, the significance of cloud, fog, and mist computing paradigms in handling geospatial big data is on the rise. Mist computing, in particular, leverages edge devices to enhance data throughput and reduce latency. MistGIS, a cutting-edge framework, has found practical applications in domains like tourism information infrastructure management and faculty information retrieval systems, simplifying data integration and retrieval. The validation of MistGIS underscored its potential to complement cloud and fog computing for geospatial big data analysis as noted by Barik, Misra, et al., (2019). Sustainable agriculture, a critical concern in a world facing a burgeoning population, presents a formidable challenge. The integration of geospatial data and technology is pivotal in mitigating ecological impacts and enhancing agricultural practices. Big data analytics, artificial intelligence, and machine learning have become imperative in optimizing agriculture by improving data accessibility and coherence. The influence of cloud computing, the Internet of Things, and data analytics has driven the agricultural industry toward digital agriculture, emphasizing precision conservation practices. The adoption of the "4 Rs" (right product, rate, time, and place) and the "7 Rs" framework significantly contribute to precision agriculture and conservation efforts. Connectivity and embracing edge computing have become paramount, especially in regions with limited bandwidth, enabling the effective harnessing of advanced agricultural technologies (Delgado et al., 2019).

Natural disasters demand efficient management, encompassing mitigation, preparedness, response, and recovery. Geospatial technologies play a vital role in this regard. Organizations like FEMA and the Copernicus Programme utilize geospatial data, but challenges in sharing, accessing, and integrating this data hinder its full potential (He & Yue, 2019). They presented a platform that leverages big data and cloud computing to enhance spatial information infrastructures, bolstering disaster data accumulation, models, and services for effective disaster risk reduction. Fog Computing, as demonstrated by the FogGIS framework, reduces latency and boosts data throughput in geospatial Big Data analytics. Its potential is showcased through the development of prototypes and the utilization of open-source compression techniques to enhance data transmission to the cloud. Leveraging open-source compression techniques and GIS, the framework can facilitate various applications such as land resource planning and decision-making, underscoring its potential in the geospatial data landscape as demonstrated by Barik et al., (2017).

The field of geological information services relies on cloud computing to handle massive-scale and complex computations. In an era of unprecedented data collection, cloud-enabled geological information services (CEGIS) address the specific requirements and challenges of this domain. The system architecture, big data management requirements, application development opportunities, and emerging trends are all explored in China by Y. Zhu et al., (2018). The challenges of processing geospatial Big Data from Internet of Spatial Things (IoST) devices in cloud computing environments have prompted the introduction of fog-assisted cloud computing. This approach aims to enhance network performance and improve data outsourcing services. GeoBD2, a novel scheme within this framework, focuses on geospatial Big Data deduplication, promising greater efficiency with lower overhead costs compared to existing deduplication schemes as demonstrated by Barik et al., (2021).

The challenge of storing rapidly growing geospatial data can be addressed through cloud storage solutions. Traditional data warehouses are augmented by cloud storage, providing cost-effective and scalable options. Middleware-like architectures can bridge the gap, enabling the retrieval of traditional geospatial data while incorporating cloud storage lineage. In this context, a prototype system exhibiting promising performance and flexibility, serving as an open-source solution for public use is demonstrated by K. Liu et al., (2016). The increasing importance of big geospatial data hosted in cloud environments is a reflection of the growing volume of remote sensing data and the trend of storing and sharing in-situ data at higher sampling rates. Cloud computing, with its scalability and reliability, is at the forefront of meeting the computational requirements for big data processing as noted by Simonis, (2018).

A novel cloud-based geospatial Linked Data (LD) management system is introduced to address the challenges associated with scaling LD systems for geospatial data. This system offers scalability and abstracts the complexities of LD publishing, dynamically scaling to match user load and providing LD-as-a-service for comprehensive LD management (Kritikos et al., 2015). In the realm of Earth observation and environmental geospatial datasets, High-Performance Computing (HPC) environments and Cloud Computing are instrumental in conducting large-scale urban growth simulations. Supported by GIS and neural network-based land transformation models, these technologies can provide valuable insights into geospatial big data as noted by Karmas et al., (2016).

GeoFog4Health, a Fog-based Spatial Data Infrastructure framework, stands out as a powerful tool for geospatial health big data analysis. Its integration with cloud computing improves data transmission and analysis, and the framework's features include lossless data compression, overlay analysis of geospatial data, and considerations such as energy savings and scalability (Barik, Dubey, et al., 2019). The introduction of BiGeo, a foundational Platform as a Service (PaaS) framework, addresses the need to efficiently handle geospatial Big Data. This framework offers comprehensive capabilities for the storage, visualization, management, analysis, service, and migration of geospatial Big Data. It promises flexibility and performance improvements, exemplified through case studies involving substantial spatial data from Sichuan Province, China (X. Liu et al., 2019).

In conclusion, the convergence of SDI, big data, and cloud computing has unleashed a new era of possibilities in the world of geospatial data. This integration empowers researchers, policymakers, and industries to explore, analyze, and leverage geospatial information on an unprecedented scale, driving innovation and sustainability across diverse domains. In this backdrop, the overarching objective of this chapter is to provide insights into the transformative impact of the convergence of SDI, big data, and cloud computing, showcasing how this integration enables unprecedented exploration, analysis, and utilization of geospatial information across various fields, fostering innovation and sustainability.

BACKGROUND

In this section, fundamental insights concerning spatial data infrastructure, big data, and the domain of cloud computing are presented.

Spatial Data Infrastructure

Spatial Data Infrastructure (SDI) represents a fundamental framework that facilitates the discovery, access, sharing, and utilization of geospatial data and related information (Rajabifard, A., Feeney, M. E. F., & Williamson, 2003). SDI is a critical enabler of decision-making processes across a wide array of domains, ranging from urban planning to environmental management.

One of the key objectives of SDI is to ensure the interoperability of geospatial data across various systems and organizations. This involves the development of standards and protocols that enable data exchange, making it possible for different stakeholders to seamlessly share and integrate geospatial information (Crompvoets et al., 2004). The Open Geospatial Consortium (OGC) plays a pivotal role in the development of such standards and specifications.

SDI is particularly vital in the context of disaster management. During crises, the availability of timely and accurate geospatial data can significantly enhance emergency response and recovery efforts (Ključanin et al., 2021). This underscores the importance of SDI as a tool for ensuring that critical information is readily accessible to relevant agencies and organizations in times of need.

Furthermore, the advent of cloud computing has introduced new possibilities for SDI. The cloud can serve as a platform for the storage, management, and dissemination of geospatial data (Waleed & Sajjad, 2023). This transition to the cloud offers scalability and accessibility, making geospatial information available to a broader audience.

Núñez-Andrés et al., (2022) have introduced the idea of a Spatial Data Infrastructure that encompasses comprehensive 3D geoinformation data specifically tailored for the analysis of fragmentary rockfalls. Building upon this concept, Vaitis et al., (2022) have proposed developing and deploying an SDI to effectively handle and disseminate marine data within the context of Greece, showcasing the versatility of SDIs across various domains. In the context of urban transportation, Grubisic, (2023) has suggested an innovative approach by advocating the implementation of an SDI-based model, harnessing the computational prowess of cloud computing to optimize public transportation systems. This forward-thinking proposition addresses transportation challenges and highlights the growing relevance of SDIs in modern urban planning and management. Furthermore, Jabbour et al., (2019) have advanced the idea that embracing a two-sided market approach can significantly benefit the formulation of industrial and pricing strategies for SDI platforms, thereby facilitating a seamless transition toward self-sustaining mechanisms. This underscored the adaptability and scalability of SDIs in supporting diverse applications.

Big Data

The concept of big data encompasses vast and ever-expanding datasets that comprise a diverse range of formats, encompassing structured, unstructured, and semi-structured data. Big data possesses an intricate character, demanding robust technologies and sophisticated algorithms for its effective handling and analysis (Oussous et al., 2018).

Spatial big data refers to a specialized category of big data that focuses on geospatial information, which encompasses a wide range of location-based data sources, such as satellite imagery, GPS data, geographical information systems, and more (Koh et al., 2022). These datasets are characterized by their immense volume, velocity, variety, and veracity, making them a crucial component of modern data-driven decision-making processes.

The integration of spatial big data with advanced analytics is revolutionizing numerous fields. GIS is at the forefront of harnessing spatial big data for applications in urban planning, environmental monitoring, disaster management, and logistics (Goodchild, 2010). For example, organizations like NASA leverage spatial big data for Earth observation, climate modeling, and space exploration. This highlights the value of spatial big data in addressing complex global challenges.

Moreover, the advent of the Internet of Things (IoT) has led to a proliferation of spatial data generated by sensors embedded in various devices. These sensors collect location-based information and transmit it to the cloud for analysis (Manogaran & Lopez, 2017). This real-time spatial big data plays a vital role in optimizing transportation systems, managing smart cities, and enhancing healthcare through remote patient monitoring.

The management and analysis of spatial big data present unique challenges. Traditional databases are often ill-suited to handle the complexity and volume of spatial data, leading to the development of specialized spatial databases and data management systems. These systems enable efficient storage, retrieval, and analysis of geospatial information.

Cloud Computing

Cloud computing is a paradigm that has revolutionized the way organizations store, access, and manage their data and applications. It offers the flexibility and scalability to meet the ever-increasing demands of the digital age (Rittinghouse & Ransome, 2016).

In essence, cloud computing involves the delivery of various computing services over the Internet, ranging from infrastructure (IaaS) to platform (PaaS) and software (SaaS) (Armbrust et al., 2010). It enables users to access resources, such as virtual machines, databases, and storage, on a pay-as-you-go basis. This cost-effective model has democratized access to high-performance computing resources, enabling even small businesses and startups to compete in the digital landscape (Dillon et al., 2010).

The cloud's scalability and elasticity allow businesses to rapidly adjust their IT resources to match their specific needs, resulting in cost savings and enhanced operational efficiency (Mell & Grance,

2011). Moreover, cloud providers often invest heavily in security measures, ensuring that data stored in the cloud is protected against breaches and cyberattacks (Ristenpart et al., 2009).

The cloud also plays a pivotal role in enabling remote work and collaboration. It provides the infrastructure for video conferencing, file sharing, and project management tools that have become essential in today's globalized and interconnected world (Singh et al., 2021).

FOCUS OF THE CHAPTER

The focus of this chapter is to explore the integration of big data in geospatial applications, emphasizing its management and analysis through cloud computing. It delves into the techniques and technologies associated with cloud-based geospatial data management and the utilization of cloud computing for large-scale geospatial data analytics. Additionally, the chapter addresses the visualization of geospatial data in cloud environments and highlights the significance of cloud-optimized geospatial formats for efficient data processing and storage.

DISCUSSIONS

This section provides an in-depth exploration of the synergies between big data and geospatial applications, with a particular focus on leveraging cloud computing for efficient data management and analytics.

Big Data in Geospatial Applications

One of the key areas where big data and geospatial technology converge is urban planning. The exponential growth of cities and the associated challenges of sustainable development demand the integration of massive amounts of geospatial data into urban planning processes (Thakuriah et al., 2017). Urban planners can use geospatial data to identify areas in need of infrastructure improvements, assess population density, and optimize public transportation routes

Furthermore, geospatial big data is instrumental in disaster management. The real-time collection and analysis of data from sources like remote sensing, weather stations, and social media can significantly improve early warning systems and disaster response (Kamel Boulos et al., 2011). This can help save lives and reduce the impact of natural and human-made disasters. It can help in identifying vulnerable areas, predicting the path of natural disasters like hurricanes or wildfires, and coordinating emergency services during crises.

The integration of big data and geospatial technology can also play a pivotal role in agriculture. Precision agriculture leverages data from sensors, satellites, and weather forecasts to optimize crop management and increase agricultural productivity (Janowicz et al., 2020). Soil quality, weather conditions, and crop health can all be monitored through satellite data and sensors, allowing for precise and sustainable farming practices.

Moreover, the healthcare sector can benefit from this fusion as well. Geospatial spatial data can be combined with healthcare data to improve the understanding of disease patterns, enhance the allocation of healthcare resources, and support public health initiatives (H, 2011; Parmanto et al., 2008). Spatial data can assist in tracking disease outbreaks, monitoring healthcare facility locations, and improving healthcare accessibility. During pandemics, geospatial data can help identify hotspots and allocate resources efficiently.

Large-scale environmental monitoring can use big spatial data for tracking changes in ecosystems, wildlife habitats, and climate patterns (Manfreda et al., 2018). For instance, satellite imagery and geospatial data can help monitor deforestation, track wildlife migration, and assess the impact of climate change on natural landscapes.

The world of transportation and logistics relies heavily on GPS data and traffic information to ensure the efficient movement of goods and people (Adam et al., 2021). These data sources provide valuable insights into the geographical structures and dynamics that underpin the industry, especially in the context of freight transportation. With this information, companies can make informed decisions to optimize their operations. They use this data not only to plan delivery routes but also to fine-tune vehicle performance, reducing emissions and operational costs.

Big data can play a crucial role in enhancing the quality and categorization of natural resource archives management (Wang & Lv, 2023). It can support sustainable management of resources like water, minerals, and forestry. By leveraging big spatial data, sustainable resource management and conservation efforts can be supported. Resource mapping and extraction planning become more precise and efficient, leading to reduced waste and environmental impact.

In the realm of retail, spatial data takes on a different dimension, where it can be used for location-based marketing, customer behavior analysis, and site selection for new stores. This can be exemplified by the use of mobile apps that harness location data to deliver personalized offers to nearby customers. Retailers can gain a profound understanding of customer preferences and shopping behaviors, tailoring their marketing strategies to individual needs. Location-based marketing can allow for more targeted promotions, enhancing the shopping experience for consumers and boosting business for retailers.

Geospatial data is the backbone of interactive maps, navigation apps, and location-based services that enrich the tourist experience. When travelers explore new destinations, these tools guide them with precision and offer valuable insights into the local culture, attractions, and amenities. Moreover, in the context of popular tourist destinations, geospatial data is an invaluable asset for crowd management. It can enable authorities to plan for high visitor volumes, ensuring the safety and satisfaction of tourists.

Law enforcement agencies have embraced spatial data for crime mapping, emergency response, and tracking trends in criminal activity. This application allows them to allocate resources effectively, concentrating efforts in areas with high crime rates and predicting potential hotspots. By employing geospatial data, law enforcement can become more efficient, responsive, and proactive in maintaining public safety and reducing criminal activity.

Cloud Computing for Geospatial Big Data

Geospatial Big Data, characterized by the volume and diversity of data sources, including satellite imagery, sensor networks, and Geographic Information Systems (GIS), presents unique challenges for analysis and storage. Cloud computing offers scalable solutions that facilitate the storage, retrieval, and processing of geospatial data on a massive scale. The cloud's dynamic nature allows organizations to elastically adapt to changing computational demands, making it a cost-effective solution for geospatial Big Data analytics. Below are the different aspects where cloud computing can be employed to manage, store, process, and visualize spatial data.

Scalability

Scalability in cloud computing can facilitate the effortless expansion or reduction of computational power and storage resources (Mell & Grance, 2011). This capability is especially vital for effectively managing extensive geospatial datasets. For instance, a weather forecasting service can seamlessly scale its infrastructure to process and analyze a sudden influx of weather data during a natural disaster. Furthermore, the cloud's scalability can allow organizations to adapt to evolving data requirements, whether for disaster management, urban planning, environmental monitoring, or precision agriculture. The cloud's computational resources can enable advanced geospatial analytics, such as spatial data mining and machine learning, which can unlock valuable insights from vast datasets.

Cost-Efficiency

Cloud computing offers cost-effective solutions by enabling organizations to pay only for the resources they utilize, minimizing the need for substantial capital expenditure. For example, an environmental monitoring agency can leverage the cloud to reduce operational costs by dynamically adjusting resource allocation based on varying data processing requirements. Cloud computing is associated with potential cost savings of up to 30% in comparison to traditional on-premises solutions (v500.com, 2021).

Data Storage

Cloud-based geospatial data management can allow for the storage and retrieval of extensive datasets on demand, reducing the need for extensive local storage infrastructure. This shift to the cloud can not only save costs but also ensure that geospatial data is readily accessible from anywhere in the world. Cloud service providers offer scalable and economically viable storage solutions like Amazon S3, Google Cloud Storage, and Azure Blob Storage (huawei, 2023), making them ideal for housing large geospatial datasets. For example, a satellite imaging company can leverage cloud storage to efficiently store and manage terabytes of high-resolution satellite images.

Data Processing

The cloud's serverless processing capabilities are well-suited for the automation of data processing tasks. Services such as AWS Lambda and Azure Functions (Poccia, 2016) can excel in efficiently processing geospatial data. Cloud-based serverless processing can automate geospatial data tasks, allowing organizations to focus on application logic. For instance, a logistics company can use cloud serverless functions to automate route optimization based on real-time geospatial data, ensuring efficient delivery routes.

Data Integration

Cloud platforms can provide a range of tools and services that can facilitate the seamless integration of geospatial data with other data types, thereby enabling in-depth analyses and insights (Yu & Sarwat, 2021). The integration of geospatial data in the cloud dismantles data silos, empowering organizations to fully harness the potential of their data assets. For instance, an urban planning department can use these capabilities to integrate geospatial data with demographic information, facilitating comprehensive city planning and development decisions. Furthermore, cloud computing can facilitate the integration of geospatial data from various sources, such as remote sensing, GPS, and GIS. With the data stored in the cloud, it can be easily combined and analyzed, leading to more comprehensive insights for decision-making processes (Dunn, 2007). Real-time data updates and collaboration among team members can also streamlined in the cloud environment.

Parallel Processing

Numerous cloud services offer support for parallel and distributed data processing, such as the utilization of Hadoop and Spark (Baraglia et al., 2010). These technologies have the potential to greatly accelerate the analysis of geospatial data. An agriculture research organization can leverage cloud-based parallel processing to analyze multi-spectral satellite imagery and derive insights for precision farming.

Geographic Information Systems

Cloud-based GIS platforms, exemplified by services like ArcGIS Online and Google Earth Engine, can foster collaborative work and geospatial data analysis within a cloud-native environment (Esri, 2023). Cloud-hosted GIS platforms not only facilitate real-time collaboration on geospatial projects but also provide access to cutting-edge mapping tools (Google Cloud, 2023b). For example, a disaster response team can utilize cloud-based GIS tools to monitor evolving situations and coordinate response efforts in real-time.

Machine Learning and AI

Cloud service providers extend their offerings to encompass machine learning and artificial intelligence services. AI-driven geospatial insights within cloud environments can empower predictive modeling (Qiu et al., 2016) and play a crucial role in supporting decision-making processes, especially in the realms of disaster management and environmental monitoring. Machine learning in the cloud can enhance geospatial data analysis, enabling the development of applications such as land cover classification and object detection (Aurélien Géron, 2019, p. 341). For instance, an insurance company can use cloud-based AI to analyze historical geospatial data and predict flood risk in specific areas, aiding in risk assessment. A wildlife conservation organization can use cloud-based machine learning pipelines to automatically detect and track endangered species in geospatial imagery.

Data Visualization

Cloud platforms offer a range of tools designed for the visualization of geospatial data, empowering the creation of interactive maps and dashboards. These tools can enhance data exploration and communication (Tableau, 2023). A public health agency can utilize cloud-based data visualization tools to display disease outbreaks geospatially, aiding in decision-making and resource allocation.

Moreover, the cloud facilitates the integration of real-time or near-real-time data feeds into geospatial visualizations. This is particularly valuable in applications like environmental monitoring, traffic management, and disaster response. Web-based mapping services have become prominent examples of geospatial data visualization in the cloud. These services enable users to interact with maps, overlay multiple layers of geospatial data, and perform analyses in a user-friendly environment. Cloud platforms provide the computational resources necessary to ensure that such services can deliver smooth and responsive user experiences, even with complex and extensive datasets.

Security and Compliance

Cloud providers are dedicated to substantial investments in the enhancement of security and compliance measures. This commitment ensures that sensitive geospatial data can be stored and processed in accordance with regulations (Mell & Grance, 2011). Data encryption, access controls, and redundancy measures (Pandey et al., 2023; Pramanik et al., 2021) can enhance data protection in the cloud. Security certifications within the cloud, such as ISO 27001 and SOC 2, establish a solid foundation for the protection of geospatial data, thereby fostering trust in cloud-based solutions (Google Cloud, 2023a). A governmental agency can store classified geospatial data in the cloud while complying with strict security standards and regulations.

Accessibility

Cloud-based solutions are designed to enable remote access to geospatial data and the associated analytical tools. This capability promotes collaboration among teams, irrespective of their physical locations (Mell & Grance, 2011). An international research consortium can use the cloud to facilitate global collaboration on climate change research by providing secure, remote access to geospatial data.

Disaster Recovery

Cloud providers present robust disaster recovery solutions, effectively mitigating the risk of data loss arising from natural disasters or unforeseen incidents (Amazon Web Services, 2023). Cloud-based disaster recovery solutions can play a pivotal role in ensuring the resilience of data and the uninterrupted continuity of businesses, particularly in high-risk geospatial data scenarios (Amazon Web Services, 2023). An emergency response organization can rely on cloud disaster recovery to ensure data resilience, enabling continuous operations during crisis situations.

Real-Time Analysis

Cloud providers are increasingly offering edge computing solutions that allow organizations to process geospatial data closer to the source (e.g., sensors or drones) for real-time analysis (Sivarajah et al., 2017). The incorporation of edge computing within the cloud minimizes latency and facilitates immediate real-time analysis of geospatial data at the source, enabling applications like autonomous vehicles and precision agriculture (Cisco, 2023). Real-time analysis of geospatial Big Data is another area where cloud computing excels. In applications such as disaster management, urban planning, or precision agriculture, cloud-based analytics can provide timely insights to support decision-making (L. Zhu et al., 2019). The cloud's processing power is especially valuable for near real-time monitoring and predictive modeling.

Data Lakes for Multi-Source Integration

Cloud-based data lakes can serve as dynamic platforms for the integration and analysis of data from a multitude of sources. Within cloud-based data lakes, data from various sources can seamlessly converge, delivering a comprehensive perspective to enhance decision-making (Microsoft, 2023). An environmental research institute can use a cloud-based geospatial data lake to integrate data from satellites, drones, and ground sensors for comprehensive environmental monitoring.

AR/VR for Geospatial Visualization

The utilization of cloud-hosted AR and VR solutions can introduce immersive geospatial encounters, with practical applications in fields such as urban planning, architecture, and geoscience research. For example, an architectural firm can use cloud-based AR/VR to create virtual walkthroughs of construction sites, facilitating design and planning reviews.

Geospatial Data Marketplaces

Cloud-based geospatial data marketplaces are emerging, allowing data providers to sell and users to purchase geospatial datasets, fostering a more open and accessible geospatial data ecosystem (Ionescu et al., 2023).

Graph Databases for Spatial Analysis

Cloud-based graph databases are being employed to represent and analyze complex geospatial relationships, allowing for more efficient route planning, social network analysis, and urban transportation optimization (tigergraph, 2023). For example, graph databases in the cloud can help e-commerce platforms recommend products or services based on the geographical proximity and preferences of users.

Geospatial Data as a Service (DaaS)

Cloud providers can offer Geospatial DaaS solutions, where organizations can access a wide range of geospatial data on-demand, including satellite imagery, weather data, and demographic information. Geospatial Data as a Service in the cloud can streamline access to diverse geospatial datasets, enabling organizations to focus on analysis rather than data acquisition (Larraondo et al., 2017). For instance, geospatial DaaS on cloud platforms can provide rapid access to critical data during disasters, aiding in relief efforts and resource allocation.

Geospatial Gamification for Education and Engagement

Cloud platforms are being used to create geospatial gamification experiences for education and public engagement, where users can learn about geography and environmental issues through interactive games and challenges. Cloud-based geospatial gamification can promote learning and public engagement by making geography and environmental education more fun and accessible.

Cloud-Optimized Geospatial Formats

Geospatial data's increasing size and complexity have rendered traditional access methods impractical. Cloud-optimized geospatial formats offer reduced latency and faster on-the-fly data processing, making them more efficient. These formats are stored on scalable cloud object storage, support parallel read requests, and provide flexibility and advanced query capabilities, reducing the necessity to download complete datasets. They also offer cost-effectiveness with options for compression. Cloud-optimized formats enable direct data access from end-user machines, reducing network latency, and efficient metadata management supports parallelized and partial data reading (Barciauskas et al., 2023).

IMPLICATIONS

The application of cloud computing for SDI and geospatial big data carries several important policy implications. These implications encompass legal, regulatory, and administrative aspects that must be addressed to ensure a successful and effective implementation of cloud computing in this context. Here are some key policy implications to consider:

Data Privacy and Security Regulations

Legal frameworks must address data privacy and security concerns related to geospatial data stored in the cloud. Regulations should require encryption, access controls, and data protection measures to safeguard sensitive information. Compliance with international standards like ISO 27001 and SOC 2 should be encouraged.

Data Ownership and Rights

Policies should define ownership and intellectual property rights regarding geospatial data stored in the cloud. Data providers, especially government agencies and private organizations, need to clarify their rights and responsibilities in data sharing and distribution.

Data Sharing and Open Data Initiatives

Governments should promote open data initiatives that encourage the sharing of non-sensitive geospatial data with the public and research institutions. Clear guidelines and mechanisms for sharing data, while protecting individual privacy and national security, should be established.

Interoperability Standards

Policies should mandate the use of interoperable standards for geospatial data in the cloud to facilitate data integration and analysis. Standards like OGC (Open Geospatial Consortium) should be promoted to ensure compatibility and data exchange.

Resource Allocation and Cost Management

Administrative policies should address the efficient allocation of resources in the cloud, including cost control. Guidelines for optimizing resource allocation and managing costs, especially for public sector organizations, are essential to prevent overspending.

Data Retention and Deletion

Legal requirements for data retention and deletion should be defined to prevent data hoarding and ensure compliance with data protection regulations. Organizations must have clear policies on how long data should be stored and when it should be deleted.

Disaster Recovery and Business Continuity

Administrative policies should mandate the use of cloud-based disaster recovery solutions, especially for critical geospatial data. Clear protocols for data recovery in the event of natural disasters or unforeseen incidents should be established.

Geospatial Data Marketplaces

Policies should govern the operation of geospatial data marketplaces, ensuring fair practices, data quality, and compliance with intellectual property rights. Regulations should also address the pricing and licensing of data in these marketplaces.

Access to Geospatial Data as a Service (DaaS)

Administrative guidelines should facilitate the use of Geospatial DaaS solutions, ensuring equitable access to diverse geospatial datasets. Policies should address data quality, pricing models, and data availability during disaster scenarios.

Data Visualization and User Experience

Policies should encourage the use of cloud-based tools for data visualization and user-friendly interfaces, especially for public-facing applications. Regulations can ensure accessibility standards are met for individuals with disabilities.

Blockchain Integration

Regulations should promote the integration of blockchain technology to enhance data integrity in the cloud. Legal frameworks must specify the legal recognition of blockchain records and their compliance with existing data protection laws.

CONCLUSION

Cloud computing can play a pivotal role in the effective management of geospatial big data. The scalability, cost-efficiency, data storage, processing, and integration capabilities of cloud platforms make them ideal for handling the volume and diversity of geospatial data sources. The cloud can enable parallel processing, GIS platforms, machine learning, data visualization, security, accessibility, and disaster recovery. Furthermore, the incorporation of edge computing and blockchain technology can ensure real-time analysis and data integrity, while data lakes, AR/VR, geospatial data marketplaces, graph databases, and Geospatial Data as a Service (DaaS) provide new opportunities and capabilities for organizations.

As we move forward, the future of big data and geospatial applications in the cloud holds exciting possibilities. With the increasing use of geospatial data, privacy and ethical concerns become more prominent. Future research can focus on developing robust privacy-preserving techniques and ethical guidelines for handling sensitive geospatial data in the cloud. As the adoption of cloud-based geospatial solutions grows, efforts can be made to establish industry standards and promote interoperability among different systems and data sources. The integration of edge computing for real-time analysis at the source of data is an evolving field. Research can further explore the potential applications of edge computing in geospatial analytics and develop more efficient edge-to-cloud data pipelines.

The application of AI and machine learning in geospatial data analysis is a promising area. Future work can focus on enhancing AI models for more accurate predictions and insights, especially in critical areas like disaster management and environmental monitoring. Research can further refine and optimize cloud-optimized geospatial formats to enhance data accessibility, reduce latency, and enable more efficient data processing.

REFERENCES

v500.com. (2021). *Is Cloud a Cost-Effective Solution?* v500. https://www.v500.com/why-cloud-is-cost-effective/

Adam, A., Finance, O., & Thomas, I. (2021). Monitoring trucks to reveal Belgian geographical structures and dynamics: From GPS traces to spatial interactions. *Journal of Transport Geography*, *91*, 102977. Advance online publication. doi:10.1016/j.jtrangeo.2021.102977

Amazon Web Services. (2023). *AWS Disaster Recovery*. AWS. https://aws.amazon.com/disaster-recovery/

Armbrust, M., Fox, A., Griffith, R., Joseph, A. D., Katz, R., Konwinski, A., Lee, G., Patterson, D., Rabkin, A., Stoica, I., & Zaharia, M. (2010). A view of cloud computing. In Communications of the ACM (Vol. 53, Issue 4). doi:10.1145/1721654.1721672

Aurélien Géron. (2019). Hands-on machine learning with Scikit-Learn, Keras and TensorFlow: concepts, tools, and techniques to build intelligent systems. O'Reilly Media.

Baraglia, R., Lucchese, C., & De Francisci Morales, G. (2010). *Large-scale Data Analysis on the Cloud*. XXIV Convegno Annuale Del CMG-Italia.

Barciauskas, A., Mandel, A., Barron, K., & Deziel, Z. (2023). *Cloud-Optimized Geospatial Formats Guide*. Cloud Native. https://guide.cloudnativegeo.org/

Barik, R. K., Dubey, H., Mankodiya, K., Sasane, S. A., & Misra, C. (2019). GeoFog4Health: A fog-based SDI framework for geospatial health big data analysis. *Journal of Ambient Intelligence and Humanized Computing, 10*(2), 551–567. doi:10.1007/s12652-018-0702-x

Barik, R. K., Dubey, H., Samaddar, A. B., Gupta, R. D., & Ray, P. K. (2017). FogGIS: Fog Computing for geospatial big data analytics. *2016 IEEE Uttar Pradesh Section International Conference on Electrical, Computer and Electronics Engineering, UPCON 2016*. IEEE. 10.1109/UPCON.2016.7894725

Barik, R. K., Misra, C., Lenka, R. K., Dubey, H., & Mankodiya, K. (2019). Hybrid mist-cloud systems for large scale geospatial big data analytics and processing: Opportunities and challenges. *Arabian Journal of Geosciences, 12*(2), 32. Advance online publication. doi:10.1007/s12517-018-4104-3

Barik, R. K., Patra, S. S., Patro, R., Mohanty, S. N., & Hamad, A. A. (2021). GeoBD2: Geospatial big data deduplication scheme in fog assisted cloud computing environment. *Proceedings of the 2021 8th International Conference on Computing for Sustainable Global Development, INDIACom 2021*. IEEE. https://doi.org/10.1109/INDIACom51348.2021.00008

Boopathi, S., Pandey, B. K., & Pandey, D. (2023). Advances in artificial intelligence for image processing: Techniques, applications, and optimization. In *Handbook of Research on Thrust Technologies?* Effect on Image Processing. doi:10.4018/978-1-6684-8618-4.ch006

Cisco. (2023). *Edge computing in the cloud*. Cisco. https://www.cisco.com/c/en/us/solutions/internet-of-things/edge-intelligence.html

Crompvoets, J., Bregt, A., Rajabifard, A., & Williamson, I. (2004). Assessing the worldwide developments of national spatial data clearinghouses. *International Journal of Geographical Information Science, 18*(7), 665–689. doi:10.1080/13658810410001702030

Delgado, J. A., Short, N. M., Roberts, D. P., & Vandenberg, B. (2019). Big Data Analysis for Sustainable Agriculture on a Geospatial Cloud Framework. In Frontiers in Sustainable Food Systems (Vol. 3). Frontiers. doi:10.3389/fsufs.2019.00054

Dillon, T., Wu, C., & Chang, E. (2010). Cloud computing: Issues and challenges. *Proceedings - International Conference on Advanced Information Networking and Applications, AINA*. IEEE. 10.1109/AINA.2010.187

Dunn, C. E. (2007). Participatory GIS - A people's GIS? In Progress in Human Geography, 31(5). doi:10.1177/0309132507081493

Esri. (2023). *ArcGIS Online*. Esri. https://www.esri.com/en-us/arcgis/products/arcgis-online/overview

Goodchild, M. F. (2010). Twenty years of progress: GIScience in 2010. *Journal of Spatial Information Science, 1*(1), 3–20. doi:10.5311/JOSIS.2010.1.2

Google Cloud. (2023a). *Google Cloud Security*. Google. https://cloud.google.com/security

Google Cloud. (2023b). *Google Earth Engine*. Google. https://cloud.google.com/earth-engine

Grubisic, F. (2023). *A spatial data infrastructure based conceptual model for an efficient public transport system* [Stockholm University, Faculty of Social Sciences]. https://www.diva-portal.org/smash/record.jsf?pid=diva2%3A1784323&dswid=-644

H, O. M. E. (2011). Geospatial mappg, analysis and simulation in health services research. In *Proceedings of Singapore Healthcare* (*Vol. 20*).

He, L., & Yue, P. (2019). A Cloud-Enabled Geospatial Big Data Platform for Disaster Information Services. *International Geoscience and Remote Sensing Symposium (IGARSS)*. IEEE. 10.1109/IGARSS.2019.8898893

Huawei. (2023). *Cloud Platforms and Big Data Storage: Scalable and Cost-Effective Solutions*. Huawei. https://forum.huawei.com/enterprise/en/Cloud-Platforms-and-Big-Data-Storage-Scalable-and-Cost-Effective-Solutions/thread/706603521027227648-667213860102352896

IonescuA.AlexandridouA.IkonomouL.PsarakisK.PatroumpasK.ChatzigeorgakidisG.SkoutasD.AthanasiouS.HaiR.KatsifodimosA. (2023). Topio Marketplace: Search and Discovery of Geospatial Data. *Advances in Database Technology - EDBT, 26*(3). doi:10.48786/edbt.2023.73

Jabbour, C., Rey-Valette, H., Maurel, P., & Salles, J. M. (2019). Spatial data infrastructure management: A two-sided market approach for strategic reflections. *International Journal of Information Management, 45*, 69–82. doi:10.1016/j.ijinfomgt.2018.10.022

Janowicz, K., Gao, S., McKenzie, G., Hu, Y., & Bhaduri, B. (2020). GeoAI: spatially explicit artificial intelligence techniques for geographic knowledge discovery and beyond. In International Journal of Geographical Information Science, 34(4). doi:10.1080/13658816.2019.1684500

Kamel Boulos, M. N., Resch, B., Crowley, D. N., Breslin, J. G., Sohn, G., Burtner, R., Pike, W., Jezierski, E., & Chuang, K.-Y. (2011). Crowdsourcing, citizen sensing and sensor web technologies for public and environmental health surveillance and crisis management: Trends, OGC standards and application examples. *International Journal of Health Geographics, 10*(1), 67. doi:10.1186/1476-072X-10-67 PMID:22188675

Karmas, A., Tzotsos, A., & Karantzalos, K. (2016). Geospatial big data for environmental and agricultural applications. In *Big Data Concepts*. Theories, and Applications. doi:10.1007/978-3-319-27763-9_10

Ključanin, S., Rezo, M., Džebo, S., & Hadžić, E. (2021). Spatial Data Infrastructure in Natural Disaster Management. *Tehnicki Glasnik, 15*(4), 455–461. Advance online publication. doi:10.31803/tg-20210108180723

Koh, K., Hyder, A., Karale, Y., & Kamel Boulos, M. N. (2022). Big Geospatial Data or Geospatial Big Data? A Systematic Narrative Review on the Use of Spatial Data Infrastructures for Big Geospatial Sensing Data in Public Health. In Remote Sensing, 14(13). doi:10.3390/rs14132996

Kritikos, K., Rousakis, Y., & Kotzinos, D. (2015). A cloud-based, geospatial linked data management system. Lecture Notes in Computer Science (Including Subseries Lecture Notes in Artificial Intelligence and Lecture Notes in Bioinformatics), 9070. Springer. doi:10.1007/978-3-662-46703-9_3

Larraondo, P. R., Pringle, S., Guo, J., Antony, J., & Evans, B. (2017). GSio: A programmatic interface for delivering Big Earth data-as-a-service. *Big Earth Data*, *1*(1–2), 173–190. doi:10.1080/20964471.2017.1397898

Liu, K., Wang, H., & Yao, Y. (2016). On storing & retrieving geospatial big-data in cloud. *Proceedings of the 2nd ACM SIGSPATIAL International Workshop on the Use of GIS in Emergency Management, EM-GIS 2016*. ACM. 10.1145/3017611.3017627

Liu, X., Hao, L., & Yang, W. (2019). Bigeo: A foundational PaaS framework for efficient storage, visualization, management, analysis, service, and migration of geospatial big data—a case study of Sichuan province, China. *ISPRS International Journal of Geo-Information*, *8*(10), 449. Advance online publication. doi:10.3390/ijgi8100449

Manfreda, S., McCabe, M. F., Miller, P. E., Lucas, R., Madrigal, V. P., Mallinis, G., Ben Dor, E., Helman, D., Estes, L., Ciraolo, G., Müllerová, J., Tauro, F., de Lima, M. I., de Lima, J. L. M. P., Maltese, A., Frances, F., Caylor, K., Kohv, M., Perks, M., & Toth, B. (2018). On the use of unmanned aerial systems for environmental monitoring. In Remote Sensing, 10(4). doi:10.3390/rs10040641

Manogaran, G., & Lopez, D. (2017). A survey of big data architectures and machine learning algorithms in healthcare. *International Journal of Biomedical Engineering and Technology*, *25*(2–4), 182. doi:10.1504/IJBET.2017.087722

Mell, P., & Grance, T. (2011). The NIST definition of cloud computing. In *Cloud Computing and Government: Background, Benefits*. Risks. doi:10.6028/NIST.SP.800-145

Microsoft. (2023). *Azure Data Lake Storage*. Microsoft. https://azure.microsoft.com/en-us/products/storage/data-lake-storage/

Núñez-Andrés, M. A., Lantada Zarzosa, N., & Martínez-Llario, J. (2022). Spatial data infrastructure (SDI) for inventory rockfalls with fragmentation information. *Natural Hazards*, *112*(3), 2649–2672. doi:10.1007/s11069-022-05282-2

Oussous, A., Benjelloun, F.-Z., Ait Lahcen, A., & Belfkih, S. (2018). Big Data technologies: A survey. *Journal of King Saud University. Computer and Information Sciences*, *30*(4), 431–448. doi:10.1016/j.jksuci.2017.06.001

Pandey, J. K., Jain, R., Dilip, R., Kumbhkar, M., Jaiswal, S., Pandey, B. K., Gupta, A., & Pandey, D. (2023). Investigating Role of IoT in the Development of Smart Application for Security Enhancement. In EAI/Springer Innovations in Communication and Computing. Springer. doi:10.1007/978-3-031-04524-0_13

Parmanto, B., Paramita, M. V., Sugiantara, W., Pramana, G., Scotch, M., & Burke, D. S. (2008). Spatial and multidimensional visualization of Indonesia's village health statistics. *International Journal of Health Geographics*, *7*(1), 30. doi:10.1186/1476-072X-7-30 PMID:18544174

Poccia, D. (2016). *AWS Lambda in Action: Event-driven serverless applications*. Simon and Schuster.

Pramanik, S., Ghosh, R., Pandey, D., Samanta, D., Dutta, S., & Dutta, S. (2021). *Techniques of Steganography and Cryptography in Digital Transformation*. IGI Global. doi:10.4018/978-1-7998-8587-0.ch002

Qiu, J., Wu, Q., Ding, G., Xu, Y., & Feng, S. (2016). A survey of machine learning for big data processing. In Eurasip Journal on Advances in Signal Processing, (1). doi:10.1186/s13634-016-0355-x

Rajabifard, A., Feeney, M. E. F., & Williamson, I. (2003). *Spatial data infrastructures: concept, nature and SDI hierarchy*. Taylor & Francis London.

Ristenpart, T., Tromer, E., Shacham, H., & Savage, S. (2009). Hey, you, get off of my cloud: Exploring information leakage in third-party compute clouds. *Proceedings of the ACM Conference on Computer and Communications Security*. ACM. 10.1145/1653662.1653687

Rittinghouse, J. W., & Ransome, J. F. (2016). Cloud Computing: Implementation, Management, and Security. In Cloud Computing: Implementation, Management, and Security. Taylor & Francis. doi:10.1201/9781439806814

Simonis, I. (2018). Geospatial BIG DATA processing in hybrid cloud environments. *International Geoscience and Remote Sensing Symposium (IGARSS), 2018-July*. IEEE. 10.1109/IGARSS.2018.8519218

Singh, R. P., Haleem, A., Javaid, M., Kataria, R., & Singhal, S. (2021). Cloud computing in solving problems of COVID-19 pandemic. *Journal of Industrial Integration and Management*, *6*(2), 209–219. doi:10.1142/S2424862221500044

Sivarajah, U., Kamal, M. M., Irani, Z., & Weerakkody, V. (2017). Critical analysis of Big Data challenges and analytical methods. *Journal of Business Research*, *70*, 263–286. doi:10.1016/j.jbusres.2016.08.001

Tableau. (2023). *Tableau*. Tableau. https://www.tableau.com/

Thakuriah, P. (Vonu), Tilahun, N. Y., & Zellner, M. (2017). Big data and urban informatics: Innovations and challenges to urban planning and knowledge discovery. In Springer Geography. Springer. doi:10.1007/978-3-319-40902-3_2

tigergraph. (2023). *Geospatial analytics with graph databases*. Tiger Graph. https://www.tigergraph.com/solutions/geospatial-analysis

Vaitis, M., Kopsachilis, V., Tataris, G., Michalakis, V. I., & Pavlogeorgatos, G. (2022). The development of a spatial data infrastructure to support marine spatial planning in Greece. *Ocean and Coastal Management*, *218*, 106025.. doi:10.1016/j.ocecoaman.2022.106025

Waleed, M., & Sajjad, M. (2023). On the emergence of geospatial cloud-based platforms for disaster risk management: A global scientometric review of google earth engine applications. *International Journal of Disaster Risk Reduction*, *97*, 104056. doi:10.1016/j.ijdrr.2023.104056

Wang, Y., & Lv, P. (2023). Digital Management Strategy of Natural Resource Archives Under Smart City Space-Time Big Data Platform. *International Journal of Data Warehousing and Mining*, *19*(4), 1–14. doi:10.4018/ijdwm.320649

Yang, C., Yu, M., Hu, F., Jiang, Y., & Li, Y. (2017). Utilizing Cloud Computing to address big geospatial data challenges. *Computers, Environment and Urban Systems*, *61*, 120–128. Advance online publication. doi:10.1016/j.compenvurbsys.2016.10.010

Yu, J., & Sarwat, M. (2021). GeoSparkViz: A cluster computing system for visualizing massive-scale geospatial data. *The VLDB Journal*, *30*(2), 237–258. doi:10.1007/s00778-020-00645-2

Zhu, L., Yu, F. R., Wang, Y., Ning, B., & Tang, T. (2019). Big Data Analytics in Intelligent Transportation Systems: A Survey. In IEEE Transactions on Intelligent Transportation Systems, 20(1). doi:10.1109/TITS.2018.2815678

Zhu, Y., Tan, Y., Luo, X., & He, Z. (2018). Big Data Management for Cloud-Enabled Geological Information Services. In Scientific Programming (Vol. 2018). doi:10.1155/2018/1327214

Chapter 17
Revealing Concepts of a Cloud Deployment Model:
A Semantic Exploration of a New Generation of the Cloud

Sohini Ghosh
Brainware University, India

Rajashri Roy Choudhury
Brainware University, India

Piyal Roy
Brainware University, India

Shivnath Ghosh
Brainware University, India

ABSTRACT

Cloud computing is a fundamental paradigm in information technology, revolutionizing computational resource access, utilization, and management by providing on-demand access to various computing services, including storage, processing power, and applications, delivered over the internet. By leveraging virtualization, resource pooling, and automation, cloud computing enables unparalleled scalability, flexibility, and cost-efficiency for businesses and individuals alike. The chapter explores the core ideas of cloud computing, summarising its essential traits, deployment strategies, and service models. Moreover, it explores the significance of cloud computing in driving innovation, facilitating digital transformation, and fostering a dynamic and interconnected technological ecosystem. Also, it discuss the advantages and disadvantages of cloud computing along with some future directions.

DOI: 10.4018/979-8-3693-0900-1.ch017

INTRODUCTION

Cloud computing can be defined as delivery of Hardware, Software, applications, services, infrastructure, storage over the Internet. Companies like Google, Amazon, Microsoft, IBM, Alibaba, provide cloud services by utilizing the concept of virtualization (Jain et al. 2016), service-oriented architecture (SOA) (Tsai et al. 2010) and parallel computing (Polze et al. 2012). We basically feed server the Hypervisor (Perez-Botero et al. 2013) which is nothing but a software which create the virtual machine. This Hypervisor often called Virtual Machine Monitor (VMM) and the Server called Host and the Virtual machine called guest. It plays a crucial role in Infrastructure as a service (I-S-S-A) solution in cloud computing. SOA is a middleware which enables user and data owner talk to each other. Parallel computing helps to make available abundant resources in cloud environments through distributed data processing, parallel task execution, parallel rendering (Liu et al. 2015) and so on.

Cloud computing offers advantages (Armbrust et al. 2010) (Namasudra et al. 2014) like rapid elasticity, resource pooling, and cost-effectiveness, but it also has drawbacks such as occasional downtime, security risks, and vendor lock-in. Access control is a major security concern due to internet-related issues like hackers. Various schemes, including gateway-based, role-based, and purpose-based access controls, aim to address these problems.

The main contributions of this paper are mentioned below:

In the first part of this paper, fundamentals of cloud computing are presented. All the issues or problems of cloud computing are discussed in this paper one by one. Many future work directions have been also explained in this paper for the cloud computing environment.

In second section we discuss the fundamental of cloud computing. Section-3 explores some related work regarding cloud security and cloud model. Section 4 and 5 presents the benefits and some issue regarding cloud computing. Many future work directions have been also explained in this paper for the cloud computing in section 6 and then we reach to our conclusion part in section 7.

FUNDAMENTALS OF CLOUD COMPUTING

History of Cloud Computing

Before the cloud computing comes into the existence there were Mainframe computer. It is basically large and costly. It is so large that the colossal hardware infrastructure of this Main frame computer was installed in a server room (a room for holding Main frame). So, it is not financially feasible for an organization to buy Main frame computer for each user. This was basically an inception of computing era. Then the personal computer comes but it cannot be connected to the database. Further came the Client -Server architecture in which all the data of client connected to the server through network. We can easily implement database using client server. It is cost effective as well as increased the performance, but it has many disadvantages like in many cases the server is prone to denial-of-service attacks, we cannot connect it through worldwide. So, after that distributed system comes into the existence. It is a combination of multiple independent system but all of them act as a single entity to user. The main problem is the system must be present physically in that geographical location. To resolve this problem Grid computing was introduced in 1990's. Before that virtualization was introduced in 1970's by IBM. Under this technology several computers can word concurrently under same environment of comput-

Fig 1: Service model in cloud computing

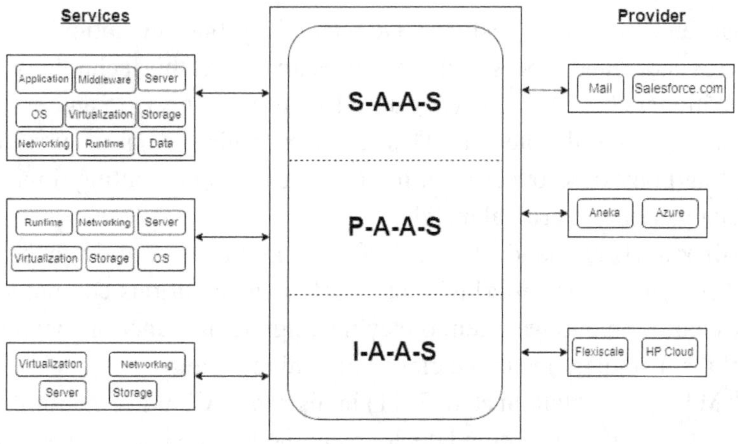

ing. To share the information worldwide and make it more effective and efficient the World Wide Web (WWW) was introduced by Tim Berners-Lee. In 1980's Cluster computing was also found. Though it was connected through a high bandwidth network, but geographical restriction still pertained.1990's Grid computing comes as a successor to this computing era. Different systems were present in completely different locations connected to the internet. In 1999, salesforce.com was the main milestone of cloud computing (Naik et al. 2013). When Google and IBM collabs with each other in 2007 from that time cloud computing become so popular and now every one of us enjoying its benefits.

Service Delivery Model

Cloud Computing can be coined by dynamic computing as it provides a virtual pool of resources to fulfill user need on demand without any barriers. There are many service provider who provides services of software, storage, resources. When there is lack of storage in user's desktop cloud computing can be beneficial, User just need internet connection to access this facility. There are some sites which remains free most of the time but consume resources. Cloud computing can be used to use these resources when they are free or when these sites are handling heavy load cloud computing can be used to avoid the failure situation. Moreover, cloud computing can access various data centers located in various geographical locations. It basically provides S-A-A-S, P-A-A-S and I-A-A-S (Manish Pokharel et al. 2009).

Deployment Model

In the context of cloud computing deployment model refers specific architecture and configuration of cloud computing to cater the organization's needs. It defines how the cloud services are provisioned, where they are located, and who has access to them. There are four type of deployment model in cloud computing such as Public Cloud, Private Cloud, Hybrid Cloud and Community Cloud.

LITERATURE REVIEW

Cloud computing has emerged as a transformative technology that revolutionizes the way businesses and individuals' access, store, and process data and applications. As this technology continues to evolve, researchers and practitioners have been investigating its various aspects to address challenges, explore opportunities, and unlock its full potential. This literature review aims to provide a comprehensive analysis of the existing body of knowledge in the field of cloud computing, highlighting key trends, latest research developments, and critical insights.

Yeshwanth Rao Bhandayker (Bhandayker et al. 2011) in his paper 'A study on the research challenges and trends of cloud computing' are offering a lot of solutions in various computer systems as well as applications. As the cloud Computing system is playing a significant function in typically all companies, they offer several of the dislike trends in the cloud computing systems.

In another study M Malathi (Malathi et al. 2011) in his paper 'Cloud computing concepts' presented the concepts of Cloud Computing like cloud deployment models, delivery models, advantages of using cloud and risks involved in it are analysed. This paper tries to bring awareness among managers and computing professionals to use Cloud computing as an alternative to large in-house data centers.

Cloud computing holds immense importance in this era due to its transformative impact on businesses, individuals, and the overall technological landscape. Hu Shuijing 'Data Security: The Challenges of Cloud Computing' (Shuijing et al. 2014) describes the great requirements in Cloud Computing, such as security key technology, standard and regulation, and discusses ways in which they may be addressed.

Ashish Singh et all (Singh et al. 2017) discussed about the basic features of the cloud computing, security issues, threats, and their solutions. Additionally, they describe several key topics related to the cloud, namely cloud architecture framework, service and deployment model, cloud technologies, cloud security concepts, threats, and attacks.

BENEFITS OF CLOUD COMPUTING

Numerous advantages are provided by cloud computing for people, companies, and organisations of all kinds. It has fundamentally changed how we use and manage technology, making it a crucial component of contemporary digital ecosystems. We shall examine some of the major advantages of cloud computing in this essay.

Cost Effectiveness

Cost effectiveness is one of the biggest benefits of cloud computing. Traditional IT infrastructures demand significant up-front expenditures for hardware, software, and upkeep. Users of cloud computing can access resources on a pay-as-you-go basis, doing away with the requirement for significant capital investments. With the help of cloud services, organisations can adjust the size of their infrastructure as necessary, ensuring they only pay for the resources they use.

Incomparable Flexibility and Scalability

Incomparable flexibility and scalability are offered by cloud computing. The cloud can smoothly scale resources up or down, helping businesses meet seasonal demand surges or expand quickly owing to expansion. This degree of adaptability makes sure that companies can quickly respond to shifting needs without being constrained by conventional on-premises systems.

Accessibility and Remote Work

In the era of remote work and mobile devices, cloud computing makes it possible to access data and apps remotely. Cloud services increase productivity and work-life balance by enabling employees to collaborate with team members and access vital information from any location with an internet connection.

ISSUES OF CLOUD COMPUTING

Scalability, flexibility, affordability, and accessibility are just a few advantages that cloud computing, a game-changing technology, has to offer. To ensure its successful installation and use, there are a number of concerns and challenges it poses as well, just like any other technology.

Security and Privacy

Data security and privacy are among the biggest issues with cloud computing. The danger of unauthorised access, data breaches, and data loss increases when sensitive data is stored in distant data centres(Boopathi et al. 2023). To safeguard customer data and defend against cyber threats, cloud service providers must incorporate strong security measures, encryption protocols, and access controls(GEORGE et al. 2021).

Downtime and Reliability

Despite its high availability goals, cloud services are not impervious to outages and downtime. Service interruptions caused by technical issues or maintenance can have an effect on how businesses operate and how customers are served. To minimise possible losses during such catastrophes, organisations must have backup plans and redundancies.

Vendor Lock-In

Moving apps and data to the cloud frequently takes a lot of work, and once a business is dependent on a specific cloud provider's ecosystem, switching to another provider can be difficult. Over time, this vendor lock-in may result in less freedom and more expenses. Businesses need to carefully plan their cloud strategy and stay away from relying too heavily on proprietary technologies.

CLOUD COMPUTING TECHNOLOGIES AND APPLICATIONS

Cloud computing is a broad category of technology and applications that fundamentally alters how organisations and people access and use computing resources. The following list of important cloud computing technologies and their uses:

Serverless Computing

Developers can run programmes using serverless computing without having to worry about managing or deploying servers. Depending on how much use an application receives, the cloud provider automatically scales the necessary resources. Event-driven applications and microservices architectures are well suited for serverless computing, which lowers operational costs and increases cost effectiveness.

Containers and Container Orchestration

Applications and their dependencies are packaged as a portable, isolated unit with containers, guaranteeing consistency across many environments. Kubernetes and other container orchestration solutions make it possible to manage, scale, and deploy containerized applications effectively. Containers facilitate scalability and quick iteration by streamlining the development and deployment process.

Cloud Storage Services

Cloud storage services are available from a number of cloud providers, including block storage, file storage, and object storage. Cloud storage services are an indispensable part of contemporary apps because they make it simple and secure for users to save and retrieve data.

FUTURE SCOPE

With numerous important sectors fostering its ongoing progress, cloud computing is primed for enormous growth and innovation in the future. Some of it are as follows:-

Integration of AI and Machine Learning

The use of AI and Machine Learning in Cloud Computing will grow. Advanced AI services from cloud providers will make it simpler for companies to use AI for a range of tasks, from data analytics to natural language processing.

Quantum Computing in the Cloud

Cloud-based quantum computing has the potential to tackle complicated issues at an exponential rate. Quantum computing is a game-changing technology. Researchers and companies will be able to access quantum processing power without owning the gear thanks to cloud providers that are likely to offer quantum computing services.

Expansion of Edge Computing

As IoT devices proliferate, edge computing will become more important. By extending their services to the network's edge, cloud providers will enable real-time data processing and lower latency for crucial applications.

Multi-Cloud and Hybrid Strategies

Hybrid and multi-cloud options will continue to be used by businesses in order to reduce vendor lock-in and optimise workloads. Future workload management and integration across many cloud platforms will be more seamless.

CONCLUSION

The future of cloud computing holds enormous growth and innovation with AI and Machine Learning integration, enabling advanced AI services for various tasks. Cloud-based quantum computing will revolutionize complex problem-solving(Pramanik et al. 2021). Edge computing will gain significance as IoT devices proliferate, ensuring real-time data processing and reduced latency. Hybrid and multi-cloud options will continue to reduce vendor lock-in and optimize workloads. Cloud computing's revolution has already transformed how individuals and companies access computing resources. Its trajectory promises continuous growth, facilitating digital transformation, and driving groundbreaking research. The inclusion of AI, machine learning, and quantum computing will open new possibilities across various industries. Multi-cloud strategies will offer adaptability, resilience, and flexibility, tailoring cloud ecosystems to unique needs and improving cost control and security(Pandey et al. 2022). Ultimately, cloud computing's future holds improved capabilities, heightened security, and transformative effects on various sectors, reshaping how we engage with the digital world.

REFERENCES

Armbrust, M., Fox, A., Griffith, R., Joseph, A. D., Katz, R., Konwinski, A., Lee, G., Patterson, D., Rabkin, A., Stoica, I., & Zaharia, M. (2010). A view of cloud computing. *Communications of the ACM*, *53*(4), 50–58. doi:10.1145/1721654.1721672

Bhandayker, Y. R. (2019). A study on the research challenges and trends of cloud computing. RESEARCH REVIEW International Journal of Multidisciplinary, 4.

Boopathi, S., Pandey, B. K., & Pandey, D. (2023). Advances in Artificial Intelligence for Image Processing: Techniques, Applications, and Optimization. In Handbook of Research on Thrust Technologies' Effect on Image Processing (pp. 73-95). IGI Global.

GEORGE, D. A. S., George, A. H., Baskar, T., & Pandey, D. (2021). XDR: The Evolution of Endpoint Security Solutions-Superior Extensibility and Analytics to Satisfy the Organizational Needs of the Future. International Journal of Advanced Research in Science [IJARSCT]. *Tongxin Jishu*, *8*(1), 493–501.

Jain, N., & Choudhary, S. (2016, March). Overview of virtualization in cloud computing. In *2016 Symposium on Colossal Data Analysis and Networking (CDAN)* (pp. 1-4). IEEE.

Liu, Z., & Zou, H. (2015, August). AzureRender: A cloud-based parallel and distributed rendering system. In 2015 IEEE 17th International Conference on High Performance Computing and Communications, 2015 IEEE 7th International Symposium on Cyberspace Safety and Security, and 2015 IEEE 12th International Conference on Embedded Software and Systems (pp. 1881-1886). IEEE. 10.1109/HPCC-CSS-ICESS.2015.328

Malathi, M. (2011, April). Cloud computing concepts. In 2011 3rd International Conference on Electronics Computer Technology (Vol. 6, pp. 236-239). IEEE. 10.1109/ICECTECH.2011.5942089

Manish Pokharel. (2009). *YoungHyun Yoon, Jong Sou Park, "Cloud Computing in System Architecture"*. IEEE.

Naik, N. D., & Modi, K. J. (2013). Evolution of IT industry towards cloud computing: A new paradigm. IJRIT Int. *J. of Research in Information Technology.*, *1*(5), 236–242.

Namasudra, S., Nath, S., & Majumder, A. Profile based access control model in cloud computing environment. In: *Proceedings of the International Conference on Green Computing, Communication and Electrical Engineering*, pp. 1-5. IEEE, Coimbatore, India (2014). 10.1109/ICGCCEE.2014.6921420

Pandey, J. K., Jain, R., Dilip, R., Kumbhkar, M., Jaiswal, S., Pandey, B. K., & Pandey, D. (2022). Investigating Role of IoT in the Development of Smart Application for Security Enhancement. In *IoT Based Smart Applications* (pp. 219–243). Springer International Publishing.

Perez-Botero, D., Szefer, J., & Lee, R. B. (2013, May). Characterizing hypervisor vulnerabilities in cloud computing servers. In *Proceedings of the 2013 international workshop on Security in cloud computing* (pp. 3-10). 10.1145/2484402.2484406

Polze, A., & Tröger, P. (2012). Trends and challenges in operating systems—From parallel computing to cloud computing. *Concurrency and Computation*, *24*(7), 676–686. doi:10.1002/cpe.1903

Pramanik, S., Ghosh, R., Pandey, D., Samanta, D., Dutta, S., & Dutta, S. (2021). Techniques of Steganography and Cryptography in Digital Transformation. In Emerging Challenges, Solutions, and Best Practices for Digital Enterprise Transformation (pp. 24-44). IGI Global. doi:10.4018/978-1-7998-8587-0.ch002

Shuijing, H. (2014, January). Data security: the challenges of cloud computing. In *2014 Sixth International Conference on Measuring Technology and Mechatronics Automation* (pp. 203-206). IEEE. 10.1109/ICMTMA.2014.52

Singh, A., & Chatterjee, K. (2017). Cloud security issues and challenges: A survey. *Journal of Network and Computer Applications*, *79*, 88–115. doi:10.1016/j.jnca.2016.11.027

Tsai, W. T., Sun, X., & Balasooriya, J. (2010, April). Service-oriented cloud computing architecture. In 2010 seventh international conference on information technology: new generations (pp. 684-689). IEEE. 10.1109/ITNG.2010.214

KEY TERMS AND DEFINITIONS

Access Control: A security measure in cloud computing that regulates and restricts user access to data and resources. Various schemes, including gateway-based, role-based, and purpose-based access controls, address security concerns.

Cloud Computing: The delivery of hardware, software, applications, services, and storage over the internet. It involves the utilization of virtualization, service-oriented architecture (SOA), and parallel computing by companies like Google, Amazon, and Microsoft.

Hypervisor: Also known as a Virtual Machine Monitor (VMM), it is software that creates and manages virtual machines, allowing multiple operating systems to run on a single physical host.

Infrastructure as a Service (IaaS): A cloud computing solution that provides virtualized computing resources over the internet, allowing users to rent virtual machines and storage rather than investing in and maintaining physical hardware.

Parallel Computing: A computing architecture where multiple processors or cores work together to solve a problem by dividing it into smaller tasks that can be processed simultaneously.

Rapid Elasticity: A characteristic of cloud computing that allows resources to be quickly and easily scaled up or down based on demand, providing flexibility and efficiency.

Serverless Computing: A cloud computing model where developers can run applications without managing or deploying servers. Resources are automatically scaled based on application usage, reducing operational costs.

Service-Oriented Architecture (SOA): A middleware framework that enables communication between users and data owners in a distributed computing environment. It facilitates the interaction between different software systems.

Vendor Lock-In: A situation where a user becomes dependent on a specific cloud service provider's ecosystem, making it challenging to switch to another provider due to integration and compatibility issues.

Virtualization: A technology that allows the creation of virtual instances of computing resources, such as servers or storage devices, enabling multiple operating systems or applications to run on a single physical machine.

Chapter 18
Implications of Blockchain Technology- Based Cryptocurrency in the cloud for the Hospitality Industry

Mohammad Badruddoza Talukder
https://orcid.org/0000-0001-7788-2732
Daffodil Institute of IT, Bangladesh

Sanjeev Kumar
https://orcid.org/0000-0002-7375-7341
Lovely Professional University, India

Iva Rani Das
https://orcid.org/0009-0006-9805-4331
Daffodil Institute of IT, Bangladesh

ABSTRACT

In various industries, blockchain technology and cryptocurrencies have gained significant importance. This study delves into the crucial role played by blockchain-based cryptocurrencies within the hospitality sector. The significance of this research lies in its aim to address inefficiencies, boost security, and adapt to the evolving landscape within the hospitality industry. The industry's heavy reliance on centralization poses challenges, including steep transaction costs, vulnerabilities in data security, and a lack of transparency. Blockchain technology and cryptocurrencies offer solutions to simplify processes, safeguard data, and enable secure, cost-efficient transactions. This paper highlights the increasing importance of blockchain-based solutions in hospitality, underscoring industry stakeholders' need to embrace these innovations. Through an analysis of implications, advantages, and obstacles, this study adds depth to our comprehension of how blockchain-based cryptocurrencies can enhance the hospitality sector's efficiency, security, and competitiveness.

DOI: 10.4018/979-8-3693-0900-1.ch018

INTRODUCTION

Blockchain technology and cryptocurrencies have moved beyond their initial origins as niche discoveries to emerge as disruptive forces across various industries (Sánchez, 2022). This study digs into the critical role that blockchain technology-based cryptocurrencies play in the hotel industry, exploring their historical evolution, recent advancements, and future possibilities. The drive for this study stems from the imperatives of eliminating inefficiencies, bolstering security, and adjusting to a dynamically shifting terrain within the hospitality business (Talukder et al., 2022). The hospitality industry, known for its sophisticated web of service providers, intermediaries, and payment systems, has several issues stemming from its centralization (Hameed et al., 2022). These difficulties include increased transaction costs, susceptibility to data breaches, and a noteworthy lack of transparency. Against this context, blockchain technology and cryptocurrencies emerge as disruptive alternatives, giving a multidimensional solution to the sector's long-standing problems. In this endeavor, we set out to investigate the numerous dimensions of this confluence. We begin by clarifying the fundamental concepts of blockchain technology and the transformational potential of cryptocurrencies. From there, we examine the historical roots of these breakthroughs, documenting their journey from conception to current popularity. This historical viewpoint provides critical insights into these technologies' rapid emergence and maturation.

While the review exposes the past, our investigation does not stop there. Instead, we turn to the present day, when recent blockchain and cryptocurrency technology developments have sparked a wave of creativity. Notably, Ethereum's introduction of smart contracts in 2015 and the following rise of Initial Coin Offerings (ICOs) have made blockchain valuable for more than just digital currencies (Hewa et al., 2021). This change emphasizes the dynamic character of blockchain technology and its capacity for constant reinvention (Brody & Couture, 2021). As we look ahead, the importance of this research becomes clearer.

Blockchain and cryptocurrency are not merely abstract concepts; they are active forces influencing the present and future of the hospitality industry (Bagloee et al., 2021). The advantages they provide, ranging from increased security and trust to simplified financial transactions, are strong reasons to study their potential in hospitality (Talukder et al., 2023). This study's significance extends beyond academic investigation; it has far-reaching ramifications for industry stakeholders. It emphasizes the importance of firms in the hotel sector adapting to and embracing blockchain-based solutions (Wang et al., 2022). As our investigation progresses, we will shed light on the consequences, benefits, and obstacles of incorporating blockchain technology-based cryptocurrencies within the sector. By doing so, we contribute to a better understanding of how these technologies may empower the industry by increasing efficiency, fortifying security, and boosting competitiveness in an increasingly digital environment. So, this study is like a lighthouse, pointing industry leaders toward a future where the hospitality industry can fully use blockchain technology and cryptocurrencies to meet the changing needs of a modern, tech-savvy clientele.

LITERATURE REVIEW

This literature study investigates the role of blockchain-based cryptocurrencies in the hospitality industry to establish context, identify significant trends, highlight difficulties and solutions, and identify research needs. Because blockchain and cryptocurrencies have evolved beyond their financial origins, this review contextualizes their historical progression and adaptation within the broader environment of the hospitality sector (Simpson & Sheller, 2022). It combines current trends and breakthroughs from academic research and industry reporting to show how new technologies transform operating processes, improve security, and upgrade visitor experiences. Furthermore, it analyzes the sector's issues, such as security, transparency, and efficiency concerns. It investigates how blockchain and cryptocurrencies have arisen as possible answers (Simpson & Sheller, 2022). This review offers the framework for further exploring this transformational convergence by identifying research gaps and providing valuable insights for academics and industry stakeholders.

Blockchain Technology in Various Industries

Blockchain technology is a decentralized and distributed ledger system that enables secure and transparent recording of transactions across a network of computers. The fundamental concept of blockchain revolves around creating a chain of blocks, where each block contains a list of transactions. These blocks are linked and secured using cryptographic hashes. Blockchain technology has found well-known uses across a wide range of industries, with each exploiting its unique qualities to overcome specific difficulties and innovate in their domains (Yaqoob et al., 2021). We will look at how blockchain technology has been used and investigated in several industries, highlighting significant findings and innovations:

Finance

Blockchain technology has led to several innovations that are changing standard banking and financial systems (Kumari & Devi, 2022). Decentralized finance platforms and blockchain-based cryptocurrencies have revolutionized the financial world, enabling direct rental, borrowing, and trading of financial assets, eliminating intermediaries, and simplifying international transactions, making it more efficient and accessible to people worldwide. Here are some of the most important uses and results:

Payment Systems

Blockchain is the core technology behind cryptocurrencies like Bitcoin, which has changed how payment systems work (Lee, 2019). It allows for safe, peer-to-peer digital transfers that cannot be hacked or shut down. Notably, blockchain transactions often have lower fees than standard banking methods. This makes them attractive to people and businesses who want to save money (Lu, 2022).

Smart Contracts

With the introduction of smart contracts, Ethereum added a new level of automation to financial agreements (Ciotta et al., 2021). Intelligent contracts are deals that follow their own set of rules. They make maintaining contracts easier without intermediaries like lawyers, banks, or escrow services. This new idea has many effects, from making complex financial swaps easier to understand to automating how insurance claims are processed (Sen et al., 2021).

Cross-Border Transactions

Blockchain technology makes it easier and faster to do deals across borders (Hongmei, 2021). Traditional foreign payments can be slow, expensive, and prone to mistakes. Blockchain-based solutions could eliminate the need for multiple currency conversions and intermediaries, making cross-border deals quicker and cheaper (Islam et al., 2022).

Financial Inclusion

One of the most essential things the finance industry has learned is that blockchain-based financial services could give people who did not have access to banks and other financial tools before those tools. The unbanked and underbanked can now use blockchain technology to secure and afford digital wallets and peer-to-peer lending platforms (Saini & India, n.d.). This could help fewer people be left out of the banking system and give people more economic power.

Supply Chain

Li et al. (2023) say that blockchain technology has brought many improvements to supply chain management, making it more transparent, secure, and efficient. Blockchain's decentralized ledger system enables real-time tracking of goods and transactions, reducing errors and fraud. Smart contracts automate processes, streamlining operations and reducing administrative overhead, leading to cost savings and improved efficiency (Javaid et al., 2022). Here are some essential uses and findings:

Provenance Tracking

Unchallengeable blockchain ledgers allow transparent supply chain tracing (Uddin, 2021). This is especially helpful in industries like food, where tracking things is very important for ensuring the quality and safety of products. By putting every step of a product's journey on the blockchain, stakeholders can easily find out about its origin, how it was handled, and how it was stored, which increases buyer trust (Kramer et al., 2021).

Reducing Counterfeits

Blockchain provides an efficient method of verifying product authenticity, which is critical in combatting counterfeiting challenges affecting numerous businesses (Yiu, 2021). By keeping product information and provenance on an irreversible blockchain, consumers and businesses may readily determine if a product is authentic or a counterfeit replica. This improves brand reputation and protects consumers from counterfeit goods.

Streamlined Processes

Smart contracts, which are an essential part of blockchain technology, make it possible to automate and improve supply chain processes, which makes them more efficient. Makam (2023) says that self-executing contracts can automate chores and start actions based on specific criteria. This feature helps reduce the need for intermediaries and the number of mistakes people make. One example of a possible benefit of smart contracts is their ability to automate the release of payments after things have been delivered as agreed. This technology speeds up the process of paying bills and reduces the need for administrative help.

Healthcare

Blockchain technology has emerged as a game-changing instrument with a wide variety of applications in the field of healthcare. One of the prominent applications is in the secure and interoperable management of electronic health records, ensuring patient privacy and efficient data sharing among healthcare providers(Cerchione et al., 2023). The following is a list of essential applications and findings:

Patient Records

Blockchain technology makes electronic health records (EHRs) safe and easy to use (Uddin, Memon, et al., 2021). Using blockchain, healthcare workers can keep a patient's health information in a way that is hard to change and protects their privacy. Patients can be granted secure access to their medical records, ensuring that healthcare providers have the most recent information (Singh et al., 2021). This interoperability makes healthcare more efficient, reduces mistakes, and protects patient privacy by making it easier for approved parties to share data.

Drug Traceability

Blockchain enables robust traceability of pharmaceuticals from manufacturing to distribution(Uddin et al., 2021). Each step in the drug supply chain is recorded on an immutable ledger, reducing the risk of counterfeit drugs entering the market. This not only safeguards patient safety but also helps pharmaceutical companies maintain the integrity of their products.

Clinical Trials

Smart contracts are crucial in managing clinical studies. They automate different parts of running a trial, such as finding patients, collecting data, and paying volunteers. This automation improves openness and efficiency, cuts administrative work, and ensures correct data. This speeds up the process of making new drugs and reduces delays (Johnson & Smith, 2023).

Real Estate

In real estate, blockchain technology has solved long-standing problems and opened new doors. Blockchain-based land registries offer immutable proof of property ownership, reducing fraud and disputes in real estate transactions. Tokenization allows individuals to invest in property with smaller budgets, increasing market liquidity. The following are some important uses and discoveries:

Property Ownership

Blockchain-based land registries provide a secure and immutable mechanism to register property ownership (Soner et al., 2021). Putting property records on a blockchain makes tampering with or disputing ownership information impossible. This minimizes the likelihood of fraud and property disputes, which have long been difficulties in real estate. Property ownership records on a blockchain provide a transparent and trustworthy source of information for property buyers and sellers (Sladi et al., 2021).

Tokenization

Blockchain technology enables the tokenization of real estate assets. This entails reflecting ownership of real estate as digital tokens on a blockchain. Tokenization allows for fractional ownership, allowing several investors to acquire property shares (Avci & Erzurumlu, 2023). This not only democratizes real estate investing but also boosts market liquidity. Investors can buy and sell property ownership tokens more efficiently than traditional real estate transactions (Bhat & Gupta, 2022).

Energy

In the energy sector, blockchain technology has introduced innovative solutions that promote sustainability, efficiency, and transparency. Blockchain enhances energy distribution by promoting renewable energy use and reducing reliance on centralized utilities. It also offers transparency and incentives for sustainable practices in the energy sector(Gawusu et al., 2022). Here are vital applications and findings:

Grid Management

Blockchain enhances energy distribution and administration. It facilitates peer-to-peer energy trading, letting people and companies buy and sell extra Energy directly to one another, eliminating dependency on centralized utilities (Soto et al., 2021). This decentralized strategy improves energy efficiency and encourages the use of renewable energy sources by pressing local energy production and consumption. Blockchain's transparent and tamper-proof ledger enables fair and secure energy transactions (Yahaya et al., 2022).

Carbon Credits

Blockchain tracks and manages carbon credits, providing a transparent and dependable method of incentivizing and verifying sustainable practices. Organizations and individuals can earn carbon credits by reducing their carbon footprint through renewable energy generation or reforestation (McAfee, 2022). These credits can then be purchased and sold on blockchain-based exchanges. Blockchain's openness and immutability safeguard the integrity of carbon credit transactions, promoting sustainable behaviors and contributing to climate change mitigation efforts.

Voting

Blockchain technology presents innovative solutions that effectively tackle concerns about security, transparency, and accessibility within elections and voting. Furthermore, blockchain enables secure remote voting, expanding accessibility for voters and potentially increasing voter turnout while maintaining the integrity of the electoral process. The following are significant applications and discoveries:

Secure Elections

Blockchain-based voting methods make voting more secure and open. Using blockchain, each vote is recorded on an immutable registry, ensuring the accuracy of electoral data. By implementing this measure, the potential for vote tampering and fraudulent activities is mitigated, enhancing public trust and faith in the integrity of the electoral system. In addition, blockchain technology enables real-time monitoring of the voting process, allowing citizens and election observers to verify the election's accuracy and impartiality (Benabdallah et al., 2022).

Remote Voting

Blockchain enables safe remote voting, making it easier for citizens to participate in elections, particularly in situations such as pandemics or for individuals unable to vote. Online voting protects the privacy and verifiability of each voter's ballot by using cryptographic techniques and verified digital identities (Mookherji et al., 2022). Not only does this increase democratic participation, but it also ensures that the voting process stays inclusive and accessible.

Intellectual Property

In intellectual property, blockchain technology has led to new ways to protect artists' rights and make it easier to get paid royalties. Smart contracts on blockchain automate royalty payments to content creators, ensuring fair compensation and reducing the complexities associated with intellectual property rights enforcement. Here are some essential uses and findings:

Copyright Protection

Blockchain creates a record of intellectual property rights that cannot be changed and is time-stamped. This gives creators and inventors a safe way to show ownership. By putting copyright information on a blockchain, artists can prove the authenticity of their work and the date it was made (Harbola et al., 2022). This protects artists, authors, and inventors against larceny and intellectual property infringement.

Royalty Distribution

Smart contracts automatically ensure content makers get royalties. With these self-executing contracts, royalties can be sent out automatically and based on existing conditions. For instance, intelligent contracts can ensure that the person who made it gets paid quickly and fairly when a piece of content is used or sold. This automation makes it easier for artists to get their proper pay (Javaid et al., 2021).

Cryptocurrencies and Their Expanding Role

Cryptocurrencies are digital or virtual currencies that use cryptography for security and operate on decentralized networks, typically based on blockchain technology. Cryptocurrencies have transcended their origins as digital currencies. They have evolved into a versatile and expansive ecosystem with applications far beyond traditional financial transactions. This evolution reflects the growing recognition of blockchain technology's potential to disrupt and innovate various industries. Here, we delve into the expanding role of cryptocurrencies:

Real Estate

Cryptocurrencies are increasingly used in real estate deals. They have perks like making international transactions faster, cutting down on paperwork, and clarifying property deals. The blockchain technology that powers cryptocurrencies can also establish tamper-proof land registries, significantly improving real estate transactions (Sanka et al., 2021). Blockchain tokenization enhances real estate investments by providing fractional ownership, making them more accessible and liquid, attracting a more comprehensive range of investors, and reducing administrative complexities.

Gaming

In the gaming industry, cryptocurrencies are utilized for in-game purchases, enabling players to buy virtual items, tokens, or assets(Aguila et al., 2022). Additionally, non-fungible tickets (NFTs), often based on cryptocurrency platforms like Ethereum, have opened new avenues for trading and owning digital assets, such as rare in-game items or unique digital collectibles. Blockchain technology ensures digital asset scarcity and provenance, creating a secure ecosystem for gamers and collectors. Integrating cryptocurrencies and NFTs could revolutionize gaming by providing actual ownership and new monetization models.

Supply Chain

Cryptocurrencies and blockchain technology are instrumental in improving transparency in supply chains(Guo et al., 2022). They enable tracking of products from origin to destination, ensuring authenticity, quality, and compliance with ethical and sustainability standards. Blockchain technology ensures digital asset scarcity and provenance, creating a secure ecosystem for gamers and collectors. Integrating cryptocurrencies and NFTs could revolutionize gaming by providing actual ownership and new monetization models.

Healthcare

Cryptocurrencies can streamline healthcare payments and insurance processes(Mamun, 2022). They provide a secure and efficient way to handle medical claims, reduce administrative costs, and mitigate fraud. Cryptocurrencies can facilitate cross-border healthcare payments, making it easier for patients to access medical services abroad and ensuring seamless and cost-effective transactions in a globalized healthcare landscape.

Non-Fungible Tokens (NFTs)

NFTs have emerged as a significant cryptocurrency-driven phenomenon, enabling the ownership and trading of unique digital assets, including art, music, virtual real estate, and more. NFTs leverage blockchain's immutability to establish provenance and ownership of digital creations (Battah et al., 2022). Moreover, NFTs have introduced new opportunities for artists and content creators to monetize their digital products directly, reducing the reliance on traditional intermediaries and expanding their reach to global audiences.

Decentralized Finance (DeFi)

The DeFi sector, built on blockchain and cryptocurrency platforms, offers various financial services, including lending, borrowing, trading, and yield farming (Wronka, 2023). DeFi protocols aim to decentralize financial intermediaries, giving users more control over their assets and financial decisions. DeFi's open, permissionless nature offers financial services to underserved individuals. It allows users to earn higher asset yields through liquidity provision and staking, potentially revolutionizing savings and investment.

Identity and Authentication

Cryptocurrencies and blockchain technology are exploring applications in digital identity verification (Gad et al., 2022). Users can have more control over their personal information while ensuring privacy and security in online interactions. Blockchain-based identity solutions can prevent identity theft and fraud by providing a tamper-proof, verifiable record of individuals' identities, streamlining user authentication across online services, and enhancing digital interaction security and efficiency.

Voting and Governance

Cryptocurrencies are integral to operating decentralized autonomous organizations (DAOs) and governance systems (Qin et al., 2022). Token holders can participate in decision-making processes, creating a more inclusive and transparent governance. Blockchain-based voting systems and decentralized autonomous vehicles (DAOs) enhance electoral integrity by recording immutable votes, reducing fraud, and allowing global communities to influence project or organization direction collectively.

Adoption of Blockchain and Cryptocurrencies in the Hospitality Industry

The literature highlights an increasing trend of blockchain technology and cryptocurrency acceptance and application within the hospitality industry (Treiblmaier et al., 2021). Hotel companies such as Marriott and InterContinental have studied blockchain's possibilities in supply chain management, improving the transparency and traceability of their food and beverage supplier networks. Furthermore, several boutique hotels and vacation rental companies have accepted cryptocurrencies as a payment method, allowing visitors to pay using digital assets. These early experiences show that blockchain and cryptocurrencies are gradually finding their place in the business, especially in supply chain optimization and as an additional payment method, boosting operational efficiency and responding to the tastes of tech-savvy clients.

Security and Privacy Concerns in Hospitality

Security and privacy issues have been prominent in the hospitality industry, with data breaches, identity theft, and fraud constituting substantial concerns. Blockchain technology, on the other hand, provides a possible solution by fundamentally rethinking how data is stored and accessible (Schulz & Feist, 2021). The immutability and decentralized characteristics of blockchain ensure that guest data and financial transactions are safe and immune to alteration (Barkel et al., 2021). Guests may be confident that their personal information will be kept private, lowering the danger of identity theft. Furthermore, smart contracts offer secure, automated, and transparent interactions, reducing the possibility of fraud. By integrating blockchain, the hospitality industry can improve data security and privacy, restoring visitor confidence and meeting regulatory compliance needs in an era when data security is critical.

Efficiency and Cost Reduction

Efficiency and cost reduction are two critical objectives for businesses and organizations across various industries. Achieving greater efficiency while minimizing costs can lead to increased profitability, improved competitiveness, and enhanced customer satisfaction(Mehmood, 2021). Blockchain's efficiency and cryptocurrencies' cost-efficiency offer businesses operational optimization and improved bottom line. However, careful planning and execution are crucial to capitalize on these benefits fully. Here are some strategies and technologies commonly used to enhance efficiency and reduce costs:

Process Automation

Automating repetitive and manual tasks through robotic process automation (RPA) and workflow automation software can significantly increase operational efficiency by reducing human error, speeding up processes, and cutting labor costs. Blockchain technology enhances trust and transparency in automated processes by providing an immutable ledger, ensuring an auditable and tamper-proof history of computerized activities.

Supply Chain Optimization

Leveraging data analytics and technologies like blockchain can streamline supply chain operations. Real-time visibility, demand forecasting, and inventory management tools help reduce wastage, lower carrying costs, and enhance supply chain efficiency(Arguelles JR & Polkowski, 2023). Blockchain technology enhances supply chain transparency, traceability, and compliance with regulatory requirements, reducing fraud, counterfeiting, and disruptions while promoting ethical sourcing practices.

Energy Efficiency

Implementing energy-efficient technologies, such as LED lighting, energy-efficient HVAC systems, and renewable energy sources, can reduce energy consumption and operational costs(Xia et al., 2021). Energy-efficient practices also contribute to sustainability goals. Blockchain-based energy management systems can enhance energy savings and sustainability by creating transparent, secure energy grids that immutably record production and consumption data.

Cloud Computing

Cloud-based solutions can significantly lower IT infrastructure and maintenance costs(Su & Chen, 2021). Cloud services offer scalability, flexibility, and reduced capital expenditure. Blockchain technology integrates with cloud computing to improve data security, trust, and transparency. This ensures decentralized, encrypted data storage and ownership among authorized parties.

Digital Transformation

Embracing digital technologies like data analytics, artificial intelligence (AI), and the Internet of Things (IoT) can optimize operations, improve decision-making, and enhance customer experiences, ultimately reducing operational costs. Integrating blockchain technology into digital transformation initiatives enhances security and transparency in data management and transactions(Alahmadi et al., 2022). Its decentralized ledger reduces data breaches and errors, allowing organizations to achieve cost-efficiency while maintaining high data security standards.

Lean Manufacturing

Applying lean principles involves minimizing waste, improving process efficiency, and optimizing resource utilization in manufacturing. This approach reduces production costs while maintaining product quality. Blockchain technology in lean manufacturing improves supply chain transparency and traceability and reduces material defects(Hader et al., 2022). It tracks raw material origin and quality, ensuring adherence to lean principles and consistent product delivery while maintaining cost-efficiency, contributing to operational excellence and competitive advantage in the manufacturing sector.

Outsourcing and Offshoring

Outsourcing non-core functions or offshoring specific tasks to regions with lower labor costs can be an effective cost-reduction strategy. However, it requires careful vendor selection and management. Blockchain technology can improve transparency and security in vendor relationships in outsourcing and offshoring processes(Khanfar et al., 2021). Smart contracts automate payment processing, reduce disputes, and improve accountability, streamlining global operations and minimizing operational risks associated with outsourcing and offshoring.

Sustainable Practices

Adopting sustainable practices, such as waste reduction, recycling, and eco-friendly materials, not only contributes to environmental responsibility but can also reduce costs over the long term (Talukder & Hossain, 2021). Blockchain integration in sustainable practices enhances transparency, verifies eco-friendly certifications, and ensures ethical material sourcing, fostering trust among environmentally conscious consumers and reducing greenwashing risks.

Telecommuting and Remote Work

Remote work arrangements reduce office space costs, commuting expenses, and associated overhead. Many organizations have adopted remote work as a cost-effective and flexible alternative. Blockchain technology can enhance remote work collaboration by providing a secure, transparent platform for sharing sensitive information and conducting transactions(Barenji & Montreuil, 2022). This reduces security risks and improves efficiency, offering cost savings and improved productivity in a decentralized work environment.

Employee Training and Development

Investing in employee training and development enhances skills and productivity, reducing errors and improving overall efficiency. A skilled workforce is adaptable to technological advancements like blockchain and cryptocurrencies, enhancing operational efficiency and customer satisfaction. Employee training and development are crucial for immediate productivity gains, long-term organizational resilience, and competitiveness (Talukder, 2020).

Transparency and Trust

Blockchain technology has become a significant tool for increasing transparency in the hospitality sector's supply chain, ensuring the authenticity and quality of products and services (Kayikci et al., 2022). Blockchain creates a tamper-resistant and verifiable trail of information by documenting every stage of the supply chain on an immutable ledger, allowing customers to trace the origin, handling, and sourcing of commodities, including food, beverages, and luxury services (Talukder et al., 2023). This increased transparency protects against fraud and counterfeit items and fosters confidence among customers who appreciate authenticity and ethical sourcing. Customers will have more trust and loyalty in hospitality firms that promote transparency and quality assurance using blockchain technology as they get access to reliable information about the products they consume.

Customer Experience and Loyalty Programs

Blockchain-based reward systems have transformed the hospitality industry, improved customer experience, and promoted client loyalty (Kathuria & Tandon, 2023). Several studies have repeatedly shown that these blockchain-enabled programs improve guest satisfaction in various ways. To begin with, blockchain assures the security and integrity of loyalty points or awards, lowering the danger of fraud or manipulation, which can undermine trust in traditional loyalty programs. Second, blockchain enables tailored and targeted rewards, adapting offers to individual preferences and actions, resulting in a more engaging and relevant customer experience. Furthermore, because visitors may independently verify the program's integrity and the fairness of prize distribution, the openness and immutability of blockchain transactions foster confidence. Overall, these improvements have resulted in higher visitor satisfaction and a stronger sense of loyalty, as guests perceive actual benefits and value in engaging in blockchain-based loyalty programs in the hotel industry.

Challenges and Regulatory Framework

According to research, the hospitality industry's adoption of blockchain technology and cryptocurrencies presents formidable regulatory challenges (Ozdemir et al., 2023). These obstacles include the ambiguous legal status and definitions of digital assets, concerns over consumer protection due to the irreversible nature of crypto transactions, complexities surrounding anti-money laundering (AML) and know-your-customer (KYC) compliance, taxation issues, potential conflicts with data privacy regulations, uncertainty surrounding the enforceability of smart contracts, and the need for harmonized rules to facilitate cross-border transactions. In light of these obstacles, the research highlights the urgent need for industry-specific regulations that recognize the unique characteristics of the hospitality industry and provide clear guidelines for its seamless integration of blockchain and cryptocurrencies, thereby ensuring innovation and stakeholders.

CASE STUDIES AND INDUSTRY REPORTS

While we cannot access specific case studies and industry reports beyond my last knowledge update in September 2021, we can provide a general overview of some noteworthy, relevant examples. Keep in mind that the landscape may have evolved since then.

Winding Tree and Lufthansa

Winding Tree, a blockchain-based travel distribution platform, partnered with Lufthansa to explore how blockchain can optimize distribution and payment processes in the airline industry. The project aimed to reduce distribution costs and increase transparency for airlines and customers.

TUI Group and Trust You

TUI, a global travel company, partnered with trust You to create a blockchain-based system for managing hotel guest reviews and ratings. This initiative aimed to enhance the trustworthiness of online reviews by preventing fraudulent submissions. TUI and TrustYou have implemented blockchain technology to manage guest reviews, creating an immutable, tamper-proof record. This transparent system enables travelers to make informed decisions based on genuine reviews, enhancing the hospitality industry.

AID Chain by AID Coin

AID Chain, developed by AID Coin, is a blockchain-based platform designed to enhance transparency and trust in charitable donations within the travel and hospitality sector. It enables donors to track their contributions and ensure they reach their intended destinations. AID Chain uses blockchain technology to secure charitable transactions, ensuring donors' contributions are used for their intended purposes. This innovation fosters trust between donors and organizations, encouraging more participation in philanthropic initiatives.

HoryouToken

HoryouToken is a cryptocurrency that promotes social good and sustainability within the travel and hospitality industry. Users can use the token for various purposes, including booking accommodations and supporting social impact projects.

These examples demonstrate the potential for blockchain and cryptocurrencies to address various issues in the hospitality and travel industries, ranging from distribution and payment efficiency to trust and transparency in reviews and charitable donations. While the performance of these initiatives varies, they give important insights and lessons for future blockchain use in the sector.

Figure 1. Framework of blockchain technology-based cryptocurrency in the hospitality industry
(Authors compilation)

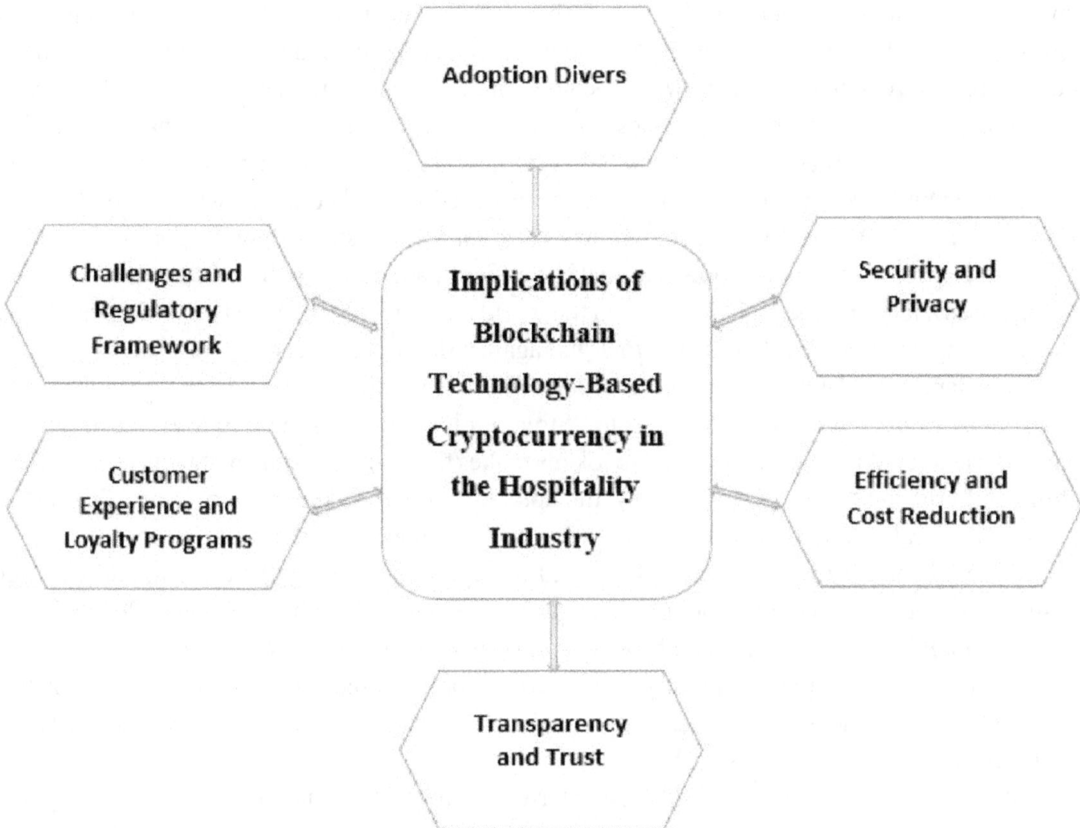

RECOMMENDATIONS

The hotel business stands to benefit significantly from the introduction of blockchain-based cryptocurrencies, but doing so successfully will need careful planning and execution. Businesses functioning in this sector would do well to seriously consider the following suggestions for improving their efficiency. Significant funds must be earmarked for robust cybersecurity procedures to protect user data and digital assets. By taking this action, we can ensure safety and build trust in our security system. Fostering alliances and encouraging collaborations within the sector is also crucial for developing industry-wide standards and best practices for implementing blockchain technology. In addition, make sure team members have access to ongoing training and education so they can fully grasp the technology and its ramifications. In addition, it is crucial to think about blockchain networks' effects on international issues and investigate eco-friendly ways to lessen their carbon imprint. Last, it is critical to see things from the user's perspective and ensure that blockchain-based systems include user-friendly features that improve the visitor experience and boost adoption rates. Using blockchain-based cryptocurrencies in the hospitality industry might improve operations, efficiency, security, and customer happiness in a dynamic global market.

CONCLUSION AND FUTURE RESEARCH DIRECTIONS

In conclusion, it can be deduced that using blockchain technology and cryptocurrencies will result in a significant and extensive hotel industry transformation. This chapter highlighted these technologies' capabilities, showed how they are used in other industries, and examined their consequences for the hotel business. People have noticed a link between the hotel industry's pressing need and blockchain technology's features, such as immutability, openness, and security. Blockchain technology has many different effects, such as ensuring that food and drink delivery lines are honest and improving loyalty programs and the guest experience (Ramos, 2021). Even so, this road of change is not without its difficulties. Existing rules are unclear and vary from country to country. This shows how important it is to have clear, industry-specific law frameworks that make it easier to adopt new practices. Because blockchain technology uses a lot of Energy, it has effects on the world that can only be fixed by coming up with new, forward-thinking solutions. Still, it is hard to argue against the benefits. Using more security measures reduces the chances of data breaches and fraudulent behavior while increasing the faith and trust of customers and critical stakeholders in the sector. Streamlining processes leads to lower costs and better working efficiencies. Also, turning assets into tokens makes them more liquid and opens new investment possibilities. In the digital age we live in now, the hotel business is on the verge of a significant change marked by decentralization, transparency, and new ideas. To maximize the benefits of blockchain and cryptocurrencies, industry leaders, researchers, and policymakers must collaborate to address regulatory issues, promote sustainability, and optimize guest experiences (Kouhizadeh et al., 2021). To move forward, the hotel business must remain flexible and open to new studies, technological advances, and changing customer needs. By participating in this project, both people and companies can learn how to handle the complicated details of blockchain technology and cryptocurrencies, allowing them to thrive in a more dynamic and connected world.

Several essential research paths could help determine where blockchain technology and cryptocurrency integration in the hospitality business are going. Future research should focus on the analysis of sustainable Blockchain solutions and environmentally sensitive agreements to reduce the ecological impact of Blockchain networks. More studies must be done to improve usability and security to make more advanced, user-friendly interfaces and safe wallet technologies. Using decentralized Finance (DeFi) in different areas, like Blockchain-based lending or insurance, can completely change how hotels finance themselves. Furthermore, researchers must examine the legal and regulatory frameworks associated with tokenized assets, such as real estate or loyalty incentives, to provide uniform and unambiguous norms. The potential influence of Blockchain technology on elements essential to the hospitality sector, such as online reputation management and guest reviews, is an intriguing topic. Blockchain experts, hotel sector professionals, and law scholars must work together to solve complex regulatory challenges and stimulate innovation in this fast-changing domain. Blockchain technology and cryptocurrency could make the hotel business much more efficient, increase trust, and make guests happier. By looking into different lines of inquiry, the industry can learn valuable things that could help with the future use of these technologies.

REFERENCES

Aguila, D. A., Bartolata, J. M., & Estrañero, J. G. (2022). *AXEing the axie infinity (AI): The AI of modern gaming, business model Strategem, and global economy towards cryptocurrency era*. College of Liberal Arts and Sciences Dasmariñas.

Alahmadi, D. H., Baothman, F. A., Alrajhi, M. M., Alshahrani, F. S., & Albalawi, H. Z. (2022). Comparative analysis of blockchain technology to support digital transformation in ports and shipping. *Journal of Intelligent Systems*, *31*(1), 55–69. doi:10.1515/jisys-2021-0131

Arguelles, J. R. P., & Polkowski, Z. (2023). Impact of Big Data on Supply Chain Performance through Demand Forecasting. *International Journal of Computations* [IJCIM]. *Information and Manufacturing*, *3*(1), 19–26.

Barenji, A. V., & Montreuil, B. (2022). Open Logistics: Blockchain-Enabled Trusted Hyperconnected Logistics Platform. *Sensors (Basel)*, *22*(13), 4699. doi:10.3390/s22134699 PMID:35808198

Battah, A., Madine, M., Yaqoob, I., Salah, K., Hasan, H. R., & Jayaraman, R. (2022). Blockchain and NFTs for trusted ownership, trading, and access of AI models. *IEEE Access : Practical Innovations, Open Solutions*, *10*, 112230–112249. doi:10.1109/ACCESS.2022.3215660

Cerchione, R., Centobelli, P., Riccio, E., Abbate, S., & Oropallo, E. (2023). Blockchain's coming to hospital to digitalize healthcare services: Designing a distributed electronic health record ecosystem. *Technovation*, *120*, 102480. doi:10.1016/j.technovation.2022.102480

Gad, A. G., Mosa, D. T., Abualigah, L., & Abohany, A. A. (2022). Emerging trends in blockchain technology and applications: A review and outlook. *Journal of King Saud University. Computer and Information Sciences*, *34*(9), 6719–6742. doi:10.1016/j.jksuci.2022.03.007

Gawusu, S., Zhang, X., Ahmed, A., Jamatutu, S. A., Miensah, E. D., Amadu, A. A., & Osei, F. A. J. (2022). Renewable energy sources from the perspective of blockchain integration: From theory to application. *Sustainable Energy Technologies and Assessments*, *52*, 102108. doi:10.1016/j.seta.2022.102108

Guo, L., Chen, J., Li, S., Li, Y., & Lu, J. (2022). A blockchain and IoT-based lightweight framework for enabling information transparency in supply chain finance. *Digital Communications and Networks*, *8*(4), 576–587. doi:10.1016/j.dcan.2022.03.020

Hader, M., Tchoffa, D., El Mhamedi, A., Ghodous, P., Dolgui, A., & Abouabdellah, A. (2022). Applying integrated Blockchain and Big Data technologies to improve supply chain traceability and information sharing in the textile sector. *Journal of Industrial Information Integration*, *28*, 100345. doi:10.1016/j.jii.2022.100345

Javaid, M., Haleem, A., Singh, R. P., Suman, R., & Khan, S. (2022). A review of Blockchain Technology applications for financial services. *BenchCouncil Transactions on Benchmarks, Standards and Evaluations*, 100073.

Khanfar, A. A. A., Iranmanesh, M., Ghobakhloo, M., Senali, M. G., & Fathi, M. (2021). Applications of blockchain technology in sustainable manufacturing and supply chain management: A systematic review. *Sustainability (Basel)*, *13*(14), 7870. doi:10.3390/su13147870

Kumar, S., Talukder, M. B., Kabir, F., & Kaiser, F. (2024). Challenges and Sustainability of Green Finance in the Tourism Industry: Evidence From Bangladesh. In Sustainable Investments in Green Finance (pp. 97-111). IGI Global.

Mamun, Q. (2022). Blockchain technology in the future of healthcare. *Smart Health (Amsterdam, Netherlands)*, *23*, 100223. doi:10.1016/j.smhl.2021.100223

Mehmood, T. (2021). Does information technology competencies and fleet management practices lead to effective service delivery? Empirical evidence from E-commerce industry. *International Journal of Technology* [IJTIM]. *Innovation and Management*, *1*(2), 14–41.

Qin, R., Ding, W., Li, J., Guan, S., Wang, G., Ren, Y., & Qu, Z. (2022). Web3-based decentralized autonomous organizations and operations: Architectures, models, and mechanisms. *IEEE Transactions on Systems, Man, and Cybernetics. Systems*, *53*(4), 2073–2082. doi:10.1109/TSMC.2022.3228530

Su, B., & Chen, C.-D. (2021). A Study of Factors Influencing the Adoption of Cloud-Based ERP System: The Perspective of Transaction Cost Economics. *International Conference on Human-Computer Interaction*, (pp. 433–443). Springer. 10.1007/978-3-030-77750-0_27

Talukder, M., Shakhawat Hossain, M., & Kumar, S. (2022). Blue Ocean Strategies in Hotel Industry in Bangladesh: A Review of Present Literatures' Gap and Suggestions for Further Study. SSRN *Electronic Journal*. doi:10.2139/ssrn.4160709

Talukder, M. B. (2020b). The Future of Culinary Tourism: An Emerging Dimension for the Tourism Industry of Bangladesh. I-Manager's. *Journal of Management*, *15*(1), 27. doi:10.26634/jmgt.15.1.17181

Talukder, M. B. (2021). An assessment of the roles of the social network in the development of the Tourism Industry in Bangladesh. *International Journal of Business, Law, and Education*, *2*(3), 85–93. doi:10.56442/ijble.v2i3.21

Talukder, M. B., & Hossain, M. M. (2021). Prospects of Future Tourism in Bangladesh: An Evaluative Study. I-Manager's. *Journal of Management*, *15*(4), 1–8. doi:10.26634/jmgt.15.4.17495

Talukder, M. B., Kabir, F., Muhsina, K., & Das, I. R. (2023). Emerging Concepts of Artificial Intelligence in the Hotel Industry: A Conceptual Paper. *International Journal of Research Publication and Reviews*, *4*(9), 1765–1769. doi:10.55248/gengpi.4.923.92451

Talukder, M. B., Kumar, S., Sood, K., & Grima, S. (2023). Information Technology, Food Service Quality and Restaurant Revisit Intention. *International Journal of Sustainable Development and Planning*, *18*(1), 295–303. doi:10.18280/ijsdp.180131

Uddin, M., Salah, K., Jayaraman, R., Pesic, S., & Ellahham, S. (2021). Blockchain for drug traceability: Architectures and open challenges. *Health Informatics Journal*, *27*(2), 14604582211011228. doi:10.1177/14604582211011228 PMID:33899576

Wronka, C. (2023). Financial crime in the decentralized finance ecosystem: New challenges for compliance. *Journal of Financial Crime*, *30*(1), 97–113. doi:10.1108/JFC-09-2021-0218

Xia, X., Wu, X., BalaMurugan, S., & Karuppiah, M. (2021). Effect of environmental and social responsibility in energy-efficient management models for smart cities infrastructure. *Sustainable Energy Technologies and Assessments*, *47*, 101525. doi:10.1016/j.seta.2021.101525

KEY TERMS AND DEFINITIONS

Blockchain Technology: A decentralized and distributed digital ledger system made possible by blockchain technology keeps records of transactions safely and openly on a network of computers. Many blocks make up this system, each with a list of transactions. These blocks are linked together using cryptographic hashes, making a chain that can't be changed. Blockchain is decentralized, which means that the ledger is not kept in one place but on many nodes across the network. This makes it safer and less likely that someone will change it. Some of the most essential features are decentralization, security through cryptography, openness, immutability, and the ability to support smart contracts. In the beginning, blockchain technology was used to power cryptocurrencies like Bitcoin. Since then, it has been used in many other fields because it is a reliable and quick way to record and confirm digital transactions.

Competitiveness: Being competitive means that a person, group, business, or country can consistently do better than rivals in a particular market or industry. It measures how well a company can make goods or provide services more quickly, creatively, and cheaply than its rivals, giving it an edge. Many different things go into making a business competitive, such as quality, productivity, innovation, adaptability, market share, and overall performance.

Cryptocurrency: Cryptocurrency is a digital or virtual currency protected by cryptography and runs on a decentralized network of computers, most of the time using blockchain technology. Cryptocurrencies are not controlled by a single government or central bank like traditional currencies are. Instead, they are often decentralized and run on a technology called blockchain, a distributed ledger maintained by a network of computers called nodes.

Decentralization: When power, decision-making, and control are spread across several entities or levels instead of being centralized in one central authority, this is called decentralization. Decisions are made in decentralized systems, which allows for a more distributed and often collaborative way of running, managing, or governing.

Efficiency: Efficiency means being able to complete a task, make a product, or provide a service while using the least amount of time, money, and effort possible. In a broad sense, efficiency means maximizing what you put in while minimizing waste, extra costs, and inputs. It is a way to rate how healthy resources are used to get a particular result.

Hospitality Industry: The hospitality industry is a broad term for a group of fields within the service industry. It includes businesses and places that provide food, lodging, entertainment, and customer service. Many different types of companies in the hospitality industry work together to meet the needs and wants of travelers, tourists, and locals. Hotels, restaurants, bars, cafes, resorts, cruise lines, theme parks, and event planning and management services are just a few of this industry's many types of businesses.

Security: Security means not being in danger, threat, or harm. It includes the steps and warnings to keep people, things, data, or computer systems safe from possible hazards, hacking, and bad behavior. Security is essential in many areas, including personal safety, national defense, information technology, the physical world, and finances.

Transparency: In the state of being open, transparent, and easy to understand, this is called transparency. In different situations, transparency means being open, being seen, and making information available to the public or other essential parties. People usually think of this idea as being honest, taking responsibility, and not having any hidden agendas or information that hasn't been shared. In many areas, transparency can help build trust, make decisions more accessible, and encourage people to act honestly.

Chapter 19
Integration of Data Science and Cloud-Based IoT Networks:
Techniques and Applications

Venkat Narayana Rao T.
Sreenidhi Institute of Science and Technology, India

M. Raghavendra Rao
https://orcid.org/0009-0001-0758-7145
Sreenidhi Institute of Science and Technology, India

S. Bhavana
Sreenidhi Institute of Science and Technology, India

ABSTRACT

In contemporary times, data science has made significant strides across various commercial domains, spanning business, finance, space science, healthcare, telecommunications, and the Internet of Things (IoT). The IoT emerges as a pivotal platform, orchestrating the convergence of people, processes, data, and physical objects to enhance our daily lives.. In light of these considerations, this chapter explores diverse frameworks for synchronized data processing, leveraging the strengths of various platforms. Numerous challenges impede the seamless integration of cloud computing, IoT, and data science collaboration. The integration of cloud and IoT offers a promising avenue to surmount these challenges, harnessing the wealth of data resources available in the cloud. This chapter presents a comprehensive overview of the technologies involved in merging data science with cloud-based IoT; this would expand the cloud capabilities and scope to scale for higher data storage and accessibility along with examining their advantages and confronting the associated challenges.

DOI: 10.4018/979-8-3693-0900-1.ch019

INTRODUCTION

The term "Internet of Things" (IoT) is a popular one in information technology. Thanks to the Internet of Things, intelligent virtual things can be made from actual objects in the future. The Internet of Things (IoT) attempts to bring everything in our surroundings under one unified infrastructure so that we may have control over them and be informed of their status(Evans, 2011).

The potential for intelligent connectivity and applications across a variety of human undertakings has significantly grown as a result of the advent of the Internet of Things (IoT). Smarter technology can give people a smart and active existence by enabling contextual awareness, sensing, and actuation abilities.

Simple examples of these products include thermostats and HVAC (Heating, Ventilation, and Air Conditioning) monitoring and control systems, which enable smart homes.But it won't be easy because there are still a lot of issues that need to be resolved and looked at from different perspectives in order for them to realize their full potential. The main objective of this review article is to provide the reader with a comprehensive study from both a technological and sociological perspective. By allowing physical things to "talk" to one another, share information, and coordinate actions, the IoT makes it possible for them to see, hear, think, and carry out tasks(Khan et al., 2012). By utilizing its supporting technologies, such as embedded devices, communication technologies, sensor networks, and Internet protocols, the IoT converts these conventional things into intelligent ones as shown in figure 1.

Emerging technologies, innovations, and service applications must expand proportionately to keep up with market demands and consumer wants in order to fulfil this potential growth. Additionally, gadgets must be created to meet consumer requirements.

The IoT, however, has a sensing layer that reduces the needs on those devices' abilities and allows their inter-connection. Purchasers of sensor facts interact with sensors or sensor owners via the data integration layer, which manages all interactions and transactions. meanwhile, converting requirements, demanding situations with information sharing, records integration and filtering, advent of new consumer services, and complexity of network architecture the usage of cloud computing is likewise developing

Figure 1. IoT based market environment

Figure 2. Layered based security framework

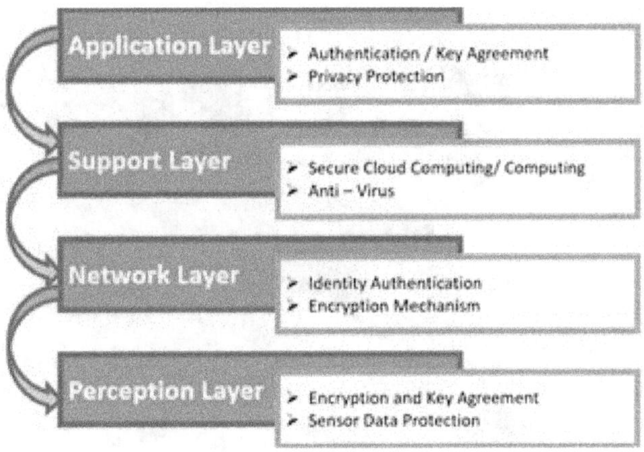

quick. New software program structures and infrastructure are made to be had inside the context of the IoT. Some of the main benefits and blessings of the internet of factors encompass the advent of new offerings with progressed overall performance and value-brought answers in addition to cost reduction (Lopez et al., 2013; Gluhak et al., 2011).

The technologies relating to internet and impending are factors taken into consideration and can be clustered into 3 categories: (1) technologies that enable "matters" to manner obtain contextual records, (2) technology that enable "aspect contextual statistics, and (3) technology to recover safety and privacy. The primary two classes can understood as practical constructing blocks essential for "intelligence" into "things", which can be certainly the structures that distinguish the IoT from the same old internet. The third class is not a functional however as a substitute a de facto requirement, without which the penetration of the IoT would be seriously decreased (Buyya et al., 2009).

RELEVANCE OF SENSORS

One of the fundamental components of the internet of things are sensors. They are deployable anyplace since they are ubiquitous systems. Additionally, they may be placed on a T-shirt, in a purse, or beneath the human skin. Some of them can be as little as 4 millimetres, yet the statistics they gather can be retrieved from great distances. They serve as an addition to human senses and have become crucial in a huge range of sectors, from production to fitness care. The key advantage of sensors is that they can predict human desires entirely solely on data gathered about their environment.

Amazon, Salesforce, Google, Yahoo, Microsoft, and other well-known cloud computing providers are just a few examples. Cloud computing providers offer a wide range of services to customers, including email, storage, infrastructure as a service, software as a service, etc. Cloud computing would provide chances and options that weren't previously available to start-ups, entrepreneurs, medium-sized organizations, and small businesses, allowing them to save billions of dollars as shown in figure 3. They will have the choice to use cloud computing and only rent the minimal amount of processing power, communication bandwidth, and storage space from a sizable cloud computing provider (Armbrust et al., 2010).

Figure 3. Cloud based environment

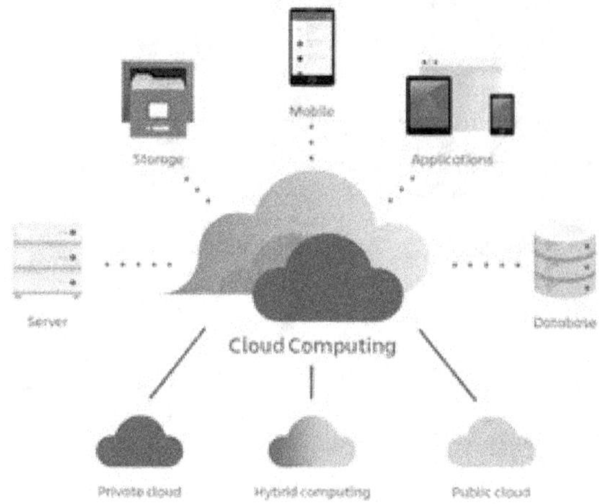

COMMUNICATION TECHNOLOGIES IN IOT

An essential component of Internet of Things-based smart farming is constant connectivity. The chain as a whole is significantly impacted by the accessibility of connectivity and the pricing of the services. The connectivity services that cell operators may offer do not in any significant way represent the market for clever farming.To meet the rising Demand, particularly in rural regions, telecom providers should provide a greater range of services as shown in figure 4.

Figure 4. IoT technologies related to range of communication

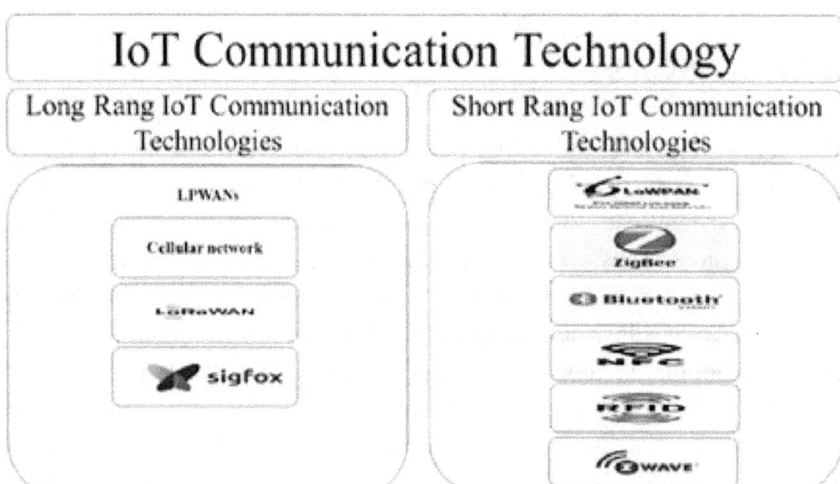

IOT INTEGRATION

Making data and packages that have been one at a time developed function well together is integration. whilst enforcing stop-to-stop IoT enterprise solutions, IoT integration refers to making the mixture of new IoT devices, IoT information, IoT structures, and IoT applications — blended with IT property (enterprise programs, legacy statistics, cellular, and SaaS) — feature nicely together. the collection of IoT integration competencies that IoT task implementers require to efficiently combine end-to-quit IoT enterprise solutions is called the IoT integration marketplace. The integration of smart devices into packaging, or even better, into the products themselves, could provide a significant cost saving and improvement in the eco-friendliness of products. It will continue to be utilized for the integration of chips and antennas into novel substrates like cloth and paper, as well as for the development of new substrates, routing systems, and bonding materials that are suited for harsh environments and environmentally friendly disposal. With the use of device-in-package (SiP) technology, several components, including antennas, sensors, active parts, and passive additives, may be integrated in a flexible and 3D manner into the packaging, enhancing tag functionality and lowering tag cost. RFID inlays with a strap coupling structure are used to create labels instead of immediately installing the integrated circuit chip and antenna.

IoT gadgets that adhere to standards degree diverse characteristics using diverse conventions and size units. Open supply standards are probably going to be one of the methods to make this facts interoperable, even whilst rival proprietary protocols are constantly being recommended. For the success of wi-fi communique technologies and, usually, for any form of device-to-machine conversation, open standards are actually essential. but, it has been mentioned that establishing interoperable standards extra quick is crucial for the deployment of IoT applications. it's far necessary to make clean the specs for a unique worldwide identification, naming, and resolver. the integration of legacy systems and the lack of convergence within the layout of not unusual reference models, reference structure for destiny networks (Takabi et al., 2010).

IOT STANDARDS

IoT standards define the requirements for IoT devices and systems. They can cover a wide range of topics, such as security, interoperability, and data formats. IoT standards are developed and maintained by various organizations and consortia that specialize in setting technical guidelines, frameworks, and best practices for the Internet of Things (Boss et al., 2009).

Some of the prominent organizations involved in the development of IoT standards include:

International Electro-technical Commission (IEC)

International standards for electrical, electronic, and related technologies are created and published by the IEC, a global organization. They are crucial in creating IoT standards for things like energy efficiency, security, and communication protocols.

IEEE

The Institute of Electrical and Electronics Engineers:

Its main professional company IEEE specializes in developing technology across some of industries, inclusive of IoT. they create standards for the IEEE 802 family, which includes ones for electricity performance, network protocols, and wireless verbal exchange.

the industrial internet Consortium (IIC) is a collection of enterprise executives, educational establishments, and IT firms that collaborates to hasten the uptake of the commercial internet of factors (IIoT). they create testbeds, reference architectures, and fine practices to inspire safety and interoperability in commercial IoT implementations (Cloud Security Alliance, 2009).

Thread Group

The Thread Group is an industry alliance focused on developing the Thread networking protocol for IoT devices in the smart home and commercial sectors. They work on defining the technical specifications and certification programs for Thread-enabled products.

Connectivity Standards Alliance

Previously known as the Zigbee Alliance, this company creates and promotes the Zigbee wireless communication standard, which is widely used in Internet of Things (IoT) applications like home automation, smart energy, and lighting control.

IOT ARCHITECTURE

The Perception Layer, Network Layer, Processing Layer, and Application Layer are the layers visible in the figure given below:

Figure 5. The IoT layers

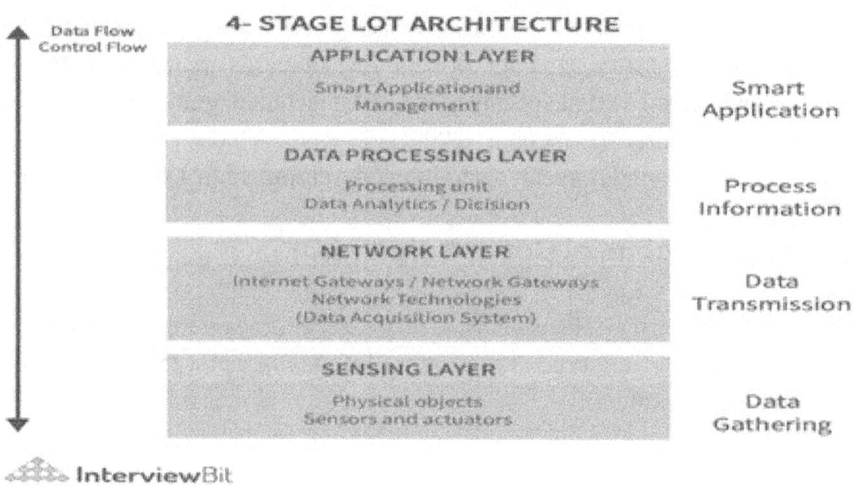

Perception/Sensing Layer

Any IoT system's first layer is built up of "matters" or endpoint gadgets that act as a hyperlink among the actual world and the virtual one. The physical layer, which includes sensors and actuators that are able to accumulating, accepting, and processing facts throughout a community, is denoted to as perception. Wi-Fi or stressed out connections can be used to attach actuators and sensors. The additives' variety and places are not limited through using the design (Pearson, 2010).

Network Layer

An outline of the data flow during the program is specified by the network layers. Data attaining Systems (DAS) and Internet/Network gateways exist in this tier. Data aggregation and conversion jobs are carried out by a DAS (congregation and combining sensor data, converting analog data to digital data, etc.). Data collected by the sensor devices need to be transferred and processed. The network layer accomplishes that task. It allows connections and communication among these gadgets and other servers, smart gadgets, and network gadgets. Moreover, it manages each device's data transmission.

Processing Layer

The IoT atmosphere's processing layer features as its brain. earlier than being transported to the statistics center, records is usually evaluated, pre-processed, and saved here. it is then retrieved by using software program packages that deal with the statistics and prepare future actions. that is where facet analytics or facet IT comes into play.

Application Layer

The application layer, which delivers the user with application explicit services, is where user interface occurs. A dashboard that displays the position of the devices in a system or a smart home application wherein users may turn on a coffee maker by touching a button in an app are two. The Internet of Things can be employed in a variety of applications, including smart homes, smart cities, and smart health (Kong, 2010).

Cloud Is the Key for Internet-Based Computing and ICT services can now be provided as a service way to cloud computing, that's the following level within the development of net-based totally computing. Cloud computing allows for the connection of pc resources, systems, commercial enterprise techniques, and infrastructure (along with servers and storage). With the upward push of cloud computing, it has emerge as less difficult to create bendy business models that let companies devour resources as their operations expand. in place of requiring a drawn-out provisioning method, cloud computing allows immediate get right of entry to to cloud shipping, unlike corporations that provide traditional internet-based services (such net website hosting). In cloud computing, every provisioning and withdrawal of resources can appear once more. users can get right of entry to cloud services and speak with apps and aid records thru APIs (software programming interfaces) as shown in figure 6.

Figure 6. Integration of cloud computing and IoT

CLOUD-BASED IOT SERVICES

Internet of Things (IoT) devices can connect with cloud services, other apps, and even other IoT devices thanks to a set of features provided by cloud platforms. Users can remotely manage, monitor, and control IoT devices using these cloud platforms. Additionally, the cloud enables IoT identity and access management (IAM) services, scalable storage, device connectivity, analytics, and reporting.

Scalable Storage

Scalable item storage offerings, like Amazon easy garage provider (Amazon S3), are supplied by cloud IoT systems, permitting corporations to without problems develop or decrease their records storage desires. IoT applications benefit from this kind of flexibility considering the fact that they frequently produce huge volumes of unstructured information that need to be stored without degrading tool overall performance.

Device Interconnection

Physical IoT devices and cloud services might also communicate without problems, reliably, and securely way to cloud-primarily based IoT platforms. A enterprise can consequently join dozens or maybe millions of IoT devices to the cloud without having to set up or clamp the vital servers and networking hardware.

Reporting and Analytics

With the help of powerful analytics tools and processing resources, cloud-based IoT systems enable businesses to obtain real-time perceptions into the enormous statistics that IoT devices generate. IoT device data can be utilized to enhance performance and create better, data-driven decisions through intricate algorithms such as predictive modelling, statistical analysis, and machine learning.

Identity and Access Management (IAM)

Identity and Access Management (IAM), an identity and authorization service, may be used to secure the data produced by IoT devices in the cloud. IAM empowers businesses to provide or restrict access to cloud services and resources for sizable numbers of users with various access requirements.

The granularity of IAM controls allows businesses to adhere to security and legal guidelines which are pertinent for preserving and access to sensitive information, in-spite of a lot IoT records being transmitted to the cloud.

IoT Cloud Platforms

Internet of things (IoT) infrastructure, merchandise, and offerings are presented by using cloud service companies (CSPs) across a wide variety that can be fully assimilated with their cloud answers. These consist of IoT platform technology, IoT Wi-Fi technology, and part synthetic intelligence (AI) computing.

AMAZON WEB SERVICES (AWS) IOT

AWS IoT and AWS IoT center only a few of Amazon net offerings' AWS) offerings are specially designed for internet of factors (IoT) programs, which includes Green grass. Agencies can also really deploy their personal internet-related devices, manipulate information securely, and benefit operational insights in actual time thanks to those services.

AWS IoT Greengrass

IoT AWS Greengrass permits customers to without difficulty deploy code at the edge in order that statistics can be processed there rather than being sent up to the cloud. by using preventing essential statistics from being shared on public networks, establishments can also enhance protection whilst lowering latency. AWS IoT Greengrass is the best select if customers need an IoT answer with pre-built additives for common use cases and want to quickly construct greater straightforward IoT packages from scratch. It gives a platform for obtaining predictive insights into patron conduct or use developments by using helping an expansion of machine learning (ML) technologies and synthetic intelligence-primarily based analytics solution (Li & Chen, 2015).

Azure IoT

A complete solution for IoT applications, Microsoft Azure's Internet of Things platform, also known as Azure IoT, enables data analysis, device management, edge computing, and back-end operations. Analytical technologies provide businesses more insight into their operations while security safeguards guarantee that all traffic is encrypted. Data Science and Internet of Things.

DATA SCIENCE AND IOT

Data science uses information gathered from IoT systems and other technologies. Through visualization and analysis, the data is then translated into value-based decision-making that helps businesses and organizations cut the competition and maintain an advantage over their competitors. The components of data science make it possible to understand and extract value from the use and deployment of the IoT.

Although companies have traditionally generated and processed data, the advent of the Internet of Things (IoT) has fundamentally altered the landscape. The methods used to evaluate data acquired through IoT systems are distinct from those used to analyze data collected in the past.

Data Science Subdomain for IoT

For numerous real-time applications that have been connected to real-time data and computing improvements, the data science employing IoT will be handled extravagantly and enormously according to the following.

Cognitive Computing

By extending this inquiry approach, cognitive computing may be able to access areas that are more challenging to access using more conventional tools like business knowledge and estimates.

Real time Processing:

Real-time data processing involves a nonstop flow of information and data production. Real-time data handling and analytics provide a company the ability to act quickly in situations where doing so within seconds is crucial.

Time Series Data Analysis

A time series is a collection of data that is organized chronologically. The most well-known method for visualizing time series data is to use a simple line diagram, where the vertical hub depicts the variable that is being estimated and the level hub plots the additions to time.

Geo Spatial Data Analysis

Geospatial data science addresses a number of important, new difficulties in innovation and financial progress.

Deep Learning

conventional system gaining knowledge of techniques have continually been progressive to address established facts and have been widely utilized by companies for credit score, buyer focusing on, beat expectation, and so on. Hand-built highlights are, realistically speak me, time-consuming, poor, and unadoptable whilst coping with unstructured material like pictures, text, speech, and recordings.

Edge Computing

Edge computing references to computation near a system chart's bend or edge. Additionally beneficial to organizations, edge computing helps them reduce expenses associated with sharing data sets through a system.

IoT vs Traditional Data Science It boils down to time by condensing the relationship between these two data developments into its simplest context. For instance, conventional data science refers to progressively simple processes that promote data agglomeration and linkage. In general, there is no deadline or expiration date to be concerned about.

IoT is continuously, easy to apply, and appears to be countless, even though one need to study and hold close records as fast as time we could. one of the distinguishing features that units the 2 technologies aside is the persevering with variable. each demand excessive flag prices and coaching periods, whereas IoT simply needs accumulated information and selections made at once. reduce or reduce the overall estimation of the data on the core of the invention with a view to prolong or lengthen the time required for data processing. The contrast of conventional records with IoT records is shown within the table.

Cloud Based IoT Networks

Edge computing, fog computing, and cloud computing, which correspond to the three layers of an IoT system (perception, distribution network, and application), are the main divisions of contemporary cloud-based IoT network. The following is a basic explanation of the three computing tiers.

Edge Computing Level

The edge computing level primarily includes edge nodes powered by mobile edge computing (MEC) technologies, such as routers, switches, and small/macro base stations.

IoT gateways hyperlink to IoT gadgets the use of an expansion of protocols, inclusive of WiFi, WirelessHART, RUBEE, second-generation 2G/3G/4G/5G, ZigBee, and Ethernet. moreover, the brink computing level is located at the IoT structures' distribution community layer, wherein it is able to, by using using MEC generation, offer real-time connection, services, and protection for IoT devices with constrained useful resource capacities on the belief layer as shown in 7.

Fog Computing Level

The distribution community layer is also where the fog computing degree is positioned. SDN controllers and SDN software servers—which can be assembled in a disbursed fashion—make up most of the people of it. these SDN controllers trade statistics with application servers and the cloud computing

Figure 7. Edge computing

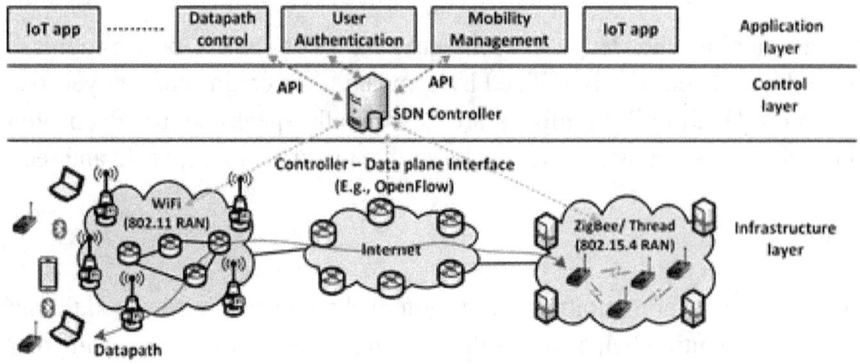

level thru northbound APIs, while southbound protocols (such OpenFlow and NetConf) are applied to connect with SDN-based totally IoT gateways. As a result, fog computing is a appropriate venue to set up IoT protection packages on the grounds that it may provide no longer simply sufficient processing assets however additionally low latency and compute-in depth packages.

Cloud Computing Level

A description for permitting universal, handy, on-call for network get admittance to a shared pool of configurable computing sources (e.g., servers, networks, garage, programs, and services) that may be rapidly implemented and launched with nominal management effort or carrier company interaction,'' according to the country wide Institute for requirements and era (NIST) in 2011. In light of this, this computing level is normally in charge of storing, analyzing, and imparting get entry to to statistics generated by means of a large quantity of IoT gadgets. In other phrases, big data storage and excessive performance computing applications must be carried out on the cloud computing stage.

Network Security Threats

The cloud environment for IoT networks and structures provides distributed computing resources, storage, and voice communication between IoT devices and programs. As a result of this surrender, several exploitable security holes are currently being used by attackers. As a consequence, we can also categorize common cyber-assaults into companies that are connected to networks as well as other companies that have the potential to significantly disrupt cloud-based IoT networks. However, in our analysis, we primarily concentrate on common network-related security risks, which are concisely summarized below i.e. figure 8.

Eavesdropping Attack

Eavesdropping Attack, sometimes referred to as data sniffing, is a dangerous cyberattack carried out by listening to IoT device interactions. Sniffers can harvest private data from communications, such as

Figure 8. Security threats

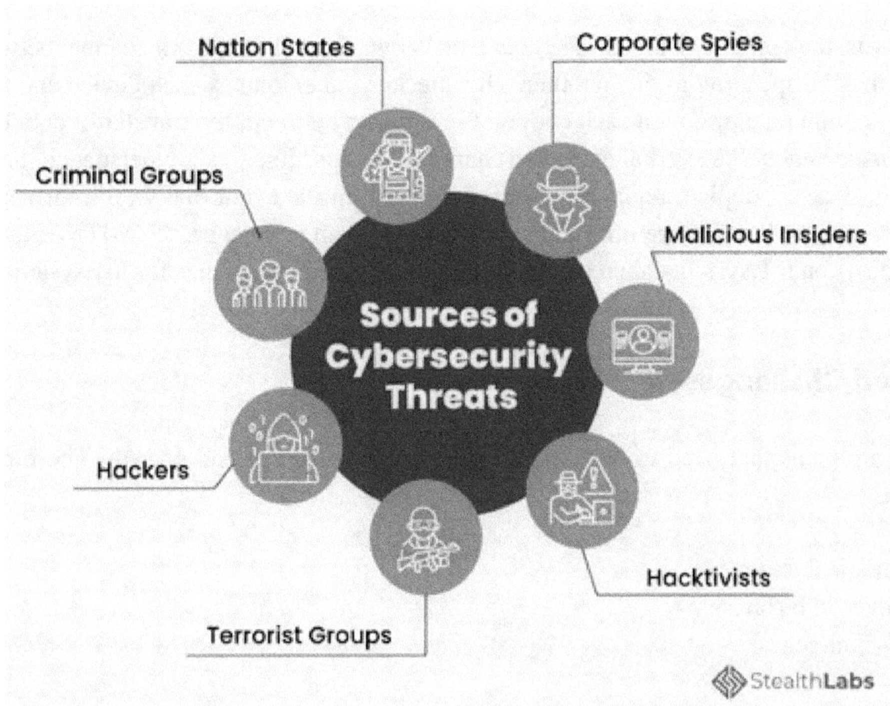

device setups or credentials, if data are being sent in an unsecured channel without encryption. Because attackers do not make network signals seem strange, eavesdropping assaults are difficult to identify and entirely avoid.

Denial-Of-Service Attack

In a cloud-based IoT system, denial-of-service (DoS) or distributed denial-of-service (DDoS) assaults are the most prevalent and deadly cyber threats. Adversaries can swiftly deplete network and computing resources with the aim of overwhelming network links and IoT devices with a huge volume of traffic, which makes the IoT communication system unavailable. A saturation assault can be launched using a variety of methods, including ICMP flooding, TCP/UDP SYN flooding, TearDrop, and Low & Slow DDoS. For instance, the Mirai botnet network was created using the more than 400,000 vendor/technology-specific IoT devices that in September 2016 flooded a French WebHost with 1 Tbps of DDoS traffic.

Spoofing Attack

A spoofing attack's antagonistic goal is to trick IoT networks and devices into believing they are receiving legal communication by seeming to be malicious traffic. Attackers might use eavesdropping to obtain information about allowed accesses, then fake attack traffic using real information such IP addresses to gain access to IoT network systems.

Man-In-The-Middle Attack

During a man-in-the-center assault (MITM), an attacker waits on the network channel between two IoT devices that may be speaking to one another. The attacker impersonates each device and relays traffic by personally communicating with each endpoint in order to intercept the transfer of data between victims. With this technique, the verbal exchange channel's two participants are persuaded that no packets are being lost, delayed, copied, replayed, spoof, or cloned. In the event that vital information, such as manipulate visitors or key change information, is gained by an adversary, the MITM attack may have disastrous effects on IoT systems, increasing insurmountable security issues for IoT systems (Vermesan et al., 2011).

IoT Enabled Challenges

IoT still has problems that need to be fixed despite its extensive use and growth. These problems are listed below:

1. Technological issues
2. Challenges in business
3. Society challenges

Technological Issues

This section will go through every technological challenge that IoT needs to solve. The following technical problems plague IoT:

Connectivity

Each IoT device is now running on a client-server architecture and linked to a single cloud server. This architecture is used for all operations. thousands of linked devices are all which can be wished for those devices for now, consequently connectivity is adequate. IoT is growing continuously, even though, as you may already be aware. It has additionally been expected that billions of devices might hook up with the internet within the destiny years (Cloud Security Alliance, 2009). the connection hassle therefore turns into at once obvious. The enormous majority of devices connected to the net cannot be related by means of an IoT device. A decentralized architecture ought to be applied that allows you to reduce the workload on the servers. the connection trouble should have a solution thanks to block chain generation.

Security

IoT is now dealing with serious security issues that are risky and unsettling for the people and government that have embraced the technology. Hackers with access to the smart devices are modifying them. This problem jeopardizes the IoT's future. IoT businesses must overcome this significant obstacle if they want to have a promising future and see the technology develop further. The firms' constant introduction of new technology is one cause of this problem. They just concentrate on utility and ignore security. In order to make IoT devices safe, it must be addressed.

Standards

Companies are not organizing their plans. The gadgets are defective because they are unable to settle on a single standard. IoT enterprises' resistance to adopting a standard is the cause of their inability to design, implement, and manage IoT systems.

Lack of Intelligent Analysis

The conclusions reached by the algorithms are flawed. The possibility that the sensor's numbers are occasionally inaccurate is extremely real. Because of this, inaccurate numbers will result in inaccurate impacts. The investigation that follows is blemished. Therefore, it is a noteworthy challenge for IoT to obtain the needed analytical abilities to evade these errors.

Compatibility

As was previously indicated, various devices utilize a variety of technologies, which puts into question a certain ubiquity. Therefore, getting out of it is a huge problem if IoT is to become the norm.

Challenges in Business

More individuals are turning to IoT investments and company startups these days. This is because it is popular and altering people's lives. It also has a promising future, making it a popular industry with the public.

All laws and regulations that apply to businesses must be complied with. Unfortunately, they are presently not functioning correctly. Therefore, the problems must be solved while addressing the obstacles.

End-to-end solution providers will be needed to supply you with all you need for your firm to meet all requirements. As a result, it would be more accurate to say that it is difficult for IoT to fully comprehend each type of IoT to conclude this part.

IoT has the following categories:

- ***Industrial IoT:***

It includes any equipment or sensors used in businesses, such as electric meters, pipeline monitors, robots, and several more Internet-connected industrial devices.

- ***Commercial IoT***:

This category includes all medical equipment, tracking equipment, and inventory controls.

- ***IoT for Consumers:***

This category includes all consumer electronics, including mobile phones, wearables, linked home devices like PCs, and various information systems.

Their description's main goal is to clarify the differences between these divisions for us. As a result, the regulatory systems may be appropriately put into place.

Society Challenges

IoT is currently confronting a number of societal challenges that are proving to be a significant hurdle for it. Although the businesses are attempting to fix them, the following problems still exist:

- Customers regularly modify their wants, therefore IoT must satisfy them.
- As new technology develops gradually, patience is required.
- It takes time and money to create new items and combine them with older ones.
- The number of users is increasing daily. IoT must therefore address each of these.
- Users may be disappointed by these problems and decide not to purchase these items.
- The users don't fully understand how these gadgets work. Therefore, if the interface is complicated, it will completely halt the product's growth.

All these issues must be resolved to keep the IoT devices secure and reliable.

viable remedies for internet of things problems

There are several difficulties associated with internet of things devices. It does not follow that we should cease producing and utilizing them, though. With simple solutions in place, these difficulties can be partially solved. A number of issues may be resolved by effective large-scale data gathering and management, user data encryption, regular IoT device testing, and the periodic release of pertinent updates (Lopez et al., 2013).

Data Collection and Management

IoT devices save a lot of information, making hacking simple. Data breaches may be prevented, however, and data can be effectively protected in line with the data privacy laws provided the right management practices are followed.

As stated in advance, garage and sharing of a big amount of data is a severe task. these may be extreme problems, but they're absolutely solvable. The advancement of generation now affords us with the next technology's 5G cellular community. This technology of mobile networks gives us with the performance required to share a huge amount of information correctly. together with it, the development of cloud computing gives you extended infrastructure to aid extra storage.

Timely and Regular Tests

checks which are completed as deliberate and with the desired modifications. earlier than being positioned in the marketplace, IoT products need to undergo rigorous checking out. assessments should not prevent at the pre-launch phase; they should go on after launch as nicely. gadgets have to be frequently inspected to make certain that flaws do not appear inside the period in-between. To make sure the product is continuously giving the high-quality carrier, recurring inspections help find out any modifications that could be required. It also guarantees that the device is mistakes-unfastened.

Strict Data Encryption

Users must understand that there is no way to guarantee 100% data security and that if they share their information on a device, it may be compromised at some point in the future. The greatest thing that can be done, though, is to encrypt data both in transit and at rest. The storage of data will have the fewest possible doors open thanks to encryption. Additionally, it ensures that only a certain number of people are permitted access to it. In addition, the user must make sure firewalls, anti-malware, and anti-virus programs are up to date and functional in order to monitor any unrelated activities.

CONCLUSION

Due to its wide range of applications and heterogeneous blend of different communications and embedded technologies in its design, the Internet of Things is a brand-new Internet revolution and a crucial study issue for researchers in embedded, computer science, and information technology.

Establishments thinking about the usage of cloud computing generation as a price-reducing and income-boosting approach should carefully assess the safety threat involved. The functionality to control danger greater effectively from a unified area is the benefit of cloud computing in data hazard management. despite the fact that cloud computing is a present day marvel that is poised to revolutionize how we use the internet, there are numerous things to consider. speedy technical improvements are resulting in the rapid emergence of several new technology, all of that have the ability to enhance human existence. the security dangers and problems associated with utilising these technology need to be carefully taken into consideration. The same is actual for cloud computing.

In general, the IoT would enable the automation of everything in our environment. This study provided a summary of the underlying assumptions of this idea, as well as its supporting technologies, protocols, applications, and recent research addressing various IoT-related issues. This should therefore give academics and practitioners who are interested in learning about IoT technologies and protocols a solid basis to comprehend the general architecture and function of the many components and protocols that make up the IoT.

In addition, several of the challenges and issues associated with the creation and application of IoT systems have been discussed. The interactions between the Internet of Things, big data analytics, cloud, and fog computing have also been a topic of discussion. We eventually emphasized the need for new "smart" autonomic management, data aggregation, and protocol adaptation services in order to achieve deeper horizontal integration across IoT services. In-depth application-use case studies were provided to show typical protocol integration situations in order to provide the essential IoT services.

REFERENCES

Alaa, M., Zaidan, A. A., Zaidan, B. B., Talal, M., & Kiah, M. L. M. (2017, November). A review of smart home applications based on Internet of Things. *Journal of Network and Computer Applications*, *97*, 48–65. doi:10.1016/j.jnca.2017.08.017

Arasteh, H., Hosseinnezhad, V., Loia, V., Tommasetti, A., Troisi, O., Shafie-khah, M., & Siano, P. (2016). IoT-based smart cities: A survey. *Proc. IEEE 16th Int. Conf. Environ. Elect. Eng. (EEEIC),* (pp. 1–6). IEEE. 10.1109/EEEIC.2016.7555867

Armbrust, M., Fox, A., Griffith, R., Joseph, A. D., Katz, R., Konwinski, A., Lee, G., Patterson, D., Rabkin, A., Stoica, I., & Zaharia, M. (2010). A View of Cloud Computing. *Communications of the ACM, 53*(4), 50–58. doi:10.1145/1721654.1721672

Atzori, L., Iera, A., & Morabito, G. (2010, October). The Internet of Things: A survey. *Computer Networks, 54*(15), 2787–2805. doi:10.1016/j.comnet.2010.05.010

Boss, G., Malladi, P., & Quan, D. (2009). *Cloud computing*. IBM. www.ibm.com/developerswork/websphere /zones/hipods/ library.html

Buyya, R., Chee Shin, Y., Venugopal, S., Broberg, J., & Brandic, I. (2009). Cloud computing and emerging IT platforms: Vision, hype, and reality for delivering computing as the 5th utility. *Future Generation Computer Systems, 25*(6), 599–616. doi:10.1016/j.future.2008.12.001

Cloud Security Alliance. (2009). *Security guidance for critical areas of focus in cloud computing(v2.1)*. CSA.

Evans, D. (2011). *The Internet of things: How the next evolution of the Internet is changing everything.* CISCO, San Jose, CA.

Gluhak, A., Krco, S., Nati, M., Pfisterer, D., Mitton, N., & Razafindralambo, T. (2011, November). A survey on facilities for experimental Internet of Things research. *IEEE Communications Magazine, 49*(11), 58–67. doi:10.1109/MCOM.2011.6069710

Gubbi, J., Buyya, R., Marusic, S., & Palaniswami, M. (2013, September). Internet of Things (IoT): A vision, architectural elements, and future directions. *Future Generation Computer Systems, 29*(7), 1645–1660. doi:10.1016/j.future.2013.01.010

Khan, R., Khan, S. U., Zaheer, R., & Khan, S. (2012). Future Internet: The Internet of Things architecture, possible applications and key challenges. Proc. 10th Int. Conf. FIT, (pp. 257–260). IEEE. 10.1109/FIT.2012.53

Kong, J. (2010). A Practical Approach to Improve the Data Privacy of Virtual Machines. *2010 IEEE 10th International Conference on Computer and Information Technology (CIT)*. IEEE. 10.1109/CIT.2010.173

Li, Y., & Chen, M. (2015). Software-defined network function virtualization: A survey. *IEEE Access : Practical Innovations, Open Solutions, 3*, 2542–2553. doi:10.1109/ACCESS.2015.2499271

Lopez, P., Fernandez, D., Jara, A. J., & Skarmeta, A. F. (2013). Survey of Internet of Things technologies for clinical environments. *Proc. 27th Int. Conf. Waina*. IEEE. 10.1109/WAINA.2013.255

Mell, P. (2011). *Timothy Grance. The NIST Definition of Cloud Computing (Draft)*. NIST.

Pearson, S. (2010). Privacy, Security and Trust Issues Arising from Cloud Computing. *2010 IEEE Second International Conference Cloud Computing Technology and Science*, (pp. 693-702). IEEE.

Sangroya, A., Kumar, S., Dhok, J., & Varma, V. (2010). Towards analyzing data security risks in cloud computing environments. *Communications in Computer and Information Science, 54*, 255–265. doi:10.1007/978-3-642-12035-0_25

Subashini S. & Kavitha V. (2011). A survey on security i issues in service delivery models of cloud computing. *Journal of Network and computer Applications, 4*(1), 1–11.

Takabi, H., Joshi, J. B. D., & Ahn, G. (2010). Security a and privacy challenges in cloud computing environments. *IEEE Security and Privacy*, *8*(6), 24–31. doi:10.1109/MSP.2010.186

Vermesan, O., Friess, P., Guillemin, P., & Gusmeroli, S. (2011). *Internet of Things Strategic Research Agenda*. River Publishers.

Yang, D., Liu, F., & Liang, Y. (2010). A survey of the Internet of Things. *Proc. 1st ICEBI*, (pp. 358–366). IEEE. 10.2991/icebi.2010.72

Chapter 20
Real-World Implementation of Cloud Computing New Technologies

Dharmesh Dhabliya
https://orcid.org/0000-0002-6340-2993
Department of Information Technology, Vishwakarma Institute of Information Technology, India

Sukhvinder Singh Dari
https://orcid.org/0000-0002-6218-6600
Symbiosis Law School, Symbiosis International University, Pune, India

Nitin N. Sakhare
https://orcid.org/0000-0002-1748-799X
Department of Computer Engineering, BRACT'S Vishwakarma Institute of Information Technology, India

Anish Kumar Dhablia
Altimetrik India Pvt. Ltd., Pune, India

Digvijay Pandey
https://orcid.org/0000-0003-0353-174X
Department of Technical Education, Government of Uttar Pradesh, India

A. Shaji George
https://orcid.org/0000-0002-8677-3682
TSM, Almarai Company, Riyadh, Saudi Arabia

A. Shahul Hameed
Department of Telecommunication, Consolidated Techniques Co. Ltd., Riyadh, Saudi Arabia

Pankaj Dadheech
https://orcid.org/0000-0001-5783-1989
Swami Keshvaand Institute of Technology, Management, and Gramothan, India

ABSTRACT

Smart cities are novel and difficult to study. Fires can kill people and destroy resources in cities near forests, farms, and open spaces. Sensor networks and UAVs are used to construct an early fire detection system to reduce fires. The suggested method uses sensors and IoT apps to monitor the surroundings. The suggested fire detection system includes UAVs, wireless sensors, and cloud computing. Image processing improves fire detection in the proposed system. Genuine detection is also improved by rules. Many current fire detection technologies are compared to the suggested system's simulation findings. The approach improves forest fire detection from 89 to 97%.

DOI: 10.4018/979-8-3693-0900-1.ch020

Table 1. Forest fire detection basics

Requirements	Specification	Reason
Prompt detection	Early detection	The prompt identification of fires and communication with the management system are both important.
Maximum Protection	Spectrum of Detection	utilising fewer sensors to monitor a larger region while also reducing overall energy consumption
Cost-effective	Notification	Warning warning distributed all over the world via email and text message Portable
Portable	Energy Usefulness	Reduced energy consumption will result in an increased lifespan for the system.

INTRODUCTION

Science is studying smart cities. This article prevents forest fires in cities. This project constructed an IoT, UAV, and image processing forest fire monitoring system. IoT devices monitor environmental indicators and analyse data to detect issues. The occurrence is confirmed via image processing. ICT, IoT, WSN, and computer automation increase urban living conditions in smart cities (Liang, L. L., et al. 2023). IT can manage transit, monitoring, and resource scheduling for cities. Smart cities may boost living standards and resource efficiency. Many governments run smart city pilot schemes to improve the environment and quality of life with smart technologies. ICT, IoT, and WSN generate intelligent apps.

To improve life, smart cities manage infrastructure and resources. In "smart cities," real-time data determines learning parameters. Smart cities use sensor internetworks and IoT for smart buildings, pollution assessment, traffic, water, public monitoring, and grid tracking.

A forests can host amphibians, birds, reptiles, etc. Forests cover 35% of the land. Forests grow from plantations and organic processes. Natural activities like fires deforest. People sometimes raise temperatures. Forest monitoring is costly and time-consuming. Forest fires threaten smart cities, the environment, economy, infrastructure, animals, and humanity worldwide. Indian forest fires are rising. In 2015, 15,937 forest fires occurred (Ozkan, O., et al. 2023) and 24,817 in 2016. The fire accelerates in a year.

Himachal Pradesh and Uttarakhand burned 17,502 acres in 2016. Human and animal extinction, ecological instability, and soil fertility loss result. Wildfires destroy ground microorganisms and nutrients and endanger neighbours. Forest fires are caused by combustible materials, environmental factors, and ignition. To protect wildlife, natural resources, and the environment, researchers have devised many forest fire prevention strategies. Wildfires are different from urban and agricultural fires and can originate for many reasons. Humans cause most wildfires. Global warming may cause forest fires. Forest conservation requires widespread public knowledge and firefighting. In Table 1, forest fire detection systems meet various standards.

The sensor-based fire detection system in Figure 1 is simple. Forest fire is shown in shot. The framework checks the snapshot and alarms for smoke or fire. Sensors, transmission channels, image processing methods, and an alert signal mechanism make up this image-processing system. The processing unit receives images from sensor nodes over a network. Fire detection and warning are done by the processing unit using RGB and YCbCr colour models. Cai Ye et al. Power supply uniformity is also ensured.

Figure 1. Fire detection system's block diagram

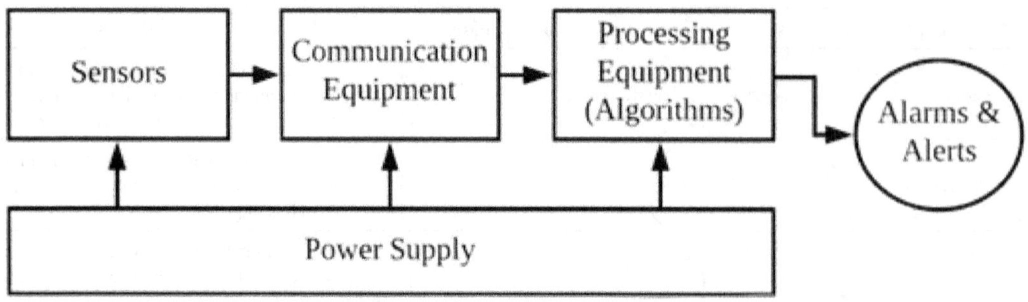

SMART CITY FIRE DETECTION WITH WSNS AND IOT

Recently, around smart cities, WSNs are used for forest fire detection. Real-time sensors monitor fire zone data and physical factors. WSNs allow you to link several devices to a scalable network and add sensors for various data collection. No towers needed; sensors can go wherever. Technological advances enable sensor recognition and communication.

IoT apps may provide realtime data. The combined IoT-dependent sensor network will predict forest fires better than satellites. Satellite fire detection may be delayed by slow scan rates and low resolution. Before forest fires spread, satellites cannot predict them. Figure 2 shows sensor data transit and position. With WSNs, woods are sensor-rich. A sensor network is formed by the nearest cluster node sending temperature, humidity, smoke, and other data to the cluster head. Field sensors use RF. Cloud gateway nodes link WSNs to the outside world. Remote users can access real-time field data through GPRS from the gateway node (Pradhan D. et al. 2022).

Homes, buildings, smart cities, even isolated hills and woodlands have sensors. Radio-connected sensor nodes report to the control room (Anand, R. et al. 2022). These sensor nodes safely transfer data to the gateway utilising repeating data relays. Gateways deliver data to servers or clouds. Cloud platforms with IoT store and analyse data for decision-making. A data analysis can cause fire alarms. Researchers studied flames using IoT and future Internet automation.

Work an Impact

The article covers WSN/IoT stationing. Disaster protection for smart cities is the goal. Real-time sensing, storage, and processing benefit controllers and service providers. This essay proposes smart city fire assessment design. Here are the main components of the proposed fire estimation architecture.

- Create a WSN, IoT, and image processing framework for forest fire detection.
- Use IoT devices to measure temperature, humidity, light, and vapour in real time.
- Image analysis for fire detection.
- Issue fire warnings quickly.

The programme evaluates, filters, and aggregates sensed data for decision-making, improving system-sensor interaction. Internet and sensors provide early fire tracking. The project seeks to quickly discover

Figure 2. Information transfer and sensor deployment

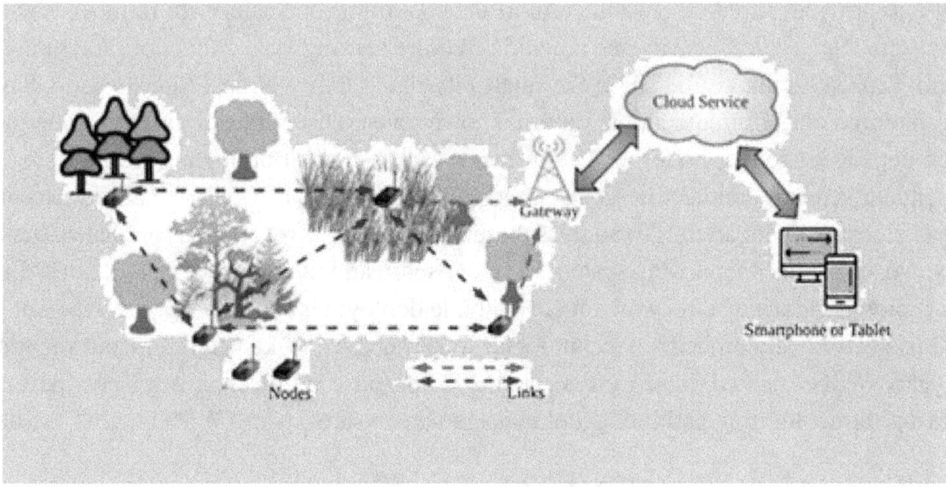

forest fires. RGB and YCbCr colour space models identify the fire zone in the proposed model. Comparing real detection rate experimental findings to current methods. The model's proper identification rate beats cutting-edge approaches.

LITERATURE REVIEW

This section discusses recent smart city and fire avoidance projects. This paper's broad literature review falls into four categories: fire revelation, image processing, and UAV fire detection.

Important WSN and IoT Stationing Research for Smart Cities

Over the past decade, IoT has changed the Internet. People and objects are connected 24/7 by IoT. Connected items generate big data. Storage and real-time processing are needed for smart device data.

Cloud computing makes remote resource processing cheap. Edge devices get compute and storage from cloud "fog" and "edge computing". S. Jain et al. (2022) summarise fog computing smart city automations. Fog system issues and smart city applications were investigated. Intelligent parking IoT and WSN were described by Aziz et al. (2022). Design, data security, privacy, and dependability were priorities. G. Jayaraman et al. (2022) recommend smart city WSN stationing to extend network life.

Sensor data needs regular storage and monitoring. The cloud stores sensor data for use. Processing all discovered data is critical due to its volume. Zhang et al. (2022) proposed real-time large data analysis. Kuthadi et al. (2022) presented a power-saving gearbox protocol. Hardware limits and energy supply are WSN's main issues due to node electronic operation and processing efficiency. Scaling a device network and picking an implementation architecture are further difficulties. WSNs have grown from star topologies and few sensor nodes to mesh networks with hundreds. Numerous fire detection research have employed different methods. Installing sensors in the research area can build the Internet of Things or Everything and monitor environmental variables. Wireless sensor networks make recording and detecting temperature, humidity, fog, brightness, and other parameters easier. The sensor network-dependent app provides rapid safety and comfort data. Comfort and safety are improved by smart city tracking systems. Smart city security and amenities require sensing, data collection, and safety research. S. Pramanik (2023) Zhang et al. (2022) fix smart city data facility issues. Microsensors have limited computing, storage, and communication. Batteries power most sensor nodes, conserving energy. Specific application-dependent sensor nodes that require exact, high-resolution metres are limited. Smart city WSN-dependent sensing architectures must choose which nodes are valuable and how to place them for energy-efficient spot locations. To address these issues, other investigations published their findings differently. No smart city monitoring system has clear setup and maintenance instructions. Generalised WSN smart city monitoring frameworks focus on node deployment and sensor management. A. Gupta et al. 2023 used RFID and embedded technologies to let people check availability and situation online. Previous years, WSNs tracked fires. Yang, J., et al. 2022 propose Wireless Sensor Network image-based event tracking. Street lighting and intelligent management systems using WSN and IoT are described.

Similar Plans to Improve Fire Detection

Forest fires damage wildlife, infrastructure, and nature. Previous forest fire reports provide proof. Nature and humanity can suffer financially and environmentally from forest fires. Several forest fire detection systems exist (Ghosh, R., et al. 2022). Standard forest fire detection requires individuals and machinery (Cao, CF., et al. 2022). Satellites, wireless sensors, and fire watchtowers detect flames (de Venâncio, P.V.A.B., et al. 2022). Fire detection is usually done via watchtowers. Notifying every fire ensures proper action. Operator fatigue, location, larger area, lack of 24/7 help, and processing speed make it a poor fire detection system.

Three items regularly disrupt WSN coverage. Poor detection ranges, uneven deployment, and insufficient sensors cover the AOI. Power shortages may cause sensor nodes to fail, reducing AOI coverage. Sensor nodes' narrow sensing radius limits coverage. Pricey, simple sensors with a broad detection range may work. Each case raises coverage issues. First option does not optimise coverage or sensing with sensor nodes closer together. The second scenario creates blind spots because to energy-intensive sensor node transmission delays (Anand, R et al. 2022).

Monitoring for Fires Through Processing of Images

Satellites spot forest fires. Multiple photographs from different dates reveal fires. Low-resolution images may hamper data extraction. Y. Li et al. (2022) developed R, G, and B detection. Forest fire IR smoke detectors. This approach measures particulates, temperature, and air quality. Use smoke particles. Khan et al. 2023 improved HSI fire pixel detection. This approach sorts pixels by brightness and blackness. Also shown is HSI colour segmentation. Lower-intensity and saturation pixels are removed to reduce false alarms. Normalised RGB helped Wang et al. (2020) avoid lighting effects. Picture analysis uses RG, GB, RB(axes). The proposed method may separate the flame zone except its centre. Colour influences fire pixels. Using RGB and YCbCrcolor models, ZG Liu et al. (2016) suggested recognising fire zones from images. Regular results can be trustworthy. Nagulan et al. (2023) partition fire pixels using YCbCr and picture statistics. This study evaluates the strategy using 750 photographs. Simulation and comparison of recommended photo classification method to current approaches. Method supposedly validates alarm rate. The uniform image partitioning method processes pictures simultaneously. Emmy

Prema et al. (2018) showed ORNAM improved image quality and reduced homogenous blocks. This layout suits grayscale photos. EWLDA feature extraction extracts global and local images (Hassan et al. 2022). This method evaluates firing zone brightness and movement. Histograms divide. Authors believe these traits may improve forest fire detection. Wu et al. (2022) created fire detection. We use RGB and HIS. Physically moving items create more false alarms but are computationally efficient. Table demonstrates parameterized colour model strengths and cons.

UAV-Based Fire Detection Similar Initiatives

Plains were better for traditional fire monitoring. But most fires happen in difficult places where wind can spread them. Modern satellites are accurate and efficient. These satellite systems are accurate with regular monitoring methods but unreliable and prone to satellite signal issues. Modern remote sensing is useful for tracking big areas. Greater spatial resolution photos are more useful and pleasant for event tracking than riskier monitoring methods. The best automation for mapping and inspecting large areas is InSAR, which monitors day and night in all conditions. Due to its restricted timeframe, InSAR cannot continuously monitor and assess fires. Satellite fire tracking is unreliable due to precision, timing, cost, and size.

Images captured in fog, cloud cover, and rain may also deceive. Previous monitoring methods were slower, less dependable, and harder to use. UAVs may quickly capture photos while flying low. Continuous operation and data collecting make UAV technology better than remote sensing and conventional monitoring. Several trials using several UAV sensor platforms showed UAVs' rapid response and easy data collection. Time and safety constraints in older event confirmation and monitoring approaches limit process data for event evaluation and monitoring. UAVs may monitor 100,000 m2 better, research show. UAVs efficiently monitor the region and verify any incident, big or small. Other approaches cost more and are less flexible than UAV surveillance. UAVs can monitor wide areas in big numbers due to their cost. Basic surface models and photos are produced by UAVs with digital cameras. Drones with various lenses map region texture. UAVs with cheaper cameras may be preferable for smart city monitoring and mapping. This area mapping method may improve satellite imaging's spatial resolution. UAVs save ground station effort and create 3D images (Mandal et al. 2021). The study found that UAVs can take centimetre-level photos (Mall. P. K. et al. 2023) Modern drones patrol with cameras.

PREFERRED ARCHITECTURE

Verification is hardest for each fire detection system to reduce false alarms. The solution addresses the difficulty of certifying a fire using affected area photographs. FIG. 3 depicts a smart city's surroundings and data collection method. It shows IoT and WSN smart city applications. IoT apps collect data from connected devices for users, businesses, and governments. WSN and IoT-dependent city fire detection is recommended. Data collecting, processing, and decision-making determine how well smart devices help the city provide services. IoT-enabled intelligent gadgets' real-time development and inter-transmission improve smart city services. Gateways deliver observation data to the cloud from devices.

The cloud can store and analyse real-time data for decision-making. Many users and controllers can obtain real-time ecological data via a network server. The smart city framework utilises IoT and WSNs. Fig. 4 shows the suggested city fire detection design. WSNs and IoT devices track fires. Smart cities

Figure 3. A smart city aided by a WSN and IoT

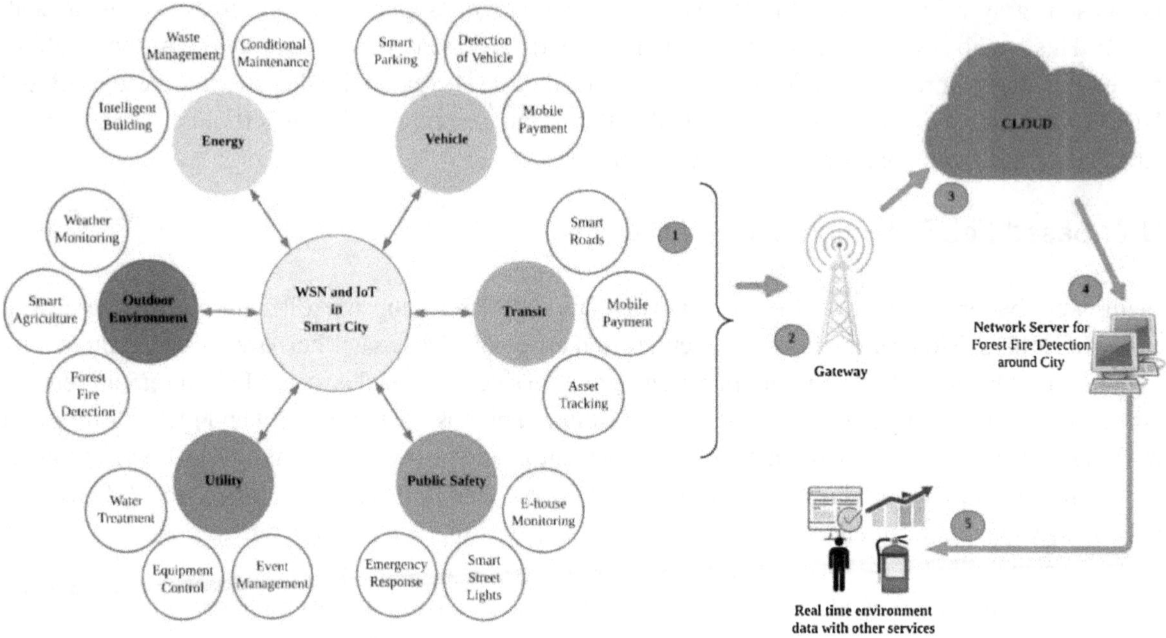

are commonly near forests or farms. Architecture shields towns from natural and man-made disasters (Mondal, D. et al. 2023) The suggested system includes sensor stationing, satellite communication, thingSpeakIoT cloud, UAV inter-network, and base station.3.1 Sensor placement

Random sensor network installation over a city is shown initially. Sensor nodes in grasslands record environmental data. Real-time temperature, humidity, fog, and brightness measurements. Radio frequency links let sensor nodes send data to sink nodes. The sink node sends sensor data to the cloud framework through GSM for real-time analysis (Gupta, A. et al. 2022). After 2–6 minutes, sensors provide real-time environmental data. Sensor nodes are listed in Section 4.

Satellite System

The area scan satellite framework is explained here. Satellite fire tracking is hampered by long scan times and limited resolution. Satellite fire surveillance is common. Satellites cannot see forest fires coming. Satellites scan the region for future development and collect climate, wind flow, etc. data. Satellite area scanning measures the area precisely. Satellite imagery maps a region and creates a real-time drone surveillance network. Satellites provide the target region's latitude and longitude to the base station for location tracking. The region is forecast for scanning using satellite latitudinal and longitudinal data.

ThingSpeakIoT Cloud—IoT-Dependent Data Analytics Platform

The platform shows and evaluates real-time sensor data. Data from the ground is safely sent to the cloud and processed in MATLAB. Our technology instantly displays live stream data and provides alarms.

Figure 4. A hypothetical integrated system for smart city fire incident detection

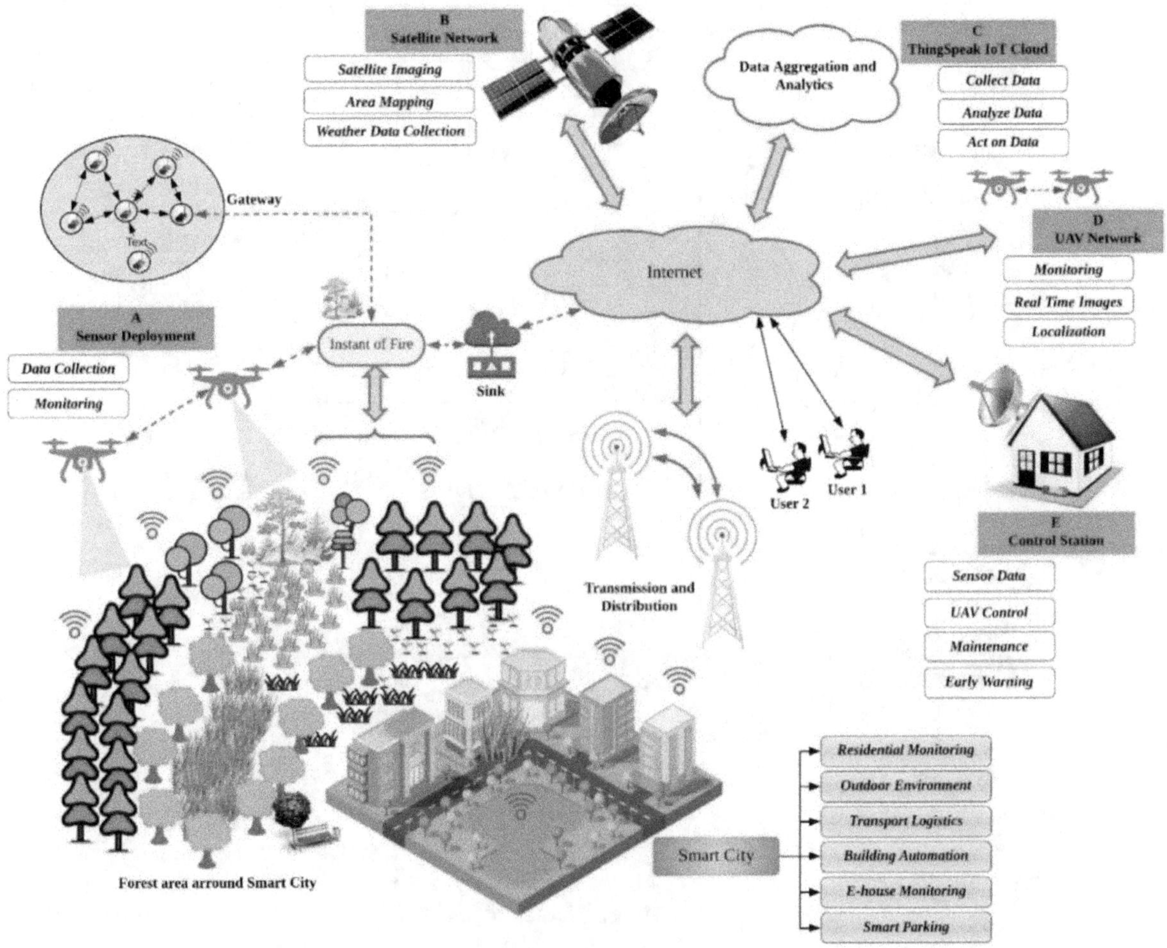

The UAV Network

After identifying the occurrence, the proposed system provides real-time photos of the affected area. UAVs help locate incidents and provide real-time fire confirmation to the control centre via picture processing. Scan begins when the server requests the monitoring mission. During mission planning, mapping software is utilised to specify checkpoint sites. The drone's flight routes are then built on the mapped region to meet the aim and sent to the base station with the latest parameter measurements. Drones take high-resolution images of the target area. The ground station sends sensed data for immediate processing. After an event occurs, its position is identified for monitoring and confirmation.

The Command Post

The base station runs the network, evaluates sensor data, and confirms fires via image processing. The control station detects events from photos. Control station sends early alerts following fire confirmation. The suggested architecture incorporates sensing, processing, and analysis. Basic fire detection is shown

Figure 5. Elements of fire detection system in smart cities

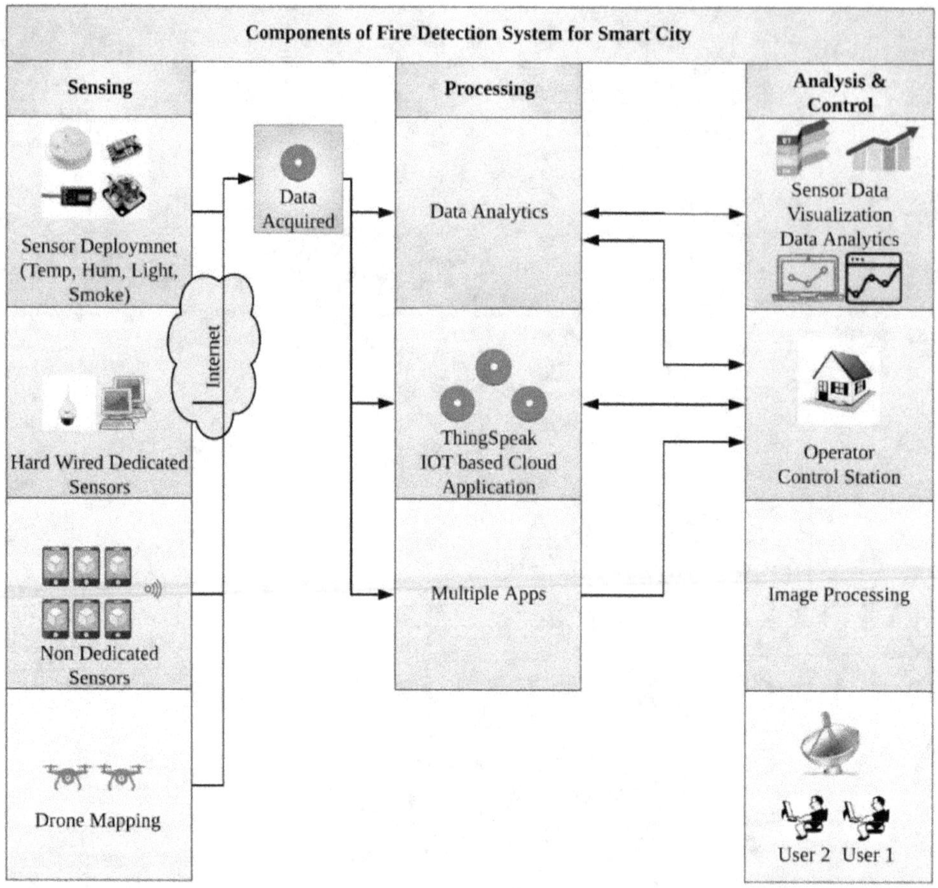

in Fig. 5. Environmental data is collected by randomly placing temperature, humidity, light, and smoke sensors outside. All sensor and sink nodes communicate directly. Data from the sink node is stored and processed by ThingSpeak. Each application's tasks are accomplished and data is analysed in the cloud. The proposed system uses sensor nodes to monitor environmental factors, including fire sources. The ThinkSpeak cloud stores data every 2–5 minutes for tracking and inquiry. Sensor data is evaluated, anomalies detected, and a decision made. Remote access to cloud data is easy. Users discover opponents and incidents early with frequent data monitoring. Final analysis uses real-time UAV data to validate the event through picture processing. Remote cloud data access is unlimited for users and controllers. A control station can guide accessories to improve communication. The suggested fire detection system leverages UAV colour photos. Photo sent to a distant station. Image detection locates fires. Control station functions include receiving, analysing, and alerting. Management prepares firefighting methods and follows orders after receiving the alarm.

MONITORING SENSING AND FUNCTIONING

Fig. 6 depicts the integrated system that is suggested for using the IoT and WSNs to detect and monitor fire.

Information Flow

WSN and IoT event tracking and monitoring schema is shown in Fig. 7. The deployment of sensor nodes begins detection. Next, we examine the need for maximum coverage with few sensors. If the goal is met, the shortest data transmission link to the sink node optimises energy efficiency. After sending data from the sink node to the base station, ThingSpeak Cloud stores it every 2–5 minutes. The cloud-based programme uses MATLAB to discover events in real-time data (Meslie, Y. et al. 2021). The control station receives the GPS coordinates of the node that caused each data anomaly. GPS coordinates and borderlines help the control station map the target zone for real-time photos.

Real-time photos and affected area location are provided to the base station. All images use the image processing algorithm. The fire confirmation image processing procedure is discussed. Image histogram equalisation starts first. Picture intensity is adjusted to improve contrast. Fire photos estimate red elements better, according to the method. To isolate fire-colored images' red regions, a threshold function is created. This work's red, blue, and green proportions may be evaluated. The proposed fire estimation system charts colour components. Loaded image is mapped with extracted edge for colour detection. Colour estimation framework based on RGB pixel outputs a picture with the chosen fire colour detection zone. Second, convert the augmented image's RGB components to YCbCr to detect fire pixels. Calculate photo mean and SD to validate fire and non-fire colour pixels. Applications jump to the next group when they see non-fire pixels. A fire alarm is activated for decision-making when fires are regulated by example photos.

Sensor Node Setup

Figure 8 displays the ambient data sensors used to detect fire in the area. Light monitors (a) measure light without taking images. Most light intensity devices are photodiodes and photo resistors. Luminescent resistors. Photo diodes generate electricity. Light reduces photo resistor resistance.

The HTS-220(b) digital temperature and humidity monitor is inexpensive. After monitoring humidity and temperature, it outputs a number on the data port. Easy to use, but data collection takes precision. The MQ2 (c) smoke monitor monitors atmospheric flammable gas and sends an analogue signal. The monitor detects 300–10,000 ppm combustible gas. The 5 V monitor uses less than 150 mA and works from -20 to 50 °C. Drain (Coordinator) nodes receive all sensing node data. (d). Thus, drain node position greatly affects WSN energy use and lifespan. Power consumption and instrument lifetime matter in Wireless Instrument Networks. Cluster leaders will receive member data. Cluster heads sent all data to the washbasin or control station. Control station data will be received. Sink Nodes link sensor nodes to data processing hubs.

Data Analysis

The UAV shoots real-time photos of anomalies detected by ThingSpeak data processing. UAVs use control centre GPS data to find and record target zones. The monitoring centre confirms fires by applying the specified image processing algorithm to incoming images. First, histogram normalisation redistributes picture luminance. To check balance, the input image is transformed to HSI while keeping Hue and Saturation.

Figure 6. An advanced idea for the use of WSNs and IoT to identify and track an occurrence

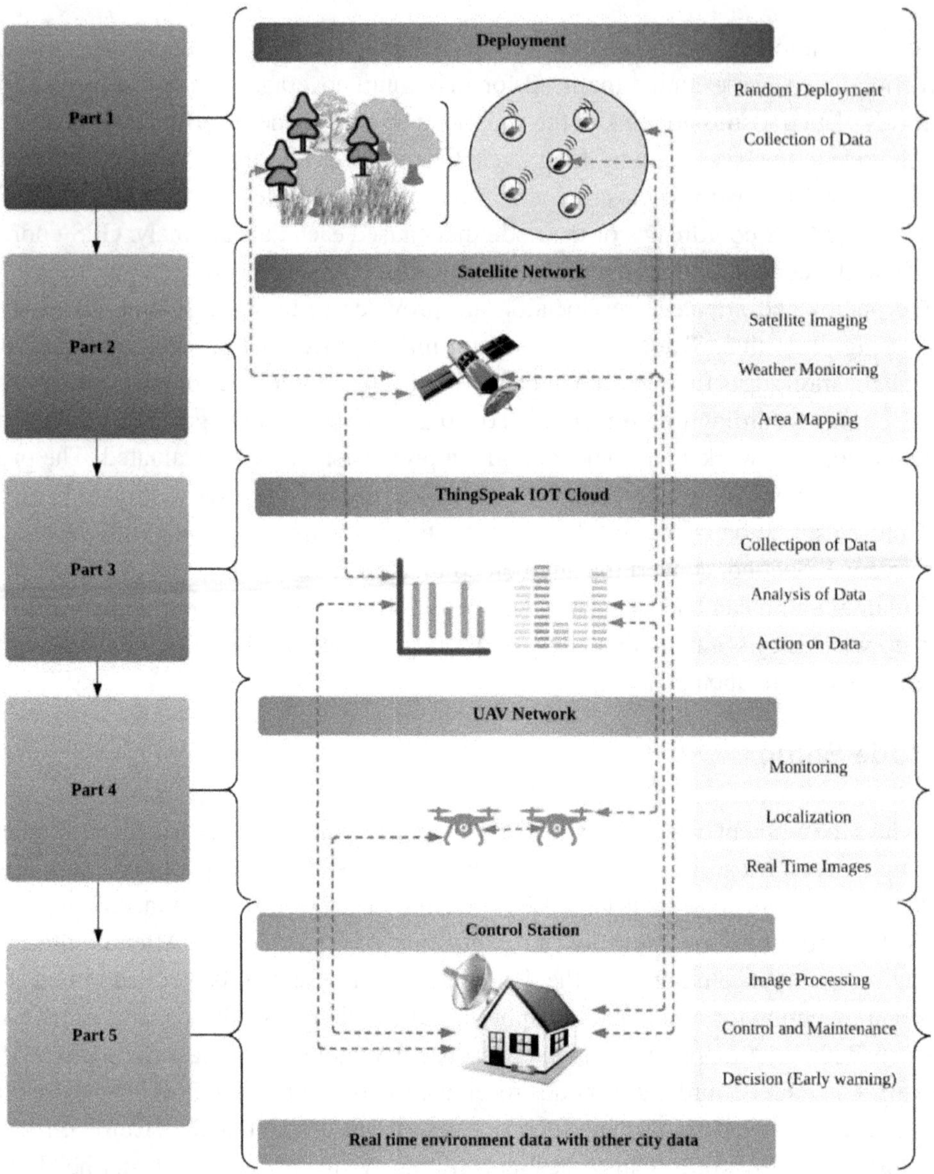

Fire Case Verification

The UAV shoots real-time photos of anomalies detected by ThingSpeak data processing. UAVs use control centre GPS data to find and record target zones. The monitoring centre confirms fires by applying the specified image processing algorithm to incoming images. First, histogram normalisation redistributes picture luminance. To check balance, the input image is transformed to HSI while keeping Hue and Saturation.

Figure 10 shows (a) initial fire incident photographs and (b) enhanced image intensity after normalisation, executed and evaluated for 4 fire images to improve image intensity. Image R, G, and B cannot be

Figure 7. Suggested event monitoring system for smart cities in a flow chart format

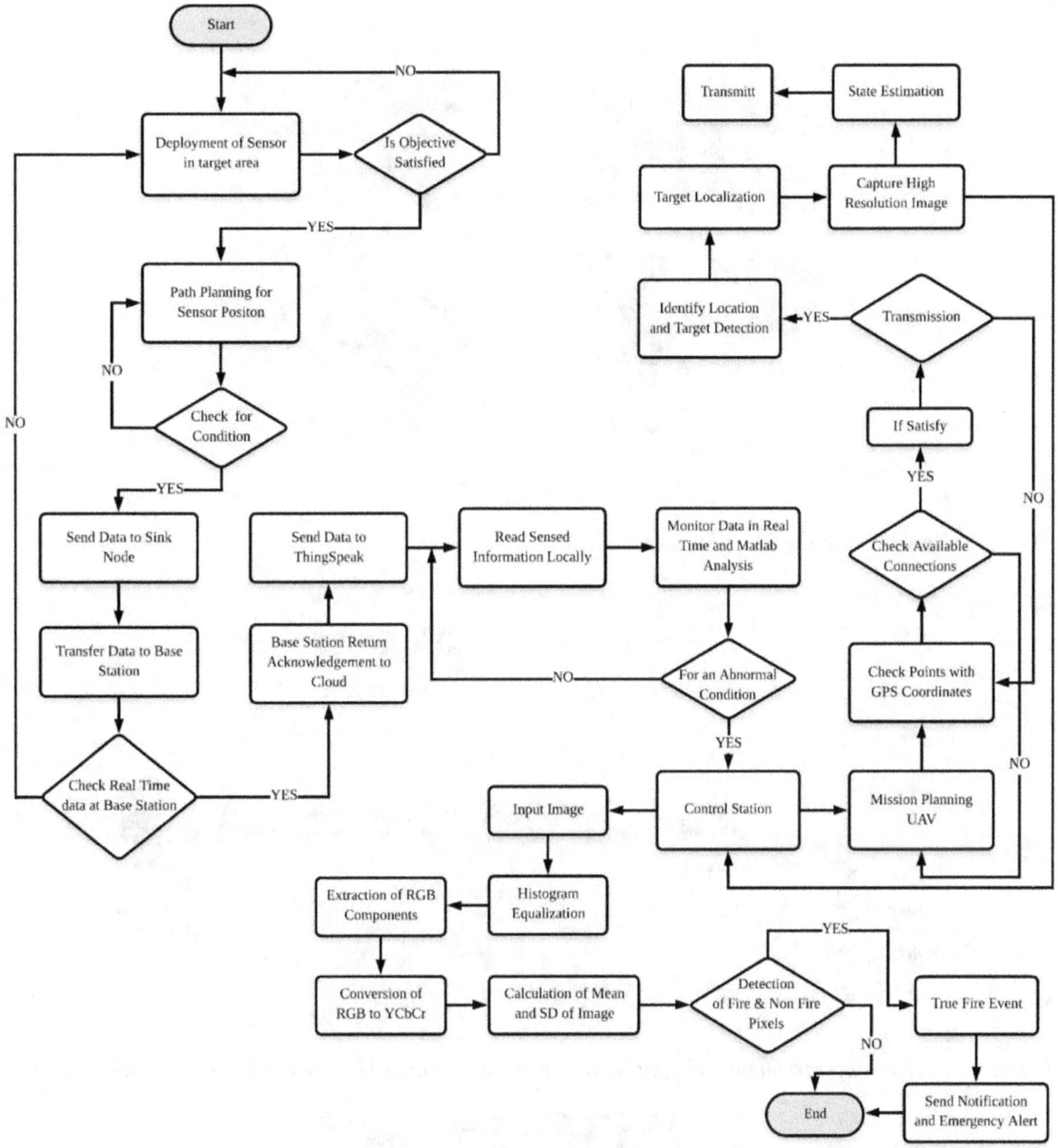

enhanced separately by histogram normalisation. Figure 10 compares images with R, G, and B histograms before and after normalisation. For luminance and pixel counts, four representative photos are taken.

Image clarity is improved by converting the RGB matrix to HSI and normalising the intensity matrix. Maintaining the HSI matrix constant converts the updated matrix back to the RGB matrix. The suggested method uses the YCbCr mechanism, which isolates picture brightness from chrominance better than any

Figure 8. The supervisor node (d) and the sensor nodes for light, temperature, humidity, and pollution (a, b, c)

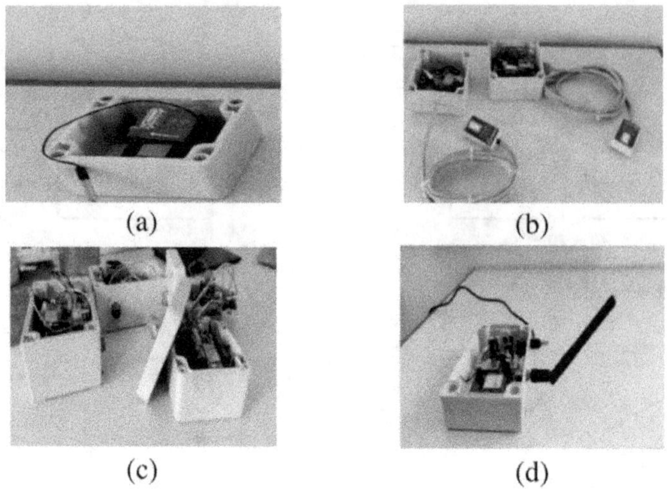

Figure 9. Operation of the ThingSpeak Cloud

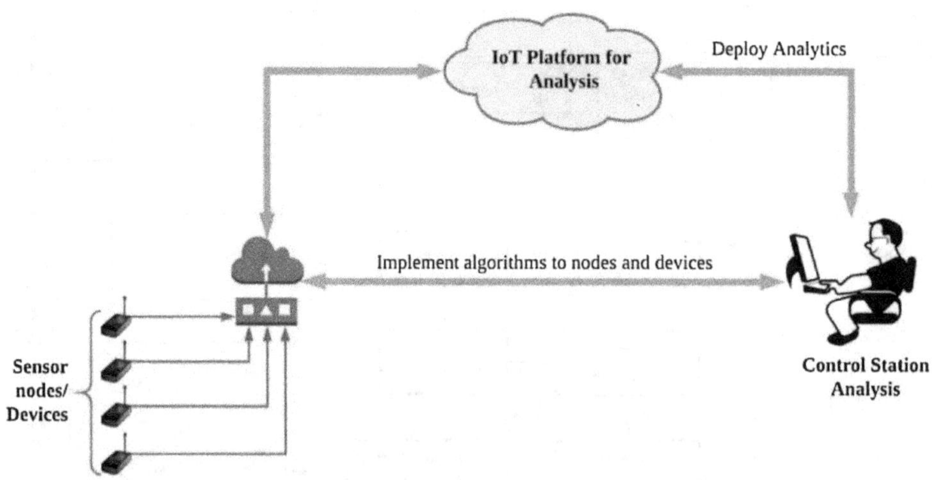

Figure 10. (a) Example of a picture without histogram equalization (b) Following the equivalence procedure

Figure 11. (a) Input RGB picture; (b) Manual fire area extraction

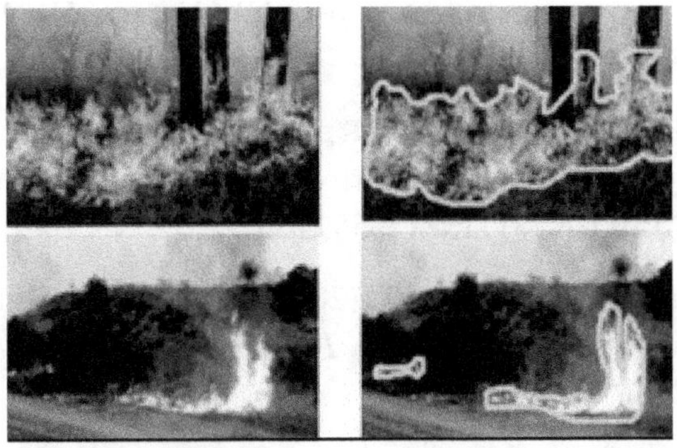

other colour model. The fire's centre is yellowish-white at its highest temperature, whereas the rest is scarlet or yellow. Following specified guidelines

Figure 10 shows (a) initial fire incident photos and (b) improved picture intensity following normalisation for 4 fire images. Histogram normalisation cannot improve images R, G, and B independently. Compare R, G, and B histogram images before and after normalisation in Figure 10. For luminance and pixel counts, four representative images are obtained.

Normalising the intensity matrix and converting RGB to HSI improves image clarity. The updated matrix becomes the RGB matrix by keeping the HSI matrix constant. The YCbCr mechanism separates picture brightness from chrominance in the suggested way. chrominance

CONCLUSION

Several nations worry about forest or wealthy community fires. Global experts believe that obtaining effective tools is the most important catastrophe mitigation measure. The study introduces a WSN-IoT infrastructure for early fire monitoring. The sensenut hardware has produced successful wireless sensor networks. Outdoor sensors collect and interpret data live. For processing, the cloud stores sensing unit data. Many graphs use ThingSpeak clouds for haze, temperature, humidity, and light strength. The system detects events by assessing real-time data and external factors. This project uses IoT and web platforms to construct a fire warning system. Global real-time data collection and monitoring is cost-effective with the design. Recommended fire incident monitoring device uses photo analysis. Several rules improve fire detection.

REFERENCES

Anand, R., Singh, J., Pandey, D., Pandey, B. K., Nassa, V. K., & Pramanik, S. (2022). Modern Technique for Interactive Communication in LEACH-Based Ad Hoc Wireless Sensor Network. In M. M. Ghonge, S. Pramanik, & A. D. Potgantwar (Eds.), *Software Defined Networking for Ad Hoc Networks*. Springer., doi:10.1007/978-3-030-91149-2_3

Aziz, A., Osamy, W., Alfawaz, O., & Khedr, A. M. (2022). EDCCS: Effective deterministic clustering scheme based compressive sensing to enhance IoT based WSNs. *Wireless Networks*, *28*(6), 2375–2391. doi:10.1007/s11276-022-02973-3

Bansal, R., Jenipher, B., Nisha, V., & Makhan, R. Kumbhkar, Pramanik, S., Roy, S. and Gupta, A. (2022). Big Data Architecture for Network Security", in Cyber Security and Network Security, Eds, Wiley, https://doi.org/ doi:10.1002/9781119812555.ch11

Cai, Y., Zhou, W., Zhang, L., Yu, L., & Luo, T. (2023). DHFNet: Dual-decoding hierarchical fusion network for RGB-thermal semantic segmentation. *The Visual Computer*. Advance online publication. doi:10.1007/s00371-023-02773-6

Cao, C. F., Yu, B., Chen, Z. Y., Qu, Y.-X., Li, Y.-T., Shi, Y.-Q., Ma, Z.-W., Sun, F.-N., Pan, Q.-H., Tang, L.-C., Song, P., & Wang, H. (2022). Fire Intumescent, High-Temperature Resistant, Mechanically Flexible Graphene Oxide Network for Exceptional Fire Shielding and Ultra-Fast Fire Warning. *Nano-Micro Letters*, *14*(1), 92. doi:10.1007/s40820-022-00837-1 PMID:35384618

Choudhary, S., Narayan, V., Faiz, M., & Pramanik, S. (2022). Fuzzy Approach-Based Stable Energy-Efficient AODV Routing Protocol in Mobile Ad hoc Networks. In M. M. Ghonge, S. Pramanik, & A. D. Potgantwar (Eds.), *Software Defined Networking for Ad Hoc Networks*. Springer., doi:10.1007/978-3-030-91149-2_6

de Venâncio, P. V. A. B., Lisboa, A. C., & Barbosa, A. V. (2022). An automatic fire detection system based on deep convolutional neural networks for low-power, resource-constrained devices. *Neural Computing & Applications*, *34*(18), 15349–15368. doi:10.1007/s00521-022-07467-z

Ghosh, R., & Kumar, A. (2022). A hybrid deep learning model by combining convolutional neural network and recurrent neural network to detect forest fire. *Multimedia Tools and Applications*, *81*(27), 38643–38660. doi:10.1007/s11042-022-13068-8

Gupta, A., Asad, A., Meena, L., & Anand, R. (2023). IoT and RFID-Based Smart Card System Integrated with Health Care, Electricity, QR and Banking Sectors. In M. Gupta, S. Ghatak, A. Gupta, & A. L. Mukherjee (Eds.), *Artificial Intelligence on Medical Data. Lecture Notes in Computational Vision and Biomechanics* (Vol. 37). Springer. doi:10.1007/978-981-19-0151-5_22

Gupta, A., Verma, A., & Pramanik, S. (2022). Advanced Security System in Video Surveillance for COVID-19. In *An Interdisciplinary Approach to Modern Network Security, S. Pramanik, A. Sharma, S. Bhatia and D. N. Le*. CRC Press. doi:10.1201/9781003147176-8

Hassan, N. M., Hamad, S., & Mahar, K. (2022). Mammogram breast cancer CAD systems for mass detection and classification: A review. *Multimedia Tools and Applications*, *81*(14), 20043–20075. doi:10.1007/s11042-022-12332-1

Jain, S., Gupta, S., Sreelakshmi, K. K., & Rodrigues, J. J. P. C. (2022). Fog computing in enabling 5G-driven emerging technologies for development of sustainable smart city infrastructures. *Cluster Computing*, *25*(2), 1111–1154. doi:10.1007/s10586-021-03496-w

Jayaraman, G., & Dhulipala, V. R. S. (2022). FEECS: Fuzzy-Based Energy-Efficient Cluster Head Selection Algorithm for Lifetime Enhancement of Wireless Sensor Networks. *Arabian Journal for Science and Engineering*, *47*(2), 1631–1641. doi:10.1007/s13369-021-06030-7

Khan, R. A., Hussain, A., Bajwa, U. I., Raza, R. H., & Anwar, M. W. (2023). Fire and Smoke Detection Using Capsule Network. *Fire Technology*, *59*(2), 581–594. doi:10.1007/s10694-022-01352-w

Kuthadi, V. M., Selvaraj, R., Baskar, S., Shakeel, P. M., & Ranjan, A. (2022). Optimized Energy Management Model on Data Distributing Framework of Wireless Sensor Network in IoT System. *Wireless Personal Communications*, *127*(2), 1377–1403. doi:10.1007/s11277-021-08583-0

Li, Y., Zhang, W., Liu, Y., & Jin, Y. (2022). A visualized fire detection method based on convolutional neural network beyond anchor. *Applied Intelligence*, *52*(11), 13280–13295. doi:10.1007/s10489-022-03243-7

Liang, L. L., Chu, S. C., Du, Z. G., & Pan, J.-S. (2023). Surrogate-assisted Phasmatodea population evolution algorithm applied to wireless sensor networks. *Wireless Networks*, *29*(2), 637–655. doi:10.1007/s11276-022-03168-6

Liu, Z. G., Yang, Y., & Ji, X. H. (2016). Flame detection algorithm based on a saliency detection technique and the uniform local binary pattern in the YCbCr color space. *Signal, Image and Video Processing*, *10*(2), 277–284. doi:10.1007/s11760-014-0738-0

Mall, P. K., Pramanik, S., Srivastava, S., Faiz, M., Sriramulu, S., & Kumar, M. N. (2023). FuzztNet-Based Modelling Smart Traffic System in Smart Cities Using Deep Learning Models. In *Data-Driven Mathematical Modeling in Smart Cities*. IGI Global. doi:10.4018/978-1-6684-6408-3.ch005

Mandal, A., Dutta, S., & Pramanik, S. (2021). Machine Intelligence of Pi from Geometrical Figures with Variable Parameters using SCILab. In D. Samanta, R. R. Althar, S. Pramanik, & S. Dutta (Eds.), *Methodologies and Applications of Computational Statistics for Machine Learning* (pp. 38–63). IGI Global. doi:10.4018/978-1-7998-7701-1.ch003

Meslie, Y., Enbeyle, W., Pandey, B. K., Pramanik, S., Pandey, D., Dadeech, P., Belay, A., & Saini, A. (2021). Machine Intelligence-based Trend Analysis of COVID-19 for Total Daily Confirmed Cases in Asia and Africa. In D. Samanta, R. R. Althar, S. Pramanik, & S. Dutta (Eds.), *Methodologies and Applications of Computational Statistics for Machine Learning* (pp. 164–185). IGI Global. doi:10.4018/978-1-7998-7701-1.ch009

Mondal, D., Ratnaparkhi, A., Deshpande, A., Deshpande, V., Kshirsagar, A. P., & Pramanik, S. (2023). Applications, Modern Trends and Challenges of Multiscale Modelling in Smart Cities. In *Data-Driven Mathematical Modeling in Smart Cities*. IGI Global. doi:10.4018/978-1-6684-6408-3.ch001

Murali, S., Govindan, V. K., & Kalady, S. (2022). Quaternion-based image shadow removal. *The Visual Computer*, *38*(5), 1527–1538. doi:10.1007/s00371-021-02086-6

Nagulan, S., Srinivasa Krishnan, A. N., Kiran Kumar, A., Vishnu Kumar, S., & Suchithra, M. (2023). An Efficient Real-Time Fire Detection Method Using Computer Vision and Neural Network-Based Video Analysis. In: Khanna, A., Gupta, D., Kansal, V., Fortino, G., Hassanien, A.E. (eds) *Proceedings of Third Doctoral Symposium on Computational Intelligence. Lecture Notes in Networks and Systems.* Springer, Singapore. 10.1007/978-981-19-3148-2_55

Ozkan, O., & Kilic, S. (2023). UAV routing by simulation-based optimization approaches for forest fire risk mitigation. *Annals of Operations Research*, *320*(2), 937–973. doi:10.1007/s10479-021-04393-6

Pradhan, D., Sahu, P. K., Goje, N. S., Myo, H., Ghonge, M. M., Tun, M., Rajeswari, R., & Pramanik, S. (2022). Security, Privacy, Risk, and Safety Toward 5G Green Network (5G-GN). Cyber Security and Network Security. Wiley. doi:10.1002/9781119812555.ch9

Pramanik, S. (2023). An Adaptive Image Steganography Approach depending on Integer Wavelet Transform and Genetic Algorithm. *Multimedia Tools and Applications*, *82*(22), 34287–34319. doi:10.1007/s11042-023-14505-y

Wang, Z., Sun, X., Zhang, X., Han, T., & Gao, F. (2020). Algorithm Improvement of Pedestrians' Red-Light Running Snapshot System Based on Image Recognition. In Q. Liang, W. Wang, X. Liu, Z. Na, M. Jia, & B. Zhang (Eds.), *Communications, Signal Processing, and Systems. CSPS 2019. Lecture Notes in Electrical Engineering* (Vol. 571). Springer. doi:10.1007/978-981-13-9409-6_207

Wu, Z., Xue, R., & Li, H. (2022). Real-Time Video Fire Detection via Modified YOLOv5 Network Model. *Fire Technology*, *58*(4), 2377–2403. doi:10.1007/s10694-022-01260-z

Yang, J., Ge, H., Yang, J., Tong, Y., & Su, S. (2022). Online multi-object tracking using multi-function integration and tracking simulation training. *Applied Intelligence*, *52*(2), 1268–1288. doi:10.1007/s10489-021-02457-5

Zhang, J., Yu, Z., Cheng, Y., Sha, X., & Zhang, H. (2022). A novel hierarchical framework to evaluate residential exposure to green spaces. *Landscape Ecology*, *37*(3), 895–911. doi:10.1007/s10980-021-01378-5

Zhang, N., Zhang, N., Zheng, Q., & Xu, Y.-S. (2022). Real-time prediction of shield moving trajectory during tunnelling using GRU deep neural network. *Acta Geotechnica*, *17*(4), 1167–1182. doi:10.1007/s11440-021-01319-1

Chapter 21
AI-Driven Cloud Computing to Revolutionize Industries and Overcome Challenges

S. Poonguzhali
https://orcid.org/0000-0002-9118-9018
VISTAS, India

A. Revathi
VISTAS, India

ABSTRACT

In recent years, the convergence of artificial intelligence (AI) and machine learning (ML) with cloud computing has sparked a revolution in the way businesses process, analyze, and utilize data. This synergy has paved the way for unprecedented advancements in various industries, from healthcare to finance, manufacturing to entertainment. This chapter explores the profound impacts of AI and ML integration in cloud computing, dissecting their implications on scalability, efficiency, security, and innovation. The integration of AI and ML algorithms within cloud computing infrastructures has led to a paradigm shift in the processing and analysis of large-scale datasets. Leveraging the extensive computational power and storage capabilities of cloud platforms, AI-driven models have demonstrated remarkable proficiency in tasks ranging from image and speech recognition to natural language processing. This has empowered businesses to extract valuable insights and automate complex processes, significantly enhancing operational efficiency.

INTRODUCTION

In the annals of technological progress, few convergences have been as transformative as the fusion of Artificial Intelligence (AI) and Machine Learning (ML) with the boundless capabilities of Cloud Computing. This unprecedented synergy has unleashed a wave of innovation and efficiency that resonates

DOI: 10.4018/979-8-3693-0900-1.ch021

across industries, reshaping the very fabric of how businesses operate and deliver value in the digital age (El Khatib et al., 2019).

Artificial Intelligence, once confined to the realms of science fiction, has evolved into a dynamic discipline with real-world applications that range from self-driving cars to personalized medical diagnoses (Dodge et al., 2022). This evolution has been propelled by the advent of Machine Learning, a subfield of AI that empowers systems to learn and adapt from data, without explicit programming. With the surge of computational power and the proliferation of vast datasets, ML algorithms have achieved feats that were once deemed improbable (Retico et al., 2021). Simultaneously, Cloud Computing has emerged as the linchpin of modern IT infrastructure. Its promise of virtually limitless computational resources and scalable storage has revolutionized how businesses manage and process data (Dozono et al., 2022). Cloud platforms have democratized access to high-performance computing, enabling even small enterprises and startups to harness computational capabilities that were once the exclusive domain of tech giants (Walsh et al., 2021).

The convergence of AI/ML and Cloud Computing stands as a watershed moment in the digital revolution. The amalgamation of AI's cognitive capabilities and ML's adaptability with the computational prowess of Cloud Computing has ushered in an era of unparalleled potential. It has not only amplified the capabilities of existing applications but also paved the way for entirely new paradigms in computing (Marshall & Lambert, 2018).

This convergence addresses a fundamental challenge faced by businesses and researchers alike: the ability to process and make sense of colossal volumes of data. Traditional computing approaches falter when confronted with the sheer scale and complexity of modern datasets (Marshall & Lambert, 2018). AI, particularly when paired with ML, provides a solution by endowing systems with the capacity to autonomously discern patterns, extract insights, and make informed decisions from this deluge of information.

Furthermore, the marriage of AI/ML and Cloud Computing has transcended the boundaries of raw processing power. It has given rise to intelligent systems that can dynamically adapt to fluctuating demands (Muhammad et al., 2018). This adaptability, driven by AI's capacity to learn and optimize, ensures that resources are allocated precisely where and when they are needed, optimizing both performance and cost-effectiveness.

In parallel, this integration addresses one of the most pressing concerns in the realm of Cloud Computing: security. The dynamic nature of cloud environments, with data traversing vast networks, necessitates robust security measures (Sharma & Singh, 2022). AI-driven security systems, equipped with anomaly detection, behavior analysis, and threat intelligence, provide a new level of vigilance against cyber threats. Encryption techniques and privacy-preserving algorithms have evolved to safeguard sensitive data, fostering trust in cloud-based services (Gill et al., 2019).

As we navigate the landscape of AI and ML within the context of Cloud Computing, it is imperative to consider the ethical dimensions that accompany this technological leap. Questions of bias in algorithms, data privacy, and responsible AI development loom large. Striking a balance between innovation and ethical responsibility is paramount to ensure that the benefits of this convergence are equitably distributed and harnessed for the betterment of society.

LITERATURE SURVEY

To provide a health monitoring system, Desai et al., (Desai et al., 2022) developed a model called "Health Cloud" which monitors the status of the health of heart patients. The author combined machine learning and cloud computing to develop this model. A prototype iOS mobile application has been developed using coreML and the dataset for it was collected from UCI repository's heart disease directory. To find the best suitable algorithm for the model, the author compared various ML algorithms such as Support Vector Machine, K Nearest Neighbors, Neural Networks, Logistic Regression and Gradient boosting and the results showed that the Logistic Regression has outperformed other algorithms in terms of latency performance, compatibility with mobile application and highest accuracy.

Another example of combining cloud and AI is prediction of covid-19, Shreshth Tuli et al., (2020) has developed an ml based prediction model, called Robust Weibull fitting, to predict the growth of covid-19 using ML and cloud computing. The dataset used in this paper is collected from thw World Health Organization (WHO). The author has used Azure B1s virtual machines with 1 GiB RAM and 64 bit MS windows server 2016. They have taken use of Health fog framework for increasing the multiple analysis tasks with FogBus. Finally, the model combined 4 iterative versions called Gaussian, Beta, Fisher-Tippet and Log normal function which resulted in an average MAPE of 12% lower than non-iteratively weighted weilbull.

To improve virtual machine (VM) migration, Ali Belgacem et al., (2023) proposed a machine learning model to improvise VM migration in cloud computing. The author's model is of two phases namely, ML preparing stage and Learning model creation stage. The cloudsim 3.0.3 toolkit was used to simulate the cloud environment components. The final results showed that the model's complexity is lower which allowed it to get the best results faster along with dynamic resource allocation automatically.

For Real-time prediction, the author, Hanjie Zhang et al., (2023) developed a model to predict in-tradialytic hypotension using ML and cloud computing infrastructure. The data was collected from 693 patients in real-time which contributed 42656 hemodialysis sessions. The model got an AUROC of 0.89 where 16% of Intradialytic hypotension was occurred. Finally, the model predicted the disease 15 to 75 minutes in advance.

Historical Context

The convergence of Artificial Intelligence, Machine Learning, and Cloud Computing finds its roots in the decades-long evolution of these individual fields.

Artificial Intelligence, conceived in the 1950s, initially aimed to replicate human intelligence in machines (Valko et al., 2022). Early pioneers like Alan Turing laid the groundwork for computational intelligence, while the Dartmouth Conference in 1956 marked the formal birth of AI as a field of study. The ensuing years saw both significant progress and periods of stagnation, as AI transitioned from symbolic reasoning to more statistically-driven approaches. Notable milestones included the development of expert systems in the 1970s and the emergence of neural networks in the 1980s (Kunduru, 2023).

Machine Learning, a subset of AI, took a data-centric approach to intelligence. Its origins can be traced back to the 1940s and 1950s with the introduction of perceptrons and early work on pattern recognition (Yathiraju, 2022). However, it was in the latter half of the 20th century that ML gained substantial traction, with advancements in algorithms like decision trees, support vector machines, and

Figure 1. Applications of AI/ML integrated Cloud computing

neural networks. The advent of big data in the 21st century provided the fertile ground on which ML truly flourished (Tiwari et al., 2021).

Cloud Computing emerged in the early 2000s, heralding a revolution in how computing resources were provisioned and accessed. Amazon Web Services (AWS) played a pioneering role by introducing Infrastructure as a Service (IaaS) in 2006, allowing businesses to rent virtual servers. This marked a fundamental shift from traditional on-premises infrastructure, as it offered scalability, elasticity, and cost-efficiency. Subsequently, other tech giants such as Microsoft and Google entered the arena, further propelling the cloud revolution (Mohammed et al., 2023).

The convergence of these fields was catalyzed by the increasing computational demands of AI and ML. Traditional on-premises infrastructure struggled to cope with the computational resources required for training and deploying sophisticated AI models (Misra et al., 2022). Cloud platforms, with their vast computational power and scalable resources, provided the ideal environment for the integration of AI/ML with Cloud Computing. This convergence not only unlocked new possibilities but also democratized access to cutting-edge AI technologies (Donahue & Hajizadeh, 2019). Some applications of AL/ML integrated cloud computing are given in Figure 1.

The historical journey of AI, ML, and Cloud Computing laid the foundation for their symbiotic relationship. This convergence represents a culmination of decades of research, experimentation, and technological advancement, culminating in a synergy that has the potential to redefine the boundaries of what is achievable in the realm of information technology.

SCALABILITY AND EFFICIENCY

Cloud Computing has revolutionized the way organizations manage their computational resources, offering unprecedented scalability and efficiency (Susila et al., 2020). The integration of Artificial Intelligence (AI) and Machine Learning (ML) within this framework has further amplified these capabilities, ushering in a new era of dynamic and adaptable computing.

Cloud Computing as an Enabler of Scalability: The essence of Cloud Computing lies in its ability to scale resources on-demand. Traditionally, businesses were constrained by the physical limitations of their own infrastructure (Zolfaghari et al., 2022). However, cloud platforms break these barriers, allowing organizations to effortlessly scale their computational resources in response to fluctuating workloads. This capability is invaluable in scenarios where computational demands are subject to rapid changes, such as during seasonal spikes in online shopping or sudden surges in web traffic (Mungoli, 2023). With just a few clicks, organizations can provision additional virtual machines or storage, ensuring uninterrupted service delivery.

Dynamic Resource Allocation and Auto-Scaling: The integration of AI and ML within Cloud Computing brings an added layer of adaptability (Kaginalkar et al., 2021). AI-driven applications possess the intelligence to monitor system performance and make real-time adjustments. Through techniques like auto-scaling, cloud resources can be dynamically allocated based on current demands. For instance, an e-commerce platform leveraging AI-powered recommendation engines can automatically scale its resources during peak shopping hours, ensuring that customers receive personalized suggestions without encountering delays. This dynamic allocation of resources optimizes performance while minimizing unnecessary costs during periods of lower demand (Gill et al., 2022).

Efficiency Gains through AI and ML: The marriage of AI and ML with Cloud Computing also leads to substantial efficiency gains. ML algorithms excel at automating repetitive tasks, optimizing processes, and identifying patterns within data. When deployed in cloud environments, these algorithms can streamline operations, leading to faster and more accurate outcomes (Sun et al., 2019). For example, in data-intensive industries like finance or healthcare, AI-powered data analytics running on cloud platforms can process vast datasets to extract insights and make informed decisions in real-time. This not only accelerates decision-making but also frees up human resources for more strategic endeavors.

Case Studies Demonstrating Enhanced Efficiency: Numerous case studies exemplify the tangible impact of this integration. One notable example is the use of AI-driven predictive maintenance in the manufacturing sector. By analyzing sensor data from machinery, AI algorithms can anticipate potential failures and schedule maintenance activities precisely when needed. When combined with the scalability of cloud resources, this approach ensures that maintenance efforts are targeted, minimizing downtime and maximizing operational efficiency (Mustapha et al., 2021). Similarly, in the realm of customer service, AI-powered chatbots operating on cloud platforms have revolutionized customer interactions. These virtual agents can handle a vast volume of inquiries in real-time, providing swift and accurate responses. The result is not only improved customer satisfaction but also substantial cost savings for businesses (Mishra & Tyagi, 2022).

In essence, the convergence of AI/ML and Cloud Computing represents a quantum leap in scalability and efficiency. The dynamic allocation of resources and the automation of tasks, underpinned by intelligent algorithms, redefine the boundaries of what is achievable in computational processing. These advancements not only enhance the capabilities of existing applications but also pave the way for entirely new paradigms in computing, driving innovation and economic growth.

Security and Privacy

The integration of Artificial Intelligence (AI) and Machine Learning (ML) in Cloud Computing has not only revolutionized processing power and efficiency but has also significantly elevated security measures (Suo et al., 2021). This convergence addresses traditional security concerns while introducing innovative approaches to safeguarding data and systems.

Traditional Security Concerns in Cloud Computing: Historically, Cloud Computing has faced scrutiny over security. Concerns such as unauthorized access, data breaches, and compliance with industry-specific regulations have been paramount. However, the integration of AI/ML introduces a new era of proactive security measures. It shifts the paradigm from reactive defenses to intelligent, anticipatory approaches.

AI-Driven Cybersecurity Solutions: AI-powered security systems are at the forefront of this revolution (Hwang, 2018). These systems utilize advanced algorithms to monitor network traffic, detect anomalies, and identify potential threats in real-time. By analyzing patterns in user behavior and network activity, AI-driven solutions can swiftly identify and respond to suspicious activities, mitigating risks before they escalate. This level of vigilance offers a formidable defense against evolving cyber threats.

Data Privacy and Encryption Advancements: Data privacy, a critical concern in the digital age, has been further bolstered by the convergence of AI/ML and Cloud Computing. Advanced encryption techniques, including homomorphic encryption and differential privacy, allow sensitive data to be processed and analyzed while remaining encrypted. This ensures that even in the event of a breach, the underlying information remains unintelligible to unauthorized parties (Spjuth et al., 2021). Additionally, the secure execution of AI models on encrypted data has become a reality, enabling organizations to derive valuable insights without compromising privacy.

Ethical Considerations and Challenges: As the capabilities of AI-driven security systems expand, ethical considerations come to the forefront. Issues of bias and fairness in algorithms, as well as concerns surrounding user consent and transparency, must be carefully addressed (Naved et al., 2022). Striking a balance between leveraging AI for enhanced security and respecting individual rights is paramount. The responsible development and deployment of AI-powered security measures ensure that the benefits are equitably distributed and do not infringe on privacy rights.

Case Studies Illustrating Enhanced Security Measures: Real-world applications exemplify the tangible impact of AI-powered security in Cloud Computing. For instance, financial institutions leverage AI algorithms to detect anomalous transactions that may indicate fraudulent activity. These algorithms continuously learn from vast datasets, adapting to new fraud patterns and minimizing false positives. In the healthcare sector, AI-driven anomaly detection is employed to safeguard patient data. By monitoring access patterns and user behavior, these systems can promptly identify and mitigate unauthorized access attempts (Bhardwaj & Kaushik, 2022).

The convergence of AI/ML and Cloud Computing not only addresses traditional security concerns but also introduces innovative solutions that fundamentally change the landscape of cybersecurity. By harnessing the power of intelligent algorithms, organizations can proactively defend against threats, ensure data privacy, and uphold ethical standards. This revolution in security measures represents a significant stride towards building trust in cloud-based services and fortifying the digital infrastructure of the modern world (Mourtzis, 2022).

Innovation and Industry Transformations

The integration of Artificial Intelligence (AI) and Machine Learning (ML) with Cloud Computing has sparked a wave of innovation, redefining how industries operate and deliver value. This convergence has not only enhanced existing applications but has also paved the way for entirely new paradigms, revolutionizing sectors across the board.

AI-Powered Applications in Various Industries: The transformative impact of AI and ML is perhaps most palpable in the diverse range of industries that have embraced this convergence. In healthcare, for example, AI-driven diagnostic tools have proven invaluable in detecting diseases and conditions with unprecedented accuracy. Likewise, in finance, algorithms leveraging ML techniques are revolutionizing risk assessment, fraud detection, and investment strategies (Muralidhara, 2017). In manufacturing, AI-powered automation is driving unprecedented levels of efficiency and precision, transforming production processes. These examples merely scratch the surface of the myriad ways in which AI/ML and Cloud Computing are reshaping industries.

Case Studies Showcasing Innovative Solutions: Examining specific case studies underscores the profound influence of this convergence. Consider the emergence of autonomous vehicles, made possible by the integration of AI algorithms with the computational capabilities of cloud platforms. These vehicles utilize real-time data processing and decision-making, revolutionizing transportation and redefining urban planning. In the realm of personalized healthcare, AI-driven models can analyze vast genomic datasets, offering tailored treatment plans and accelerating drug discovery. These innovations not only improve patient outcomes but also represent significant strides towards a more efficient and effective healthcare system (Akter et al., 2022).

Economic and Societal Impacts of AI-Driven Transformations: The economic and societal ramifications of these innovations are far-reaching. Industries that harness the power of AI/ML in conjunction with Cloud Computing are positioned to achieve unprecedented levels of productivity and competitiveness. This, in turn, fuels economic growth and job creation. Moreover, advancements in areas such as personalized medicine and renewable energy, driven by this convergence, hold the promise of addressing some of society's most pressing challenges. By revolutionizing how we approach healthcare, energy, transportation, and more, this synergy contributes to a more sustainable and inclusive future.

Fostering an Ecosystem of Innovation: The integration of AI/ML and Cloud Computing has not only catalyzed innovation within individual industries but has also given rise to a burgeoning ecosystem of startups, research initiatives, and collaborative ventures. These endeavors leverage the accessibility and scalability of cloud platforms to develop cutting-edge applications and services (Stein, Campitelli, & Mezzio, 2020). The democratization of technology through cloud-based resources empowers even nascent companies to pioneer groundbreaking solutions, leveling the playing field and promoting a culture of continuous innovation.

Ethical Considerations

As the integration of Artificial Intelligence (AI) and Machine Learning (ML) with Cloud Computing propels technological advancement, it brings forth a host of ethical considerations that demand careful scrutiny. Balancing innovation with ethical responsibility is paramount to ensure the responsible development and deployment of these transformative technologies.

Bias and Fairness in Algorithms: One of the foremost ethical concerns in AI/ML is the potential for bias in algorithms. AI systems learn from historical data, which may contain implicit biases. If not addressed, these biases can perpetuate existing inequalities and lead to discriminatory outcomes (Stein, Campitelli, & Mezzio, 2020). It is imperative that developers and organizations implement measures to detect and mitigate bias, ensuring that AI systems are fair and just in their decision-making processes.

Data Privacy and User Consent: The convergence of AI/ML and Cloud Computing hinges on the collection and analysis of vast amounts of data. This raises significant privacy concerns, particularly regarding sensitive personal information. Striking a balance between leveraging data for innovation and respecting individual privacy rights is a critical ethical challenge. Obtaining informed consent from users for data collection and processing is a cornerstone of responsible AI development.

Responsible AI Development and Deployment Practices: Ensuring the responsible development and deployment of AI systems requires a holistic approach. This encompasses transparent documentation of algorithms and methodologies, adherence to industry best practices, and robust testing procedures. Moreover, organizations must establish mechanisms for ongoing monitoring and evaluation to detect and rectify ethical issues that may arise during the lifecycle of an AI system.

Transparency and Explainability: The black-box nature of some AI models poses a significant ethical challenge. Understanding how these models arrive at their decisions is crucial, particularly in high-stakes applications such as healthcare or finance. Efforts to develop interpretable AI models, as well as mechanisms to provide explanations for their decisions, are essential for building trust and accountability (Dube et al., 2019).

Ensuring Accessibility and Inclusivity: The benefits of AI/ML integrated with Cloud Computing should be accessible to all, irrespective of factors such as economic status, geography, or physical ability. Ethical considerations extend to ensuring that these technologies do not exacerbate existing disparities, but rather, are leveraged to bridge gaps and create opportunities for marginalized communities.

Adherence to Regulatory and Ethical Frameworks: Compliance with existing regulations and ethical frameworks is a cornerstone of responsible AI deployment. This includes adherence to data protection laws, industry-specific guidelines, and ethical standards set forth by professional organizations. Organizations must proactively engage with regulatory bodies and stakeholders to navigate the evolving landscape of AI ethics.

Continuous Education and Ethical Awareness: Fostering a culture of ethical awareness and responsibility is a collective endeavor. This involves providing education and training to developers, data scientists, and stakeholders involved in AI projects. By instilling a deep understanding of ethical considerations, organizations can ensure that responsible practices are ingrained in the development process.

Technical Challenges and Future Trends

The integration of Artificial Intelligence (AI) and Machine Learning (ML) with Cloud Computing has propelled innovation, but not without encountering a set of technical challenges. Understanding and addressing these hurdles is essential to ensure the continued advancement and sustainable growth of this transformative convergence.

Complexity of AI/ML Models in Cloud Environments: The complexity of deploying and managing AI/ML models within cloud environments is a substantial technical challenge. These models often require specialized hardware, optimized software frameworks, and large-scale computational resources.

Ensuring seamless integration and performance optimization in the cloud ecosystem demands continuous research and development efforts.

Resource Requirements for Training and Deployment: The training of sophisticated AI models, particularly deep learning architectures, demands substantial computational resources. Cloud platforms must offer the necessary infrastructure to facilitate the training process efficiently. Additionally, the deployment of trained models for real-time inference requires careful consideration of latency, scalability, and cost-effectiveness.

Optimizing for Cost and Energy Efficiency: Balancing computational power with cost-effectiveness and energy efficiency is a critical technical consideration. Cloud providers and organizations must employ strategies such as auto-scaling, resource allocation algorithms, and energy-aware computing to optimize the utilization of resources while minimizing operational expenses and environmental impact.

Ensuring Data Security in Cloud-Based AI/ML Systems: The dynamic nature of cloud environments, with data traversing vast networks, introduces unique security challenges. Ensuring data integrity and confidentiality, particularly in multi-tenant environments, requires robust encryption techniques and access controls. Additionally, organizations must implement rigorous identity and access management protocols to safeguard sensitive information.

Interoperability and Standardization: As the landscape of AI/ML tools and frameworks continues to evolve, ensuring interoperability and standardization becomes imperative. Seamless integration between various components of the AI/ML stack, including data preprocessing, model training, and deployment, is crucial for the efficient development and deployment of applications.

FUTURE TRENDS

Advancements in Federated Learning: Federated Learning, a paradigm where models are trained across decentralized devices or servers holding local data samples, is poised to play a pivotal role. This approach addresses privacy concerns by keeping data localized, while still benefiting from collaborative model training. The trends of AI and cloud computing are given in Figure 2.

Edge Computing and AI at the Edge: Edge Computing, which involves processing data closer to its source, is gaining prominence. Combining AI with Edge Computing allows for real-time decision-making and reduced reliance on centralized cloud resources. This trend is particularly relevant for applications like IoT, autonomous vehicles, and augmented reality.

Explainable AI and Ethical AI Frameworks: Advancements in Explainable AI aim to make AI models more interpretable and transparent, addressing concerns regarding trust and accountability. Additionally, the development of ethical AI frameworks will play a crucial role in ensuring responsible AI development and deployment.

Quantum Computing and AI: The intersection of Quantum Computing and AI holds promise for solving complex problems that are currently beyond the capabilities of classical computing. Quantum AI algorithms may revolutionize fields such as optimization, cryptography, and material science.

APPLICATIONS OF AI/ML IN CLOUD COMPUTING

1: Healthcare - IBM Watson for Oncology

Figure 2. Trends of AI and cloud computing

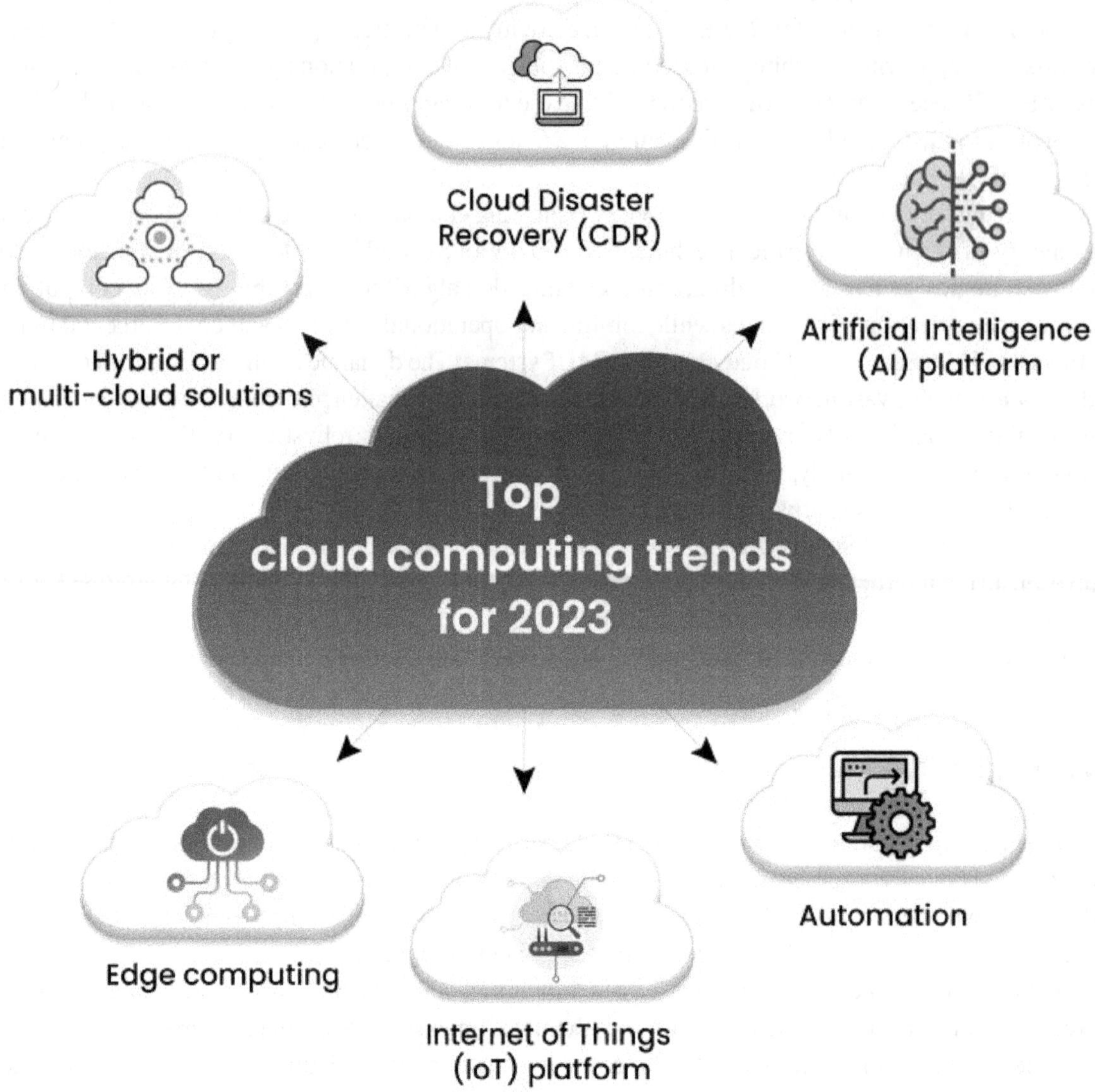

In the field of healthcare, the integration of AI and Cloud Computing has yielded groundbreaking advancements. IBM Watson for Oncology exemplifies this synergy. By leveraging the computational power of the cloud, Watson analyzes vast volumes of medical literature, clinical trial data, and patient records to assist oncologists in making treatment decisions. This AI-powered system provides personalized treatment recommendations based on the latest research, enabling clinicians to deliver more targeted and effective care to cancer patients.

2: Finance - Fraud Detection with Amazon SageMaker

In the financial sector, the marriage of AI/ML with Cloud Computing has revolutionized fraud detection. Amazon SageMaker, a cloud-based machine learning platform, exemplifies this transformation. By utilizing SageMaker's robust suite of ML tools and the scalability of AWS cloud resources, financial institutions can deploy sophisticated fraud detection models. These models analyze transactional data in real-time, identifying suspicious activities and mitigating fraudulent transactions before they occur. This integration not only enhances security but also reduces financial losses for both institutions and customers.

3: Manufacturing - Predictive Maintenance with Google Cloud AI

Predictive maintenance in manufacturing has been revolutionized by the convergence of AI/ML and Cloud Computing. Google Cloud AI provides a powerful platform for implementing these solutions. By utilizing IoT sensors to gather real-time data from machinery, and leveraging Google's cloud infrastructure, manufacturers can apply machine learning algorithms to predict when equipment is likely to fail. This enables proactive maintenance measures, minimizing downtime, reducing maintenance costs, and optimizing overall operational efficiency.

4: Retail - Personalized Recommendations with Azure Machine Learning

In the retail industry, personalized customer experiences have become a cornerstone of success. Microsoft Azure Machine Learning, integrated with Cloud Computing, has transformed how retailers engage with their customers. By analyzing customer behavior, purchase history, and preferences, retailers can deploy recommendation engines that provide tailored product suggestions. This not only enhances customer satisfaction but also drives increased sales and customer loyalty, demonstrating the profound impact of AI-powered personalization in the retail sector.

5: Autonomous Vehicles - NVIDIA and NVIDIA Drive AGX

The convergence of AI, ML, and Cloud Computing is revolutionizing the automotive industry, particularly in the development of autonomous vehicles. NVIDIA's Drive AGX platform is at the forefront of this transformation. By harnessing the computational capabilities of cloud resources, coupled with on-board AI processors, Drive AGX enables vehicles to process massive amounts of sensor data in real-time. This allows for advanced perception, mapping, and decision-making capabilities, paving the way for safer and more efficient autonomous transportation systems.

These applications exemplify how the integration of AI and ML with Cloud Computing has revolutionized various industries, showcasing the practical applications and tangible impacts of this convergence. Each example highlights the transformative potential of leveraging AI/ML in conjunction with the computational power and scalability of cloud platforms.

SOLUTIONS AND RECOMMENDATIONS

Complexity of AI/ML Models in Cloud Environments:

Solution: Develop specialized tools and frameworks that streamline the deployment of AI models in cloud environments. Provide pre-configured environments optimized for specific AI tasks. Offer comprehensive documentation and tutorials for users to navigate the complexities.

Resource Requirements for Training and Deployment:

Solution: Implement auto-scaling capabilities that dynamically allocate resources based on the computational demands of AI/ML tasks. Provide cost-effective pricing models for training and deployment, such as spot instances or reserved instances. Offer specialized hardware configurations for accelerated model training.

Optimizing for Cost and Energy Efficiency:

Solution: Utilize auto-scaling and resource optimization algorithms to ensure that computational resources are used efficiently. Implement energy-efficient hardware and explore renewable energy sources for data centers. Provide cost monitoring and budgeting tools to help users manage expenses.

Ensuring Data Security in Cloud-Based AI/ML Systems:

Solution: Implement robust encryption mechanisms to protect data both in transit and at rest. Utilize secure access controls and multi-factor authentication to prevent unauthorized access. Regularly audit and monitor access logs for any suspicious activities.

Interoperability and Standardization:

Solution: Encourage collaboration between AI/ML tool providers to establish interoperable standards and protocols. Develop open-source initiatives that promote standardized interfaces and data formats. Provide compatibility layers for popular AI frameworks to ensure seamless integration.

Advancements in Federated Learning:

Solution: Invest in research and development of federated learning techniques that enable secure and efficient model training across decentralized devices. Offer platforms and tools that facilitate federated learning implementations, providing resources for model aggregation and synchronization.

Edge Computing and AI at the Edge:

Solution: Develop specialized edge computing platforms that seamlessly integrate with cloud environments. Provide tools for deploying and managing AI models on edge devices. Offer latency-aware solutions that optimize the distribution of workloads between edge and cloud resources.

Explainable AI and Ethical AI Frameworks:

Solution: Invest in research to develop interpretable AI models that provide transparent explanations for their decisions. Implement ethical AI frameworks that incorporate fairness, accountability, and transparency (FAT) principles. Offer tools for auditing and validating AI systems for compliance with ethical guidelines.

Quantum Computing and AI:

Solution: Foster collaboration between quantum computing experts and AI researchers to explore applications of quantum algorithms in AI tasks. Provide specialized quantum computing platforms that facilitate experimentation and development of quantum AI algorithms.

By implementing these solutions, organizations and cloud providers can address the challenges posed by the integration of AI/ML with Cloud Computing, enabling the realization of the full potential of this transformative convergence.

CONCLUSION AND FUTURE DIRECTIONS

The integration of Artificial Intelligence (AI) and Machine Learning (ML) with Cloud Computing marks a pivotal moment in the evolution of information technology. This convergence has not only amplified the capabilities of existing applications but has also paved the way for entirely new paradigms in computing. The amalgamation of AI's cognitive capabilities and ML's adaptability with the computational prowess of Cloud Computing has ushered in an era of unparalleled potential.

From healthcare to finance, manufacturing to retail, the transformative impacts of this convergence are evident across diverse industries. AI-powered diagnostic tools are revolutionizing healthcare, while fraud detection algorithms are fortifying the financial sector. Predictive maintenance is optimizing manufacturing processes, and personalized recommendations are reshaping retail experiences. Autonomous vehicles, empowered by AI and Cloud Computing, are on the cusp of revolutionizing transportation. The benefits extend beyond industry-specific applications. Scalability, efficiency, security, and privacy have been elevated to new heights, driven by intelligent algorithms and dynamic cloud resources. Ethical considerations, once confined to theoretical discourse, have now become central to responsible AI development and deployment. However, this transformative convergence is not without its challenges. The complexity of deploying AI/ML models in cloud environments, resource optimization, and ensuring data security remain critical technical considerations. Ethical dilemmas surrounding bias, privacy, and transparency demand vigilant attention. Striking a balance between innovation and ethical responsibility is paramount.

As we look to the future, the landscape of AI/ML integrated with Cloud Computing is poised for further evolution. Advancements in federated learning, quantum computing, and edge computing hold promise for unlocking new frontiers. Explainable AI and ethical frameworks will continue to shape responsible development practices. In conclusion, the integration of AI/ML with Cloud Computing represents a monumental shift in how industries operate, innovate, and serve society. By navigating technical challenges and ethical considerations, we can harness the full potential of this convergence. With responsible development practices and a steadfast commitment to ethical principles, we stand on the brink of a future where the possibilities of AI/ML integrated with Cloud Computing are limited only by our imagination and ethical compass.

REFERENCES

Akter, S., Michael, K., Uddin, M. R., McCarthy, G., & Rahman, M. (2022). Transforming business using digital innovations: The application of AI, blockchain, cloud and data analytics. *Annals of Operations Research, 308*(1-2), 1–33. doi:10.1007/s10479-020-03620-w PMID:35935743

Belgacem, A., Mahmoudi, S., & Ferrag, M. A. (2023). A machine learning model for improving virtual machine migration in cloud computing. *The Journal of Supercomputing*, *79*(9), 1–23. doi:10.1007/s11227-022-05031-z

Bhardwaj, A., & Kaushik, K. (2022). Predictive analytics-based cybersecurity framework for cloud infrastructure. *International Journal of Cloud Applications and Computing*, *12*(1), 1–20. doi:10.4018/IJCAC.297106

Desai, F., Chowdhury, D., Kaur, R., Peeters, M., Arya, R., Wander, G., Gill, S. S., & Buyya, R. (2022). HealthCloud: A system for monitoring health status of heart patients using machine learning and cloud computing. *Internet of Things : Engineering Cyber Physical Human Systems*, *17*, 100485. doi:10.1016/j.iot.2021.100485

Dodge, J., Prewitt, T., Tachet des Combes, R., Odmark, E., Schwartz, R., Strubell, E., & Buchanan, W. (2022, June). Measuring the carbon intensity of AI in cloud instances. In *Proceedings of the 2022 ACM Conference on Fairness, Accountability, and Transparency* (pp. 1877-1894). ACM. 10.1145/3531146.3533234

Donahue, L., & Hajizadeh, F. (2019). Artificial intelligence in cloud marketing. *Artificial Intelligence and machine learning for business for non-engineers*, 77-88. Routledge.

Dozono, K., Amalathas, S., & Saravanan, R. (2022). The impact of cloud computing and artificial intelligence in digital agriculture. In *Proceedings of Sixth International Congress on Information and Communication Technology: ICICT 2021, London,* Volume 1 (pp. 557-569). Springer Singapore. 10.1007/978-981-16-2377-6_52

Dube, P., Suk, T., & Wang, C. (2019, October). AI gauge: Runtime estimation for deep learning in the cloud. In *2019 31st International Symposium on Computer Architecture and High Performance Computing (SBAC-PAD)* (pp. 160-167). IEEE.

El Khatib, M. M., Al-Nakeeb, A., & Ahmed, G. (2019). Integration of cloud computing with artificial intelligence and Its impact on telecom sector—A case study. *iBusiness, 11*(01), 1.

Gill, S. S., Tuli, S., Xu, M., Singh, I., Singh, K. V., Lindsay, D., Tuli, S., Smirnova, D., Singh, M., Jain, U., Pervaiz, H., Sehgal, B., Kaila, S. S., Misra, S., Aslanpour, M. S., Mehta, H., Stankovski, V., & Garraghan, P. (2019). Transformative effects of IoT, Blockchain and Artificial Intelligence on cloud computing: Evolution, vision, trends and open challenges. *Internet of Things : Engineering Cyber Physical Human Systems, 8*, 100118. doi:10.1016/j.iot.2019.100118

Gill, S. S., Xu, M., Ottaviani, C., Patros, P., Bahsoon, R., Shaghaghi, A., Golec, M., Stankovski, V., Wu, H., Abraham, A., Singh, M., Mehta, H., Ghosh, S. K., Baker, T., Parlikad, A. K., Lutfiyya, H., Kanhere, S. S., Sakellariou, R., Dustdar, S., & Uhlig, S. (2022). AI for next generation computing: Emerging trends and future directions. *Internet of Things : Engineering Cyber Physical Human Systems, 19*, 100514. doi:10.1016/j.iot.2022.100514

Hwang, T. (2018). Computational power and the social impact of artificial intelligence. *arXiv preprint arXiv:1803.08971.*

Kaginalkar, A., Kumar, S., Gargava, P., & Niyogi, D. (2021). Review of urban computing in air quality management as smart city service: An integrated IoT, AI, and cloud technology perspective. *Urban Climate, 39*, 100972. doi:10.1016/j.uclim.2021.100972

Kunduru, A. R. (2023). Artificial intelligence usage in cloud application performance improvement. *Central Asian Journal of Mathematical Theory and Computer Sciences, 4*(8), 42–47.

Marshall, T. E., & Lambert, S. L. (2018). Cloud-based intelligent accounting applications: Accounting task automation using IBM watson cognitive computing. *Journal of Emerging Technologies in Accounting, 15*(1), 199–215. doi:10.2308/jeta-52095

Mishra, S., & Tyagi, A. K. (2022). The role of machine learning techniques in internet of things-based cloud applications. *Artificial intelligence-based internet of things systems*, 105-135.

Misra, S., Tyagi, A. K., Piuri, V., & Garg, L. (Eds.). (2022). *Artificial Intelligence for Cloud and Edge Computing*. Springer. doi:10.1007/978-3-030-80821-1

Mohammed, S., Fang, W. C., & Ramos, C. (2023). Special issue on "artificial intelligence in cloud computing". *Computing, 105*(3), 507–511. doi:10.1007/s00607-021-00985-z

Mourtzis, D. (2022). Introduction to cloud technology and Industry 4.0. In *Design and Operation of Production Networks for Mass Personalization in the Era of Cloud Technology* (pp. 1–12). Elsevier. doi:10.1016/B978-0-12-823657-4.00011-7

Muhammad, T., Munir, M. T., Munir, M. Z., & Zafar, M. W. (2018). Elevating Business Operations: The Transformative Power of Cloud Computing. *International Journal Of Computer Science And Technology*, *2*(1), 1–21.

Mungoli, N. (2023). Scalable, Distributed AI Frameworks: Leveraging Cloud Computing for Enhanced Deep Learning Performance and Efficiency. *arXiv preprint arXiv:2304.13738*.

Muralidhara, P. (2017). The evolution of cloud computing security: addressing emerging threats. *International journal of computer science and technology*, *1*(4), 1–33.

Mustapha, U. F., Alhassan, A. W., Jiang, D. N., & Li, G. L. (2021). Sustainable aquaculture development: A review on the roles of cloud computing, internet of things and artificial intelligence (CIA). *Reviews in Aquaculture*, *13*(4), 2076–2091. doi:10.1111/raq.12559

Naved, M., Fakih, A. H., Venkatesh, A. N., Vijayakumar, P., & Kshirsagar, P. R. (2022, May). Supervise the data security and performance in cloud using artificial intelligence. In AIP Conference Proceedings (Vol. 2393, No. 1). AIP Publishing.

Retico, A., Avanzo, M., Boccali, T., Bonacorsi, D., Botta, F., Cuttone, G., Martelli, B., Salomoni, D., Spiga, D., Trianni, A., Stasi, M., Iori, M., & Talamonti, C. (2021). Enhancing the impact of Artificial Intelligence in Medicine: A joint AIFM-INFN Italian initiative for a dedicated cloud-based computing infrastructure. *Physica Medica*, *91*, 140–150. doi:10.1016/j.ejmp.2021.10.005 PMID:34801873

Sharma, A., & Singh, U. K. (2022). Modelling of smart risk assessment approach for cloud computing environment using AI & supervised machine learning algorithms. *Global Transitions Proceedings*, *3*(1), 243–250. doi:10.1016/j.gltp.2022.03.030

Spjuth, O., Frid, J., & Hellander, A. (2021). The machine learning life cycle and the cloud: Implications for drug discovery. *Expert Opinion on Drug Discovery*, *16*(9), 1071–1079. doi:10.1080/17460441.2021.1932812 PMID:34057379

Stein, M., Campitelli, V., & Mezzio, S. (2020). Managing the impact of cloud computing. *The CPA Journal*, *90*(6), 20–27.

Sun, W., Liu, J., & Yue, Y. (2019). AI-enhanced offloading in edge computing: When machine learning meets industrial IoT. *IEEE Network*, *33*(5), 68–74. doi:10.1109/MNET.001.1800510

Suo, K., Shi, Y., Hung, C. C., & Bobbie, P. (2021, March). Quantifying context switch overhead of artificial intelligence workloads on the cloud and edges. In *Proceedings of the 36th Annual ACM Symposium on Applied Computing* (pp. 1182-1189). ACM. 10.1145/3412841.3441993

Susila, N., Sruthi, A., & Usha, S. (2020). Impact of cloud security in digital twin. *Advances in Computers*, *117*(1), 247–263. doi:10.1016/bs.adcom.2019.09.005

Tiwari, S., Bharadwaj, S., & Joshi, S. (2021). A study of impact of cloud computing and artificial intelligence on banking services, profitability and operational benefits. *Turkish Journal of Computer and Mathematics Education*, *12*(6), 1617–1627.

Tuli, S., Tuli, S., Tuli, R., & Gill, S. S. (2020). Predicting the growth and trend of COVID-19 pandemic using machine learning and cloud computing. *Internet of Things : Engineering Cyber Physical Human Systems*, *11*, 100222. doi:10.1016/j.iot.2020.100222

Valko, N. V., Goncharenko, T. L., Kushnir, N. O., & Osadchyi, V. V. (2022, March). Cloud technologies for basics of artificial intelligence study in school. In *CTE Workshop Proceedings* (Vol. 9, pp. 170-183). CTE. 10.55056/cte.113

Walsh, P., Bera, J., Sharma, V. S., Kaulgud, V., Rao, R. M., & Ross, O. (2021, November). Sustainable AI in the Cloud: Exploring machine learning energy use in the cloud. In *2021 36th IEEE/ACM International Conference on Automated Software Engineering Workshops (ASEW)* (pp. 265-266). IEEE.

Yathiraju, N. (2022). Investigating the use of an Artificial Intelligence Model in an ERP Cloud-Based System. *International Journal of Electrical. Electronics and Computers*, *7*(2), 1–26.

Zhang, H., Wang, L. C., Chaudhuri, S., Pickering, A., Usvyat, L., Larkin, J., Waguespack, P., Kuang, Z., Kooman, J. P., Maddux, F. W., & Kotanko, P. (2023). Real-time prediction of intradialytic hypotension using machine learning and cloud computing infrastructure. *Nephrology, Dialysis, Transplantation*, *38*(7), gfad070. doi:10.1093/ndt/gfad070 PMID:37055366

Zolfaghari, B., Yazdinejad, A., Dehghantanha, A., Krzciok, J., & Bibak, K. (2022). The dichotomy of cloud and iot: Cloud-assisted iot from a security perspective. *arXiv preprint arXiv:2207.01590.*

Compilation of References

Aarthee, S., & Prabakaran, R. (2023). Energy-Aware Heuristic Scheduling Using Bin Packing MapReduce Scheduler for Heterogeneous Workloads Performance in Big Data. *Arabian Journal for Science and Engineering*, *48*(2), 1891–1905. doi:10.1007/s13369-022-06963-7

Abidin, S., Swami, A., Ramirez-Asís, E., Alvarado-Tolentino, J., Maurya, R. K., & Hussain, N. (2022). Quantum cryptography technique: A way to improve security challenges in mobile cloud computing (MCC). *Materials Today: Proceedings*, *51*, 508–514. doi:10.1016/j.matpr.2021.05.593

Acaru, S. F., Abdullah, R., Lai, D. T. C., & Lim, R. C. (2022). Hydrothermal biomass processing for green energy transition: Insights derived from principal component analysis of international patents. *Heliyon*, *8*(9), e10738. doi:10.1016/j.heliyon.2022.e10738 PMID:36177226

Adam, A., Finance, O., & Thomas, I. (2021). Monitoring trucks to reveal Belgian geographical structures and dynamics: From GPS traces to spatial interactions. *Journal of Transport Geography*, *91*, 102977. Advance online publication. doi:10.1016/j.jtrangeo.2021.102977

Adewojo, A. A., & Bass, J. M. (2023). A Novel Weight-Assignment Load Balancing Algorithm for Cloud Applications. *SN Computer Science*, *4*(3), 270. doi:10.1007/s42979-023-01702-7

Admin. (2023). A Comprehensive Guide to Digital Scalability with Cloud Computing. *Best Urdu Poetry for U*. https://www.besturdupoetryforu.com/2023/06/a-comprehensive-guide-to-digital.html

Agarwal, R., Baghel, N., & Khan, M. A. (2020). *Load Balancing in Cloud Computing using Mutation Based Particle Swarm Optimization*. 2020 International Conference on Contemporary Computing and Applications (IC3A), Lucknow, India. 10.1109/IC3A48958.2020.233295

Agarwal, M., & Srivastava, G. M. S. (2021). Opposition-based learning inspired particle swarm optimization (OPSO) scheme for task scheduling problem in cloud computing. *Journal of Ambient Intelligence and Humanized Computing*, *12*(10), 9855–9875. doi:10.1007/s12652-020-02730-4

Agrawal, D., El Abbadi, A., Das, S., & Elmore, A. J. (2011). Database Scalability, Elasticity, and Autonomy in the Cloud. International conference on database systems for advanced applications, (pp. 2-15), Springer. 10.1007/978-3-642-20149-3_2

Aguila, D. A., Bartolata, J. M., & Estrañero, J. G. (2022). *AXEing the axie infinity (AI): The AI of modern gaming, business model Strategem, and global economy towards cryptocurrency era*. College of Liberal Arts and Sciences Dasmariñas.

Ahmad, S., Mishra, S., & Sharma, V. (2023). Green computing for sustainable future technologies and its applications. *Contemporary Studies of Risks in Emerging Technology, Part A*, 241–256. Emerald. doi:10.1108/978-1-80455-562-020231016

Ahmad, A.-S., & Andras, P. (2019). Scalability analysis comparisons of cloud-based software services. *Journal of Cloud Computing (Heidelberg, Germany)*, *8*(1), 1–17.

Ahmed, M., & Haskell-Dowland, P. (2021). *Secure Edge Computing: Applications, Techniques and Challenges*. CRC Press. doi:10.1201/9781003028635

Ajah, I. A., & Nweke, H. F. (2019). Big data and business analytics: Trends, platforms, success factors and applications. *Big Data and Cognitive Computing*, *3*(2), 32. doi:10.3390/bdcc3020032

Akherfi, K., Gerndt, M., & Harroud, H. (2018). Mobile cloud computing for computation offloading: Issues and challenges. *Applied Computing and Informatics*, *14*(1), 1–16. doi:10.1016/j.aci.2016.11.002

Akhtar, S. M. F. (2018). *Big Data Architect's Handbook*. Packt.

Akhtar, T., Haider, N. G., & Khan, S. M. (2022). *A Comparative Study of the Application of Glowworm Swarm Optimization Algorithm with other Nature-Inspired Algorithms in the Network Load Balancing Problem*. Engineering, Technology & Applied Science Research. doi:10.48084/etasr.4999

Akter, S., Michael, K., Uddin, M. R., McCarthy, G., & Rahman, M. (2022). Transforming business using digital innovations: The application of AI, blockchain, cloud and data analytics. *Annals of Operations Research*, *308*(1-2), 1–33. doi:10.1007/s10479-020-03620-w PMID:35935743

Alaa, M., Zaidan, A. A., Zaidan, B. B., Talal, M., & Kiah, M. L. M. (2017, November). A review of smart home applications based on Internet of Things. *Journal of Network and Computer Applications*, *97*, 48–65. doi:10.1016/j.jnca.2017.08.017

Alabdulrazzaq, H., & Alenezi, M. N. (2022). Performance evaluation of cryptographic algorithms: DES, 3DES, blowfish, twofish, and threefish. *International Journal of Communication Networks and Information Security*, *14*(1), 51–61. doi:10.17762/ijcnis.v14i1.5262

Alahmadi, D. H., Baothman, F. A., Alrajhi, M. M., Alshahrani, F. S., & Albalawi, H. Z. (2022). Comparative analysis of blockchain technology to support digital transformation in ports and shipping. *Journal of Intelligent Systems*, *31*(1), 55–69. doi:10.1515/jisys-2021-0131

Alankar, B., Sharma, G., Kaur, H., Valverde, R., & Chang, V. (2020). Experimental Setup for Investigating the Efficient Load Balancing Algorithms on Virtual Cloud. *Sensors, 20*(24), 7342. doi:10.3390/s20247342

Aldossary, M. (2021). A Review of Dynamic Resource Management in Cloud Computing Environments. *Computer Systems Science and Engineering*, *36*(3), 461–476. doi:10.32604/csse.2021.014975

Alguliyev, R., Imamverdiyev, Y., & Abdullayeva, F. (2019). PSO-based Load Balancing Method in Cloud Computing. *Automatic Control and Computer Sciences*, *53*(1), 45–55. doi:10.3103/S0146411619010024

Ali, M. (2010). A Guide to Dynamic Load Balancing in Distributed Computer Systems. *IJCSNS International Journal of Computer Science and Network Security, 10*(6).

Ali, S., & Shirazi, F. (2023). The Paradigm of Circular Economy and an Effective Electronic Waste Management. *Sustainability, 15*(3), 1998. doi:10.3390/su15031998

Alipourfard, O. (2017). Cherrypick: Adaptively unearthing the best cloud configurations for big data analytics. *14th {USENIX} Symposium on Networked Systems Design and Implementation ({NSDI} 17)*. Usenix.

Alli, A. A., Kassim, K., Mutwalibi, N., Hamid, H., & Ibrahim, L. (2021). Secure Fog-Cloud of Things: Architectures, Opportunities and Challenges. In M. Ahmed & P. Haskell-Dowland (Eds.), *Secure Edge Computing* (1st ed., pp. 3–20). CRC Press. doi:10.1201/9781003028635-2

Alonso-Calvo, R., Crespo, J., Garcia-Remesal, M., Anguita, A., & Maojo, V. (2010). On distributing load incloud computing: A real application for very-large image datasets. *Procedia Computer Science*, *1*(1), 2669–2677. doi:10.1016/j.procs.2010.04.300

Alouffi, B., Hasnain, M., Alharbi, A., Alosaimi, W., Alyami, H., & Ayaz, M. (2021). A Systematic Literature Review on Cloud Computing Security: Threats and Mitigation Strategies. *IEEE Access : Practical Innovations, Open Solutions*, *9*, 57792–57807. doi:10.1109/ACCESS.2021.3073203

Alsaidy, S. A., Abbood, A. D., & Sahib, M. A. (2022). Heuristic initialization of PSO task scheduling algorithm in cloud computing. *Journal of King Saud University. Computer and Information Sciences*, *34*(6), 2370–2382. doi:10.1016/j.jksuci.2020.11.002

Amazon Web Services. (2023). *AWS Disaster Recovery*. AWS. https://aws.amazon.com/disaster-recovery/

Anandharajan, T., & Bhagyaveni, M. (2011). Co-operative scheduled energy aware load-balancing technique for an efficient computational cloud. *International Journal of Computational Science*, *8*(2).

Anand, R., Singh, J., Pandey, D., Pandey, B. K., Nassa, V. K., & Pramanik, S. (2022). Modern Technique for Interactive Communication in LEACH-Based Ad Hoc Wireless Sensor Network. In M. M. Ghonge, S. Pramanik, & A. D. Potgantwar (Eds.), *Software Defined Networking for Ad Hoc Networks*. Springer. doi:10.1007/978-3-030-91149-2_3

Anand, S., Gupta, S., Fatnani, S., Sharma, V., & Jain, D. (2010). Article: Semantic Cloud for Mobile Technology. *International Journal of Computer Applications*, *8*(12), 1–4. doi:10.5120/1260-1795

Andola, N., Prakash, S., Yadav, V. K., Raghav, Venkatesan, S., & Verma, S. (2022). A secure searchable encryption scheme for cloud using hash-based indexing. *Journal of Computer and System Sciences*, *126*, 119–137. doi:10.1016/j.jcss.2021.12.004

Ansari, N., & Sun, X. (2018). Mobile edge computing empowers internet of things. *IEICE Transactions on Communications*, *101*(3), 604–619. doi:10.1587/transcom.2017NRI0001

Anthony, T. (2010). Cloud Computing A Practical Approach. McGraw-Hill.

Apple Environmental Progress. (2020). *Apple's Environmental Progress Report*. Apple. https://www.apple.com/environment/pdf/Apple_Environmental_Progress_Report_2021.pdf

Apple. (2018). *Apple now globally powered by 100 percent renewable energy*. Apple. https://www.apple.com/newsroom/2018/04/apple-now-globally-powered-by-100-percent-renewable-energy/

Arasteh, H., Hosseinnezhad, V., Loia, V., Tommasetti, A., Troisi, O., Shafie-khah, M., & Siano, P. (2016). IoT-based smart cities: A survey. *Proc. IEEE 16th Int. Conf. Environ. Elect. Eng. (EEEIC)*, (pp. 1–6). IEEE. 10.1109/EEEIC.2016.7555867

Aref, S., Kadum, J., & Kadum, A. (2022). Optimization of Max-Min and Min-Min Task Scheduling Algorithms Using G.A in Cloud Computing. *2022 5th International Conference on Engineering Technology and its Applications (IICETA)*, Al-Najaf, Iraq. 10.1109/IICETA54559.2022.9888542

Arguelles, J. R. P., & Polkowski, Z. (2023). Impact of Big Data on Supply Chain Performance through Demand Forecasting. *International Journal of Computations* [IJCIM]. *Information and Manufacturing*, *3*(1), 19–26.

Armbrust, M., Fox, A., Griffith, R., Joseph, A. D., Katz, R., Konwinski, A., Lee, G., Patterson, D., Rabkin, A., Stoica, I., & Zaharia, M. (2010). A view of cloud computing. In Communications of the ACM (Vol. 53, Issue 4). doi:10.1145/1721654.1721672

Armbrust, M., Fox, A., Griffith, R., Joseph, A. D., Katz, R., Konwinski, A., Lee, G., Patterson, D., Rabkin, A., Stoica, I., & Zaharia, M., (2010). A view of cloud computing, Communications. *ACM Magazine, 53*, 50-58.

Armbrust, M., Das, T., Sun, L., Yavuz, B., Zhu, S., Murthy, M., Torres, J., van Hovell, H., Ionescu, A., Łuszczak, A., Świtakowski, M., Szafrański, M., Li, X., Ueshin, T., Mokhtar, M., Boncz, P., Ghodsi, A., Paranjpye, S., Senster, P., & Zaharia, M. (2020). Delta lake: High-performance ACID table storage over cloud object stores. *Proceedings of the VLDB Endowment International Conference on Very Large Data Bases, 13*(12), 3411–3424. doi:10.14778/3415478.3415560

Armbrust, M., Xin, R. S., Lian, C., Huai, Y., Liu, D., Bradley, J. K., Meng, X., Kaftan, T., Franklin, M. J., Ghodsi, A., & Zaharia, M. (2015). Spark SQL: relational data processing in spark. In: *Proceedings of the 2015 ACM SIGMOD International Conference on Management of Data*, (pp. 1383–1394). ACM. 10.1145/2723372.2742797

Arockiam, L., Monikandan, S., & Parthasarathy, G. (2017). Cloud Computing: A Survey. *International Journal of Computer and Communication Technology*, 21–28. doi:10.47893/IJCCT.2017.1393

Ashari, A., & Setiawan, H. (2011). Cloud Computing: Solusi ICT? *Jurnal Sitem Informasi, JSI., 3*(2), 336–345.

Aske, A., & Zhao, X. (2018, August). Supporting multi-provider serverless computing on the edge. In *Workshop Proceedings of the 47th International Conference on Parallel Processing* (pp. 1-6). ACM. 10.1145/3229710.3229742

Assunção, M. D., Calheiros, R. N., Bianchi, S., Netto, M. A. S., & Buyya, R. (2015). Big Data Computing and Clouds: Trends and Future Directions. *Journal of Parallel and Distributed Computing, 79–80*, 3–15. doi:10.1016/j.jpdc.2014.08.003

Ateya, A. A., Mahmoud, M., Zaghloul, A., Soliman, N. F., & Muthanna, A. (2022). Empowering the internet of things using light communication and distributed edge computing. *Electronics (Basel), 11*(9), 1511. doi:10.3390/electronics11091511

Attaran, M., & Woods, J. (2019). Cloud computing technology: Improving small business performance using the Internet. *Journal of Small Business and Entrepreneurship, 31*(6), 495–519. doi:10.1080/08276331.2018.1466850

Atzori, L., Iera, A., & Morabito, G. (2010, October). The Internet of Things: A survey. *Computer Networks, 54*(15), 2787–2805. doi:10.1016/j.comnet.2010.05.010

Aurélien Géron. (2019). Hands-on machine learning with Scikit-Learn, Keras and TensorFlow: concepts, tools, and techniques to build intelligent systems. O'Reilly Media.

Awasthi, K., & Awasthi, S. (2023). Green Computing: A Sustainable and Eco-friendly Approach for Conservation of Energy (A Contribution to Save Environment). *Sustainable Computing: Transforming Industry 4.0 to Society 5.0*, 319–333. Springer. doi:10.1007/978-3-031-13577-4_20

AWS. (n.d.). *Home.* Amazon. https://aws.amazon.com/

Aziz, A., Osamy, W., Alfawaz, O., & Khedr, A. M. (2022). EDCCS: Effective deterministic clustering scheme based compressive sensing to enhance IoT based WSNs. *Wireless Networks, 28*(6), 2375–2391. doi:10.1007/s11276-022-02973-3

Babu, S. Z. D., Pandey, D., Naidu, G. T., Sumathi, S., Gupta, A., Bader Alazzam, M., & Pandey, B. K. (2022, July). Analysation of Big Data in Smart Healthcare. In *Artificial Intelligence on Medical Data: Proceedings of International Symposium, ISCMM 2021* (pp. 243-251). Singapore: Springer Nature Singapore.

Baek, J., Vu, Q., Liu, J., Huang, X., & Xiang, Y. (2015). A secure cloud computing based framework for big data information management of smart grid. *IEEE Transactions on Cloud Computing, 3*(2), 233–244. doi:10.1109/TCC.2014.2359460

Bansal, R., Jenipher, B., Nisha, V., & Makhan, R. Kumbhkar, Pramanik, S., Roy, S. and Gupta, A. (2022). Big Data Architecture for Network Security", in Cyber Security and Network Security, Eds, Wiley, https://doi.org/doi:10.1002/9781119812555.ch11

Bansal, R., Obaid, A. J., Gupta, A., Singh, R., & Pramanik, S. (2021). Impact of Big Data on Digital Transformation in 5G Era. *2nd International Conference on Physics and Applied Sciences (ICPAS 2021).* IOP. , 2021.10.1088/1742-6596/1963/1/012170

Baraglia, R., Lucchese, C., & De Francisci Morales, G. (2010). *Large-scale Data Analysis on the Cloud.* XXIV Convegno Annuale Del CMG-Italia.

Barciauskas, A., Mandel, A., Barron, K., & Deziel, Z. (2023). *Cloud-Optimized Geospatial Formats Guide*. Cloud Native. https://guide.cloudnativegeo.org/

Barenji, A. V., & Montreuil, B. (2022). Open Logistics: Blockchain-Enabled Trusted Hyperconnected Logistics Platform. *Sensors (Basel)*, *22*(13), 4699. doi:10.3390/s22134699 PMID:35808198

Baresi, L., Filgueira Mendonça, D., & Garriga, M. (2017). Empowering low-latency applications through a serverless edge computing architecture. In Service-Oriented and Cloud Computing: 6th IFIP WG 2.14 European Conference, ESOCC 2017, Oslo, Norway, September 27-29, 2017 [Springer International Publishing.]. *Proceedings*, *6*, 196–210.

Baresi, L., & Mendonça, D. F. (2019, June). Towards a serverless platform for edge computing. In *2019 IEEE International Conference on Fog Computing (ICFC)* (pp. 1-10). IEEE. 10.1109/ICFC.2019.00008

Barik, R. K., Patra, S. S., Patro, R., Mohanty, S. N., & Hamad, A. A. (2021). GeoBD2: Geospatial big data deduplication scheme in fog assisted cloud computing environment. *Proceedings of the 2021 8th International Conference on Computing for Sustainable Global Development, INDIACom 2021*. IEEE. https://doi.org/10.1109/INDIACom51348.2021.00008

Barik, R. K., Dubey, H., Mankodiya, K., Sasane, S. A., & Misra, C. (2019). GeoFog4Health: A fog-based SDI framework for geospatial health big data analysis. *Journal of Ambient Intelligence and Humanized Computing*, *10*(2), 551–567. doi:10.1007/s12652-018-0702-x

Barik, R. K., Dubey, H., Samaddar, A. B., Gupta, R. D., & Ray, P. K. (2017). FogGIS: Fog Computing for geospatial big data analytics. *2016 IEEE Uttar Pradesh Section International Conference on Electrical, Computer and Electronics Engineering, UPCON 2016*. IEEE. 10.1109/UPCON.2016.7894725

Barik, R. K., Misra, C., Lenka, R. K., Dubey, H., & Mankodiya, K. (2019). Hybrid mist-cloud systems for large scale geospatial big data analytics and processing: Opportunities and challenges. *Arabian Journal of Geosciences*, *12*(2), 32. Advance online publication. doi:10.1007/s12517-018-4104-3

Barlette, Y., & Baillette, P. (2022). Big data analytics in turbulent contexts: Towards organizational change for enhanced agility. *Production Planning and Control*, *33*(2-3), 105–122. doi:10.1080/09537287.2020.1810755

Barroso, L. A., Hölzle, U., & Ranganathan, P. (2019). *The datacenter as a computer: Designing warehouse-scale machines*. Springer Nature. doi:10.1007/978-3-031-01761-2

Basan, M. (2023). 13 Cloud Security Best Practices & [eSecurity Planet. Retrieved from https://www.esecurityplanet.com/cloud/cloud-security-best-practices/]. *Trends in Pharmacological Sciences*, *2023*.

Bashir, S., Mustafa, S., Ahmad, R. W., Shuja, J., Maqsood, T., & Alourani, A. (2023). Multi-factor nature inspired SLA-aware energy efficient resource management for cloud environments. *Cluster Computing*, *26*(2), 1643–1658. doi:10.1007/s10586-022-03690-4

Bastiaanssen, W. G. M., Menenti, M., Feddes, R. A., & Holtslag, A. A. M. (1998). A remote sensing surface energy balance algorithm for land (SEBAL). 1. Formulation. *Journal of Hydrology (Amsterdam)*, *212-213*, 198–212. doi:10.1016/S0022-1694(98)00253-4

Basu, K., Maqousi, A., & Ball, F. (2020). Architecture of an end-to-end energy consumption model for a Cloud Data Center. *2020 12th International Symposium on Communication Systems, Networks and Digital Signal Processing, CSNDSP 2020*. IEEE. 10.1109/CSNDSP49049.2020.9249479

Battah, A., Madine, M., Yaqoob, I., Salah, K., Hasan, H. R., & Jayaraman, R. (2022). Blockchain and NFTs for trusted ownership, trading, and access of AI models. *IEEE Access : Practical Innovations, Open Solutions*, *10*, 112230–112249. doi:10.1109/ACCESS.2022.3215660

Bauspiess, F., & Damm, F. (1992). Requirements for Cryptographic Hash Functions. *Computers & Security*, *11*(5), 427–437. doi:10.1016/0167-4048(92)90007-E

Bebortta, S., Das, S. K., Kandpal, M., Barik, R. K., & Dubey, H. (2020). Geospatial serverless computing: Architectures, tools and future directions. *ISPRS International Journal of Geo-Information*, *9*(5), 311. doi:10.3390/ijgi9050311

Begam, G. S., Sangeetha, M., & Shanker, N. R. (2022). Load Balancing in DCN Servers through SDN Machine Learning Algorithm. *Arabian Journal for Science and Engineering*, *47*(2), 1423–1434. doi:10.1007/s13369-021-05911-1

Belgacem, A. (2022). Dynamic resource allocation in cloud computing: Analysis and taxonomies. *Computing*, *104*(3), 681–710. doi:10.1007/s00607-021-01045-2

Belgacem, A., Mahmoudi, S., & Ferrag, M. A. (2023). A machine learning model for improving virtual machine migration in cloud computing. *The Journal of Supercomputing*, *79*(9), 1–23. doi:10.1007/s11227-022-05031-z

Beloglazov, A., & Buyya, R. (2012). Optimal online deterministic algorithms and adaptive heuristics for energy and performance efficient dynamic consolidation of virtual machines in Cloud data centers. *Concurrency and Computation*, *24*(13), 1397–1420. doi:10.1002/cpe.1867

Bemthuis, R., Iacob, M. E., & Havinga, P. (2020). A design of the resilient enterprise: A reference architecture for emergent behaviors control. *Sensors (Basel)*, *20*(22), 6672. doi:10.3390/s20226672 PMID:33233426

Bessant, Y. A., Jency, J. G., Sagayam, K. M., Jone, A. A. A., Pandey, D., & Pandey, B. K. (2023). Improved parallel matrix multiplication using Strassen and Urdhvatiryagbhyam method. *CCF Transactions on High Performance Computing*, *5*(2), 1–14. doi:10.1007/s42514-023-00149-9

Bhandayker, Y. R. (2019). A study on the research challenges and trends of cloud computing. RESEARCH REVIEW International Journal of Multidisciplinary, 4.

Bharany, S., Sharma, S., Khalaf, O. I., Abdulsahib, G. M., Al Humaimeedy, A. S., Aldhyani, T. H. H., Maashi, M., & Alkahtani, H. (2022). A Systematic Survey on Energy-Efficient Techniques in Sustainable Cloud Computing. *Sustainability, 14*(10), 6256. doi:10.3390/su14106256

Bhardwaj, A., & Kaushik, K. (2022). Predictive analytics-based cybersecurity framework for cloud infrastructure. *International Journal of Cloud Applications and Computing*, *12*(1), 1–20. doi:10.4018/IJCAC.297106

Bhimani, J., Yang, Z., Leeser, M., & Mi, N. (2017). Accelerating big data applications using lightweight virtualization framework on enterprise cloud. In: High Performance Extreme Computing Conference (HPEC), (pp. 1–7). IEEE. doi:10.1109/HPEC.2017.8091086

Bijapure, S., & Borse, Y. (2023). Cloud security threats and solutions: A survey. *Wireless Personal Communications*, *128*(1), 387–413. doi:10.1007/s11277-022-09960-z

Boopathi, S., Pandey, B. K., & Pandey, D. (2023). Advances in Artificial Intelligence for Image Processing: Techniques, Applications, and Optimization. In Handbook of Research on Thrust Technologies' Effect on Image Processing (pp. 73-95). IGI Global.

Boopathi, S., Pandey, B. K., & Pandey, D. (2023). Advances in artificial intelligence for image processing: Techniques, applications, and optimization. In *Handbook of Research on Thrust Technologies?* Effect on Image Processing. doi:10.4018/978-1-6684-8618-4.ch006

Boss, G., Malladi, P., & Quan, D. (2009). *Cloud computing*. IBM. www.ibm.com/developerswork/websphere /zones/ hipods/ library.html

Brataas, G., Herbst, N., Ivansek, S., & Polutnik, J. (2017). Scalability Analysis of Cloud Software Services. *2017 IEEE International Conference on Autonomic Computing (ICAC)*, (pp. 285-292). IEEE. 10.1109/ICAC.2017.34

Brataas, G., Stav, E., Lehrig, S., Becker, S., Kopčak, G., & Huljenic, D. (2013). CloudScale: scalability management for cloud systems. *Proceedings of the 4th ACM/SPEC International Conference on Performance Engineering*, (pp. 335-338). ACM. 10.1145/2479871.2479920

Braun, T. D., Siegel, H. J., Beck, N., Boloni, L. L., Maheswaran, M., Reuther, A. I., Robertson, J. P., Theys, M. D., Yao, B., Hensgen, D., & Freund, R. F. (2001). A comparison of eleven static heuristics for mapping a class of independent tasks onto heterogeneous distributed computing systems. *Journal of Parallel and Distributed Computing*, *61*(6), 2669–2677. doi:10.1006/jpdc.2000.1714

Buyya, R., Yeo, C., & Venugopal, S. (2008). Market-oriented cloud computing: Vision, hype, and reality for delivering IT services as computing utilities. *10th IEEE International Conference on High Performance Computing and Communications, (HPCC '08)*. IEEE. 10.1109/HPCC.2008.172

Buyya, R., Yeo, C. S., Venugopal, S., Broberg, J., & Brandic, I. (2009). Cloud computing and emerging IT platforms: Vision, hype, and reality for delivering computing as the 5th utility. *Future Generation Computer Systems*, *25*(6), 599–616. doi:10.1016/j.future.2008.12.001

Cáceres, J., Vaquero, L. M., Rodero-Merino, L., Polo, A., & Hierro, J. J. (2010). Service scalability over the cloud. Handbook of Cloud Computing, (pp. 357-377). Springer. doi:10.1007/978-1-4419-6524-0_15

Cai, Y., Zhou, W., Zhang, L., Yu, L., & Luo, T. (2023). DHFNet: Dual-decoding hierarchical fusion network for RGB-thermal semantic segmentation. *The Visual Computer*. Advance online publication. doi:10.1007/s00371-023-02773-6

Canaj, E., & Xhuvani, A. (2018). Big Data in Cloud Computing: A Review of Key Technologies and Open Issues. Springer. doi:10.1007/978-3-319-75928-9_45

Canbaloğlu, G., Treur, J., & Wiewiora, A. (2023). Computational Modeling of Multilevel Organizational Learning: From Conceptual to Computational Mechanisms. In A. Shukla, B. K. Murthy, N. Hasteer, & J. P. Van Belle (Eds.), *Computational Intelligence. Lecture Notes in Electrical Engineering* (Vol. 968). Springer. doi:10.1007/978-981-19-7346-8_1

Cao, B., Zhang, L., Li, Y., Feng, D., & Cao, W. (2019). Intelligent offloading in multi-access edge computing: A state-of-the-art review and framework. *IEEE Communications Magazine*, *57*(3), 56–62. doi:10.1109/MCOM.2019.1800608

Cao, C. F., Yu, B., Chen, Z. Y., Qu, Y.-X., Li, Y.-T., Shi, Y.-Q., Ma, Z.-W., Sun, F.-N., Pan, Q.-H., Tang, L.-C., Song, P., & Wang, H. (2022). Fire Intumescent, High-Temperature Resistant, Mechanically Flexible Graphene Oxide Network for Exceptional Fire Shielding and Ultra-Fast Fire Warning. *Nano-Micro Letters*, *14*(1), 92. doi:10.1007/s40820-022-00837-1 PMID:35384618

Cao, J., Zhang, Q., Shi, W., Cao, J., Zhang, Q., & Shi, W. (2018). Challenges and opportunities in edge computing. Edge Computing. *PRiMER: Peer-Reviewed Reports in Medical Education Research*, 59–70.

Cao, Z., Zhou, X., Wu, X., Zhu, Z., Liu, T., Neng, J., & Wen, Y. (2023). Data Center Sustainability: Revisits and Outlooks. *IEEE Transactions on Sustainable Computing*, 1–13. doi:10.1109/TSUSC.2023.3281583

Carillo, K. D. A. (2017). Let's stop trying to be "sexy"–preparing managers for the (big) data-driven business era. *Business Process Management Journal*, *23*(3), 598–622. doi:10.1108/BPMJ-09-2016-0188

Carvalho, G., Cabral, B., Pereira, V., & Bernardino, J. (2021). Edge computing: Current trends, research challenges and future directions. *Computing*, *103*(5), 993–1023. doi:10.1007/s00607-020-00896-5

Cassel, G. A. S., Rodrigues, V. F., da Rosa Righi, R., Bez, M. R., Nepomuceno, A. C., & da Costa, C. A. (2022). Serverless computing for Internet of Things: A systematic literature review. *Future Generation Computer Systems*, *128*, 299–316. doi:10.1016/j.future.2021.10.020

Castro, P., Ishakian, V., Muthusamy, V., & Slominski, A. (2019). The rise of serverless computing. *Communications of the ACM*, *62*(12), 44–54. doi:10.1145/3368454

Cebula, D. (2022). *How to Build Scalable Cloud Architecture?* Net Guru. https://www.netguru.com/blog/how-to-build-scalable-cloud-architecture

Cerchione, R., Centobelli, P., Riccio, E., Abbate, S., & Oropallo, E. (2023). Blockchain's coming to hospital to digitalize healthcare services: Designing a distributed electronic health record ecosystem. *Technovation*, *120*, 102480. doi:10.1016/j.technovation.2022.102480

Chandarana, P., & Vijayalakshmi, M. (2014). Big data analytics frameworks. In: *Proceedings of the International Conference on Circuits*, (pp. 430–434). IEEE.

Chang, B. R., Tsai, H. F., Chen, C. Y., Huang, C. F., & Hsu, H. T. (2015). Implementation of secondary index on cloud computing NoSQL database in big data environment. *Scientific Programming*, *2015*, 19. doi:10.1155/2015/560714

Chan, W. K., Mei, L., & Zhang, Z. (2009). Modeling and testing of cloud applications. *Proceedings of 2009 IEEE Asia-Pacific Services Computing Conference (APSCC 2009)*, (Singapore, December 7-11, 2009), IEEE Computer Society Press. 10.1109/APSCC.2009.5394131

Chen, L., Dang, Q., Chen, M., Sun, B., Du, C., & Lu, Z. (2023). BertHTLG: Graph-Based Microservice Anomaly Detection Through Sentence-Bert Enhancement. In L. Yuan, S. Yang, R. Li, E. Kanoulas, & X. Zhao (Eds.), Lecture Notes in Computer Science: Vol. 14094. *Web Information Systems and Applications. WISA 2023*. Springer. doi:10.1007/978-981-99-6222-8_36

Chen, S. L., Chen, Y. Y., & Kuo, S. H. (2017). CLB: A novel load balancing architecture and algorithm for cloud services. *Computers & Electrical Engineering*, *58*, 154–160. doi:10.1016/j.compeleceng.2016.01.029

Chen, Z., Gu, J., & Yan, H. (2023). HAE: A Hybrid Cryptographic Algorithm for Blockchain Medical Scenario Applications. *Applied Sciences (Basel, Switzerland)*, *13*(22), 12163. doi:10.3390/app132212163

Chieu, T. C., Mohindra, A., & Karve, A. A. (2011). Scalability and Performance of Web Applications in a Compute Cloud. *2011 IEEE 8th International Conference on e-Business Engineering*, (pp. 317-323). IEEE. 10.1109/ICEBE.2011.63

Chitturi, A. K., & Swarnalatha, P. (2020). Exploration of various cloud security challenges and threats. In *Soft Computing for Problem Solving: SocProS 2018* (Vol. 2, pp. 891–899). Springer Singapore. doi:10.1007/978-981-15-0184-5_76

Choudhary, A., Govil, M. C., Singh, G., Awasthi, L. K., & Pilli, E. S. (2022). Energy-aware scientific workflow scheduling in cloud environment. *Cluster Computing*, *25*(6), 3845–3874. doi:10.1007/s10586-022-03613-3

Choudhary, S., Narayan, V., Faiz, M., & Pramanik, S. (2022). Fuzzy Approach-Based Stable Energy-Efficient AODV Routing Protocol in Mobile Ad hoc Networks. In M. M. Ghonge, S. Pramanik, & A. D. Potgantwar (Eds.), *Software Defined Networking for Ad Hoc Networks*. Springer. doi:10.1007/978-3-030-91149-2_6

Chun, B. G., & Maniatis, P. (2009). Augmented smartphone applications through clone cloud execution. *Proceedings of the 12th conference on Hot topics in operating systems*, Berkeley, CA, USA.

Chun, B., Ihm, S., Maniatis, P., Naik, M., & Patti, A. (2011). Clonecloud: Elastic execution between mobile device and cloud. *Proceedings of the sixth conference on Computer systems*. ACM. 10.1145/1966445.1966473

Cicconetti, C., Conti, M., Passarella, A., & Sabella, D. (2020). Toward distributed computing environments with serverless solutions in edge systems. *IEEE Communications Magazine*, *58*(3), 40–46. doi:10.1109/MCOM.001.1900498

Cinque, M. (2023). *Real-Time FaaS: serverless computing for Industry 4.0.* SOCA. doi:10.1007/s11761-023-00360-0

Cisco. (2023). *Edge computing in the cloud.* Cisco. https://www.cisco.com/c/en/us/solutions/internet-of-things/edge-intelligence.html

Cisco. (n.d.). *Mobile Consumers reach for the Cloud.* IBSG Cisco.

Cloud Security Alliance. (2009). *Security guidance for critical areas of focus in cloud computing(v2.1).* CSA.

Cole, T., Bhardwaj, A. K., Garg, L., & Shrivastava, D. P. (2019). Investigation into cloud computing adoption within the hedge fund industry. [JCIT]. *Journal of Cases on Information Technology*, *21*(3), 1–25. doi:10.4018/JCIT.2019070101

Coppolino, L., D'Antonio, S., Mazzeo, G., & Romano, L. (2017). Cloud security: Emerging threats and current solutions. *Computers & Electrical Engineering*, *59*, 126–140. doi:10.1016/j.compeleceng.2016.03.004

Crompvoets, J., Bregt, A., Rajabifard, A., & Williamson, I. (2004). Assessing the worldwide developments of national spatial data clearinghouses. *International Journal of Geographical Information Science*, *18*(7), 665–689. doi:10.1080/13658810410001702030

Cuervo, E., & Balasubramanian, A. (2010). MAUI: Making Smartphones Last Longer with Code offload. *Proceedings of the 8th International Conference on Mobile systems, applications, and services*, (pp. 49-62). ACM. 10.1145/1814433.1814441

Dai, P., Luo, J., Zhao, K., Xing, H., & Wu, X. (2023). Stacked denoising autoencoder for missing traffic data reconstruction via mobile edge computing. *Neural Computing & Applications*, *35*(19), 14259–14274. doi:10.1007/s00521-023-08475-3

Dai, Y., Xu, D., Maharjan, S., Qiao, G., & Zhang, Y. (2019). Artificial intelligence empowered edge computing and caching for internet of vehicles. *IEEE Wireless Communications*, *26*(3), 12–18. doi:10.1109/MWC.2019.1800411

Damblin, G., Couplet, M., & Iooss, B. (2013). Numerical studies of space filling designs: Optimization of Latin Hypercube Samples and subprojection properties. *Journal of Simulation*, *7*(4), 276–289. doi:10.1057/jos.2013.16

Dave, A., Patel, B., & Bhatt, G. (2016). Load balancing in cloud computing using optimization techniques: A study. *Proceedings of the International Conference on Communication and Electronics Systems, ICCES 2016*. IEEE. 10.1109/CESYS.2016.7889883

David, S., Duraipandian, K., Chandrasekaran, D., Pandey, D., Sindhwani, N., & Pandey, B. K. (2023). Impact of blockchain in healthcare system. In *Unleashing the Potentials of Blockchain Technology for Healthcare Industries* (pp. 37–57). Academic Press. doi:10.1016/B978-0-323-99481-1.00004-3

de Venâncio, P. V. A. B., Lisboa, A. C., & Barbosa, A. V. (2022). An automatic fire detection system based on deep convolutional neural networks for low-power, resource-constrained devices. *Neural Computing & Applications*, *34*(18), 15349–15368. doi:10.1007/s00521-022-07467-z

Deb, M., & Choudhury, A. (2021). Hybrid cloud: A new paradigm in cloud computing. *Machine Learning Techniques and Analytics for Cloud Security*, 1-23.

Dede, E., Sendir, B., Kuzlu, P., Weachock, J., Govindaraju, M., & Ramakrishan, L. (2016). Processing Cassandra datasets with Hadoop-streaming based approaches. *IEEE Transactions on Services Computing*, *9*(1), 46–58. doi:10.1109/TSC.2015.2444838

Deft. (2014). Scalability in cloud computing: using virtualization to save money. *Deft.* https://deft.com/blog/scalability-in-cloud-computing/

Dehdouh, K., Bentayeb, F., Boussaid, O., & Kabachi, N. (2015). Using the column oriented NoSQL model for implementing big data warehouses. In: *Proceedings of the International Conference on Parallel and Distributed Processing Techniques and Applications (PDPTA).* The Steering Committee of the World Congress in Computer Science, Computer Engineering and Applied Computing (WorldComp).

Delgado, J. A., Short, N. M., Roberts, D. P., & Vandenberg, B. (2019). Big Data Analysis for Sustainable Agriculture on a Geospatial Cloud Framework. In Frontiers in Sustainable Food Systems (Vol. 3). Frontiers. doi:10.3389/fsufs.2019.00054

Delimitrou, C., & Kozyrakis, C. (2014). Quasar: Resource-efficient and qos-aware cluster management. In ACM SIGARCH [ACM.]. *Computer Architecture News*, *42*(1), 127–144. doi:10.1145/2654822.2541941

DELL ESG Report. (2023). *Dell ESG Report FY23.* DELL. https://www.dell.com/en-us/dt/corporate/social-impact/esg-resources/reports/fy23-esg-report.htm#scroll=off

Desai, F., Chowdhury, D., Kaur, R., Peeters, M., Arya, R., Wander, G., Gill, S. S., & Buyya, R. (2022). HealthCloud: A system for monitoring health status of heart patients using machine learning and cloud computing. *Internet of Things : Engineering Cyber Physical Human Systems*, *17*, 100485. doi:10.1016/j.iot.2021.100485

Dewan, M., Mudgal, A., Pandey, P., Raghav, Y. Y., & Gupta, T. (2023). Predicting Pregnancy Complications Using Machine Learning. In D. Satishkumar & P. Maniiarasan (Eds.), *Technological Tools for Predicting Pregnancy Complications* (pp. 141–160). IGI Global. doi:10.4018/979-8-3693-1718-1.ch008

Dey, N. S., Reddy, S. P. K., & Lavanya, G. (2023, October). Serverless Computing: Architectural Paradigms, Challenges, and Future Directions in Cloud Technology. In *2023 7th International Conference on I-SMAC (IoT in Social, Mobile, Analytics and Cloud)(I-SMAC)* (pp. 406-414). IEEE. 10.1109/I-SMAC58438.2023.10290253

Dhanalakshmii, G., & George, G. V. (2022). An Enhanced Data Integrity for the E-Health Cloud System using a Secure Hashing Cryptographic Algorithm with a Password Based Key Derivation Function2 (KDF2). *Int J Eng Trends Technol*, *70*(9), 290–297. doi:10.14445/22315381/IJETT-V70I9P229

Dharaniya, R., Saranya, V. S., Sarath Babu, N., & Zaid, S. A. (2023). AI Agents at Different Data Centers to Minimize the Energy Spending. *2023 9th International Conference on Advanced Computing and Communication Systems, ICACCS 2023*, (pp. 813–818). IEEE. 10.1109/ICACCS57279.2023.10113130

Dillon, T., Wu, C., & Chang, E. (2010). Cloud computing: Issues and challenges. *Proceedings - International Conference on Advanced Information Networking and Applications, AINA*. IEEE. 10.1109/AINA.2010.187

Dinakarrao, S. M. P. (2019). Lightweight Node-level Malware Detection and Network-level Malware Confinement in IoT Networks. 2019 Design, Automation & Test in Europe Conference & Exhibition (DATE). IEEE.

Ding, D., Fan, X., Zhao, Y., Kang, K., Yin, Q., & Zeng, J. (2020). Q-learning based dynamic task scheduling for energy-efficient cloud computing. *Future Generation Computer Systems*, *108*, 361–371. doi:10.1016/j.future.2020.02.018

Dinh, H. T., Lee, C., Niyato, D., & Wang, P. (2011). A survey of Mobile Cloud Computing: Architecture, Applications and Approaches. *Wireless Communications and Mobile Computing.*

Dinh, H. T., Lee, C., Niyato, D., & Wang, P. (2013). A survey of mobile cloud computing: Architecture, applications, and approaches. *Wireless Communications and Mobile Computing*, *13*(18), 1587–1611. doi:10.1002/wcm.1203

Dodge, J., Prewitt, T., Tachet des Combes, R., Odmark, E., Schwartz, R., Strubell, E., & Buchanan, W. (2022, June). Measuring the carbon intensity of AI in cloud instances. In *Proceedings of the 2022 ACM Conference on Fairness, Accountability, and Transparency* (pp. 1877-1894). ACM. 10.1145/3531146.3533234

Dogani, J., Khunjush, F., Mahmoudi, M. R., & Seydali, M. (2023). Multivariate workload and resource prediction in cloud computing using CNN and GRU by attention mechanism. *The Journal of Supercomputing*, *79*(3), 3437–3470. doi:10.1007/s11227-022-04782-z

Donahue, L., & Hajizadeh, F. (2019). Artificial intelligence in cloud marketing. *Artificial Intelligence and machine learning for business for non-engineers*, 77-88. Routledge.

Donald, A. C., Oli, S. A., & Arockiam, L. (2013). Mobile cloud security issues and challenges: A perspective. *International Journal of Engineering and Innovative Technology*, *3*(1), 401. https://www.researchgate.net/profile/A-Cecil-Donald/publication/260981217

Dozono, K., Amalathas, S., & Saravanan, R. (2022). The impact of cloud computing and artificial intelligence in digital agriculture. In *Proceedings of Sixth International Congress on Information and Communication Technology: ICICT 2021, London,* Volume 1 (pp. 557-569). Springer Singapore. 10.1007/978-981-16-2377-6_52

Duan, Y., Fu, G., Zhou, N., Sun, X., Narendra, N., & Hu, B. (2015). Everything as a Service (XaaS) on the Cloud: Origins, Current and Future Trends. *2015 IEEE 8th International Conference on Cloud Computing*. IEEE. 10.1109/CLOUD.2015.88

Duan, S., Wang, D., Ren, J., Lyu, F., Zhang, Y., Wu, H., & Shen, X. (2022). Distributed artificial intelligence empowered by end-edge-cloud computing: A survey. *IEEE Communications Surveys and Tutorials*.

Dube, P., Suk, T., & Wang, C. (2019, October). AI gauge: Runtime estimation for deep learning in the cloud. In *2019 31st International Symposium on Computer Architecture and High Performance Computing (SBAC-PAD)* (pp. 160-167). IEEE.

Duisters, H. (2023). *Scaling Startups In The Cloud: Ways To Make That Journey*. ProShore. https://proshore.eu/ways-to-scale-startups-in-the-cloud/

Dunn, C. E. (2007). Participatory GIS - A people's GIS? In Progress in Human Geography, 31(5). doi:10.1177/0309132507081493

Dushyant, K., Muskan, G., Gupta, A., & Pramanik, S. (2022). Utilizing Machine Learning and Deep Learning in Cyber security: An Innovative Approach. In M. M. Ghonge, S. Pramanik, R. Mangrulkar, & D. N. Le (Eds.), *Cyber security and Digital Forensics*. Wiley. doi:10.1002/9781119795667.ch12

Dutta, P., & Shome, S. (2023). A new belief entropy measure in the weighted combination rule under DST with faulty diagnosis and real-life medical application. *International Journal of Machine Learning and Cybernetics*, *14*(4), 1179–1203. doi:10.1007/s13042-022-01693-6

Earney, S. (2023a). *How edge computing is transforming enterprises.* Xailient. https://xailient.com/blog/how-edge-computing-is-transforming-enterprises/

Earney, S. (2023b). *What are the top seven edge computing use cases?* Xailient. https://xailient.com/blog/what-are-the-top-7-edge-computing-use-cases/

Ebinazer, E., Silambarasan, N. S., & Mary Saira Bhanu, S. (2021). ESKEA: Enhanced symmetric key encryption algorithm based secure data storage in cloud networks with data deduplication. *Wireless Personal Communications*, *117*(4), 3309–3325. doi:10.1007/s11277-020-07989-6

EDHEC. (2019). *Three ways educators are using big data.* EDHEC. https://master.edhec.edu/news/threeways-educators-are-using-bigdata-analytics-improve-learning-process#

Ekong, M. O., George, W. K., Pandey, B. K., & Pandey, D. (2023). Enhancing the Fundamentals of Industrial Safety Management in TVET for Metaverse Realities. In *Applications of Neuromarketing in the Metaverse* (pp. 19–41). IGI Global. doi:10.4018/978-1-6684-8150-9.ch002

El Khatib, M. M., Al-Nakeeb, A., & Ahmed, G. (2019). Integration of cloud computing with artificial intelligence and Its impact on telecom sector—A case study. *iBusiness, 11*(01), 1.

Elmagzoub, M. A., Syed, D., Shaikh, A., Islam, N., Alghamdi, A., & Rizwan, S. (2021). A survey of swarm intelligence based load balancing techniques in cloud computing environment. In Electronics (Switzerland). doi:10.3390/electronics10212718

Elsaid, M. E., Abbas, H. M., & Meinel, C. (2022). Virtual machines pre-copy live migration cost modeling and prediction: A survey. *Distributed and Parallel Databases*, *40*(2–3), 441–474. doi:10.1007/s10619-021-07387-2

Ermetic Team. (2022). *Lessons Learned in Cloud Security from Lapsus$ Surfacing*. Ermetic. https://ermetic.com/blog/cloud/lessons-learned-in-cloud-security-from-lapsus-surfacing/

Eskandani, N., & Salvaneschi, G. (2021, May). The wonderless dataset for serverless computing. In *2021 IEEE/ACM 18th International Conference on Mining Software Repositories (MSR)* (pp. 565-569). IEEE. 10.1109/MSR52588.2021.00075

Esri. (2023). *ArcGIS Online*. Esri. https://www.esri.com/en-us/arcgis/products/arcgis-online/overview

European Commission. (2022). *Green cloud and green data centres - Shaping Europe's digital future*. EC. https://digital-strategy.ec.europa.eu/en/policies/green-cloud

Evans, D. (2011). *The Internet of things: How the next evolution of the Internet is changing everything.* CISCO, San Jose, CA.

Falatah, M. M., & Batarfi, O. A. (2014). Cloud scalability considerations. *International Journal of Computer Science and Engineering Survey*, *5*(4), 37–47. doi:10.5121/ijcses.2014.5403

Fan, X., Cao, J., & Mao, H. (2012). *A Survey on Mobile Cloud Computing*. ZTE Corporation.

Fan, Q., & Ansari, N. (2018). Application aware workload allocation for edge computing-based IoT. *IEEE Internet of Things Journal*, *5*(3), 2146–2153. doi:10.1109/JIOT.2018.2826006

Fan, X., Cao, J., & Mao, H. (2011). A survey of mobile cloud computing. *ZTE Communications*, *9*(1), 4–8.

Fan, X., Xiang, C., Gong, L., He, X., Chen, C., & Huang, X. (2019, May). UrbanEdge: Deep learning empowered edge computing for urban IoT time series prediction. In *Proceedings of the ACM Turing Celebration Conference* (pp. 1-6). ACM. 10.1145/3321408.3323089

Farnga, M. (2018). Cloud Security Architecture and Implementation-A practical approach. arXiv preprint arXiv:1808.03892. https://doi.org//arXiv.1808.03892 doi:10.48550

Farshad, A. (2006). *Mobile Service Clouds: A Self-Managing Infrastructure for Autonomic Mobile Computing Services.* Self-Managed Networks, Systems, and Services.

Fatima, E., & Ehsan, S. (2023). Data Centers Sustainability: Approaches to Green Data Centers. *4th International Conference on Communication Technologies, ComTech 2023*, (pp. 105–110). IEEE. 10.1109/ComTech57708.2023.10165494

Fatima, S., & Ahmad, S. (2021). Quantum key distribution approach for secure authentication of cloud servers. [IJCAC]. *International Journal of Cloud Applications and Computing*, *11*(3), 19–32. doi:10.4018/IJCAC.2021070102

Ferdman, M., Adileh, A., Kocberber, O., Volos, S., Alisafaee, M., Jevdjic, D., Kaynak, C., Popescu, A. D., Ailamaki, A., & Falsafi, B. (2012). Clearing the clouds: a study of emerging scale-out workloads on modern hardware. In ACM SIGPLAN Notices, 47, 37–48. ACM. doi:10.1145/2150976.2150982

Ferguson, A. D., Bodik, P., Kandula, S., Boutin, E., & Fonseca, R. (2012). Jockey: guaranteed job latency in data parallel clusters. In *Proceedings of the 7th ACM European conference on Computer Systems*, (pp. 99–112). ACM. 10.1145/2168836.2168847

Flower, Z. (2020). Top 6 complexity challenges of operating a cloud at scale. *Tech Target.* https://www.techtarget.com/searchcloudcomputing/tip/Top-6-complexity-challenges-of-operating-a-cloud-at-scale

Forman, G. H., & Zahorjan, J. (1994). The Challenges of Mobile Computing. *Computer*, *27*(4), 38–47. doi:10.1109/2.274999

Foster, I., Zhao, Y., Raicu, I., & Lu, S. (2009). Cloud Computing and Grid Computing 360-Degree Compared. *Proceedings of Workshop on Grid Computing Environments (GCE)*, (pp. 1-10). ACM.

Foster, S., Hawking, P., & Stein, A. (2004). Change Management: The Forgotten Critical Success Factor in Enterprise Wide System Implementations. *Proc. Of the 15th Australasian Conference on Information Systems (ACIS).* IEEE.

Fouzar, Y., Lakhssassi, A., & Ramakrishna, M. (2023). A Novel Hybrid Multikey Cryptography Technique for Video Communication. *IEEE Access : Practical Innovations, Open Solutions*, *11*, 15693–15700. doi:10.1109/ACCESS.2023.3242616

Fusaro, D., Olivastri, E., Evangelista, D., Imperoli, M., Menegatti, E., & Pretto, A. (2023). Pushing the Limits of Learning-Based Traversability Analysis for Autonomous Driving on CPU. In I. Petrovic, E. Menegatti, & I. Marković (Eds.), *Intelligent Autonomous Systems 17. IAS 2022. Lecture Notes in Networks and Systems* (Vol. 577). Springer. doi:10.1007/978-3-031-22216-0_36

Gad, A. G., Mosa, D. T., Abualigah, L., & Abohany, A. A. (2022). Emerging trends in blockchain technology and applications: A review and outlook. *Journal of King Saud University. Computer and Information Sciences*, *34*(9), 6719–6742. doi:10.1016/j.jksuci.2022.03.007

Gaffoor, Z., Pietersen, K., Bagula, A., Jovanovic, N., Kanyerere, T., & Wanangwa, G. (2021). *Big Data Analytics and Modelling*. Research Gate.

Gai, K., Wu, Y., Zhu, L., Xu, L., & Zhang, Y. (2019). Permissioned blockchain and edge computing empowered privacy-preserving smart grid networks. *IEEE Internet of Things Journal*, *6*(5), 7992–8004. doi:10.1109/JIOT.2019.2904303

Galloway, J. M., Smith, K. L., & Vrbsky, S. S. (2011). Power aware load balancing for cloud computing. *Proceedings of the World Congress on Engineering and Computer Science*, (vol. 1, pp. 19–21).

Garg, S., Singh, A., Batra, S., Kumar, N., & Yang, L. T. (2018). UAV-empowered edge computing environment for cyber-threat detection in smart vehicles. *IEEE Network*, *32*(3), 42–51. doi:10.1109/MNET.2018.1700286

Gawusu, S., Zhang, X., Ahmed, A., Jamatutu, S. A., Miensah, E. D., Amadu, A. A., & Osei, F. A. J. (2022). Renewable energy sources from the perspective of blockchain integration: From theory to application. *Sustainable Energy Technologies and Assessments*, *52*, 102108. doi:10.1016/j.seta.2022.102108

GEORGE, D. A. S., George, A. H., Baskar, T., & Pandey, D. (2021). XDR: The Evolution of Endpoint Security Solutions-Superior Extensibility and Analytics to Satisfy the Organizational Needs of the Future. International Journal of Advanced Research in Science [IJARSCT]. *Tongxin Jishu*, *8*(1), 493–501.

Gewirtz, D. (2018). *Volume, velocity, and variety.* ZDNet. https://www.zdnet.com/article/volume-velocity-and-varietyunderstanding-the-three-vs-of-big-data/

Gezimati, M., & Singh, G. (2023). Advances in terahertz technology for cancer detection applications. *Optical and Quantum Electronics*, *55*(2), 151. doi:10.1007/s11082-022-04340-0 PMID:36588663

Ghazanfari-Rad, S., & Ebneyousef, S. (2023). A Survey of Renewable Energy Approaches in Cloud Data Centers. *2023 8th International Conference on Technology and Energy Management, ICTEM 2023*. IEEE. 10.1109/ICTEM56862.2023.10083820

Ghezelbash, R., Maghsoudi, A., Shamekhi, M., Pradhan, B., & Daviran, M. (2023). Genetic algorithm to optimize the SVM and *K*-means algorithms for mapping of mineral prospectivity. *Neural Computing & Applications*, *35*(1), 719–733. doi:10.1007/s00521-022-07766-5

Ghomi, M., Zare, E. N., Alidadi, H., Pourreza, N., Sheini, A., Rabiee, N., Mattoli, V., Chen, X., & Makvandi, P. (2023). A multifunctional bioresponsive and fluorescent active nanogel composite for breast cancer therapy and bioimaging. *Advanced Composites and Hybrid Materials*, *6*(1), 51. doi:10.1007/s42114-022-00613-0

Ghosh, S., & Banerjee, C. (2018). Dynamic time quantum priority based round robin for load balancing in cloud environment. *Proceedings - 2018 4th IEEE International Conference on Research in Computational Intelligence and Communication Networks, ICRCICN 2018*, (pp. 33–37). IEEE. 10.1109/ICRCICN.2018.8718694

Ghosh, R., & Kumar, A. (2022). A hybrid deep learning model by combining convolutional neural network and recurrent neural network to detect forest fire. *Multimedia Tools and Applications*, *81*(27), 38643–38660. doi:10.1007/s11042-022-13068-8

Ghosh, R., Mohanty, S., Pattnaik, P. K., & Pramanik, S. (2020). Performance Analysis Based on Probablity of False Alarm and Miss Detection in Cognitive Radio Network. *International Journal of Wireless and Mobile Computing*, *20*(4), 390. doi:10.1504/IJWMC.2021.117530

Ghosh, R., Mohanty, S., Pattnaik, P., & Pramanik, S. (2020). A Performance Assessment of Power-Efficient Variants of Distributed Energy-Efficient Clustering Protocols in WSN. *International Journal of Interactive Communication Systems and Technologies*, *10*(2), 1–14. doi:10.4018/IJICST.2020070101

Ghosh, R., & Pramanik, S. (2021). A Novel Performance Evaluation of Resourceful Energy Saving Protocols of Heterogeneous WSN to Maximize Network Stability and Lifetime. *International Journal of Interdisciplinary Telecommunications and Networking*, *13*(2), 72–88. doi:10.4018/IJITN.2021040106

Gill, S. S., Tuli, S., Xu, M., Singh, I., Singh, K. V., Lindsay, D., Tuli, S., Smirnova, D., Singh, M., Jain, U., Pervaiz, H., Sehgal, B., Kaila, S. S., Misra, S., Aslanpour, M. S., Mehta, H., Stankovski, V., & Garraghan, P. (2019). Transformative effects of IoT, Blockchain and Artificial Intelligence on cloud computing: Evolution, vision, trends and open challenges. *Internet of Things : Engineering Cyber Physical Human Systems*, *8*, 100118. doi:10.1016/j.iot.2019.100118

Gill, S. S., Xu, M., Ottaviani, C., Patros, P., Bahsoon, R., Shaghaghi, A., Golec, M., Stankovski, V., Wu, H., Abraham, A., Singh, M., Mehta, H., Ghosh, S. K., Baker, T., Parlikad, A. K., Lutfiyya, H., Kanhere, S. S., Sakellariou, R., Dustdar, S., & Uhlig, S. (2022). AI for next generation computing: Emerging trends and future directions. *Internet of Things : Engineering Cyber Physical Human Systems*, *19*, 100514. doi:10.1016/j.iot.2022.100514

Gisin, N., Ribordy, G., Tittel, W., & Zbinden, H. (2002). Quantum cryptography. *Reviews of Modern Physics*, *74*(1), 145–195. doi:10.1103/RevModPhys.74.145

Gluhak, A., Krco, S., Nati, M., Pfisterer, D., Mitton, N., & Razafindralambo, T. (2011, November). A survey on facilities for experimental Internet of Things research. *IEEE Communications Magazine*, *49*(11), 58–67. doi:10.1109/MCOM.2011.6069710

Godhrawala, H., & Sridaran, R. (2023). A dynamic Stackelberg game based multi-objective approach for effective resource allocation in cloud computing. *International Journal of Information Technology : an Official Journal of Bharati Vidyapeeth's Institute of Computer Applications and Management*, *15*(2), 803–818. doi:10.1007/s41870-022-00926-9

Golightly, L., Chang, V., Xu, Q. A., Gao, X., & Liu, B. S. C. (2022). Adoption of cloud computing as innovation in the organization. *International Journal of Engineering Business Management*, *14*. doi:10.1177/18479790221093992

Goodchild, M. F. (2010). Twenty years of progress: GIScience in 2010. *Journal of Spatial Information Science*, *1*(1), 3–20. doi:10.5311/JOSIS.2010.1.2

Google cloud, (2023), Available: https://cloud.google.com/appengine/docs/the-appengine-environments

Google Cloud. (2020). *BigQuery*. Google. https://cloud.google.com/bigquery

Google Cloud. (2023a). *Google Cloud Security*. Google. https://cloud.google.com/security

Google Cloud. (2023b). *Google Earth Engine*. Google. https://cloud.google.com/earth-engine

Google. (n.d.). *About OS Images*. Google. https://cloud.google.com/compute/docs/images

Grubisic, F. (2023). *A spatial data infrastructure based conceptual model for an efficient public transport system* [Stockholm University, Faculty of Social Sciences]. https://www.diva-portal.org/smash/record.jsf?pid=diva2%3A1784323&dswid=-644

Gruschka, N., & Jensen, M. (2010). Attack surfaces: A taxonomy for attacks on cloud services. *Proc. 2010 IEEE 3rd Int. Conf. Cloud Comput. CLOUD 2010,* (pp. 276–279). IEEE. 10.1109/CLOUD.2010.23

Guan, L., Ke, X., Song, M., & Song, J. (2011). A survey of research on mobile cloud computing. In S. Xu, W. Du, & R. Lee (Eds.), *2011 10th IEEE/ACIS International Conference on Computer and Information Science* (pp. 387–392). Washington, DC: IEEE. 10.1109/ICIS.2011.67

Gubbi, J., Buyya, R., Marusic, S., & Palaniswami, M. (2013, September). Internet of Things (IoT): A vision, architectural elements, and future directions. *Future Generation Computer Systems*, *29*(7), 1645–1660. doi:10.1016/j.future.2013.01.010

Guest, O., & Martin, A. E. (2023). On Logical Inference over Brains, Behaviour, and Artificial Neural Networks. *Computational Brain & Behavior*, *6*(2), 213–227. doi:10.1007/s42113-022-00166-x

Guo, L., Chen, J., Li, S., Li, Y., & Lu, J. (2022). A blockchain and IoT-based lightweight framework for enabling information transparency in supply chain finance. *Digital Communications and Networks*, *8*(4), 576–587. doi:10.1016/j.dcan.2022.03.020

Guo, Y., Gong, Y., Fang, Y., Khargonekar, P. P., & Geng, X. (2014). Energy and network aware workload management for sustainable data centers with thermal storage. *IEEE Transactions on Parallel and Distributed Systems*, *25*(8), 2030–2042. doi:10.1109/TPDS.2013.278

Gupta, A., Asad, A., Meena, L., & Anand, R. (2023). IoT and RFID-Based Smart Card System Integrated with Health Care, Electricity, QR and Banking Sectors. In M. Gupta, S. Ghatak, A. Gupta, & A. L. Mukherjee (Eds.), *Artificial Intelligence on Medical Data. Lecture Notes in Computational Vision and Biomechanics* (Vol. 37). Springer. doi:10.1007/978-981-19-0151-5_22

Gupta, A., & Namasudra, S. (2022). A Novel Technique for Accelerating Live Migration in Cloud Computing. *Automated Software Engineering*, *29*(1), 1–21. doi:10.1007/s10515-022-00332-2

Gupta, A., Verma, A., & Pramanik, S. (2022). Advanced Security System in Video Surveillance for COVID-19. In *An Interdisciplinary Approach to Modern Network Security, S. Pramanik, A. Sharma, S. Bhatia and D. N. Le*. CRC Press. doi:10.1201/9781003147176-8

Gupta, T., Pandey, P., & Raghav, Y. Y. (2023). Impact of Social Media Platforms on the Consumer Decision-Making Process in the Food and Grocery Industry. In T. Tarnanidis, M. Vlachopoulou, & J. Papathanasiou (Eds.), *Influences of Social Media on Consumer Decision-Making Processes in the Food and Grocery Industry* (pp. 119–139). IGI Global. doi:10.4018/978-1-6684-8868-3.ch006

Gür, T. M. (2018). Review of electrical energy storage technologies, materials and systems: Challenges and prospects for large-scale grid storage. *Energy & Environmental Science*, *11*(10), 2696–2767. doi:10.1039/C8EE01419A

H, O. M. E. (2011). Geospatial mappg, analysis and simulation in health services research. In *Proceedings of Singapore Healthcare (Vol. 20)*.

Hader, M., Tchoffa, D., El Mhamedi, A., Ghodous, P., Dolgui, A., & Abouabdellah, A. (2022). Applying integrated Blockchain and Big Data technologies to improve supply chain traceability and information sharing in the textile sector. *Journal of Industrial Information Integration*, *28*, 100345. doi:10.1016/j.jii.2022.100345

Haghshenas, K., Setz, B., Blosch, Y., & Aiello, M. (2023). Enough hot air: The role of immersion cooling. *Energy Informatics*, *6*(1), 1–18. doi:10.1186/s42162-023-00257-4

Hajvali, M., Adabi, S., Rezaee, A., & Hosseinzadeh, M. (2023). Decentralized and scalable hybrid scheduling-clustering method for real-time applications in volatile and dynamic Fog-Cloud Environments. *Journal of Cloud Computing (Heidelberg, Germany)*, *12*(1), 66. doi:10.1186/s13677-023-00428-4

Halak, B., Yilmaz, Y., & Shiu, D. (2022). Comparative analysis of energy costs of asymmetric vs symmetric encryption-based security applications. *IEEE Access : Practical Innovations, Open Solutions*, *10*, 76707–76719. doi:10.1109/ACCESS.2022.3192970

Hamdan, S., Ayyash, M., & Almajali, S. (2020). Edge-computing architectures for internet of things applications: A survey. *Sensors (Basel)*, *20*(22), 6441. doi:10.3390/s20226441 PMID:33187267

Harauzek, D. (2022). *Cloud Computing: Challenges of cloud computing from business users perspective-vendor lock-in.* LinkedIn.

Hartmann, M., Hashmi, U. S., & Imran, A. (2022). Edge computing in smart health care systems: Review, challenges, and research directions. *Transactions on Emerging Telecommunications Technologies*, *33*(3), e3710. doi:10.1002/ett.3710

Hassan, N. M., Hamad, S., & Mahar, K. (2022). Mammogram breast cancer CAD systems for mass detection and classification: A review. *Multimedia Tools and Applications*, *81*(14), 20043–20075. doi:10.1007/s11042-022-12332-1

Hassan, N., Yau, K. L. A., & Wu, C. (2019). Edge computing in 5G: A review. *IEEE Access : Practical Innovations, Open Solutions*, *7*, 127276–127289. doi:10.1109/ACCESS.2019.2938534

Hazra, A., Rana, P., Adhikari, M., & Amgoth, T. (2023). Fog computing for next-generation Internet of Things: Fundamental, state-of-the-art and research challenges. *Computer Science Review*, *48*, 100549. doi:10.1016/j.cosrev.2023.100549

He, L., & Yue, P. (2019). A Cloud-Enabled Geospatial Big Data Platform for Disaster Information Services. *International Geoscience and Remote Sensing Symposium (IGARSS)*. IEEE. 10.1109/IGARSS.2019.8898893

Henke, N., & Jacques Bughin, L. (2016). *The age of analytics: Competing in a data-driven world*. McKinsey.

Hercigonja, Z. (2016). Comparative analysis of cryptographic algorithms. *International Journal of Digital Technology & Economy*, *1*(2), 127–134.

Hesaraki, A. F., Dellaert, N. P., & de Kok, T. (2023). Online scheduling using a fixed template: The case of outpatient chemotherapy drug administration. *Health Care Management Science*, *26*(1), 117–137. doi:10.1007/s10729-022-09616-1 PMID:36319888

Hlaing, Y. T. H., & Yee, T. T. (2019). Static independent task scheduling on virtualized servers in cloud computing environment. *2019 International Conference on Advanced Information Technologies (ICAIT)*. IEEE. 10.1109/AITC.2019.8920865

Horizontal vs. Vertical Scaling in the Cloud. (2021). Cloud Checkr. https://cloudcheckr.com/cloud-automation/horizontal-vertical-cloud-scaling/

Hou, M., Zhou, L., & Sun, J. (2023). Deep-learning-based 3D super-resolution MRI radiomics model: Superior predictive performance in preoperative T-staging of rectal cancer. *European Radiology*, *33*(1), 1–10. doi:10.1007/s00330-022-08952-8 PMID:35726100

HP. (2023). *What is Cloud Scalability?* HP. https://tinyurl.com/3yt9w9xa

Hsu, C.-J., Nair, V., Freeh, V.W., & Menzies, T. (2017). *Low level augmented Bayesian optimization for finding the best cloud VM*.

Huang, B., Boehm, M., Tian, Y., Reinwald, B., Tatikonda, S., & Frederick, R. R. (2015). Resource elasticity for largescale machine learning. In *Proceedings of the 2015 ACM SIGMOD International Conference on Management of Data*, (pp. 137–152). ACM. 10.1145/2723372.2749432

Huang, D. (2011). Mobile cloud computing. IEEE ComSoc Multimedia Communications Technical Committee (MMTC). *E-Letter*, *6*(10), 27–31.

Huang, P., Copertaro, B., Zhang, X., Shen, J., Löfgren, I., Rönnelid, M., Fahlen, J., Andersson, D., & Svanfeldt, M. (2020). A review of data centers as prosumers in district energy systems: Renewable energy integration and waste heat reuse for district heating. *Applied Energy*, *258*, 114109. doi:10.1016/j.apenergy.2019.114109

Huang, T., Lan, L., Fang, X., An, P., Min, J., & Wang, F. (2015). Promises and challenges of big data computing in health sciences. *Big Data Res.*, *2*(1), 2–11. doi:10.1016/j.bdr.2015.02.002

Huang, X., Lin, Y., Zhang, Z., Guo, X., & Su, S. (2022). A gradient-based optimization approach for task scheduling problem in cloud computing. *Cluster Computing*, *25*(5), 3481–3497. doi:10.1007/s10586-022-03580-9

Huawei. (2023). *Cloud Platforms and Big Data Storage: Scalable and Cost-Effective Solutions*. Huawei. https://forum.huawei.com/enterprise/en/Cloud-Platforms-and-Big-Data-Storage-Scalable-and-Cost-Effective-Solutions/thread/706603521027227648-667213860102352896

Hung, T. C., Hy, P. T., Hieu, L. N., & Phi, N. X. (2019). MMSIA: Improved max-min scheduling algorithm for load balancing on cloud computing. *ACM International Conference Proceeding Series*, (pp. 60–64). ACM. 10.1145/3310986.3311017

Hwang, T. (2018). Computational power and the social impact of artificial intelligence. *arXiv preprint arXiv:1803.08971*.

Hwang, K., & Chen, M. (2017). *Big-data analytics for cloud, IoT and cognitive computing*. John Wiley & Sons.

IBM Data Breach Report. (2022). IBM. https://www.ibm.com/reports/data-breach

IBM. (2022). *IBM 2022 ESG Report and Addendum.* IBM. https://www.ibm.com/impact/files/reports-policies/2022/IBM_2022_ESG_Report_and_Addendum.pdf

IBM. (n.d.). *Home.* IBM. https://cloud.ibm.com/

International Energy Agency. (2022). *Data Centres and Data Transmission Networks.* IEA. https://www.iea.org/energy-system/buildings/data-centres-and-data-transmission-networks

IonescuA.AlexandridouA.IkonomouL.PsarakisK.PatroumpasK.ChatzigeorgakidisG.SkoutasD.AthanasiouS.HaiR.Katsifodimos A. (2023). Topio Marketplace: Search and Discovery of Geospatial Data. *Advances in Database Technology - EDBT, 26*(3). doi:10.48786/edbt.2023.73

Ivan, C., Vasile, R., & Dadarlat, V. (2019). Serverless computing: An investigation of deployment environments for web apis. *Computers*, *8*(2), 50. doi:10.3390/computers8020050

Iyyanar, P., Anand, R., Shanthi, T., Nassa, V. K., Pandey, B. K., George, A. S., & Pandey, D. (2023). A Real-Time Smart Sewage Cleaning UAV Assistance System Using IoT. In *Handbook of Research on Data-Driven Mathematical Modeling in Smart Cities* (pp. 24–39). IGI Global.

Jabbour, C., Rey-Valette, H., Maurel, P., & Salles, J. M. (2019). Spatial data infrastructure management: A two-sided market approach for strategic reflections. *International Journal of Information Management*, *45*, 69–82. doi:10.1016/j.ijinfomgt.2018.10.022

Jadon, K. S., Bhadoria, R. S., & Tomar, G. S. (2016). A review on costing issues in big data analytics. *Proc. 2015 International Conference on Computational Intelligence and Communication Networks (CICN)*, Jabalpur, India.

Jain, N., & Choudhary, S. (2016, March). Overview of virtualization in cloud computing. In *2016 Symposium on Colossal Data Analysis and Networking (CDAN)* (pp. 1-4). IEEE.

Jain, S., Gupta, S., Sreelakshmi, K. K., & Rodrigues, J. J. P. C. (2022). Fog computing in enabling 5G-driven emerging technologies for development of sustainable smart city infrastructures. *Cluster Computing*, *25*(2), 1111–1154. doi:10.1007/s10586-021-03496-w

Jalaparti, V., Ballani, H., Costa, P., Karagiannis, T., & Rowstron, A. (2012). Bridging the tenant-provider gap in cloud services. In *Proceedings of the Third ACM Symposium on Cloud Computing*. ACM. 10.1145/2391229.2391239

Janowicz, K., Gao, S., McKenzie, G., Hu, Y., & Bhaduri, B. (2020). GeoAI: spatially explicit artificial intelligence techniques for geographic knowledge discovery and beyond. In International Journal of Geographical Information Science, 34(4). doi:10.1080/13658816.2019.1684500

Jasim, O. K., Abbas, S., El-Horbaty, E.-S. M., & Salem, A.-B. M. (2014). Cryptographic cloud computing environment as a more trusted communication environment. [IJGHPC]. *International Journal of Grid and High Performance Computing*, *6*(2), 38–51. doi:10.4018/ijghpc.2014040103

Javaid, M., Haleem, A., Singh, R. P., Suman, R., & Khan, S. (2022). A review of Blockchain Technology applications for financial services. *BenchCouncil Transactions on Benchmarks, Standards and Evaluations*, 100073.

Jayapoorani, S., Pandey, D., Sasirekha, N. S., Anand, R., & Pandey, B. K. (2023). Systolic optimized adaptive filter architecture designs for ECG noise cancellation by Vertex-5. *Aerospace Systems*, *6*(1), 163–173. doi:10.1007/s42401-022-00177-3

Jayaprakash, J. (2022). Cloud Data Encryption and Authentication Based on Enhanced Merkle Hash Tree Method. *Computers, Materials & Continua*, *72*(1). doi:10.32604/cmc.2022.021269

Jayaraman, G., & Dhulipala, V. R. S. (2022). FEECS: Fuzzy-Based Energy-Efficient Cluster Head Selection Algorithm for Lifetime Enhancement of Wireless Sensor Networks. *Arabian Journal for Science and Engineering*, *47*(2), 1631–1641. doi:10.1007/s13369-021-06030-7

Jayasingh, R., & Kumar, J. (2022). Speckle noise removal by SORAMA segmentation in Digital Image Processing to facilitate precise robotic surgery. *International Journal of Reliable and Quality E-Healthcare*, *11*(1), 1–19. Advance online publication. doi:10.4018/IJRQEH.295083

Jena, R. K. (2015). Multi Objective Task Scheduling in Cloud Environment Using Nested PSO Framework. *Procedia Computer Science*, *57*, 1219–1227. doi:10.1016/j.procs.2015.07.419

Jiang, F., Wang, K., Dong, L., Pan, C., Xu, W., & Yang, K. (2020). Deep-Learning-Based Joint Resource Scheduling Algorithms for Hybrid MEC Networks. *IEEE Internet of Things Journal*, *7*(7), 6252–6265. doi:10.1109/JIOT.2019.2954503

Kaffes, K., Yadwadkar, N. J., & Kozyrakis, C. (2021). *Practical scheduling for real-world serverless computing*. arXiv preprint arXiv:2111.07226.

Kaginalkar, A., Kumar, S., Gargava, P., & Niyogi, D. (2021). Review of urban computing in air quality management as smart city service: An integrated IoT, AI, and cloud technology perspective. *Urban Climate*, *39*, 100972. doi:10.1016/j.uclim.2021.100972

Kakati, S., Mazumdar, N., & Nag, A. (2022). Green Cloud Computing for IoT Based Smart Applications. In *Green Mobile Cloud Computing* (pp. 201–212). Springer International Publishing. doi:10.1007/978-3-031-08038-8_10

Kalinaki, K., Namuwaya, S., Mwamini, A., & Namuwaya, S. (2023). Scaling Up Customer Support Using Artificial Intelligence and Machine Learning Techniques. In *Contemporary Approaches of Digital Marketing and the Role of Machine Intelligence* (pp. 23–45). IGI Global. doi:10.4018/978-1-6684-7735-9.ch002

Kalinaki, K., Thilakarathne, N. N., Mubarak, H. R., Malik, O. A., & Abdullatif, M. (2023). Cybersafe Capabilities and Utilities for Smart Cities. In *Cybersecurity for Smart Cities* (pp. 71–86). Springer. doi:10.1007/978-3-031-24946-4_6

Kamel Boulos, M. N., Resch, B., Crowley, D. N., Breslin, J. G., Sohn, G., Burtner, R., Pike, W., Jezierski, E., & Ch uang, K.-Y. (2011). Crowdsourcing, citizen sensing and sensor web technologies for public and environmental health surveillance and crisis management: Trends, OGC standards and application examples. *International Journal of Health Geographics*, *10*(1), 67. doi:10.1186/1476-072X-10-67 PMID:22188675

Kandukuri, B. R., & Rakshit, A. (2009). Cloud security issues. In *2009 IEEE International Conference on Services Computing* (pp. 517-520). IEEE. https://doi.org/10.1109/SCC.2009.84

Kansal, N. J., & Chana, I. (2012). Existing load balancing techniques in cloud computing: A systematic review. *Journal of Information Systems & Communication*, *3*(1), 87–91.

Karmas, A., Tzotsos, A., & Karantzalos, K. (2016). Geospatial big data for environmental and agricultural applications. In *Big Data Concepts*. Theories, and Applications. doi:10.1007/978-3-319-27763-9_10

Karpagam, M., Geetha, K., & Rajan, C. (2020). A modified shuffled frog leaping algorithm for scientific workflow scheduling using clustering techniques. *Soft Computing*, *24*(1), 637–646. doi:10.1007/s00500-019-04484-4

Kashyap, S., & Singh, A. (2023). Prediction-based scheduling techniques for cloud data center's workload: A systematic review. *Cluster Computing*, *26*(5), 1–27. doi:10.1007/s10586-023-04024-8

Katal, A., Dahiya, S., & Choudhury, T. (2023). Energy efficiency in cloud computing data centers: A survey on software technologies. *Cluster Computing*, *26*(3), 1845–1875. doi:10.1007/s10586-022-03713-0 PMID:36060618

Katal, A., Wazid, M., & Goudar, R. H. (2013). Big data: Issues, challenges, tools and good practices. *Proc. 6th Int. Conf. Contemporary Computing*, Noida, India. 10.1109/IC3.2013.6612229

Kaur, A. (2017). Particle Swarm Optimization based Dynamic Load Balancing in Cloud Environment. *International Journal on Computer Science and Engineering*.

Kaur, K., Bharany, S., Badotra, S., Aggarwal, K., Nayyar, A., & Sharma, S. (2023). Energy-efficient polyglot persistence database live migration among heterogeneous clouds. *The Journal of Supercomputing*, *79*(1), 265–294. doi:10.1007/s11227-022-04662-6

Kaur, S., Kaur, G., & Shabaz, M. (2022). A secure two-factor authentication framework in cloud computing. *Security and Communication Networks*, *2022*, 1–9. doi:10.1155/2022/7540891

Kazemzadeh, E., Fuinhas, J. A., Salehnia, N., & Osmani, F. (2023). The effect of economic complexity, fertility rate, and information and communication technology on ecological footprint in the emerging economies: A two-step stirpat model and panel quantile regression. *Quality & Quantity*, *57*(1), 737–763. doi:10.1007/s11135-022-01373-1

Khalil, I., Khreishah, A., & Azeem, M. (2014). Cloud Computing Security: A Survey. *Computers*, *3*(1), 1–35. doi:10.3390/computers3010001

Khan, R., Khan, S. U., Zaheer, R., & Khan, S. (2012). Future Internet: The Internet of Things architecture, possible applications and key challenges. Proc. 10th Int. Conf. FIT, (pp. 257–260). IEEE. 10.1109/FIT.2012.53

Khan, A. R., Othman, M., Madani, S. A., & Khan, S. U. (2013). A survey of mobile cloud computing application models. *IEEE Communications Surveys and Tutorials*, *16*(1), 393–413. doi:10.1109/SURV.2013.062613.00160

Khanfar, A. A. A., Iranmanesh, M., Ghobakhloo, M., Senali, M. G., & Fathi, M. (2021). Applications of blockchain technology in sustainable manufacturing and supply chain management: A systematic review. *Sustainability (Basel)*, *13*(14), 7870. doi:10.3390/su13147870

Khanh, P. T., Ngọc, T. H., & Pramanik, S. (2023). Future of Smart Agriculture Techniques and Applications. In A. Khang & I. G. I. Global (Eds.), *Advanced Technologies and AI-Equipped IoT Applications in High Tech Agriculture*. doi:10.4018/978-1-6684-9231-4.ch021

Khan, L. U., Yaqoob, I., Tran, N. H., Kazmi, S. A., Dang, T. N., & Hong, C. S. (2020). Edge-computing-enabled smart cities: A comprehensive survey. *IEEE Internet of Things Journal*, *7*(10), 10200–10232. doi:10.1109/JIOT.2020.2987070

Khan, M. W., Khan, S. Y., Altaf, S., & Ali, M. W. (2021). A REVIEW OF THE SECURITY ISSUES IN CLOUD COMPUTING AND ITS REMEDIAL ACTION. *INFORMATION TECHNOLOGY IN INDUSTRY*, *9*(1), 444–455. doi:10.17762/itii.v9i1.150

Khan, N., & Al-Yasiri, A. (2016). Identifying cloud security threats to strengthen cloud computing adoption framework. *Procedia Computer Science*, *94*, 485–490. doi:10.1016/j.procs.2016.08.075

Khan, R. A., Hussain, A., Bajwa, U. I., Raza, R. H., & Anwar, M. W. (2023). Fire and Smoke Detection Using Capsule Network. *Fire Technology*, *59*(2), 581–594. doi:10.1007/s10694-022-01352-w

Khurana, D., Koli, A., Khatter, K., & Singh, S. (2023). Natural language processing: State of the art, current trends and challenges. *Multimedia Tools and Applications*, *82*(3), 3713–3744. doi:10.1007/s11042-022-13428-4 PMID:35855771

Kilgore, G. (2023). *Carbon Footprint of Data Centers & Data Storage Per Country*. Eight Billion Trees. https://8billiontrees.com/carbon-offsets-credits/carbon-ecological-footprint-calculators/carbon-footprint-of-data-centers/

Kimball, R., & Ross, M. (2013). *The data warehouse toolkit: The definitive guide to dimensional modeling* (3rd ed.). John Wiley & Sons.

Kineber, A. F., Oke, A. E., Alyanbaawi, A., Abubakar, A. S., & Hamed, M. M. (2022). Exploring the Cloud Computing Implementation Drivers for Sustainable Construction Projects—A Structural Equation Modeling Approach. *Sustainability, 14*(22), 14789. doi:10.3390/su142214789

Kirvan, P. (2021). How to effectively plan cloud storage scalability. *Tech Target.* https://www.techtarget.com/searchstorage/tip/How-to-effectively-plan-cloud-storage-scalability

Kjorveziroski, V., Bernad Canto, C., Juan Roig, P., Gilly, K., Mishev, A., Trajkovikj, V., & Filiposka, S. (2021). *IoT serverless computing at the edge: Open issues and research direction.* Transactions on Networks and Communications.

Klein, A., Mannweiler, C., Schneider, J., & Schotten, H. D. (2010). Access schemes for mobile cloud computing. In *2010 Eleventh International Conference on Mobile Data Management* (pp. 387–392). IEEE. 10.1109/MDM.2010.79

Ključanin, S., Rezo, M., Džebo, S., & Hadžić, E. (2021). Spatial Data Infrastructure in Natural Disaster Management. *Tehnicki Glasnik, 15*(4), 455–461. Advance online publication. doi:10.31803/tg-20210108180723

Koh, K., Hyder, A., Karale, Y., & Kamel Boulos, M. N. (2022). Big Geospatial Data or Geospatial Big Data? A Systematic Narrative Review on the Use of Spatial Data Infrastructures for Big Geospatial Sensing Data in Public Health. In Remote Sensing, 14(13). doi:10.3390/rs14132996

Kohli, V., Chougule, A., Chamola, V., & Yu, F. R. (2022, May). MbRE IDS: an AI and edge computing empowered framework for securing intelligent transportation systems. In *IEEE INFOCOM 2022-IEEE Conference on Computer Communications Workshops (INFOCOM WKSHPS)* (pp. 1-6). IEEE. 10.1109/INFOCOMWKSHPS54753.2022.9798390

Kokilavani, T., & Amalarethinam, D. (2011). Load balanced min-min algorithm for static meta-task scheduling in grid computing. *International Journal of Computer Applications*, *20*(2), 24–31. doi:10.5120/2403-3197

Koliopoulos, A., Yiapanis, P., Tekiner, F., Nenadic, G., & Keane, J. (2015). A parallel distributed weka framework for big data mining using spark. In: *2015 IEEE International Congress Big Data (BigData Congress),* (pp. 9–16). IEEE. 10.1109/BigDataCongress.2015.12

Kong, J. (2010). A Practical Approach to Improve the Data Privacy of Virtual Machines. *2010 IEEE 10th International Conference on Computer and Information Technology (CIT).* IEEE. 10.1109/CIT.2010.173

Kong, L., Tan, J., Huang, J., Chen, G., Wang, S., Jin, X., Zeng, P., Khan, M., & Das, S. K. (2022). Edge-computing-driven internet of things: A survey. *ACM Computing Surveys*, *55*(8), 1–41. doi:10.1145/3555308

Kosta, Aucinas, Hui, Mortier, & Zhang. (2012). Thinkair: Dynamic resource allocation and parallel execution in cloud for mobile code offloading. *INFOCOM IEEE Proceedings*, 945-953.

Kounev, S. (2023, April). Serverless Computing Revisited: Evolution, State-of-the-Art, and Performance Challenges. In *Companion of the 2023 ACM/SPEC International Conference on Performance Engineering* (pp. 309-310). ACM. 10.1145/3578245.3584856

Kovachev, D., Cao, Y., & Klamma, R. (2011). *Mobile cloud computing: A comparison of application models*. arXiv preprint.

Kratzke, N., & Quint, P.-C. (2017). Understanding cloud-native applications after 10 years of cloud computing - A systematic mapping study. *Journal of Systems and Software*, *126*, 1–16. doi:10.1016/j.jss.2017.01.001

Krishnasamy, K. G., Periasamy, S., Periasamy, K., Prasanna Moorthy, V., Thangavel, G., Lamba, R., & Muthusamy, S. (2023). A Pair-Task Heuristic for Scheduling Tasks in Heterogeneous Multi-cloud Environment. *Wireless Personal Communications*, *131*(2), 773–804. doi:10.1007/s11277-023-10454-9

Kritikos, K., Rousakis, Y., & Kotzinos, D. (2015). A cloud-based, geospatial linked data management system. Lecture Notes in Computer Science (Including Subseries Lecture Notes in Artificial Intelligence and Lecture Notes in Bioinformatics), 9070. Springer. doi:10.1007/978-3-662-46703-9_3

Kruekaew, B., & Kimpan, W. (2022). Multi-Objective Task Scheduling Optimization for Load Balancing in Cloud Computing Environment Using Hybrid Artificial Bee Colony Algorithm with Reinforcement Learning. *IEEE Access : Practical Innovations, Open Solutions*, *10*, 17803–17818. doi:10.1109/ACCESS.2022.3149955

Kumar, R. (2020). Sustainable Supply Chain Management in the Era of Digitialization. In Handbook of Research on Social and Organizational Dynamics in the Digital Era (pp. 446–460). IGI Global. doi:10.4018/978-1-5225-8933-4.ch021

Kumar, S., Talukder, M. B., Kabir, F., & Kaiser, F. (2024). Challenges and Sustainability of Green Finance in the Tourism Industry: Evidence From Bangladesh. In Sustainable Investments in Green Finance (pp. 97-111). IGI Global.

Kumar, A., Kan, S. B., Pandey, S. K., Shankar, A., Maple, C., Mashat, A., & Malibari, A. A. (2023). Development of a cloud-assisted classification technique for the preservation of secure data storage in smart cities. *Journal of Cloud Computing (Heidelberg, Germany)*, *12*(1), 92. doi:10.1186/s13677-023-00469-9

Kumari, A., Behera, R. K., Sahoo, B., & Misra, S. (2022, July). Role of serverless computing in healthcare systems: Case studies. In *International Conference on Computational Science and Its Applications* (pp. 123-134). Cham: Springer International Publishing. 10.1007/978-3-031-10542-5_9

Kumar, M. S., Sankar, S., Nassa, V. K., Pandey, D., Pandey, B. K., & Enbeyle, W. (2021). Innovation and creativity for data mining using computational statistics. In *Methodologies and Applications of Computational Statistics for Machine Intelligence* (pp. 223–240). IGI Global. doi:10.4018/978-1-7998-7701-1.ch012

Kumar, P., & Kumar, R. (2019). Issues and challenges of load balancing techniques in cloud computing: A survey. *ACM Computing Surveys*, *51*(6), 1–35. doi:10.1145/3281010

Kumar, R., & Goyal, R. (2019). On cloud security requirements, threats, vulnerabilities and countermeasures: A survey. *Computer Science Review*, *33*, 1–48. doi:10.1016/j.cosrev.2019.05.002

Kumar, S., & Goudar, R. H. (2012). Cloud Computing – Research Issues, Challenges, Architecture, Platforms and Applications: A Survey. *International Journal of Future Computer and Communication*, *356–360*, 356–360. doi:10.7763/IJFCC.2012.V1.95

Kumar, S., Pal, S., Singh, S., Singh, V. P., Singh, D., Saha, T. K., Gupta, H., & Jaiswal, P. (2023). Energy Efficient Model for Balancing Energy in Cloud Datacenters Using Dynamic Voltage Frequency Scaling (DVFS) Technique. *Lecture Notes in Networks and Systems*, *479*, 533–540. doi:10.1007/978-981-19-3148-2_45

Kunduru, A. R. (2023). Artificial intelligence usage in cloud application performance improvement. *Central Asian Journal of Mathematical Theory and Computer Sciences*, *4*(8), 42–47.

Kuthadi, V. M., Selvaraj, R., Baskar, S., Shakeel, P. M., & Ranjan, A. (2022). Optimized Energy Management Model on Data Distributing Framework of Wireless Sensor Network in IoT System. *Wireless Personal Communications*, *127*(2), 1377–1403. doi:10.1007/s11277-021-08583-0

Kuyoro, S. O., Ibikunle, F., & Awodele, O. (2011). Cloud computing security issues and challenges. [IJCN]. *International Journal of Computer Networks*, *3*(5), 247–255. http://eprints.lmu.edu.ng/1390/

Kwekha-Rashid, A. S., Abduljabbar, H. N., & Alhayani, B. (2023). Coronavirus disease (COVID-19) cases analysis using machine-learning applications. *Applied Nanoscience*, *13*(3), 2013–2025. doi:10.1007/s13204-021-01868-7 PMID:34036034

Lamas-Linares, A., & Kurtsiefer, C. (2007). Breaking a quantum key distribution system through a timing side channel. *Optics Express*, *15*(15), 9388–9393. doi:10.1364/OE.15.009388 PMID:19547285

Laprinth, X. (2018). *Better, Faster, Stronger.* LaprinthX,. https://laptrinhx.com/better-faster-smarter-elt-vs-etl-2084402419/

Larraondo, P. R., Pringle, S., Guo, J., Antony, J., & Evans, B. (2017). GSio: A programmatic interface for delivering Big Earth data-as-a-service. *Big Earth Data*, *1*(1–2), 173–190. doi:10.1080/20964471.2017.1397898

Larsen, M. L. (2023). Bottom-up market-facilitation and top-down market-steering: Comparing and conceptualizing green finance approaches in the EU and China. *Asia Europe Journal*, *21*(1), 61–80. doi:10.1007/s10308-023-00663-z PMID:36741919

Lee, D., & Rowe, J. (2020). *Software, servers, systems, sensors, and science: Facebook's recipe for hyperefficient data centers*. Facebook. https://tech.facebook.com/engineering/2020/1/hyperefficient-data-centers/

Lei, Q. (2023). Artificial Intelligence Empowered Traffic Control for Internet of Things with Mobile Edge Computing. *Journal of Circuits, Systems, and Computers*, *32*(08), 2350048. doi:10.1142/S0218126623500482

Liang, L. L., Chu, S. C., Du, Z. G., & Pan, J.-S. (2023). Surrogate-assisted Phasmatodea population evolution algorithm applied to wireless sensor networks. *Wireless Networks*, *29*(2), 637–655. doi:10.1007/s11276-022-03168-6

Liao, H., Zhou, Z., Zhao, X., Zhang, L., Mumtaz, S., Jolfaei, A., Ahmed, S. H., & Bashir, A. K. (2019). Learning-based context-aware resource allocation for edge-computing-empowered industrial IoT. *IEEE Internet of Things Journal*, *7*(5), 4260–4277. doi:10.1109/JIOT.2019.2963371

Liladhar, R. R., & Ujwal, A. L. (2010). Article: Implementation of Cloud Computing on Web Application. [Published By Foundation of Computer Science.]. *International Journal of Computer Applications*, *2*(8), 28–32. doi:10.5120/685-964

Lin, H. C., ShivnathBabu, J. S. C., & Parekh, S.S. (2009). *Automated Control in Cloud Computing: Opportunities and Challenges*. Proc. of the 1st Workshop on Automated control for data centers and clouds, New York, NY, USA.

Liu, Y. (2023). *Leveraging Emerging Technologies towards Energy-Efficient and High-Performance Computing*. Handle. https://hdl.handle.net/10657/15006

Liu, Z., & Zou, H. (2015, August). AzureRender: A cloud-based parallel and distributed rendering system. In 2015 IEEE 17th International Conference on High Performance Computing and Communications, 2015 IEEE 7th International Symposium on Cyberspace Safety and Security, and 2015 IEEE 12th International Conference on Embedded Software and Systems (pp. 1881-1886). IEEE. 10.1109/HPCC-CSS-ICESS.2015.328

Liu, K., Wang, H., & Yao, Y. (2016). On storing & retrieving geospatial big-data in cloud. *Proceedings of the 2nd ACM SIGSPATIAL International Workshop on the Use of GIS in Emergency Management, EM-GIS 2016*. ACM. 10.1145/3017611.3017627

Liu, X., Hao, L., & Yang, W. (2019). Bigeo: A foundational PaaS framework for efficient storage, visualization, management, analysis, service, and migration of geospatial big data—a case study of Sichuan province, China. *ISPRS International Journal of Geo-Information*, *8*(10), 449. Advance online publication. doi:10.3390/ijgi8100449

Liu, Z. G., Yang, Y., & Ji, X. H. (2016). Flame detection algorithm based on a saliency detection technique and the uniform local binary pattern in the YCbCr color space. *Signal, Image and Video Processing*, *10*(2), 277–284. doi:10.1007/s11760-014-0738-0

Li, Y., & Chen, M. (2015). Software-defined network function virtualization: A survey. *IEEE Access : Practical Innovations, Open Solutions*, *3*, 2542–2553. doi:10.1109/ACCESS.2015.2499271

Li, Y., Lin, Y., Wang, Y., Ye, K., & Xu, C. (2022). Serverless computing: State-of-the-art, challenges and opportunities. *IEEE Transactions on Services Computing*, *16*(2), 1522–1539. doi:10.1109/TSC.2022.3166553

Li, Y., Zhang, W., Liu, Y., & Jin, Y. (2022). A visualized fire detection method based on convolutional neural network beyond anchor. *Applied Intelligence*, *52*(11), 13280–13295. doi:10.1007/s10489-022-03243-7

Lloyd, W., Ramesh, S., Chinthalapati, S., Ly, L., & Pallickara, S. (2018, April). Serverless computing: An investigation of factors influencing microservice performance. In *2018 IEEE international conference on cloud engineering (IC2E)* (pp. 159-169). IEEE. doi:10.1109/IC2E.2018.00039

Lo, H.-K., & Lütkenhaus, N. (2007). Quantum cryptography: from theory to practice. arXiv preprint quant-ph/0702202 (2007).

Lopez, P., Fernandez, D., Jara, A. J., & Skarmeta, A. F. (2013). Survey of Internet of Things technologies for clinical environments. *Proc. 27th Int. Conf. Waina*. IEEE. 10.1109/WAINA.2013.255

Lu, Y., & Xu, X. (2019). Cloud-based manufacturing equipment and big data analytics to enable on-demand manufacturing services. *Robotics and Computer-integrated Manufacturing*, *57*, 92–102. doi:10.1016/j.rcim.2018.11.006

Lv, Z., Song, H., Basanta-Val, P., Steed, A., & Jo, M. (2017). Nextgeneration big data analytics: State of the art, challenges, and future research topics. *IEEE Transactions on Industrial Informatics*, *13*(4), 1891–1899. doi:10.1109/TII.2017.2650204

Machiraju, S., & Gaurav, S. (2018). *Power BI Data Analysis and Visualization*. De-G Press. doi:10.1515/9781547400720

Mahajan, H. B., Rashid, A. S., Junnarkar, A. A., Uke, N., Deshpande, S. D., Futane, P. R., Alkhayyat, A., & Alhayani, B. (2023). Integration of Healthcare 4.0 and blockchain into secure cloud-based electronic health records systems. *Applied Nanoscience*, *13*(3), 2329–2342. doi:10.1007/s13204-021-02164-0 PMID:35136707

Maheshwari, S., Gautam, P., & Jaggi, C. K. (2021). Role of Big Data Analytics in supply chain management: Current trends and future perspectives. *International Journal of Production Research, 59*(6), 1875-1900.

Maheshwari, S., Raychaudhuri, D., Seskar, I., & Bronzino, F. (2018). Scalability and Performance Evaluation of Edge Cloud Systems for Latency Constrained Applications. *IEEE/ACM Symposium on Edge Computing (SEC)*, (pp. 286-299). ACM. 10.1109/SEC.2018.00028

Makrani, H. M. (2018). Compressive Sensing on Storage Data: An Effective Solution to Alleviate I/0 Bottleneck in Data-Intensive Workloads. *2018 IEEE 29th International Conference on Applicationspecific Systems, Architectures and Processors (ASAP)*. IEEE. 10.1109/ASAP.2018.8445131

Makrani, H. M. (2014). Evaluation of software-based fault tolerant techniques on embedded OS's components. *Proceedings of the International Conference on Dependability (DEPEND'14)*. IEEE.

Makrani, H. M. (2019). XPPE: cross-platform performance estimation of hardware accelerators using machine learning. *Proceedings of the 24th Asia and South Pacific Design Automation Conference*. ACM. 10.1145/3287624.3288756

Makrani, H. M., & Homayoun, H. (2017). Memory requirements of hadoop, spark, and MPI based big data applications on commodity server class architectures. *2017 IEEE International Symposium on Workload Characterization (IISWC)*. IEEE. 10.1109/IISWC.2017.8167763

Malathi, M. (2011, April). Cloud computing concepts. In 2011 3rd International Conference on Electronics Computer Technology (Vol. 6, pp. 236-239). IEEE. 10.1109/ICECTECH.2011.5942089

Malik, M. (2019). ECoST: Energy-Efficient Co-Locating and Self Tuning MapReduce Applications. *Proceedings of the 48th International Conference on Parallel Processing*. ACM. 10.1145/3337821.3337834

Malik, M., Tullsen, D. M., & Homayoun, H. (2017). Co-Locating and concurrent fine-tuning MapReduce applications on micro servers for energy efficiency. *2017 IEEE International Symposium on Workload Characterization (IISWC)*. IEEE. 10.1109/IISWC.2017.8167753

Malla, P. A., & Sheikh, S. (2023). Analysis of QoS aware energy-efficient resource provisioning techniques in cloud computing. *International Journal of Communication Systems*, *36*(1), e5359. doi:10.1002/dac.5359

Mallika, C., & Selvamuthukumaran, S. (2017). Hadoop framework: analyzes workload predicition of data from cloud computing. In: *2017 International Conference on IoT and Application (ICIOT)*, (pp. 1–6). IEEE. 10.1109/ICIOTA.2017.8073624

Mall, P. K., Pramanik, S., Srivastava, S., Faiz, M., Sriramulu, S., & Kumar, M. N. (2023). FuzztNet-Based Modelling Smart Traffic System in Smart Cities Using Deep Learning Models. In *Data-Driven Mathematical Modeling in Smart Cities*. IGI Global. doi:10.4018/978-1-6684-6408-3.ch005

Mampage, A., Karunasekera, S., & Buyya, R. (2022). A holistic view on resource management in serverless computing environments: Taxonomy and future directions. *ACM Computing Surveys*, *54*(11s), 1–36. doi:10.1145/3510412

Mamun, Q. (2022). Blockchain technology in the future of healthcare. *Smart Health (Amsterdam, Netherlands)*, *23*, 100223. doi:10.1016/j.smhl.2021.100223

Mandal, A., Dutta, S., & Pramanik, S. (2021). Machine Intelligence of Pi from Geometrical Figures with Variable Parameters using SCILab. In D. Samanta, R. R. Althar, S. Pramanik, & S. Dutta (Eds.), *Methodologies and Applications of Computational Statistics for Machine Learning* (pp. 38–63). IGI Global. doi:10.4018/978-1-7998-7701-1.ch003

Mandal, R., Mondal, M. K., Banerjee, S., Srivastava, G., Alnumay, W., Ghosh, U., & Biswas, U. (2023). MECpVmS: An SLA aware energy-efficient virtual machine selection policy for green cloud computing. *Cluster Computing*, *26*(1), 651–665. doi:10.1007/s10586-022-03684-2

Manfreda, S., McCabe, M. F., Miller, P. E., Lucas, R., Madrigal, V. P., Mallinis, G., Ben Dor, E., Helman, D., Estes, L., Ciraolo, G., Müllerová, J., Tauro, F., de Lima, M. I., de Lima, J. L. M. P., Maltese, A., Frances, F., Caylor, K., Kohv, M., Perks, M., & Toth, B. (2018). On the use of unmanned aerial systems for environmental monitoring. In Remote Sensing, 10(4). doi:10.3390/rs10040641

Manganelli, M., Soldati, A., Martirano, L., & Ramakrishna, S. (2021). Strategies for Improving the Sustainability of Data Centers via Energy Mix, Energy Conservation, and Circular Energy. *Sustainability*, *13*(11), 6114. doi:10.3390/su13116114

Manish Pokharel. (2009). *YoungHyun Yoon, Jong Sou Park, "Cloud Computing in System Architecture"*. IEEE.

Manogaran, G., & Lopez, D. (2017). A survey of big data architectures and machine learning algorithms in healthcare. *International Journal of Biomedical Engineering and Technology*, *25*(2–4), 182. doi:10.1504/IJBET.2017.087722

Mansouri, Y., & Babar, M. A. (2021). A review of edge computing: Features and resource virtualization. *Journal of Parallel and Distributed Computing*, *150*, 155–183. doi:10.1016/j.jpdc.2020.12.015

Marshall, T. E., & Lambert, S. L. (2018). Cloud-based intelligent accounting applications: Accounting task automation using IBM watson cognitive computing. *Journal of Emerging Technologies in Accounting*, *15*(1), 199–215. doi:10.2308/jeta-52095

Marston, S., Li, Z., Bandyopadhyay, S., Zhang, J., & Ghalsasi, A. (2011). Cloud Computing – The business perspective. *Decision Support Systems*, *51*(1), 176–189. doi:10.1016/j.dss.2010.12.006

Matallah, H., & Belalem, G. (2017). Experimental comparative study of NoSQL databases: HBASE versus MongoDB by YCSB. *Computer Systems Science and Engineering*, *32*(4), 307–317.

Mayyas, A. T., Ruth, M. F., Pivovar, B. S., Bender, G., & Wipke, K. B. (2019). *Manufacturing Cost Analysis for Proton Exchange Membrane Water Electrolyzers*. OSTI. doi:10.2172/1557965

McGrath, G., & Brenner, P. R. (2017, June). Serverless computing: Design, implementation, and performance. In *2017 IEEE 37th International Conference on Distributed Computing Systems Workshops (ICDCSW)* (pp. 405-410). IEEE. 10.1109/ICDCSW.2017.36

Medara, R., & Singh, R. S. (2022). A Review on Energy-Aware Scheduling Techniques for Workflows in IaaS Clouds. *Wireless Personal Communications*, *125*(2), 1545–1584. doi:10.1007/s11277-022-09621-1

Mehmood, T. (2021). Does information technology competencies and fleet management practices lead to effective service delivery? Empirical evidence from E-commerce industry. *International Journal of Technology* [IJTIM]. *Innovation and Management*, *1*(2), 14–41.

Mell, P. & Grance, T. (2011). *The NIST definition of Cloud Computing. v15.3*. NIST.

Mell, P., & Grance, T. (2011). *The NIST Definition of Cloud Computing (Technical report)*. National Institute of Standards and Technology: U.S. Department of Commerce. Special publication 800-145.

Mell, P. (2011). *Timothy Grance. The NIST Definition of Cloud Computing (Draft)*. NIST.

Mell, P. (2012). What's special about cloud security? *IT Professional*, *14*(4), 6–8. doi:10.1109/MITP.2012.84

Mell, P., & Grance, T. (2011). The NIST definition of cloud computing. In *Cloud Computing and Government: Background, Benefits*. Risks. doi:10.6028/NIST.SP.800-145

Mell, P., & Grance, T. (2011). The NIST definition of cloud computing. *National Institute of Standards and Technology, NIST Special Publication USA*, *53*(6), 50–50.

Menasce, D. A., & Ngo, P. (2009). Understanding cloud computing: Experimentation and capacity planning. *Computer Measurement Group Conference*. George Mason University.

Meneguette, R., De Grande, R., Ueyama, J., Filho, G. P. R., & Madeira, E. (2021). Vehicular edge computing: Architecture, resource management, security, and challenges. *ACM Computing Surveys*, *55*(1), 1–46. doi:10.1145/3485129

Meng, S., Dou, W., Zhang, X., & Chen, J. (2014). KASR: A keyword-aware service recommendation method on MapReduce for big data applications. *IEEE Transactions on Parallel and Distributed Systems*, *25*(12), 3221–3231. doi:10.1109/TPDS.2013.2297117

Meslie, Y., Enbeyle, W., Pandey, B. K., Pramanik, S., Pandey, D., Dadeech, P., Belay, A., & Saini, A. (2021). Machine Intelligence-based Trend Analysis of COVID-19 for Total Daily Confirmed Cases in Asia and Africa. In D. Samanta, R. R. Althar, S. Pramanik, & S. Dutta (Eds.), *Methodologies and Applications of Computational Statistics for Machine Learning* (pp. 164–185). IGI Global. doi:10.4018/978-1-7998-7701-1.ch009

Microsoft. (2022). *Microsoft Project Natick Phase 2*. Microsoft. https://natick.research.microsoft.com/

Microsoft. (2023). *Azure Data Lake Storage*. Microsoft. https://azure.microsoft.com/en-us/products/storage/data-lake-storage/

Microsoft. (n.d.). *Azure*. Microsoft. https://azure.microsoft.com/

Miller, J., Bowman, C., Harish, V., & Quinn, S. (2016). Open source big data analytics frameworks written in scala. In: *2016 IEEE International Congress on Big Data (BigData Congress),* (pp. 389–393). IEEE. 10.1109/BigDataCongress.2016.61

Miller, R. (2020). *Microsoft: Servers in Our Underwater Data Center Are Super-Reliable.* Data Center Frontier. https://www.datacenterfrontier.com/design/article/11428732/microsoft-servers-in-our-underwater-data-center-are-super-reliable

Mishra, S., & Tyagi, A. K. (2022). The role of machine learning techniques in internet of things-based cloud applications. *Artificial intelligence-based internet of things systems*, 105-135.

Misra, S., Tyagi, A. K., Piuri, V., & Garg, L. (Eds.). (2022). *Artificial Intelligence for Cloud and Edge Computing.* Springer. doi:10.1007/978-3-030-80821-1

Mladen, A. (2008). Cloud Computing Issues, Research and Implementations. *Proceedings of the ITI 2008 30th Int. Conf. on Information Technology Interfaces.* IEEE.

Mohammad, O. K. (2019). Detailed quantum cryptographic service and data security in cloud computing. *Advances in Data Science, Cyber Security and IT Applications: First International Conference on Computing.* Springer.

Mohammad, O. K. (2015). Securing cloud computing environment using a new trend of cryptography. In *2015 International Conference on Cloud Computing (ICCC),* (pp. 1-8). IEEE.

Mohammed, S., Fang, W. C., & Ramos, C. (2023). Special issue on "artificial intelligence in cloud computing". *Computing, 105*(3), 507–511. doi:10.1007/s00607-021-00985-z

Mohanty, S. K., Premsankar, G., & Di Francesco, M. (2018). An Evaluation of Open Source Serverless Computing Frameworks. *CloudCom, 2018*, 115–120. doi:10.1109/CloudCom2018.2018.00033

Mondal, D., Ratnaparkhi, A., Deshpande, A., Deshpande, V., Kshirsagar, A. P., & Pramanik, S. (2023). Applications, Modern Trends and Challenges of MultiscaleModelling in Smart Cities. In *Data-Driven Mathematical Modeling in Smart Cities.* IGI Global. doi:10.4018/978-1-6684-6408-3.ch001

Montazerolghaem, A., Yaghmaee, M. H., & Leon-Garcia, A. (2020). Green Cloud Multimedia Networking: NFV/SDN Based Energy-Efficient Resource Allocation". *IEEE Transactions on Green Communications and Networking, 4*(3), 873–889. doi:10.1109/TGCN.2020.2982821

Montesinos, L., Salinas-Navarro, D. E., & Santos-Diaz, A. (2023). Transdisciplinary experiential learning in biomedical engineering education for healthcare systems improvement. *BMC Medical Education, 23*(1), 207. doi:10.1186/s12909-023-04171-x PMID:37013525

Morton, K., Balazinska, M., & Grossman, D. (2010). Paratimer: a progress indicator for mapreduce dags. In *Proceedings of the 2010 ACM SIGMOD International Conference on Management of data*, (pp. 507–518). ACM. 10.1145/1807167.1807223

Moudud-Ul-Huq, S., Asaduzzaman, M., & Biswas, T. (2020). Role of cloud computing in global accounting information systems. *The Bottom Line (New York, N.Y.), 33*(3), 231–250. doi:10.1108/BL-01-2020-0010

Mourtzis, D. (2022). Introduction to cloud technology and Industry 4.0. In *Design and Operation of Production Networks for Mass Personalization in the Era of Cloud Technology* (pp. 1–12). Elsevier. doi:10.1016/B978-0-12-823657-4.00011-7

Muhammad, T., Munir, M. T., Munir, M. Z., & Zafar, M. W. (2018). Elevating Business Operations: The Transformative Power of Cloud Computing. *International Journal Of Computer Science And Technology, 2*(1), 1–21.

Mukherjee, K., & Sahoo, G. (2010). Article: Cloud Computing: Future Framework for e-Governance. *International Journal of Computer Applications, 7*(7), 31–34. doi:10.5120/1262-1613

Mulat, W. W., Mohapatra, S. K., Sathpathy, R., & Dhal, S. K. (2022). *Improving Throttled Load Balancing Algorithm in Cloud Computing*, (pp. 369–377). Springer. doi:10.1007/978-981-19-0332-8_27

Mungoli, N. (2023). Scalable, Distributed AI Frameworks: Leveraging Cloud Computing for Enhanced Deep Learning Performance and Efficiency. *arXiv preprint arXiv:2304.13738.*

Muralidhara, P. (2017). The evolution of cloud computing security: addressing emerging threats. *International journal of computer science and technology*, *1*(4), 1–33.

Murali, S., Govindan, V. K., & Kalady, S. (2022). Quaternion-based image shadow removal. *The Visual Computer*, *38*(5), 1527–1538. doi:10.1007/s00371-021-02086-6

Murino, T., Monaco, R., Nielsen, P. S., Liu, X., Esposito, G., & Scognamiglio, C. (2023). Sustainable Energy Data Centres: A Holistic Conceptual Framework for Design and Operations. *Energies, 16*(15), 5764. doi:10.3390/en16155764

Mustapha, U. F., Alhassan, A. W., Jiang, D. N., & Li, G. L. (2021). Sustainable aquaculture development: A review on the roles of cloud computing, internet of things and artificial intelligence (CIA). *Reviews in Aquaculture*, *13*(4), 2076–2091. doi:10.1111/raq.12559

Nadeem, M. A. (2016). Cloud computing: Security issues and challenges. *Journal of Wireless Communications*, *1*(1), 10–15. doi:10.21174/jowc.v1i1.73

Nagulan, S., Srinivasa Krishnan, A. N., Kiran Kumar, A., Vishnu Kumar, S., & Suchithra, M. (2023). An Efficient Real-Time Fire Detection Method Using Computer Vision and Neural Network-Based Video Analysis. In: Khanna, A., Gupta, D., Kansal, V., Fortino, G., Hassanien, A.E. (eds) *Proceedings of Third Doctoral Symposium on Computational Intelligence. Lecture Notes in Networks and Systems.* Springer, Singapore. 10.1007/978-981-19-3148-2_55

Naik, N. D., & Modi, K. J. (2013). Evolution of IT industry towards cloud computing: A new paradigm. IJRIT Int. *J. of Research in Information Technology.*, *1*(5), 236–242.

Nakamura, V. A., Souza, C. S., & Araujo, A. C. (2023). Mass-flowering native species are key in the structure of an urban plant-hummingbird network. *Urban Ecosystems*, *26*(4), 929–940. Advance online publication. doi:10.1007/s11252-023-01346-8

Namasudra, S., Nath, S., & Majumder, A. Profile based access control model in cloud computing environment. In: *Proceedings of the International Conference on Green Computing, Communication and Electrical Engineering*, pp. 1-5. IEEE, Coimbatore, India (2014). 10.1109/ICGCCEE.2014.6921420

Namazi, M. (2019). Mitigating the Performance and Quality of Parallelized Compressive Sensing Reconstruction Using Image Stitching. *Proceedings of the 2019 on Great Lakes Symposium on VLSI.* ACM. 10.1145/3299874.3317991

Naved, M., Fakih, A. H., Venkatesh, A. N., Vijayakumar, P., & Kshirsagar, P. R. (2022, May). Supervise the data security and performance in cloud using artificial intelligence. In AIP Conference Proceedings (Vol. 2393, No. 1). AIP Publishing.

Neeraja, J., Yadwadkar, B. H., Gonzalez, J. E., Smith, B., & Katz, R. H. (2017). Selecting the best VM across multiple public clouds: a data-driven performance modeling approach. In *Proceedings of the 2017 Symposium on Cloud Computing*, (pp. 452–465). ACM.

Neshatpour, K. (2018). Design Space Exploration for Hardware Acceleration of Machine Learning Applications in MapReduce. *2018 IEEE 26th Annual International Symposium on Field-Programmable Custom Computing Machines (FCCM).* IEEE. 10.1109/FCCM.2018.00055

Ngọc, T. H., Khanh, P. T., & Pramanik, S. (2023). Smart Agriculture using a Soil Monitoring System. In A. Khang & I. G. I. Global (Eds.), *Advanced Technologies and AI-Equipped IoT Applications in High Tech Agriculture*. doi:10.4018/978-1-6684-9231-4.ch011

Nguyen, T. M. T., Sfaxi, M. A., & Ghernaouti-Hélie, S. (2006). Integration of quantum cryptography in 802.11 networks. In *First International Conference on Availability, Reliability and Security (ARES'06)*, (pp. 8). IEEE. 10.1109/ARES.2006.75

Niemiec, M. (2019). Error correction in quantum cryptography based on artificial neural networks. *Quantum Information Processing*, *18*(6), 174. doi:10.1007/s11128-019-2296-4

Nisticò, G. (2023). Three-Dimensional Reconstruction of Coronal Features: A Python Tool for Geometric Triangulation. *Solar Physics*, *298*(3), 36. doi:10.1007/s11207-023-02122-9

Niu, Y., Ying, L., Yang, J., Bao, M., & Sivaparthipan, C. B. (2021). Organizational business intelligence and decision making using big data analytics. *Information Processing & Management*, *58*(6), 102725. doi:10.1016/j.ipm.2021.102725

Nodarakis, N., Sioutas, S., Tsakalidis, A., & Tzima, G., (2016). *Using Hadoop for Large Scale Analysis on Twitter: A Technical Report.*

nOps (2023). *What is Scalability in Cloud Computing? Types, Benefits, and Practical Advice.* nOps. https://www.nops.io/blog/cloud-scalability/

Novakovi, D., Vasic, N., Novakovic, S., Kostic, D., & Bianchini, R. (2013). Deepdive: Transparently identifying and man- aging performance interference in virtualized environments. In *Presented as part of the 2013 USENIX Annual Technical Conference (USENIX ATC 13).* USENIX.

Núñez-Andrés, M. A., Lantada Zarzosa, N., & Martínez-Llario, J. (2022). Spatial data infrastructure (SDI) for inventory rockfalls with fragmentation information. *Natural Hazards*, *112*(3), 2649–2672. doi:10.1007/s11069-022-05282-2

Nye, J. S. (2023). Get Smart: Combining Hard and Soft Power. In *Soft Power and Great-Power Competition. China and Globalization*. Springer. doi:10.1007/978-981-99-0714-4_8

OCI. (n.d.). *Home. OCI.* https://www.oracle.com/cloud/

Odeh, A., Keshta, I., & Abu Al-Haija, Q. (2022). Analysis of Blockchain in the Healthcare Sector: Application and Issues. *Symmetry*, *14*(9), 1760. doi:10.3390/sym14091760

Olavsrud, T. (2016). *Data and analytic trends that will dominate 2016.* CIO. https://www.cio.com/article/3023838/analytics/21-data-and-analytics-trends-that-will-dominate-2016.html

Oliveira, D., & Ogasawara, E. (2010). Article: Is Cloud Computing the Solution for Brazilian Researchers? *International Journal of Computer Applications*, *6*(8), 19–23. doi:10.5120/1096-1432

Oman, M., & Stearns, I. F. (2022). *Clean energy projects begin to power Google data centers.* Google Cloud. https://cloud.google.com/blog/topics/sustainability/clean-energy-projects-begin-to-power-google-data-centers

Opara-Martins, J., Sahandi, R., & Tian, F. (2016). Critical analysis of vendor lock-in and its impact on cloud computing migration: A business perspective. *Journal of Cloud Computing (Heidelberg, Germany)*, *5*(1), 1–18. doi:10.1186/s13677-016-0054-z

Ortar, N., Taylor, A. R. E., Velkova, J., Brodie, P., Johnson, A., Marquet, C., Pollio, A., & Cirolia, L. (2023). *Powering "smart" futures: data centres and the energy politics of digitalisation. 10*, 125–168. https://shs.hal.science/halshs-03907750

Ortiz, J. L. R., Oneto, L., & Anguita, D. (2015). Big data analytics in the cloud: Spark on hadoop vs MPI/OpenMP on Beowulf. *Procedia Computer Science*, *53*, 121–130. doi:10.1016/j.procs.2015.07.286

Oussous, A., Benjelloun, F. Z., Lahcen, A. A., & Belfkih, S. (2017). Big data technologies: A survey. *Journal of King Saud University. Computer and Information Sciences.*

Oussous, A., Benjelloun, F.-Z., Ait Lahcen, A., & Belfkih, S. (2018). Big Data technologies: A survey. *Journal of King Saud University. Computer and Information Sciences, 30*(4), 431–448. doi:10.1016/j.jksuci.2017.06.001

Ozkan, O., & Kilic, S. (2023). UAV routing by simulation-based optimization approaches for forest fire risk mitigation. *Annals of Operations Research, 320*(2), 937–973. doi:10.1007/s10479-021-04393-6

Padhy, R.P., Patra, M., & Satapathy, S.C., (2011). Cloud Computing: Security Issues & Research Challenges. *IJCSITS, 1*(2), 136-146.

Pandey, B. K., Pandey, D., Nassa, V. K., George, S., Aremu, B., Dadeech, P., & Gupta, A. (2022, July). Effective and secure transmission of health information using advanced morphological component analysis and image hiding. In *Artificial Intelligence on Medical Data: Proceedings of International Symposium, ISCMM 2021* (pp. 223-230). Singapore: Springer Nature Singapore.

Pandey, D. Pandey, Wairya, S., Agarwal, G., Dadeech, P. S. ,Dogiwal, R., & Pramanik, S. (2022). Application of Integrated Steganography and Image Compressing Techniques for Confidential Information Transmission. Cyber Security and Network Security. Wiley. ,. doi:10.1002/9781119812555.ch8

Pandey, J. K., Jain, R., Dilip, R., Kumbhkar, M., Jaiswal, S., Pandey, B. K., Gupta, A., & Pandey, D. (2023). Investigating Role of IoT in the Development of Smart Application for Security Enhancement. In EAI/Springer Innovations in Communication and Computing. Springer. doi:10.1007/978-3-031-04524-0_13

Pandey, B. K., & Pandey, D. (2023). Parametric optimization and prediction of enhanced thermoelectric performance in co-doped CaMnO3 using response surface methodology and neural network. *Journal of Materials Science Materials in Electronics, 34*(21), 1589. doi:10.1007/s10854-023-10954-1

Pandey, B. K., Pandey, S. K., & Pandey, D. (2011). A survey of bioinformatics applications on parallel architectures. *International Journal of Computer Applications, 23*(4), 21–25. doi:10.5120/2877-3744

Pandey, D., Pandey, B. K., & Wairya, S. (2021). Hybrid deep neural network with adaptive galactic swarm optimization for text extraction from scene images. *Soft Computing, 25*(2), 1563–1580. doi:10.1007/s00500-020-05245-4

Pandey, D., Wairya, S., Pradhan, B., & Wangmo. (2022). Understanding COVID-19 response by twitter users: A text analysis approach. *Heliyon, 8*(8), e09994. doi:10.1016/j.heliyon.2022.e09994 PMID:35873536

Pandey, J. K., Jain, R., Dilip, R., Kumbhkar, M., Jaiswal, S., Pandey, B. K., & Pandey, D. (2022). Investigating Role of IoT in the Development of Smart Application for Security Enhancement. In *IoT Based Smart Applications* (pp. 219–243). Springer International Publishing.

Pan, J., & McElhannon, J. (2017). Future edge cloud and edge computing for internet of things applications. *IEEE Internet of Things Journal, 5*(1), 439–449. doi:10.1109/JIOT.2017.2767608

Parmanto, B., Paramita, M. V., Sugiantara, W., Pramana, G., Scotch, M., & Burke, D. S. (2008). Spatial and multidimensional visualization of Indonesia's village health statistics. *International Journal of Health Geographics, 7*(1), 30. doi:10.1186/1476-072X-7-30 PMID:18544174

Patel, Y. S., Mehrotra, N., & Soner, S. (2015). Green cloud computing: A review on Green IT areas for cloud computing environment. *2015 1st International Conference on Futuristic Trends in Computational Analysis and Knowledge Management, ABLAZE 2015*, (pp. 327–332). IEEE. 10.1109/ABLAZE.2015.7155006

Patel, K. D., & Bhalodia, T. M. (2019). An Efficient Dynamic Load Balancing Algorithm for Virtual Machine in Cloud Computing. *2019 International Conference on Intelligent Computing and Control Systems (ICCS)*, Madurai, India. 10.1109/ICCS45141.2019.9065292

Patibandla, R. L., Kurra, S. S., & Mundukur, N. B. (2012). *An Overview of Environmental Scalability and Security in Hybrid Cloud Infrastructure Designs*. Distributed Computing and Internet Technology: 8th International Conference, ICDCIT 2012, Bhubaneswar, India.

Patil, R., Chaudhery, T. S., Qureshi, M. A., Sawant, V., & Dalvi, H. (2021, August). Serverless Computing and the Emergence of Function-as-a-Service. In *2021 International Conference on Recent Trends on Electronics, Information, Communication & Technology (RTEICT)* (pp. 764-769). IEEE. 10.1109/RTEICT52294.2021.9573962

Paulson, L. D. (2003). Low-Power Chips for High-Powered Handhelds. *Computer*, *36*(1), 21–23. doi:10.1109/MC.2003.1160049

Pearson, S. (2010). Privacy, Security and Trust Issues Arising from Cloud Computing. *2010 IEEE Second International Conference Cloud Computing Technology and Science,* (pp. 693-702). IEEE.

Peng, S., Liu, R., & Wang, F. (2017). *New Research on Key Technologies of Unstructured Data Cloud Storage*. Francis Academic Press.

Peng, X., Bhattacharya, T., Cao, T., Mao, J., Tekreeti, T., & Qin, X. (2022). Exploiting Renewable Energy and UPS Systems to Reduce Power Consumption in Data Centers. *Big Data Research*, *27*, 100306. doi:10.1016/j.bdr.2021.100306

Perez-Botero, D., Szefer, J., & Lee, R. B. (2013, May). Characterizing hypervisor vulnerabilities in cloud computing servers. In *Proceedings of the 2013 international workshop on Security in cloud computing* (pp. 3-10). 10.1145/2484402.2484406

Pfarr, F., Buckel, T., & Winkelmann, A. (2014). Cloud Computing Data Protection--A Literature Review and Analysis. In *2014 47th Hawaii International Conference on System Sciences* (pp. 5018-5027). IEEE. 10.1109/HICSS.2014.616

Poccia, D. (2016). *AWS Lambda in Action: Event-driven serverless applications*. Simon and Schuster.

Polze, A., & Tröger, P. (2012). Trends and challenges in operating systems—From parallel computing to cloud computing. *Concurrency and Computation*, *24*(7), 676–686. doi:10.1002/cpe.1903

Pons, X., & Ninyerola, M. (2008). Mapping a topographic global solar radiation model implemented in a GIS and refined with ground data. *International Journal of Climatology*, *28*(13), 1821–1834. doi:10.1002/joc.1676

Pradeep, K., & Pravakar, D. (2022). *Exploration on Task Scheduling using Optimization Algorithm in Cloud computing*. 2022 6th International Conference on Trends in Electronics and Informatics (ICOEI), Tirunelveli, India. 10.1109/ICOEI53556.2022.9777120

Pradhan, D., Sahu, P. K., Goje, N. S., Myo, H., Ghonge, M. M., Rajeswari, R., & Pramanik, S. (2022). Security, Privacy, Risk, and Safety Toward 5G Green Network (5G-GN)", in Cyber Security and Network Security. Wiley. doi:10.1002/9781119812555.ch9

Pradhan, A., Bisoy, S. K., Kautish, S., Jasser, M. B., & Mohamed, A. W. (2022). Intelligent Decision-Making of Load Balancing Using Deep Reinforcement Learning and Parallel PSO in Cloud Environment. *IEEE Access : Practical Innovations, Open Solutions*, *10*, 76939–76952. doi:10.1109/ACCESS.2022.3192628

Pramanik, S., & Obaid, A. J., & Bandyopadhyay, S.K. (2023). Applications of Big Data in Clinical Applications. *Al-Kadhum 2nd International Conference on Modern Applications of Information and Communication Technology, AIP Conference Proceedings.* AIP. 10.1063/5.0119414

Pramanik, S., Galety, M. G., & Samanta, N. P. Joseph, (2022). Data Mining Approaches for Decision Support Systems. *3rd International Conference on Emerging Technologies in Data Mining and Information Security*. IEEE.

Pramanik, S., Ghosh, R., Pandey, D., Samanta, D., Dutta, S., & Dutta, S. (2021). *Techniques of Steganography and Cryptography in Digital Transformation*. IGI Global. doi:10.4018/978-1-7998-8587-0.ch002

Pramanik, S., Niranjanamurthy, M., & Panda, S. N. (2022). Using Green Energy Prediction in Data Centers for Scheduling Service Jobs. ICRITCSA 2022, Bengaluru.

Pramanik, S., Pandey, D., Joardar, S., Niranjanamurthy, M., Pandey, B. K., & Kaur, J. (2023, October). An overview of IoT privacy and security in smart cities. In AIP Conference Proceedings (Vol. 2495, No. 1). AIP Publishing. doi:10.1063/5.0123511

Pramanik, S., Sagayam, K. M., & Jena, O. P. (2021). Machine Learning Frameworks in Cancer Detection. ICCSRE 2021, Morocco. doi:10.1051/e3sconf/202129701073

Pramanik, S., Samanta, D., Ghosh, R., Bandyopadhyay, S. K. (2021). A New Combinational Technique in Image Steganography. *International Journal of Information Security and Privacy, 15*(3), IGI Global. doi:10.4018/IJISP.2021070104

Pramanik, S. (2023). An Adaptive Image Steganography Approach depending on Integer Wavelet Transform and Genetic Algorithm. *Multimedia Tools and Applications, 2023*(22), 34287–34319. Advance online publication. doi:10.1007/s11042-023-14505-y

Pramanik, S., & Bandyopadhyay, S. (2023). Identifying Disease and Diagnosis in Females using Machine Learning. In I. G. I. John Wang (Ed.), *Encyclopedia of Data Science and Machine Learning*. Global. doi:10.4018/978-1-7998-9220-5.ch187

Pratt, M. (2021). Top Ten edge computing use cases and examples. *TechTarget.* https://www.techtarget.com/searchcio/feature/4-edge-computing-use-cases-delivering-value-in-the-enterprise

Praveenkumar, S., Veeraiah, V., Pramanik, S., Basha, D., Lira, S. M., Neto, A. V., De Albuquerque, V. H. C., & Gupta, A. (2023). Prediction of Patients' [Springer]. *Incurable Diseases Utilizing Deep Learning Approaches, ICICC*, 2023.

Pring. (2009). *Forecast: Sizing the cloud; understanding the opportunities in cloud services, Gartner Inc.* Tech.

Ptiček, M., & Vrdoljak, B. (2017). *MapReduce research on warehousing of big data*. Mipro. doi:10.23919/MIPRO.2017.7973634

Qi, H., & Gani, A. (2012). Research on Mobile Cloud Computing: Review,Trend and Perspectives. *Proceedings of the Second International Conference on Digital Information and Communication Technology and its Applications (DICTAP)*. IEEE. 10.1109/DICTAP.2012.6215350

Qing-hail, B., Wen, Z., Peng, J., & Xul, L. (2012). Research on design principles of elliptic curve public key cryptography and its implementation. *Int. Conf. on Computer Science and Service System*, Nanjing, China.

Qin, R., Ding, W., Li, J., Guan, S., Wang, G., Ren, Y., & Qu, Z. (2022). Web3-based decentralized autonomous organizations and operations: Architectures, models, and mechanisms. *IEEE Transactions on Systems, Man, and Cybernetics. Systems, 53*(4), 2073–2082. doi:10.1109/TSMC.2022.3228530

Qiu, J., Wu, Q., Ding, G., Xu, Y., & Feng, S. (2016). A survey of machine learning for big data processing. In Eurasip Journal on Advances in Signal Processing, (1). doi:10.1186/s13634-016-0355-x

Qiu, T., Chi, J., Zhou, X., Ning, Z., Atiquzzaman, M., & Wu, D. O. (2020). Edge computing in industrial internet of things: Architecture, advances and challenges. *IEEE Communications Surveys and Tutorials, 22*(4), 2462–2488. doi:10.1109/COMST.2020.3009103

Radmanesh, S. A., Haji, A., & Fatahi Valilai, O. (2023). Blockchain-Based Architecture for a Sustainable Supply Chain in Cloud Architecture. *Sustainability, 15*(11), 9072. doi:10.3390/su15119072

Radu, L. D. (2017). Green Cloud Computing: A Literature Survey. *Symmetry, 9*(12), 295. doi:10.3390/sym9120295

Raghav, Y. Y., & Vyas, V. (2019). *A comparative analysis of different load balancing algorithms on different parameters in cloud computing.* 2019 3rd International Conference on Recent Developments in Control, Automation & Power Engineering (RDCAPE), Noida, India. 10.1109/RDCAPE47089.2019.8979122

Raghav, Y. Y., & Gulia, S. (2023). The Rise of Artificial Intelligence and Its Implications on Spirituality. In S. Chakraborty (Ed.), *Investigating the Impact of AI on Ethics and Spirituality* (pp. 165–178). IGI Global. doi:10.4018/978-1-6684-9196-6.ch011

Raghav, Y. Y., & Vyas, V. (2023a). ACBSO: A hybrid solution for load balancing using ant colony and bird swarm optimization algorithms. *International Journal of Information Technology : an Official Journal of Bharati Vidyapeeth's Institute of Computer Applications and Management, 15*(5), 1–11. doi:10.1007/s41870-023-01340-5

Raghav, Y. Y., & Vyas, V. (2023b). A Comparative Analysis Report of Nature-Inspired Algorithms for Load Balancing in Cloud Environment. In *Women in Soft Computing* (pp. 47–63). Springer Nature Switzerland.

Raghav, Y. Y., Vyas, V., & Rani, H. (2022). Load balancing using dynamic algorithms for cloud environment: A survey. *Materials Today: Proceedings, 69*, 349–353. doi:10.1016/j.matpr.2022.09.048

Rahman, A., Islam, M. J., Band, S. S., Muhammad, G., Hasan, K., & Tiwari, P. (2023). Towards a blockchain-SDN-based secure architecture for cloud computing in smart industrial IoT. *Digital Communications and Networks, 9*(2), 411–421. doi:10.1016/j.dcan.2022.11.003

Rai, P., & Rawat, Y. (2023). Trends and Challenges in Green Computing. *Sustainable Digital Technologies*, 109–134. Taylor & Francis. doi:10.1201/9781003348313-6

Rajabifard, A., Feeney, M. E. F., & Williamson, I. (2003). *Spatial data infrastructures: concept, nature and SDI hierarchy*. Taylor & Francis London.

Rajeswari, V., & Gobinath, G. S. R. A. R. (2021). Securing an E-Health Care Information Systems on Cloud Environments with Big Data Approach. *Design Engineering (London)*, 6986 6991.

Ran, Y., Hu, H., Zhou, X., & Wen, Y. (2019). DeepEE: Joint optimization of job scheduling and cooling control for data center energy efficiency using deep reinforcement learning. *Proceedings - International Conference on Distributed Computing Systems, 2019-July*, (pp. 645–655). IEEE. 10.1109/ICDCS.2019.00070

Randles, M. (2009). A Comparative Experiment in Distributed Load Balancing. *Second International Conference on Developments in eSystems Engineering*. Semantic Scholar.

Randles, M., & Lamb, D. A. (2010). A Comparative Study into Distributed Load Balancing Algorithms for Cloud Computing. *IEEE 24th International Conference on Advanced Information Networking and Applications Workshops*. IEEE.

Ranjan, J., & Foropon, C. (2021). Big data analytics in building the competitive intelligence of organizations. *International Journal of Information Management, 56*, 102231. doi:10.1016/j.ijinfomgt.2020.102231

Rao, T. R., Mitra, P., Bhatt, R., & Goswami, A. (2019). The big data system, components, tools, and technologies: A survey. *Knowledge and Information Systems, 60*(3), 1165–1245. doi:10.1007/s10115-018-1248-0

Ray, P. P. (2016). A survey of IoT cloud platforms. *Future Computing and Informatics Journal, 1*(1-2), 35–46. doi:10.1016/j.fcij.2017.02.001

Ray, P. P. (2018). An Introduction to Dew Computing: Definition, Concept and Implications. *IEEE Access : Practical Innovations, Open Solutions*, *6*, 723–737. doi:10.1109/ACCESS.2017.2775042

Reddy, K.V., Thirumal-Rao, B., Reddy, L.R.R., & SaiKiran, P., (2011). Research Issues in Cloud Computing. *Global Journal of Computer Science and Technology, 11*(11).

Reddy, M. I., Rao, P. V., Kumar, T. S., & K, S. R. (2023). Encryption with access policy and cloud data selection for secure and energy-efficient cloud computing. *Multimedia Tools and Applications*, 1–27. doi:10.1007/s11042-023-16082-6

Reepu, S., Kumar, M. G., Chaudhary, K. G., Gupta, S., & Gupta, A. (2023). Information Security and Privacy in IoT. In J. Zhao, V. V. Kumar, R. Natarajan & T. R. Mahesh (eds.) Handbook of Research in Advancements in AI and IoT Convergence Technologies. IGI Global.

Ren, J., Zhang, D., He, S., Zhang, Y., & Li, T. (2019). A survey on end-edge-cloud orchestrated network computing paradigms: Transparent computing, mobile edge computing, fog computing, and cloudlet. *ACM Computing Surveys*, *52*(6), 1–36. doi:10.1145/3362031

Retico, A., Avanzo, M., Boccali, T., Bonacorsi, D., Botta, F., Cuttone, G., Martelli, B., Salomoni, D., Spiga, D., Trianni, A., Stasi, M., Iori, M., & Talamonti, C. (2021). Enhancing the impact of Artificial Intelligence in Medicine: A joint AIFM-INFN Italian initiative for a dedicated cloud-based computing infrastructure. *Physica Medica*, *91*, 140–150. doi:10.1016/j.ejmp.2021.10.005 PMID:34801873

Revathi, T. K., Sathiyabhama, B., Sankar, S., Pandey, D., Pandey, B. K., & Dadeech, P. (2022). An intelligent model for coronary heart disease diagnosis. *Networking Technologies in Smart Healthcare: Innovations and Analytical Approaches*, 234. Taylor & Francis.

Rezakhani, M., Sarrafzadeh-Ghadimi, N., Entezari-Maleki, R., Sousa, L., & Movaghar, A. (2023). Energy-aware QoS-based dynamic virtual machine consolidation approach based on RL and ANN. *Cluster Computing*. doi:10.1007/s10586-023-03983-2

Ristenpart, T., Tromer, E., Shacham, H., & Savage, S. (2009). Hey, you, get off of my cloud: Exploring information leakage in third-party compute clouds. *Proceedings of the ACM Conference on Computer and Communications Security*. ACM. 10.1145/1653662.1653687

Rittinghouse, J. W., & Ransome, J. F. (2016). Cloud Computing: Implementation, Management, and Security. In Cloud Computing: Implementation, Management, and Security. Taylor & Francis. doi:10.1201/9781439806814

Roenigk, M., Baldonado, O., & Jani, D. (2021). *How OCP revolutionized the open hardware community - Tech at Meta*. Facebook. https://tech.facebook.com/engineering/2021/11/open-compute-project/

Rudenko, A., Reiher, P., Popek, G. J., & Kuenning, G. H. (1998). Saving portable computer battery power through remote process execution. *Journal of ACM SIGMOBILE on Mobile Computing and Communications Review*, *2*(1), 19–26. doi:10.1145/584007.584008

Ruiz, M. D., Gómez-Romero, J., Fernandez-Basso, C., & Martin-Bautista, M. J. (2021). Big data architecture for building energy management systems. *IEEE Transactions on Industrial Informatics*, *18*(9), 5738–5747. doi:10.1109/TII.2021.3130052

Sahinoglu, M., & Cueva-Parra, L. (2011). Cloud computing. Wiley interdisciplinary reviews: Computational statistics, 3(1), 47-68. Wiley.

Saidi, K., & Bardou, D. (2023). Task scheduling and VM placement to resource allocation in Cloud computing: Challenges and opportunities. *Cluster Computing*, *26*(5), 3069–3087. doi:10.1007/s10586-023-04098-4

Saif, M. A. N., Niranjan, S. K., Murshed, B. A. H., Ghanem, F. A., & Ahmed, A. A. Q. (2023). CSO-ILB: Chicken swarm optimized inter-cloud load balancer for elastic containerized multi-cloud environment. *The Journal of Supercomputing*, *79*(1), 1111–1155. doi:10.1007/s11227-022-04688-w

Saif, S., & Wazir, S. (2018). Performance analysis of big data and cloud computing techniques: A survey. *Procedia Computer Science*, *132*, 118–127. doi:10.1016/j.procs.2018.05.172

Salami, Y., Khajevand, V., & Zeinali, E. (2023). Cryptographic Algorithms: A Review of the Literature, Weaknesses and Open Challenges. *J. Comput. Robot*, *16*(2), 46–56.

Salles, A. C., Lunardi, G. L., & Thompson, F. (2022). A Framework Proposal to Assess the Maturity of Green IT in Organizations. *Sustainability*, *14*(19), 12348. doi:10.3390/su141912348

Samarati, P., & De Capitani di Vimercati, S. (2016). Cloud security: Issues and concerns. In *Encyclopedia of cloud computing* (pp. 205–219). Wiley. doi:10.1002/9781118821930.ch17

Sampé, J., Vernik, G., Sánchez-Artigas, M., & García-López, P. (2018, December). Serverless data analytics in the IBM cloud. In *Proceedings of the 19th International Middleware Conference Industry* (pp. 1-8). ACM. 10.1145/3284028.3284029

Sangaiah, A. K., Javadpour, A., Ja'fari, F., Pinto, P., Zhang, W., & Balasubramanian, S. (2023). A hybrid heuristics artificial intelligence feature selection for intrusion detection classifiers in cloud of things. *Cluster Computing*, *26*(1), 599–612. doi:10.1007/s10586-022-03629-9

Sangroya, A., Kumar, S., Dhok, J., & Varma, V. (2010). Towards analyzing data security risks in cloud computing environments. *Communications in Computer and Information Science*, *54*, 255–265. doi:10.1007/978-3-642-12035-0_25

Santos, M. Y., & Costa, C. (2016). Data warehousing in big data: from multidimensional to tabular data models. In: *Proceedings of the Ninth International C* Conference on Computer Science and Software Engineering*, (pp. 51–60). ACM. 10.1145/2948992.2949024

Sarathi, T. V., Reddy, J. S. N., Shiva, P., Saha, R., Satpathy, A., & Addya, S. K. (2022, July). A Preliminary Study of Serverless Platforms for Latency Sensitive Applications. In *2022 IEEE International Conference on Electronics, Computing and Communication Technologies (CONECCT)* (pp. 1-6). IEEE. DOI: 10.1109/CONECCT55679.2022.9865790

Saravanan, G., Neelakandan, S., Ezhumalai, P., & Maurya, S. (2023). Improved wild horse optimization with levy flight algorithm for effective task scheduling in cloud computing. *Journal of Cloud Computing (Heidelberg, Germany)*, *12*(1), 24. doi:10.1186/s13677-023-00401-1

Sarkar, S., Choudhary, G., Shandilya, S. K., Hussain, A., & Kim, H. (2022). Security of zero trust networks in cloud computing: A comparative review. *Sustainability (Basel)*, *14*(18), 11213. doi:10.3390/su141811213

SAS. (2023). *SAS: Analytics, Business Intelligence and Data Management*. SAS. https://www.sas.com/en_in/home.html

Sayadi, H. (2018). Customized machine learning-based hardware assisted malware detection in embedded devices. *2018 17th IEEE International Conference On Trust, Security And Privacy In Computing And Communications/12th IEEE International Conference On Big Data Science And Engineering (TrustCom/BigDataSE)*. IEEE. 10.1109/TrustCom/BigDataSE.2018.00251

Sayadi, H. (2017). Machine learning-based approaches for energy efficiency prediction and scheduling in composite cores architectures. *2017 IEEE International Conference on Computer Design (ICCD)*. IEEE. 10.1109/ICCD.2017.28

Sayadi, H., Makrani, H. M., Dinakarrao, S. M. P., Mohsenin, T., Sasan, A., Rafatirad, S., & Homayoun, H. (2019). *2SMaRT: A Two-Stage Machine Learning-Based Approach for Run-Time Specialized Hardware-Assisted Malware Detection. 2019 Design, Automation & Test in Europe Conference & Exhibition (DATE)*. IEEE.

Sayadi, H., Manoj, S. P. D., Amir Houmansadr, A., Rafatirad, S., & Homayoun, H. (2018). Comprehensive assessment of run-time hardware-supported malware detection using general and ensemble learning. *CF '18: Proceedings of the 15th ACM International Conference on Computing Frontiers,* (pp. 212–215). ACM. 10.1145/3203217.3203264

Scalability: What every business using the cloud needs to know. (2023). Hack Mamba. https://dev.to/hackmamba/scalability-what-every-business-using-the-cloud-needs-to-know-54ci

Scarani, V., Iblisdir, S., Gisin, N., & Acin, A. (2005). Quantum cloning. *Reviews of Modern Physics*, *77*(4), 1225–1256. doi:10.1103/RevModPhys.77.1225

Schleier-Smith, J., Holz, L., Pemberton, N., & Hellerstein, J. M. (2020). *A faas file system for serverless computing*. arXiv preprint arXiv:2009.09845.

Schuler, L., Jamil, S., & Kühl, N. (2021, May). AI-based resource allocation: Reinforcement learning for adaptive auto-scaling in serverless environments. In *2021 IEEE/ACM 21st International Symposium on Cluster, Cloud and Internet Computing (CCGrid)* (pp. 804-811). IEEE. 10.1109/CCGrid51090.2021.00098

Searchbusinessanalytics. (2023). *Big data Analytics*. Serious Business Analytics.\: https://searchbusinessanalytics.techtarget.com/definition/big-data-analytics

Semenkov, K., Mengazetdinov, N., & Poletykin, A. (2019). Extending Operation Lifespan of Instrumentation and Control Systems with Virtualization Technologies. *Proceedings - 2019 International Russian Automation Conference, RusAutoCon 2019*. IEEE. 10.1109/RUSAUTOCON.2019.8867595

Sennan, S., Kirubasri, Alotaibi, Y., Pandey, D., & Alghamdi, S. (2022). EACR-LEACH: Energy-Aware Cluster-based Routing Protocol for WSN Based IoT. *CMC-COMPUTERS MATERIALS & CONTINUA, 72*(2), 2159-2174

Senyo, P. K., Effah, J., & Addae, E. (2016). Preliminary insight into cloud computing adoption in a developing country. *Journal of Enterprise Information Management*, *29*(4), 505–524. doi:10.1108/JEIM-09-2014-0094

Shafiei, H., Khonsari, A., & Mousavi, P. (2022). Serverless computing: A survey of opportunities, challenges, and applications. *ACM Computing Surveys*, *54*(11s), 1–32. doi:10.1145/3510611

Shafik, W., & Kalinaki, K. (2023). Smart City Ecosystem: An Exploration of Requirements, Architecture, Applications, Security, and Emerging Motivations. In Handbook of Research on Network-Enabled IoT Applications for Smart City Services (pp. 75–98). IGI Global. doi:10.4018/979-8-3693-0744-1.ch005

Shahrad, M., Fonseca, R., Goiri, I., Chaudhry, G., Batum, P., Cooke, J., & Bianchini, R. (2020). Serverless in the wild: Characterizing and optimizing the serverless workload at a large cloud provider. In *2020 USENIX annual technical conference (USENIX ATC 20)* (pp. 205-218). ACM.

Shahzad, F. (2014). State-of-the-art survey on cloud computing security challenges, approaches and solutions. *Procedia Computer Science*, *37*, 357–362. doi:10.1016/j.procs.2014.08.053

Shaikh, E., Mohiuddin, I., Alufaisan, Y., & Nahvi, I. (2019, November). Apache spark: A big data processing engine. *In 2019 2nd IEEE Middle East and North Africa COMMunications Conference (MENACOMM)* (pp. 1-6). IEEE. 10.1109/MENACOMM46666.2019.8988541

Shakerkhan, K. O., & Abilmazhinov, E. T. (2019). Development of a Method for Choosing Cloud Computing on the Platform of Paas for Servicing the State Agencies. *International Journal of Modern Education & Computer Science*, *11*(9), 14–25. doi:10.5815/ijmecs.2019.09.02

Shamsuddin, S. M., & Hasan, S. (2015). Data science vs. big data @ UTM big data centre. *Proc. of 2015 IEEE Int. Conf. Science in Information Technology*. IEEE. 10.1109/ICSITech.2015.7407766

Shao, X., Zhang, Z., Song, P., Feng, Y., & Wang, X. (2022). A review of energy efficiency evaluation metrics for data centers. *Energy and Building*, *271*, 112308. doi:10.1016/j.enbuild.2022.112308

Sharma, S., (2015). *An extended classification and comparison of NoSQL big data models.*

Sharma, A., & Singh, U. K. (2022). Modelling of smart risk assessment approach for cloud computing environment using AI & supervised machine learning algorithms. *Global Transitions Proceedings*, *3*(1), 243–250. doi:10.1016/j.gltp.2022.03.030

Sharma, D. K., Singh, N. C., Noola, D. A., Doss, A. N., & Sivakumar, J. (2022). A review on various cryptographic techniques & algorithms. *Materials Today: Proceedings*, *51*, 104–109. doi:10.1016/j.matpr.2021.04.583

Sharma, K., Shetty, A., Jain, A., & Dhanare, R. K. (2021, January). A Comparative Analysis on Various Business Intelligence (BI), Data Science and Data Analytics Tools. In *2021 International Conference on Computer Communication and Informatics (ICCCI)* (pp. 1-11). IEEE. 10.1109/ICCCI50826.2021.9402226

Sharma, S., Tim, U. S., Wong, J., Gadia, S., & Sharma, S. (2014). A brief review on leading big data models. *Data Science Journal*, *13*(0), 138–157. doi:10.2481/dsj.14-041

Shi, J., Zou, J., Lu, J., Cao, Z., Li, S., & Wang, C. (2014). MRTuner: A toolkit to enable holistic optimization for MapReduce jobs. *Proceedings of the VLDB Endowment International Conference on Very Large Data Bases*, *7*(13), 1319–1330. doi:10.14778/2733004.2733005

Shuijing, H. (2014, January). Data security: the challenges of cloud computing. In *2014 Sixth International Conference on Measuring Technology and Mechatronics Automation* (pp. 203-206). IEEE. 10.1109/ICMTMA.2014.52

Shukla, P., & Pandey, S. (2023). MAA: Multi-objective artificial algae algorithm for workflow scheduling in heterogeneous fog-cloud environment. *The Journal of Supercomputing*, *79*(10), 11218–11260. doi:10.1007/s11227-023-05110-9

Shurpali, S. (2020). *Role of Edge Computing in Connected and Autonomous Vehicles.* eInfo Chips. https://www.einfochips.com/blog/role-of-edge-computing-in-connected-and-autonomous-vehicles/

Simonis, I. (2018). Geospatial BIG DATA processing in hybrid cloud environments. *International Geoscience and Remote Sensing Symposium (IGARSS), 2018-July*. IEEE. 10.1109/IGARSS.2018.8519218

Singh, S., Madaan, G., Kaur, J., Swapna, H. R., Pandey, D., Singh, A., & Pandey, B. K. (2023). Bibliometric Review on Healthcare Sustainability. Handbook of Research on Safe Disposal Methods of Municipal Solid Wastes for a Sustainable Environment, 142-161. Research Gate.

Singh, A. K., & Kumar, J. (2023). A privacy-preserving multidimensional data aggregation scheme with secure query processing for smart grid. *The Journal of Supercomputing*, *79*(4), 3750–3770. doi:10.1007/s11227-022-04794-9

Singh, A., & Chatterjee, K. (2017). Cloud security issues and challenges: A survey. *Journal of Network and Computer Applications*, *79*, 88–115. doi:10.1016/j.jnca.2016.11.027

Singh, A., & Dutta, K. (2013). A genetic algorithm based task scheduling for cloud computing with fuzzy logic. *Ieie Transactions on Smart Processing & Computing*, *2*(6), 367–372.

Singh, A., Dutta, K., & Gupta, H. (2014). A survey on load balancing algorithms for cloud computing. *Int. J. Comput. Appl*, *6*(4), 66–72.

Singh, A., & Hemalatha, M. (2012). Cloud Computing for Academic Environment. *International Journal of Information and Communication Technology Research*, *2*(2), 98–101.

Singh, A., & Shrivastava, M. (2012). Overview of Attacks on Cloud Computing. *Int. J. Eng. Innov. Technol.*, *1*(4), 321–323.

Singh, D., & Reddy, C. K. (2015). A survey on platforms for big data analytics. *Journal of Big Data, 2*(1), 8. doi:10.1186/s40537-014-0008-6 PMID:26191487

Singh, J., Pandey, D., & Singh, A. K. (2023). *Event detection from real-time twitter streaming data using community detection algorithm.* Multimed Tools Appl. doi:10.1007/s11042-023-16263-3

Singh, J., & Walia, N. K. (2023). A Comprehensive Review of Cloud Computing Virtual Machine Consolidation. *IEEE Access : Practical Innovations, Open Solutions, 11*, 1–1. doi:10.1109/ACCESS.2023.3314613

Singh, R. P., Haleem, A., Javaid, M., Kataria, R., & Singhal, S. (2021). Cloud computing in solving problems of COVID-19 pandemic. *Journal of Industrial Integration and Management, 6*(2), 209–219. doi:10.1142/S2424862221500044

Singh, S., Jeong, Y. S., & Park, J. H. (2016). A survey on cloud computing security: Issues, threats, and solutions. *Journal of Network and Computer Applications, 75*, 200–222. doi:10.1016/j.jnca.2016.09.002

Sinha, M., Chacko, E., Makhija, P., & Pramanik, S. (2021). Energy Efficient Smart Cities with Green IoT. In C. Chakrabarty (Ed.), *Green Technological Innovation for Sustainable Smart Societies: Post Pandemic Era.* Springer. doi:10.1007/978-3-030-73295-0_16

Siriwardhana, Y., Porambage, P., Liyanage, M., & Ylianttila, M. (2021). A survey on mobile augmented reality with 5G mobile edge computing: Architectures, applications, and technical aspects. *IEEE Communications Surveys and Tutorials, 23*(2), 1160–1192. doi:10.1109/COMST.2021.3061981

Sivarajah, U., Kamal, M. M., Irani, Z., & Weerakkody, V. (2017). Critical analysis of Big Data challenges and analytical methods. *Journal of Business Research, 70*, 263–286. doi:10.1016/j.jbusres.2016.08.001

Smith, S. (2022). Maximizing Cloud Computing Benefits in the Age of Big Data. *INTERNATIONAL JOURNAL OF COMPUTER SCIENCE AND TECHNOLOGY, 6*(1), 103–118.

Sneha, T., V., Singh, P., & Pandey, P. (2023). Green Cloud Computing: Goals, Techniques, Architectures, and Research Challenges. *2023 International Conference on Advancement in Computation and Computer Technologies, InCACCT 2023*, (pp. 438–443). IEEE. 10.1109/InCACCT57535.2023.10141845

Sohaib Ajmal, M., Iqbal, Z., Zeeshan Khan, F., Bilal, M., & Majid Mehmood, R. (2021). Cost-based Energy Efficient Scheduling Technique for Dynamic Voltage and Frequency Scaling System in cloud computing. *Sustainable Energy Technologies and Assessments, 45*, 101210. doi:10.1016/j.seta.2021.101210

Soma, S., & Rukmini, S. (2023). Virtual Machine and Container Live Migration Algorithms for Energy Optimization of Data Centre in Cloud Environment: A Research Review. *Lecture Notes in Networks and Systems, 528*, 637–647. doi:10.1007/978-981-19-5845-8_45

Spjuth, O., Frid, J., & Hellander, A. (2021). The machine learning life cycle and the cloud: Implications for drug discovery. *Expert Opinion on Drug Discovery, 16*(9), 1071–1079. doi:10.1080/17460441.2021.1932812 PMID:34057379

Sridhar, S. D. S. S., & Smys, S. (2016). A survey on cloud security issues and challenges with possible measures. In *International conference on inventive research in engineering and technology* (*Vol. 4*). Research Gate. https://www.researchgate.net/publication/304157460

Srivastav, A. L., Markandeya, Patel, N., Pandey, M., Pandey, A. K., Dubey, A. K., Kumar, A., Bhardwaj, A. K., & Chaudhary, V. K. (2023). Concepts of circular economy for sustainable management of electronic wastes: challenges and management options. *Environmental Science and Pollution Research, 30*(17), 48654–48675. doi:10.1007/s11356-023-26052-y

Stein, M., Campitelli, V., & Mezzio, S. (2020). Managing the impact of cloud computing. *The CPA Journal, 90*(6), 20–27.

Strumberger, I., Bacanin, N., Tuba, M., & Tuba, E. (2019). Resource Scheduling in Cloud Computing Based on a Hybridized Whale Optimization Algorithm. *Applied Sciences (Basel, Switzerland)*, *9*(22), 4893. doi:10.3390/app9224893

Su, B., & Chen, C.-D. (2021). A Study of Factors Influencing the Adoption of Cloud-Based ERP System: The Perspective of Transaction Cost Economics. *International Conference on Human-Computer Interaction*, (pp. 433–443). Springer. 10.1007/978-3-030-77750-0_27

Subashini S. & Kavitha V. (2011). A survey on security i issues in service delivery models of cloud computing. *Journal of Network and computer Applications, 4*(1), 1–11.

Sundararajan, A. D. D., & Rajashree, R. (2022). A Comprehensive Survey on Lightweight Asymmetric Key Cryptographic Algorithm for Resource Constrained Devices. *ECS Transactions*, *107*(1), 7457–7468. doi:10.1149/10701.7457ecst

Sundar, K., Sasikumar, S., Jayakumar, C., Nagarajan, D., & karthick, S. (2023). Quantum cryptography based cloud security model (QC-CSM) for ensuring cloud data security in storage and accessing. *Multimedia Tools and Applications*, *82*(27), 1–16. doi:10.1007/s11042-023-15463-1

Sun, W., Liu, J., & Yue, Y. (2019). AI-enhanced offloading in edge computing: When machine learning meets industrial IoT. *IEEE Network*, *33*(5), 68–74. doi:10.1109/MNET.001.1800510

Suo, K., Shi, Y., Hung, C. C., & Bobbie, P. (2021, March). Quantifying context switch overhead of artificial intelligence workloads on the cloud and edges. In *Proceedings of the 36th Annual ACM Symposium on Applied Computing* (pp. 1182-1189). ACM. 10.1145/3412841.3441993

Susila, N., Sruthi, A., & Usha, S. (2020). Impact of cloud security in digital twin. *Advances in Computers*, *117*(1), 247–263. doi:10.1016/bs.adcom.2019.09.005

Sustainability, G. (2023). *Sustainable Innovation & Technology - Google Sustainability*. Google. https://sustainability.google/reports/google-2023-environmental-report

Swarnakar, S., Kumar, R., Krishn, S., & Banerjee, C. (2020). Improved Dynamic Load Balancing Approach in Cloud Computing. *2020 IEEE 1st International Conference for Convergence in Engineering (ICCE)*, (pp. 195-199). IEEE. 10.1109/ICCE50343.2020.9290602

Syu, J. H., Lin, J. C. W., Srivastava, G., & Yu, K. (2023). A Comprehensive Survey on Artificial Intelligence Empowered Edge Computing on Consumer Electronics. *IEEE Transactions on Consumer Electronics*, 1. doi:10.1109/TCE.2023.3318150

Szameitat, A. J., Lepsien, J., Cramon, D. Y., Sterr, A., & Schubert, T. (2006). Task-order coordination in dual-task performance and the lateral prefrontal cortex: An event-related fMRI study. *Psychological Research*, *70*(6), 541–552. doi:10.1007/s00426-005-0015-5 PMID:16142491

Tableau. (2023). *Tableau*. Tableau. https://www.tableau.com/

Tabrizchi, H., & Kuchaki Rafsanjani, M. (2020). A survey on security challenges in cloud computing: Issues, threats, and solutions. *The Journal of Supercomputing*, *76*(12), 9493–9532. doi:10.1007/s11227-020-03213-1

Takabi, H., Joshi, J. B. D., & Ahn, G. (2010). Security a and privacy challenges in cloud computing environments. *IEEE Security and Privacy*, *8*(6), 24–31. doi:10.1109/MSP.2010.186

Talaat, F. M., Ali, H. A., Saraya, M. S., & Saleh, A. I. (2022). Effective scheduling algorithm for load balancing in fog environment using CNN and MPSO. *Knowledge and Information Systems*, *64*(3), 773–797. doi:10.1007/s10115-021-01649-2

Talukder, M., Shakhawat Hossain, M., & Kumar, S. (2022). Blue Ocean Strategies in Hotel Industry in Bangladesh: A Review of Present Literatures' Gap and Suggestions for Further Study. SSRN *Electronic Journal*. doi:10.2139/ssrn.4160709

Talukder, M. B. (2020b). The Future of Culinary Tourism: An Emerging Dimension for the Tourism Industry of Bangladesh. I-Manager's. *Journal of Management*, *15*(1), 27. doi:10.26634/jmgt.15.1.17181

Talukder, M. B. (2021). An assessment of the roles of the social network in the development of the Tourism Industry in Bangladesh. *International Journal of Business, Law, and Education*, *2*(3), 85–93. doi:10.56442/ijble.v2i3.21

Talukder, M. B., & Hossain, M. M. (2021). Prospects of Future Tourism in Bangladesh: An Evaluative Study. I-Manager's. *Journal of Management*, *15*(4), 1–8. doi:10.26634/jmgt.15.4.17495

Talukder, M. B., Kabir, F., Muhsina, K., & Das, I. R. (2023). Emerging Concepts of Artificial Intelligence in the Hotel Industry: A Conceptual Paper. *International Journal of Research Publication and Reviews*, *4*(9), 1765–1769. doi:10.55248/gengpi.4.923.92451

Talukder, M. B., Kumar, S., Sood, K., & Grima, S. (2023). Information Technology, Food Service Quality and Restaurant Revisit Intention. *International Journal of Sustainable Development and Planning*, *18*(1), 295–303. doi:10.18280/ijsdp.180131

Taviti Naidu, G., & Ganesh, K. V. B. (2023). Technological Innovation Driven by Big Data, in In H. Ahmed (ed.) Advanced Bioinspiration Methods for Healthcare Standards, Policies, and Reform. IGI Global. doi:10.4018/978-1-6684-5656-9

Tesla. (2021). *Tesla Impact Report*. Tesla. https://www.tesla.com/ns_videos/2021-tesla-impact-report.pdf

Thakuriah, P. (Vonu), Tilahun, N. Y., & Zellner, M. (2017). Big data and urban informatics: Innovations and challenges to urban planning and knowledge discovery. In Springer Geography. Springer. doi:10.1007/978-3-319-40902-3_2

Thota, C., Manogaran, G., Lopez, D., & Sundarasekar, R. (2021). Architecture for big data storage in different cloud deployment models. In Research Anthology on Architectures, Frameworks, and Integration Strategies for Distributed and Cloud Computing (pp. 178-208). IGI Global. doi:10.4018/978-1-7998-5339-8.ch009

Tian, Y.-C., & Gao, J. (2023). *Virtualization and Cloud*, 447–499. Springer. doi:10.1007/978-981-99-5648-7_12

Tianfield, H. (2012). Security issues in cloud computing. In *2012 IEEE International Conference on Systems, Man, and Cybernetics (SMC)* (pp. 1082-1089). IEEE. https://doi.org/10.1109/ICSMC.2012.6377874

tigergraph. (2023). *Geospatial analytics with graph databases*. Tiger Graph. https://www.tigergraph.com/solutions/geospatial-analysis

Tiwari, R., Sille, R., Salankar, N., & Singh, P. (2022). Utilization and Energy Consumption Optimization for Cloud Computing Environment. *Lecture Notes on Data Engineering and Communications Technologies*, *73*, 609–619. doi:10.1007/978-981-16-3961-6_50

Tiwari, S., Bharadwaj, S., & Joshi, S. (2021). A study of impact of cloud computing and artificial intelligence on banking services, profitability and operational benefits. *Turkish Journal of Computer and Mathematics Education*, *12*(6), 1617–1627.

Tsai, W. T., Sun, X., & Balasooriya, J. (2010, April). Service-oriented cloud computing architecture. In 2010 seventh international conference on information technology: new generations (pp. 684-689). IEEE. 10.1109/ITNG.2010.214

Tuli, S., Tuli, S., Tuli, R., & Gill, S. S. (2020). Predicting the growth and trend of COVID-19 pandemic using machine learning and cloud computing. *Internet of Things : Engineering Cyber Physical Human Systems*, *11*, 100222. doi:10.1016/j.iot.2020.100222

Uddin, M., Salah, K., Jayaraman, R., Pesic, S., & Ellahham, S. (2021). Blockchain for drug traceability: Architectures and open challenges. *Health Informatics Journal*, *27*(2), 14604582211011228. doi:10.1177/14604582211011228 PMID:33899576

Ugorji, B., Abouzakhar, N., & Sapsford, J. (2013). Cloud Security: A Review of Recent Threats and Solution Models. In *ICCSM2013-Proceedings of the International Conference on Cloud Security Management: ICCSM 2013* (p. 115). Academic Conferences Limited. https://core.ac.uk/download/pdf/19772349.pdf

Ullah Khan, H., Ali, F., & Nazir, S. (2022). Systematic analysis of software development in cloud computing perceptions. *Journal of Software (Malden, MA)*, *2485*, e2485. doi:10.1002/smr.2485

UNITAR. (2020). *GEM 2020 - E-Waste Monitor*. UNITAR. https://ewastemonitor.info/gem-2020/

v500.com. (2021). *Is Cloud a Cost-Effective Solution?* v500. https://www.v500.com/why-cloud-is-cost-effective/

Vaitis, M., Kopsachilis, V., Tataris, G., Michalakis, V. I., & Pavlogeorgatos, G. (2022). The development of a spatial data infrastructure to support marine spatial planning in Greece. *Ocean and Coastal Management*, *218*, 106025.. doi:10.1016/j.ocecoaman.2022.106025

Valko, N. V., Goncharenko, T. L., Kushnir, N. O., & Osadchyi, V. V. (2022, March). Cloud technologies for basics of artificial intelligence study in school. In *CTE Workshop Proceedings* (Vol. 9, pp. 170-183). CTE. 10.55056/cte.113

Vallati, C., Virdis, A., Mingozzi, E., & Stea, G. (2016). Mobile-edge computing come home connecting things in future smart homes using LTE device-to-device communications. *IEEE Consumer Electronics Magazine*, *5*(4), 77–83. doi:10.1109/MCE.2016.2590100

Van Eyk, E., Toader, L., Talluri, S., Versluis, L., Uţă, A., & Iosup, A. (2018). Serverless is more: From paas to present cloud computing. *IEEE Internet Computing*, *22*(5), 8–17. doi:10.1109/MIC.2018.053681358

Vandervelden, T., De Smet, R., Steenhaut, K., & Braeken, A. (2022). Symmetric-key-based authentication among the nodes in a wireless sensor and actuator network. *Sensors (Basel)*, *22*(4), 1403. doi:10.3390/s22041403 PMID:35214305

Venkatraman, S.K.F., Kaspi, S., & Venkatraman, R., (2016). *SQL versus NoSQL Movement with Big Data Analytics*.

Vergilio, T., & Ramachandran, M. (2018, January). PaaS-BDP a multi-cloud architectural pattern for big data processing on a platform-as-a-service model. In *COMPLEXIS 2018-Proceedings of the 3rd International Conference on Complexity, Future Information Systems and Risk* (pp. 45-52). SciTePress. 10.5220/0006632400450052

Verma, S., & Bala, A. (2021). Auto-scaling techniques for IoT-based cloud applications: A review. *Cluster Computing*, *24*(3), 2425–2459. doi:10.1007/s10586-021-03265-9

Vermesan, O., Friess, P., Guillemin, P., & Gusmeroli, S. (2011). *Internet of Things Strategic Research Agenda*. River Publishers.

Victo Sudha George, G. (2021). A Review of Classifying and Securing Sensitive Customer Data on Cloud Environments using Cryptographic Algorithms. *Design Engineering (London)*, 12424–12444.

Vidya Chellam, V., Veeraiah, V., Khanna, A., Sheikh, T. H., Pramanik, S., & Dhabliya, D. (2023). *A Machine Vision-based Approach for Tuberculosis Identification in Chest X-Rays Images of Patients, ICICC 2023*. Springer.

Vinodhini, V., Kumar, M. S., Sankar, S., Pandey, D., Pandey, B. K., & Nassa, V. K. (2022). IoT-based early forest fire detection using MLP and AROC method. *International Journal of Global Warming*, *27*(1), 55–70. doi:10.1504/IJGW.2022.122794

VM Ware. (n.d.). *Home*. VM Ware. https://www.vmware.com/

VMware. (2023). *How do you determine optimal cloud scalability?* VMware. https://www.vmware.com/topics/glossary/content/cloud-scalability.html

VMware. (2023). *Server Virtualization and Consolidation*. VMware, Inc. https://www.vmware.com/solutions/consolidation.html

Vyshnova, J. (2023). *How to Ensure Cloud Scalability in 2023*. Dinarys. https://dinarys.com/blog/how-to-ensure-cloud-scalability

Wadhwa, H., & Aron, R. (2023). Optimized task scheduling and preemption for distributed resource management in fog-assisted IoT environment. *The Journal of Supercomputing*, *79*(2), 2212–2250. doi:10.1007/s11227-022-04747-2

Waleed, M., & Sajjad, M. (2023). On the emergence of geospatial cloud-based platforms for disaster risk management: A global scientometric review of google earth engine applications. *International Journal of Disaster Risk Reduction*, *97*, 104056. doi:10.1016/j.ijdrr.2023.104056

Walsh, P., Bera, J., Sharma, V. S., Kaulgud, V., Rao, R. M., & Ross, O. (2021, November). Sustainable AI in the Cloud: Exploring machine learning energy use in the cloud. In *2021 36th IEEE/ACM International Conference on Automated Software Engineering Workshops (ASEW)* (pp. 265-266). IEEE.

Wang, H., Niu, D., & Li, B. (2019, April). Distributed machine learning with a serverless architecture. In *IEEE INFOCOM 2019-IEEE Conference on Computer Communications* (pp. 1288-1296). IEEE. 10.1109/INFOCOM.2019.8737391

Wang, I., Liri, E., & Ramakrishnan, K. K. (2020, November). Supporting iot applications with serverless edge clouds. In *2020 IEEE 9th International Conference on Cloud Networking (CloudNet)* (pp. 1-4). IEEE. DOI: 10.1109/CloudNet51028.2020.9335805

Wang, J., Rao, C., Goh, M., & Xiao, X. (2023). Risk assessment of coronary heart disease based on cloud-random forest. *Artificial Intelligence Review*, *56*(1), 203–232. doi:10.1007/s10462-022-10170-z

Wang, L., von Laszewski, G., Younge, A., He, X., Kunze, M., Tao, J., & Fu, C. (2010). Cloud Computing: A Perspective Study. *New Generation Computing*, *28*(2), 137–146. doi:10.1007/s00354-008-0081-5

Wang, S. C., Yan, K.-Q., Liao, W.-P., & Wang, S.-S. (2010). *Towards a load balancing in a three-level cloud computing network* (Vol. 1). IEEE.

Wang, X., Wen, Q., Yang, J., Xiang, J., Wang, Z., Weng, C., Chen, F., & Zheng, S. (2022). A review on data centre cooling system using heat pipe technology. *Sustainable Computing : Informatics and Systems*, *35*, 100774. doi:10.1016/j.suscom.2022.100774

Wang, Y., & Lv, P. (2023). Digital Management Strategy of Natural Resource Archives Under Smart City Space-Time Big Data Platform. *International Journal of Data Warehousing and Mining*, *19*(4), 1–14. doi:10.4018/ijdwm.320649

Wang, Z., & Cai, X. (2023). Teaching mechanism empowered by virtual simulation: Edge computing–driven approach. *Digital Communications and Networks*, *9*(2), 483–491. doi:10.1016/j.dcan.2022.03.016

Wang, Z., Sun, X., Zhang, X., Han, T., & Gao, F. (2020). Algorithm Improvement of Pedestrians' Red-Light Running Snapshot System Based on Image Recognition. In Q. Liang, W. Wang, X. Liu, Z. Na, M. Jia, & B. Zhang (Eds.), *Communications, Signal Processing, and Systems. CSPS 2019. Lecture Notes in Electrical Engineering* (Vol. 571). Springer. doi:10.1007/978-981-13-9409-6_207

Warner, B., Ratner, E., & Lendasse, A. (2023). Edammo's Extreme AutoML Technology – Benchmarks and Analysis. In: Björk, KM. (eds) *Proceedings of ELM 2021. ELM 2021.Proceedings in Adaptation, Learning and Optimization*. Springer, Cham. 10.1007/978-3-031-21678-7_15

Wei, B., Su, G., & Liu, F. (2023). Dynamic Assessment of Spatiotemporal Population Distribution Based on Mobile Phone Data: A Case Study in Xining City, China. *International Journal of Disaster Risk Science*, *14*(4), 649–665. doi:10.1007/s13753-023-00480-3

Welsch, C. (2022). *As the world goes digital, datacenters that make the cloud work look to renewable energy sources.* Microsoft. https://news.microsoft.com/europe/features/as-the-world-goes-digital-datacenters-that-make-the-cloud-work-look-to-renewable-energy-sources/

Wen; Y., Zhang; W., & Luo, H. (2012). Energy-Optimal Mobile Application Execution: Taming Resource-Poor Mobile Devices with Cloud Clones. *INFOCOM IEEE Proceedings*, (pp. 2716-2720). IEEE.

Wirajing, M. A. K., & Nchofoung, T. N. (2023). The role of education in modulating the effect of ICT on governance in Africa. *Education and Information Technologies*, *28*(9), 11987–12020. doi:10.1007/s10639-023-11631-w PMID:37361761

Wronka, C. (2023). Financial crime in the decentralized finance ecosystem: New challenges for compliance. *Journal of Financial Crime*, *30*(1), 97–113. doi:10.1108/JFC-09-2021-0218

Wu, C., & Buyya, R. (2015). *Cloud Data Centers and Cost Modeling: A complete guide to planning, designing and building a cloud data center.* Morgan Kaufmann.

Wu, Y., Cai, C., Bi, X., Xia, J., Gao, C., Tang, Y., & Lai, S. (2023). Intelligent resource allocation scheme for cloud-edge-end framework aided multi-source data stream. *EURASIP Journal on Advances in Signal Processing*, *2023*(1), 1–20. doi:10.1186/s13634-023-01018-x

Wu, Z., Xue, R., & Li, H. (2022). Real-Time Video Fire Detection via Modified YOLOv5 Network Model. *Fire Technology*, *58*(4), 2377–2403. doi:10.1007/s10694-022-01260-z

Xiang, H., Wu, K., Chen, J., Yi, C., Cai, J., & Niyato, D. (2023). Edge Computing Empowered Tactile Internet for Human Digital Twin: Visions and Case Study. arXiv preprint arXiv:2304.07454.

Xiao, L., Li, Q., & Liu, J. (2016). Survey on secure cloud storage. *Journal of Data Acquis Process*, *31*(3), 464–472.

Xia, X., Wu, X., BalaMurugan, S., & Karuppiah, M. (2021). Effect of environmental and social responsibility in energy-efficient management models for smart cities infrastructure. *Sustainable Energy Technologies and Assessments*, *47*, 101525. doi:10.1016/j.seta.2021.101525

Xiong, S., Li, B., & Zhu, S. (2023). DCGNN: A single-stage 3D object detection network based on density clustering and graph neural network. *Complex & Intelligent Systems*, *9*(3), 3399–3408. doi:10.1007/s40747-022-00926-z

Xu, D., Li, T., Li, Y., Su, X., Tarkoma, S., Jiang, T., Crowcroft, J., & Hui, P. (2021). Edge intelligence: Empowering intelligence to the edge of network. *Proceedings of the IEEE*, *109*(11), 1778–1837. doi:10.1109/JPROC.2021.3119950

Xu, H., Xu, S., Wei, W., & Guo, N. (2023). Fault tolerance and quality of service aware virtual machine scheduling algorithm in cloud data centers. *The Journal of Supercomputing*, *79*(3), 2603–2625. doi:10.1007/s11227-022-04760-5

Yadav, A. K., Misra, M., Braeken, A., & Liyanage, M. (2023), A Secure Blockchain-based Authentication and Key Agreement Protocol for 5G Roaming. *IEEE Consumer Communications and Networking Conference (CCNC) 2023.* IEEE. 10.1109/CCNC51644.2023.10059918

Yadav, A. K., Braeken, A., & Misra, M. (2023). Symmetric key-based authentication and key agreement scheme resistant against semi-trusted third party for fog and dew computing. *The Journal of Supercomputing*, *79*(10), 1–39. doi:10.1007/s11227-023-05064-y

Yang, C., Huang, Q., Li, Z., Liu, K., & Hu, F. (2017). Big Data and cloud computing: Innovation opportunities and challenges. *International Journal of Digital Earth, 10*(1), 13–53. doi:10.1080/17538947.2016.1239771

Yang, C., Yu, M., Hu, F., Jiang, Y., & Li, Y. (2017). Utilizing Cloud Computing to address big geospatial data challenges. *Computers, Environment and Urban Systems, 61*, 120–128. Advance online publication. doi:10.1016/j.compenvurbsys.2016.10.010

Yang, D., Liu, F., & Liang, Y. (2010). A survey of the Internet of Things. *Proc. 1st ICEBI*, (pp. 358–366). IEEE. 10.2991/icebi.2010.72

Yang, J., Ge, H., Yang, J., Tong, Y., & Su, S. (2022). Online multi-object tracking using multi-function integration and tracking simulation training. *Applied Intelligence, 52*(2), 1268–1288. doi:10.1007/s10489-021-02457-5

Yang, L., Cao, J., Tang, S., Li, T., & Chan, A. T. S. (2012). A Framework for Partitioning and Execution of Data Stream Applications in Mobile Cloud Computing. *5th International Conference on Cloud Computing (CLOUD)*. IEEE. 10.1109/CLOUD.2012.97

Yang, L., Zhang, H., Li, M., Guo, J., & Ji, H. (2018). Mobile edge computing empowered energy efficient task offloading in 5G. *IEEE Transactions on Vehicular Technology, 67*(7), 6398–6409. doi:10.1109/TVT.2018.2799620

Yathiraju, N. (2022). Investigating the use of an Artificial Intelligence Model in an ERP Cloud-Based System. *International Journal of Electrical. Electronics and Computers, 7*(2), 1–26.

Yi, Z., Zilin, Z., & Yuhe, Z. (2023). *Application status and development of artificial intelligence technology in large data center.* Spie. doi:10.1117/12.2683016

Youseff, L., Butrico, M., & Da Silva, D. (2008). Toward a unified ontology of cloud computing. *Grid Computing Environments Workshop*. IEEE. 10.1109/GCE.2008.4738443

Yu, J., & Sarwat, M. (2021). GeoSparkViz: A cluster computing system for visualizing massive-scale geospatial data. *The VLDB Journal, 30*(2), 237–258. doi:10.1007/s00778-020-00645-2

Yu, T., Liu, Q., Du, D., Xia, Y., Zang, B., Lu, Z., & Chen, H. (2020, October). Characterizing serverless platforms with serverlessbench. In *Proceedings of the 11th ACM Symposium on Cloud Computing* (pp. 30-44). ACM. 10.1145/3419111.3421280

Yu, Y. (2016). Mobile edge computing towards 5G: Vision, recent progress, and open challenges. *China Communications, 13*(2, Supplement2), 89–99. doi:10.1109/CC.2016.7405725

Zeyu, H., Geming, X., Zhaohang, W., & Sen, Y. (2020, June). Survey on edge computing security. In *2020 International Conference on Big Data, Artificial Intelligence and Internet of Things Engineering (ICBAIE)* (pp. 96-105). IEEE.

Zhang, H., Wang, L. C., Chaudhuri, S., Pickering, A., Usvyat, L., Larkin, J., Waguespack, P., Kuang, Z., Kooman, J. P., Maddux, F. W., & Kotanko, P. (2023). Real-time prediction of intradialytic hypotension using machine learning and cloud computing infrastructure. *Nephrology, Dialysis, Transplantation, 38*(7), gfad070. doi:10.1093/ndt/gfad070 PMID:37055366

Zhang, J., Yu, Z., Cheng, Y., Sha, X., & Zhang, H. (2022). A novel hierarchical framework to evaluate residential exposure to green spaces. *Landscape Ecology, 37*(3), 895–911. doi:10.1007/s10980-021-01378-5

Zhang, K., Zhu, Y., Leng, S., He, Y., Maharjan, S., & Zhang, Y. (2019). Deep learning empowered task offloading for mobile edge computing in urban informatics. *IEEE Internet of Things Journal, 6*(5), 7635–7647. doi:10.1109/JIOT.2019.2903191

Zhang, N., Zhang, N., Zheng, Q., & Xu, Y.-S. (2022). Real-time prediction of shield moving trajectory during tunnelling using GRU deep neural network. *Acta Geotechnica, 17*(4), 1167–1182. doi:10.1007/s11440-021-01319-1

Zhang, W., Xie, H., Cao, B., & Cheng, A. M. K. (2014). Energy-Aware Real-Time Task Scheduling for Heterogeneous Multiprocessors with Particle Swarm Optimization Algorithm. *Mathematical Problems in Engineering, 2014*, 1–9. doi:10.1155/2014/287475

Zhang, X. (2010). *Towards an elastic application model for augmenting computing capabilities of mobile platforms.* Mobile Wireless Middleware, Operating Systems, and Applications.

Zhang, X., & Huang, P. (2023). *Data Centers as Prosumers in Urban Energy Systems.* Springer., doi:10.1007/978-981-99-1222-3_4

Zhang, X., & Yue, W. T. (2020). *Integration of on-premises and cloud-based software: the product bundling perspective.* Forthcoming in Journal of the Association for Information Systems.

Zhang, Y., Zhao, Y., Dai, S., Nie, B., Ma, H., Li, J., Miao, Q., Jin, Y., Tan, L., & Ding, Y. (2022). Cooling technologies for data centres and telecommunication base stations – A comprehensive review. *Journal of Cleaner Production, 334*, 130280. doi:10.1016/j.jclepro.2021.130280

Zhao, S., Miao, J., & Zhao, J. (2023). *A comprehensive and systematic review of the banking systems based on pay-as-you-go payment fashion and cloud computing in the pandemic era.* Inf Syst E-Bus Manage. doi:10.1007/s10257-022-00617-9

Zhou, A., Li, S., Ma, X., & Wang, S. (2022). Service-Oriented Resource Allocation for Blockchain-Empowered Mobile Edge Computing. *IEEE Journal on Selected Areas in Communications*, *40*(12), 3391–3404. doi:10.1109/JSAC.2022.3213343

Zhu, L., Yu, F. R., Wang, Y., Ning, B., & Tang, T. (2019). Big Data Analytics in Intelligent Transportation Systems: A Survey. In IEEE Transactions on Intelligent Transportation Systems, 20(1). doi:10.1109/TITS.2018.2815678

Zhu, Y., Tan, Y., Luo, X., & He, Z. (2018). Big Data Management for Cloud-Enabled Geological Information Services. In Scientific Programming (Vol. 2018). doi:10.1155/2018/1327214

Ziyath, S. P. M., & Subramaniyan, S. (2022). An Improved Q-Learning-Based Scheduling Strategy with Load Balancing for Infrastructure-Based Cloud Services. *Arabian Journal for Science and Engineering*, *47*(8), 9547–9555. doi:10.1007/s13369-021-06279-y

Zolfaghari, B., Yazdinejad, A., Dehghantanha, A., Krzciok, J., & Bibak, K. (2022). The dichotomy of cloud and iot: Cloud-assisted iot from a security perspective. *arXiv preprint arXiv:2207.01590.*

Zolfaghari, R., Sahafi, A., Rahmani, A. M., & Rezaei, R. (2022). An energy-aware virtual machines consolidation method for cloud computing: Simulation and verification. *Software, Practice & Experience*, *52*(1), 194–235. doi:10.1002/spe.3010

About the Contributors

Musau Abdullatif is a passionate technophile with research interests in cloud computing, virtualization, ICT for development, Artificial Intelligence, data mining, and wireless and mobile computing. With a deep-rooted fascination for cutting-edge technologies, bridging the digital divide and empowering underserved communities is a dream come true.

Munir Ahmad, Ph.D. in Computer Science, brings over 24 years of invaluable expertise in the realm of spatial data development, management, processing, visualization, and quality assurance. His unwavering commitment to open data, crowdsourced data, volunteered geographic information, and spatial data infrastructure has solidified him as a seasoned professional and a trusted trainer in cutting-edge spatial technologies. With a profound passion for research, Munir has authored more than 30 publications in his field, culminating in the award of his Ph.D. in Computer Science from Preston University Pakistan in 2022. His dedication to propelling the industry forward and sharing his extensive knowledge defines his mission. Connect with Munir to delve into the world of Spatial Data, GIS, and GeoTech. #SpatialData #GIS #GeoTech

Aitizaz Ali is member of IEEE Communication Society. He has published more than twenty research papers in IEEE Transactions, IEEE Access, CMC, Senors and Applied Science. His research area includes cybersceurity, Blockchain and AI.

Asmat Ali is PhD in Remote Sensing & GIS. He is Director of Cartography and GIS at Survey of Pakistan. He is also Project Director Feasibility Study for Establishment of National Spatial Data Infrastructure (NSDI) for Pakistan. In, 1998 he earned Professional Master Degree in Geoinformatics from Faculty of Geo-Information Science and Earth Observation (ITC), University of Twente, Enschede The Netherlands. The title of his IFA was, "DIGITAL PRODUCTION LINE IN THE CONTEXT OF SURVEY OF PAKISTAN". Later on, he got MSc Degree in Geo-information Science and Earth Observation, with Specialization in Geo-Information Management from the same university. The title of his MSc thesis was, "POTENTIAL OF PUBIC PRIVATE PARTNERSHIP FOR NSDI IMPLEMENTATION IN PAKISTAN". In 2022, he got PhD degree in Remote Sensing and GIS from PMAS-Arid Agriculture University Rawalpindi, Pakistan. The title of his dissertation was "SPATIAL DATA INFRASTRUCTURE AS THE MEANS TO ASSEMBLE GEOGRAPHIC INFORMATION NECESSARY FOR EFFECTIVE AGRICULTURAL POLICIES IN PAKISTAN". He has 35 years of experience in geospatial information production and management discipline as practitioner, trainer and educator. He has served on several operational, administrative and instructional appointments. He was in-charge of the team which started GIS mapping and digital cartography at Survey of Pakistan in 1999. His more than 30 research papers including four book chapters and articles on Spatial Data Infrastructure (SDI), GIS, Remote Sensing, E-governance, as well as Land Administration have been published in various internationally renowned journals and conferences. In 2008, SDI Asia-Pacific identified him as FOCAL POINT FOR SDI DEVELOPMENT IN PAKISTAN. GSDI in 2016, acknowledged and awarded him as SDI IMPLEMENTER FROM PAKISTAN. He is on the visiting faculty of Bahria University Islamabad and PMAS- Arid Agriculture University Rawalpindi, Pakistan.

Biswajit Biswal is an Associate Professor of Computer Science at South Carolina State University. He holds Ph.D. in Computer and Information Systems Engineering from Tennessee State University, an M.S. in Electrical Engineering from NYU Tandon School of Engineering, and a B.E. in Medical Electronics Engineering from India. His research interests are machine learning, data mining, cybersecurity, cloud computing, RF signal detection (Drones), IoT, and big data analysis. He has many technical papers published in conferences and journals. He has served as a technical reviewer in many conferences and journals. He is also a senior member of IEEE.

Sachin Chaudhary completed his Graduation from MJPRU, and Post Graduation from AKTU, Moradabad, U.P. Currently Pursuing his Ph.D. in Computer Science and Engineering from Govt. Recognized University. Presently, he is working as an Assistant Professor in the Department of Computer Science and Applications, IIMT University, Meerut, U.P, India. He has been awarded as Excellence in teaching award 2019. He is the reviewer member of some reputed journals. He has published several book chapters and research papers of national and international reputed journals.

Pankaj Dadheech is currently working as a Professor & Deputy Head in the Department of Computer Science & Engineering (NBA Accredited), Swami Keshvanand Institute of Technology, Management & Gramothan (SKIT), Jaipur, Rajasthan, India (Accredited by NAAC A++ Grade). He has more than 18 years of experience in teaching. He is currently working a Professor & Dy. HOD in the Department of Computer Science & Engineering (NBA Accredited), Swami Keshvanand Institute of Technology, Management & Gramothan (SKIT), Jaipur, Rajasthan, India. He has published 25 Patents at Intellectual Property India, Office of the Controller General of Patents, Design and Trade Marks, Department of Industrial Policy and Promotion, Ministry of Commerce and Industry, Government of India. He has published 8 International Patents (USA, South African, Australian, Germany) & 2 Copyrights. He has 73 publications in various International & National Journals, 63 papers in various National & International conferences. He has published 9 Books & 35 Book Chapters.

Iva Rani Das is a dynamic individual, currently pursuing her MPhil in the Marketing Department of Dhaka University. Alongside her academic pursuits, she holds key positions as an Assistant Director at the Daffodil Institute of Technology and serves as Guest Faculty in the Business Faculty at the Asian Institute of Business and Technology. Her scholarly achievements extend beyond the classroom, with publications in esteemed national and international journals. Iva's dedication to education and research makes her a driving force in the fields of business and marketing.

Sateesh Gorikapudi received M.Tech. from Acharya Nagarjuna University, Guntur in 2009. Currently, he is a Research Scholar in the School of Computer Science and Engineering, VIT-AP University, Andhra

Pradesh, India and pursuing his Ph.D. work in the field of Internet of Things. His main areas of research include the Internet of Things, Wireless Sensor Networks and Nature Inspired Optimization Techniques.

Ankur Gupta has received the B.Tech and M.Tech in Computer Science and Engineering from Ganga Institute of Technology and Management, Kablana affiliated with Maharshi Dayanand University, Rohtak in 2015 and 2017. He is an Assistant Professor in the Department of Computer Science and Engineering at Vaish College of Engineering, Rohtak, and has been working there since January 2019. He has many publications in various reputed national/ international conferences, journals, and online book chapter contributions (Indexed by SCIE, Scopus, ESCI, ACM, DBLP, etc). He is doing research in the field of cloud computing, data security & machine learning. His research work in M.Tech was based on biometric security in cloud computing.

Shaziya Islam Associate Professor in CSE at Rungta College Of Engineering & Technology, Bhilai

Ramesh Kait obtained Master's degree (Master of Computer Science) and PhD (Computer Science & Applications) from Kurukshetra University, Kurukshetra and during research his dissertation topic, "Optimizations of Security Techniques for Wireless Networks". Presently, He is working as Assistant Professor in the Department of Computer Science and Applications, Kurukshetra University, Kurukshetra, Haryana, India. He has presented and published more than seventy papers in International and National Conferences/Journals. His research interests are Wireless networks, VANET and Security in Cloud and Fog Computing, Artificial Intelligence and Machine Learning.

Kassim Kalinaki (MIEEE) is a passionate technologist, researcher, and educator with more than ten years of experience in industry and academia. He received his Diploma in Computer engineering from Kyambogo University, a BSc in computer science and engineering, and an MSc. Computer Science and Engineering from Bangladesh's Islamic University of Technology (IUT). Since 2014, He has been lecturing at the Islamic University in Uganda (IUIU), where he most recently served as the Head of Department Computer Science department (2019-2022). Currently, he's pursuing his Ph.D. in Computer Science at the School of Digital Science at Universiti Brunei Darussalam (UBD) since January 2022 and is slated to complete in August 2025. He's the founder and principal investigator of Borderline Research Laboratory (BRLab) and his areas of research include Ecological Informatics, Data Analytics, Computer Vision, ML/DL, Digital Image Processing, Cybersecurity, IoT/AIoMT, Remote Sensing, and Educational Technologies. He has authored and co-authored several published peer-reviewed articles in renowned journals and publishers, including in Springer, Elsevier, Taylor and Francis, Emerald and IEEE.

Shobhana Kashyap is a Research Scholar in Department of CSE in Dr. B. R. Ambedkar National Institute of Technology, Jalandhar Punjab, India since 2019. She has completed her master's from Thapar University, Patiala India. Her current research is concerned with Machine Learning and Cloud Computing. She has two year teaching experience and written papers for national and international conferences.

Palak Keshwani is working as an Assistant Professor at ICFAI University, Raipur. She has more than 10 years of teaching experience. She has published her research in various national and international journals . Her research interest includes Wireless Sensor Networks, Image Processing,Cloud Computing etc.

Hari Kishan Kondaveeti received his B.Tech degree in Information Technology from Acharya Nagarjuna University, India in 2009. He completed his M.Tech, in Computer Science and Engineering from the JNTUK University, India in 2012 and then joined the Department of CS & SE, AUCE (A), Andhra University, India and got a Doctor of Philosophy (Ph.D.) in the field of Computer Science and Engineering. He worked as Research Associate in a research project funded by Naval Science and Technological Laboratory, India when he was at Andhra University. Currently, he is working as Associate Professor at the School of Computer Science and Engineering, VIT-AP University, Andhra Pradesh, India, and acting as a Coordinator of Engineering Clinics. He is an IBM Certified Data Science Professional and NASSCOM Associate Analyst certified faculty and handling multiple Data Analytics courses. His research interests include Digital Image Processing, Machine Learning, Data Analytics, Remote Sensing, and IoT. In recent years, he is focusing on collaborating actively with researchers in several other disciplines and trying to develop interdisciplinary projects.

Kugonza Julius holds a master's degree in Business Administration (Data Science Major) from Manipal Academy of Higher Education-India, Masters in Economic policy and a bachelor's degree in statistics from Makerere University, Uganda. He is also a trade policy design and negotiation fellow from the University of Adelaide, Australia. Julius has over 10 years' experience in the public, CSO and private sectors. He currently works as the Head of business intelligence and Analysis unit at Uganda Revenue Authority. He begun his career at Uganda Bureau of Statistics.He is also a senior research fellow at Pride data solutions (Policy Thinktank). He is also currently a Consultant- Informal Cross Border Trade (ICBT) for the United Nations Economic Commission for Africa. He has also previously worked as a Consultant-Applied Statistician/Power BI Developer for GIZ-South Africa. He also previously worked at a Consultant-Trade Statistics Trainer for JICA. Julius' research interests are in the areas of Regional Integration, Disruptive Technologies, IFFs and Environment

Bhupendra Kumar completed his Graduation and Post Graduation from Chaudhary Charan Singh University, Meerut, U.P. and Ph.D. in Computer Science and Engineering from Mewar University, Hapur. Presently, he is working as a Professor in the Department of Computer Science and Applications, IIMT University, Meerut, U.P. He has been a huge teaching experience of 19 years. He is the reviewer member of some reputed journals. He has published several book chapters and research papers of national and international reputed journals.

Sanjeev Kumar is an accomplished expert in Food and Beverage. He currently holds the positions of Professor at the Lovely Professional University, Punjab, India. With over a decade of experience in the field, food Service Industry, his research focuses on Alcoholic beverages, Event management and Sustainable Management Practices, Metaverse and Artificial Intelligence. He has published more than 35 research papers, articles and chapters in Scopus Indexed, UGC Approved and peer reviewed Journals and books. Dr. Sanjeev Kumar participated and acted as resource person in various National and International conferences, seminars, research workshops and industry talks and his work has been widely cited.

Valli Kumari Vatsavayi, professor of computer science and systems engineering,andhra university. She is an active consultant to several government/public sector/private organisations. She successfully completed six consultant projects for Naval Science and Technological Laboratories and two projects of DST, Govt of India. She has successfully managed the computerisation of Integrated Common Entrance

Test (ICET) for MCA/ MBA in AP State, on behalf of Convener and APSCHE from 2009 to 2011 and Education Common Entrance Test (EdCET) from 2012 to 2014. She is a member of IEEE, ACM, CRSI and CSI. She is the founder Vice-Chair of IEEE Vizag Bay Subsection. She is also the Executive Member of Andhra Pradesh State Knowledge Mission and state nodal officer for Digital India Week, 2015.

L. Shyamala working as Associate professor in VIT, Chennai campus from 2016 onwards. She did her B.E in ECE at Madras university, PG and Ph.D in CEG, Anna University. Her area of interest for research includes Cloud computing, Data analytics. and networks. Published 20 papers in journals and attended 5 international conferences

Ranjan Kumar Mondal is an Assistant Professor in the department of Computer Science and Engineering, School of Engineering, Swami Vivekananda University, Barrackpore, West Bengal. He received his M.Tech in Computer Science and Engineering from University of Kalyani, Kalyani, Nadia; and B.Tech in Computer Science and Engineering from Government College of Engineering and Textile Technology, Berhampore, Murshidabad, West Bengal under West Bengal University of Technology, West Bengal, India. His research interests include Cloud Computing, Wireless and Mobile Communication Systems.

Balakumar Muniandi is an Associate Professor of Practice in the Department of Electrical and Computer Engineering. He worked as a Postdoctoral research associate in Electrical and Computer science Engineering (ECE), University of Massachusetts, where he developed an energy-efficient Cellular Neuromorphic Computing (CNN) chip in deep sub-micron process for DARPA, USA by collaborating with BAE systems. He was also worked as an R&D Engineer in Hsinchu Science Park (Silicon Valley of Taiwan), Taiwan. During his PhD, he is a key person in Indo-Taiwan bilateral project for developing "MPPT based solar battery charger system". His research interest mainly focuses on power management circuits, battery chargers, mixed signal IC designs, GaN gate driver, smart battery management system for electric vehicles and Neuromorphic computing.

Sempala Abdul-Karim Nasser is a fast learner, researcher, innovator, passionate technologist and business orientated with more than five years of experience in the IT industry and much interest in Cybersecurity, sensing technologies and Artificial intelligence. He received a BIT in Islamic University In Uganda (IUIU) and worked at as research assistant. Currently, he is doing Masters in Information Technology Management at IUIU, area of research in Cybersecurity and working with Uganda Revenue Authority.

Ronald Nsubuga holds a Master of Business Administration and a Bachelor of Statistics from Makerere University - Uganda. He is also finalizing a Master of Science in Business Analytics at Manipal Academy of Higher Education - India. He has professionally worked as a Consultant with the United Nations Economic Commission for Africa, United Nations Development Programme and the International Organization for Migration. He has also worked previously with AMREF Health Africa, International Non-Government Organization, as a Monitoring and Evaluation Specialist. He has also previously worked with Pride Data Solutions, a policy think tank, as a Development Researcher. Ronald's research interests are in the areas of Artificial Intelligence, regional integration, international trade, migration among many others.

Rajneesh Panwar graduated and post graduated in Mathematics and Computer Application from Ch. Charan Singh University, Meerut (U.P.) and received his M. Tech. in Computer Science from Shobhit University, Meerut. Presently, he is working as an Assistant Professor in the School of Computer Science and Application IIMT University, Meerut, U.P. He qualifies GATE 2021 and UGC-NET June 2020 and December 2020. He has published several book chapters and research papers of national and international repute.

Kaushikkumar Patel is a distinguished leader known for his exceptional contributions at the intersection of finance and technology. As a key figure at TransUnion, he leverages Big Data to transform decision-making processes and financial strategies, with expertise spanning Data Analytics, FinTech, and Digital Transformation. Based in the United States, Mr. Patel is renowned for his strategic insights in addressing complex challenges like data privacy and risk assessment, ensuring compliance in dynamic financial landscapes. An influential thought leader, Mr. Patel's work has been internationally recognized, earning him the prestigious ET Leadership Excellence Award for his groundbreaking achievements in Data-Driven Financial Strategies. His unique blend of technical prowess and strategic acumen establishes him as a visionary in his field, continually pushing the boundaries of what's possible in finance and technology.

Kiran Peddireddy is a Technical Lead with over 16 years of experience in Data Engineering, Data Analysis, and Product Design. He has worked for companies such as Cox Automotive and Pratt and Whitney, where he led the design and development of several successful products. Kiran has experience in data warehousing, ETL, and data modeling techniques, and has developed end-to-end data pipeline systems in AWS environments. He is certified in AWS Solutions Architecture, SAS Platform Engineering, and Salesforce Specialization. Kiran is also an active member of several industry communities and has authored technical publications, including books on enterprise data integration and streaming and digital transformation using Salesforce CRM.

Sabyasachi Pramanik is a professional IEEE member. He obtained a PhD in Computer Science and Engineering from Sri Satya Sai University of Technology and Medical Sciences, Bhopal, India. Presently, he is an Associate Professor, Department of Computer Science and Engineering, Haldia Institute of Technology, India. He has many publications in various reputed international conferences, journals, and book chapters (Indexed by SCIE, Scopus, ESCI, etc). He is doing research in the fields of Artificial Intelligence, Data Privacy, Cybersecurity, Network Security, and Machine Learning. He also serves on the editorial boards of several international journals. He is a reviewer of journal articles from IEEE, Springer, Elsevier, Inderscience, IET and IGI Global. He has reviewed many conference papers, has been a keynote speaker, session chair, and technical program committee member at many international conferences. He has authored a book on Wireless Sensor Network. He has edited 8 books from IGI Global, CRC Press, Springer and Wiley Publications.

Piyal Roy is working as an Assistant Professor at Computer Science and Engineering Department at Brainware University, West Bengal, India.

Nitin Nandkumar Sakhare received B. E. Computer degree in Computer Engineering from Vishwakarma Institute of Information Technology, Pune affiliated to Savitribai Phule Pune University, formerly known as Pune University, in 2012 and Master's degree in Computer Engineering from Sinhgad College of Engineering, Pune affiliated to Savitribai Phule Pune University, formerly known as Pune University, in 2012. Nitin Nandkumar He is currently working toward the Ph.D. degree at the Department of Computer Science and Engineering, KL University, Vijaywada, Andhra Pradesh. He is currently working as an assistant professor in the department of Computer Engineering of Vishwakarma Institute of Information Technology, Pune. His research interests include Data Science, Machine Learning, Computer Networking and Internet of Things.

Kewal Krishan Sharma is a professor in computer sc. in IIMT University, Meerut, U.P, India. He did his Ph.D. in computer network with this he has MCA, MBA and Law degree also. He did variously certification courses also. He has an overall experience of around 33 year in academic, business and industry. He wrote a number of research papers and books.

Vikas Sharma completed his Graduation and Post Graduation from Chaudhary Charan Singh University, Meerut, U.P. Currently Pursuing his Ph.D. in Computer Science and Engineering from Govt. Recognized University. Presently, he is working as an Assistant Professor in the Department of Computer Science and Applications, IIMT University, Meerut, U.P. He has been awarded as Excellence in teaching award 2019. He is the reviewer member of some reputed journals. He has published several book chapters and research papers of national and international reputed journals.

Avtar Singh is working as an Assistant Professor in Department of CSE in Dr. B. R. Ambedkar National Institute of Technology, Jalandhar Punjab, India. He received the B.Tech and M.Tech degree in Computer Science Engineering from the Electro Technical University, Saint Petersburg Russia (LETI) in 1999 and 2001 respectively. In 2001, he served more than 5 years in IT industry Bangalore and leading educational institutions in year 2006. His research areas of interests include Cloud Computing, Internet of Things (IoT), Parallel and Distributed Computing and Machine Learning. He is a member of IEEE and ACM organization. He has written number of papers for national and international journals and conferences. He is currently guiding 4 research scholars at Ph.D. levels and three master's students. He has published extensively in these areas and has supervised 10 Master's students. He has organized five STC events.

Mohammad Badruddoza Talukder is an Associate Professor and head of the Department of Tourism and Hospitality Management, Daffodil Institute of Information Technology (at the National University), Dhaka, Bangladesh. He completed his Ph.D. in Hotel Management at the School of Hotel Management and Tourism, Lovely Professional University, India. He holds a bachelor's and a master's degree in Hotel Management from India. He has been teaching various courses in the Department of Tourism and Hospitality at various universities in Bangladesh since 2009. His research areas include tourism management, hotel management, hospitality management, food and beverage management, and accommodation management, where he has published research papers in well-known journals in Bangladesh and abroad. Dr. Talukder is one of the executive members of the Tourism Educators Association of Bangladesh. He has led training and counseling for various hospitality organizations in Bangladesh. As an administrator, Dr. Talukder served as a debate advisor at the University coordinator for courses and exams in the Department of Tourism and Hotel Management. He has experience as a manager in various business-class hotels in Bangladesh. He is one of the certified trainers for the food and beverage service department of the SIEP project from Bangladesh. He became an honorary facilitator at Bangladesh Tourism Board's Bangabandhu International Tourism and Hospitality Training Institute.

Udithaa Terala completed her intermediate from Sree Vidya Niketan college, Tirupati in 2022. Currently, she is doing B.tech in the School of Computer Science and Engineering And pursuing her 2nd year in VIT-AP University, Andhra Pradesh, India . Her main areas of research include Artificial Intelligence (AI), Data Science and Big Data, Cybersecurity, Internet of Things (IoT),Cloud Computing and Distributed Systems,Software Engineering.

Tin Tin Ting received her BSc and PhD in Computer Sciences from University of Science, Malaysia. Ting joined Gemalto as telecommunication software engineer in Singapore before joined academic industry after her PhD graduation. She has more than 12 years of lecturing, supervising projects, and research. Her research interests including big data analytics, information systems engineering, educational systems, psycho-academic research, and software engineering. Ting received her professional certification in project management from PMI and data analytics from SAS. Currently, Ting is attached to INTI International University responsible primary in research and postgraduate supervision. At the same time, Ting serves as freelance lecturer in Monash University, Tunku Abdul Rahman University College, Methodist College Kuala Lumpur, and Ace Education.

Tarun Kumar Vashishth is an active academician and researcher in the field of computer science with 21 years of experience. He earned Ph.D. Mathematics degree specialized in Operations Research; served several academic positions such as HoD, Dy. Director, Academic Coordinator, Member Secretary of Department Research Committee, Assistant Center superintendent and Head Examiner in university examinations. He is involved in academic development and scholarly activities. He is member of International Association of Engineers, The Society of Digital Information and Wireless Communications, Global Professors Welfare Association, International Association of Academic plus Corporate (IAAC), Computer Science Teachers Association and Internet Society. His research interest includes Cloud Computing, Artificial Intelligence, Machine Learning and Operations Research; published more than 20 research articles with 1 book and 10 book chapters in edited books. He is contributing as member of editorial and reviewers boards in conferences and various computer journals published by CRC Press, Taylor and Francis, Springer, IGI global and other universities.

Index

A

B

C

D

E

F

G

H

I

J

L

M

N

O

P

Q

R

S

T

U

V

W

Ensure Quality Research is Introduced to the Academic Community

Become an Reviewer for IGI Global Authored Book Projects

The overall success of an authored book project is dependent on quality and timely manuscript evaluations.

Applications and Inquiries may be sent to:

development@igi-global.com

Applicants must have a doctorate (or equivalent degree) as well as publishing, research, and reviewing experience. Authored Book Evaluators are appointed for one-year terms and are expected to complete at least three evaluations per term. Upon successful completion of this term, evaluators can be considered for an additional term.

If you have a colleague that may be interested in this opportunity, we encourage you to share this information with them.

www.ingramcontent.com/pod-product-compliance
Lightning Source LLC
LaVergne TN
LVHW080117011026
849160LV00013B/1122